T0254631

Pro SQL Server 2008
Administration

987654321

Ken Simmons and Sylvester Carstarphen

Apress®

Pro SQL Server 2008 Administration

Copyright © 2009 by Ken Simmons and Sylvester Carstarphen

All rights reserved. No part of this work may be reproduced or transmitted in any form or by any means, electronic or mechanical, including photocopying, recording, or by any information storage or retrieval system, without the prior written permission of the copyright owner and the publisher.

ISBN-13 (pbk): 978-1-4302-2373-3

ISBN-13 (electronic): 978-1-4302-2374-0

9 8 7 6 5 4 3 2 1

Trademarked names may appear in this book. Rather than use a trademark symbol with every occurrence of a trademarked name, we use the names only in an editorial fashion and to the benefit of the trademark owner, with no intention of infringement of the trademark.

Lead Editor: Jonathan Gennick
Technical Reviewer: Rodney Landrum
Editorial Board: Clay Andres, Steve Anglin, Mark Beckner, Ewan Buckingham, Tony Campbell, Gary Cornell, Jonathan Gennick, Michelle Lowman, Matthew Moodie, Jeffrey Pepper, Frank Pohlmann, Ben Renow-Clarke, Dominic Shakeshaft, Matt Wade, Tom Welsh
Project Manager: Beth Christmas
Copy Editor: Kim Benbow
Associate Production Director: Kari Brooks-Copony
Production Editor: Laura Esterman
Compositor: Jill Flores
Proofreader: Kim Burton
Indexer: Becky Hornyak
Artist: April Milne
Cover Designer: Kurt Krames
Manufacturing Director: Tom Debolski

Distributed to the book trade worldwide by Springer-Verlag New York, Inc., 233 Spring Street, 6th Floor, New York, NY 10013. Phone 1-800-SPRINGER, fax 201-348-4505, e-mail orders-ny@springer-sbm.com, or visit http://www.springeronline.com.

For information on translations, please contact Apress directly at 2855 Telegraph Avenue, Suite 600, Berkeley, CA 94705. Phone 510-549-5930, fax 510-549-5939, e-mail info@apress.com, or visit http://www.apress.com.

Apress and friends of ED books may be purchased in bulk for academic, corporate, or promotional use. eBook versions and licenses are also available for most titles. For more information, reference our Special Bulk Sales–eBook Licensing web page at http://www.apress.com/info/bulksales.

The information in this book is distributed on an "as is" basis, without warranty. Although every precaution has been taken in the preparation of this work, neither the author(s) nor Apress shall have any liability to any person or entity with respect to any loss or damage caused or alleged to be caused directly or indirectly by the information contained in this work.

The source code for this book is available to readers at http://www.apress.com.

I want to dedicate this book to my wife Susan and son Nathan. Writing a book takes a lot of time and hard work, and they have definitely given me the support and encouragement I needed throughout the process.
—Ken Simmons

This book is dedicated to my loving wife, Kimberly, who motivated me when I was tired, encouraged me when I was down, and never complained when I spent all weekend writing. Thanks for all of your support. I love you.
—Sylvester Carstarphen

Contents at a Glance

PART 1 ▪▪▪ Introducing Microsoft SQL Server 2008

PART 2 ▪▪▪ Getting Started

PART 3 ▪▪▪ Administering Microsoft SQL Server 2008

PART 4 ▦ ▦ ▦ Troubleshooting and Tuning

PART 5 ▦ ▦ ▦ Conclusion

Contents

PART 1 ■ ■ ■ Introducing Microsoft SQL Server 2008

PART 2 ▪▪▪ Getting Started

PART 3 ▪▪▪ Administering Microsoft SQL Server 2008

PART 4 ■■■ Troubleshooting and Tuning

PART 5 ▪▪▪ Conclusion

About the Authors

 **KEN SIMMONS** is a database administrator/developer specializing in MSSQL Server and .NET. He has been working in the IT industry since 2000 and currently holds certifications for MCP, MCAD, MCSD, MCDBA, and MCTS for SQL 2005.

Ken is highly active in the in the online community and often participates in the SQL forums on MSDN and SQLServerCentral.com. He enjoys sharing tips by writing articles for SQLServerCentral.com and MSSQLTips.com. He has also formed a SQL Server users group in Columbus, Georgia, to provide a local faucet for SQL Server professionals to come together to share knowledge and resources. When he is not working, Ken enjoys traveling with his wife Susan and son Nathan, and can often be found on a cruise ship, at a Disney resort, or at the beach in his hometown of Pensacola, Florida.

 **SYLVESTER CARSTARPHEN** is a senior database administrator for a CRM company, where he is leading its performance-tuning efforts on its VLDBs. Sylvester started his database administration career almost six years ago at a Fortune 500 company, where he rapidly progressed from DBAI, DBAII, and senior DBA to manager (working manager) of database support in four years. His role consisted of managing six SQL Server DBAs in an environment of 100+ SQL Server instances with 150+ application databases. In search of opportunities to increase his performance-monitoring and tuning skills, Sylvester took on a new role with the CRM company to help solve its major performance issues.

Sylvester possesses a bachelor's degree in computer science from Wofford College in South Carolina and a master's degree in applied computer science with a concentration in software development from Columbus State University, Georgia. Sylvester enjoys playing video games and spending time with his wife, Kimberly, and his American Staffordshire terrier.

About the Technical Reviewer

 **RODNEY LANDRUM** has been working with SQL Server technologies for longer than he can remember. (He turned 40 in May of 2009, so his memory is going.) He writes regularly about many SQL Server technologies, including Integration Services, Analysis Services, and Reporting Services. He has authored three books on Reporting Services and is working on a fourth book at present, expanding several popular articles on his DBA Script Thumb idea. He is a regular contributor to *SQL Server Magazine* online, SQLServerCentral.com, and Simple-Talk, the latter of which he sporadically blogs on about SQL and his plethora of geek tattoos. Rodney also speaks regularly on SQL topics at such events as SQL Saturday in Florida, his home state. His day job finds him overseeing the health and well-being of a large SQL Server infrastructure in Pensacola, Florida. He swears he owns the expression, "Working with databases on a day-to-day basis," and anyone who disagrees is itching to lose at an arm-wrestling match.

Acknowledgments

First of all, I would like to thank Jonathan Gennick for giving me an opportunity to write this book. He, along with everyone else at Apress, has been really supportive throughout this process. Beth Christmas did an awesome job keeping the project on track. She was even able to push me a little to get the book out sooner than I anticipated. It is unbelievable how Kim Benbow was able to catch all the little details to make sure the terminology remained consistent throughout the book. I would also like to thank the production editor, Laura Esterman, and everyone else at Apress who has worked on the book.

I want to thank Sylvester Carstarphen, the coauthor, for stepping in and helping me with the book. I didn't want to take on such a large topic by myself, and he improved the book in many areas by adding his expertise and experience to the mix. I also knew I could count on him to keep the book on schedule, even if it meant working a lot of late nights and sacrificing his weekends.

I was also lucky to have Rodney Landrum, a well-known author, MVP, and all-around smart guy, as a technical reviewer. I have known Rodney for about ten years now, and he was the first one on my list when Jonathan asked me if I had anyone in mind for a technical editor. He has done a great job making sure the content is accurate throughout.

Ken Simmons

First and foremost, I have to thank Ken for asking me to work with him on this book. It is an opportunity of a lifetime and I would still be waiting on such an opportunity if it wasn't for him. Ken, I owe you one—a big one.

I would also like to thank all of the DBAs I have worked with over the years. I have learned a lot from each of you. Specifically, I would like to thank Steven Cush for introducing me to SQL Server and sharing his DBA knowledge and skills. And thank you to the DBAs I'm currently working with, Jan, JD, and Michelle, for always listening to my ideas about chapter content and providing good feedback.

Lastly, I have to thank my family and friends for always supporting me in everything that I do.

Sylvester Carstarphen

Introduction

SQL Server administration is an extensive subject that covers everything from the critical decisions you need to make before installing SQL Server to managing and tuning queries running on existing systems. Even though complete books can and have been dedicated to many of the topics covered throughout this book, we think that it is important for database administrators to have a "go-to" guide when they need to make those important administrative decisions. With that in mind, we set out to write a book that database administrators could keep on their desks to assist them in the planning phases of database administration and help them through its troubleshooting aspects, as well as provide them with a source of reference on the many topics critical to database administration. Our goal is to ensure that, after reading this book, you will be prepared to face the challenges that database administrators encounter on a daily basis.

Who Should Read This Book

This book is for junior and seasoned database administrators who are looking to develop their knowledge and skill set in Microsoft SQL Server 2008. This book is highly focused on database administration and the new techniques introduced in SQL Server 2008.

How the Book Is Structured

We have put a lot of thought into the organization of this book. We want to ensure the chapters are presented in the order that database administrators encounter critical choices, giving you the comprehension and proficiency needed to make tactical decisions. Instead of just writing about new features and how to use them, we dive into the details about when and why to use these new features and how they impact the database administrator. This book also focuses on database administration to allow the content to be thoroughly covered.

Downloading the Code

You can download the source code for the book at the Apress web site's Source Code page located at www.apress.com/book/sourcecode. The code is broken into .sql files by chapter.

You can download the sample databases used in this book from the CodePlex web site at www.codeplex.com/MSFTDBProdSamples. You will want to download the SQL Server 2008 product sample databases and follow the installation instructions.

Contacting the Authors

You can contact Ken Simmons by emailing him at cyberjunkyks@yahoo.com, or you can visit his blog at http://cybersql.blogspot.com. You can contact Sylvester Carstarphen by emailing him at sqllazywriter@gmail.com or visiting his blog at http://sqllazywriter.blogspot.com. There will be a tag on both blogs (called Pro SQL Server 2008 Administration) that you can use to filter posts directly related to the book. Please include the book title in any emails to help us identify questions or comments about the book.

Introducing Microsoft
SQL Server 2008

CHAPTER 1

■ ■ ■

New Feature Overview

The release of Microsoft SQL Server 2008 has introduced many new features that increase scalability, manageability, availability, programmability, and security across the enterprise. With many organizations focused on consolidation and virtualization, this couldn't have come at a better time. As the demand for data keeps growing and security and compliance keep tightening, the role of the database administrator (DBA) has become an increasingly critical part of the organization. It is important for every DBA to have a good understanding of the tools available to help maintain a highly available, secure environment.

This book will cover the techniques you need to understand in order to implement and manage a successful database environment. After a brief overview of some of the enhancements, you will learn how to make intelligent decisions when choosing an installation or upgrade path. You will also learn how to manage a secure and consistent database environment by implementing policies across the organization. By learning how to automate tedious administrative tasks, you will be able to focus on more important tasks, like performance tuning, which will also be covered in detail. Finally, we will be looking to see what the future holds for database administration along with giving you the resources necessary to excel as a DBA.

This chapter will present an overview of several new features available in SQL Server 2008. Although the main focus of the book is database administration, having a basic understanding of many of the new features available in SQL Server is essential to effectively managing a successful database environment. That being said, some topics are introduced here only to give you an awareness of their existence, while others have an enormous impact on database administration and will be covered in great detail throughout the book.

Figure 1-1 shows the same expanded view of the Management Studio Object Explorer in SQL Server 2005 (left) and SQL Server 2008 (right). Even at a quick glance, you can see there are several new features available in SQL Server 2008. You should also note that there are a couple of features in the SQL Server 2005 Object Explorer that are no longer in SQL Server 2008, such as the Activity Monitor and the Full-Text Search service. The functionality has not been removed; it has just been relocated. To start the Activity Monitor, you now have to right-click on the SQL Server instance and select it from the context menu. The Full-Text Search service is now fully managed using the SQL Server Configuration Manager.

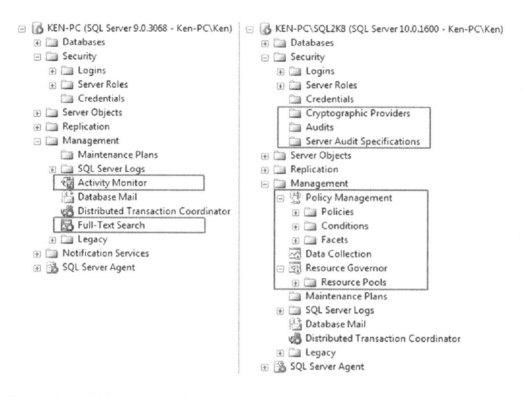

Figure 1-1. *Available features in the Management Studio Object Explorer when using SQL Server 2008 (right) compared to SQL Server 2005 (left)*

Scalability Enhancements

Scalability seems to be a word we keep hearing more and more these days. Companies want to get the most they can out of their hardware, and query performance plays a major role. The more efficiently SQL Server can execute a query, the more queries it can execute against the given hardware. Scalability enhancements can be categorized into three key areas: filtered indexes and statistics, table and query hints, and query performance and processing.

Filtered Indexes and Statistics

Filtered indexes are non-clustered indexes that can be created on a defined subset of rows within a table. If you've ever wanted to index only some of the rows in a table, now you can. For example, if you have a field that stores a wide variety of dates, and your application only queries dates after 1975, you can create an index that includes only those dates. Creating a filtered index will reduce the disk space required to store the index, as well as the time it takes to rebuild the index.

Filtered statistics are automatically created for filtered indexes, but you can also create filtered statistics independently in order to optimize a query plan on a subset of rows. The ability to create filtered indexes and statistics ultimately leads to more efficient queries in addition to reduced index maintenance and storage overhead.

Table and Query Hints

A few improvements have been made in SQL Server 2008 to enhance common table and query hints. The OPTIMIZE FOR query hint has been enhanced by adding the UNKNOWN option. When you use the OPTIMIZE FOR query hint by itself, the query optimizer optimizes a query based on the initial value assigned to a local variable. When you supply the UNKNOWN option, you instruct the query optimizer to use statistical data to determine the value for a local variable instead of using the initial value during the optimization phase.

The capability to use table hints as query hints has also been added in SQL Server 2008. The new FORCESEEK table hint has also been added, which allows you to force an index seek on a table in the execution plan. The FORCESEEK table hint is useful when a query plan may be using an index scan to access the data, causing an excessive number of reads.

Query Performance and Processing

Several enhancements have been made in SQL Server 2008 to improve query performance and processing. You can use some of the enhancements to find and tune process-intensive queries, while the others provide an automatic benefit courtesy of the query optimizer.

The LOCK_ESCALATION option has been added to the ALTER TABLE statement to allow you to disable lock escalation on the table. Disabling lock escalation can greatly reduce lock contention on partitioned tables, as it will allow you to configure locks to escalate to the partitions instead of to the whole table.

You can use Dynamic Management Views (DMVs) to return hash values for similar queries. Finding similar hash values will allow you to locate and tune similar queries by comparing execution plans.

Plan guides can now accept XML Showplan output as a parameter, which simplifies the process of applying a fixed query plan. A few new system functions and counters have been added for plan guides as well.

Parallel query processing has been improved to provide an automatic benefit when querying partitioned tables and objects.

Optimized bitmap filtering automatically improves data warehouse queries by removing non-qualifying rows early in a query plan.

Manageability Enhancements

There have been some nice features added in SQL Server 2008 to enhance your management capabilities. You can use many of the new features, such as SQL Server Audit and the Data Collector, to provide you with more insight into your servers. In addition, you can use features, such as Policy-Based Management and the Resource Governor, to attain greatly needed granular control over your environment.

Auditing

SQL Server Audit is a new feature that captures data for a specific group of server or database actions. Audits can be defined using event actions or by using action groups, which is a predefined group of actions. SQL Server Audit uses extended events to capture data, such as CPU utilization and deadlocks. The extended events method is used by the server to capture generic events. In certain situations, you can use extended events to correlate events between SQL Server, the application, and the operating system (OS). You can save the event results to a target destination, such as a text file, Windows security log, or Windows application log.

Change Data Capture

Change Data Capture is a feature that can be used to capture insert, update, and delete statements applied to a table. The data being inserted, updated, or deleted is captured in a format that mirrors the original table along with metadata explaining the action. Change Data Capture is useful when managing a data warehouse environment. For example, you can enable Change Data Capture on a large table that is used to feed a reporting server. The changes to the large table will then be captured in a separate table, and instead of processing an entire dataset every time you want to update the reporting server, you only have to process the data in the table that is tracking the changes.

Change Tracking

Change Tracking allows you to capture information about row changes in a table. Unlike Change Data Capture, Change Tracking does not capture the data that was changed. Change Tracking does, however, capture the Data Manipulation Language (DML) information about the change along with columns that were affected. The primary key is the only data element that is captured as a result of Change Tracking. Change Tracking has to be enabled at the database level and can then be enabled on specified tables. Enabling Change Tracking has no impact to the table definition, and no triggers are created on the table being tracked. Change Tracking functions are used in order to retrieve the information about the changes and can be incorporated into standard Transact-SQL (T-SQL) statements.

Backup Compression

Backup compression is a long awaited feature that is now available in SQL Server 2008 right out of the box. Although you need Enterprise Edition to create a compressed backup, you can restore a compressed backup in any edition of SQL Server 2008.

Backing up a database using backup compression takes significantly less time because fewer pages have to be written to disk. While this sounds good, the trade-off is higher CPU usage while the backup is being compressed. However, you can regulate CPU usage by using the Resource Governor to run the backup in a low-priority session.

The percentage of disk space saved by using backup compression depends on the type of data being compressed. Dividing the `backup_size` and `compressed_backup_size` columns in the `backupset` table in the `msdb` database will allow you to calculate the percentage of disk space savings. Since encrypted data usually doesn't have high compression ratios, using backup compression with Transparent Data Encryption will likely be ineffective and not worth the CPU hit.

Data Collector

The Data Collector is a component in SQL Server 2008 that allows you to collect data across database servers and store the information in a central location known as the *management data warehouse.* The management data warehouse is a relational set of tables that can be used to store data collected from a variety of sources. The type and frequency of the data collection is completely configurable and can be viewed using a collection set report in SQL Server Management Studio. Data sources must be configured for data collection, and data can come from various places, such as DMVs, performance monitor (PerfMon) counters, and SQL traces. The Data Collector comes with three system collection sets: disk usage, server activity, and query statistics. Although you can configure custom collection sets as well, the need for this will be rare due to the extensive amount of metrics that can be gathered using the predefined system collection sets.

Central Management Servers

You can create a central management server in SQL Server 2008 in order to maintain a collection or grouping of servers, much like registered servers in previous versions. Unlike registered servers, the server you designate as a central management server stores all of the information about the participating servers in the msdb database. Since the information is stored in the msdb database, you can share the collection of servers contained in the central management server among all the DBAs in the organization. When you register a server using a central management server, you must use Windows authentication (username and passwords are not allowed).

One of the major benefits you gain when using a central management server is the ability to execute a single query against all of the registered servers in a server group. You can configure the result set to include each server name along with the login name that executed the query. You can also configure the query results to be returned as multiple independent result sets or merged and returned as a single result set. Using a central management server also provides you with the capability to create and evaluate policies across a server group, which is essential when using Policy-Based Management to administer your environment.

Policy-Based Management

You can now use SQL Server Management Studio to create policies to manage objects in SQL Server. A policy consists of two parts: a check condition and a filter condition. The *check condition* is the condition the policy is actually validating, and the *filter condition* specifies the target object for the policy.

Administrators can either force target objects to comply with a given policy and rollback the changes, or allow the policy to be violated and review the violations later. You can create custom policies or import one of the predefined policies provided by Microsoft that corresponds with Best Practice Analyzer rules and default settings in the Surface Area Configuration tool. For example, you can import a predefined policy that will allow you to check the data and log file location, the database AutoShrink configuration, and even the last successful backup date.

Resource Governor

Resource Governor is a new feature that can be used to limit the amount of CPU and memory used by predefined requests to the database. Min and Max settings can be used to limit the resources in a resource pool. The interesting thing about the Resource Governor is that if no CPU or memory pressure is detected by the server, the Max threshold will be ignored. As soon as another query comes along with a higher priority, the Resource Governor will throttle lower priority work down to the Max settings, as needed, to relieve pressure. It is a good idea to always leave the Min settings at zero because the Resource Governor will reserve the minimum amount of defined CPU and memory even if it is not needed.

PowerShell

PowerShell is a powerful scripting tool that allows database administrators to write more robust scripts when T-SQL may not be a viable solution. PowerShell is now integrated into SQL Server 2008 and can even be executed in a job step using SQL Server Agent. Select Power-Shell as the step type and insert the script, just as you would with T-SQL or an ActiveX script. There is an extensive script library located at http://powershell.com/ that includes several SQL Server scripts along with many other system-related scripts that can help you manage your environment.

Availability Enhancements

Availability is becoming more of a concern with many organizations wanting to achieve four and five nines. Since achieving four nines allows for less than one hour of downtime per year and achieving five nines allows for less than six minutes per year, living up to this type of expectation is not an easy task. There have been improvements in many areas, including database mirroring, clustering, and peer-to-peer replication to help achieve this goal. Some enhancements in SQL Server 2008 even have a positive impact on availability, even though availability is not their primary function. For example, while backup compression was primarily added to SQL Server to provide space savings and reduced backup times, it also reduces the time it takes to restore a database, which ultimately leads to less downtime if a disaster is encountered.

Database Mirroring

Database mirroring was introduced in SQL Server 2005 to provide highly available redundant databases. Database mirroring has been given performance enhancements in SQL Server 2008, through it can now automatically recover from corrupted pages.

Automatic recovery from a corrupted page consists of one mirroring partner requesting the unreadable page from the other. If a query is executed that contains data that resides on a corrupted page, an error will be raised and a new page will be copied from the mirror to replace the corrupted page. In most cases, by the time the query is executed again, the page will have been restored from the mirror, and the query will execute successfully.

One of the most prominent performance enhancements is stream compression between the principal and the mirror server to minimize network bandwidth. This feature will add more value to networks having latency issues by reducing the amount of traffic that is being sent between servers. If you have a high-speed network with plenty of bandwidth, the effects of stream compression may hardly be noticeable at all. Your server may experience higher CPU utilization as a result of stream compression because it takes more cycles to compress and decompress the files. Also, the server will be processing more transactions per second, requiring more CPU cycles.

Log send buffers are used more efficiently by appending log records of the next log-flush operation to the most recently used log cache if it contains sufficient free space. Write-ahead events have been enhanced by asynchronously processing incoming log records and log records that have already been written to disk. In a failover, read-ahead during the undo phase is enhanced by the mirror server sending read-ahead hints to the principal to indicate the pages that will be requested so the principal server can put it in the copy buffer.

Clustering

The SQL Server clustering installation process has changed from SQL Server 2005 where you only ran the install on one node and the binaries were pushed to the other node. In SQL Server 2008, you install a one-node cluster and then run the install on the other nodes, adding them one by one. Any time you want to add or remove a node, the setup is run from the node that is being added or removed, thus reducing the need for downtime. This approach also allows for rolling upgrades, service packs, and patches.

Several changes have been made in Windows Server 2008 to enhance failover clustering. While these are not necessarily SQL Server changes, SQL Server does reap the benefits. The new Windows Server 2008 Cluster Validation tool allows you to run through validation tests on your cluster configuration to ensure the cluster is configured correctly without having to search the hardware compatibility list (HCL) to ensure the server configuration will be supported. Windows Server 2008 also supports up to 16 node clusters, enabling SQL Server 2008 to take full advantage of this architecture.

■**Caution** While Windows Server 2008 no longer requires clustered nodes to be on the same subnet, this feature is not currently supported in SQL Server 2008.

Peer-to-Peer Replication

The concept of peer-to-peer replication was introduced in SQL Server 2005 so that multiple servers could act as both a publisher and subscriber while maintaining a full, usable dataset. In SQL Server 2008, you now have the ability to add and remove nodes without impacting the application. The capability to detect conflicts prevents issues such as application inconsistency that may have otherwise been overlooked. The Topology Wizard allows for visual configuration, while improved replication monitoring eases replication management.

Hot-Add CPU

It is now possible to hot-add CPUs to SQL Servers that reside on compatible hardware. This is a critical addition to the ability to hot-add memory, introduced in SQL Server 2005. Combining both of these features increases the ability to perform hardware changes without impacting the application or more importantly the end user. This also supports a pay-as-you-grow scenario, allowing you to add hardware resources as they become necessary. This provides flexibility when capacity planning and budgeting, allowing minimal hardware to be deployed in order to meet the needs of the current workload instead of purchasing and deploying additional hardware up front on a system that may or may not need the extra resources.

Programmability Enhancements

Several programming enhancements have been added to SQL Server 2008. New data types allow for a more granular and precise storage, including date, time, and spatial data. The addition of the *user-defined table* type is a key new feature that enables passing entire tables to procedures and functions by implementing another new feature, known as *table-valued functions*. Full-Text Search has undergone an architecture overhaul, enabling it to be a fully integrated database feature.

Some manageability improvements also apply to programming. Unstructured data, such as images and documents, are now supported by using FILESTREAM to store the data on the file system. Partition switching is another useful feature that allows you to quickly switch your partition from one table to another while maintaining data integrity.

A couple of new features allow you to take advantage of space savings. Rarely used columns can be defined as *sparse columns* and will not use any space to store NULL data in the data pages or the indexes. Compressed storage of tables and indexes allows both row and page compression for tables and indexes. Several T-SQL enhancements have been made as well. The INSERT statement has been enhanced with a new feature called *row constructors* that allows you to specify multiple INSERT sets in the VALUES clause. The new MERGE statement allows you to perform an INSERT, UPDATE, or DELETE in a single statement based on the results of a JOIN. GROUPING SETS is a new operator that allows you to generate the union of multiple, pre-aggregated result sets. Let's not forget about variables; they can now be declared and set in the same operation while the use of compound operators make for simplified code logic.

■**Note** The primary focus of this book is on administration, and we will not be going into great detail with T-SQL. Thus we will demonstrate a few of the concepts previously listed, as the new syntax may be used in code samples throughout the book.

Variables

When it comes to working with variables, a few enhancements have been made that align variable usage in SQL Server with other programming languages, such as VB.Net and C#. You can now declare and initialize your variables in a single line of code. You can also take advantage of compound operators when using variables in mathematical operations. Both of these new variable enhancements result in shorter, cleaner, and altogether more elegant code.

- *Variable initialization*: The following sample allows you to declare and set your variables with a single line of code (Declare @x int = 1).

- *Compound operators*: Compound operators allow you to perform mathematical operations on a variable without having to reference the variable twice. Table 1-1 shows a sample of how you would use the new compound operator syntax along with the equivalent syntax prior to SQL Server 2008.

Table 1-1. *Compound Operator Syntax Comparison*

Compound Operator	SQL Server 2005
Set @x+=1	Set @x = @x + 1
Set @x-=1	Set @x = @x - 1
Set @x*=2	Set @x = @x * 2

Putting it all together, Table 1-2 shows a simple code sample that performs a loop, increments a variable, and prints the output. The table shows the code sample for both SQL Server 2005 and SQL Server 2008. The SQL Server 2008 version is very similar to the code you would see in VB.Net.

Table 1-2. *Variable Enhancement Code Comparison*

SQL Server 2008	SQL Server 2005
Declare @x int = 1	Declare @x int
	Set @x = 1
While @x <= 10	While @x <= 10
Begin	Begin
Print @x	Print @x
Set @x+=1	Set @x = @x + 1
End	End

Transact-SQL Row Constructors

Row constructors provide a syntax enhancement to the INSERT statement, allowing multiple value lists to be supplied, provided each value list is separated from the previous one by a comma. Listing 1-1 demonstrates a code sample that uses three different methods to insert three records into the @DateRecords table variable. The reason we say that row constructors are a *syntax* enhancement is that, while you will get better performance using row constructors over multiple INSERT statements, the row constructor sample in Listing 1-1 will produce exactly the same execution plan as the UNION ALL method. Thus the enhancement is one of syntax more than of performance.

Listing 1-1. *Row Constructors Compared to Prior Methods of Inserting Multiple Rows*

```
DECLARE @DateRecords TABLE (RecordID int, StartDate Datetime)

--Multiple inserts using UNION ALL
INSERT INTO @DateRecords
SELECT 1,'1/1/2008'
UNION ALL
SELECT 2,'1/2/2008'
UNION ALL
SELECT 3,'1/3/2008'

--Multiple inserts using single statements
INSERT INTO @DateRecords VALUES(4,'1/4/2008')
INSERT INTO @DateRecords VALUES(5,'1/5/2008')
INSERT INTO @DateRecords VALUES(6,'1/6/2008')

--Multiple inserts using row constructors
INSERT INTO @DateRecords
VALUES(7,'1/7/2008'),
      (8,'1/8/2008'),
      (9,'1/9/2008')

--Display INSERT results
SELECT * FROM @DateRecords
```

Table-Valued Parameters

Table-valued parameters are exposed through the new user-defined table type in SQL Server 2008. Table-valued parameters provide an easy way to pass an entire dataset or table to functions and procedures. This prevents you from having to loop through a dataset calling a stored procedure multiple times for each row in the dataset.

Following are some of the benefits from using table-valued parameters:

- Does not acquire locks for the initial population of data from a client
- Reduces round trips to the server
- Supports unique constraints and primary keys
- Strongly typed

Alas, most good things come with a price. When you use table-valued parameters, keep the following restrictions in mind:

- SQL Server does not maintain statistics on columns of table-valued parameters
- Parameters are passed to the routines as READONLY values
- Cannot be the target of a SELECT INTO or INSERT EXEC statement

Listing 1-2 provides an example of all the steps needed to create and execute a table-valued function. First, we do some cleanup work just in case we run the script multiple times, but the real work begins in the second section of the script where we create the user-defined table type CustomerPreferenceTableType. Once we have the user-defined table type, we create the CustomerPreferences_Insert stored procedure, which accepts a parameter that we defined using the CustomerPreferencesTableType data type. Next, we create a variable that uses the CustomerPreferencesTableType data type, load some sample data to the variable, and then execute the CustomerPreferences_Insert stored procedure passing the variable we just created. Finally, we query the CustomerPreferences table to show that multiple records were actually inserted into the table with only a single call to the insert stored procedure.

Listing 1-2. *Sample Script Demonstrating the Use of Table-Valued Parameters*

```
USE tempdb

--1. Prep work
--Drop objects
IF OBJECT_ID('CustomerPreferences') IS NOT NULL
  DROP TABLE CustomerPreferences;
GO

IF OBJECT_ID('CustomerPreferences_Insert') IS NOT NULL
  DROP PROCEDURE CustomerPreferences_Insert;
GO

IF  EXISTS (SELECT * FROM sys.types st
               JOIN sys.schemas ss
                ON st.schema_id = ss.schema_id
            WHERE st.name = N'CustomerPreferenceTableType'
              AND ss.name = N'dbo')
  DROP TYPE [dbo].[CustomerPreferenceTableType]
GO

--Create table to hold results from procedure
CREATE TABLE CustomerPreferences
(CustomerID INT, PreferenceID INT)

GO

--2. Create table type
CREATE TYPE CustomerPreferenceTableType AS TABLE
( CustomerID INT,
  PreferenceID INT );
GO

--3. Create procedure
CREATE PROCEDURE CustomerPreferences_Insert
 @CustomerPrefs CustomerPreferenceTableType READONLY
```

```
AS
SET NOCOUNT ON

INSERT INTO CustomerPreferences
SELECT *
FROM  @CustomerPrefs;

 GO

--4. Execute procedure

--Table variable
DECLARE @CustomerPreference
AS CustomerPreferenceTableType;

--Insert data into the table variable
INSERT INTO @CustomerPreference
    Values (1,1),(1,2),(1,3);

--Pass the table variable data to a stored procedure
EXEC CustomerPreferences_Insert @CustomerPreference;

--View the results inserted using the table-valued function
SELECT * FROM CustomerPreferences
```

MERGE Statement

You can use the MERGE statement to perform INSERT, UPDATE, or DELETE actions in a single state-ment based on the results of a TABLE JOIN. This functionality is very useful when writing stored procedures that insert records into a table if they do not exist, and update records if they do exist. You can use the optional OUTPUT clause to return information about which operation actually occurred.

■**Note** The MERGE statement must be terminated with a semicolon, or you will receive an error message during execution.

Listing 1-3 shows three executions of a MERGE statement. Execute the listing on your own system, and take some time to understand the results. It may help to execute each MERGE state-ment individually so that you can see the effect of each. You can view the results in Figure 1-2.

Listing 1-3. *Three Different Uses of the MERGE Statement*

```
--Prep work
DECLARE @DateRecords TABLE (RecordID int, StartDate Datetime)

INSERT INTO @DateRecords VALUES(1,'1/1/2008'),
                               (2,'1/2/2008'),
                               (3,'1/4/2008'),
                               (5,'1/5/2008')

 --Display original dataset
SELECT * FROM @DateRecords ORDER BY RecordID

--Sample UPDATE WHEN MATCHED
MERGE @DateRecords AS Target
 USING (Select '1/4/2008') as Source (StartDate)
 ON (Target.StartDate = Source.StartDate)
 WHEN MATCHED THEN
   UPDATE SET StartDate = '1/3/2008'
 WHEN NOT MATCHED THEN
   INSERT (RecordID, StartDate)
     VALUES (4,'1/4/2008')
     OUTPUT deleted.*, $action, inserted.*;

--Display changed result set
SELECT * FROM @DateRecords ORDER BY RecordID

--Sample INSERT WHEN NOT MATCHED
MERGE @DateRecords AS target
 USING (Select '1/4/2008') as Source (StartDate)
 ON (target.StartDate = Source.StartDate)
 WHEN MATCHED THEN
   DELETE
 WHEN NOT MATCHED THEN
   INSERT (RecordID, StartDate)
     VALUES (4,'1/4/2008')
     OUTPUT deleted.*, $action, inserted.*;

--Display changed result set
SELECT * FROM @DateRecords ORDER BY RecordID

--Running the same query again will result
--in a Delete now that the record exists.
MERGE @DateRecords AS target
 USING (Select '1/4/2008') as Source (StartDate)
 ON (target.StartDate = Source.StartDate)
 WHEN MATCHED THEN
   DELETE
```

```
WHEN NOT MATCHED THEN
   INSERT (RecordID, StartDate)
     VALUES (4,'1/4/2008')
     OUTPUT deleted.*, $action, inserted.*;

--Display changed result set
SELECT * FROM @DateRecords ORDER BY RecordID
```

The first record set in Figure 1-2 shows the original result set we will be working with prior to using any MERGE statements. The second record set shows the actions that took place as a result of the first MERGE statement in the script and is returned by adding the OUTPUT clause to the MERGE statement. As you can see, since a match was found between the target and the source, RecordID 3 was updated from 1/4/2008 to 1/3/2008. If no match was found between the target and the source, 1/4/2008 would have been inserted into the target. You can see that this is exactly what occurred by viewing the new query results displayed in the third record set. You can apply the same logic to the remaining record sets to follow the chain of events that occur throughout the script in Listing 1-3.

	RecordID	StartDate			
1	1	2008-01-01 00:00:00.000			
2	2	2008-01-02 00:00:00.000			
3	3	2008-01-04 00:00:00.000			
4	5	2008-01-05 00:00:00.000			

	RecordID	StartDate	$action	RecordID	StartDate
1	3	2008-01-04 00:00:00.000	UPDATE	3	2008-01-03 00:00:00.000

	RecordID	StartDate
1	1	2008-01-01 00:00:00.000
2	2	2008-01-02 00:00:00.000
3	3	2008-01-03 00:00:00.000
4	5	2008-01-05 00:00:00.000

	RecordID	StartD...	$action	RecordID	StartDate
1	NULL	NULL	INSERT	4	2008-01-04 00:00:00.000

	RecordID	StartDate
1	1	2008-01-01 00:00:00.000
2	2	2008-01-02 00:00:00.000
3	3	2008-01-03 00:00:00.000
4	4	2008-01-04 00:00:00.000
5	5	2008-01-05 00:00:00.000

	RecordID	StartDate	$action	RecordID	StartDate
1	4	2008-01-04 00:00:00.000	DELETE	NULL	NULL

	RecordID	StartDate
1	1	2008-01-01 00:00:00.000
2	2	2008-01-02 00:00:00.000
3	3	2008-01-03 00:00:00.000
4	5	2008-01-05 00:00:00.000

Figure 1-2. *Results returned using the script in Listing 1-3*

GROUPING SETS Operator

The script we will be reviewing in Listing 1-4 covers the new GROUPING SETS operator. This new operator allows you to group aggregated result sets that would normally be accomplished by combining the results of two GROUP BY statements using UNION ALL. As you can see in Listing 1-4, the code is much cleaner using GROUPING SETS rather than using the alternative UNION ALL syntax. You can view the results of Listing 1-4 in Figure 1-3. We have only included the result sets returned using GROUPING SETS, since the UNION ALL queries would only produce duplicate results.

Listing 1-4. *Script Demonstrating the New GROUPING SETS Operator*

```
DECLARE @DateRecords TABLE (RecordID int, StartDate Datetime)

INSERT INTO @DateRecords
VALUES(1,'1/1/2008'),
      (2,'1/2/2008'),
      (3,'1/4/2008'),
      (4,'1/4/2008')


--GROUP BY using GROUPING SETS
SELECT RecordID, StartDate
FROM @DateRecords
GROUP BY  GROUPING SETS (RecordID, StartDate)

--Equivalent to the previous query
SELECT NULL AS RecordID, StartDate
FROM @DateRecords
GROUP BY StartDate
UNION ALL
SELECT RecordID, NULL AS StartDate
FROM @DateRecords
GROUP BY  RecordID, StartDate

--Include all records by using MAX
SELECT MAX(RecordID) MaxRecordID, MAX(StartDate) MaxStartDate
FROM @DateRecords
GROUP BY  GROUPING SETS (RecordID,StartDate)

--Equivalent to the previous query
SELECT MAX(RecordID) MaxRecordID, StartDate
FROM @DateRecords
GROUP BY StartDate
UNION ALL
SELECT RecordID, MAX(StartDate)
FROM @DateRecords
GROUP BY  RecordID, StartDate
```

Figure 1-3. *Results returned using the new GROUPING SETS operator in Listing 1-4*

Listing 1-5 provides the new `ROLLUP` and `CUBE` syntax introduced in SQL Server 2008. You should make sure to use the new syntax whenever writing new code and change any existing code whenever possible because the old syntax has been deprecated and will be removed in a future release. There is also a new `GROUPING_ID` function you can use to return more information about the grouping level than you can get with the existing `GROUPING` function. The results of Listing 1-5 can be seen in Figure 1-4.

Listing 1-5. *New Syntax Used with ROLLUP, CUBE, and GROUPING_ID*

```
DECLARE @DateRecords TABLE (RecordID int, StartDate Datetime)

INSERT INTO @DateRecords
VALUES(1,'1/1/2008'),
      (2,'1/2/2008'),
      (3,'1/4/2008'),
      (4,'1/4/2008')

--Old ROLLUP deprecated syntax
SELECT MAX(RecordID) MaxRecordID, StartDate
FROM @DateRecords
GROUP BY  StartDate WITH ROLLUP
```

```
--New Syntax
SELECT MAX(RecordID) MaxRecordID, StartDate
FROM @DateRecords
GROUP BY ROLLUP(StartDate)

--New GROUPING_ID function
SELECT RecordID, StartDate, GROUPING_ID(RecordID,StartDate) GroupingID
FROM @DateRecords
GROUP BY CUBE(RecordID, StartDate)
ORDER BY GROUPING_ID(RecordID,StartDate)
```

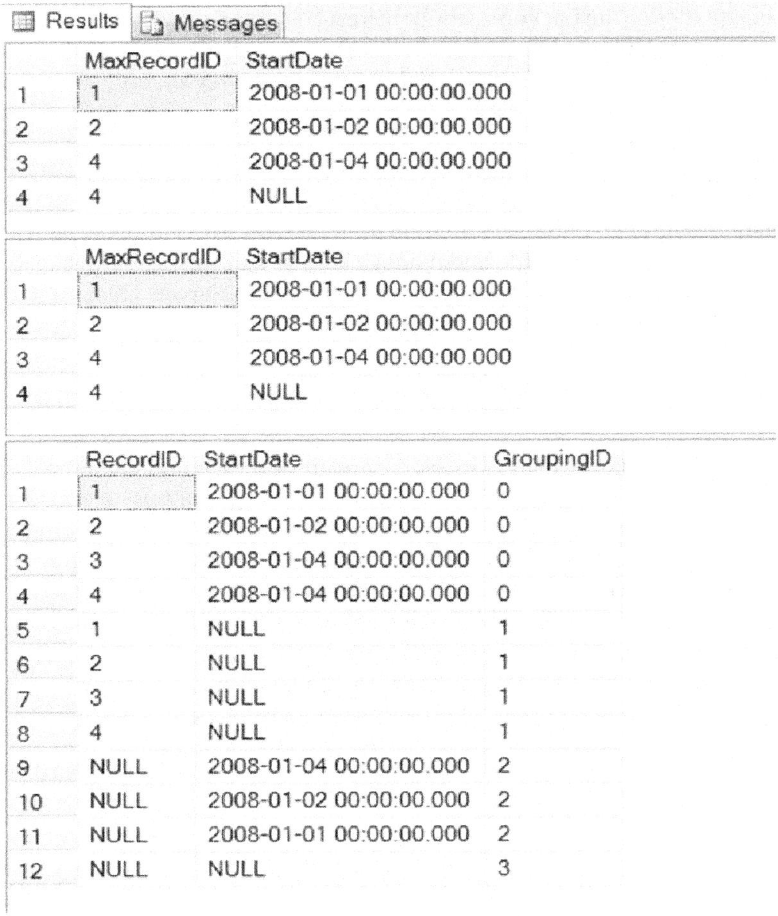

▦ Results | ▣ Messages

	MaxRecordID	StartDate
1	1	2008-01-01 00:00:00.000
2	2	2008-01-02 00:00:00.000
3	4	2008-01-04 00:00:00.000
4	4	NULL

	MaxRecordID	StartDate
1	1	2008-01-01 00:00:00.000
2	2	2008-01-02 00:00:00.000
3	4	2008-01-04 00:00:00.000
4	4	NULL

	RecordID	StartDate	GroupingID
1	1	2008-01-01 00:00:00.000	0
2	2	2008-01-02 00:00:00.000	0
3	3	2008-01-04 00:00:00.000	0
4	4	2008-01-04 00:00:00.000	0
5	1	NULL	1
6	2	NULL	1
7	3	NULL	1
8	4	NULL	1
9	NULL	2008-01-04 00:00:00.000	2
10	NULL	2008-01-02 00:00:00.000	2
11	NULL	2008-01-01 00:00:00.000	2
12	NULL	NULL	3

Figure 1-4. *Query results returned by Listing 1-5*

Security Enhancements

Microsoft has made some key additions to security management by introducing the new Transparent Data Encryption and Extensible Key Management technologies. These new features along with the auditing enhancements are an integral part of meeting the growing compliance needs of the organization.

Transparent Data Encryption

Transparent Data Encryption enables the database administrator to store the data, log, and backup files in a secure manner by automatically encrypting and decrypting the data as it is read from and written to the disk. The database uses a database encryption key, and without the correct certificate, the data files or the backups cannot be restored to another server. This process is implemented at the data layer and is transparent to front-end applications. This does not mean that the data is encrypted between the application and the server, only the pages containing the data on the server.

Extensible Key Management

Extensible Key Management provides an enhanced method for managing encryption keys. It enables third-party software vendors to provide and manage keys by supporting hardware security module (HSM) products that can be registered and used with SQL Server. This provides many advantages, including the physical separation of data and keys.

Summary

As you can see, SQL Server 2008 is a feature-heavy release. There are several enhancements that not only make database administration easier, but that would be almost impossible to implement in earlier releases without purchasing third-party tools. Many of the features presented in this chapter require the Enterprise Edition of SQL Server 2008 in order to take full advantage of their functionality. A breakdown of features by edition will be provided in the next chapter, where we will be going over decisions that need to be made before a SQL Server install. Many of these new features will change the way DBAs manage data by removing limitations and providing the more industrial level tools needed to meet today's business needs. It's perfectly acceptable to drive a nail with a hammer, but we sure would rather use a nail gun to build a house.

CHAPTER 2

▪▪▪

Pre-Installation Considerations

Unfortunately, in most production environments, you do not have enough time to preplan the installation of SQL Server. In addition to ensuring your current production environment performs as expected, you provide server specifications for new systems. This requires a lot of research to determine things such as how much RAM the server will need; what type and how powerful the CPUs should be; and the layout, size, and RAID (redundant array of independent disks) levels of your storage system, along with many other considerations. In addition to providing server specs, you also have to manage the implementation of processes and procedures after the installation is complete. If there is a lack of preparation and research time, you sometimes make the wrong assumptions or decisions when providing your recommendations. Although bypassing some research up front will save time initially, there may be an extreme cost to you and the company by not taking the time to preplan properly. For the next two chapters, we are going to talk about some of the things that you definitely want to consider before installing SQL Server 2008.

Choosing a SQL Server Edition

Microsoft SQL Server provides multiple editions to help organizations with different performance and price requirements to accomplish their goals. Table 2-1 gives a brief summary of these editions, which we will then talk about in more detail.

Based on the requirements received (that is, making a big assumption that you will actually receive good requirements), you can determine which edition of SQL Server enables you to fulfill those requirements. The editions range from the fully loaded SQL Server Enterprise Edition with all the bells and whistles to the stripped-down Express Editions that lack a large number of features. However, each edition provides applications with the features needed to have SQL Server as a backend. As always, the fully loaded option costs more than the stripped-down alternative; so instead of always going with the best edition on the market, do a little research and choose the edition needed to complete the requirements for the application. (The Developer Edition is not listed in Table 2-1 because it contains the same features as Enterprise Edition.)

Table 2-1. *SQL Server Edition Feature Comparison*

Feature	Enterprise	Standard	Workgroup	Web	Express
Resource Governor	√	x	x	x	x
Filtered indexes and statistics	√	x	x	x	x
Spatial support	√	√	√	√	√
FILESTREAM support	√	√	√	√	√
Change Data Capture and Change Tracking	√	x	x	x	x
Policy-Based Management	√	√	√	√	√
Performance data collection	√	√	√	√	x
Enhanced date and time support	√	√	√	√	√
Sparse column support	√	x	x	x	x
Data/backup compression	√	x	x	x	x
Enhanced SQL Server Audit	√	x	x	x	x
Transparent data encryption	√	x	x	x	x

Enterprise Edition

Enterprise Edition is the fully loaded, production-licensed edition of SQL Server. This edition provides the performance, scalability, security, and availability needed to perform as the data layer for enterprise-wide applications. Enterprise Edition runs on servers with x86 (or 32-bit systems), x64 (or 64-bit systems), and IA64 (or Itanium 64-bit chip set systems). Enterprise Edition is used on applications where you identify the features of that edition as a necessity to meet the requirements or future requirements for SQL Server. Unfortunately, the costs of licenses are too expensive to justify the purchase of the edition if the organization will not be taking advantage of the features that it provides.

■**Note** Microsoft provides you with the option to purchase licenses per processor or per CAL for Enterprise Edition. CAL stands for client access license, which gives users access to services on a server. Microsoft's web site provides the cost of SQL Server 2008 licenses.

Please spend time narrowing down the application requirements and thoroughly evaluating the editions prior to recommending the purchase of an edition. The company that employs you will appreciate it.

All the features that Microsoft provides are generally available in the Enterprise Edition. The good and bad news for you, the database administrator, is that all features available in SQL Server 2008 will be at your disposal. What does that mean? It means that you will assume all the risk associated with implementing the new features in your production environment. While figuring out the effective use of new features like the Resource Governor, there may be some mishaps or problems that arise from issues or situations that you did not think through or simply did not think about. Remember to always test (even though you do not have real test environments to test in) and to always know when and how to use the new features instead of using them because they are there. (We will discuss when and how to use the new features throughout this book.).

Standard Edition

Standard Edition is another licensed production system without all the features of the Enterprise Edition, but it is built to provide ease of use and manageability. Standard Edition runs on servers with x86 (or 32-bit systems) and x64 (or 64-bit systems). Standard Edition is run in environments where you have determined that the features provided only in the Enterprise Edition are not needed to accomplish the current and future requirements of all applications running on the server. Let's be honest: Asking for or receiving detailed requirements from management, customers, or clients probably will not happen. (You will be lucky if you can make them out through the beer stains on the napkin.) Therefore, when it comes down to determining the version that meets the bare-bones requirements you receive, you may have to go back to the requirements provider to ensure all the documentation is accurate and complete. Try asking the requirements provider a series of questions in different ways to help you determine what the real requirements are for the application. That way you will feel comfortable supporting the application on the edition of SQL Server chosen. Standard Edition is significantly cheaper than Enterprise Edition so be wary of management wanting to install Standard Edition even though the application needs Enterprise Edition features.

■ **Note** Microsoft provides you with the option to purchase licenses per processor or per CAL for the Standard Edition.

Stand your ground and make the application owner or management sign off on the functionality that you will not be able to provide if they insist on purchasing the cheaper edition. That way, when the blame game starts and people start pointing fingers, you can pull out your documentation and utilize your get-out-of-jail-free card.

In the Standard Edition, Microsoft has included many of the features required to manage a production environment in small to midsized organizations, and maybe even larger organizations, depending on the requirements of the application.

Highlights of the Standard Edition include the following:

- High availability
  - Clustering
  - Mirroring
  - Log shipping
  - Replication

- Manageability features
  - Central management servers
  - Policy-Based Management
  - Standard performance reports
- Management tools
  - All management tools

Overall, the Standard Edition is not a bad choice when you do not have to utilize the greater number of features available in the Enterprise Edition. Remember, a "nice-to-have" is completely different than a feature that is absolutely necessary. The cost difference does not justify the purchase of the Enterprise Edition if the features are just nice-to-haves.

Note Standard Edition for Small Businesses includes all features and functionality of the Standard Edition, but contains licenses for a business environment with less than 75 computers.

Developer Edition

The Developer Edition contains all of the features of the Enterprise Edition, but it is licensed for nonproduction systems. The Developer Edition runs on servers with x86 (or 32-bit systems), x64 (or 64-bit systems), and IA64 (or Itanium 64-bit chip set systems). This edition is ideal for developers or administrators looking to install and test out SQL Server 2008.

Developer Edition offers a great introductory platform for validating your application's functionality with the new version of SQL Server 2008, along with providing a playground for trying out features. While doing this, make a detailed evaluation of the features that your production environment requires. If the organization is planning to purchase the Standard Edition, then experiment with the features of Enterprise Edition by using the Developer Edition. That will help you determine if the production environment needs the features that the Standard Edition does not support. Likewise, if the organization is purchasing Enterprise Edition, then use the Developer Edition to evaluate what supporting your production environment would be like without all the features available in the Enterprise Edition.

For example, Enterprise Edition is required to take advantage of backup compression, a wonderful enhancement added by Microsoft. However, if the largest database supported by an instance of SQL Server is not that large, then how much value does the backup compression feature actually provide for that instance? By experimenting with the Developer Edition, not only do you get to use the backup compression feature, but you can also familiarize yourself with the commands and syntax of backup compression. You can also utilize the Developer Edition to generate documentation of the backup and restore processes with and without compression for comparison purposes. Documenting the results of your test prepares support for your recommendation of the next edition of SQL Server to purchase.

Workgroup Edition

The Workgroup Edition is a licensed production system with fewer features than the Standard and Enterprise Editions. The primary purpose of the Workgroup Edition is to provide data management and reporting platform for business applications running at branch locations. The Workgroup Edition runs on servers with x86 (or 32-bit systems) and x64 (or 64-bit systems). Workgroup Edition is installed in environments where you or the organization has determined that there is a benefit to separate instances of SQL Server residing at the organization's multiple branches.

■**Note** Microsoft provides you with the option to purchase licenses per processor or per CAL for the Workgroup Edition.

The Workgroup Edition includes the core database components of SQL Server along with remote synchronization, security, and management capabilities for supporting the branch applications. Following are some of the highlights of this edition:

- High availability
    - Log shipping
    - Subscriber in replication
- Manageability features
    - Policy-Based Management
    - Policy-Based Configuration
- Management tools
    - All management tools

Remember, the Workgroup Edition was created to satisfy specific organizational requirements. When it comes to validating the features and functionality of this edition, follow the same rules previously described. Document the feature information by using the Developer Edition, or from reading books or online content, to ensure that the Workgroup Edition will fulfill the business requirements that have been provided to you.

Web Edition

The purpose for the Web Edition, as the name implies, is for web-hosting companies that need to provide their customers with highly available and scalable solutions for a low cost. Web Edition runs on servers with x86 (or 32-bit systems) and x64 (or 64-bit systems). Web Edition has no restrictions on the amount of memory the instance can support or a cap on the size of databases. That increases its scalability options for web-hosting companies. The price is per processor, per month under the general guideline of the Service Provider Licensing Agreement (SPLA). Once again, this edition targets specific organizational requirements and should be researched further to determine if you can benefit from using this version.

The Web Edition includes the core database components of SQL Server and closely resembles the Workgroup Edition. For example, here are some of the highlights:

- High availability
  - Log shipping
  - Subscriber in replication
- Manageability
  - Policy-Based Management
  - Policy-Based Configuration
- Management tools
  - SQL Server Management Studio (Basic Version)
  - All other tools

Express Edition

A free version of SQL Server, the Express Edition, comes in three forms: SQL Server Express (the basic package with no extra tools), Express with Tools, and Express with Advanced Services. Regardless of which form you buy, Express Edition is the free version of SQL Server 2008 designed to help those who are not database administrators on a daily basis but who need a database backend to support their desktop and web applications. Express Edition runs on both x86 (or 32-bit systems) and x64 (or 64 bit systems), but it does not provide any advanced features. Express Edition supports one processor, 4 GB of storage, and 1 GB of memory. Express with Tools contains the core database engine, SQL Server Management Studio, and is the main edition of Express Edition. Express with Advanced Services includes all the features of Express with Tools, but it adds Full-Text Search and reporting services.

The bare SQL Server Express Edition includes only the core SQL Server database engine. The main usage of SQL Server Express Edition is in deployment scenarios. You can package your application and include SQL Server Express Edition for your deployment.

Surprisingly, the Express Edition does contain some of the new Enterprise Edition features and supports some high-availability solutions. Following are the highlights of this edition:

- High availability
  - Witness in database mirroring
  - Subscriber only in replication
  - Utilize SQL Server Change Tracking
- Manageability
  - Policy-Based Management
  - Policy-Based Configuration
- Management tools
  - SQL Server Management Studio (Basic Version)
  - SQLCMD utility

Overall, we would say that for a free edition of SQL Server, Express Edition contains a large number features, as well as a core engine that makes it a viable option to install and play with.

As we wrap up the section on editions, we want to encourage you to make time to evaluate the features and functionality of each edition as it applies to your situation before providing a recommendation on which SQL Server edition to purchase. For some of you, it is a no-brainer: You will have to utilize the Enterprise Edition for a number of reasons. However, there are a large number of you who might think you need the Enterprise Edition, but you do not have the evidence to support that decision. Install the Developer Edition, try out the new features, and document your results. That way, when the time comes to discuss with management or the application owner the edition that will be purchased, you will have documentation, hard facts, and solid analysis to support your recommendation and why so much money should be spent on the Enterprise Edition.

Determining Hardware Requirements

Now that you have determined the edition of SQL Server 2008 that best fits your requirements, the process of figuring out the specifications for the hardware begins. The commonly used industry term for this process is "specing" or "spec'ing out" the server. To *spec out* the server is to create a document that contains specifications for the server (both brand and model), the CPU requirements (how fast and how many), and the storage and memory requirements. (There are additional things that will be included in this document, like NIC cards, but that is outside the scope of this book.)

Spec'ing out servers is a process that definitely is an art and not a science. So many key factors drive decisions such that the slightest change in the business requirements can dramatically change two different server specifications. Some of you currently work in an environment where documentation occurs during downtime, so the organization probably does not have a method of ensuring that all of you follow the same process. For discussion purposes, let us assume that most organizations have a documented process for creating the specifications of servers. Unfortunately, if you were to take hold of 100 companies' plans, you would probably find a large number of differences, specifically in the interpretation of business requirements and then transformed into physical hardware requirements. With all the variation that exists in the industry, it would be unwise for us to tell you how to spec out your server. The goal of this section is to provide you with tips and things to think about during the decision-making process at your organization.

Before you get started, there are a number of questions that should be answered regarding the software before you can realistically provide hardware requirements. If you lack such answers about the software requirements, then you are either going to have to research the answers to these questions or make intelligent guesses.

Some questions that you may want to consider are the following:

- What types of requests will the application be supporting (such as online transaction processing, online analytical processing, and so on)?

- How many concurrent users does the application expect?

- What is the expected response time of the application?

- What is the application usage pattern? What is the frequency of reads compared to writes? How does it use `tempdb`?

- What is the maximum number of transactions per second?

- What is the combined spaced needed to support all of the databases on that server?

- What are the future growth plans for the application over the next 3 to 5 years?

- What is the projected growth of the data over the next 3 to 5 years?

- What is the skill set of the developers writing the application? If this is an upgrade, then what is the performance of the current application? If this is a new application or internally built, then what is the reputation of the company or group? Do the developers follow normalization and indexing practices? Do they use stored procedures to access data? Figure out what you can about the developers.

- What are the availability requirements? It always helps to know if you will be purchasing more than one server.

- What is your budget?

Feel free to add as many questions to this list as you feel is necessary. The more information you know about the environment, the closer you will be to ensuring that your recommendation meets and exceeds your business requirements.

One other thing you need to know before getting started is what the minimum requirements are for the available SQL Server editions. See Table 2-2 for a brief summary of those requirements by edition.

Table 2-2. *SQL Server Edition Minimum Requirements*

Edition	Memory	Processor
Enterprise (64-bit) IA64	Minimum: 512 MB Recommended: 2.048 GB Maximum: OS Max	Processor Type: Itanium Processor Speed: Minimum Recommended 1.0 GHz or faster
Enterprise (64-bit)	Minimum: 512 MB Recommended: 2.048 GB Maximum: OS Max	Processor Type: See web site Processor Speed Minimum 1.4 GHz, Recommended 2.0 GHz or faster
Standard (64-bit)	Minimum: 512 MB Recommended: 2.048 GB Maximum: OS Max	Processor Type: See web site Processor Speed: Minimum 1.4 GHz, Recommended 2.0 GHz or faster
Developer (64-bit)	Minimum: 512 MB Recommended: 2.048 GB Maximum: OS Max	Processor Type: 1.4 GHz Processor Speed: Minimum 1.4 GHz, Recommended 2.0 GHz or faster
Workgroup (64-bit)	Minimum: 512 MB, Recommended: 2.048 GB, Maximum: OS Max	Processor Type: 1.4 GHz Processor Speed Minimum 1.4 GHz, Recommended 2.0 GHz or faster
Web (64-bit)	Minimum: 512 MB Recommended: 2.048 GB Maximum: OS Max	Processor Type: See web site Processor Speed: Minimum 1.4 GHz, Recommended 2.0 GHz or faster
Express with Tools (64-bit)	Minimum: 512 MB Recommended: 1 GB Maximum: 1 GB	Processor Type: See web site Processor Speed: Minimum 1.4 GHz, Recommended 2.0 GHz or faster

(continued)

Edition	Memory	Processor
Express with Advanced Services (64-bit)	Minimum: 512 MB Recommended: 1 GB Maximum: 1 GB	Processor Type: See web site Processor Speed: Minimum 1.4 GHz, Recommended 2.0 GHz or faster
Enterprise (32-bit)	Minimum: 512 MB Recommended: 2.048 GB Maximum: OS Max	Processor Type: Pentium III or higher Processor Speed: Minimum 1.0 GHz, Recommended 2.0 GHz or faster
Standard (32-bit)	Minimum: 512 MB Recommended: 2.048 GB Maximum: OS Max	Processor Type: Pentium III or higher Processor Speed: Minimum 1.0 GHz, Recommended 2.0 GHz or faster
Developer(32-bit)	Minimum: 512 MB Recommended: 2.048 GB Maximum: OS Max	Processor Type: Pentium III or higher Processor Speed: Minimum 1.0 GHz, Recommended 2.0 GHz or faster
Workgroup (32-bit)	Minimum: 512 MB Recommended: 2.048 GB Maximum: OS Max	Processor Type: Pentium III or higher Processor Speed: Minimum 1.0 GHz, Recommended 2.0 GHz or faster
Web (32-bit)	Minimum: 512 MB Recommended: 2.048 GB Maximum: OS Max	Processor Type: Pentium III or higher Processor Speed: Minimum 1.0 GHz, Recommended 2.0 GHz or faster
Express with Tools (32-bit)	Minimum: 512 MB Recommended: 1.024 GB Maximum: 1.024 GB	Processor Type: Pentium III or higher Processor Speed: Minimum 1.0 GHz, Recommended 2.0 GHz or faster
Express with Advanced Services (32-bit)	Minimum: 512 MB Recommended: 1.024 GB Maximum: 1.024 GB	Processor Type: Pentium III or higher Processor Speed: Minimum 1.0 GHz, Recommended 2.0 GHz or faster

Determining CPU Needs

Determining the amount of CPU needed to handle the workload of the application or applications running on a server can sometimes be a little challenging. We would love to provide you with absolute metrics, but there are too many variables to provide that level of detail. Instead, we would like to discuss some of the factors that contribute to the amount of CPU needed and walk through a process that helps you build servers that resemble the server(s) you have in-house.

Deriving a Baseline Specification

To begin, you need baseline information for comparing your questions. If an external vendor developed the application you will be supporting, then hopefully they provided recommendations for CPU needs based upon users, workload, and so on. If you are purchasing a server for consolidation or to upgrade existing hardware, then utilize the existing hardware to determine usage statistics. If you are implementing a brand-new application in your environment with no supporting documentation, then find an application that closely resembles the expected usage patterns and user base and use its SQL Server for your baseline. As a last resort, go out on the web, find an application that is similar in functionality and features, and use its user and workload recommendations.

■**Tip** Strive to use comparable servers from your own environment. Your environment already supports the number of users, typical transactions per second, and the quality of servers that run your existing applications. Management is also accustomed to the cost of those servers. Trust your existing servers to provide a good baseline server speciation.

Consider Future Utilization

Now that you have a baseline server to start from, start looking at the causes of increased CPU utilization. Do not forget to pay close attention to how high the CPU usage is within your baseline and compare that to the level where you would like to keep the CPU usage of the new server. For example, if your baseline server constantly runs at 80% CPU utilization and the new server should run at 50% or lower, then make sure to consider that factor when determining how much CPU is needed.

Here are some questions to think about when deriving a new server specification from an existing, baseline server:

- What is the difference in the number of concurrent users?

- What is the transaction per second difference?

- What is the response time difference?

- Are the application usage patterns the same?

- Did the quality of the developers change?

I hope that these questions stimulated your mind with even more questions to consider. Please add as many questions to this list as possible. Try to consider all the factors and think through all of the scenarios that can affect CPU utilization.

Example Using the CPU Questions

Let's say that your baseline server runs on average at 60% CPU utilization. Your company plans to upgrade the application, and you are getting ready to purchase a new server to support that upgrade. Because of the new features of the application:

- Your user base is going to increase by 1½ times what it is now.

- Your transactions per second are going to double.

Knowing about these increases, you can consider them in light of some additional requirements that you have pertaining to the new server:

- You want to keep the same response time.

- You want your system running at 40% CPU utilization instead of 60%.

Finally, you also know a couple of additional facts:

- The usage pattern of the application will stay the same.
- The vendor still has not figured out how to partition its tables or any other performance improvement technique.

Reviewing this scenario definitely shows you the need to purchase more CPU than what currently exists in your baseline server. How much to increase the CPU? We cannot tell you that. As the DBA, you have to determine the importance of each answer and factor in what it will mean to the increase or decrease in CPU utilization for the new server. This method will take some getting used to, and the process may not be perfect the first couple of times through. As you fine-tune your questions and establish what the answers mean for the CPU, you will begin to develop a consistent method for determining the amount of CPU needed for any new server that you are spec'ing out.

Disk Subsystems

Determining the design, size, and utilization of the disk subsystem is either complex or extremely simple. Unbelievably, there are still DBAs out there who support systems with one physical hard drive that contains the operating system files, the data, log, and backup files for SQL Server. In some instances, servers were set up this way because of budget reasons. In other instances, servers were set up this way due to the lack of knowledge in the spec'ing out phase of the disk subsystem. The goal of this section is to provide you with some information and tips about determining the space needed to store the database. We also hope to help with terminology and to present options for laying out the data, log, tempdb, and backup files on the server.

For those who have had conversations with server administrators or hardware specialists, you know they use terms not commonly used in the database world. If you are not prepared and do not understand these terms when discussing a disk subsystem, then you may miss out on a key design decision. Therefore, here is a brief list of some common terms and their definitions to help you with that conversation.

- *Physical hard drive*: The actual tangible unit attached to a server.
- *Logical hard drive*: Provides usable storage capacity on one or more physical disk drives.
- *Local disks*: Disks that are controlled and connected to the hard disk controller.
- *Spindle*: Responsible for turning the hard disk platters. This is another way to reference a physical hard drive.
- *Logical unit number (LUN)*: The number assigned to a logical unit.
- *Disk subsystem*: The disks on the system.
- *RAID level*: Used to simultaneously use multiple disks for better performance.
- *Storage area network (SAN)*: Architecture used to attach remote computer storage devices to servers.
- *Disk array*: A disk storage system that contains multiple disk drives.
- *Hot standby*: Also known as a *hot spare*, it refers to a physical disk that resides in the disk array waiting for another disk to fail so it can fill in.

The first decision probably made for you by the organization is how the disk subsystem is attached to the server. Generally, any established company has already made the strategic decision to purchase a SAN, use a fiber channel to connect to the disk array, or to use local disks. So we are not going to spend any time discussing how the disk will be attached to your SQL Server. For the most part, you will need to fit in with whatever storage infrastructure your organization has already chosen.

Database Sizing

Choosing the sizes of your disks is a different matter. It is absolutely within your purview to specify how much disk space your database will need for log files, data files, and so forth. There are multiple ways to propose the estimated sizes of your databases. One method is to guess, but the method that we like the most takes you back to the baseline server. This method is a lot easier if you are upgrading the server, have a good comparable server in your environment, or have specification documents from a vendor.

Note If you are not upgrading and do not have vendor specification documents, then do not worry. We have another method to show you after this one.

Estimating Size from a Baseline

Starting with your baseline, here are some of the questions that you may want to ask:

- What is the expected user difference?
- How large are the current databases (applies to upgrading only)?
- How many years did it take to accumulate that amount of data (applies to upgrading only)?
- What is the difference between the data retention policies for the baseline and new databases?
- How many years is your data projection for?
- Are there any projected data retention policy changes?
- Is there a difference between the data storage practices used by the application your baseline database supports vs. the new application that you are installing?

As we said before, please add your own questions to this list. The questions listed here are to help stimulate ideas. The more questions you come up with, the better your database size estimation will be. Do not forget to determine how much each answer factors into the final recommendation for the sizing of your disks.

Estimating Size Based Upon Row and Column Sizes

If the previous method does not work for you, then Microsoft provides some information about sizing your database. The size of a database consists of the sum of the individual sizes of the tables within that database. The size of a table is determined by the number of indexes, the types of indexes, and/or the heap if the table does not have any indexes.

Following is a brief summary of Microsoft's size estimation process. First, for each table, you must calculate the amount of space required to store data on the heap:

1. Calculate the space used to store data in the leaf-level pages.

2. Calculate the space used to store index information in the table's clustered index, if there is one.

3. Total the calculated values.

Next, you must estimate the size of each nonclustered index upon the table:

1. Calculate the space used to store index information in the leaf level of the nonclustered index.

2. Calculate the space used to store index information in the non-leaf levels of the non-clustered index.

3. Total the calculated values.

Repeat the preceding two processes for each table in your database. Sum all the values together. When you have gone over every table and index, you will have a reasonable estimate of the amount of disk space that you need to allocate to your database.

■**Note** Detailed instructions on computing row, column, and index sizes can be found at http://msdn.microsoft.com/en-us/library/ms187445.aspx.

Regardless of the method used to determine the projected size of your databases, you still have to figure out the sizes for the log, tempdb, and backup drives. The backup drive will have to be large enough to store the database backup file. It will also need to be large enough to hold multiple copies of the backup file if holding multiple backups is part of your backup strategy. The backup drive also needs room for transaction log backups, if you plan to back up your log files.

The size of the log drive should be 25% of the database drive, and the tempdb drive should also be 25% of the database drive. Once you have determined the sizes of your new database and the sizes of the drives needed for any additional files, the next step is for you to determine the RAID levels for the drives and how you want them configured.

■**Tip** If given a choice between small fast drives or the large slower drives, choose the small fast drives. Smaller faster drives outperform larger slower drives.

Determining RAID Levels

Hopefully, there is still some flexibility in the decision-making process for the RAID levels of the physical disks. Which level you choose depends upon your requirements for fault toler-ance and performance. Cost is also a significant factor. If you want the best in both fault tolerance and performance, then be prepared to pay for it.

Understanding RAID Levels

There are three basic RAID levels that are used on SQL Server: RAID 1, RAID 0, and RAID 5. Also commonly used is a combination of 1 and 0, which is called RAID 10. Following are descriptions of these levels:

- *RAID 0 (striped disks)*: Stripes data across multiple drives; no redundancy.

- *RAID 1 (mirrored disks)*: Each drive has its data copied to another drive; good redun-dancy.

- *RAID 5 (striped disks with distributed parity)*: Stripes data across multiple drives, and parity information for one drive is distributed across all drives; good redundancy.

- *RAID 10 (mirrored and striped)*: Data is striped across multiple drives and then copied to another drive; good redundancy.

RAID 0

Of the three RAID levels previously listed, RAID 0, or striped, is the best for input and output (IO) performance. When the disk subsystem is set up on RAID 0, the disk controller ensures the striping of data occurs evenly across all disks in an array. Unfortunately, if one disk fails in the array, then the data stored within those disks are lost. RAID 0 has no fault tolerance, we don't use it on systems that are required to be available, and data loss is unacceptable. RAID 0 is the cheapest of the listed RAID levels because of the lack of redundancy. You do not have to purchase additional drives which means all the drives in a RAID 0 array are used.

RAID 1

RAID 1, or mirrored disks, copies all data written to the primary disk to a secondary disk. Both disks are available for reads, which makes RAID 1 very fast for data retrieval. Because data writes occur to multiple disks, then a failure in the primary or a secondary disk does not cause data loss or application unavailability. That is the reason why RAID 1 provides redun-dancy within the disk array. The redundancy provided by RAID 1 is what makes this option expensive. In order to set up RAID 1, every physical drive purchased for writes has to have an additional drive in order to copy the data. You can see how the cost for using this RAID level increases rapidly.

RAID 5

RAID 5, or striped disks with distributed parity, stripes data across multiple drives and writes parity bits across all drives. Data retrieval on RAID 5 is very fast, but writes are extremely costly. Because of the parity bit, when one command writes to disk, one write occurs to write the data to disk, and then a parity write occurs to write to the parity drive, followed by a check to ensure that a disk failure did not occur during the write operation. A single write command potentially costs four IO; that is costly in an environment with heavy writes.

On the other side, the parity bits ensure that, in the event of drive failure, the re-creation of the data stored on that disk occurs without loss of availability to the application or data loss. The redundancy of RAID 5 is good as long as you don't lose multiple drives. It is good practice to use a hot-swappable drive in RAID 5. A hot-swappable drive is one that is part of the array, unused until a failure occurs in one of the disks. That drive has all the data from the failed drive re-created on it, and then it steps in and becomes a part of the array. RAID 5 is a relatively inexpensive option for providing redundancy. Writes occur on all drives, minimizing the need for extra drives not used for writing. At a minimum, RAID 5 requires three drives, which means 33% of each drive will be used for parity.

RAID 10

RAID 10 combines the benefits of RAID 1 and RAID 0 to create an awesome RAID level. RAID 10 stripes data across mirrored drives. Therefore, the mirroring occurs first and then stripes data across the mirrored or secondary drives to improve performance. Be careful not to confuse RAID 01 with RAID 10. The implementation of RAID 01 occurs by striping first and then mirroring the striped set. RAID 10 provides the benefit of striping to RAID 1 while creating the needed redundancy for RAID 0, making the combination of the two RAID levels nice complements to one another. Clearly, you can see the cost of RAID 10 over the previously discussed RAID levels. At a minimum, RAID 10 needs four drives, and the numbers quickly increase from there. Luckily, hard drives are getting cheaper, making this option more feasible in today's environments.

Choosing Your RAID Level and Laying Out Your Files

Now that you understand RAID levels, we can discuss the layout of SQL Server's files and the RAID levels of the drives that will support them. Here are a couple of things to keep in the back of your mind:

- The RAID level selected may increase the cost of your disk subsystem. So know your budget as you read the tips for laying out your SQL Server files.

- The size of the system that you are designing may not require you to implement all of the tips that we provide. If you are creating a system for a couple of users with low transactions per second, then it is probably overkill to implement everything we suggest in this section.

We like to set up all of our servers the same, but that decision of how you set up your own servers is left up to you. Depending on the disk subsystem that you have at your organization, you may not have much decision-making power when it comes to determining the RAID levels of whatever new server you are configuring. In some environments, SAN administrators predetermine the RAID levels for the drives. Do not get upset—there is no reason to worry about decisions you have no control over. Just worry about what you do have control over.

- Place your data, log, tempdb, and backups on separate physical drives.

- Set the RAID level on your data drive to RAID 10, or set it to 1 if the budget does not permit 10.

- Set the RAID level on your log drive to RAID 1.

- Set the RAID level on your `tempdb` drive to RAID 10, or set it to 1 if the budget does not permit 10.

- Set the RAID level on your backup drive to RAID 5.

Right now, not everyone in the industry agrees with setting up your data drives on RAID 1 or RAID 10. There are people who would like to place data files on a RAID 5 disk array. We have supported databases on both setups and could argue both ways. Our preference is RAID 10 or 1, and that is why we listed those RAID levels in the section. If you have the time, then do your own research so you can make an informed decision.

Final Disk Storage Configuration

After the drives are set up, there are just a few more things that we recommend you doing to ensure your disk subsystem is ready for production:

- Ensure your disk subsystem can handle your SQL Server IO production load by utilizing IO subsystem stress tools.

- Create separate `tempdb` files for every physical processor. (Multiple cores count as multiple processors, but hyper-threading technology does not.)

- Make sure the disk offset of your drives are set up to 64 KB. (Feel free to research disk offsets and how and why to validate your disk offset online.)

Proper configuration of your physical and logical disk is essential to SQL Server running effectively. Make enough time to test the IO subsystem of your SQL Server before the server goes into Production. Validate the correctness of your supplied configuration options. We have reviewed newly built servers and identified partitions that were on the same physical drive with different logical drive letters instead of separate physical drives with different logical drive letters. So, verify the settings or get the server administrator to show you how if you do not know. Learn to use the physical disk monitors in Performance Monitor (covered later on in this book) to proactively monitor your disk subsystem. That way, you are the first one to know when your disk starts to become a bottleneck. Take advantage of the information and implement or verify that these tips are in place on your server(s).

Determining Memory Requirements

Generally, we try to purchase as much memory as a server will hold. The more memory you have, that much more of your database can be stored in memory, decreasing the amount of time it takes to retrieve data from the disk. Unfortunately, when budgets are tight, nobody has the luxury of spending extra money.

When accurately trying to determine the amount of memory needed for a new server, we always resort to our baseline servers and start asking questions. The following questions are not meant to be the only questions asked. They are designed to get you thinking about the changes within your application that would affect the amount of memory needed. For the following set of questions, we are going to add a little more reasoning around each question and why it is important to memory contributions:

- What is the difference in the number of concurrent users between your baseline database and the new one you are configuring? The more concurrent users there are, the greater the need to keep frequently accessed data in memory. The greater the memory, the more data that are kept in memory, preventing physical disk reads.

- What is the transaction per second difference? If transactions increase, then the amount of data needed to process the requests likely will increase. The more memory you have, the more data pages you can keep in memory instead of on physical disk.

- Is the quality of the developers different? If you have developers who do not take advantage of proper database practices, then their queries will pull entire tables into memory for table scans. Depending on the amount of data, the performance of those queries maybe poor, and their execution may hog memory for an extended period of time, forcing other frequently accessed data to be removed from memory.

- What is the difference between the size of your baseline database and the system you are implementing? What about expected growth? The bigger the database, the more memory you want. Generally, larger databases require larger data sets in memory to fulfill user queries. The more memory you have, the more queries you can process without having to go to a physical disk.

As we said before, please add any questions you would like to the preceding list. Figure out how the answers to these questions will factor into the overall increase or decrease of needed memory. Never underestimate the amount of memory you need. In fact, you should overestimate when it comes to memory. After all, what is the worst thing that would happen if your entire database were in memory? Our guess is that you would have some happy customers.

Choosing the Server

There are a number of vendors that build servers that allow enough customization in their server models to build a SQL Server to meet and exceed the needs of any application. No one pays us to advertise for one company or the next, so we really do not have a vendor preference. And in many cases, an organization will have a standard vendor that you will be required to use, except in the rare case when requirements dictate otherwise.

When researching models provided by your hardware vendor, make sure you pay attention to the maximum memory, CPU, and so forth that each model supports. Leave yourself a bit of headroom for future expansion. That way, if one of the requirements was wrong, some of the requirements changed after ordering the server, or one of your best guesses was a little off, you have some wiggle room in the currently ordered hardware. We would prefer to go back to management and request additional money to buy more memory instead of requesting money to purchase a new server because the server cannot handle any additional memory.

Another important note about server vendors is that they are building most of their servers with 64-bit support. Following are some of the benefits of a 64-bit SQL Server compared to a 32-bit SQL Server:

- Larger, directly addressable space, increasing the memory available for processing complex queries

- Enhanced parallelism and support for up to 64 processors, which increases scalability

- Capability to handle a larger number of concurrent users with improved response time

- Improvements within the bus architecture, increasing the amount of data passed through to processor and cache, in turn improving performance

There are some benefits to putting SQL Server 2008 on a 64-bit server, especially when the hardware that you purchase is designed to run 64-bit applications. When the time comes to pick out the server, find the model that is big enough to meet your minimum requirements and large enough to handle any unexpected changes with the application. After you have determined the model of the server to use, finish preparing your neatly formatted document, including all of the specifications that you have just determined. Congratulations, your server specification document is complete.

Documenting a repeatable process for consistently spec'ing out new servers ensures that the decision-making process for all new servers will cover the same considerations. The old way of undocumented, intelligent analysis does not work if you want all DBAs performing this task the same way. Sit down with your team, go over the questions that should be considered, and determine the factor of increase or decrease based on the response to each question.

Creating a sound, server specification document will not only save you time when spec'ing out servers, but it will also save support time when you are up and running in production. Spend the time to do the work, and document the process so that that you can repeat it and improve it going forward.

SQL Server Consolidation

Consolidating SQL Server instances onto a single or multiple servers has become increasingly popular with 64-bit hardware. 64-bit servers have enabled you to utilize servers with up to 32 processors and the maximum amount of RAM supported by the operating system directly without having to use other technologies to address the memory. That kind of power within a single server has helped organizations easily make the switch to consolidated setups.

What does it mean to consolidate your SQL Server? To consolidate your SQL Server is to combine multiple, separate database servers into one bigger, more powerful database server. The consolidation process can be smooth and simple or extremely complex, depending on the applications that the individual database servers are supporting. The purpose of this section is to provide you with some benefits of SQL Server consolidation along with tips and things to watch out for if you are thinking about consolidation.

For those of you scratching your head trying to figure out why in the world one would want to consolidate multiple SQL Server instances, let's review some of the pros and cons.

Benefits of server consolidation include the following:

- Reduces the amount of management required to support physical servers

- Decreases the number of SQL Server licenses needed

- Increases the application uptime and availability

- Increases performance within the applications

But there's a cloud to go along with every silver lining. Drawbacks to consolidation include the following:

- Management of the consolidated server is more challenging in terms of maintenance windows, patching, scheduled jobs, and so on.
- When the consolidated server goes down, then all the applications on that server are down.
- The upfront cost of purchasing a big beefy server, which includes the license and hardware, is expensive. You may want to consider purchasing a redundant server for the consolidated server. When you have multiple applications on one server, you definitely don't want to loose that server for any period of time.

Although there are a couple of issues to think about before deciding to consolidate, we definitely think exploring the benefits of SQL Server consolidation in your environment is a worthwhile task. We're going to provide you with some lessons that we have learned while supporting consolidated environments:

Do not put mission-critical applications on a consolidated server. We suggest that you deal with those applications individually.

Write clearly documented guidelines for applications to abide by in prior to adding the application to the consolidated server. For example, application users can have database owner rights to their database only. Do not allow users to have system administrator rights because that impacts more than just the application they are using.

Name your automated processes with some form of application identification. In a consolidated server environment, multiple applications will likely have their jobs that need to run. Identifying jobs for an application without any form of identification can be time consuming. That is not the situation you want to be in, especially when you have management on your back about rerunning a process.

Watch out for out-of-control applications and set up a policy for removing that application from the consolidated server. Remember, one bad application impacts all the other applications on that server.

Only add one application/database at a time to the consolidated server. This enables you to monitor the server after the addition of an application to ensure that the server resources are at a manageable level.

Determine what the normal resource utilization should be. Make sure you know when you need to stop adding applications.

Group similar application types and functionality together on the same consolidated database server. In most cases, similar applications have similar usage patterns, maintenance windows, and other similarities that enable the support of those groups of applications easier.

Spend some time monitoring an application before adding it to your consolidated server. That way, you estimate the amount of resources it will consume on the consolidated server. You do not want to wait until the addition of the application to the server to realize that it will negatively influence the resources on the consolidated server.

Create service level agreements for every application on the server. With that information, you will know the order in which to get applications back up in case of emergency.

If you are considering consolidating your SQL Server instances but would like more information about the servers in your environment to help identify hardware and software similarities, then use the Microsoft Assessment and Planning (MAP) toolkit. MAP will provide you with detailed reports of all the instances of SQL Server installed in your environment. MAP scans the network and collects detailed information from each computer using Windows Management Instrumentation (WMI) calls, Remote Registry service, and Simple Network Management Protocol (SNMP). MAP then stores the collected information in a SQL Server database for later reporting.

Before consolidating your SQL Server instances, you may also want to consider ensuring the compatibility of the features on the various SQL Server instances. Apparently, the features selected during installation can dictate how SQL Server stores information within the data files. When databases are set up on editions containing those features, they cannot be migrated to a SQL Server that does not support them. Running the `sys.dm_db_persisted_sku_features` dynamic management view will allow you to compare the features that are restricted by the edition. If the view does not return results, then the database does not contain any edition-specific features.

Do not get discouraged after reviewing the preceding tips. Consolidating SQL Server is not always complex, and it provides benefits to you and the organization. Look at your database environment and identify servers that have minimal CPU utilization and low transactions/batches per second. Start with small, low-impact servers and then determine if you want mission-critical applications on a consolidated server. Make sure you have thought through and tested your high-availability plan. Having a server go down and being without one application is stressful, but losing ten applications at the same time without a recovery plan is just plain madness. So spend a little time up front to document and test your recovery plan before adding databases to the consolidated server. Who knows? With the money you save the company in license fees and server maintenance, you may actually see the benefit in your paycheck. Well, we can dream can't we?

Consolidation with Virtual Servers

Virtual servers are becoming increasingly popular for SQL Server installations, especially for development and sandbox environments. Virtual servers enable you to consolidate multiple SQL Server instances onto one host, creating a consolidated server. The smaller the server, the more likely it is a candidate for virtualization. Servers within the two processor/4 GB of RAM range are easily virtualizable, while servers within the four processor/8 to 16 GB of RAM range are candidates for virtualization, but require a little more planning and effort. Try avoiding servers larger than the preceding requirements if possible. If you decide to use virtual servers for your production environment, we strongly recommend that you test the disk subsystem to ensure that the virtual server performs at acceptable levels. Use techniques discussed earlier in this chapter and performance counters discussed in Chapter 14 to monitor the performance of your subsystem. Just keep in mind that virtualizing servers within your environment may be an option to explore when building out your new environments.

Summary

There are many decisions that must be made prior to installing SQL Server. At a minimum, you have to determine which edition of SQL Server to install, the hardware that SQL Server will run on, and whether to add the database to an existing consolidated server. We know planning and preparing is something that you do not have enough time to do. Remember your Five P's: Proper Planning Prevents Poor Performance. Repeat that phrase to encourage yourself during the times when properly preparing for an installation doesn't seem likely.

You may have noticed that this chapter covers pre-installation from the hardware and software considerations. Another major pre-installation consideration is ensuring that your system meets the availability requirements of post-production. The next chapter is going to focus on high availability and the various solutions that are available in SQL Server 2008. The solution implemented to keep your system available is as important as the hardware and software you choose. So make time to prepare for all of these considerations before installing SQL Server 2008.

CHAPTER 3

Choosing a High-Availability Solution

High availability has become an increasingly popular subject in SQL Server. Not only have there been entire books dedicated to high availability, but we have seen specialized books written on each topic that falls under the high-availability umbrella. Needless to say, we will not be going into great detail here, but it is important to understand how each of SQL Server's high-availability solutions can play a role in your environment. This chapter will give an overview of each solution to help differentiate what factors play a role in designing the best, overall solution for your organization. By the end of this chapter, you should be armed with the information necessary to make an informed decision on the best usage scenarios for each high-availability technique offered in SQL Server 2008.

What Exactly Is High Availability Anyway?

First of all, it is important to understand what high availability actually means. The terms *high availability* and *disaster recovery* are often confused or thought of as the same thing. Just because you have implemented a high-availability solution does not mean that you are prepared for a disaster. High availability generally covers hardware or system-related failures, while disaster recovery (DR) can be used in the event of a catastrophic failure due to environmental factors. While some of the high-availability options may help you when designing your DR strategy, they are not the be-all and end-all solution.

The goal of high availability is to provide an uninterrupted user experience with zero data loss; but high availability can have many different meanings, depending on who you ask. According to Microsoft's SQL Server 2008 Books Online, "a high-availability solution masks the effects of a hardware or software failure and maintains the availability of applications so that the perceived downtime for users is minimized." (For more information, see `http://msdn.microsoft.com/en-us/library/bb522583.aspx`.) Many times users will say they need 100% availability, but what, exactly, does that mean to the user? Does being 100% available mean that the data is 100% available during business hours, Monday through Friday, or that the data is available 24/7? High availability is about setting expectations and then living up to them. That's why one of the most important things to do when dealing with high availability is to define those expectations in a Service Level Agreement (SLA) that can be agreed upon and signed by all parties involved.

Some of the things you should cover in the SLA are maintenance windows, the amount of recovery time allowed to bring the system back online due to a catastrophic failure, and the amount of acceptable data loss, if any. Defining a maintenance window allows you to apply service packs, patches, and upgrades to the system to ensure optimal performance and maintain compliance. Having a maintenance window allows you to do this in a tested and planned fashion. A drop-dead time should be determined so that a back out plan can be executed if problems are encountered, ensuring system availability by the end of the maintenance window.

Defining the amount of time allowed to recover from a disaster along with the maximum allowed data loss will help you determine what techniques you may need to use to ensure that your SLAs are met. Every organization wants 100% availability 100% of the time; but when presented with the cost of a system that would even come close to achieving this goal, they are usually willing to negotiate attainable terms. It is important to have an understanding of what it means for a system to be unavailable. Is it a minor inconvenience because users within your organization will not be able to log their time, or are you losing thousands of dollars in revenue every hour the system is down? Answering these kinds of questions will allow you to justify the cost of an appropriate solution. Each high-availability method brings unique characteristics to the table, and unfortunately there is no cookie-cutter solution. In the next few sections, we will discuss the individual techniques used to achieve your high-availably needs.

Failover Clustering

Failover clustering is a technique that uses a cluster of SQL Server instances to protect against failure of the instance currently serving your users. Failover clustering is based on a hardware solution comprised of multiple servers (known as *nodes*) that share the same disk resources. One server is active and owns the database. If that server fails, then another server in the cluster will take over ownership of the database and continue to serve users.

Key Terms

When discussing high availability, each technique has its own set of key terms. At the beginning of each section, we will list the terms used for each solution. Here are some of the terms you need to be familiar with when setting up a failover cluster:

- *Node*: Server that participates in the failover cluster.

- *Resource group*: Shared set of disks or network resources grouped together to act as a single working unit.

- *Active node*: Node that has ownership of a resource group.

- *Passive node*: Node that is waiting on the active node to fail in order to take ownership of a resource group.

- *Heartbeat*: Health checks sent between nodes to ensure the availability of each node.

- *Public network*: Network used to access the failover cluster from a client computer.

- *Private network*: Network used to send heartbeat messages between nodes.

- *Quorum*: A special resource group that holds information about the nodes, including the name and state of each node.

Failover Clustering Overview

You can use failover clustering to protect an entire instance of SQL Server. Although the nodes share the same disks or resources, only one server may have ownership (read and write privileges) of the resource group at any given time. If a failover occurs, the ownership is transferred to another node, and SQL Server is back up in the time it takes to bring the databases back online. The failover usually takes anywhere from a few seconds to a few minutes, depending on the size of the database and types of transactions that may have been open during the failure.

In order for the database to return to a usable state during a failover, it must go through a Redo phase to roll forward logged transactions and an Undo phase to roll back any uncommitted transactions. Fast recovery is an Enterprise Edition feature that was introduced in SQL Server 2005 that allows applications to access the database as soon as the Redo phase has completed. Also, since the cluster appears on the network as a single server, there is no need to redirect applications to a different server during a failover. The network abstraction combined with fast recovery makes failing over a fairly quick and unobtrusive process that ultimately results in less downtime during a failure.

The number of nodes that can be added to the cluster depends on the edition of the operating system (OS) as well as the edition of SQL Server, with a maximum of 16 nodes using SQL Server 2008 Enterprise Edition running on Windows Server 2008. Failover clustering is only supported in the Enterprise and Standard Editions of SQL Server. If you are using the Standard Edition, you are limited to a 2-node cluster. Since failover clustering is also dependant on the OS, you should be aware of the limitations for each edition of the OS as well. Windows Server 2008 only supports the use of failover clustering in its Enterprise, Datacenter, and Itanium Editions. Windows Server 2008 Enterprise and Datacenter Editions both support a 16-node cluster, while the Itanium edition only supports an 8-node cluster.

In order to spread the workload of multiple databases across servers, every node in a cluster can have ownership of its own set of resources and its own instance of SQL Server. Every server that owns a resource is referred to as an *active node*, and every server that does not own a resource is referred to as a *passive node*. There are two basic types of cluster configurations: a single-node cluster and a multi-node cluster. A multi-node cluster contains two or more active nodes, and a single-node cluster contains one active node with one or more passive nodes. Figure 3-1 shows a standard single-node cluster configuration commonly referred to as an active/passive configuration.

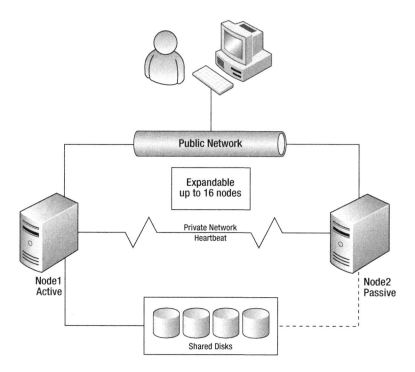

Figure 3-1. *Common single-node (active/passive) cluster configuration*

So if multiple active nodes allow you to utilize all of your servers, why wouldn't you make all the servers in the cluster active? The answer: Resource constraints. In a 2-node cluster, if one of the nodes has a failure, the other available node will have to process its normal load as well as the load of the failed node. For this reason, it is considered best practice to have one passive node per active node in a failover cluster. Figure 3-2 shows a healthy multi-node cluster configuration running with only two nodes. If Node 1 has a failure, as demonstrated in Figure 3-3, Node 2 is now responsible for both instances of SQL Server. While this configuration will technically work, if Node 2 does not have the capacity to handle the workload of both instances, your server may slow to a crawl, ultimately leading to unhappy users in two systems instead of just one.

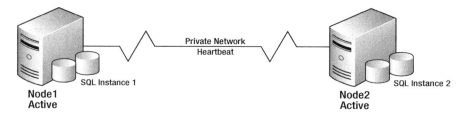

Figure 3-2. *Multi-node (active/active) cluster configuration*

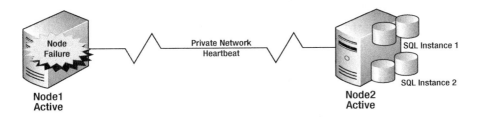

Figure 3-3. *Multi-node (active/active) cluster configuration after failure*

So, how does all of this work? A heartbeat signal is sent between the nodes to determine the availability of one another. If one of the nodes has not received a message within a given time period or number of retries, a failover is initiated and the primary failover node takes ownership of the resources. It is the responsibility of the quorum drive to maintain a record of the state of each node during this process. Heartbeat checks are performed at the OS level as well as the SQL Server level. The OS is in constant contact with the other nodes, checking the health and availability of the servers. For this reason, a private network is used for the heartbeat between nodes to decrease the possibility of a failover occurring due to network-related issues. SQL Server sends messages known as LooksAlive and IsAlive. LooksAlive is a less intrusive check that runs every 5 seconds to make sure the SQL Server service is running. The IsAlive check runs every 60 seconds and executes the query Select @@ServerName against the active node to make sure that SQL Server can respond to incoming requests.

Implementation

Before you can even install SQL Server, you have to make sure that you have configured a solid Windows cluster at the OS and hardware levels. One of the major pain points you used to have when setting up a failover cluster is searching the Hardware Compatibility List (HCL) to ensure that the implemented hardware solution would be supported. This requirement has been removed in Windows Server 2008. You can now run the new cluster validation tool to perform all the required checks that will ensure you are running on a supported configuration. Not only can the cluster validation tool be used to confirm the server configuration, it can be used to troubleshoot issues after setup as well.

From a SQL Server perspective, the installation process is pretty straightforward. If you are familiar with installing a failover cluster in SQL Server 2005, it has completely changed in SQL Server 2008. First you run the installation on one node to create a single-node cluster. Then you run the installation on each remaining node, choosing the Add Node option during setup. In order to remove a node from a cluster, you run setup.exe on the server that needs to be removed and select the Remove Node option. The new installation process allows for more granular manageability of the nodes, allowing you to add and remove nodes without bringing down the entire cluster. The new installation process also allows you to perform patching and rolling upgrades with minimal downtime.

Do not be afraid of failover clustering. It takes a little extra planning up front, but once it has been successfully implemented, managing a clustered environment is really not much different than any other SQL environment. Just as the SQL instance has been presented to the application in a virtual network layer, it will be presented to the administrator this way as well. As long as you use all the correct virtual names when connecting to the SQL instance, it will just be administration as usual.

Pros and Cons of Failover Clustering

As with any other technology solution, failover clustering brings certain benefits, but at a cost. Benefits of failover clustering include the following:

- Zero data loss
- Protection of the entire instance
- Fast recovery
- Automatic failover

The price you pay for these benefits is as follows:

- Failover clustering does not protect against disk failure.
- No standby database is available for reporting.
- Special hardware is required.
- Failover clustering is generally expensive to implement.
- There is no duplicate data for reporting or disaster recovery.

Database Mirroring

The technique of database mirroring can be summed up very simply: It's the practice of keeping two separate copies of your database in synchronization with each other so that if you lose one copy, you can continue work with the other. Mirroring is commonly used at the disk level in RAID arrays. The concept is much the same when it comes to databases.

Key Terms

Just as failover clustering has its own terminology, database mirroring has its own conventions that you need to be familiar with. Study the list to follow because some of the same terms are used in other aspects of information technology, but with slightly different meanings. Using the correct terminology for SQL Server will help make sure everyone has the same understanding when discussing high availability. The key terms to be familiar with include the following:

- *Principal*: Source server containing the functionally active database in the mirrored pair.
- *Mirror*: Target server containing the destination database in the mirrored pair.
- *Witness*: Optional server that monitors the principal and mirror servers.
- *Partner*: Opposite server when referring to the principal and mirror servers.
- *Endpoint*: Object that is bound to a network protocol that allows SQL Servers to communicate across the network.

Database Mirroring Overview

Database mirroring was introduced in SQL Server 2005 and provides two levels of protection: high-performance mode and high-safety mode. Both modes have the same concept, but the order in which a transaction is committed is slightly different. With high-performance mode, the transaction is committed on the principal server before the mirror. This enables the application to move forward without having to wait for the transaction to commit on the mirror. With high-safety mode, the transaction is committed on the mirror before committing on the principal. This causes the application to wait until the transaction has been committed on both servers before moving forward. Both high-performance and high-safety modes require the principal database to be set to full recovery. We will look at each mode individually and discuss the pros and cons of using each technique.

Implementation

Database mirroring has a much easier implementation process when compared to failover clustering. It requires no special hardware configuration and can be applied and managed completely through SQL Server. Here are the basic steps you must perform in order to set up database mirroring:

1. Create endpoints for database communication.

2. Backup the database on the principal server.

3. Restore the database on the mirror server.

4. Set the principal server as a partner on the mirror server.

5. Set the mirror server as a partner on the principal server.

One of the downsides of database mirroring compared to failover clustering is that you must set up database mirroring for each database, whereas once you set up failover clustering, the entire instance is protected. Since mirroring is configured for each individual database, you must make sure that any external data needed by the mirror database is also copied to the mirror server. For example, you need to copy logins from the `master` database to the `master` database on the mirror server, and also make sure that any jobs needed by the mirror database are on the mirror server. Also, since database mirroring makes a copy of the database, you will need to use twice as much disk space than you would with failover clustering. On the upside, having a duplicate copy of the database makes database mirroring a far better solution than failover clustering when you are worried about disaster recovery and disk failure. SQL Server 2008 even includes a new feature that will repair corrupt data pages by copying them from the partner once the corruption has been detected.

Snapshots for Reporting

In order to use a mirrored database as a reporting solution, you must also use the database snapshot feature, which requires the Enterprise Edition of SQL Server 2008. You can use database snapshots in conjunction with database mirroring in order to provide a static reporting solution by taking regular snapshots of the mirror database. Users are unable to connect directly to the mirror database to perform queries, but you can create a snapshot of the mirror database at any given time, which will allow users to connect to the snapshot database.

The snapshot database starts out relatively small, but as changes are made to the mirror database, the original data pages are added to the snapshot database in order to provide the data as it appeared when the snapshot was created. After some time of copying the original data pages, the snapshot database could become rather large, but never larger than the size of the original database at the time the snapshot was created. In order to keep the data current and the size of the snapshot to a minimum, you should refresh the snapshot periodically by creating a new snapshot and directing the traffic there. Then you can delete the old snapshot as soon as all the open transactions have completed. The snapshot database will continue to function after a failover has occurred; you will just lose connectivity during the failover while the databases are restarted. A failover could, however, place an additional load on the production system. Since it is now being used for processing the data for the application and serving up reporting requests, you may need to drop the snapshots and suspend reporting until another server is brought online.

Redirection in the Event of a Failure

Transparent client redirect is a feature provided in the Microsoft Data Access Components (MDAC) that works with database mirroring to allow client applications to automatically redirect in the case of a failover. When connecting to a database that participates in database mirroring, MDAC will recognize there is a mirror database and store the connection information needed to connect to the mirror database, along with the principal database. If a connection to the principal database fails, the application will try to reconnect. If the application is unable to reconnect to the principal database, a connection to the mirror database is attempted. There is one major caveat when working with transparent client redirect: The application must connect to the principal database before a failover has occurred in order to receive the connection information about the mirror. If the application cannot connect to the principal server, it will never be redirected to the mirror, meaning the failure must occur during an active application session. This can be mediated by storing two possible connection strings in the application.

High-Safety Mode

You can use high-safety mode in database mirroring to provide a duplicate copy of the principal database on a mirror server in a synchronous fashion so there is no chance of data loss between the principal and the mirror. In order for a transaction to commit on the principal database, it must first commit on the mirror. High-safety mode is supported in the Enterprise and Standard Editions of SQL Server, with one caveat being that the principal and the mirror must be running the same edition.

In order to provide the highest level of availability, you can use a witness server to verify connectivity between the principal and the mirror (see Figure 3-4). The witness server is not a requirement for high-safety mode, but it is a requirement for automatic failover capabilities. The witness server runs an instance of SQL Server that consumes very little resources and can even run using SQL Server Workgroup and Express Editions. Using a witness provides a communication check between the principal and the mirror, similar to the heartbeat in failover clustering. This communication check provides the ability for the mirror to assume the role of the principal should the principal become unavailable. The witness is not a single point of failure and does not actually perform the failover; it just provides verification to the mirror server that the principal server is down. If the witness server crashes, database mirroring is still operational and completely functioning between the principal and the mirror, and you will just lose the ability to automatically fail over. The reason for this behavior is to prevent unnecessary failovers due to network connectivity. In order for a server to become a principal server, it has to be able to communicate with at least one other server; therefore, the only purpose of the witness is to answer the question, "Is the principal down?" In order to automatically recover from a failure, the witness and the mirror servers must agree that the principal is actually down.

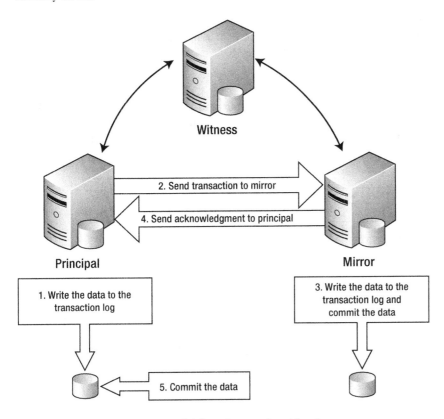

Figure 3-4. *Database mirroring high-safety mode with witness server*

High-Performance Mode

You can use high-performance mode in database mirroring to perform asynchronous operations between the principal and mirror databases. High-performance mode supports only a manual failover with the possibility of data loss. There is no need to use a witness server in high-performance mode because there is no automatic failover capability. Since the principal database does not have to wait for acknowledgment from the mirror server in order to keep processing requests, high-performance mode could increase application performance if you have a slow network connection or latency issues between the principal and mirror servers. Asynchronous processing also means that the mirror server can be several minutes behind when processing a high volume of transactions, which may or may not be acceptable, depending on the requirements agreed upon in the SLA. High-performance mode is only supported if you are using the Enterprise Edition of SQL Server.

■**Tip** SQL Server 2008 introduces the capability to compress the individual transactions being transmitted to the mirror database to help improve performance on slow networks with bandwidth limitations. This may increase performance enough to allow you to implement high-safety mode when using database mirroring in SQL Server 2008 on networks that may have prevented you from using high-performance mode in SQL Server 2005.

Figure 3-5 shows the typical configuration of database mirroring using high performance mode. Notice the order of operations using high performance mode that allows the application to perform requests without having to wait for the transactions to commit on the mirror.

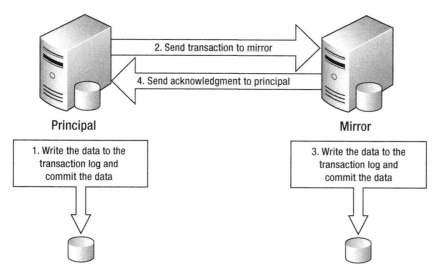

Figure 3-5. *Database mirroring high-performance mode*

Pros and Cons of Database Mirroring

As always, there are trade-offs to think about. The benefits of database mirroring include the following:

- No special hardware or windows configurations
- No distance limitations
- Duplicate data for disaster recovery
- Possible reporting solution using database snapshots of the mirror

Following are some restrictions and drawbacks of database mirroring to be aware of:

- Requires more disk space to store duplicate data
- Must be configured separately for each database
- May cause application performance issues on slow networks (high-performance mode)

In addition, keep in mind the following differences between high-safety mode and high-performance mode:

- High-safety mode ensures zero data loss. High-performance mode trades the chance of some data loss for increased performance.
- High-safety mode can cause application performance issues on slower networks. High-performance mode avoids performance issues by not waiting for the mirror to commit first (hence, the risk of data loss).
- Recovery is faster in high-safety mode because no uncommitted transactions need to be applied or undone.
- For the same reason, failover can be automatic in high-safety mode, but not in high-performance mode.

Copying Data with Log Shipping

One way to think of *log shipping* is as a poor man's approach to mirroring. The end goal is much the same as for database mirroring—to keep a second copy of a database in case the first copy is lost or damaged. The difference is that log shipping achieves its goal by making clever use of SQL Server's built-in backup and recovery functionality. Log shipping may have a few advantages over database mirroring, depending on your needs. For one thing, you can log ship to multiple servers, whereas you can only mirror to a single server. You can also use log shipping between different editions of SQL Server, while it is recommended that all servers are running the same edition when using database mirroring. You can also control the interval that the transactions are applied to when using log shipping because the databases are kept in sync by applying an entire transaction log at once instead of applying individual transactions.

Key Terms

The key terms in log shipping are pretty self explanatory, but once again it is best to know the correct terminology for each high-availability solution. Terms to know include the following:

- *Primary*: Server containing the source database sending the transaction logs.
- *Secondary*: Server containing the target database receiving the transaction logs.
- *Monitor*: Server that tracks information related to log shipping such as backup and restore times and sends alerts in the case of a failure.

Log Shipping Overview

Log shipping consists of a primary server copying the transaction logs of one or more data-bases and restoring them on one or more secondary servers. You can use a monitor server to track information about the status of log shipping. During the setup process, an alert job is configured on the monitor to send a failure notification if the primary and secondary data-bases are past the configured sync threshold. The monitor can be the same server as the primary or secondary, but it should be located on a different server to increase the chances of receiving an alert if the primary or secondary server has issues. All servers involved in log ship-ping must be running the Enterprise, Standard, or Workgroup Edition of SQL Server. You can also configure log compression with log shipping to reduce the network bandwidth needed to transfer the logs, but this requires the Enterprise Edition of SQL Server 2008.

Implementation

As with database mirroring, you must configure log shipping for each database, and log ship-ping does not provide protection at the instance level. For this reason, you must also copy any data that may be needed by the secondary database, such as logins and jobs. Unlike database mirroring, log shipping relies on copying the entire transaction log instead of sending and committing single transactions. The recovery model for the primary database can be full or bulk-logged. (Database mirroring must use the full recovery model.) Also, there is no option that provides automatic failover using log shipping; it is purely a manual process referred to as a *role change*. During a role change, you manually bring online the secondary server, and it assumes the "role" of the primary server.

Log shipping uses a fairly fundamental process. One database makes normal transaction log backups, while another database is in constant restore mode. You would take the following actions during a typical log shipping setup process:

1. Take a full backup of the primary database.

2. Restore that backup on the secondary server, leaving the database in a state to accept further restores.

3. Create a job on the primary server to back up the transaction logs for the primary data-base.

4. Create a job on the secondary server to copy transaction logs.

5. Create a job on the secondary server to restore the transaction logs.

6. Create an alert job on the monitor to indicate a failure if the databases are out of sync beyond the configured threshold.

You can use network load balancing to mask the role change from the application. Using network load balancing allows both servers to appear on the network with the same IP address. The client applications can connect to the primary server using the virtual IP address, and if a role change occurs, you can use network load balancing to transfer the traffic to the new primary server without having to modify the application. While network load balancing still does not provide automatic failover, it does make the role change a faster process, since the applications will be ready to use the database as soon as the role change has occurred. Figure 3-6 shows a typical configuration using log shipping with network load balancing.

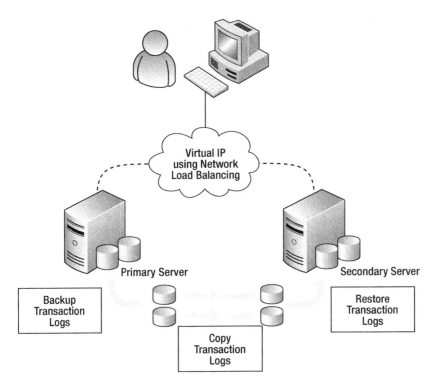

Figure 3-6. *Log shipping configuration and workflow*

There are two types of role changes: planned and unplanned. A planned role change occurs when the primary and secondary servers are still online. This is obviously the best kind of role change, since you are not in emergency mode trying to get the database back online. An unplanned role change occurs when the primary server crashes, and you bring the secondary server online to service the requests.

Restoring to the Secondary Server

You can restore the database on the secondary server using two different options, NORECOVERY and STANDBY. Using the NORECOVERY option will place the database in a loading state and will not allow any connections to the database. Using the STANDBY option will place the database in a read-only state that will allow connectivity, but any time a new log is restored, all the connections to the database must be dropped or the restore will fail. If you are trying to use log shipping as a reporting solution as well as a high-availability solution, we don't think your users will enjoy getting kicked out of the database every 15 minutes while the transaction logs are restored. One way to avoid this is by setting a load delay of 12 hours or so to bypass log restores during business hours. The logs will continue copying to the secondary server, and only the ones older than the load delay will be applied. After business hours, the load delay can be reset to 15 minutes or so to allow the logs to catch up with the primary server, which will ensure that no logs are restored during business hours. Using a load delay works well with systems that require static, day-old reporting capabilities. Another benefit of using a load delay is that it protects against human errors, such as users deleting the wrong records in a table. If you set a load delay of four hours and a user calls you about a mistake that was made two hours ago, the transaction log containing the mistake has not yet been applied to the secondary server, so you can recover the data from there.

Pros and Cons of Log Shipping

Log shipping is a fairly inexpensive way to get data from point A to point B. It was officially released in SQL Server 2000, but homegrown implementations were used prior to its release. Because log shipping works by copying transaction logs across the network, there is no way to ensure zero data loss. Also, the latency between the primary database and the secondary database can be significant. If log shipping is all your budget will allow, and you have set the proper expectations with your management, log shipping can be configured in several different ways to provide a flexible solution for high availability and recovery.

The benefits of log shipping include the following:

- No special hardware or windows configurations

- No distance limitations

- Duplicate data for disaster recovery

- Limited reporting capabilities

Restrictions and drawbacks of log shipping are that it

- Requires more disk space to store duplicate data

- Must be configured separately for each database

- Does not fail over automatically

- Will likely result in some data loss in the event that a failover occurs

Making Data Available Through Replication

Replication refers to the technology behind creating and maintaining duplicate copies of database objects, such as tables. For example, you can create a copy of a key table—say, a customer table—in several reporting databases located at different regional offices of your company. You can synchronize those copies manually or automatically. If automatically, you can schedule synchronizations to occur at specific times of day. You can even go so far as to force all replicated copies to be kept fully up to date as transactions against the master copy occur.

Replication is best thought of as a way to make business data available in different databases or at different locations. The idea is to give different applications access to the same data or to make data conveniently available for reporting. Replication isn't really intended as a high-availability mechanism, though it does sometimes get used as one.

Key Terms

As with every other high-availability technique discussed in this chapter, replication has its own way of referring to the participating servers and objects. Here is a list of key terms that you should be familiar with while reading this section and when talking about replication in SQL Server:

- *Publisher*: Source server containing the primary database
- *Subscriber*: Target server receiving the publication
- *Distributor*: Server used to keep track of the subscriptions and manages the activity between the publisher and the subscriber
- *Articles*: Database objects that are being replicated
- *Publications*: Collection of articles
- *Agents*: Executables used to help perform replications tasks

Replication Overview

Replication offers a wide variety of options and methods of implementation. Unlike anything else discussed thus far, replication allows you to copy data at the object level instead of the database level. Unfortunately, replication requires several up front design considerations that may prevent you from deploying it in your environment, especially if you are supporting a vendor-supplied application. For example, each table that is published using transactional replication must have a primary key; or when using identity columns in a multi-node replication topology, each node must be configured to use a distinct range of values.

Replication is a good solution when working with disconnected data sources or subsets of data. It allows users in separate locations the ability to work with their own subscription database and sync back up with the publisher on a periodic basis by using a push or pull subscription. In a *push* subscription, the distributor pushes the data to the subscriber; in a *pull* subscription, the subscriber pulls the data. Replication supports the distribution of publications to many subscribers. The replicated data is first sent from the publisher and then stored on the distributor until the transactions are sent to the subscriber. You can configure the distributor to run on the same server as the publisher, but this will add extra overhead to the server. The publisher will run more efficiently if the distributor is on a separate server. The subscription database is not required to be read-only and remains in a completely functional state, allowing normal operations to occur.

Replication uses executables called *replication agents* to support certain replication actions that are performed. Different replication agents are used depending on the type of replication that is implemented. The three basic types of replication are known as *snapshot*, *merge*, and *transactional*. Each replication type has different capabilities that will be discussed in the following sections. Replication is supported in all editions of SQL Server with the exception that publishing is not allowed in SQL Server Express or SQL Server Compact 3.5 SP1.

> **Note** If you are looking purely from a high-availability standpoint, in our opinion, replication is usually a poor choice. We have always thought of replication as a way of combining or sharing disconnected data sets and not as a high-availability technique. You will generally notice the lack of the word failover when dealing with replication. That is because high availability is not the primary function of replication; it's more of a side effect. However, replication does allow more granular capabilities for transferring data and may prove to be the best solution in certain situations.

Snapshot Replication

Snapshot replication runs on a periodic basis and copies the entire publication to the subscriber every time it is run. It lays the foundation for transactional and merge replication by sending the initial publication to the subscriber. No updates can be performed on a table while the snapshot agent copies the data from the publisher to the distributor. The entire table is locked during the process. To boost the speed of the snapshot generation process, parallel processing is available in SQL Server 2008 when scripting objects and bulk copying data. SQL Server 2008 also allows for interrupted snapshot delivery, meaning that if the delivery of the snapshot is interrupted during initialization, only the data that has not been copied will be transferred when the snapshot is resumed. Figure 3-7 shows the configuration of snapshot replication.

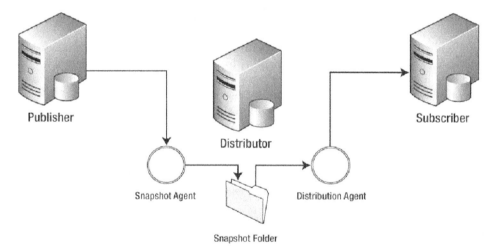

Figure 3-7. *Snapshot replication configuration*

Transactional Replication

Transactional replication is most often preferred when high availability is a concern because it provides the highest level of precision by using distributed transactions to ensure consistency. Transactional replication works by sending an initial snapshot to the subscriber and then keeping the subscriber up to date by sending only specific marked transactions. The snapshot is periodically resent on a scheduled basis, and transactions are used to update subscribers between snapshots. SQL Server 2008 allows the initial snapshot to be created from any backup that has been taken after the publication has been enabled for initialization with a backup.

The transactions are stored in the distribution database until they have been applied to all the subscribers. The transactions are applied to the subscribers in the order they were received on the publisher to ensure accuracy. It is important to note that transactions cannot be cleared from the transaction log on the publisher until they have been sent to the distributor. If connectivity is lost between the publisher and the distributor, this could cause excessive growth in the transaction log. Also, some database administrators like to disable auto growth and put a cap on the size of the data files. This could also lead to a failure in the case of excessive transaction log growth. Figure 3-8 shows the configuration of transactional replication.

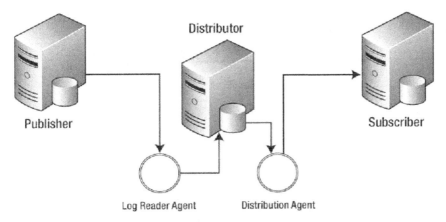

Figure 3-8. *Transactional replication configuration*

Tip You need to make sure to size the drives appropriately to account for the possibility of excessive file growth due to connection issues so you will not suffer an outage due to lack of disk space.

Updateable Subscriptions

You can use updateable subscriptions in transactional replication to allow the subscriber to update the publications and synchronize them with the publisher. Triggers are added to the subscription database that fire when data needs to be sent to the publisher. The two types of updateable subscriptions are known as immediate updating and queued updating.

Immediate updating uses the Microsoft Distributed Transaction Coordinator (MSDTC) to apply a two-phase commit transaction. Along with the triggers that are created on the subscriber to transmit data changes to the publisher, stored procedures are created on the publisher to update the data. The triggers on the subscriber use the MSDTC to call the stored procedures on the publisher to update the data. If there is any conflict due to out-of-date data on the subscriber, the entire transaction is rolled back at the publisher and the subscriber. Once the change has been made to the publisher, the publisher will then distribute the changes to any other subscribers. Figure 3-9 demonstrates transactional replication with immediate updating.

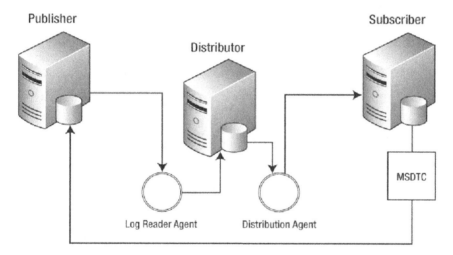

Figure 3-9. *Transactional replication with immediate updating*

Queued updating works similarly to immediate updating, except instead of making a two-phase commit, it uses the MSreplication_queue to store the transactions. The queue reader agent then reads the transactions from the MSreplication_queue and calls the stored procedures on the publisher to update the data. If a conflict is encountered, it is resolved by the rules defined in the conflict resolution policy set when the publication was created. Just as in immediate updating, the changes are then distributed to the other subscribers. The benefit of using queued updating is that the subscriber does not have to be connected in order to make changes to the database. Figure 3-10 demonstrates transactional replication with queued updating.

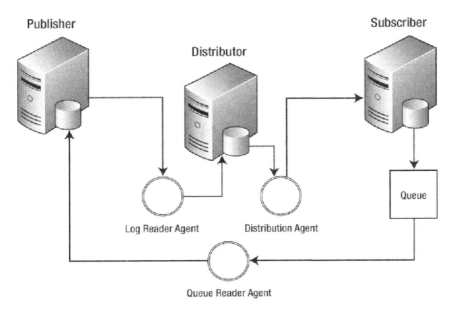

Figure 3-10. *Transactional replication with queued updating*

Peer-to-Peer Replication

Peer-to-peer replication was introduced in SQL Server 2005 and is an important feature when using replication as a high-availability aid. It is a special form of transactional replication that maintains an almost real-time copy of the data across multiple servers. The servers participating in peer-to-peer replication are referred to as nodes because each server is a publisher and a subscriber. Since the data is propagated to all of the servers in the topology, you can easily take a server out of the mix to perform maintenance by redirecting the traffic to another server. One of the downfalls is that you never know where a transaction is in the process of replicating to the other servers in the topology.

SQL Server 2008 has enhanced peer-to-peer replication by allowing you to add and remove servers without interrupting the other servers in the topology. Conflict detection has also been provided in SQL Server 2008, allowing you to catch conflicts that may have otherwise been overlooked in SQL Server 2005. The topology wizard has also been added in SQL Server 2008 to enable visual configuration of peer-to-peer replication. Figure 3-11 shows a typical peer-to-peer transactional replication configuration.

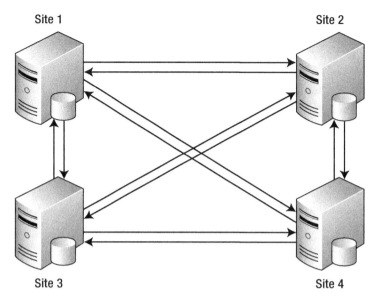

Figure 3-11. *Peer-to-peer transactional replication configuration*

Merge Replication

You can use merge replication to allow publishers and subscribers to make changes to data independently and then merge the results. The merge process is not immediate and depends on the push and pull processes to combine the data. One of the benefits of merge replication is that you can write custom code to handle conflicts. With transactional replication, either the publisher or subscriber is deemed the winner, and their transaction is applied, or the conflict is logged and human intervention is required. Writing custom code allows you to apply complex business logic so that no human intervention will be required when a conflict is encountered.

The merge agent watches for conflicting changes, and the conflict resolver determines what change will be applied. You can track conflicts at the column level or the row level. Column-level conflicts occur if multiple updates have been made to the same column in a row by multiple servers; row-level conflicts occur when multiple updates have been made to any column in a given row. Figure 3-12 shows the configuration of merge replication.

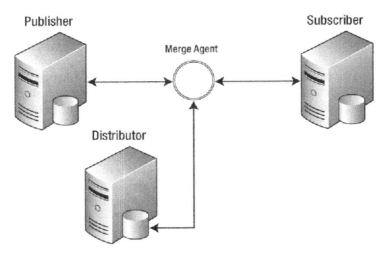

Figure 3-12. *Merge replication configuration*

Pros and Cons of Replication

Instead of going into the benefits and restrictions of each type of replication and various configurations, we will summarize the benefits and restrictions of replication as a whole. The benefits of replication include the following:

- No distance limitations
- Duplicate data for disaster recovery
- Disconnected data manipulation and synchronization

Restrictions and drawbacks are as follows:

- Possible data loss
- Possible data conflicts
- No automatic failover
- Requires special database design considerations

Other High-Availability Techniques

High availability is not limited to the techniques already discussed in this chapter. You should utilize anything that can attribute to less downtime and a better end-user experience. There are third-party solutions to supplement SQL Server, such as geographically disbursed clusters.

Geographically disbursed clustering allows you to break the network limitations in failover clustering and place the nodes in separate geographic locations. Hardware configurations, such as drive mirroring and RAID levels, provide fault tolerance and protect against a single disk failure.

Other capabilities in SQL Server can be used to help ensure availability as well. Change Data Capture will allow you to capture changes that have been made in certain tables and ship them off to another server. Having a good backup solution is always your last line of defense when dealing with high availability. If all else fails, you can always restore from a recent backup. No matter how much money you spend on the hardware and software, it is critical to have the appropriate level of knowledge to support it. If you do not have the proper comprehension to spring into action when the time comes, you could make costly mistakes. A lack of knowledge could cause something that may have taken a few minutes to possibly take a few days, and in certain situations, valuable data could be lost that may never be recovered.

High Availability Feature Comparison

Table 3-1 can be used as a quick reference when comparing the features of the major high-availability techniques. You can quickly narrow down which solution you may need in your environment by highlighting the required features. For example, if zero data loss is required, then that leaves you with failover clustering and high-safety mirroring. If you require protection against disk failure, the only remaining option is high-safety mirroring. Sometimes the best solution is a combination of high-availability techniques. You can find out more about combining high-availability techniques by reading the article "High Availability: Interoperability and Coexistence" at SQL Server Books Online (http://msdn.microsoft.com/en-us/library/bb500117.aspx).

Table 3-1. *High Availability Feature Comparison*

Feature	Failover Clustering	Mirroring (High Performance)	Mirroring (High Safety)	Log Shipping	Replication
Instance Level Protection	Yes	No	No	No	No
Duplicate Copy of Database	No	Yes	Yes	Yes	Yes
User Error Protection	No	No	No	Yes	No
Reporting Capabilities	No	Yes	Yes	Yes	Yes
Fast Recovery	Yes	No	Yes	No	No
Automatic Failover	Yes	No	Yes	No	No
Zero Data Loss	Yes	No	Yes	No	No
Distance Limitations	Yes	No	No	No	No
Requires Special Hardware	Yes	No	No	No	No
Protects Against Disk Failure	No	Yes	Yes	Yes	Yes

DON'T MESS WITH THE SERVER

I can't tell you how many times we have seen a server crash because someone thought they could fit in some server patches or update some drivers during a quick reboot. Everything that happens on a server should be thought of in a worst-case scenario. What happens if I apply this patch and the server dies? Is this a chance I am willing to take 30 minutes before hundreds of users start trying to login to a production system?

Make sure you have plenty of maintenance time and a good backout plan no matter how trivial you think a change may be. After all, what's the point of taking the time and money to research and implement high availability when a simple bad decision could bring an environment to its knees? That is why it is so important to create an SLA and stick to it. All maintenance on the server should be performed during the defined maintenance window instead of doing something just because you had to reboot the server anyway.

Not to pick on the hardware people, but unplanned maintenance may be happening in your environment without you even knowing it. Server administrators have different priorities than database administrators. They may need updated firmware or drivers in order to use the latest versions of their monitoring tools. There are several patches a month that need to be applied to servers, and the server administrators may be getting a lot of pressure to keep the systems up to date. Many times if you call a system administrator to perform a quick reboot, you may be getting a little more than you expected.

While we are on the subject of patching, make sure not to patch all your servers at once. Make sure to patch all of your nonproduction systems well in advance to provide a sufficient "burn in" time. Also, if it is at all possible, stagger your production patches as well. There is always the possibility that something will get overlooked on the test systems that will be a show-stopper in production. We have seen an application go down because all production servers were patched, and the only way to back out was to reinstall SQL Server to a patch level that was supported by the application.

Our rule of staggering changes goes for configuration changes as well. We saw someone try to make a "quick change" to a table by adding a new column in the middle of the table. If you have ever seen what happens in the background to achieve such a change, you know it could take quite a while, depending on the size of the table. SQL Server creates a new temporary table to store the data, inserts the data from the old table, drops the old table, and then renames the new table to the original table name. They didn't understand why this was taking so long in production (on a table with a few million records) when it only took a few seconds on the test system in a table with significantly fewer records.

The bottom line is this: Don't mess with the server. You can't use a production server, which you expect to participate in a highly available system, as a playground. If you have to think twice about doing something, that's one time too many.

Summary

Microsoft SQL Server 2008 offers many different techniques to help you implement and maintain the highest available solution possible. Many of the features offered by these techniques can be combined to ensure an even higher level of availability. Having the knowledge necessary to understand what technologies are available and determining how they will be implemented in your environment is key to the successful deployment of any application. Now that we've covered many of the things you should consider during the planning stages, you will finally be able to get your hands dirty. The next section will cover the ins and outs of installing and upgrading SQL Server 2008.

PART 2

Getting Started

CHAPTER 4

Installing Microsoft SQL Server 2008

The past two chapters discussed which edition of SQL Server 2008 to install, identifying and selecting the hardware requirements, and figuring out the high-availability solution to implement, if any. In an effort to help stimulate thought and effort into planning the installation of your system, there was an adequate amount of information presented. You have finally reached the point where you can validate your pre-installation considerations and install SQL Server 2008. There are three installation methods discussed throughout this chapter:

- Installing SQL Server using the GUI version of setup.exe

- Installing SQL Server from the command line

- Installing SQL Server using a configuration file

Installing SQL Server from the GUI version of setup.exe is the method that many of you use to complete your installations. Fortunately (or unfortunately, depending on your point of view), Microsoft has modified the setup installation process, forcing you to pay attention to the verbiage on each screen and be knowledgeable about the installation process. How many of you have previously installed SQL Server versions just by clicking on Next repeatedly until the install was complete? However, you no longer have that luxury. Beginning with SQL Server 2008, you need to know what options you want installed and where to find those options within the Installation Center.

Command-line installation allows you to pass parameters to the install executable in order to configure SQL Server 2008. Once you have determined the configuration options and the SQL Server features that you want, you can pass those as parameters to the command-line, and the installation process will proceed without any further user interaction.

You also have the option to install based upon a configuration that you record in a text file called a *configuration file*. This type of installation accepts a configuration file parameter at the command line, pointing to a file that specifies the tools and configuration options you want for that installation of SQL Server. Installing SQL Server using a configuration file also requires no user interaction. For those of you who want to deploy multiple instances of SQL Server 2008 throughout your organization with the same configuration, then pay close attention to the sections titled, "Command-Line Installation" and "Configuration File Installation."

User Accounts

Before installing SQL Server 2008, we recommend spending some time identifying the type of login you want used for each one of the services. The selected components during install will create services to run them. You can set up all the services to run under one user account or have separate accounts for each one of the services. We prefer to set up restrictive accounts for each service, which only give rights to perform the tasks needed. This minimizes the chances of compromising all SQL Server components in the event that one of the user passwords is cracked. The user accounts can be one of three types: a domain user account, a built-in system account, or a local user account.

Use domain accounts if

- The service will be accessing files from another server (via sending or picking up).

- The service has to utilize network services.

Use local user accounts if

- The service will not access any of the servers.

- The server is not a member of the domain.

Use built-in system accounts if

- The service needs predefined rights on the local server or network.

Based on the needs of your service, choose the best type of account for your purposes. Remember, the security of your system depends on the decisions that you make. Don't rush this process; figure out what the best security policy is for you.

Preparation and Prerequisites

Before you start the install, there are a couple of terms used throughout SQL Server Books Online and the verbiage within setup that you should be familiar with:

- *SQL Server Installation Center*: The first screen that you will see after clicking on setup.exe. It contains the categories needed to navigate through the various installation methods.

- *Database engine configuration*: A screen you will come across when installing the database engine. It contains options for determining the security method for the SQL Server instance, the location of files, and the enabling of FILESTREAM.

After you have inserted the SQL Server 2008 disk or navigated out to the network share where the SQL Server 2008 files are stored, you can double-click on setup.exe and start the installation process.

Note   We are walking through the installation of Enterprise Edition in this chapter.

When the installation process starts, SQL Server 2008 will check for some prerequisites for the application to install on the server/machine. The first prerequisite checks that you are likely to encounter are for the Microsoft .NET Framework and an update to the Windows Installer. (SQL Server 2008 requires you to have Microsoft .NET Framework 3.5 service pack 1 and Windows Installer 4.5 installed on your server/ machine.) Figure 4-1 shows you the prerequisite message.

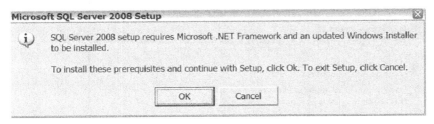

Figure 4-1. *The SQL Server 2008 message that requires you to install Microsoft .NET Framework and an update to the Windows Installer*

Caution You need to ensure that any applications running on the sever or computer where SQL 2008 is being installed will continue to function properly with .NET Framework 3.5 service pack 1. You don't want to break other applications by blindly installing the new framework. If SQL Server is on a server/machine by itself, then upgrading the framework should result in minimal risk to your environment.

After you have made the decision to install the prerequisites, follow the instructions on the screen to download and install the missing applications. Unfortunately, installing prerequisites, such as the .NET Framework, may require a reboot. Make sure you have scheduled downtime on the server prior to installing any prerequisite applications. Once you have installed the prerequisites, setup.exe will finish its initial validations and launch the SQL Server Installation Center.

SQL Server Installation Center

SQL Server Installation Center does not resemble any of the previous SQL Server versions. Keep in mind that SQL Server 2008 will not allow you to "Next" your way through the installation process. The initial screen of the SQL Server Installation Center requires you to read the options and select the category that best suits what you are looking for. Figure 4-2 shows you the default menu of SQL Server Installation Center.

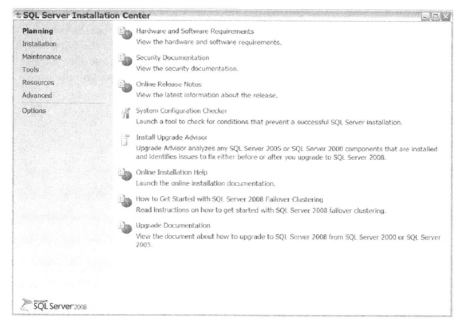

Figure 4-2. *The various options available within the SQL Server Installation Center*

As you can see from Figure 4-2, the SQL Server Installation Center has seven main categories to choose from: Planning, Installation, Maintenance, Tools, Resources, Advanced, and Options. Because each category has a series of different options, we want to review each of the categories with you to help you better understand how they work.

Planning

The Planning category within the SQL Server Installation Center incorporates links that take you to MSDN to review hardware and software requirements, security considerations, online release notes, online installation help, upgrade documentation, and information on how to get started with SQL Server 2008 failover clustering.

We've already covered hardware, software, and security requirements in the pre-installation process in Chapter 2. Hopefully, you followed our advice and started the planning process before beginning the actual installation. If you've arrived at the installation stage without any proper planning, then we encourage you to read or re-read Chapter 2 and plan your installation.

The Planning category also provides a System Configuration Checker and an installation Upgrade Advisor. The System Configuration Checker scans the machine where the installation of SQL Server 2008 exists and determines if there are stipulations that would cause SQL Server not to install properly. In order to continue on the installation path, the System Configuration Checker cannot fail on any of the items needed for the install. The System Configuration Checker will provide hints or suggestions for getting rid of any of the obstacles that are in your way.

The Upgrade Advisor identifies potential problems that may exist on your server/machine with components from SQL Server 2000 and SQL Server 2005. The feature determines if issues exist to address before or after an upgrade to SQL Server 2008. To run the Upgrade Adviser, first install it by clicking on the link, accepting the license agreement, and following the remaining instructions on the screen. Once the Upgrade Advisor install has completed, you are ready to utilize the Upgrade Advisor. (We cover the Upgrade Advisor in detail in Chapter 5.)

■**Note** This chapter focuses upon a fresh install of SQL Server 2008. Chapter 5 covers upgrading from a previous release.

Installation

The Installation category contains the wizards that will guide you through the various installation options available within SQL Server 2008. From this option, you can install SQL Server 2008 or add additional features to an existing installation. You can upgrade to SQL Server 2008 from SQL Server 2000 or SQL Server 2005, install SQL Server 2008 failover clustering, or add an additional node to an existing cluster. There is also an option to run Microsoft Update to check your machine for the latest and greatest patches. See Figure 4-3 for a glimpse of the installation options.

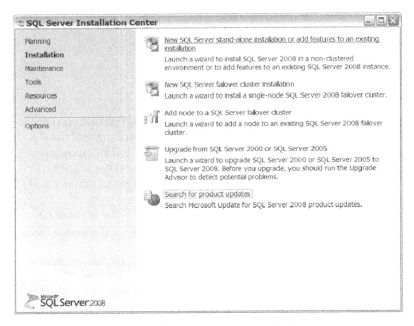

Figure 4-3. *The options available under the Installation category*

Maintenance

The Maintenance category provides options for modifying your SQL Server 2008 installation. (Figure 4-4 shows the Maintenance screen.) It provides selections for upgrading the edition of SQL Server 2008 that's currently installed (allowing you to move from, say, Standard Edition to Enterprise Edition), a choice to repair a corrupt SQL Server 2008 installation, and an option to remove a node from a SQL Server cluster.

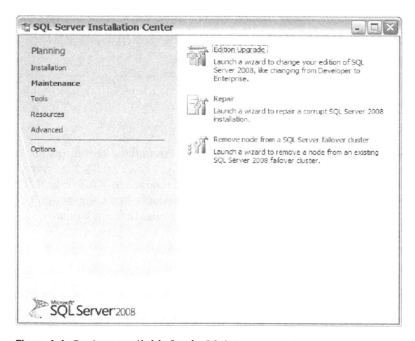

Figure 4-4. *Options available for the Maintenance category*

Remember that Chapter 2 covered the various editions of SQL Server 2008 that you can install. Some of you may have determined during your pre-installation planning that the SQL Server 2008 Workgroup Edition would fulfill your business requirements, and you may have installed that edition. If your requirements have changed, and you now need the Standard or Enterprise Edition, then you can use the Edition Upgrade option to modify your edition. You can do that without having to re-install SQL Server.

The Repair option resembles any other application repair processes. In the event of corruption within the core application files, you run the repair wizard and follow the instructions on the screen while it walks you through the repair process.

Earlier, in Figure 4-3, you saw the option to add additional nodes to a SQL Server cluster. It's here in the Maintenance category, though, where you remove unwanted nodes. (You can see that option in Figure 4-4.) Just as with earlier options, selecting the Remove Node from a SQL Server Failover Cluster option will launch a wizard that walks you through the process of removing the node.

Tools

The Tools category in the SQL Server Installation Center provides you with the means for ensuring no restrictions exist that would prevent you from installing SQL Server 2008. It allows you to identify all SQL Server 2000, 2005, and 2008 features and components. Finally, it provides a method for upgrading SQL Server 2005 SQL Server Integration Services (SSIS) packages to SQL Server 2008 SSIS packages. Figure 4-5 shows the screen and the options at your disposal.

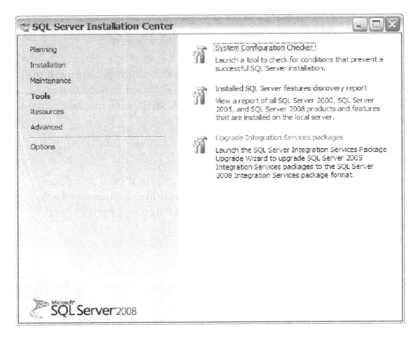

Figure 4-5. *The Tools category of SQL Server Installation Center*

The System Configuration Checker exists in the Tools category as well as in the Planning category. The designers of the Installation Center must have wanted to ensure that the System Configuration Checker wasn't overlooked or lost.

Selecting the Installed SQL Server Features Discovery Report option provides you with a detailed report of information about SQL Server products installed on the server. Reviewing that report is an excellent method for validating the features from SQL Server 2000, 2005, or 2008 that are currently installed. The report will display the product, instance, features, edition, version, and clustering, if it exists. (See Figure 4-6 for an example.)

Microsoft SQL Server 2008 Setup Discovery Report

Product	Instance	Instance ID	Feature	Language	Edition	Version	Clustered
Sql Server 2005			Tools	1033	Standard Edition	9.2.3054	No
Sql Server 2005			ToolsClient	1033	Standard Edition	9.2.3054	No
Sql Server 2005			ToolsClient\Connectivity	1033	Standard Edition	9.2.3054	No
Sql Server 2005			ToolsDocument	1033	Standard Edition	9.2.3054	No
Sql Server 2005			ToolsDocument\BOL	1033	Standard Edition	9.2.3054	No

Figure 4-6. *A sample Microsoft SQL Server 2008 Features Setup Discovery Report*

The Upgrade Integration Services Packages option is a wizard that walks you through the process of upgrading your SQL Server 2005 SSIS packages to the SQL Server 2008 SSIS packages format. Upgrading SSIS packages will be covered in Chapter 5, so for now just be aware of the location of this option.

Resources

The Resources category contains links to various SQL Server 2008 informational web pages. From this category, you can quickly access SQL Server 2008 Books Online, SQL Server TechCenter, SQL Server Developer Center, and several other links. This category provides great links to increase your knowledge on SQL Server 2008 (see Figure 4-7).

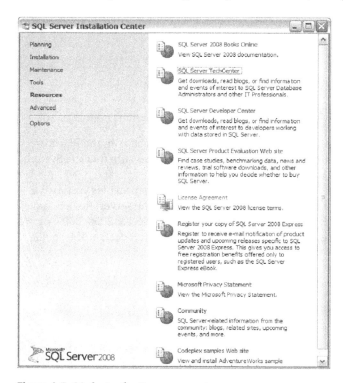

Figure 4-7. *Links in the Resources category*

Advanced

The Advanced category provides options for more complex installs, such as from a configuration file. The category also provides an Advanced Cluster Preparation wizard. Figure 4-8 shows the category screen.

The configuration file install selection allows you to install SQL Serve 2008 based on an existing configuration file. We will discuss configuration file installs later on in this chapter (see the "Configuration File Installation" section).

The other two options in this category pertain to wizards for preparing SQL Server 2008 for failover clustering installation, as well as for completing the setup of failover clustering. Detailed clustering installation information is not covered in this book, but please don't forget the location of these options, especially if you want to set up clustering in your environment.

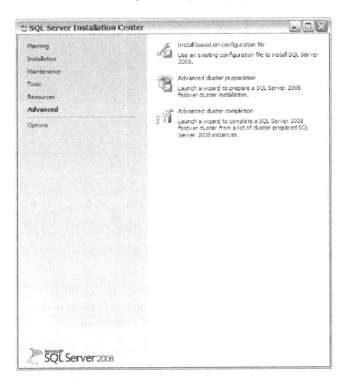

Figure 4-8. *The Advanced category screen*

Options

The Options category allows you to specify the architecture of SQL Server to install or to change the location of the installation files. The edition of SQL Server 2008 that you are installing, along with the hardware of the target PC or server, will determine the architecture options available (see Figure 4-9).

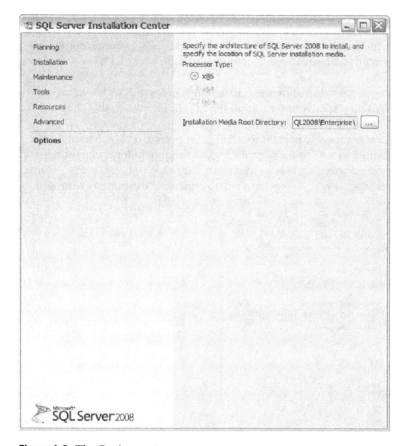

Figure 4-9. *The Options category screen*

The Processor Type options available for the Enterprise Edition are x86, x64, or IA64. Grayed out options are not supported by your server. The installation media will likely default to the location you clicked on in the setup file. If you would like to change the installation media location, then the options category is where you should make that change.

Installing Your First Instance

Now that you understand the layout of the SQL Server Installation Center and what is contained within each category, you can begin the installation process. In this section, we show how to install the SQL Server 2008 software and create your first database instance on a given server. The next major section, called "Installing More Than One Instance," shows you how to install a second and subsequent instances on the same server.

Checking System Configuration

The first thing usually run is the System Configuration Checker. As stated earlier, this exists in both the Tools and Planning categories in the SQL Server Installation Center. After selecting the System Configuration Checker, a process will start scanning your server/computer to validate your configurations. See Figure 4-10 for an example of System Configuration Checker results.

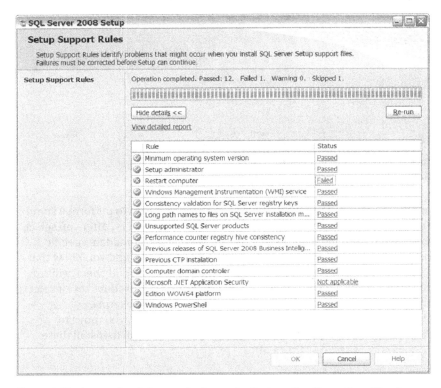

Figure 4-10. *A sample of the results from the System Configuration Checker*

Each rule may receive one of four statuses: Passed, Failed, Warning, or Not Applicable (option skipped because it does not apply). Passed means that the rule met the installation requirements. The Failed status, also symbolized by a red X icon, indicates problems that were identified during the scan. You must fix all failures before the setup process can continue. Click on the Failed link for information about each error and for help in resolving the issues. Figure 4-10 displayed a failure message on the Restart Computer rule because of a failure to restart the computer after an application install. The Failed link indicated the need to restart the computer in order to continue the installation process.

Review warnings even though they identify rules that did not fail. The Not applicable status indicates options that do not apply to your machine or server. After resolving any Failed statuses, or if nothing fails, you should receive a summary of the Setup Support Rules, as shown in Figure 4-11.

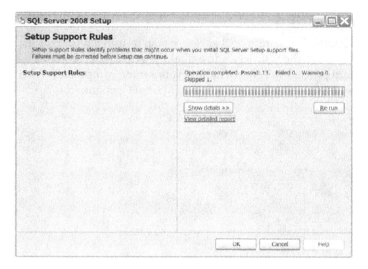

Figure 4-11. *After the successful completion of the System Configuration Checker*

After completing the System Configuration Checker, you can move on to perform a stand-alone installation. The option to do that is located in the Installation category. After you select the stand-alone installation option, the installer will run another check to validate specific rules. Since you have already executed the System Configuration Checker, and you know that your system is ready for the install, further delays will be minimal. This second check will run successfully, and you can proceed to the Product Key section. Enter your product key or select a free edition to install. Click Next after the selection and accept the license terms.

Once you've entered your product key and accepted the license terms, you move to the Setup Support Files installation page, shown in Figure 4-12. Click Install to install these support files.

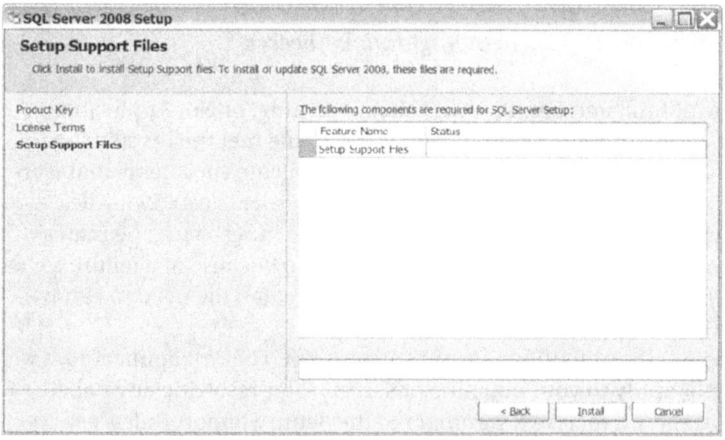

Figure 4-12. *The Setup Support Files installation screen*

The validations of the remainder of the System Configuration Checker rules occur on the summary screen once the installation of the setup support files is complete. All of the rules should pass, as shown in Figure 4-13, unless you've skipped checking your system configuration earlier as we suggested.

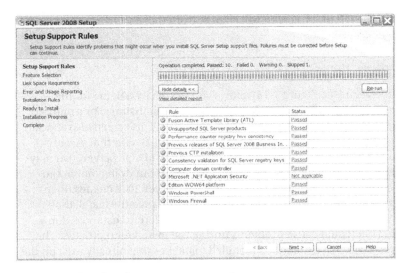

Figure 4-13. *Passing the setup support rules*

Choosing Your Features

Click Next and look at the Feature Selection screen (shown in Figure 4-14), which lists the options available to install. We don't cover all options in this chapter. We do, however, cover installing the database engine and many of the shared features.

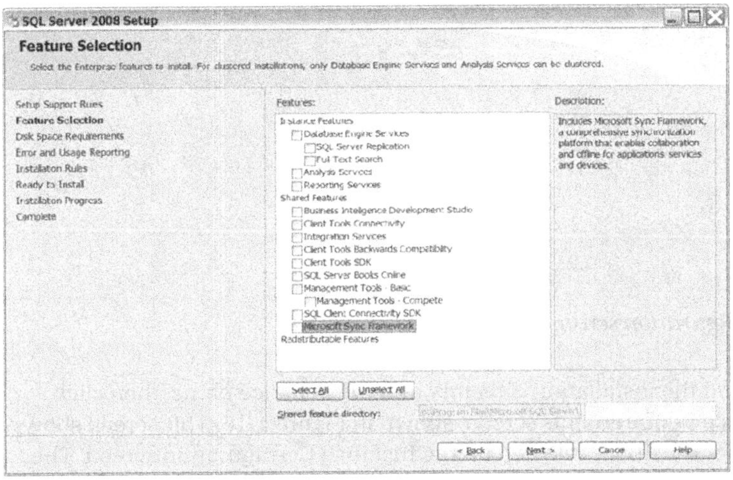

Figure 4-14. *The selectable features available for install*

Select the features that you want to install. If you are trying to determine what the functionality of a feature is, then highlight the feature and review the displayed description. The feature's description should provide you with enough information to help you determine whether to install it.

Once you select all the features that you want installed, click Next. If you select Database Engine Services, the steps on the left of the screen will change from those shown in Figure 4-14 to those in Figure 4-15 in the next section.

Configuring the Instance

The Instance Configuration screen (see Figure 4-15) allows you to specify a name for the instance of SQL Server that you are installing. You can specify a default instance or a named instance, depending on the pre-installation decisions that you made. This screen also allows you to change the location of the root directory for the instance of SQL Server that you are installing. Therefore, if you are installing a named or second instance of SQL Server, you may want to change the installation directory of the files. We'll talk later about doing that in the section called "Installing More Than One Instance." Luckily, SQL Server 2008 creates directories based upon the instance name by default. So if you forget to change the installation directory of the files, then SQL Server will make sure the files from different instances don't reside in the same location. That would cause problems during the installation process. The Instance Configuration screen will also display any installed instances that already exist on the server or machine.

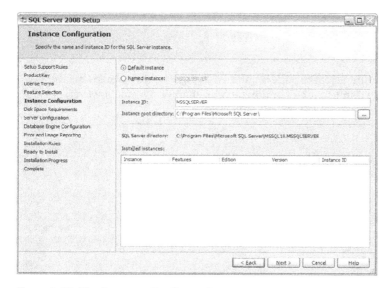

Figure 4-15. *The Instance Configuration screen*

After you have determined the installation directory and the instance name, then click Next to arrive at the Disk Space Requirements screen, shown in Figure 4-16. This screen shows you the disk usage summary of the drives selected on the Instance Configuration screen. The summary shows the chosen drives, the required space from each of those drives, and the available space on each. Then the drive summary breaks down the required space into separate sections, allowing you to see how much space each component of the install will consume. You'll see a green check mark icon by each drive with enough space. If you see any red X icons, you should free up space before moving on.

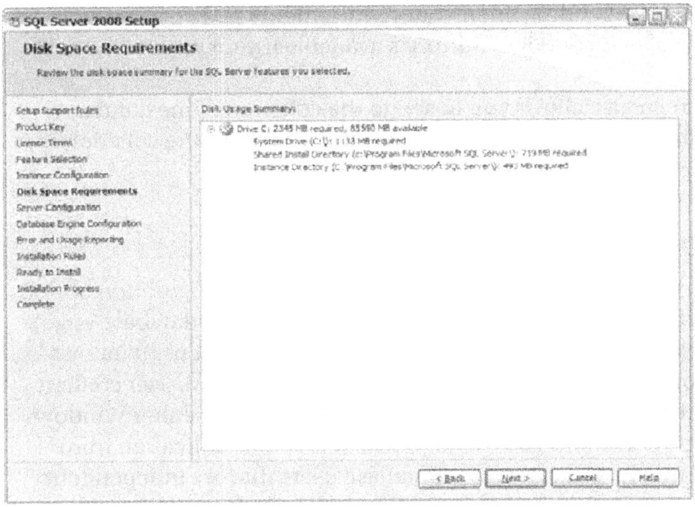

Figure 4-16. *A sample Disk Space Requirements screen*

After selecting Next from the Disk Space Requirements screen, the Server Configuration page (see Figure 4-17) is where you determine the service account names and passwords to be used for the database engine, as well as the other services you want installed.

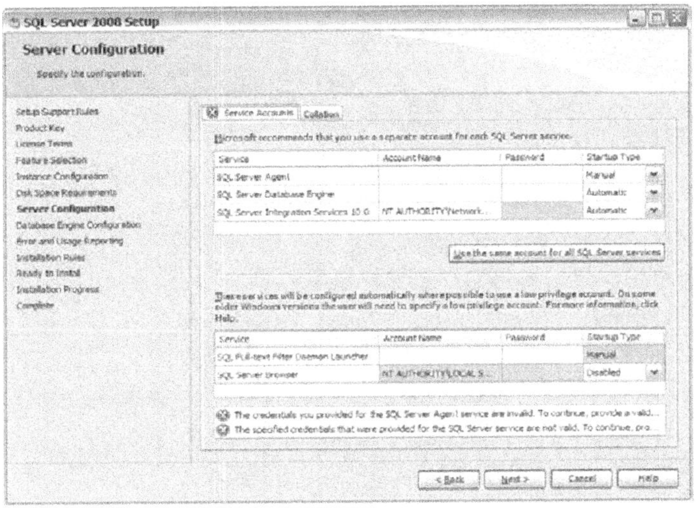

Figure 4-17. *The Service Accounts tab in the Server Configuration screen*

For each service, populate the account name, the password, and the startup type. The startup type configures the behavior of the service after the restart of your server. An option exists to use the same account for all services that you are installing. In the "User Accounts" section at the beginning of this chapter, we provided recommendations for account names and usage for the different services. Depending upon your requirements and environment, the Use Same Accounts for All SQL Server Services button is available if your environment fits that model.

The Server Configuration screen also allows you to set up the collation of the database engine. Based on your application needs and business requirements, choose the collation that meets those needs and select Next.

Configuring the Database Engine

After you have completed the server configuration, the Database Engine Configuration options shown in Figure 4-18 are next. First, decide the authentication mode for your database engine. You can choose between Windows Authentication Mode or Mixed Mode options. Windows authentication allows users to connect to SQL Server 2008 using their Windows user credentials. Mixed mode authentication allows users to connect to SQL Server using either Windows authentication or SQL Server authentication. You manage SQL Server authentication from within the database engine. Essentially, you can create database users that are independent from any existing Windows user accounts.

If you select mixed mode authentication, then SQL Server forces you to create a password for the system administrator (SA) account. Choose a strong password for the SA account!

In SQL Server 2008, administrators for the server at the Windows level are not necessarily administrators within SQL Server. You can use the Specify SQL Server Administrators option shown in Figure 4-18 to designate certain Windows users and groups as SQL Server administrators.

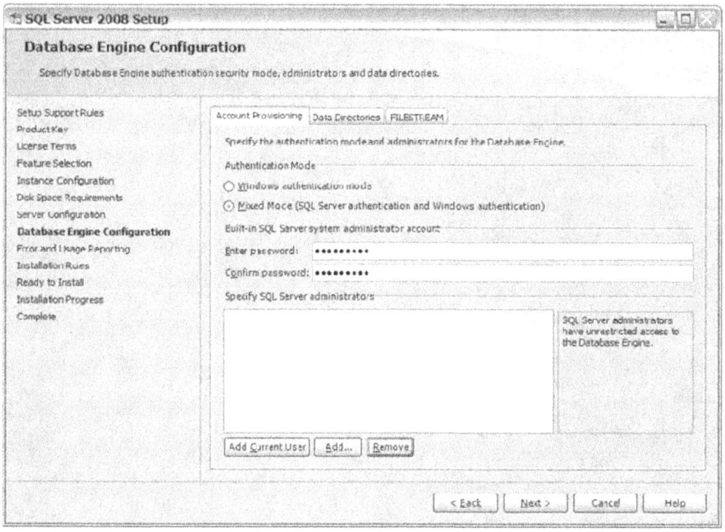

Figure 4-18. *The Account Provisioning tab in the Database Engine Configuration screen*

■Note If you do not designate any Windows users (or groups) as having SQL Server administration rights, then you will need to login into SQL Server using the SA account and create at least one administrative user from within SQL Server. If you forget to grant a Windows user access and misplace the SA password, then you will not to be able to log in to SQL Server.

The next tab within the Database Engine Configuration screen is Data Directories (shown in Figure 4-19), which helps you apply the best practice of laying out your database files to multiple locations. In historical versions of SQL Server, the option did not exist to place `tempdb` and backups in separate directories during the install. Therefore, after you would finish the installation process, part of your post-configuration process included moving `tempdb` and your backup directory to separate drives. With the options available within the installation process, you can now place your files in the directories of your choice from the beginning and save time post-installation.

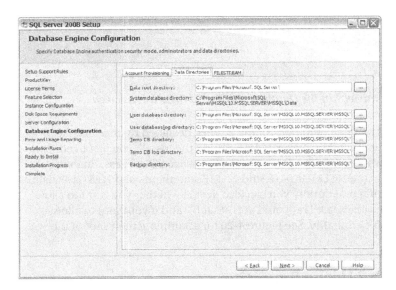

Figure 4-19. *The Data Directories tab within the Database Engine Configuration screen*

Remember, we discussed file layouts and placement in Chapter 2. Create the directories for data, log, `tempdb` data, `tempdb` log, and backup directories on the disks specified in your previous documentation. Populate the fields in Figure 4-19 with the appropriate paths.

The final tab for database engine configuration concerns FILESTREAM (shown in Figure 4-20). The FILESTREAM option is a new feature in SQL Server 2008 that allows binary large objects (or BLOBs) data to be stored as files within the file system. According to Microsoft, you should use FILESTREAM when storing files that will consistently be greater than 1 MB, and when fast-read access of large varbinary (max) files is important.

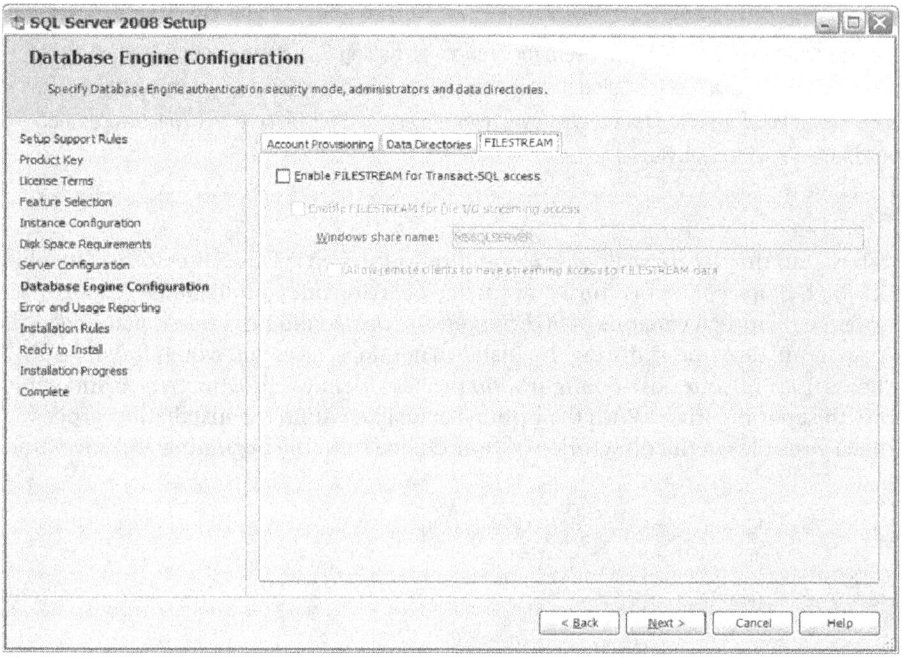

Figure 4-20. *The FILESTREAM tab within the Database Engine Configuration screen*

FILESTREAM data is stored in data containers, or file groups, designed to interface the database engine and file system together. Nevertheless, during the install, you just need to worry about whether you want to enable FILESTREAM for Transact-SQL access. Enabling FILESTREAM permits you to execute INSERT, UPDATE, and DELETE statements on FILESTREAM data via Transact-SQL. After selecting that option, you can also decide whether you want to allow access to FILESTREAM functions like ReadFile() and WriteFile(), and if you want to allow remote users to have similar functionality. See Figure 4-20 for a sample screen shot of the options you have available.

Allowing for Error and Usage Reporting

After database engine configuration comes the Error and Usage Reporting screen, shown in Figure 4-21. This screen allows you to select the information you would like to send to Microsoft to help improve their product. The options include sending Windows and SQL Server error reports, as well as sending feature usage data, including hardware configuration and usages of the software and services. It's up to you as the administrator to determine whether and how much to report to Microsoft.

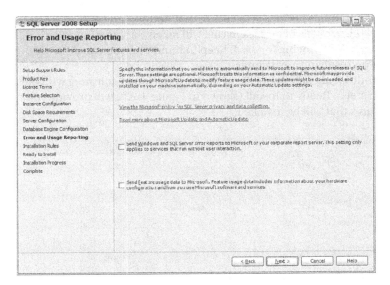

Figure 4-21. *Options available for error and usage reporting*

Validating and Installing

Now that you have selected any Error Usage and Reporting options that you want to enable, you can click Next and let the Installation Rules validation process begin. Figure 4-22 shows the output from that process.

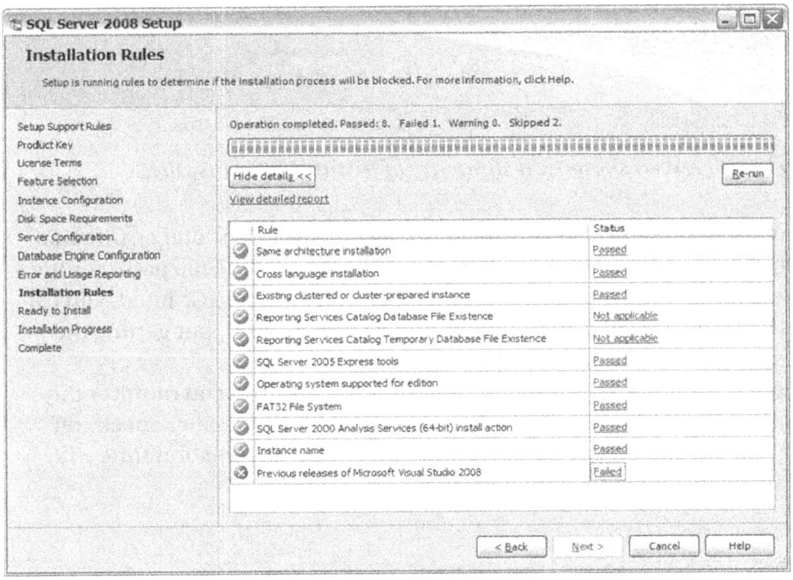

Figure 4-22. *Example results of the Installation Rules test showing a Failed status*

The purpose of the Installation Rules process is to ensure that nothing prevents the installation from completing successfully. Just as before, each rule will receive a status, and you must correct all Failure statuses before moving forward. Keep in mind that you can click the Failed links to see suggestions on resolving any failures.

After resolving any outstanding rule failures, click on the Next button to continue with the installation process. The next screen, Ready to Install (shown in Figure 4-23), will provide you with a summary of all the features that will be installed.

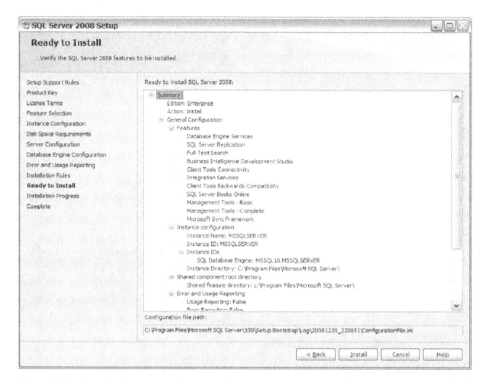

Figure 4-23. *The Ready to Install screen showing a summary of features to be installed*

Review the Ready to Install screen closely. Validate all of your selections and ensure that all of the components you want installed are selected. Also, confirm that the file paths for the data, log, backup, `tempdb` data, and log files all point to the correct locations. Granted, you can always go back, add missing components, and move your data files around, but getting the details correct now will save you time in the future.

Once you have reviewed the summary, click on the Install button. You can monitor the process from the Installation Progress screen shown in Figure 4-24. The installer checks off each feature with either a Failed or Success status during the process. Installation time will vary, depending on the speed of your server or computer.

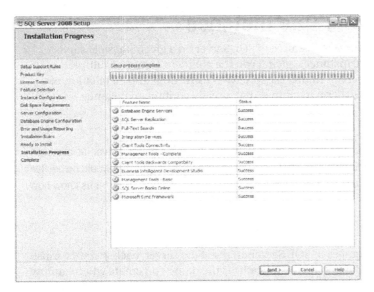

Figure 4-24. *The Installation Progress screen showing successful process completion*

Finally, you'll reach the Complete screen, shown in Figure 4-25. This screen provides two important pieces of information: the destination of the log files and information about the setup process and potential next steps. If issues occurred during the install, or if you are curious about the installation process, then spend a little time reading the log files. We hope that your last screen looks similar to Figure 4-25, indicating a successful database engine install.

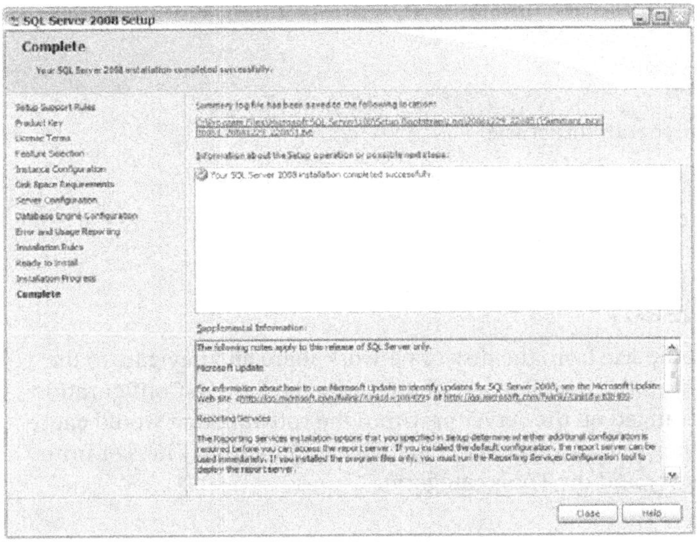

Figure 4-25. *The Complete screen after a successful install of SQL Server 2008*

Installing More Than One Instance

You're not limited to installing just one instance of SQL Server on a given physical server machine. You can install up to 50 instances, giving you the ability to support multiple instances of SQL Server on one server. In this section, we walk through the installation of a separate instance of SQL Server 2008 on machines that already contain an instance.

■**Caution** We have never supported a server with more than three instances of SQL Server installed on it, so we are not familiar with the performance metrics on a server with 50 instances. We would be hesitant to place a server in production with that many instances on it. If you try it out, then please let us know how it goes.

When creating multiple instances of SQL Server on the same server, each instance must have a separate instance ID. By default, the instance ID is the name you create when naming your instance. Although SQL Server shares some common files, the data files, which have the same names, must exist in separate folders. By default, SQL Server creates separate directories for each instance and places instance-specific program and data files into those directories. The rest of this section discusses a few points that will get you ready to install multiple SQL Server instances.

Preparing to Install Another Instance

Prior to installing an instance of SQL Server 2008 on a server, you will need to determine how you would like the instance set up. That way, when prompted with questions during the install, you know exactly how to address each question. Some pre-planning addresses questions like the following:

- What is the instance name?
- What should be the instance root directory?
- Where should program files be located?
- Where do you want your data files?

Getting Your System Ready

To get started, double-click on setup.exe from the disk or network share and navigate to the SQL Server Installation Center. From the Installation Center, rerun the System Configuration Checker to ensure nothing has changed on the server or within the software that would cause your installation to fail. (Remember, you can access the System Configuration Checker from two locations: the Planning category and the Tools category).

After the System Configuration Checker has completed its scan, we like to run the Install SQL Server Features Setup Discovery Report, which you first saw back in Figure 4-6. Figure 4-26 shows a more complete discovery report that includes a SQL Server 2008 instance name. The discovery report helps you review and validate the components and instance names that currently exist on your machine.

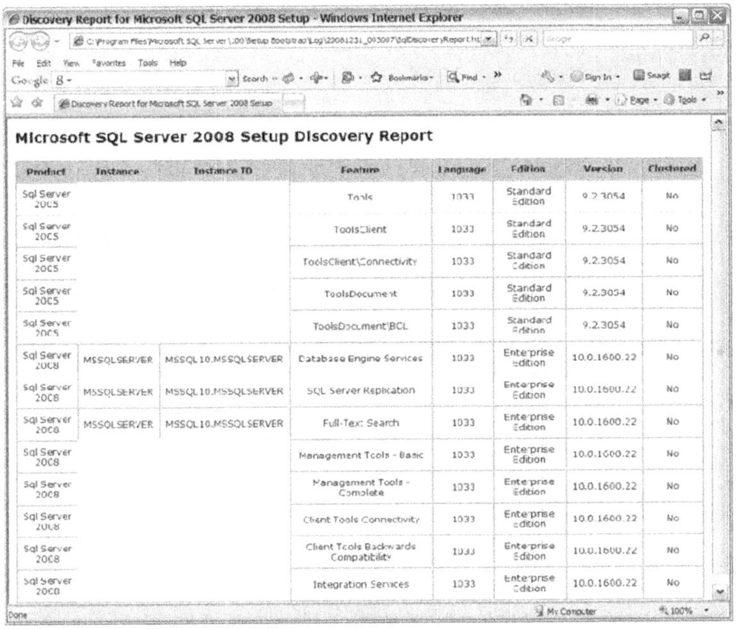

Figure 4-26. *A discovery report showing a SQL Server 2008 installation*

After you have reviewed the discovery report and determined the file locations and instance name that you would like to use for the new instance you want to create, then proceed to the New SQL Server Stand-Alone Installation or Add Features to an Existing Installation link under the Installation category. Once you click on this link, the System Configuration Checker, mentioned earlier, runs to make sure that your new install can proceed without error. Since you already should have executed the complete System Configuration Checker, you should not have any problems going through this mini system check process. Once the setup support files have installed, the System Configuration Checker will scan your system. After the scan completes successfully, you will land on the screen shown in Figure 4-27, asking about the type of installation you want. Because you are trying to install a separate instance of SQL Server, you should select the option to perform a new installation of SQL Server 2008.

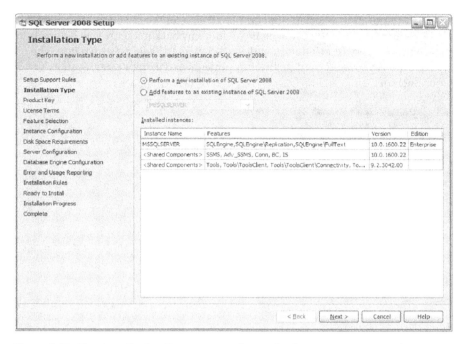

Figure 4-27. *The Installation Type screen asking whether you want to perform a new install or add features to an existing install*

Note The Installation Type screen in Figure 4-27 also shows you the instance and any other shared components installed on the machine. Keep this screen in mind when you are looking to add additional features to an existing instance.

After your selection, you advance to a series of steps similar to those that we reviewed earlier. You insert your product key, accept the license agreement, and choose the features that you want installed on your new instance. Figure 4-28 shows the Feature Selection screen. Notice that the Shared Feature Directory options are grayed out, preventing you from modifying the location of the shared files. That's because you already have the shared files installed, and you cannot move them as part of installing a new instance.

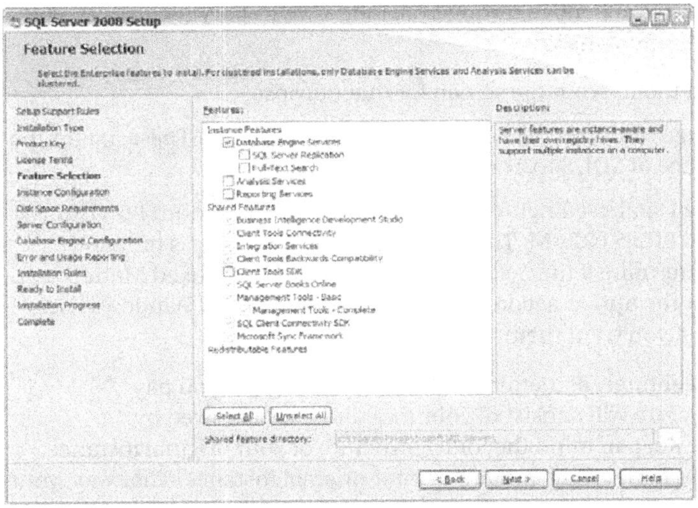

Figure 4-28. *The Feature Selection screen showing installed shared features and the Shared Feature Directory field grayed out*

Configuring the Instance

Next, you have to configure the instance, which you do from the screen shown in Figure 4-29. Using the planning documentation you already created, you can easily supply the values for the instance name, instance ID and the instance root directory. You will also see installed instances on your server listed at the bottom of the screen to ensure you do not duplicate instance names or IDs.

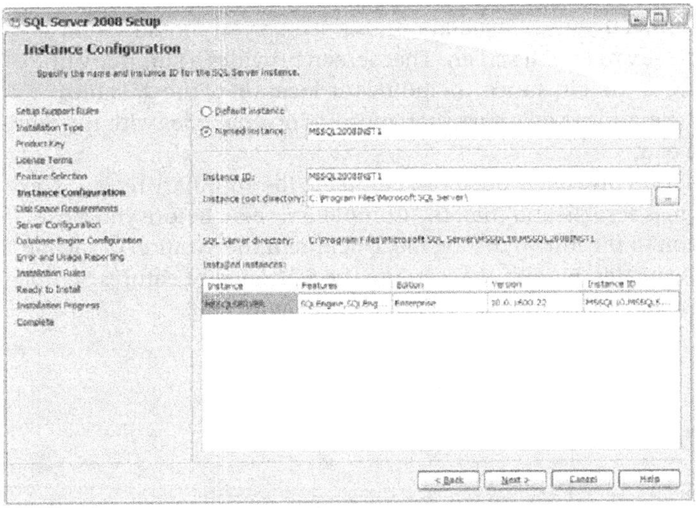

Figure 4-29. *The Instance Configuration screen showing a currently installed instance of SQL Server 2008*

After configuring the instance, you'll move through the following steps, which are essentially the same as for installing your first instance:

1. Review disk space requirements from the screen for that purpose.

2. Plug in usernames and passwords on the Server Configuration screen. These are for the services of the new instance of SQL Server that you are installing.

3. Visit the three tabs on the Database Engine Configuration screen: Account Provisioning, Data Directories, and FILESTREAM. The Account Provisioning tab is the same from the initial install; determine if the instance will be Windows or Mixed Mode authentication and select the option accordingly. Do not forget to add Windows users to the administrator role if you want them administering the instance.

The Data Directories tab is definitely something that we would suggest you pay attention to. The default file structure will consist of your root directory followed by \MSSQL10.InstanceName\Data. Keep in mind the folder structure of your original instance. You may want to lay out your files in the same pattern as your original instance. That way, your file structure is consistent, making it easy for you and anyone else to determine where your files are located.

Tip The projected input and output (IO) usage for an instance will determine the placement of the instance files. For low usage, you may want to use the same drives for the instances, separating the files into multiple folders by instance name. For high IO, you may want to utilize a separate disk subsystem. Regardless of the method used, use the IO subsystem stress tools discussed in Chapter 2 to ensure that your disk subsystem can deal with the IO of the newly added instances.

The FILESTREAM tab, Error and Usage Reporting, Installation Rules, and Ready to Install screens are the same as for your initial instance installation. One screen you should spend a little extra time reviewing is the Ready to Install screen. That screen provides a summary of the components you are installing for that instance, including the location of the data files, the instance name, and other information. Make sure that information coincides with the outcome you expect before you proceed.

Click Next to start the installation processes once you complete the summary review. Next you will see the Installation Progress screen, and then the Complete screen. Before you close the Complete screen, pay attention to the link to the log file. Document the location of the log file just in case you need to review it later. Finally, you can run the SQL Server Features Setup Discovery Report and see the newly installed instance, as shown in Figure 4-30.

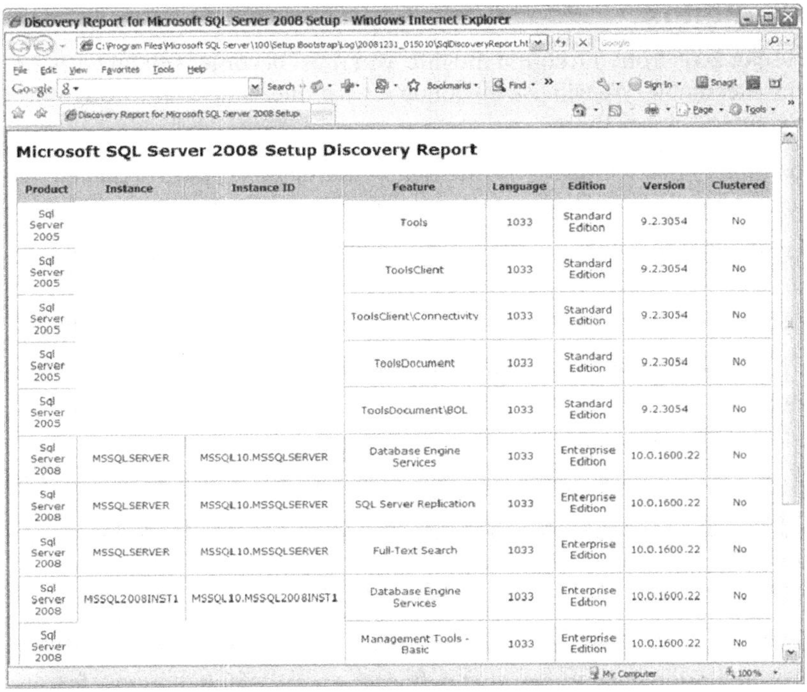
Microsoft SQL Server 2008 Setup Discovery Report

Product	Instance	Instance ID	Feature	Language	Edition	Version	Clustered
Sql Server 2005			Tools	1033	Standard Edition	9.2.3054	No
Sql Server 2005			ToolsClient	1033	Standard Edition	9.2.3054	No
Sql Server 2005			ToolsClient\Connectivity	1033	Standard Edition	9.2.3054	No
Sql Server 2005			ToolsDocument	1033	Standard Edition	9.2.3054	No
Sql Server 2005			ToolsDocument\BOL	1033	Standard Edition	9.2.3054	No
Sql Server 2008	MSSQLSERVER	MSSQL10.MSSQLSERVER	Database Engine Services	1033	Enterprise Edition	10.0.1600.22	No
Sql Server 2008	MSSQLSERVER	MSSQL10.MSSQLSERVER	SQL Server Replication	1033	Enterprise Edition	10.0.1600.22	No
Sql Server 2008	MSSQLSERVER	MSSQL10.MSSQLSERVER	Full-Text Search	1033	Enterprise Edition	10.0.1600.22	No
Sql Server 2008	MSSQL2008INST1	MSSQL10.MSSQL2008INST1	Database Engine Services	1033	Enterprise Edition	10.0.1600.22	No
Sql Server 2008			Management Tools - Basic	1033	Enterprise Edition	10.0.1600.22	No

Figure 4-30. *The SQL Server Features Setup Discovery Report showing the installation of a second instance*

Command-Line Installation

Command-line installs provide an effective method of ensuring consistency among the SQL Server installations within your environment. Once you've defined parameters and their values, you can run installs from the command line to ensure that every SQL Server installation is identical. Think about it—what better way to make sure that all database administrators within your organization follow the same rules and install SQL Server instances identically than to provide a method for executing the same install script with the same commands and values for multiple servers?

■ **Note** While command-line installs are very useful, we do recommend that you do your first few installs through the GUI. Doing so helps you get familiar with the available install options. It's a matter of learning one thing at a time. Learn to install SQL Server, and then learn the command-line installer. Don't try to learn both at once.

Learning the Parameters

In order to install SQL Server 2008 from the command line, you must become familiar with the parameters passed to the executable. We will use the following parameter options throughout the section to discuss command-line installs.

- Q: An optional parameter that allows for no interaction during the install. It is called Quiet mode.

- QS: An optional parameter that allows the setup to run without user input but show progress.

- ACTION: A required parameter that tells the executable what you are getting ready to do, such as install, upgrade, and so on.

- FEATURES: The required parameter that defines the components you want installed.

- CONFIGURATIONFILE: An optional parameter that identifies the configuration file to use for the install.

- INSTANCENAME: The required parameter that identifies the name of the instance.

- INSTANCEDIR: An optional parameter that defines the location of components for a given instance.

- INSTANCEID: An optional parameter that allows you to change the default instance ID.

- INSTALLSHAREDDIR: An optional parameter that defines the non-default directory for 64-bit shared components.

- INSTALLSHAREDWOWDIR: An optional parameter that defines the non-default for 32-bit shared components.

- AGTSVCACCOUNT: The required parameter that specifies the user account for a SQL Server Agent.

- AGTSVCPASSWORD: The required parameter for the password of the SQL Server Agent.

- AGTSVCSTARTUPTYPE: The optional parameter that determines how the SQL Server Agent starts after a reboot. The values are automatic, disabled, or manual.

- BROWSERSVCSTARTUPTYPE: The optional parameter that determines how the SQL Server Browser service starts after a reboot. The values are automatic, disabled, or manual.

- SQLSVCACCOUNT: The required parameter that specifies the user account for the SQL Server service.

- SQLSVCPASSWORD: The required parameter for the password of the SQL Server service.

- SQLSVCSTARTUPTYPE: The optional parameter that determines how SQL Server service starts after a reboot. The values are automatic, disabled, or manual.

- ISSVCACCOUNT: The required parameter that specifies the user account for Integration service. The default value is NT Authority\Network Service.

- ISSVCPassword: The required parameter for the password of Integration service.

- ISSVCSTARTUPTYPE\: The optional parameter that determines how Integration service starts after a reboot.

- SQLCOLLATION: An optional parameter that specifies the collation of your SQL Server instance. The default value is SQL_Latin1_General_CP1_CS_AS.

- SQLSYSADMINACCOUNTS: The required parameter that allows you to grant user access to SQL Server for members of the sysAdmin group.

- SECURITYMODE: An optional parameter that identifies the authentication method for your SQL Server instance. Windows authentication is the default value if a parameter is not supplied. SQL is a supported value.

- SAPWD: The required parameter for when Mixed Mode authentication is selected. It sets the password for the SA account.

- INSTALLSQLDATADIR: The optional parameter that defines the location for the data files. The default location is Program Files%\Microsoft SQL Server\.

- SQLBACKUPDIR: An optional parameter that specifies the location of the backup directory. The default value is INSTALLSQLDATADIR\INSTANCEID\MSSQL\Backup.

- SQLTEMPDBDIR: The optional parameter that defines the location for the data files of tempdb. The default value is INSTALLSQLDATADIR\INSTANCEID\MSSQL\Data.

- SQLTEMPDBLOGDIR: The optional parameter that defines the location for the log files of tempdb. The default value is INSTALLSQLDATADIR\INSTANCEID\MSSQL\Data.

- SQLUSERDBDIR: The optional parameter that defines the location for the data files of user databases. The default value is INSTALLSQLDATADIR\INSTANCEID\MSSQL\Data.

- SQLUSERDBLOGDIR: The optional parameter that defines the location for the log files of user databases. The default value is INSTALLSQLDATADIR\INSTANCEID\MSSQL\Data.

- USESYSDB: The optional parameter that specifies the location of the system databases to use for the installation. Do not add the \Data extension to the file path.

- FILESTREAMLEVEL: The optional parameter that enables or disables the FILESTREAM feature. The values are 0 – disable, 1 – Enable T-SQL Access, 2 – Enable T-SQL access and I/O streaming access, and 3 – Remote access to FILESTREAM data. The default value is 0.

- FILESTREAMSHARENAME: The optional parameter that specifies the directory where FILESTREAM data will be stored.

- ERRORREPORTING: An optional parameter that determines if you will participate in Microsoft error reporting or not. The supported values are 1 or 0 and enabled or disabled.

- SQMREPORTING: The optional parameter that determines if you will participate in Microsoft error reporting or not for feature usage. The supported values are 1 or 0 and enabled or disabled.

- INDICATEPROGRESS: An optional parameter that allows the log file to be written to the screen.

- PID: Surprisingly, an optional parameter that sets the product key. If you do not provide a product key, the evaluation product key for the Enterprise Edition will be used.

- HIDECONSOLE: The optional parameter that determines the visibility of the console window.

This list of parameters may look a little overwhelming, but if you have installed SQL Server 2008 already from the GUI, then the parameter names and choices really make sense. We even list the parameters in the order that you make decisions within the GUI installer.

Passing Parameters to the Installer

The installer executable is setup.exe. You use the same executable for all types of installs, whether GUI-based or command-line based. You can pass parameters in several formats. Some parameters are simple switches. You pass these by just listing them after the command line. For example, you can specify the Q parameter if you want your install to proceed silently, with no status or progress messages displayed. Here's how to do that:

```
setup.exe /Q
```

That's it. Just specify the Q parameter, and you turn on the "silent" switch. Also notice that you precede parameter names with forward slash characters.

Next, some parameters allow for true/false values. Specifying the parameter name without following text implies that a parameter is set to true. Excluding a parameter implies the parameter value is false. You can explicitly specify true/false for some of the parameters. For example:

```
setup.exe /Q=true /QS=false
```

Other parameters require that you pass specific numeric or text values. Pass numeric values simply by specifying a number. Pass text values by placing those values within quotes. For example:

```
setup.exe /FILESTREAMLEVEL=0 /INSTALLSQLDATADIR="C:\ScrapFiles"
```

Technically, you do not have to enclose text values within quotes unless those values contain spaces or other special characters. Use quotes if you have any doubts about needing them. You can also quote numeric values, if you like.

Running a Command-Line Install

Now that you're familiar with the parameters and how to pass them, you can begin to put together your first command-line install. The following subsections walk you through an example.

First, though, you may want to "cheat" and run the System Configuration Checker from the Planning category in the SQL Server Installation Center. Yes, that's in the GUI, but we like to run it anyway. We like it because the resulting report helps us identify and head off problems that would cause installation failures.

Choosing the Level of Silence

The first thing you have to decide is whether you want to see the status of the installation as it proceeds, or whether you want the installation to run silently. Specify /Q as a parameter to get a quiet install, or one that runs without user interaction and status bars. Specify /QS if you want to see status bars only, while avoiding user input.

When developing a new command-line script, we generally execute the script using the /QS parameter to enable us to monitor the progress of the install. As our comfort level increases with our installation script, we modify the script to use /Q.

Specifying the Action and the Components

Next, you have to specify the action to perform. For this discussion, you are installing SQL Server 2008. Therefore, the action portion of the process is /ACTION=Install. After the action, you have to determine the components that you want installed. The available options are as follows:

- SQL: Installs the database engine, replication, and Full-Text components.
- SQLENGINE: Just installs the database engine services.
- REPLICATION: Installs SQL Server replication. The database engine has to be specified in order to install replication.
- FULLTEXT: Installs the Full-Text Search service. The database engine has to be specified in order to install Full-Text components.
- Tools: Installs client tools and SQL Server Books Online.
- BC: Installs backward compatibility.
- BOL: Installs SQL Server Books Online.
- BIDS: Installs Business Intelligence Development Studio.
- Conn: Installs client tools connectivity.
- SSMS: Installs Management Tools (Basic).
- ADV_SSMS: Installs Management Tools (Complete).
- SDK: Installs the Software Development Toolkit.

For this walkthrough, let's install the database engine and the tools. To do that, specify install /Features = SQL, Tools.

Configuring the Instance

After the feature selection, you should set up the instance name and instance ID. For this example, specify the instance name using /INSTANCENAME=MSSQLCMDLINE. The instance ID is an optional parameter that you can change here if you want. For example, you can specify something like /INSTANCEID=MSSQLCMDLINEID.

In the GUI setup, options exist to change the location of the instance root directory. You can do the same thing from the command-line installer using the /INSTALLSHAREDDIR option. For example:

/INSTALLSHAREDDIR="c:\program files\SQLCMDINSTALL"

   or

/INSTALLSHAREDWOWDIR="c:\program files\SQLCMDINSTALL"

Which of these parameters to use depends upon the hardware and edition of SQL Server 2008 you are installing. (Use the WOW version of the parameter for 32-bit systems). Personally, using the default locations for the shared file directories is a good choice.

Next, you have to populate the usernames and passwords for the services that you are installing. However, you do not need to populate the password parameter for services using system accounts in the form NT Authority\Network Service. The following list shows the parameters used to specify the usernames and passwords for the services, along with their startup types:

- /AGTSVCACCOUNT="NT Authority\ Network Service"

- /AGTSVCPASSWORD

- /AGTSVCSTARTUPTYPE=automatic

- /BROWSERSVCSTARTUPTYPE=manual

- /SQLSVCACCOUNT="Domain\UserName"

- /SQLSVCPASSWORD=P@55w0rd!

- /SQLSVCSTARTUPTYPE=automatic

- /ISSVCACCOUNT="NT Authority\ Network Service"

- /ISSVCPassword

- /ISSVCSTARTUPTYPE=automatic

- /SQLSYSADMINACCOUNTS="Domain\UserName"

After setting up usernames and passwords for your services, your next step is to set up the collation for SQL Server. You set the collation using the /SQLCOLLATION parameter. For example:

```
setup.exe /SQLCOLLATION="SQL_Latin1_General_CP1_CI-AI"
```

Next, you set up the authentication mode for the SQL Server instance. Specify /SECURITYMODE=SQL for Mixed Mode authentication. Once you set the authentication level to mixed, you have to set up the SA passwords by using the /SAPWD="P@ssw0rd!" parameter.

Specifying the Data Directories

After getting all the instance-related items out of the way, you can set up the data directories for the database files. The following list shows one approach that you might take:

```
/SQLUSERDBDIR="g:\sqldata\"

/SQLUSERDBLOGDIR="h:\sqlLogs\"

/SQLBACKUPDIR="j:\backups\"

/SQLTEMPDBDIR="i:\sqldata\"

/SQLTEMPDBLOGDIR="i:\sqldata\"
```

After setting up the data directories, decide if you want to turn on FILESTREAM. Specify /FILESTREAMLEVEL=1 to enable it. Finally, decide if want to participate in Microsoft reporting. There are two reporting parameters: /ERRORREPORTING and /SQMREPORTING. Set these parameters to 1 if you want to enable their corresponding reporting options.

Running Your Install

Now put all the parameters together and install SQL Server. Following is an example command line:

```
setup.exe /QS /ACTION=install /FEATURES=SQL /INSTANCENAME=MSSQLCMDLN _
 /SQLSVCACCOUNT="NT AUTHORITY\Network Service" /SQLSYSADMINACCOUNTS="NT_
 AUTHORITY\Network Service" /SQLSVCSTARTUPTYPE="automatic" /AGTSVCACCOUNT="NT_
AUTHORITY\Network Service" /AGTSVCSTARTUPTYPE="automatic" /SQLCOLLATION=_
"SQL_Latin1_General_CP1_CI_AI" /SECURITYMODE=SQL /SAPWD="P@ssw0rd!"_
/SQLUSERDBDIR="c:\sqldata" /SQLUSERDBLOGDIR="c:\sqlLogs" SQLBACKUPDIR=_
"c:\backups"    /SQLTEMPDBDIR="c:\sqldata" /SQLTEMPDBLOGDIR="c:\sqldata"_
 /FILESTREAMLEVEL=1 /ERRORREPORTING=0 /SQMREPORTING=0
```

■ **Note** Make sure there are no spaces before or after the equals (=) sign for any of the parameters. Place the entire command in one line before pasting it in the command line. You can use batch files to execute the command.

Having a command, you can now execute it. First, navigate using the command line to the directory containing setup.exe. Then paste in the command line that you have created and watch it run. Do not be alarmed if you receive some errors. The messages are pretty straightforward and are easy to debug. The script that we are supplying works in our environment, so you should be able to run it with only a few modifications for your environment. Do not forget: The supplied script uses NT Authority\Network Service for service accounts, which do not require passwords, does not include a product key, and the folder directories may not exist. So you will have to modify the script to include those items to work on your system.

After you start the command-line install, a series of checks and validation will occur. The /QS parameter in our example causes the installer to open a GUI window, from which you can monitor installation progress. Figure 4-31 shows the progress screen that you'll see during the installation of support files.

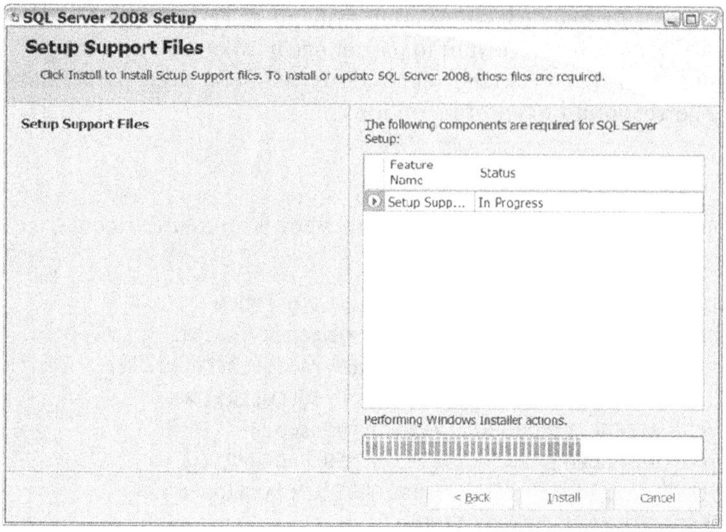

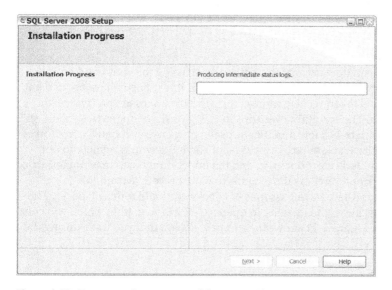

Figure 4-31. *The Setup Support Files screen during a command-line installation*

Figure 4-32 shows the progress screen for the subsequent instance install.

Figure 4-32. *Progress of a command-line installation*

If an error occurs during the install, then the GUI will close and the installer will display an error message in the command-line window (see Figure 4-33).

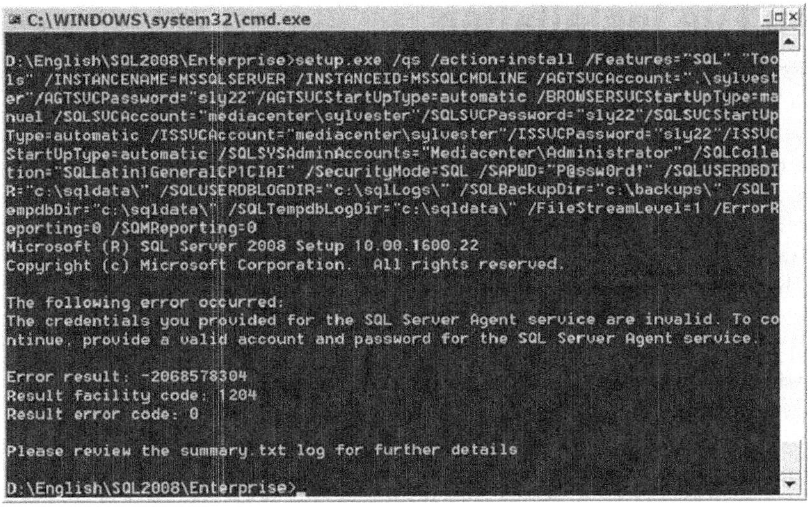

Figure 4-33. *Encountering an error during a command-line install*

For even more detail about the error, you can review the summary.txt file (see Figure 4-34) in the shared install directory. That file is located in \Program Files\Microsoft SQL Server\100\ Setup Bootstrap\Log.

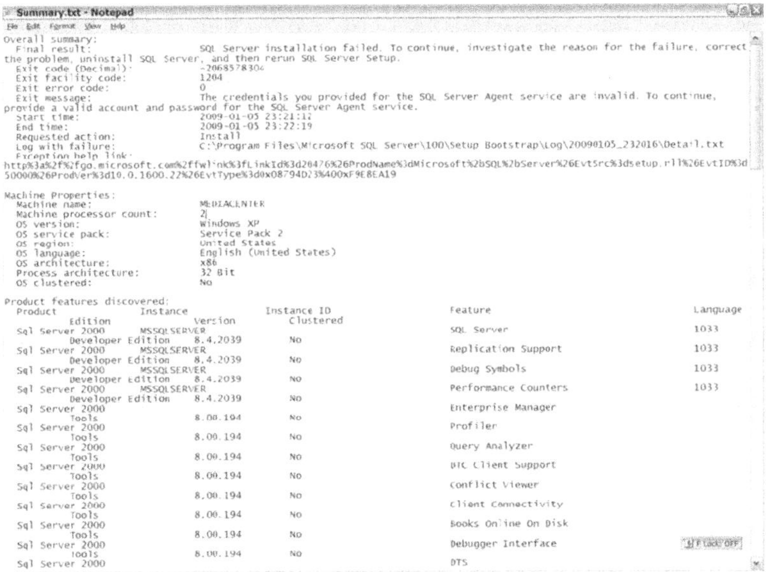

Figure 4-34. *Sample summary file following an error*

Configuration File Installation

Installing SQL Server from a configuration file is another option available to you in SQL Server 2008. Configuration file installs are command-line installs with a parameter change that points setup.exe to a file containing the installation parameters. One major advantage of a configuration file install is that successful completion of a SQL Server 2008 install, such as from the GUI, creates a configuration file for you. The file is placed in the following folder: Program Files\ Microsoft SQL Server\100\Setup Bootstrap\Log\TimeOfSuccessfulInstall. So you can install SQL Server 2008 from the GUI version of setup.exe, and then utilize the configuration file created by the installer to install SQL Server 2008 consistently on any other server that you build.

Configuration file installs are extremely simple compared to command-line installs and require only a couple of changes to implement. Since you understand the command-line parameters, reviewing and modifying a configuration file, like Listing 4-1, is not a challenging task.

Listing 4-1. *Sample Configuration File*

```
;SQLSERVER2008 Configuration File
[SQLSERVER2008]

; Specifies the instance ID for the SQL Server features you have specified. _
SQL Server directory structure, registry structure, and service names will _
reflect the instance ID of the SQL Server instance.

INSTANCEID="MSSQLCMDLINE"

; Specifies a setup workflow, like INSTALL, UNINSTALL, or UPGRADE._
 This is a required parameter.

ACTION="Install"

; Specifies features to install, uninstall, or upgrade. The list of top-level _
features include SQL, AS, RS, IS, and Tools. The SQL feature will install _
the database engine, replication, and Full-Text. The Tools feature will install _
Management Tools, Books Online, Business Intelligence Development Studio, _
and other shared components.

FEATURES=SQLENGINE,REPLICATION,FULLTEXT

; Displays the command-line parameters usage

HELP="False"

; Specifies that the detailed setup log should be piped to the console.

INDICATEPROGRESS="False"

; Setup will not display any user interface.
```

```
QUIET="False"

; Setup will display progress only without any user interaction.

QUIETSIMPLE="True"

; Specifies that setup should install into WOW64. This command-line argument _
is not supported on an IA64 or a 32-bit system.

X86="False"

; Specifies the path to the installation media folder where setup.exe is located.

MEDIASOURCE="D:\English\SQL2008\Enterprise\"

; Specifies if errors can be reported to Microsoft to improve future SQL Server
releases. Specify 1 or True to enable and 0 or False to disable this feature.

ERRORREPORTING="False"

; Specifies the root installation directory for native shared components.

INSTALLSHAREDDIR="C:\Program Files\Microsoft SQL Server"

; Specifies the installation directory.

INSTANCEDIR="C:\Program Files\Microsoft SQL Server"

; Specifies that SQL Server feature usage data can be collected and sent to
 Microsoft. Specify 1 or True to enable and 0 or False to disable this feature.

SQMREPORTING="False"

; Specifies a default or named instance. MSSQLSERVER is the default instance
 for non-Express Editions and SQLExpress for Express Editions. This parameter_
 is required when installing the SQL Server Database Engine (SQL),
 Analysis Services (AS), or Reporting Services (RS).

INSTANCENAME="MSSQLCMDLINE"

; Agent account name

AGTSVCACCOUNT="NT AUTHORITY\NETWORK SERVICE"

; Auto-start service after installation.

AGTSVCSTARTUPTYPE="Manual"
```

```
; Startup type for Integration services.

ISSVCSTARTUPTYPE="Automatic"

; Account for Integration services: Domain\User or system account.

ISSVCACCOUNT="NT AUTHORITY\NetworkService"

; Controls the service startup type setting after the service has been created.

ASSVCSTARTUPTYPE="Automatic"

; The collation to be used by Analysis Services.

ASCOLLATION="Latin1_General_CI_AS"

; The location for the Analysis Services data files.

ASDATADIR="Data"

; The location for the Analysis Services log files.

ASLOGDIR="Log"

; The location for the Analysis Services backup files.

ASBACKUPDIR="Backup"

; The location for the Analysis Services temporary files.

ASTEMPDIR="Temp"

; The location for the Analysis Services configuration files.

ASCONFIGDIR="Config"

; Specifies whether or not the MSOLAP provider is allowed to run in process.

ASPROVIDERMSOLAP="1"

; Startup type for the SQL Server service.

SQLSVCSTARTUPTYPE="Automatic"

; Level to enable FILESTREAM feature at (0, 1, 2 or 3).

FILESTREAMLEVEL="0"
```

```
; Set to "1" to enable RANU for SQL Server Express.

ENABLERANU="False"

; Specifies a Windows collation or a SQL collation to use for the database engine.

SQLCOLLATION="SQL_Latin1_General_CP1_CI_AS"

; Account for SQL Server service: Domain\User or system account.

SQLSVCACCOUNT="NT AUTHORITY\Network Service"

; Windows account(s) to provision as SQL Server system administrators.

SQLSYSADMINACCOUNTS="NT AUTHORITY\Network Service"

; Provision current user as a database engine system administrator for
SQL Server 2008 Express.

ADDCURRENTUSERASSQLADMIN="False"

; Specify 0 to disable or 1 to enable the TCP/IP protocol.

TCPENABLED="1"

; Specify 0 to disable or 1 to enable the Named Pipes protocol.

NPENABLED="0"

; Startup type for Browser Service.

BROWSERSVCSTARTUPTYPE="Automatic"

; Specifies how the startup mode of the report server NT service. When
Manual - Service startup is manual mode (default).
Automatic - Service startup is automatic mode.
Disabled - Service is disabled

RSSVCSTARTUPTYPE="Automatic"

; Specifies which mode report server is installed in.
Default value: "FilesOnly"

RSINSTALLMODE="FilesOnlyMode"
```

Notice that the configuration file options look similar to the parameters used in the previous section's command-line install. Before installing SQL Server 2008 with a configuration file, review the file to ensure that the options you want installed are enabled. If you are installing SQL Server 2008 from a configuration file created by a previous GUI install that you are happy with, then you only have to change a couple of the configuration options.

You have to modify the configuration file to change your GUI install, where you supply all the options, to a command-line install that uses the /Q or /QS parameters. Change the either QUIET or QUIETSIMPLE option to true in the configuration file. Both of those options are set to false during a GUI install.

After modifying the QUIET and QUIETSIMPLE options within the configuration file, you may want to validate that the INSTANCENAME and INSTANCEID will not cause a conflict on the server. Besides those two changes, you should be able to execute a configuration file install using the configuration file from the previous install without problems.

To perform a configuration file installation, open a command prompt and navigate to the directory where the setup.exe file exists. Then execute setup.exe /CONFIGURATIONFILE="file path and file name" and sit back and watch the installation run without you inputting anything. If you are using Mixed Mode authentication or if the service account users need passwords, then adding additional parameters for the appropriate passwords is required. For example, the SA password is required in Mixed Mode authentication. So to install SQL Server 2008 using a configuration file with the SA password parameter supplied, you need to execute setup.exe /CONFIGURATIONFILE="file path and file name" /SAPWD="Password". Then you are all set. Figure 4-35 is a sample command-line interface when the configurations file installation starts.

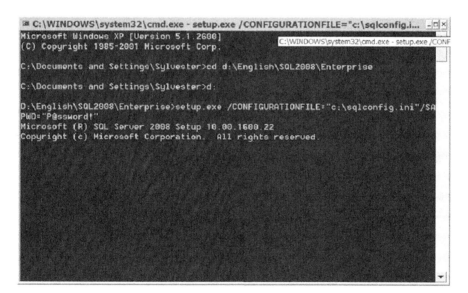

Figure 4-35. *The command-line interface executing a configuration file installation*

Figure 4-36 shows the progress screen that you will see in QUIETSIMPLE mode during the install.

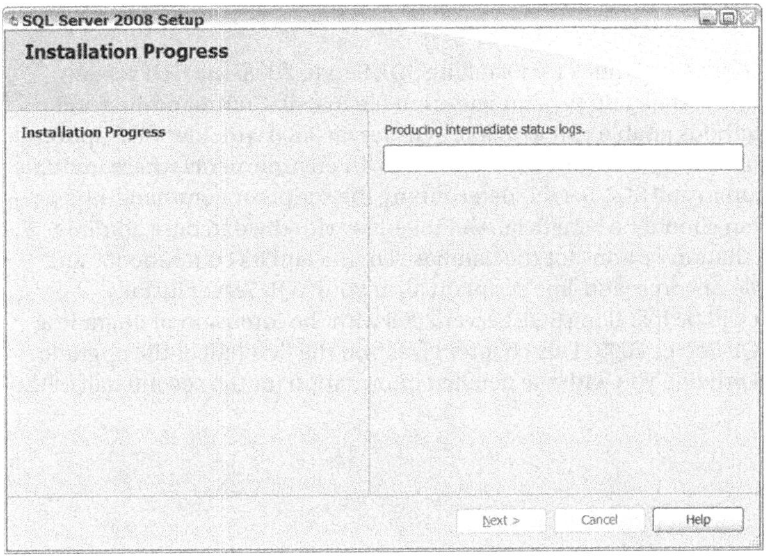

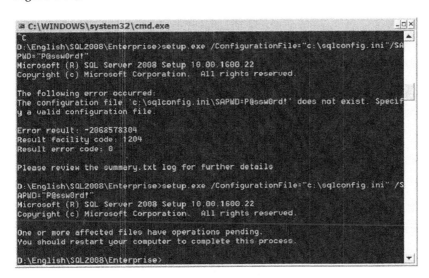

Figure 4-36. *Installation progress of a configuration file installation with QUIETSIMPLE option set to true*

The completion of the install shows messages in the command-line window (see Figure 4-37).

Figure 4-37. *The completion of a configuration file installation*

Summary

In this chapter, we reviewed three methods for installing SQL Server 2008: the GUI version of setup.exe, a command-line install, and the configuration file install. Command-line and configuration file install methods enable you to install SQL Server 2008 with identical options and decrease the amount of user time required for the install. In environments where multiple members of the organization install SQL Server, determining the script for command-line or configuration file installation should be beneficial. Get together with the database administration team, agree on installation options for the database engine and its components, and utilize that configuration file or command-line script on all of your SQL Server installs.

A large number of you will be installing SQL Server 2008 with the intension of upgrading from SQL Server 2000 or SQL Server 2005. This chapter gives you the first half of the upgrade process, but Chapter 5 will provide you with the detailed information for the second half of the migration process.

CHAPTER 5

■■■

Upgrading to Microsoft SQL Server 2008

There are several things that need to be addressed when upgrading to SQL Server 2008. Once you have decided to upgrade, you have to make sure that all the features implemented in the prior version are compatible with SQL Server 2008. We will be discussing several tools in this chapter to help guide you through the upgrade process. This chapter will also explain the different upgrade strategies to help you decide the best method for your environment. Finally, we will look at configuration changes that need to be made after the upgrade to ensure that you are taking full advantage of the features offered in SQL Server 2008.

Upgrade Tools

There are two main tools available to assist you in the upgrade process to SQL Server 2008. These tools help you to resolve any possible compatibility and performance issues that might exist. These tools are the Upgrade Advisor and the Upgrade Assistant.

Microsoft SQL Server 2008 Upgrade Advisor

The Microsoft SQL Server 2008 Upgrade Advisor analyzes your SQL Server 2000 and SQL Server 2005 instances and identifies configuration items that may impact your upgrade process. The Upgrade Advisor then provides links to web pages that will provide you with the information needed to resolve the conflicts before the upgrade.

The Upgrade Advisor can be installed from the first page of the SQL Server 2008 install screen or downloaded from the following URL: www.microsoft.com/downloads/details. aspx?familyid=F5A6C5E9-4CD9-4E42-A21C-7291E7F0F852&displaylang=en.

The install is pretty straightforward (accepting the defaults should be fine). Once you have completed the install, use the following steps to produce your analysis report:

1. Open the application and select Launch Upgrade Advisor Analysis Wizard.

2. This brings you to the Welcome screen, as shown in Figure 5-1. Select Next to continue.

Figure 5-1. *Upgrade Advisor Analysis Wizard Welcome screen*

3. Enter the server name and select the components you would like to analyze, as shown in Figure 5-2. Select Next to continue.

Figure 5-2. *Upgrade Advisor server and components selection*

4. This brings you to the authentication page, shown in Figure 5-3, from where you can select the instance name and enter your credentials. Select Next to continue.

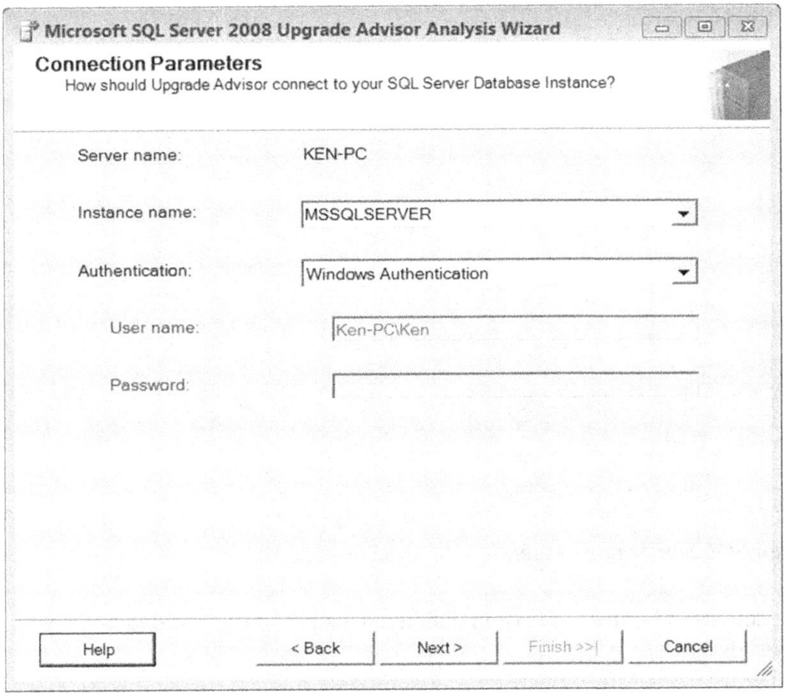

Figure 5-3. *Upgrade Advisor authentication*

5. After authenticating, you can now select the databases you would like to analyze. Figure 5-4 shows three databases selected. You may also choose to analyze trace or batch files as well. Select Next to continue. If you have selected other components (refer to Figure 5-2), such as Analysis Services or Reporting Services, there will be authentication screens for each of those as well. Also, if you have selected Data Transformation Services (DTS) packages or SQL Server Integration Services (SSIS), you will be given the option to analyze packages for the server or select a path containing package files on subsequent screens.

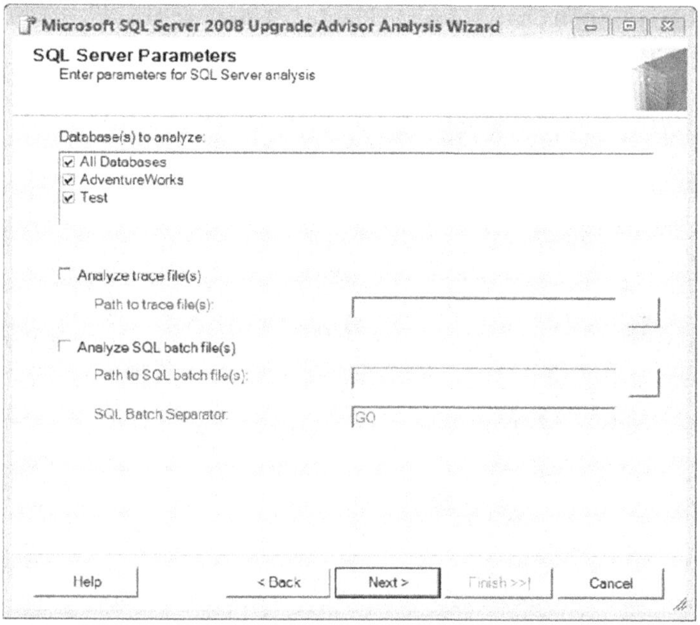

Figure 5-4. *Upgrade Advisor SQL Server parameters*

6. The confirmation screen in Figure 5-5 is then displayed. Confirm the options and select Run to begin the analysis.

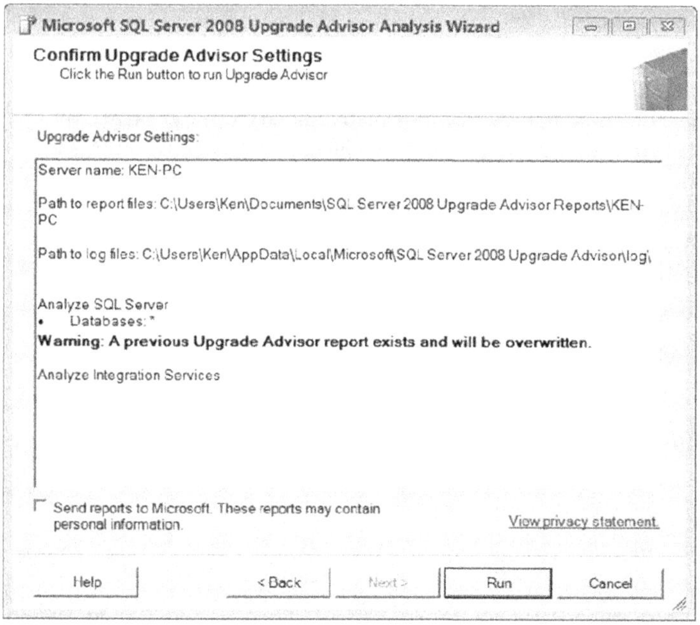

Figure 5-5. *Upgrade Advisor confirmation screen*

7. Figure 5-6 shows the analysis in progress. As you can see, certain rules are analyzed for each selected component.

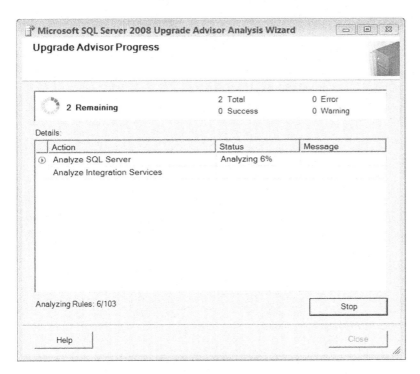

Figure 5-6. *Upgrade Advisor rule analysis*

8. After the analysis has completed, warnings will be displayed for those components needing attention. Figure 5-7, for example, shows a warning pertaining to SQL Server itself. Select Launch Report to display an analysis showing the details behind the warning.

Figure 5-7. *Upgrade Advisor rule analysis completed*

9. Figure 5-8 shows a detailed analysis report. Notice the red circles with X-marks in the Importance column. This report is showing that you will encounter a problem relating to a change in storage format for types xs:dateTime, xs:date, and xs:time. Three objects are affected. Click the Show Affected Objects link, and you'll get the screen shown in Figure 5-9, which lists those objects. Click the Tell Me More About This Issue and How to Resolve It link if you want to see the Upgrade Advisor help page explaining how to resolve the problem.

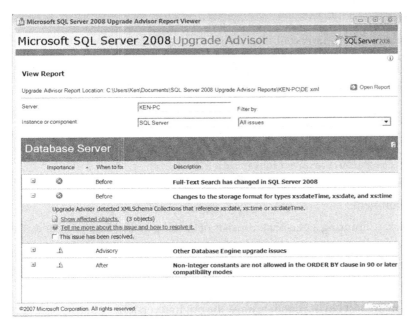

Figure 5-8. *Upgrade Advisor analysis report*

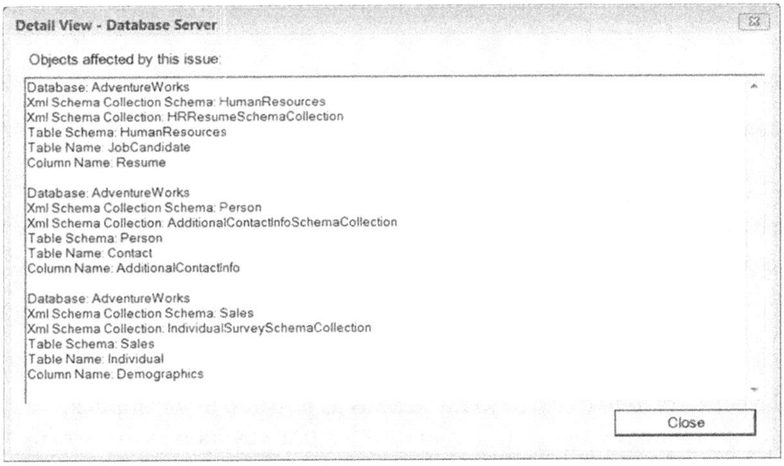

Figure 5-9. *Upgrade Advisor affected objects*

Upgrade Advisor is helpful in planning an upgrade, and you'll find yourself returning to it often. You don't have to rerun reports, however. You can review the reports again without rerunning the analysis by selecting Launch Upgrade Advisor Report Viewer from the application home screen.

Upgrade Assistant

The Upgrade Assistant is a free third-party tool you can use to determine how a database will perform after it has been upgraded from SQL Server 2000 or SQL Server 2005 to SQL Server 2008. The Upgrade Assistant also identifies compatibility issues that may not have been detected using the Upgrade Advisor. The Upgrade Assistant will create a baseline by running a trace on the SQL Server 2000 or SQL Server 2005 database that is going to be upgraded. It will then run the trace against the upgraded SQL Server 2008 database in a controlled test environment and generate a report comparing the two traces. The Upgrade Assistant and user guide can be downloaded from the scalability experts download page located at www.scalabilityexperts.com/default.asp?action=article&ID=45.

Following is a list of the general steps involved when running the Upgrade Assistant:

1. Set up a test environment.

2. Capture a playback. (Capturing a playback consists of backing up the databases and running a trace.)

3. Restore the database to the test environment using the original version of SQL Server.

4. Run the Upgrade Advisor as described in the previous section and resolve any conflicts.

5. Replay the trace on the test environment against the original version.

6. Restore the database on a SQL Server 2008 instance.

7. Replay the trace against the SQL Server 2008 instance.

8. Compare the traces and analyze the results using the report viewer.

Caution The Upgrade Assistant should be run in a test environment to ensure that the tests will not affect the production system. A production system may be used to capture adequate trace information, but the capture process could impact performance just as any trace on a production server could. More importantly, the Upgrade Assistant takes a backup of all of the databases (including the system databases) on the instance during the capture process. This backup by the Upgrade Assistant will break the backup sequence of each of the databases and could impact any high-availability processes you have in place.

When capturing a playback, try to perform as many actions as possible in the application to generate a trace with proper coverage. You should start the trace as soon as the backup process has completed to prevent transactions from occurring that will cause rerunning the playback on the test system to fail. Since the initial playback process backs up all the databases on the instance, make sure you have sufficient disk space to store the backups and the trace file. The trace file is generated in the same location as the backup files. You can use a network share if the server does not have enough disk space. You must be a member of the sysadmin role to capture a playback.

Tip You can take any databases offline that you do not want backed up as a result of the playback process.

SQL Server Integration Services

SQL Server Integration Services (SSIS) was introduced in SQL Server 2005 and uses a completely different architecture than its predecessor Data Transformation Services (DTS). SSIS provides a much more robust environment for moving and transforming data, but it also provides difficulties when upgrading packages from SQL Server 2000. You basically have two choices: You can rewrite each package to run in SSIS or use the old DTS DLLs to continue running each package. If you have a small number of fairly simple packages, it may be easy enough to rewrite the packages manually. If not, there are a few tools available to help you with the conversion process.

Running DTS in SQL Server 2008

SQL Server 2008 provides the ability to run and manage DTS packages by downloading a couple of add-ons. We would use this approach as a last resort and use the upgrade as an opportunity to migrate your packages to SSIS. SSIS performs much more efficiently, and the add-ons may not be available in the next version of SQL Server. For more information, search for the topic "How to: Install Support for Data Transformation Services Packages" in SQL Server Books Online or MSDN (http://msdn.microsoft.com).

Runtime Support

In order to run DTS packages in SQL Server 2008, you must install the runtime support add-on. To install runtime support for DTS packages in SQL Server 2008, download and install the Microsoft SQL Server 2005 backward compatibility components from the Microsoft SQL Server 2008 Feature Pack web page from the Download Center located at www.microsoft.com/downloads/details.aspx?FamilyID=228de03f-3b5a-428a-923f-58a033d316e1&DisplayLang=en.

Design-Time Support

In order to design and manage DTS Packages in SQL Server 2008, you must install the design-time support add-on. To install design-time support for DTS packages in SQL Server 2008, download the Microsoft SQL Server 2000 DTS designer components from the Feature Pack for Microsoft SQL Server 2005 web page from the Download Center located at www.microsoft.com/downloads/details.aspx?FamilyID=50b97994-8453-4998-8226-fa42ec403d17&displaylang=en.

DTS Package Migration Wizard

The DTS Package Migration Wizard is installed when you select Integration Services as a feature during your SQL Server 2008 install. The Migration Wizard allows you to upgrade existing DTS packages to an SSIS format, as long as all the objects are compatible. The Upgrade Advisor can be used to identify some of the issues that need to be resolved before migrating the packages.

■**Note** DTS xChange is a third-party tool that can be used to migrate DTS packages to SSIS. DTS xChange does a better job than the DTS Migration Wizard. It can also convert packages that the Migration Wizard will be unable to convert. DTS xChange is not a free tool, but if you have many complex DTS packages to convert, it may be well worth the investment. The demo version can be used to migrate up to five packages and can be downloaded from the Pragmatic Works web site at www.pragmaticworks.com.

Use the following steps to convert DTS packages to SSIS using the DTS Package Migration Wizard:

1. Start the DTS Package Migration Wizard in one of three ways.

   • Navigate to the Legacy folder under Management in SQL Server Management Studio. Right-click Data Transformation Services and select Migration Wizard.

   • Open an Integration Services project in the Business Intelligence Development Studio (BIDS). Right-click on SSIS Packages in the Solution Explorer and select Migrate DTS 2000 Package.

   • Start the DTSMigrationWizard.exe located in the C:\Program Files\Microsoft SQL Server\100\DTS\Binn folder.

2. Select the source of the packages.

3. Select the destination for the packages.

4. Select the available packages from the source that you wish to migrate.

5. If any of the packages are password protected, you will be prompted for their passwords. It is not possible to migrate a package that has been password protected without knowing the password. If none of the packages is password protected, the wizard will skip this step.

6. You can specify a log file to capture any errors that were encountered during the migration.

7. The packages are then upgraded one by one, and you can view the progress of each migration. If a package cannot be migrated, you can opt to end the migration process for the remaining packages or to skip just the package that cannot be migrated.

8. Once the migration process is complete, open the packages using BIDS and check for any validation errors. If possible, run each package to make sure it executes successfully and that the results are as you expect.

Upgrade Strategies

Once you have determined that your databases are compatible with SQL Server 2008, you are ready to perform an upgrade. There are two ways to perform an upgrade. The first is known as an *in-place upgrade*, and as the name implies, it upgrades an entire instance "in place" by converting the data files to the new format. The second approach is known as a *side-by-side upgrade*, which consists of installing a second instance of SQL Server and moving the data files to the new version. Both methods have their pros and cons, and the best method for one application may not be the best method for another. An in-place upgrade provides simplicity but lacks the flexibility offered by a side-by-side upgrade.

In-Place Upgrade

An in-place upgrade can be used to upgrade an instance of SQL Server 2000 or SQL Server 2005 directly to SQL Server 2008. Search for "Version and Edition Upgrades" on MSDN for specifics on the supported upgrade paths for each version and edition.

One of the benefits of performing an in-place upgrade is that you can use the same server and instance names. This may save you from having to track down all the connections to the database and point them to a new server or instance name. It is a fairly simple process, much like performing an installation. You do not need extra disk space to make a copy of the data files because they will be converted to the new format during the upgrade. The downside is that there is a point during the upgrade process where there is no turning back. The only back out is to reinstall the prior version of SQL Server and restore the databases from a backup that was made prior to the upgrade. You cannot restore a backup of a database that has been converted to SQL Server 2008 on a previous version. If you determine that a problem has been caused a week later by the upgrade, you will have to restore the database from a backup prior to the upgrade and hope you have a way to recover the transactions that have occurred since the upgrade.

Caution It is important to have a tested backup in a safe location, since that is the only way to back out of an in-place upgrade. You may want to take an image of the server as well and store it in a safe location to reduce the backout time.

The steps to performing an in-place upgrade include the following:

1. Make sure you have current backups in a safe location.

2. Run SQL Server setup.exe. Install any prerequisites and exit the install. If a reboot is required due to the prerequisites, reboot and run setup.exe again.

3. From the SQL Server Installation Center, select Upgrade from SQL Server 2000 or SQL Server 2005, as shown in Figure 5-10.

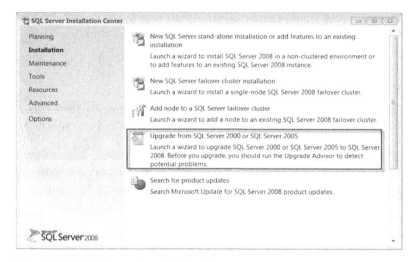

Figure 5-10. *SQL Server Installation Center*

4. SQL Server will install any required support files, and you may be required to reboot and start setup.exe again.

5. The System Configuration Checker will run a discovery and setup log files will be created for the installation. The Setup Support Rules screen, shown in Figure 5-11, identifies any problems that you may encounter when installing the setup support files. These errors will need to be resolved in order to continue.

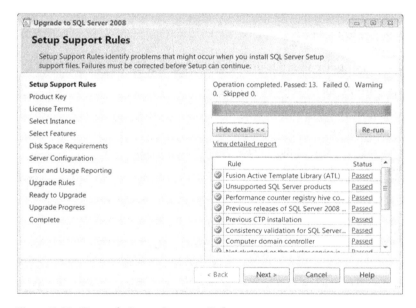

Figure 5-11. *Upgrade Setup Support Rules*

6. On the Product Key screen (see Figure 5-12), enter the product key or indicate that you are upgrading to a free version.

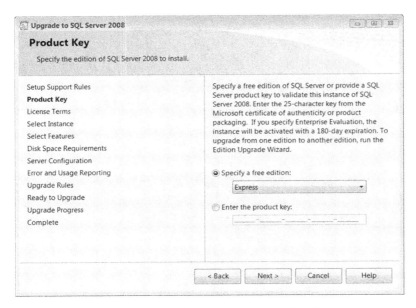

Figure 5-12. *Upgrade to a free edition or enter a product key.*

7. Accept the license agreement, as shown in Figure 5-13.

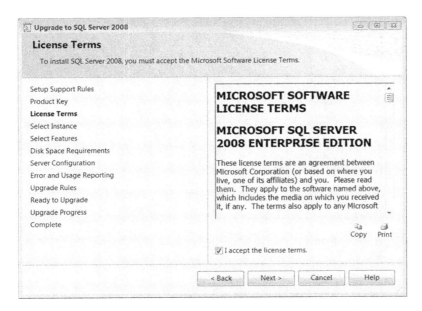

Figure 5-13. *Upgrade license agreement*

8. Select the instance of SQL Server you will be upgrading. You'll be presented with a list like that shown in Figure 5-14.

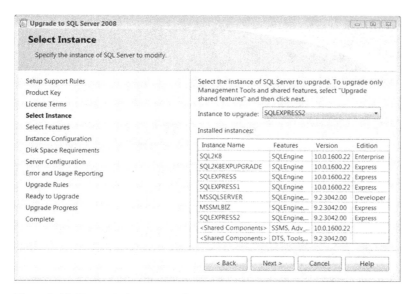

Figure 5-14. *Upgrade instance selection*

9. The feature selections will be preselected and cannot be changed. The checklist of features will be grayed out, as shown in Figure 5-15. If you need to add additional features, you will need to rerun setup.exe after the upgrade.

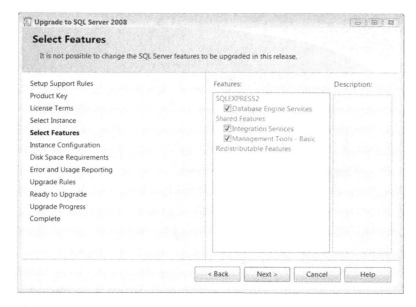

Figure 5-15. *Upgrade features selection*

10. Specify the name of the new instance. In Figure 5-16, we specified SQLEXPRESS2 as our instance name.

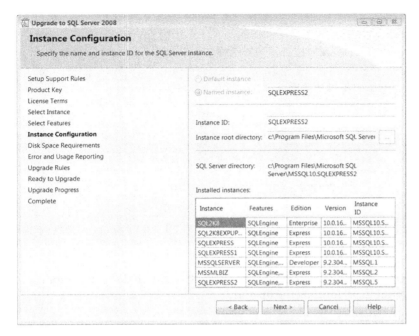

Figure 5-16. *Upgrade the instance configuration*

11. Continue through the upgrade screens, validating the disk space requirements and selecting Error and Usage Reporting.

12. The installer will do a final check to make sure the upgrade process will not be blocked. You'll be presented with upgrade rules like those in Figure 5-17. You'll be able to see which rules you pass, and which require some action on your part.

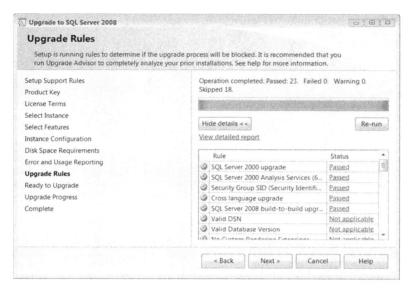

Figure 5-17. *Upgrade rules*

13. The Ready to Upgrade screen in Figure 5-18 allows you to verify all the features that will be upgraded prior to performing the upgrade.

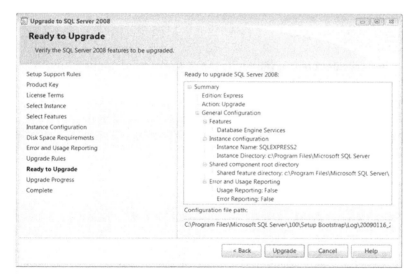

Figure 5-18. *Upgrade features verification*

14. Next, the Upgrade Progress screen in Figure 5-19 allows you to view the status of the upgrade as it progresses.

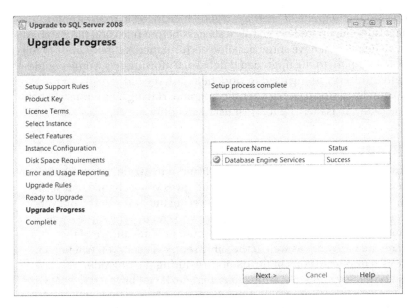

Figure 5-19. *Upgrade Progress screen*

15. Review the log file after the upgrade has completed. The installer will provide a link to the log file on the Complete screen, shown at the upper right of Figure 5-20.

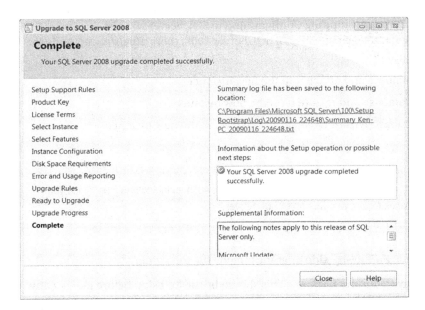

Figure 5-20. *Upgrade completion*

Once you have completed the upgrade, it is always a good idea to log in to the application and run some tests to make sure the upgrade was truly a success before releasing the database back into production. It will help if you have some baseline performance statistics prior to the upgrade that you can use to compare to the upgraded database. Unfortunately, some people are reluctant to change and think everything used to work better on the old version. In rare cases, some queries may actually perform worse after the upgrade. Having a baseline will help you determine if there is actually an issue, or if it is just user perception.

Side-by-Side Upgrade

A side-by-side upgrade consists of installing SQL Server 2008 and moving the databases from the old instance to the new instance. The side-by-side method gives you a chance to test the effects SQL Server 2008 will have on an application before severing the ties with the old version. The new instance can be installed on a second server, or you can use the same server provided it meets the install requirements. Generally, you should take advantage of the upgrade process to upgrade the hardware as well. If the same server is used, you will need sufficient disk space to store a duplicate copy of the databases during the upgrade.

Log shipping can also be useful when performing an upgrade. If you have a large database, you can set up log shipping in advance to keep the databases in sync on the new system while the old system is still active. This will keep the downtime to a minimum, since you can keep your system online while you wait for a large data file to copy to a new server. You can copy the database to the new server and perform the upgrade in advance, so the application will only need to be offline while you restore a few transaction logs on the new server. More information about this approach can be found in SQL Server Books Online by searching for the topics "Migrating a SQL Server 2000 Log Shipping Configuration to SQL Server 2008" or "Migrating a SQL Server 2005 Log Shipping Configuration to SQL Server 2008."

Once you have installed the new instance of SQL Server 2008, there are three methods for moving the databases to the new instance:

- Detach the old database and attach it to the new instance.

- Back up the old database and restore it on the new instance.

- Use the Copy Database Wizard to copy the database to the new instance.

■**Note** You will also need to copy any objects outside the database, such as logins and jobs, since you cannot restore system databases to a newer version of SQL Server.

The steps to performing a side-by-side upgrade include the following:

1. Make sure you have a current backup. (This should be the first step before making any modifications to any databases.)

2. Script the logins.

3. Script the jobs.

4. Install SQL Server 2008.

5. Copy the database to the new instance by using one of the methods previously listed. (These will be described in detail in the subsections that follow.)

6. Create the logins on the new instance by running the login script.

7. Create the jobs on the new instance by running the job script.

8. Check database connectivity and functionality.

Installing SQL Server 2008 in this side-by-side approach is no different from doing a fresh install (described in Chapter 4). However, with a side-by-side upgrade, you also have to worry about migrating your database afterward. The following sections cover the three ways to perform that migration.

The Detach/Attach Migration Method

We prefer the detach and attach method when permanently moving databases to a new instance of SQL Server. By moving each file itself instead of a copy of the file at any given point in time, you can be sure you have captured the exact state of the database as it existed on the previous instance. Since the database is detached, it will be inaccessible for any transactions, ensuring that no data will be committed on the old system during the upgrade. Detaching the database also helps to validate that all the connections have been reconfigured to point to the new system. If a connection was missed and is still pointing to the old instance, you will encounter an error instead of actually making a connection that you think is pointing to the new instance.

You can use the sp_detach_db stored procedure to detach a database. You should also set the database to single-user mode and immediately roll back any transactions before trying to detach the database. Listing 5-1 contains a script invoking sp_detach_db that you can use to detach a database.

Listing 5-1. *T-SQL Script to Detach a Database*

```
USE [master]
GO
ALTER DATABASE [DatabaseName] SET SINGLE_USER WITH ROLLBACK IMMEDIATE
GO
EXEC master.dbo.sp_detach_db 'DatabaseName'
GO
```

To attach a database in SQL Server 2008, you should use the CREATE DATABASE statement with the FOR ATTACH clause. This statement and clause replace the sp_attach_db stored procedure that was previously used to attach a database. The sp_attach_db stored procedure has been deprecated and will be removed in a future release. You will also need to specify the locations of the data files that are going to be attached. The complete syntax for attaching a database is shown in Listing 5-2.

Listing 5-2. *T-SQL Script to Attach a Database*

```
USE [master]
GO
CREATE DATABASE [DatabaseName] ON
( FILENAME = N'C:\MSSQL\DATA\DatabaseName.mdf' ),
( FILENAME = N'C:\MSSQL\DATA\DatabaseName_log.ldf' )
 FOR ATTACH
GO
```

Alternatively, you can detach and attach databases using the GUI in SQL Server Management Studio. To detach a database using the GUI, you can right-click on the database you want to detach, select Tasks, and then select Detach from the context menu. This will bring up the Detach Databases screen. Select OK to detach the database. To attach a database using the GUI, you can right-click on the Databases folder and select Attach from the context menu. This will bring you to the Attach Databases screen. Selecting Add will bring up the Locate Database Files screen, which will allow you to navigate to the data file you would like to attach. Once you have selected the data file, select OK to close the Locate Database Files screen and OK once again on the Attach Databases screen to close the screen and attach the database.

Backup/Restore Migration Method

Using the backup and restore method is a good way to copy the database to the new instance without impacting the availability of the current database. All you need to do is take a full backup of the current database, copy that backup to the new location, and restore it (backup and restore will be covered in Chapters 11 and 12). SQL Server will upgrade the database during the restore process. The result will be a SQL Server 2008 database that you will not be able to move back to an earlier release.

■**Note** You won't be able to move a 2008 database back to an earlier release, even when you are running that database in a prior compatibility mode. You cannot back up and restore to go from 2008 to an earlier release, nor can you detach and attach. You can only move a database forward. You cannot migrate backward.

Copy Database Wizard Migration Method

You can use the Copy Database Wizard to provide a user-friendly interface to copy your database to an upgraded instance of SQL Server 2008. You are given the option to make a copy of the database or completely move the database. You may also choose to copy the database by using the detach and attach method, or by using SQL Management Objects (SMO). If you use the detach and attach method from the wizard, make sure there are no users trying to access the database before running the wizard. If you use SMO, the database will remain online during the entire process. You can also choose to move any database-related objects, such as logins and jobs. We should point out that while you can copy logins using the Copy Database Wizard, for security reasons, the wizard creates the login on the destination server with a random password and then disables the login.

Note The Copy Database Wizard creates a SQL Server Agent job that executes an SSIS package. Make sure you have Integration Services installed and the SQL Server Agent running on the destination server prior to executing the Copy Database Wizard.

Use the following steps to upgrade a database using the Copy Database Wizard:

1. Start the Copy Database Wizard by right-clicking the Management folder in the SQL Server 2008 Management Studio Object Explorer and selecting Copy Database. As you can see in Figure 5-21, you can use the Copy Database Wizard to move or copy databases from an instance of SQL Server 2000 or later to SQL Server 2008. Select Next to continue.

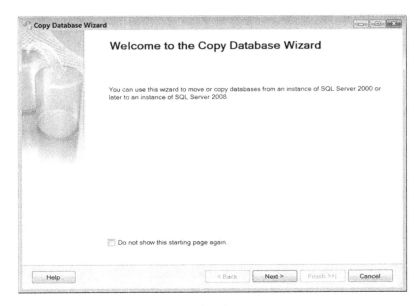

Figure 5-21. *Copy Database Wizard Welcome screen*

2. Choose the source server and instance name that contains the database you will be upgrading. See Figure 5-22 for an example. Provide the appropriate authentication and select Next to continue.

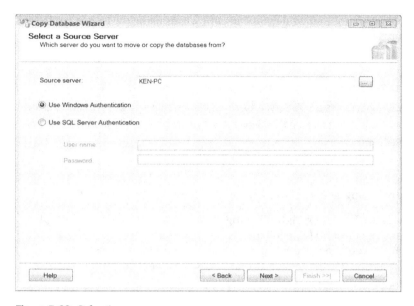

Figure 5-22. *Selecting a source server*

3. Choose the destination server and instance name that will host the new database. The destination server in Figure 5-23 is KEN-PC\SQL2K8. Provide the appropriate authentication and select Next to continue.

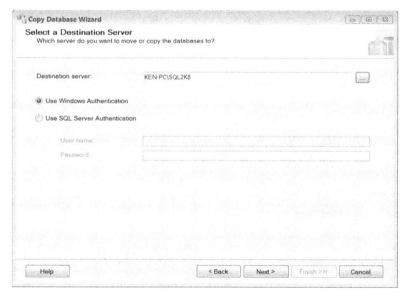

Figure 5-23. *Selecting a destination server*

4. Choose the method that should be used to transfer the database to the new server and select Next to continue. If you use the detach and attach method, the database will be offline during the process. Taking the database offline can be a good thing if you want to make sure no data is being processed during the upgrade; but if you are making a copy of the database for test purposes, you may need to use SMO to ensure that the database remains online, as shown in Figure 5-24.

Figure 5-24. *Selecting a transfer method*

5. Select the database or databases from the source server that you would like to transfer (see Figure 5-25), and select Next to continue. Pay special attention to the option that you choose to transfer the database. If you select Move, the database will no longer exist on the source server after the wizard has completed. Also notice that there is no option to move or copy the system databases to the new instance.

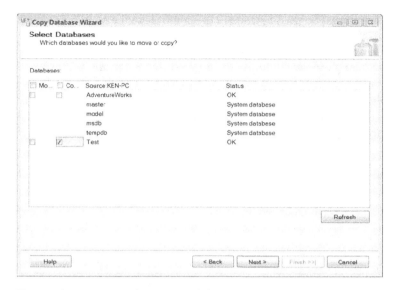

Figure 5-25. *Copy Database Wizard database selection*

6. Specify the name and location of the destination database. As you can see in
   Figure 5-26, you have the option of stopping the transfer or dropping the database
   if it already exists on the destination server. Select the appropriate option and select
   Next to continue. This step will be repeated for each database that has been selected
   for transfer to the destination server.

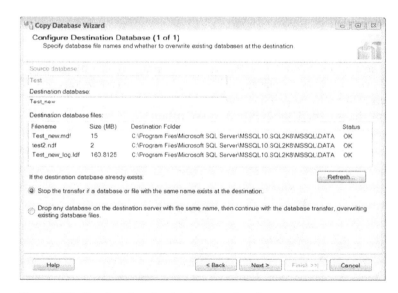

Figure 5-26. *Configuring the destination database*

7. On the left side of the screen, select the related server objects that you would like to transfer to the new instance (shown in Figure 5-27) and click the arrow to move them to the right side of the screen. Once you have selected to move the objects, you can click the ellipsis to the right of each object to specify detailed copy instructions for each object type, as shown in Figure 5-28. Select Next to continue.

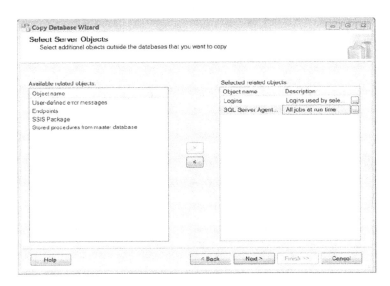

Figure 5-27. *Select related server objects*

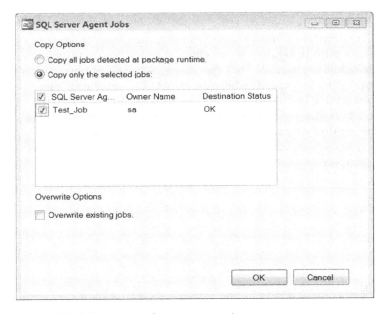

Figure 5-28. *Select server objects copy options*

8. As shown in Figure 5-29, specify the name of the SSIS package that will be created to transfer the databases. (This name will also be used for the SQL Server Agent job that will be created.) Configure the appropriate logging options by choosing Windows Event Log or Text File from the drop-down menu. If you choose to log to a text file, you can also choose the path where you would like to store the logs. Select Next to continue.

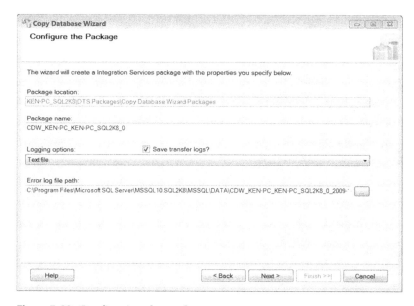

Figure 5-29. *Configuring the package*

9. You can choose to execute the package immediately following the wizard or schedule the package to run at a later time. In Figure 5-30, we chose to run the package immediately. If you choose to schedule the package, click the Change Schedule button to open the New Job Schedule dialog box and specify when you would like to execute the package. Select the proxy account that will be used to perform the transfer. There must be a proxy account available to the user with the SQL Server Integration Services package execution permission on the destination server. You can create a new proxy account if needed by expanding the SQL Server Agent, right-clicking on the Proxies folder, and selecting New Proxy. Select Next to continue.

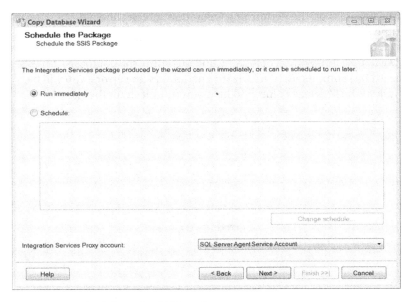

Figure 5-30. *Scheduling the SSIS package*

10. Review the options you have selected on the Complete the Wizard screen (shown in Figure 5-31) and select Finish to start the transfer.

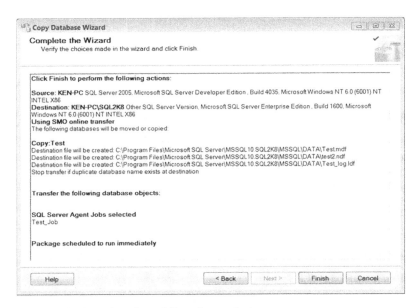

Figure 5-31. *Copy Database Wizard completion*

11. You can monitor the progress on the Performing Operation screen shown in Figure 5-32. The time it takes to complete the transfer depends on the size of the databases being transferred and the options that were chosen during the wizard process. For example, SMO will take longer than detaching and attaching the databases. Click Close once the wizard has completed. If the wizard encounters any errors, you will be able to select the link in the Message column to help you troubleshoot the issue.

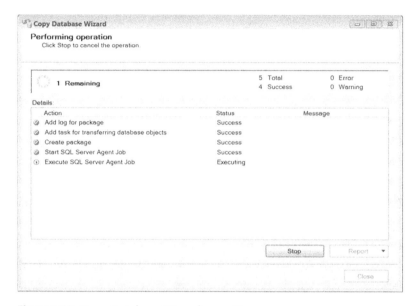

Figure 5-32. *Copy Database Wizard operation progress*

Post-Upgrade Procedures

In order to take advantage of everything that SQL Server 2008 has to offer, there are a few steps that need to be taken after an upgrade has occurred. We will discuss each change that needs to be made and explain how it benefits you after the upgrade. Following are the steps that you should perform after any upgrade:

- Change the compatibility level
- Check the integrity of the objects in your database
- Correct inaccurate row and page counts for tables and indexes
- Set your page verification method to CHECKSUM
- Update statistics

Changing Compatibility Level

The first thing you should do after the upgrade is change the compatibility level of the database, assuming it is supported by the application. We have had some vendors allow us to upgrade the database, as long as we left the compatibility level set to the prior version. When upgrading a database to SQL Server 2008, the database maintains the current compatibility level. In order to take advantage of the new features offered in SQL Server 2008, you should change the compatibility level to SQL Server 2008 (100).

Note If the database compatibility level is below SQL Server 2000 (80), it will be changed automatically to SQL Server 2000 (80) during the upgrade, which is the minimum level supported in SQL Server 2008.

To view the current compatibility level, you can query the sys.databases catalog view:

```
Select name, compatibility_level FROM sys.databases
```

The ALTER DATABASE command replaces the sp_dbcmptlevel procedure that was previously used to change the compatibility level. You can also change the compatibility level in the Options tab of the Database Properties dialog box that is displayed by right-clicking the database and selecting Properties.

Run the following statement to change the compatibility level to SQL Server 2008:

```
ALTER DATABASE [DatabaseName] SET COMPATIBILITY_LEVEL = 100
```

Caution Changing the compatibility level while the database is currently in use could result in the generation of an incorrect query plan and unpredictable queries. The faulty query plan may also be stored in the cache and used for multiple queries. It is recommended that you change the compatibility level when the database is in single-user mode.

Checking Object Integrity

The next thing you should do is run DBCC commands to test for object integrity. The DBCC CHECKDB command checks the integrity of the objects in a database and should be run on a regular basis. One thing that this command does not check in databases created in versions prior to SQL Server 2005 is the integrity of the data in the columns. Adding the DATA_PURITY option causes the CHECKDB command to look for column values that are invalid or out of range. Any database that was created in SQL Server 2005 or later will include the DATA_PURITY check by default; but if the database is being upgraded from an earlier version, you must run the command with the DATA_PURITY option at least once and fix any issues. Once the command has executed successfully and the issues have been resolved, an entry is made in the database header and the DATA_PURITY option will be included by default as a part of the normal CHECKDB operation.

The following command should be executed to perform a CHECKDB with DATA_PURITY:

```
DBCC CHECKDB ([DatabaseName]) WITH DATA_PURITY
```

Correct Row and Page Counts

The DBCC UPDATEUSAGE command corrects inaccurate row and page counts for tables and indexes. Invalid counts are common in previous versions of SQL Server and can skew the results of certain commands, such as sp_spaceused. You should always run the UPDATEUSAGE command on databases that have been upgraded from SQL Server 2000. You do not need to run the command on a regular basis unless frequent Data Definition Language (DDL) modifications are made in the database.

The following command should be executed to update the usage counts for a given database:

```
DBCC UPDATEUSAGE ([DatabaseName])
```

Setting the Page Verification Method

When upgrading a database, the PAGE_VERIFY option will remain the same as it was in the prior version. You should make sure this option is set to CHECKSUM after the upgrade. The CHECKSUM option was introduced in SQL Server 2005 and provides the highest level of integrity for the data files. When the CHECKSUM option is enabled, a checksum of the whole page is computed and stored in the page header when the page is written to disk. When the page is read from disk, the checksum is recalculated and compared with the value in the header.

To view the current PAGE_VERIFY option, you can query the sys.databases catalog view:

```
SELECT name, page_verify_option_desc FROM sys.databases
```

Use the ALTER DATABASE command to change the PAGE_VERIFY option to CHECKSUM:

```
ALTER DATABASE [DatabaseName] SET PAGE_VERIFY CHECKSUM WITH NO_WAIT
```

Updating Statistics

Updating the statistics after the upgrade allows the database engine to take advantage of the enhancements made in SQL Server 2008 to optimize query performance. The statistics that reside in the database were created with an earlier version of SQL Server. By recreating them with SQL Server 2008, you are allowing SQL Server to create more intelligent statistics to work with. This ultimately results in a better execution plan and faster, more efficient queries.

To update statistics, run the following script against each of the databases that have been upgraded:

```
USE [DatabaseName]
GO
sp_msforeachtable 'UPDATE STATISTICS ON ? WITH FULLSCAN; '
```

Summary

Several processes and tools are in place to help make your upgrade a success. Using the tools provided, you should be able to find and resolve any issues and conflicts that would prevent a successful upgrade. Understanding all the upgrade options will also prevent costly mistakes during the upgrade. Remember, the best upgrade method depends on the circumstances; what may work for some systems may not be the best strategy for others. Understanding all the available upgrade paths will ultimately lead to a seamless and painless upgrade.

CHAPTER 6

Post-Installation

After you have installed or upgraded your environment to SQL Server 2008, we recommend spending some time configuring your instance to ensure that SQL Server runs optimally and is secure. There are many configuration options and different post-installation processes and procedures utilized across the globe by various database administrators. We cannot cover every scenario and describe the best configuration setting for all the different types of applications, but we would like to discuss the more important options and describe situations where you can take advantage of the settings.

SQL Server Configuration Manager

SQL Server 2008 Configuration Manager is a tool supplied by Microsoft to set up connection protocols, determine the connectivity from client computers, and to mange the service accounts for the installed instances on a server. This tool allows you to configure all instances of SQL Server 2005 or older installed on your server. Once the tool is launched, it is fairly simple to navigate through the available options and modify any configuration options that need to be altered. Figure 6-1 shows the SQL Server Configuration Manager window.

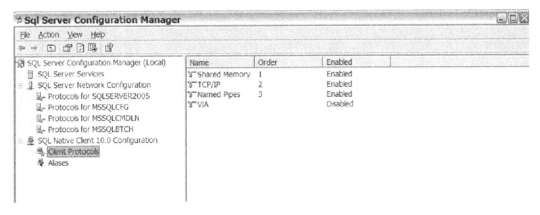

Figure 6-1. *SQL Server Configuration Manager after it is launched*

As you can see from Figure 6-1, the Configuration Manager allows you to configure multiple instances of SQL Server, including SQL Server 2005. The figure also shows the three major configuration setting categories: SQL Server Services, SQL Server Network Configuration, and SQL Native Client 10.0 Configuration.

SQL Server Services

The SQL Server Services section lists the SQL Server services installed on your server for each instance. The window displays the name of each service, its current state, the start mode, the login name that the service starts as, what type of service it is, and the process ID (see Figure 6-2).

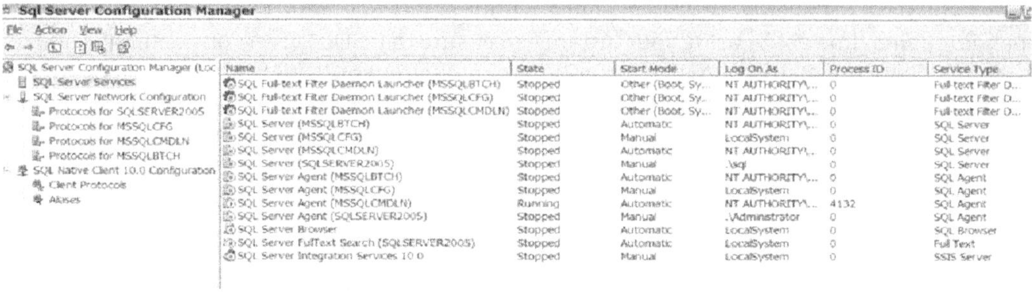

Figure 6-2. *A list of SQL Server services in the Configuration Manager*

From the SQL Server Services section, you can easily start, stop, and restart any service listed. You can also modify the properties of the services using the SQL Server Properties dialog shown in Figure 6-3. Within the dialog, all services have three tabs: Log On, Service, and Advanced, which contain configurable options that were set up during the install. The database engine service actually has an additional tab, FILESTREAM, which is also configurable from the Properties dialog.

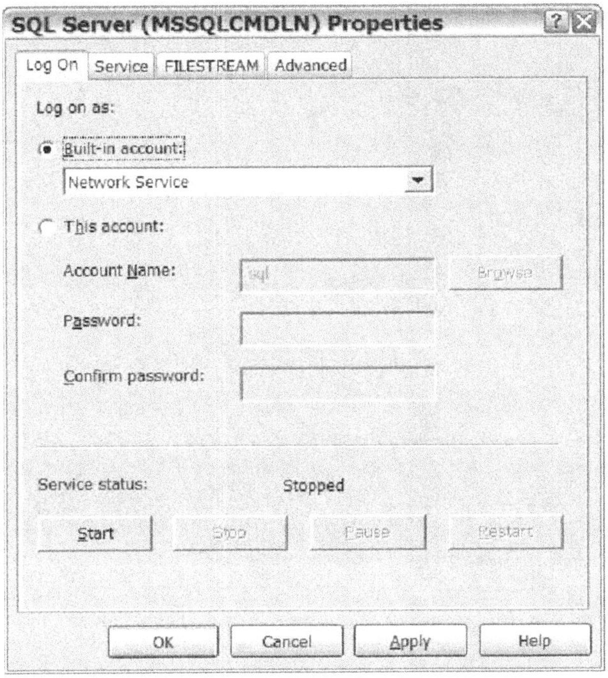

Figure 6-3. *Log On tab of the SQL Server Properties dialog*

The Log On tab is the location from which you change the user account that a service uses. That login name could be a built-in account or a local or domain account. There is a drop-down list that makes it easy to select any of the system accounts. The process for choosing domain or user accounts works just as it always has. You can type the name in or browse the domain or computer for the username that you are looking for. So if during the install you selected an account that you do not want to use, or you need to change the account for any reason, then navigate to the Log On tab to make that change.

The Service tab (see Figure 6-4) provides information about an instance. The Service tab reminds you of the location in which SQL Server binary files are located, the host name, the instance name, the service type, start mode, and the current state. The only changeable option from this tab is the start mode. The start mode determines the service action after a reboot occurs. The available options for Start Mode are Automatic, Disabled, or Manual. Unless you installed an unutilized service, then you probably want to leave the service in Automatic mode. That way, if the server reboots unexpectedly, the services needed for your environment to run properly will start when the server starts.

Figure 6-4. *The Service tab of the SQL Server Properties dialog*

The FILESTREAM tab shown in Figure 6-5 is almost identical to the FILESTREAM tab in the GUI version of the installation process. The FILESTREAM tab allows you to enable or disable FILESTREAM for Transact-SQL access. After you enable FILESTREAM, you have the option to enable FILESTREAM for file input and output (IO) streaming access. If you select the FILESTREAM option for file IO streaming access, then you need to add the Windows share name. The last configuration option that you have to decide is whether to allow remote clients to have streaming access to FILESTREAM data. For those of you who were not ready to enable FILESTREAM data during the installation process, you enable that option in the Configuration Manager after installation.

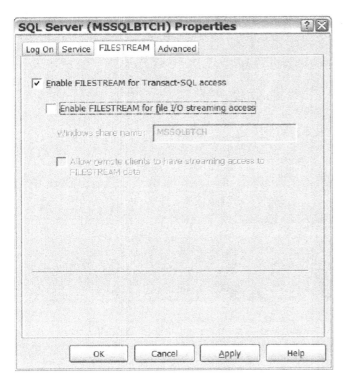

Figure 6-5. *The FILESTREAM tab within the SQL Server Properties dialog*

The Advanced tab shown in Figure 6-6 is a mixture of information about the instance and configurable options for the instance. This tab provides useful information such as whether the instance is clustered, the data path, version, service pack level, and much more. The tab also allows you to enable reporting, change the startup parameters, and modify the dump directory. When you want to review instance information about the server without logging into SQL Server Management Studio, the Advanced tab within SQL Server Configuration Manager allows you to view many of the common options for an instance.

Figure 6-6. *The Advanced tab within the SQL Server Properties dialog*

SQL Server Network Configuration

The SQL Server Network Configuration section allows you to determine the available protocols for use in connecting to an instance of SQL Server 2008. Before we dive too deep into the different types of protocols, let's go ahead and define the terms that will be used throughout this section:

- *Protocol*: A method that controls the connection and data transfer between two computer endpoints.

- *Shared Memory*: Protocol used for connecting to SQL Server from a client on the same server.

- *Named Pipes*: Protocol used for connecting to SQL Server on local networks.

- *TCP/IP (Transmission Control Protocol/Internet Protocol)*: Most widely used protocol for communicating over the Internet. This protocol is used for connecting to SQL Server on local networks and interconnected networks.

- *Virtual Interface Adapter (VIA)*: Protocol used for communicating with virtual hardware.

SQL Server 2008 allows you to enable four protocols: Shared Memory, Named Pipes, TCP/IP, and VIA. When you select the protocols for an instance, the protocol and its status exist on the right side of the screen (see Figure 6-7).

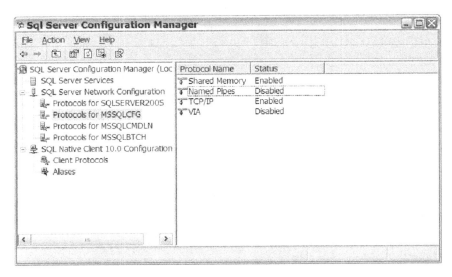

Figure 6-7. *Enabled protocols for the MSSQLCFG instance*

The Shared Memory protocol is the easiest to utilize because there are no configuration options. From the Properties dialog of the Shared Memory protocol (see Figure 6-8), the only options you have are to enable or disable the protocol. The Shared Memory protocol connects to a SQL Server instance on the same server. If you are unable to connect to SQL Server from other machines across your network, then remote into your server and see if you can connect to SQL Server locally. As long as the Shared Memory protocol is enabled, the client will attempt to connect to SQL Server using that protocol. If you are able to connect to SQL Server locally, then you will know that the problem exists with the configuration of the other protocols, not SQL Server.

Figure 6-8. *The Properties dialog for enabling and disabling the Shared Memory protocol*

The Named Pipes protocol is easy to enable or disable, but it can be a little trickier to configure when you are not using the default instance or default pipe. SQL Server has a pre-configured named pipes file, which is used by default unless you specify another file name. The default pipe name is sql\query. In order to connect to a specific named pipe other than the default pipe, you have to either enable the SQL Server Browser service, create an alias for the named pipes connection on the client, or create a custom connection string on the client. Then the client has to utilize that alias name within the connection string when connecting to the database server. Figure 6-9 shows the Properties dialog for the Named Pipes protocol.

■**Note** You can create your own named pipes configuration file and select it from within the Configuration Manager. However, creating named pipe configuration files are outside the scope of this book.

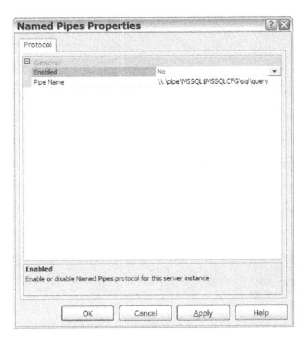

Figure 6-9. *Configuration options for the Named Pipes protocol*

TCP/IP is a frequently used communication protocol that is easy to enable, but can be complex to configure and set up. Luckily, the SQL Server Configuration Manager only allows you to modify minimal settings—changing the parameters incorrectly can cause SQL Server to be unreachable. Before you alter any of the settings, consult with a network person if you are unfamiliar with the choices presented to you.

The Protocol tab (see Figure 6-10) under the TCP/IP Properties dialog consists of three configurable options: the ability to enable TCP/IP along with the Keep Alive and Listen All properties. Obviously, the enabled option allows you to enable or disable the TCP/IP options. The Listen All choice allows the database engine to accept connections on all the enabled valid IP addresses for the server.

Figure 6-10. *The Protocol tab in the TCP/IP Properties dialog*

The Keep Alive selection allows you to determine how long SQL Server waits before validating that a connection is still active. How does this process work? At the designated interval, SQL Server will send a Keep Alive packet to the other end of the connection. Upon receiving the acknowledgement packet, SQL Server keeps that connection open. If the acknowledgment packet isn't received, then SQL Server closes that connection, returns, and then frees the resources. The default interval for sending Keep Alive packets is 30,000 milliseconds, or 30 seconds. Before changing the default time or enabling this process, check with the network engineers at your organization to ensure that the choices selected are in line with theirs.

The IP Addresses tab (see Figure 6-11) lists all the IP addresses for your machine, including a loopback (127.0.0.1). The dialog shows you which IP addresses are active or enabled, as well as the TCP port that it uses for connection. The default instance of SQL Server still connects to port 1433. If you have multiple instances of SQL Server on a server and you have not set up the port used to connect to the instance, then the TCP Dynamic Ports option will show 0, indicating that the instance uses dynamic ports. Using dynamic ports simply means that the instance will choose an available port when the service starts. This also implies that the instance does not guarantee to have the same port every time. In an environment where the applications are configured to talk to a certain port, or port-specific firewall rules are in place, you definitely do not want the port changing on you. Consider defining a port for your database instances.

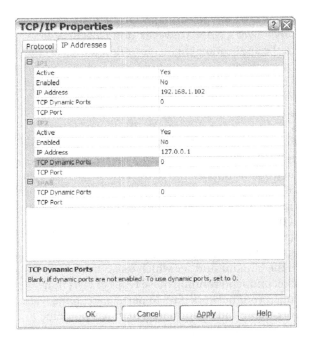

Figure 6-11. *The IP Addresses tab in the TCP/IP Properties dialog*

One thing to be aware of when configuring TCP/IP is that properties are read once when the SQL Server service starts. Any changes made in the TCP/IP Properties dialog will not take effect until you stop and start the SQL Server service. Figure 6-12 shows the message you will receive after changes to remind you that you need to restart your service for those changes to take effect.

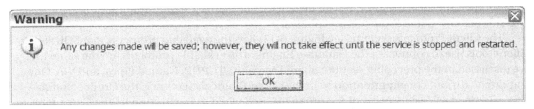

Figure 6-12. *The warning message received after changes are made in the TCP/IP Properties dialog*

We have supported applications that performed better when using TCP/IP over named pipes. We are not network engineers, so pretending to explain to you why performance was better in those instances would not be beneficial. However, named pipes was comparable to TCP/IP on fast LAN networks. Unfortunately, we haven't always supported databases on the fastest networks, and the bulk of our applications communicated via WAN traffic, where named pipes doesn't compete with TCP/IP in terms of performance. We encourage you to test in your environment the difference between your application connecting to SQL Server via TCP/IP and named pipes, especially if your network has performance problems or the application servers connect to the database server over a WAN. However, don't just disable TCP/IP or named pipes without checking with the application engineers or developers to validate the connection protocol used by the application.

How do you determine if performance is better with one protocol over the other? Utilizing testing tools that simulate user activity has always worked best for us. You can simulate a series of steps or user processes with a number of users and measure response times of the application. If the organization does not own or possess testing tools, then get a stopwatch and a group of people and simulate the work of a testing tool. First, develop a script or a series of steps that you want to execute from the application. Next, run the script measuring the amount of time it takes to execute a command from the application to the amount of time that it takes for the response to complete. Measure the time of each step and store that information as your baseline. Then start running your script, enabling and disabling the different protocols while paying close attention to the amount of time that it takes each step to complete. Feel free to have multiple users running through the script during the baseline period and your future tests in order to simulate multiple users using the application. After the tests are complete, compare the results of each protocol run with the baseline and see which one is best.

Because manual tests are not perfect, we recommend running these types of tests multiple times before making the final change. Pull in your network guys to participate in the tests. Oftentimes, they have tools to measure network traffic and performance that may pinpoint problems or help measure the responses of your tests. We know this method is not perfect and requires effort to pull off. However, when you have no other tools and need a method to measure your application performance, this process works.

SQL Native Client Configuration

The various settings under SQL Native Client Configuration section of the Configuration Manager determines how client applications will connect to SQL Server 2008. Modifications within this section will influence how the client tools on the server or machine connect to SQL Server. Modifying client configuration on the server where the instance resides only modifies the configuration for the local instance, not all instances. The Native Client Configuration section has two subsections: Client Protocols and Aliases.

The Client Protocols section (see Figure 6-13) lists the available protocols that SQL Server Client tools use to connect to the Database Engine. The available protocols are the same that we discussed in the preceding section: Shared Memory, TCP/IP, Named Pipes, and VIA. One important attribute to pay attention to in the Client Protocols section is the Order column—this column specifies the order of the protocols used when trying to connect the Client tools to SQL Server.

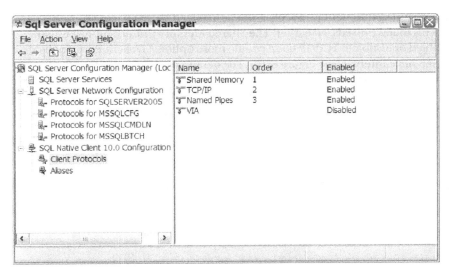

Figure 6-13. *Client protocols supported by SQL Native Client Configuration*

You can arrange the order of the enabled protocols, except for the Shared Memory protocol. That protocol will always be number 1 when enabled. Figure 6-14 shows the Client Protocols Properties dialog that you use for changing protocol order.

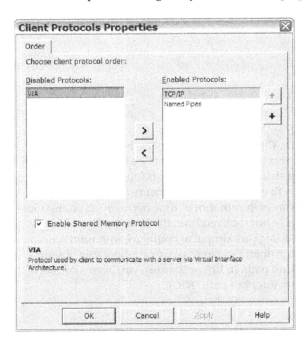

Figure 6-14. *The dialog in which the order of protocols is changed*

The work of configuring the client protocols is not as involved as that of configuring the network protocols that we discussed earlier. The Shared Memory protocol only has two options again: enabled or disabled. TCP/IP has a couple more options: Default Port, Enabled, Keep Alive, and Keep Alive Interval (see Figure 6-15). The default port is the one that the Client tools will utilize when connecting to SQL Server. If the default instance does not use the default port (port 1433), then modify the setting in the Default Port option.

Figure 6-15. *The TCP/IP Properties in the Client Configuration section*

If you are connecting to a named instance, then the client will query the SQL Server Browser service to determine the port to connect to. If the Browser service is not running, then the port number must exist in the connection string. The Keep Alive option determines how long it will take an idle connection to send the Keep Alive packet to ensure that the connection is still active. The Keep Alive Interval option shows the amount of time between resubmissions of the Keep Alive packet when transmissions are not received from the Client tools.

The Named Pipes and the VIA protocol settings are simple to configure with minimal decision points. In the Named Pipes protocol properties, you have two configurable options (enabled or disabled) and the path to the default path. In VIA properties, you have a couple of options, the default server and default network interface card (NIC).

As you can see, the SQL Server Configuration Manager has a number of configurable options that can affect the way that SQL Server and its components start and are communicated with. From within the Configuration Manager, you have the power to prevent SQL Server or any of its components from starting and from being reachable from applications. So before making modifications to any of the options within the Configuration Manager, ensure you are aware of the impact of the changes that you make.

Configuring the Instance

Another important aspect of post-installation involves configuring the instance(s) of your SQL Server. Configuring SQL Server focuses on modifying settings or options to help SQL Server perform optimally. Throughout this section, our objective is to discuss some of our favorite configurable options. The intention is not to configure your environment; however, we would like to provide you with enough information about the settings so you can make intelligent decisions to meet your application's needs.

Before starting the configuration discussion, we would like to point out that there are generally two methods of modifying configuration options in SQL Server: You can use the SQL Server Management Studio GUI interface, or you can invoke the stored procedure sp_configure in a query window. When both methods of amending a configuration option exist, we will show you both the GUI version and code version for the change.

Viewing Advanced Options

By default, SQL Server does not let you view all of the available configuration options. You are initially limited to the most basic choices. Thus the first command to run in your query window is the following:

```
sp_configure 'show advanced options', 1;GO reconfigure
```

This statement allows us to view the advanced options when executing the sp_configure query. That way, we can ensure all the options discussed in subsequent subsections are viewable.

Viewing Configuration Settings

There are three basic methods of viewing the configuration options and their minimum, maximum, and currently configured value:

- Executing the stored procedure sp_configure

- Querying the sys.configurations system view

- Right-clicking on the instance name and selecting Properties from the pop-up menu

Figure 6-16 displays the results of executing the sp_configure stored procedure.

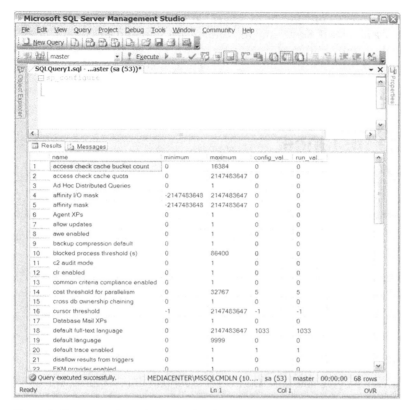

Figure 6-16. *A snapshot of the results of sp_configure*

Figure 6-17 shows the results of querying the sys.configurations system view.

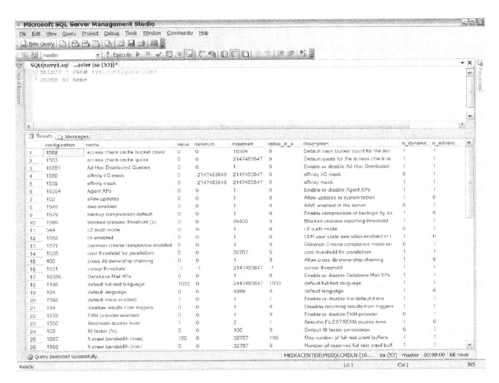

Figure 6-17. *The results of the sys.configurations system view*

Figure 6-18 shows the Server Properties window.

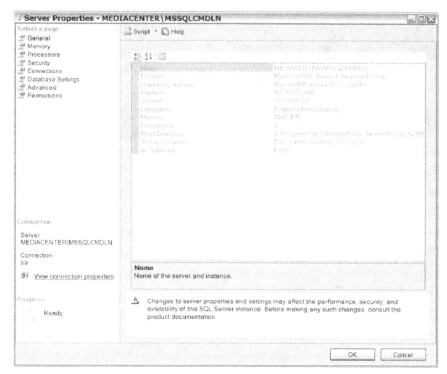

Figure 6-18. *A sample of the Server Properties window*

Visually, you can easily identify the similarities and differences among the screenshots. We encourage you to review the results of the sys.configuration system view. The system view provides you with similar information as the other views, with the advantage of a description of the configuration option. After reviewing the descriptions, you should have a better understanding of the usages of the option and determine if you need to do more research before enabling or disabling the option.

ALLOWING UPDATES TO SYSTEM TABLES

The Allow Updates configuration option exists in SQL Server 2000 solely to allow administrators to update system tables. Even though that configuration option still exists in SQL Server 2008, the ability to directly update system tables is no longer supported. Executing sys.sp_configure 'allow updates', 1 will run and complete successfully, although it provides no additional functionality to the user. When you attempt to reconfigure the server, the reconfiguration will fail (if WITH OVERRIDE is not specified), informing you that updates to the system catalog are not supported. Plan to remove the Allow Updates configuration option from all scripts and processes because it may be removed from a future version of SQL Server.

Specifying Maximum and Minimum Server Memory

Determining the maximum and minimum amounts of memory each instance of SQL Server requires can be easy or complex, depending on the server and what applications are running on it. If you have a single instance of SQL Server on a server without any other applications (excluding applications like virus scan and other essential apps), then you want to dedicate as much memory as possible to SQL Server while still leaving enough memory for the operating system to run effectively. Depending on the amount of memory that server has, we generally like to leave at least 1 or 2 GB for Windows. Figure out the best setting for maximum memory where both SQL Server and the operating system are happy. In Chapter 14, we discuss methods for monitoring your memory. That should help you determine if your instance needs more memory.

You can specify memory allocation from the Memory section of the Server Properties dialog for your instance (see Figure 6-19). You can see that the minimum server memory has been left at 0 MB, whereas the maximum has been set at 8192 MB (which is 8 GB).

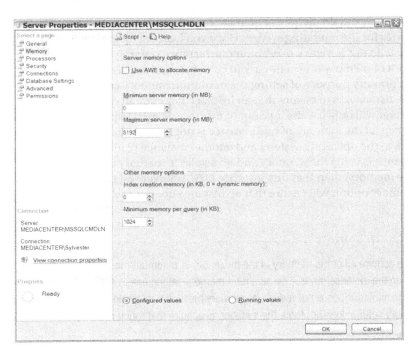

Figure 6-19. *The Memory section of the Server Properties dialog*

You also have the option to invoke a stored procedure to specify memory allocation. The following invocation of `sys.sp_configure` requests the same 0 to 8192 MB allocation as was shown in Figure 6-19:

```
EXEC sys.sp_configure N'max server memory (MB)', N'8192'
GO
```

Configuring your maximum amount of memory on servers that have multiple instances of SQL Server or other applications will increase the complexity and importance of your task. Do not forget that SQL Server is a memory hog; it allocates as much memory to the buffer as needed to process or handle the workload. If you have multiple instances of SQL Server reserving memory without restrictions or limitations, then one instance will likely be starved or not have as much memory as it needs. To help eliminate that as a potential problem, you should set minimum and maximum memory allocations.

When determining the maximum amount of memory for each instance, we usually revert to the requirements documentation for information about the applications that will be running on each instance. During the pre-installation phase, you gather information about the number of users, the anticipated transaction per second, the size of the databases, and so on. With that information, settle on the amount of maximum memory that you want to allocate to each instance. When the applications are highly similar in terms of transactions per second, database sizes, and the like, you should divide the memory equally among the instances after leaving a couple of gigabytes for the operating system. Once you have set up the maximum memory configuration, you do not have to worry about one instance starving another.

The minimum amount of memory is usually easy to configure and does not require as much consideration. The primary purpose of setting the minimum memory configuration on a server that has multiple instances is to ensure that an instance has enough memory to perform as expected. SQL Server will only use the amount of memory needed to process requests from the applications. When all the memory of one instance is not being utilized, that instance may release memory back to the operating system, and another instance could reserve the memory. If the other instance is using the memory and no available memory remains for the instance that released the memory, then that first instance of SQL Server will perform poorly. Setting the minimum memory option will ensure that an instance does not release too much of its memory.

■**Note** SQL Server does not acquire all of the memory in the maximum or minimum memory configuration settings immediately when the instance starts. The minimum memory setting ensures that an instance, having acquired more than the minimum, does not reduce its memory below the minimum that you specify. However, the minimum memory setting does not force the instance to acquire that much memory at startup.

Enabling Address Windows Extensions

Address Windows Extensions (AWE) is one of the configuration options that you should be aware of if you are running on 32-bit operating systems. Enabling AWE allows a 32-bit SQL Server to use more than 2 or 3 GB of RAM. You can enable AWE from the Server Properties dialog, as previously shown in Figure 6-19.

AWE is not applicable in 64-bit operating systems because 64-bit architecture does not have the same memory restrictions as 32-bit systems. There are additional configurations that you may want to consider prior to enabling AWE. The following list describes some configuration options:

How much memory do you have? If your server only has 4 GB of memory, do you need to enable AWE?

Do you need to enable /3gb? The /3gb switch in the boot.ini file allows processes to use more than 3 GB of memory.

Is the /pae switch enabled on your server? To take advantage of 4 GB of memory, you must enable the /pae switch.

Can you enable the Lock Pages in Memory option? Lock Pages in Memory identifies accounts that use a process to keep data pages in memory. That minimizes the amount of paging to virtual memory on disk. You have to enable Lock Pages in Memory on 32-bit systems in order to turn on AWE.

Unfortunately, those configuration options are system dependent and are difficult to cover in such a small section. So I encourage you to look for AWE in SQL Server Books Online or see the topic "Awe-Enabled Option" at http://msdn.microsoft.com/en-us/library/ ms190731.aspx for more details.

Specifying the Backup Compression Default

The Backup Compression Default option enables you to compress backups without specifying the WITH COMPRESSION or WITH NO_COMPRESSION options to your backup statements. By default, SQL Server 2008 Enterprise Edition disables backup compression during the installation process. If you have determined that backup compression is your preferred choice for performing backups, then enable compression by default to remove the requirement of specifying that you want your databases compressed each and every time you initiate a backup.

You can specify backup compression by default from the Database Settings section of the Server Properties dialog, shown in Figure 6-20.

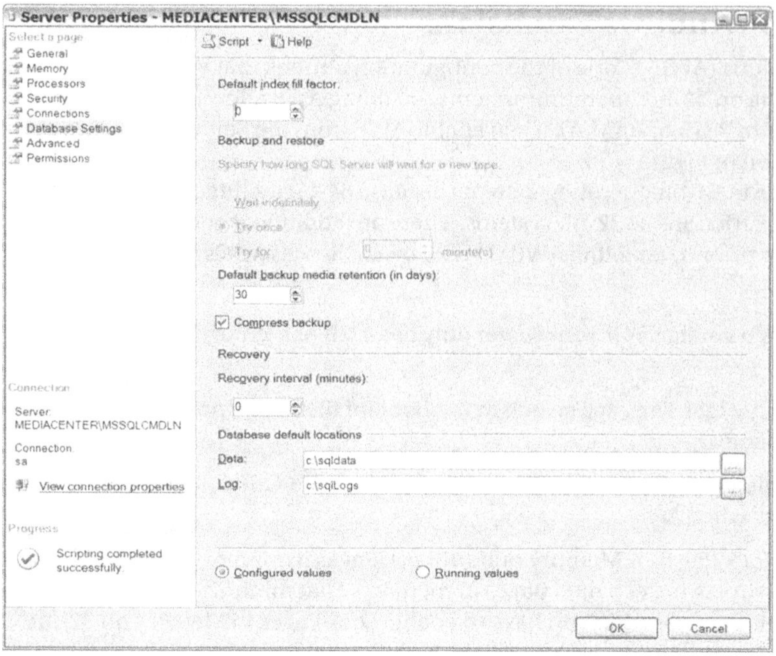

Figure 6-20. *The Database Settings section of the Server Properties dialog*

And you can specify compression by default through a stored procedure call. For example, the following will enable compression by default:

```
EXEC sys.sp_configure N'backup compression default', N'1'
GO
RECONFIGURE WITH OVERRIDE
GO
```

Specifying compression by default can save you time by eliminating one possible avenue for mistake. Imagine yourself on the night when you have to back up the database before applying a major change. You execute the backup command that you have been running for years, and it runs for hours. Too late, you realize that you forgot to include compression as part of that command. What makes matters worse is the fact that your server doesn't have enough space to keep that uncompressed backup on the server. So you have to back up the database again, after having lost time that you dearly need for the major change that your boss wants in place by 8:00 AM. Don't put yourself in the position of having to request compression each and every time you make a backup. Enable compression by default if you prefer to compress your backups.

Note We will discuss backup compression in more detail in Chapter 11.

Enabling Login Failure Auditing

We like to track successful and failed logins on the SQL Server instances that we support. Monitoring the failed login attempts to SQL Server enables you to identify and track down unwanted login activity against it. We also track successful logins to help identify who was logged into the system when unexpected actions occur. You can enable login auditing from the Security section of the Server Properties dialog, as shown in Figure 6-21.

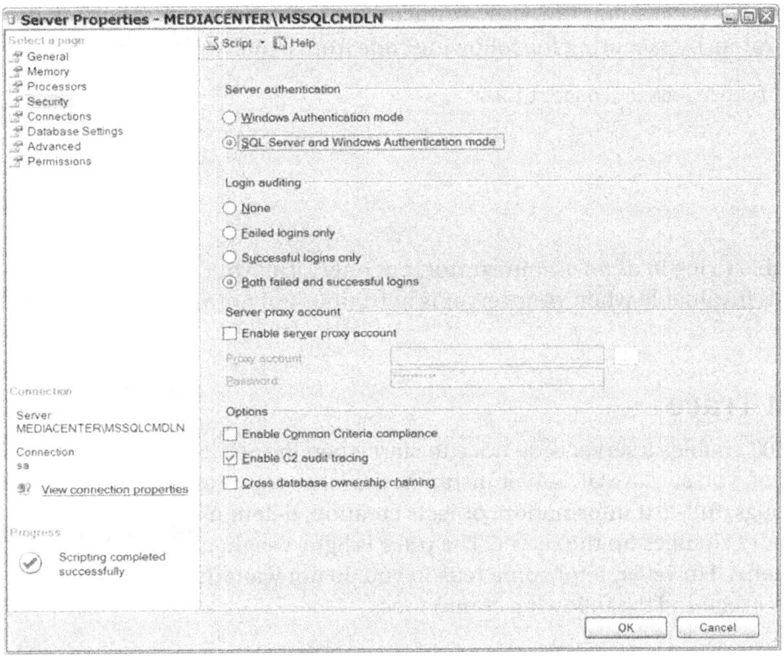

Figure 6-21. *The Security section of the Server Properties dialog*

You may also invoke auditing via a call to the xp_instance_regwrite stored procedure. (That extended stored procedure allows you to write directly to your system registry.) For example:

```
USE [master]
GO
EXEC xp_instance_regwrite N'HKEY_LOCAL_MACHINE',_
N'Software\Microsoft\MSSQLServer\MSSQLServer', N'AuditLevel', _ REG_DWORD, 3
GO
```

Unfortunately, many of us (myself included) work in environments where we do not get 100% control over who has access to SQL Server. Someone in management has forced you to grant Insert, Update, and Delete permissions to non-DBA personal, and you are terrified about the mistakes that they can make. Logging successful logins to SQL Server allows you to identify when such individuals are in your system and can help you narrow down which individuals to pursue when all the data is deleted from a table and no one owns up to it.

Enabling Dedicated Administrator Connections

SQL Server 2008 provides a method for members of the `sysadmin` group to connect to an unresponsive instance of SQL Server, even when other connections are failing. This feature improves the database administrator's ability to troubleshoot problems within SQL Server.

By default, in order to utilize a dedicated administrator connection, you must connect on the server itself through SQLCMD or SQL Server Management Studio. Luckily, Microsoft allows you to enable remote dedicated administrator connections, which will allow you to connect to the dedicated administrator connection from across the network. Enable remote dedicated connections for administrators by executing the following code from a query window:

```
EXEC sys.sp_configure 'remote admin connections' ,1
GO

RECONFIGURE
GO
```

You should now be able to log in as an administrator, not only locally but across the network as well. This ability is invaluable when your server is in trouble and normal logins are not going through.

Disabling Default Trace

By default, SQL Server 2008 enables a server-side trace to start when the SQL Server service starts for an instance. When you start a SQL Server instance, the trace captures some database options, errors and warnings, full-text information, objects creation, deletion and alters, as well as security and memory changes on the server. The trace is light-weight and should not cause performance problems. However, if for some reason you do not want this trace running, then you can disable it by executing the following commands:

```
EXEC sys.sp_configure 'default trace enabled' ,0
GO

RECONFIGURE
GO
```

Think twice before disabling the trace because it can help you capture events when they occur. How many times have you been asked questions about who performed a certain action or at what time the action occurred? If you do not have a trace running at the time the action occurred, you will be unable to provide an adequate answer to such questions. With the default trace, however, such questions may be easily answered.

Enabling Use of the CLR (Common Language Runtime)

The `clr enabled` option within SQL Server 2008 allows SQL Server to run assemblies. By default, the option is disabled, or set to zero. That means assembly executions aren't allowed or permitted to run within SQL Server 2008. You can enable the use of the CLR as follows:

```
EXEC sys.sp_configure 'clr enabled' ,1
GO

RECONFIGURE
GO
```

Changes to the `clr enabled` option are effective immediately. You do not need to restart your service. Disabling CLR after it has been enabled causes any application domains that include user assemblies to unload immediately following the `RECONFIGURE` statement.

Choosing Lightweight Pooling

Lightweight pooling is an option available in SQL Server 2008 that can potentially help in multiprocessor environments that experience heavy context switching. Lightweight pooling potentially increases throughput, which can increase performance.

Enable lightweight pooling by executing the following code:

```
EXEC sys.sp_configure sp_configure 'lightweight pooling', '1'
GO

RECONFIGURE
GO
```

Unfortunately, you cannot enable common language runtime after the enabling of lightweight pooling. So spend a little time contemplating your need for the CLR prior to enabling lightweight pooling. If you do enable the feature, SQL Server will generate a message to remind you that you also must disable the use of the CLR.

■**Caution** We have experienced problems with our linked server queries failing after our having enabled lightweight pooling. Our particular problems became apparent upon restart of our services. If you are working in an environment with linked servers, then make sure you test thoroughly before enabling lightweight pooling.

Enabling a Query Governor Cost Limit

Have you ever identified resource-intensive queries on your system that cause all sorts of performance problems? We especially get annoyed with users who execute queries and forget the `where` clause and the `nolock` hint on the largest table in our Very Large Databases (VLDB). To avoid such problems, you can specify a maximum limit in seconds for queries executed against your server. Such a limit is termed a *query governor cost limit*. Before you can specify a limit in seconds, you must enable the option as follows:

```
EXEC sys.sp_configure 'query governor cost limit' ,1
GO

RECONFIGURE
GO
```

We know this option sounds great, and it can definitely be a method for improving performance. However, we encourage you to consider the consequences of preventing certain processes from running against your server. Believe me, we're on your side—we would love to make developers write better code, and preventing a process from running is one way to force developers to write that code better. Unfortunately, your boss's boss, who really needs the results from a long-running query, may not be as understanding. Make sure you set a query limit decision wisely. The Resource Governor that was added in SQL Server 2008 actually provides much more flexibility when dealing with resource-intensive queries.

xp_cmdshell

xp_cmdshell is a configurable option that allows you to disable or enable the use of the extended stored procedure xp_cmdshell. xp_cmdshell is used to execute command-line statements from within the database engine. If you need it though, you can enable xp_cmdshell by executing the following code:

```
EXEC sys.sp_configure 'xp_cmdshell' ,1
GO

RECONFIGURE
GO
```

Be careful! By default, the xp_cmdshell stored procedure is disabled during install and should remain disabled if it is not required by the application. Think about it—once a user gains access to your system, he has the power to cause all sorts of havoc on your server.

Miscellaneous Configuration Options

In this section, we describe a set of configuration options requiring more expertise before enabling on your SQL Server. Most of these setting have a direct impact on how your SQL Server will process queries, and we strongly recommend testing, and hopefully load testing, before enabling these options in your production environment. To be honest, we do not tweak all of the configuration options we describe here, but we think they are important to know about. Here's the list:

- *Blocked Process Threshold*: Amount of time a process is blocked before a blocked process report is generated. The threshold is measured in seconds, and alerts can be generated when these events are triggered.

  ```
  EXEC sys.sp_configure 'blocked process threshold' ,1
  GO

  RECONFIGURE
  GO
  ```

- *Cursor Threshold*: Threshold used to determine if the cursor will be processed synchronously (wait on all the rows to be returned) or asynchronously (allows users to get data from cursor while it retrieves the data), depending on the amount of rows returned for the result set.

```
EXEC sys.sp_configure 'cursor threshold' ,1
GO

RECONFIGURE
GO
```

- *Cost Threshold for Parallelism*: Threshold used to figure out when a query should be executed in parallel versus serially. In other words, when this threshold is surpassed, the query will be executed using parallelism.

```
EXEC sys.sp_configure 'cost threshold for parallelism' ,1
GO

RECONFIGURE
GO
```

- *Maximum Degree of Parallelism*: Threshold used to determine the maximum number of processors that can be used to process a single query during a parallel execution.

```
EXEC sys.sp_configure 'max degree of parallelism' ,1
GO

RECONFIGURE
GO
```

- *Query Wait*: Threshold in seconds that determines the amount of time a query waits on resources before it times out. By default, the query wait time is set to wait 25 times of the estimated cost of query.

```
EXEC sys.sp_configure 'query wait' ,60
GO

RECONFIGURE
GO
```

- *User Connections*: Sets the number of user connections for an instance of SQL Server.

```
EXEC sys.sp_configure 'user connections' ,1000
GO

RECONFIGURE
GO
```

Preproduction Tasks

Once you have configured your SQL Server instances, you will want to continue to prepare your server for production. Depending on your environment, configuring SQL Server for production will require various processes and procedures. The following sections will provide you with some of the steps that we go through prior to deployment of our SQL Server instances into production from a server and database perspective.

Server Tasks

Following are some things you should do, or at least consider doing, from a server level prior to placing your server into production:

- *Apply Patches*: Before your new SQL Server is added to production, ensure that the patch level of the server is at its correct level. We are not recommending that you install a service pack that your environment is not ready for, but consider applying less risky patches like security patches. Applying currently available patches before going live in production should increase the uptime of your new SQL Server because you will only have to bring the server down afterward to apply new patches as they are released by Microsoft.

- *Test Your IO Subsystem*: In Chapter 2, we discussed the importance of testing your IO subsystem before SQL Server is placed into production. If you have not simulated a workload on your IO subsystem, then we encourage you to go out on the Web and download some free testing tools. Do not wait until SQL Server is running in production to identify problems with the setup and configuration of your IO subsystem. Spend a little time up front, learn how to effectively utilize an IO-testing tool, and make sure that your system is ready for production.

- *Run the Best Practices Analyzer*: SQL Server 2000 and SQL Server 2005 both had applications published by Microsoft that compared the SQL Server and Windows configuration settings against Microsoft's recommended best practices to determine if there were potential issues. In SQL Server 2008, use some of the predefined policies of Policy Based Management (see Chapter 7) to ensure that your SQL Server instance is in line with Microsoft best practices. You can also review the options checked by SQL Server 2005's Best Practices Analyzer and ensure that you are following the best practice items that you are concerned about. Make the time to validate your server against Microsoft's best practices, even if doing so requires more work than you would prefer. The amount of time that a best practices check can potentially save you in the long run is well worth the effort.

Database Tasks

Following are some tasks that you should perform for each database that you plan to deploy into production. The tasks are not mandatory, but they can prove beneficial and can save you headaches down the road.

- *Size data and log files*: When creating new databases, options exist to determine the initial size of the database data and log files to the size of your choice. If you have a general idea about the expected size of the database, then take advantage of this option and allocate space for the data and log files, respectively. By initializing the data and log files to a projected size, you will minimize the number of data and log file growths because of the database needing more space. Saving data and log file growths will ultimately save CPU cycles and disk IO, dedicating more resources to processing application requests.

- *Enable Autogrowth*: Many database administrators argue that you should not set up your database data and log files to autogrow by a certain percentage or fixed size. We have heard many administrators say that you should monitor your files enough so that you can grow them when necessary. Our advice to you is to set up the autogrowth option in whatever way that enables you to keep production running (see Figure 6-22 for an example). If you manage multiple servers and are constantly fighting fires, chances are that you don't have time to monitor data and log files to grow them manually. So set up the autopilot and ensure that your production databases keep running.

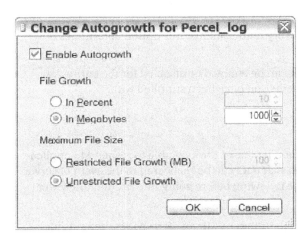

Figure 6-22. *Autogrowth options for a log file*

The flip side of that coin is to periodically review the autogrowth setting that you have set up to ensure that you are not wasting large amounts of space and increasing disk defragmentation. Growing your database and log files by 10% to 20% may have made sense when your database was 10 to 20 GB. Now that your database is 100 GB, you may want to consider revising some of those percentages. Regardless of what option you select, make sure you educate yourself enough to understand what options are available to you in the event that you manage the data growth. Keep in mind, your data drive and log drive may be running out of space because of the autogrowth option selected. Modifying how your database and log files grow may buy you some more time before needing to purchase additional space.

- *Disable autoshrink*: Shrinking your data or log files is a process that removes any unused free space from those files. Configuring the database to automatically shrink the data and log files is simply a bad idea. The main reason why we do not like to enable this option stems from the lack of control over when the process will start. Unfortunately, we have seen this option cause problems in our environment.

- *Set key database options*: In SQL Server, options are available that allow you to configure the behavior of a database. Following are some of the options that we frequently specify.

  Auto Create Statistics: Automatically creates statistics on columns without indexes that are used in the where clause of queries.

  Auto Update Statistics: Automatically updates statistics needed by queries by the optimizer based on changes within the data.

  Cursor Default: Allows cursors created within a single procedure or trigger to be referenced by any process using that connection.

  Parameterization: Determines how queries will be parameterized via default rules for the database or all queries in the database.

  Recovery: Based on your data recovery requirements, this option determines how the transaction log will be used.

  SQL Options: Various options that can be enabled or disabled for the entire database, depending on the requirements you have been supplied with.

Maintenance and Monitoring

Database administrators must ensure that their databases are available to respond to application queries at the required response rate and that data can be recovered in the event of server failure. To that end, you should at least do the following before going into production with a new server and database:

- *Create a backup and recovery strategy*: Fortunately, Microsoft provides methods for backing up and maintaining your databases. However, at a minimum, before going into production, you definitely want to create a backup strategy that meets the business requirements. (We cover backups, restores, and maintaining your databases in depth in Chapters 11, 12, and 13.)

- *Create a plan to maintain indexes and integrity*: Commands and features exist to maintain indexes and check the integrity of your databases. You should put together a plan to accomplish these. (See Chapter 13 for more information about ongoing maintenance.)

- *Create processes to monitor your server*: Setting up processes to monitor and capture SQL Server performance is critical to supporting and base-lining the application. In a perfect world, organizations would purchase software to aid in the monitoring of your server. Unfortunately, purchasing software is not always an option, but expectations still exist for you to proactively monitor your system to identify problems. In Chapter 14, we discuss monitoring your server and the different methods and tactics that can be used if you don't have another application to assist you. Regardless of the method used to monitor your server, strive to have processes in place prior to placing your server into production.

Summary

As we conclude this chapter, we hope that you have a better understanding of the configuration options that we consider prior to putting SQL Server into production. Prior to amending options in the SQL Server Configuration Manager, SQL Server, or the databases, spend some time understanding the impact of the changes on your system. As a database administrator, part of your responsibilities include availability and performance. Modifying configuration options incorrectly will negatively impact the system availability or its performance. Be careful: Test the changes if you can on servers that resemble your own production environment as much as possible.

We encourage you to develop a checklist prior to deploying SQL Server 2008 into production to include the SQL Server Configuration Manager, SQL Server, and database options that you would like reviewed along with the preproduction considerations. That way all database administrators within the organization have a consistent way of ensuring the review and modification of configuration options.

Administering Microsoft
SQL Server 2008

CHAPTER 7

Multi-Server Administration

With the number of database servers increasing and the tolerance for errors decreasing in today's organizations, it is has become necessary to define and maintain database standards across the enterprise. One of the problems prior to SQL Server 2008 has been making sure those standards are being followed. As a DBA, you would have to go out to each server and run queries using system tables to ensure that each server was in compliance. You can now use Policy-Based Management to ensure that your standards are being followed. By using central management servers, you can use a single server as an access point to all the servers in the organization. Central management servers enable you to evaluate policies and execute queries against registered server groups with a single click. You can also use the new Dynamic Management Views and functions introduced with SQL dependency reporting to locate object dependencies between servers.

Policy-Based Management

Policy-Based Management is a new feature in SQL Server 2008 that allows you to define and implement policies across the organization. Policy-Based Management was initially called the Declarative Management Framework but was changed before the final release of SQL Server 2008. First, we will show you how to manually create a policy and then move on to some of the more automated ways of creating a policy.

There are a few key terms you should be familiar with when discussing Policy-Based Management:

- *Target*: Object that is being managed by a policy
- *Facet*: Group of logical properties that can be applied to a target
- *Condition*: A check that is evaluated by a policy
- *Policy*: A condition that is applied to a given set of objects
- *Category*: Group of policies that help you manage policy enforcement

When you look at the Policy Management node in SQL Server Management Studio, you see three folders: Policies, Conditions, and Facets. The folder structure forms a sort of hierarchy of the objects required to use Policy-Based Management. Facets are required in order to create conditions, and conditions are required in order to create policies.

Manually Creating a Policy

To manually create a policy you must first create a condition, and then you will be able to create a policy that uses that condition. Once you have created a policy, you can then place it in the appropriate category and apply it to one or more targets.

Let's start by creating a condition that will be used in a policy. In this example, we will create a condition that checks to see if a database is using the full recovery model. To create a new condition, right-click the Conditions folder and select New Condition. (The Conditions folder is located under Policy Management in the Management node of the Object Explorer in SQL Server Management Studio.) This will bring you to the Create New Condition dialog box, as shown in Figure 7-1.

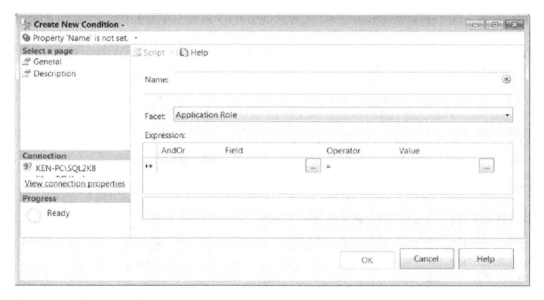

Figure 7-1. *Policy-Based Management Create New Condition dialog box*

Create the new condition by entering the following information:

- *Name*: In the Name field, enter **Full Recovery Model**. Notice that the dialog box title now says "Create New Condition – Full Recovery Model," and the error displayed under the title bar changes from saying that the name is not set to saying that the ExpressionNode is not set.

- *Facet*: Before you set the expression, change the Facet field to Database Maintenance by selecting it from the drop-down list.

- *Expression*: Click the cell in the Field column and select @RecoveryModel from the drop-down list. Leave the equals sign (=) in the Operator column. You can see all the available operators by clicking on the drop-down list. Click the drop-down list in the Value column and select Full. Notice that the Value column changes to reflect the values that are appropriate for the attribute that has been selected in the Field column. For example, if you change the field to @LastBackupDate, a calendar control would be displayed in the Value drop-down list. You can also enter multiple expressions using AND/OR logic by selecting the next row and entering the appropriate information.

• *Description*: Optionally you can enter a description by selecting the Description page on the left and entering it in the text box provided. Select the Description page and type a brief description, such as **Condition to check to make sure a database recovery model is set to Full**.

Once you've entered all the information correctly, the errors are removed from the top of the dialog box, and the status changes to Ready as shown in Figure 7-2.

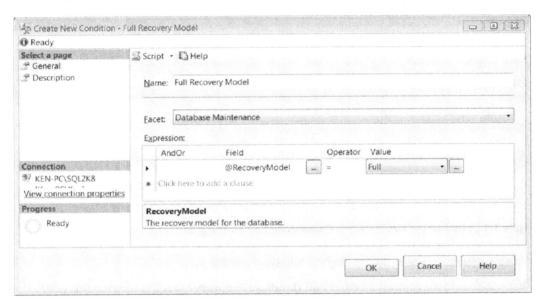

Figure 7-2. *Completed Policy-Based Management Create New Condition dialog box*

Click OK to finish creating the condition. You should now see the new condition under the Conditions folder in Policy-Based Management.

Now that you have created a condition, you are ready to create a policy that can use the condition. To create a new policy, right-click the Policies folder and select New Policy. (The Policies folder is located under Policy Management in the Management node of the Object Explorer in SQL Server Management Studio.) This will bring you to the Create New Policy dialog box as shown in Figure 7-3.

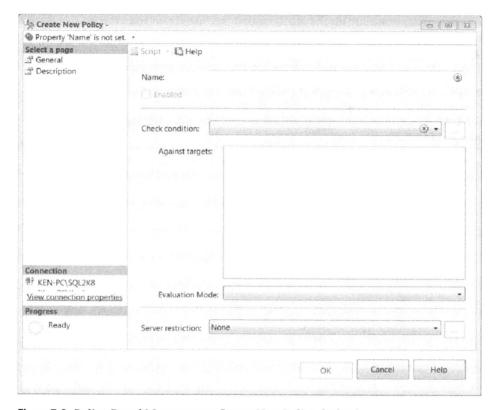

Figure 7-3. *Policy-Based Management Create New Policy dialog box*

Create the new policy by entering the following information:

- *Name*: In the Name field enter **Full Database Recovery Model**. Notice the title now says "Create New Policy – Full Database Recovery Model," and the error displayed now states that the Condition is not set instead of the Name.

- *Check Condition*: Set the Check Condition option by clicking the drop-down list and selecting Full Recovery Model. If this is your first time using Policy-Based Management, it should be the only thing in the drop-down you are allowed to select. Once the condition has been selected, you can click the ellipsis next to the drop-down list to edit or review the condition directly from the policy.

- *Against Targets*: Once the condition has been set, the target is automatically set to Every Database. You can exclude databases by clicking the drop-down menu next to Every and selecting New Condition (see the completed policy later in Figure 7-5). This will allow you to create a condition you can use to exclude certain databases based on given properties exposed in the database facet. For example, you may want to create a condition that will exclude read-only databases from a policy that verifies all databases are using the full recovery model.

- *Evaluation Mode*: Use this drop-down list to select the evaluation mode. For this example, we will be using On Demand. Selecting On Schedule will enable you to either assign an existing schedule to run the policy or create a new one. Also, selecting On Schedule will allow you to enable the policy by selecting the Enabled check box located directly under the policy name. Only enabled policies will be run by the scheduled job that will be created to check the policies. Valid evaluation modes are On Demand, On Change: Prevent, On Change: Log Only, and On Schedule. The evaluation modes displayed in the drop-down list depend on the facet you are using in the condition. All facets support On Change and On Schedule, but On Change: Prevent relies on the facet being able to use Data Definition Language (DDL) triggers to roll back the transaction. On Change: Log Only relies on the ability of the facet change to be captured by an event.

- *Server Restriction*: You can create a condition to exclude servers from the policy by using the server facet. For example, you could create a condition that only evaluates the policy on SQL Servers that are running the Enterprise or Standard Edition. For this example, we will not be using a server restriction.

Select the Description page, as shown in Figure 7-4, to configure the remaining options.

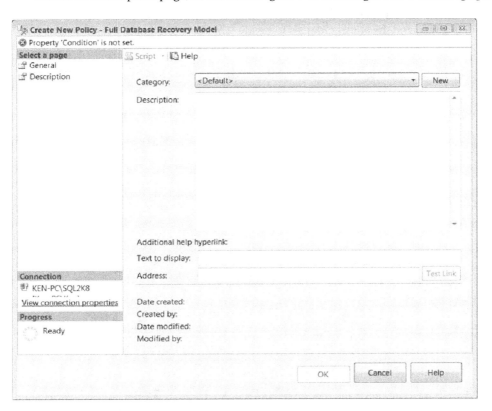

Figure 7-4. *Create New Policy dialog box Description page*

The remaining options in Figure 7-4 are as follows:

- *Category*: For this example, we will leave the category set to Default. To change the category, you would click the drop-down menu and select a defined category or click the New button to create a new category. We will show you how to manage categories later in this section.

- *Description*: Optionally, you can define a description by entering it in the text box provided. Enter a brief description, such as **Policy to make sure a database recovery model is set to Full**.

- *Text to Display*: Type the text that will be displayed as a hyperlink when the policy has been violated. For this example, type something such as **Choosing a Recovery Model**.

- *Address*: Type the address for the hyperlink. This could be a hyperlink to MSDN explaining why you should use the policy or even to an internal web site that lists the standards for the organization. For this example, type `http://msdn.microsoft.com/en-us/library/ms175987.aspx`, which will take you to an article on MSDN about choosing a recovery model. Click the Test Link button to open a browser and validate the link.

Once you have entered all of the information correctly, the errors are removed from the top of the dialog box, and the status changes to Ready. The completed policy is shown in Figure 7-5.

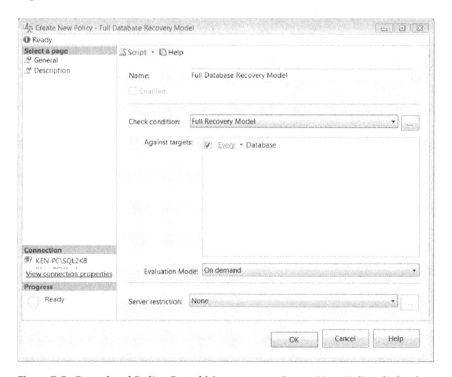

Figure 7-5. *Completed Policy-Based Management Create New Policy dialog box*

Click OK to finish creating the policy. You should now see the new policy under the Policies folder in Policy-Based Management.

Now that you have created a policy, you are ready to evaluate that policy against the targets. Right-click the policy you just created named Full Database Recovery Model and select Evaluate from the context menu. The policy will be evaluated against the defined targets, and the Evaluate Policies dialog box will be displayed as shown in Figure 7-6. Notice that one of my targets did not comply with the policy and is displayed with a red X, indicating the failure.

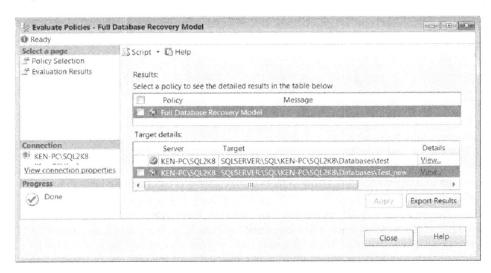

Figure 7-6. *Evaluate Policies dialog box*

Click on the View hyperlink in the Target Details column to display comprehensive information about why the policy failed. After clicking the View hyperlink, you will be able to see the Results Detailed View dialog box, as shown in Figure 7-7. The Results Detailed View will not only show you the expected value for the condition that was used, you will also be able to see the actual value to determine why the condition failed. You will also see the description you entered for the policy, along with the hyperlink information you defined when creating the policy. Close the Results Detailed View dialog and return to the Evaluate Policies dialog box.

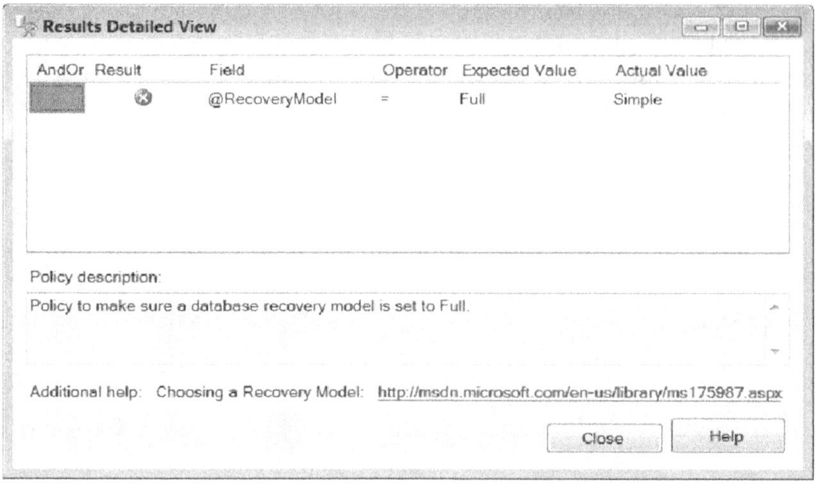

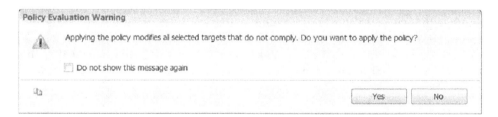

Figure 7-7. *Results Detailed View dialog box*

Policy-Based Management allows you to fix certain violations by checking boxes next to messages indicating noncompliance in the Evaluate Policies dialog box and selecting Apply. Not all policies can be automatically corrected. For example, there is a predefined policy that you must manually address stating that data and log files for a given database cannot be located on the same drive. There are too many variables involved in moving data files for SQL Server to automatically move them for you. You will know that you cannot automatically correct a policy failure if there is no check box that will allow you to select the policy in violation.

If you have selected policy violations that you wish to automatically correct, then click the Apply button. Your result will be a confirmation box, as shown in Figure 7-8, warning you that all noncompliant selected targets will be modified. Select Yes to accept and apply the changes.

Figure 7-8. *Policy Evaluation Warning message box*

To manage policy categories, right-click on Policy Management in the SQL Server Management Studio Object Explorer and select Manage Categories from the context menu. This will display the Manage Policy Categories dialog box, shown in Figure 7-9. Here you can add categories and specify whether the database subscriptions to a category will be mandated. If a category is mandated, it will be evaluated against all targets; if not you will have to specifically designate the targets that will be evaluated. All policies must be assigned to a category, and if no category is specifically chosen, the policy will be assigned to the Default category. One thing to note about the Default category is that you cannot remove the Mandate Database Subscriptions check box. All policies that remain in the Default category will be mandated against all targets.

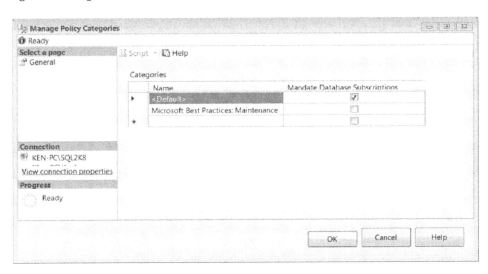

Figure 7-9. *Manage Policy Categories dialog box*

That's all there is to manually creating and executing a policy. Since Microsoft provides predefined policies, you may never have to manually create a policy, but it is the best way to become familiar with the available options. One other thing that should be noted is that policies are stored in the msdb database, so once you have created a new policy, you should make sure the msdb is backed up.

Exporting Current State As Policy

Many policies can be exported based on the current state of a facet. Once you have configured the facet, you can export the current state of the facet as a policy. This section will walk you through exporting a Surface Area Configuration policy using the current state.

If you are familiar with SQL Server 2005, you may have noticed that the Surface Area Configuration tool is not available when you install SQL Server 2008. The configuration of the Database Engine features are now managed using the Surface Area Configuration facet in Policy-Based Management. In SQL Server Management Studio, right-click on the server instance you would like to configure and select Facets from the context menu. This will bring up the View Facets dialog box. Change the Facet option to Surface Area Configuration, as shown in Figure 7-10.

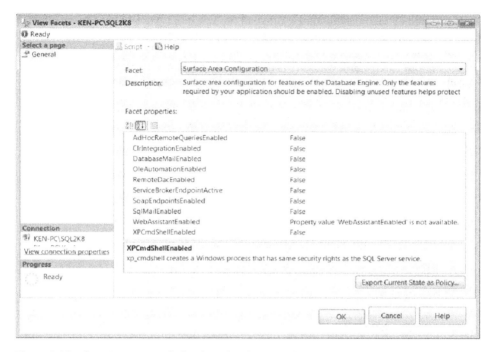

Figure 7-10. *The View Facets dialog box displays available facets for an object.*

From the View Facets dialog, you can configure the values and select OK to apply the new configurations. You can also export the current configurations as a policy to the local server or to a file that you can import and apply to multiple servers across the organization. Click on the Export Current State as Policy button on the View Facets dialog box to bring up the Export as Policy dialog box, shown in Figure 7-11.

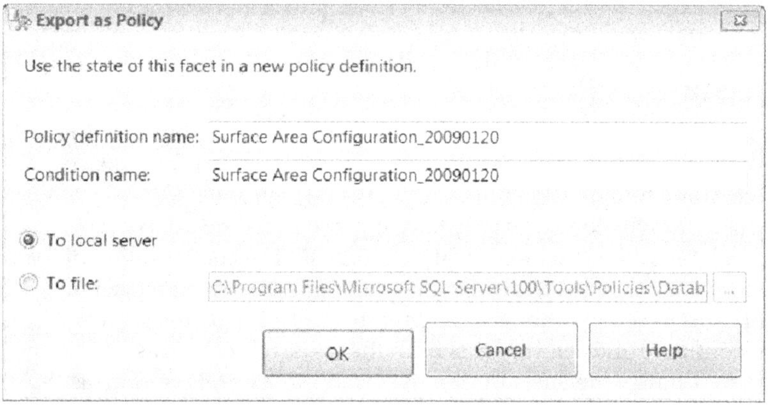

Figure 7-11. *Export as Policy dialog box*

The Export as Policy dialog box allows you to name the policy and condition that will be created. By default, the policy and condition name will be FacetName_YYYYMMDD. For this demonstration, save the policy to the local server and click OK. Click OK again to close the View Facets dialog box.

You should now be able to see the new policy and condition that was created in the Policy Management node in SQL Server Management Studio. You can manage and evaluate the policy using the same methods as if you created it manually. You can use other objects to export current state as policy as well. For example, if you right-click on a database and select Facets, it will bring up the View Facets dialog box with a drop-down list of available facets for the database object.

Importing a Predefined Policy

We mentioned earlier that you could import predefined policies provided by Microsoft that correspond with Best Practice Analyzer rules and default settings in the Surface Area Configuration tool. Microsoft provides these policies in the form of XML files as a part of the normal installation process. The XML files are located in the Polices folder in the Tools directory where you installed SQL Server. Importing a predefined policy is nice because it not only creates the policy, but all the conditions required as well. You also know that the policy is based on Microsoft best practices and has been tested by someone other than yourself. You may also want to create your own custom policies and deploy them as well. This section will walk you through the steps required to import a policy.

For this example, we will be importing a policy that checks to make sure the data and log files are not stored on the same drive. Right-click on the Policies folder located under the Policy Management node in SQL Server Management Studio, and then select Import Policy from the context menu. This will open the Import dialog box, as shown in Figure 7-12.

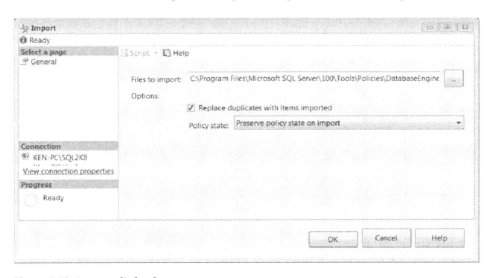

Figure 7-12. *Import dialog box*

From the Files to Import field, click the ellipsis to navigate to the C:\Program Files\ Microsoft SQL Server\100\Tools\Policies\DatabaseEngine\1033\ directory and select the Data and Log File Location.xml file. (If you made custom installation changes, your files may be in a different directory). Select the Replace Duplicates with Items Imported check box to overwrite any policies and conditions that have the same name of the policy you are importing. You can choose to preserve the state of the policy being imported, enable the policy on import, or, disable the policy on import. For this example, select Preserve Policy State on Import and select OK to import the policy.

You can now see the new policy and the conditions that were created under the Policy Management node in SQL Server Management Studio. The new policy is called Data and Log File Location (see Figure 7-13). The policy uses two conditions: one that checks to make sure the files are on separate logical drives (called Data and Log Files on Separate Drives), and one that places a server restriction on the policy (called Enterprise or Standard Edition). As you can see in Figure 7-13, you can use a condition as a check condition or a server restriction. By placing a server restriction on the policy, it will only be evaluated against servers that meet the condition defined for the restriction.

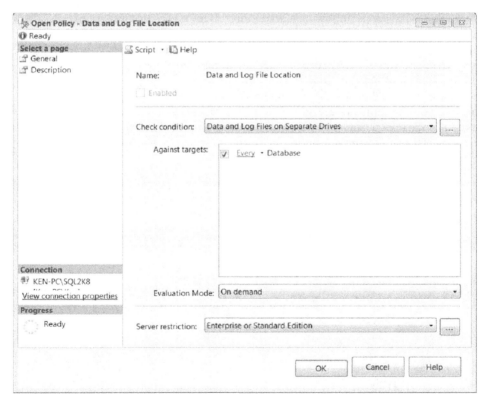

Figure 7-13. *Data and Log File Location Policy General Tab*

As you can see, importing a predefined policy is an easy way to make sure your servers are using Microsoft best practices or standards that you have implemented within your organization. You can see the final policy in Figures 7-13 and 7-14. Figure 7-13 shows the general options that were automatically created when you imported the policy.

All the category, description, and hyperlink information is also prepopulated with the policy, as shown in Figure 7-14, making it easy to reference the documentation as to why this policy should be implemented.

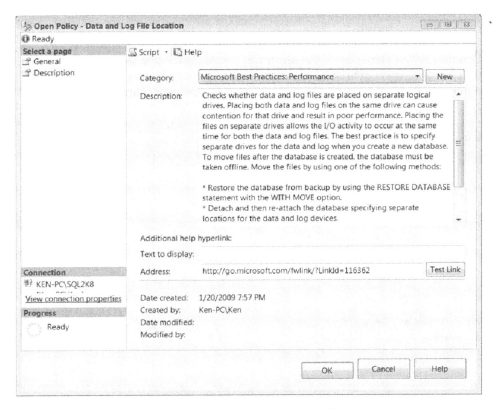

Figure 7-14. *Data and Log File Location Policy Description Tab*

Central Management Servers

Central management servers are new in SQL Server 2008 and are the hub of multi-server administration. Central management servers provide you with a central location to execute multi-server queries and evaluate policies against defined server groups. Central management servers are managed using the Registered Servers window in SQL Server Management Studio. A central management server is a designated database instance that maintains a collection or grouping of SQL Servers, much like registered server groups.

Creating a Central Management Server

You must designate a SQL Server 2008 instance as a central management server, but you can register and manage previous versions of SQL Server with the central management server, including the ability to evaluate policies. The central management sever maintains the information needed to connect to each server. Windows authentication is the only method of connecting to each registered server, which means that no usernames or passwords are stored on the central management server. Using Windows authentication also means that you may have different levels of security access on each server, depending on how your account is configured on that individual server.

Let's start by configuring a SQL Server 2008 instance as a central management server. Right-click on the Central Management Servers folder located in the Registered Servers window in SQL Server Management Studio, and select Register Central Management Server from the context menu. This will bring you to the New Server Registration dialog box, as shown in Figure 7-15.

Figure 7-15. *Dialog box used to create a central management server*

Enter the name of the SQL Server instance that will be designated as the central management server, along with the appropriate connection information in the New Server Registration dialog box. Notice that you can use SQL Server authentication to create the central management server; the Windows authentication rule only applies to the registered servers being managed by the central management server. Click Test to test the connection. If the connection is successful, click Save to create the central management server.

The next thing you need to do is create a server group to organize the servers you will be registering and managing. Right-click on the central management server you just created and select New Server Group from the context menu. This will bring up the New Server Group Properties dialog box, as shown in Figure 7-16. Enter **Production** as the group name and enter a group description, such as **Production SQL Server Group**. Click OK to close the dialog box and create the group.

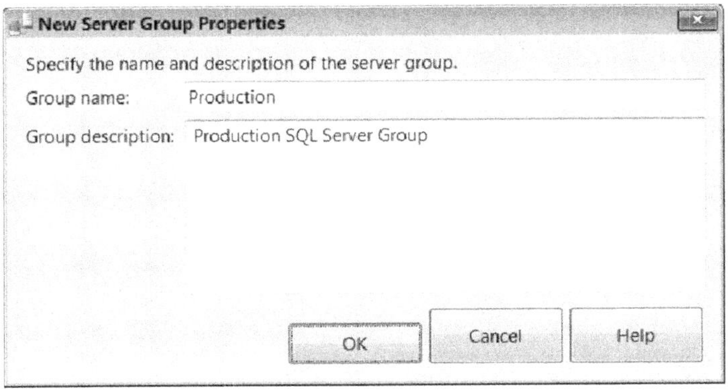

Figure 7-16. *New Server Group Properties dialog box*

Now we need to add a few servers to the group in order to take advantage of the centralized management features offered by the central management server. Right-click on the Production group you just created and select New Server Registration from the context menu. This will open the New Server Registration dialog box, as shown in Figure 7-17. This is similar to the dialog box that was used to register the central management server with one small exception: The Authentication selection is preset to Windows Authentication and cannot be changed. Click Test to test the connection. If the connection is successful, click Save to complete the registration. We will repeat the process a couple of times to add a few servers to the Production group in order to demonstrate the benefits of using a central management server.

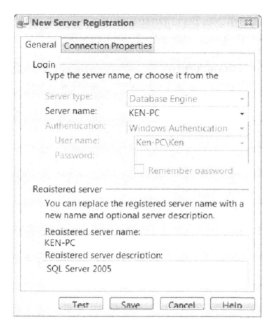

Figure 7-17. *Dialog box used to register a server to be managed by a central management server*

■**Note** A central management server cannot be registered to be a part of its own group.

You can see the final central management server configuration we have created for this example in Figure 7-18. We are using an instance of SQL Server 2008 named KEN-PC\SQL2K8 as the central management server. There are three registered instances of SQL Server in the Production group, each a different version:

KEN-PC is running an instance of SQL Server 2005 Developer Edition.

KEN-PC\SQL2K is running an instance of SQL Server 2000 Developer Edition.

KEN-PC\SQLEXPRESS1 is running an instance SQL Server 2008 Express Edition.

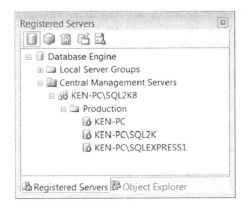

Figure 7-18. *Sample central management server configuration*

Right-clicking a server group provides you with a couple of options you can execute against all the servers in the group. Two options that are particularly interesting are New Query and Evaluate Policies. Being able to run a single query against multiple servers and having the ability to evaluate policies from a single location, regardless of the version and edition of SQL Server, is where the true power lies in central management servers.

Running Multi-Server Queries

One of the appealing new features in SQL Server 2008 is the ability to execute a single query against multiple servers. This can save many hours of mundane work during your career as a DBA. How many times have you written a script that you needed to run on each of your servers? You would not only waste time running the script on each server, but if you needed a centralized result set, you would have to manually combine the results as well. Multi-server queries are not just for selecting data either—think about it from a deployment perspective. For example, you can push a new stored procedure to all the servers in a given group. For that matter, you could even create a new database on every server in the group just by running a single statement. Any script you can write that is compatible with the different versions and editions of all the instances in the group is fair game for execution as a multi-server query.

To run a multi-server query, right-click on a server group and select New Query from the context menu. We will be using the Production group created in the previous section. Clicking New Query from the context menu will open a new query editor window. Your status bar should be a light shade of pink instead of the yellow color that is normally displayed. The status bar will also show the number of servers that the query will execute against by displaying the number of connections made and the number of servers in the group. For example, if you have four servers in a group, you should see Connected (4/4) in the status bar if you are able to make a connection to all four servers. Another interesting thing that happens is that the database drop-down menu is limited to only the databases that are shared by all the servers in the group.

Now we are ready to execute a query. We will execute a simple query to return the name of all the user databases in the server group. For example:

```
Select name From sysaltfiles Where dbid > 4
```

Since we have a SQL 2000 instance in the group, we will use the `sysaltfiles` table instead of the `sys.sysaltfiles` table that was not available until SQL 2005. Figure 7-19 shows a result set after executing the query against a group of servers.

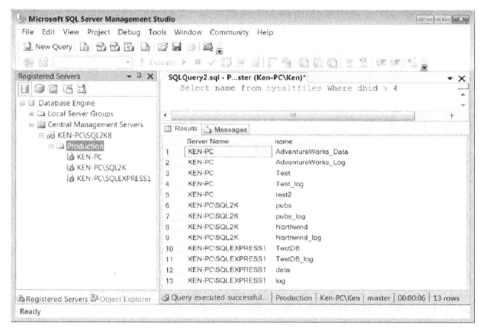

Figure 7-19. *Multi-server query result set*

If you look at the status bar in Figure 7-19, you can see a couple of interesting data elements. The status bar shows the name of the group the query is executing against, the user who is executing the query, and the database the query will be executed against. You also may have noticed that the query includes the name of each server as a part of the result set, even though we did not specifically add it to the query.

You can also run multi-server queries using local server groups by registering the servers and running a query against a specific group. The benefit of using a local server group to run a multi-server query is that you can include the central management server in the local server group. Remember that a central management server cannot be a part of the group it is managing, so there is no way to include the server that is managing the groups in the result set. Another benefit to using local server groups to run multi-server queries is that you can register the servers using Windows authentication or SQL Server authentication. The downside to using local server groups is that the groups that are created are local to each DBA. A central management server allows DBAs to share a common registered server group.

Configuring Multi-Server Query Options

Multi-server query results have three configurable options. Adding the server name to the results is one of them, and you've seen that option already in Figure 7-19. The complete list of options is as follows:

- Add login name to the results

- Add server name to the results

- Merge results into one result set

The default configuration is to add the server name and merge the results. To change the multi-server result options, follow these steps:

1. Select Options from the Tools Menu in SQL Server Management Studio.

2. Navigate to Multiserver Results options using the tree menu in the Options dialog box. Expand the Query Results node, expand the SQL Server node and then select Multi-server Results, as shown in Figure 7-20.

3. Change the options to the desired configuration and click OK.

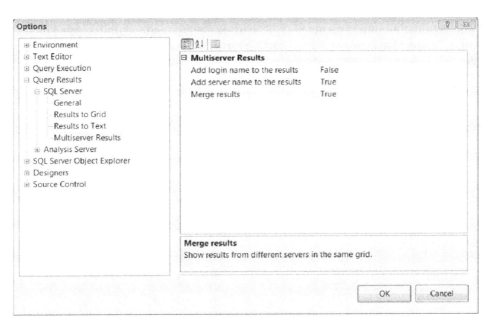

Figure 7-20. *Multiserver Results configuration options*

If the result set is being merged, the column headers are derived from the first server that returns the results. If a result set is returned by a subsequent server that does not have the same number of columns or the column names do not match, an error will be returned indicating that the result sets cannot be merged. Also, if one of the servers is missing an object used in the query, the result sets cannot be merged and an error is returned.

If you do not merge the results, each result set will have its own schema and column set, meaning the number of columns or column names do not have to match. You will, however, receive an error if one of the objects in the query does not exist on one of the servers in the group. Since each result set is individually returned, this is more of an informational message indicating that the server does not contain the object and does not stop the query from executing on the remaining servers.

Evaluating Policies

You can evaluate policies against registered servers or an entire server group using central management servers. The great thing about evaluating policies against multiple servers is that you can simply click a check box to apply the necessary changes to the noncompliant servers.

■**Note**   Only certain policies will be valid with each version. For example, since Database Mail was introduced in SQL Server 2005, it would not be a valid to perform a check on a SQL 2000 server that required Database Mail to be enabled. You may want to add a server restriction on policies that are version or edition specific to prevent excessive failures.

To evaluate a policy against multiple servers, right-click on a server group and select Evaluate Policies from the context menu. We will be using the Production group created in the "Creating a Central Management Server" section earlier in this chapter. This will bring up the Evaluate Policies dialog box, as shown in Figure 7-21. Notice that the group name that we will be evaluating is displayed in the title of the dialog box; in our case the title is Evaluate Policies - Production.

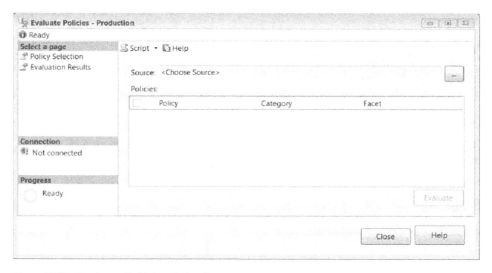

Figure 7-21. *Evaluate Policies dialog box*

Now you need to choose the source for the policy or policies you would like to evaluate. Click the ellipsis next to the Source field to bring up the Select Source dialog box shown in Figure 7-22.

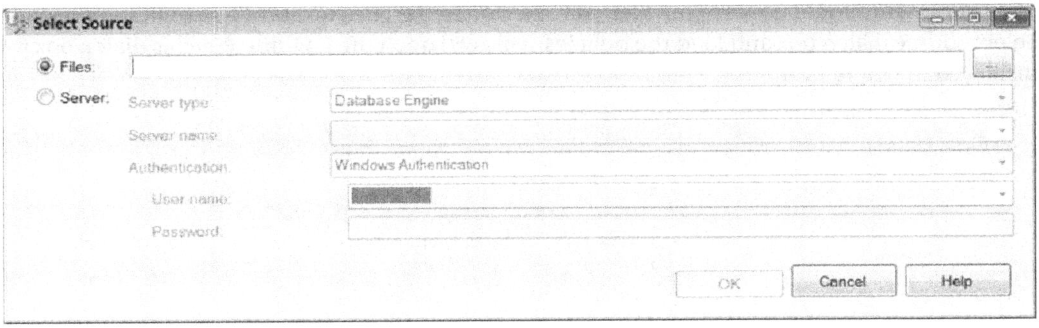

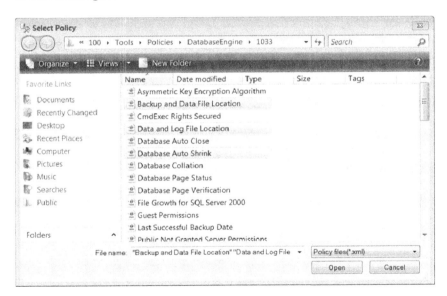

Figure 7-22. *Select Source dialog box*

As you can see in Figure 7-22, you have the ability to use files or a server that contains policies as a source to obtain the policy information to evaluate. If you choose to use a server as the source, you can enter the connection information for any server that contains a valid policy. (The policies will be displayed in the Evaluate Policies dialog box, as shown in Figure 7-25.) If you read the "Policy-Based Management" section at the beginning of this chapter, you know that Microsoft provides several predefined policy files we can also use. In the Select Source dialog, select the ellipsis next to the Files text box to open the Select Policy dialog box, as shown in Figure 7-23.

Figure 7-23. *Select Policy dialog box*

One nice feature is that you are allowed to select multiple policy files to evaluate. Navigate to the C:\Program Files\Microsoft SQL Server\100\Tools\Policies\DatabaseEngine\1033\ directory if you are not already there, and then select a couple of polices you would like to evaluate by holding the Ctrl key and clicking each policy. Figure 7-23 shows the policies we have selected. Once you have selected the policies, click Open to return to the Select Source

dialog box. You should now see the files you selected in the Files text box. Click OK to close the
Select Source dialog box and load the policies. This will open the Loading Policies dialog box,
displayed in Figure 7-24.

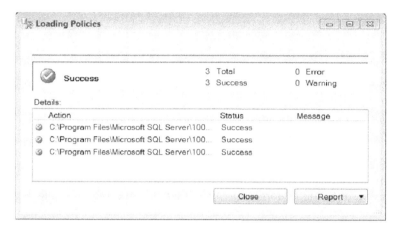

Figure 7-24. *Loading Policies dialog box*

Once you have successfully loaded the policies, click Close to return to the Evaluate
Policies dialog box, which will now show all the policies you included in the Select Source
dialog box (see Figure 7-25).

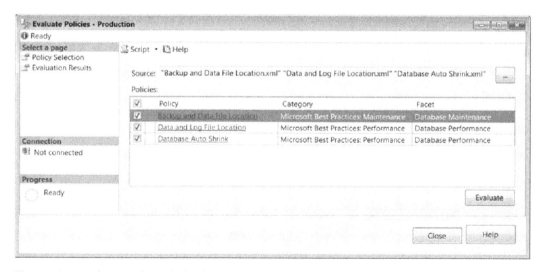

Figure 7-25. *Evaluate Polices dialog box with selected policies*

You can review each policy configuration and description by selecting the policy name
link from the Policy column. Make sure each policy that you would like to evaluate is checked
and click Evaluate. This will evaluate each policy and take you to the Evaluate Policies results
page, as shown in Figure 7-26.

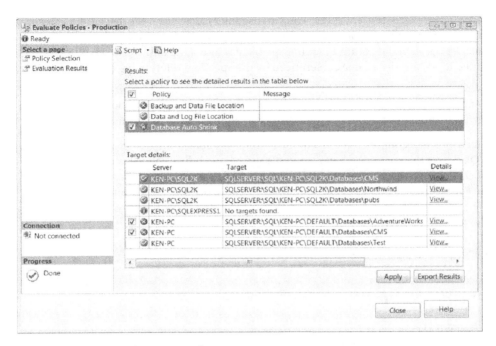

Figure 7-26. *Policy evaluation results*

Each policy that succeeds against all the servers will be indicated with a green check mark, and any policy that has a noncompliant server will be displayed with a red X. If you select a specific policy, you can see the results in the Target details table. Also, certain policies that contain failures have a check box beside them. This check box indicates that SQL Server can automatically apply changes to the server that will make them compliant with the policy. If you select the check box beside the policy, it will automatically check all the noncompliant servers. You can uncheck any server you do not wish to be affected by the changes and click Apply. Click Close to exit the evaluation. There you have it—in just a few clicks, you are able evaluate and manage policies across multiple servers in the organization.

SQL Dependency Reporting

Another issue that you face when administering SQL Server instances across an organization is determining object dependencies between servers and databases. If you have to make changes to objects in a database, it is hard to establish a list of items that may be affected (especially if the referencing objects are on another server). SQL Server 2008 introduces a new catalog view and two new dynamic management functions that can be used to help determine object dependencies:

- `sys.sql_expression_dependencies`: You can use the `sys.sql_expression_dependencies` catalog view to report dependency information for a given database. Cross-database entities are returned only when a valid four-part or three-part name is specified.

- `sys.dm_sql_referenced_entities`: You can use the `sys.dm_sql_referenced_entities` dynamic management function to return one row for each user-defined entity referenced by name in the definition of the specified referencing entity. The result set is limited to the entities that are referenced by the specified referencing entity.

- `sys.dm_sql_referencing_entities`: You can use the `sys.dm_sql_referencing_entities` dynamic management function to return one row for each user-defined entity in the current database that references another user-defined entity by name.

First, let's look at a couple of queries that can help you determine object dependencies between SQL Server instances. We have created a stored procedure called `CrossServerSelect` on the SQL Server 2008 instance named KEN-PC\SQL2K8 that references the `Person.Address` table in the `AdventureWorks` database located on the default SQL Server instance named KEN-PC. The `CrossServerSelect` stored procedure executes a simple query using the four-part naming convention, as shown in Listing 7-1.

Listing 7-1. *CrossServerSelect Stored Procedure Definition*

```
Create Procedure CrossServerSelect
AS

Select Distinct City
FROM [KEN-PC].AdventureWorks.Person.Address
GO
```

Now we know there is an object on the KEN-PC\SQL2K8 instance that references the KEN-PC instance. Let's look at a couple of ways you can identify that dependency. One way is to use the `sys.sql_expression_dependencies` catalog view, as shown in Listing 7-2. This code should be executed from the context of the database that contains the object that is doing the referencing. In this case, that is the Test database on the KEN-PC\SQL2K8 instance. The results of Listing 7-2 can be seen in Figure 7-27.

Listing 7-2. *Returns All Referencing Dependencies in the Current Database*

```
SELECT @@SERVERNAME LocalServer,
              OBJECT_NAME (referencing_id) referencing_object_name,
              referenced_server_name,
              referenced_database_name,
              referenced_schema_name,
              referenced_entity_name
FROM sys.sql_expression_dependencies
```

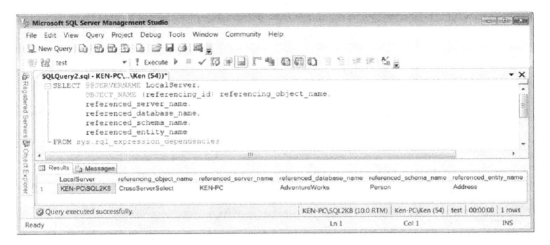

Figure 7-27. *Results of all referencing dependencies in the current database*

Another way to display cross-server dependencies is by using the sys.dm_sql_referenced_ entities dynamic management function, as shown in Listing 7-3. You are required to provide the sys.dm_sql_referenced_entities function with two parameters: the referencing entity name and the referencing class. The object name we will be using is the dbo.CrossServer- Select stored procedure created earlier in this section. The referencing class can be one of three types: OBJECT, DATABASE_DDL_TRIGGER, or SERVER_DDL_TRIGGER. In this case, we are using the OBJECT class. We are executing the code in Listing 7-3 against the Test database on the KEN-PC\SQL2K8 instance. The results of Listing 7-3 can be seen in Figure 7-28.

Note You are required to provide the schema name along with the referencing entity name if you are using the OBJECT class.

Listing 7-3. *Returns Entities Referenced by the dbo.CrossServerSelect Object*

```
SELECT @@SERVERNAME LocalServer,
            referenced_server_name,
            referenced_database_name,
            referenced_schema_name,
            referenced_entity_name
FROM sys.dm_sql_referenced_entities ('dbo.CrossServerSelect','OBJECT')
```

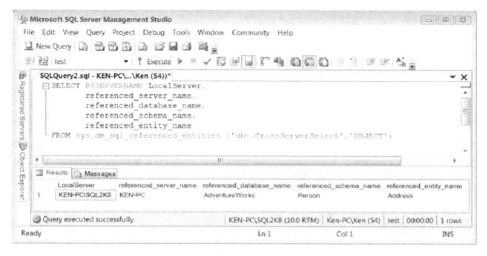

Figure 7-28. *Results of entities referenced by the dbo.CrossServerSelect object*

Now that you have seen how to display dependencies between servers, let's look at an example using the sysjobshistory table in the msdb database that doesn't require you to have multiple instances or any special setup configurations. Let's start by taking a look at all of the objects that reference the sysjobshistory table by running the code in Listing 7-4. The results of Listing 7-4 are shown in Figure 7-29.

Listing 7-4. *Returns Objects That Reference the sysjobshistory Table by Using the sys.sql_expression_dependencies Catalog View*

```
USE msdb
GO

SELECT OBJECT_NAME(referencing_id) AS referencing_entity_name,
            referenced_database_name AS database_name,
            referenced_schema_name,
            referenced_entity_name
FROM sys.sql_expression_dependencies
WHERE referenced_entity_name = 'sysjobshistory'
```

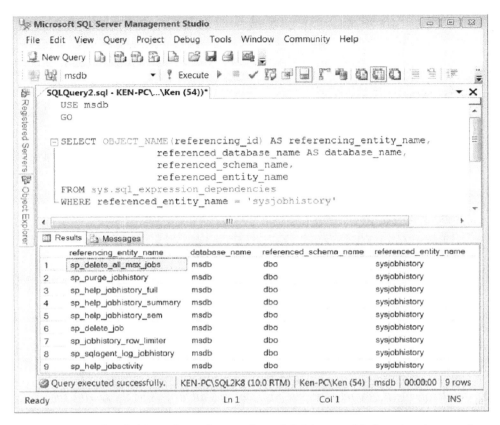

Figure 7-29. *Results of objects that reference the sysjobshistory table by using the sys.sql_ expression_dependencies catalog view*

In this case you could also use the sys.dm_sql_referencing_entities function, as shown in Listing 7-5, since you are only returning referencing entities in the current database. The sys.dm_sql_referencing_entities function does not have a column to display the referenced object or database. There is no need to have a column for the referenced object, since you are supplying the referenced object name as a parameter. There is no referenced database column because the sys.dm_sql_referencing_entities function only returns dependencies for the current database. The results of Listing 7-5 are shown in Figure 7-30.

Listing 7-5. *Returns Objects That Reference the sysjobshistory Table by Using the sys.dm_sql_ referencing_entities Dynamic Management Function*

```
USE msdb
GO

SELECT referencing_entity_name
FROM sys.dm_sql_referencing_entities ('dbo.sysjobhistory','OBJECT')
```

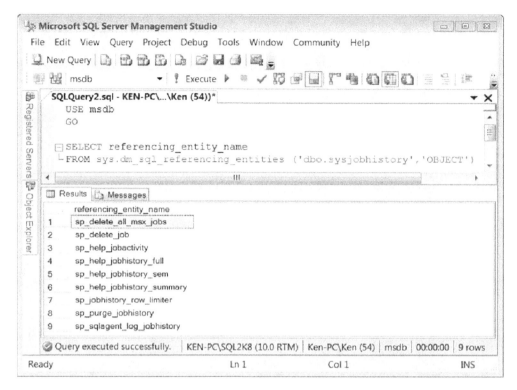

Figure 7-30. *Results of objects that reference the sysjobshistory table by using the sys.dm_sql_ referencing_entities dynamic management function*

It is important to note that the new functionality provided by dependency reporting will not catch everything. You must use the proper three- or four-part notation when referencing the object. Let look at an example using the sp_help_job function in the msdb database. If you run the code in Listing 7-6, you can see there are seven entities referenced by the sp_help_job procedure. The results can be viewed in Figure 7-31.

Listing 7-6. *Returns Entities Referenced by the sp_help_job Procedure*

```
USE msdb
GO

SELECT referenced_schema_name,
            referenced_entity_name,
            referenced_minor_name
FROM sys.dm_sql_referenced_entities ('dbo.sp_help_job','OBJECT')
```

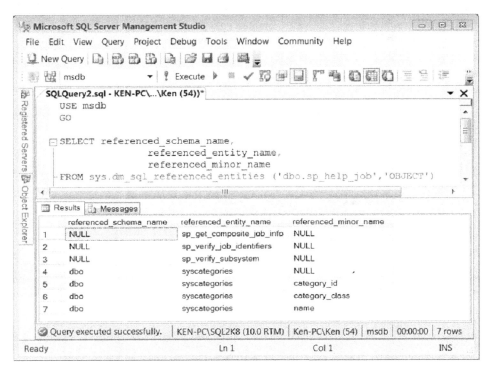

Figure 7-31. *Results of the entities referenced by the sp_help_job procedure*

Now let's review a couple of lines in the sp_help_job stored procedure by executing sp_helptext 'sp_help_job'. If you look at the code block starting on line 238 (shown in Figure 7-32), you will see that sp_help_job executes the sp_get_composite_job_info stored procedure. If you refer to Figure 7-31, you will see that it is the first line in the result set.

Figure 7-32. *Lines 237–250 of the sp_help_job stored procedure executes the sp_get_composite_job_info stored procedure.*

Now look at line 142 of the code shown in Figure 7-33. You can see that the sp_help_job stored procedure is calling the sp_help_jobserver stored procedure using dynamic SQL. If you look back at the dependency results displayed in Figure 7-31, because sp_help_jobserver is called using dynamic SQL, it is not displayed as a dependency of the sp_help_job stored procedure.

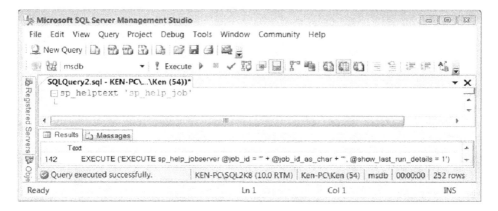

Figure 7-33. *Line 142 of the sp_help_job stored procedure executes the sp_help_jobserver stored procedure using dynamic SQL.*

Summary

This chapter has shown you many of the new features in SQL Server 2008 that will help you manage all of your database servers from a central environment. You can use Policy-Based Management to ensure that policies and procedures are being followed and use a central management server to easily evaluate those policies. Central management servers also ease routine administrative tasks by allowing you to execute queries and scripts against server groups. Finally, we discussed the benefits of SQL dependency reporting when moving or making schema changes to database objects. Implementing these new features requires a little more setup and research than you may have done with previous versions of SQL Server, but taking a little more time in the beginning will save a lot of time in the long run.

CHAPTER 8

Managing Security Within the Database Engine

Managing security within the Database Engine is one of the most important tasks for a database administrator. Controlling access to SQL Server and the roles and rights that each user has within SQL Server, as well as the security of the data, are the main security concerns. Throughout this chapter, our goal is to discuss security in the manner in which we believe security measures are encountered: Windows security, SQL Server security, database security, and then protecting the physical data itself.

Note Security starts with the physical security of the equipment, network security, and detailed information about Windows security. But detailed information outside of Windows authentication and discussing the available options in the SQL Server Configuration Manager is beyond of the scope of this book.

Security Language

In SQL Server 2005, Microsoft introduced several new security features and changed the verbiage used when discussing security. Granted, terms like *users*, *roles*, and *permissions* still exist, but new words like *principals*, *schemas*, and *securables* emerged into discussions. SQL Server 2008 utilizes the same verbiage, so we want to make sure you are clear on the new terms and what they mean. Figure 8-1 provides a good visual representation of the security features and how they relate to each other. You may find it helpful to refer back to Figure 8-1 throughout the chapter as we discuss these features.

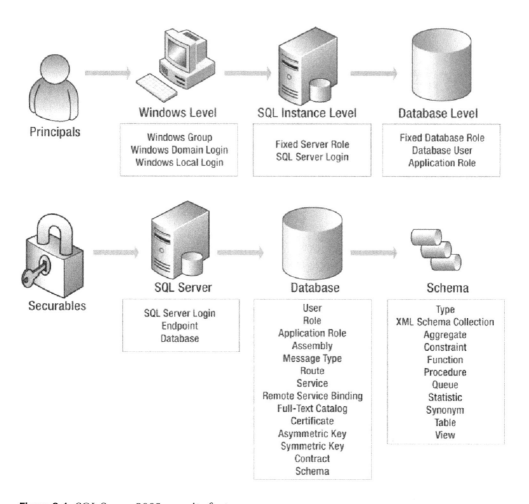

Figure 8-1. *SQL Server 2008 security features*

Principals

Principals are entities or objects that can request and access objects within SQL Server. There are three basic types: Window's principals, SQL Server principals, and database principals. The following list briefly defines the three types:

- Windows-level principals are generally domain and local server user accounts that authenticate to SQL Server using Windows authentication.

- SQL Server–level principals are SQL Server logins that authenticate to SQL Server using SQL Server authentication.

- Database-level principals are database users, database roles, or application roles.

Keep in mind, you have to map Windows and SQL Server principals to database principals in order to access the objects within a database.

Securables

Securables are the objects within SQL Server that can be controlled and managed through SQL Server security. SQL Server 2008 distinguishes between three scopes, which are nested hierarchies of securables:

- *Server scope* securables consist of endpoints, logins, and databases. Server securables are objects that exist at the server level, not the database level.

- *Database scope* securables entail users, roles, assemblies, and other objects that do not belong to specific schemas.

- *Schema scope* securables are types, XML schemas, and objects. Objects are the tables, views, stored procedures, and other creatable objects within a schema.

Schemas

Database schemas exist in SQL Server 2000 as single users, but in both SQL Server 2005 and SQL Server 2008, you can assign multiple users to a schema. The schema container can consist of many different objects, such as tables, views, and stored procedures. Schemas are database specific, meaning their names must be unique within a database. Schemas are not new; they are simply the owner of objects like sys. or dbo. However, Microsoft has expanded schemas in SQL Server 2005 and SQL Server 2008 to enhance security. We will dive into schema security when discussing database security later on in this chapter.

Creating SQL Server Principals

This section will discuss the server-level principals provided for you in SQL Server 2008. Once again, those principals are SQL Server logins and SQL Server roles. We also will touch on user creation for certificates, asymmetric keys, credentials, and Windows principals.

Creating Logins for SQL Server

SQL Server 2008 supports both Windows and SQL Server authentication. SQL Server authentication does the username and password validation for users attempting to gain access to SQL Server, while Windows handles the user validation for Windows-authenticated users. In order to use SQL Server authentication, you must configure your instance of SQL Server to utilize Mixed Mode authentication. Mixed Mode authentication means that the instance will support both Windows authentication and SQL Server authentication. While you can configure SQL Server to enable only Windows authentication, there is no way to enable SQL Server to use only SQL Server authentication without allowing Windows authentication as well.

Creating SQL Server logins using T-SQL follows the same basic syntax as credentials, certificates, asymmetric keys, Windows principals, and SQL Server–authenticated logins. The following syntax in Listing 8-1 shows you how to create SQL Server logins.

Listing 8-1. *Syntax for Creating SQL Server Logins*

```
CREATE LOGIN loginName {WITH PASSWORD OPTIONS, Additional Options
| FROM SOURCE}
```

When creating a SQL Server login, you have to specify the login name, and depending on the type of SQL Server login you are creating, specify password options or another source with which to associate the username. The available password options allow you to supply a password in standard text or a hash value. If you supply a password in standard text, then SQL Server will convert the password to hash before storing it within the database. So don't worry about your password being compromised if you create an account with a password in standard text.

The password options available to you when creating SQL Server logins are as follows:

- `MUST_CHANGE`: Specifies that users must change their password when they login.

- `CHECK_EXPIRATION`: Determines if the password expiration policy is enforced. The default value is OFF.

- `CHECK_POLICY`: Specifies if the Windows policies of the computer/server running SQL Server are enforced on the login. The default value is ON.

- `CREDENTIAL`: Identifies the name of the credential to associate to the login.

- `DEFAULT_DATABASE`: Specifies the default database for the new login. If you do not specify the default database parameter, SQL Server will assign the master database as the default database for the login.

- `Default_Language`: Specifies the default language for the new login. If you do not supply the default language parameter, SQL Server will use the default language for the instance of SQL Server.

- `SID`: Allows you to specify the `uniqueidentifier` that will be assigned to the newly created login. SQL Server will assign a random `uniqueidentifier` if you do not supply this parameter in the `Create Login` statement. The `SID` option is only valid for SQL Server logins.

The available sources in the `FROM SOURCE` clause are certificates, asymmetric keys and Windows. We will discuss associating SQL Server logins to certificates and asymmetric keys in the upcoming section "Associating Logins with Certificates and Asymmetric Keys." We will also discuss creating SQL Server logins for Windows principals in the next section.

Creating SQL Server Logins for Windows Principals

SQL Server 2008 permits Windows principals, local Windows users, or domain groups and users to gain access to SQL Server without resupplying a password. In order for Windows principals to access SQL Server, SQL Server uses Windows to confirm the identity of the user. Windows authentication is more secure and is the default authentication method for SQL Server. We recommend using Windows authentication whenever possible.

Creating Windows users and groups is outside of the scope of this book. However, after the creation of a Windows principal, granting access to that user within SQL Server is not complex. Using the syntax from Listing 8-1, in order to create a SQL Server user for a Windows user, you specify the SQL Server login name that you want to create, specify that the source is Windows, and then define the Windows options. The available Windows options allow you to define the default database and default languages if you want. The following code example creates a SQL Server login for a Windows principal.

```
USE MASTER
GO


CREATE LOGIN [mediacenter\sql] FROM WINDOWS WITH DEFAULT_DATABASE =_
 AdventureWorks2008;
GO
```

■**Note** Unlike previous versions of SQL Server, SQL Server 2008 starts restricting access to SQL Server for Windows users during the installation process. By default, you have to grant access to Windows users or groups to SQL Server 2008 in order for the user to have any access to SQL Server. Historically, users within the Windows administrator group would have administrator access to SQL Server, but that is no longer the case. Remember in Chapter 4, during the installation process, you were given the opportunity to grant Windows users access to SQL Server. If access is not granted to Windows users during the installation process, then you will have go through a process similar to the preceding example to grant those users or groups access to SQL Server.

Creating SQL Server–Authenticated Logins

When creating SQL Server–authenticated logins, the usernames and passwords are stored within the database. Unlike Windows authentication, users have to supply their usernames and passwords to log in to SQL Server.

To create a SQL Server–authenticated login using the syntax in Listing 8-1, specify the login name and the password. Remember, you can provide a hash password or a standard text password. If you are creating a password for a person, you may want to utilize the MUST_CHANGE option. That way, you can provide the user with a simple password like Abc123#@ and require them to change it when they login. Finally, determine the default database, the default language, and whether you want the password policy and password expiration enabled. In order to enable password expiration, then you must enable the password policy. Review the following SQL Server script to create a standard SQL Server login.

```
USE MASTER
GO


CREATE LOGIN apressSecurity WITH PASSWORD = 'P@ssw0rd!' ,CHECK_POLICY_
 = ON, CHECK_EXPIRATION = ON, DEFAULT_DATABASE = Adventureworks2008;
```

Associating Logins with Certificates and Asymmetric Keys

In SQL Server 2008, you can associate SQL Server logins to certificates and asymmetric keys. Mapping a SQL Server user to a certificate or asymmetric key controls the application rights and access levels in SQL Server. We will review certificates and asymmetric keys in detail later on in this chapter. Here we briefly discuss and provide an example of associating users to Certificates and Asymmetric Keys.

■Note SQL Server logins enclosed in double pound signs (##) represent internal logins created from certificates. The installation process will create users like ##MS_PolicyEventProcessingLogin##, so do not be alarmed when you see them on your server.

Referring back to Listing 8-1, you can see that creating SQL Server logins for certificates and asymmetric keys are fairly simple, assuming you have a certificate or key already in place. You specify the login name that you would like to create, then reference the certificate or asymmetric key that you are associating the user to, and you are all set. Make sure the key or certificate that you are associating the user to resides in the master database. Review the following example of a certificate creation followed by a user that is created using the certificate.

```
Use master;
GO

CREATE CERTIFICATE apressCert
ENCRYPTION BY PASSWORD = '5qlS3rvErROcks'
WITH SUBJECT = 'book',
START_DATE = '01/01/2009',
EXPIRY_DATE = '12/31/2010'
GO

CREATE LOGIN apressCertUsr
FROM CERTIFICATE apressCert
```

Linking Credentials to Logins

SQL Server 2008 allows you to create SQL Server logins and associate them to credentials. Credentials contain authentication information for connecting to resources outside of SQL Server. Credentials generally contain Windows username and password information used internally by SQL Server to access an outside resource. You can associate credentials to Windows and SQL Server–authenticated logins; however, the information stored within a credential allows SQL Server–authenticated users to connect to resources outside of SQL Server. Picture this: A user connects to SQL Server using their SQL Server login account, and then they need to perform an action on the server using the credential that they are associated with to access that resource. SQL Server will use the username and password from the credential to fulfill the request. You can map multiple SQL Server logins to the same credential.

In this example, you are going to link a credential to a SQL Server login. Following the syntax in Listing 8-1, you can see that linking a login to a credential is straightforward. The first thing you do is supply the username that you want associated to the credential and the password, and then specify the credential name that you are assigning the user to. (See the following code sample.) The example also shows you how to create a credential.

```
CREATE CREDENTIAL apressCred
WITH IDENTITY = 'sylvester',
SECRET = 'password'
go

CREATE LOGIN apressCredUsr
WITH PASSWORD = 'P@ssw0rd!',
CREDENTIAL = apressCred
GO
```

Generally, we recommend that you use Windows authentication because it provides the benefits of user administration and increased security. In most organizations, domain accounts or local server accounts have password policies in place that force users to have strong passwords as well as modify their passwords in a predetermined amount of time. Luckily, if you are unable to use Windows authentication, SQL Server 2008 has the ability to set password expiration and enforce strong passwords for SQL accounts.

■Note According to SQL Server Books Online, strong passwords have a minimum of eight characters, have numbers, characters, and symbols, are not found in the dictionary, are not the names of commands, are not a username, are not the name of a person, are significantly different than the last password, are not the computer name, are changed regularly, contain or start with a space, and start with a $ or @ sign. SQL Server 2008 can enforce the same password policy as Windows 2003, which is not quite the same as what Books Online recommends. If you choose to enforce the same password policy as Windows 2003, then each password must not contain all or part of the account name, the password must be eight characters long, must include a capital letter, a lower case letter, a number, and a non-alphanumeric character.

Enabling the password enforcement policy adds additional security to SQL Server accounts. Still, we recommend using Windows authentication when possible. Removing additional user account administration from your long list of daily tasks enables you to spend more time doing fun DBA stuff, like tuning queries and solving performance problems. No one enjoys the repetitive task of constantly resetting user passwords.

SQL Server–Level Roles

SQL Server 2008 has predefined roles or groups that enable you to manage permissions for SQL Server logins throughout the server. Microsoft defines the server roles, and you cannot create additional roles beyond what Microsoft has defined. Logins added to sever-level roles have the ability to add or delete other users from the role. The available server-level roles are as follows:

- SysAdmin: Allows users to perform any activity on the server.

- ServerAdmin: Permits users to manage configuration options on the server and shut down SQL Server.

- SecurityAdmin: Gives users the ability to grant, revoke, and deny server- and database-level permissions. They can also manage users and passwords, as well as reset passwords of other users.

- ProcessAdmin: Allows users to end processes running on an instance.

- SetupAdmin: Creates linked servers.

- BulkAdmin: Performs bulk-insert statements.

- DiskAdmin: Manages the disk files.

- DBCreator: Creates, alters, or drops any databases.

- Public: The default role that server logins belong to.

Adding Logins to Server-Level Roles

In T-SQL, adding logins to server-level roles occurs via a stored procedure sp_addsrvrolemember. The stored procedure expects two parameters: a login name for the user that you want added to the role and the name of the role. Try the following code sample to add a login to a server-level role.

```
EXEC master..sp_addsrvrolemember @loginame = N'apressSecurity',_
 @rolename = N'serveradmin'
GO
EXEC master..sp_addsrvrolemember @loginame = N'apressSecurity', _
@rolename = N'securityadmin'
GO
EXEC master..sp_addsrvrolemember @loginame = N'apressSecurity',_
 @rolename = N'processadmin'
GO
EXEC master..sp_addsrvrolemember @loginame = N'apressSecurity',_
 @rolename = N'dbCreator'
GO
```

Removing Logins from Server-Level Roles

In T-SQL, removing logins from server-level roles also occur via a stored procedure sp_dropsrvrolemember. The stored procedure also takes two parameters; a login name that you want removed from the server-level role and the role name that you want to remove the login name from.

Database Security

The database principals include database users, database roles, and application roles. These principals control a user's rights within the database. Keep in mind that you must map Windows and SQL Server principals to database principals for the Windows and SQL Server principals to have access to the objects within the database.

Creating Database Users

Database users are one type of principal that you can grant permissions for accessing objects within the database. The permissions granted to a user will determine their capabilities within the database (we will talk about permissions later on in this chapter). Server principals have no rights in databases until you assign them to a database principal, and for the purposes of this discussion, that database principal is a database user.

Assigning server principals to database principals is not a complex task. You've probably done it naturally without thinking about the proper verbiage used to describe the process. Review the following syntax to see how you create a database user.

```
CREATE USER username
[ { {FOR | FROM}
   {LOGIN loginName
      |  CERTIFICATE certificateName
      |  ASYMMETRIC KEY asymmetricKeyName
   }
   |   WITHOUT LOGIN
]
WITH DEFAULT_SCHEMA = schemaName
```

Using the preceding syntax, you create a database user by first supplying a name. Next, specify the server login name that you want to associate to the user. If you do not specify the server login name, then SQL Server will try to map the user to a server login with the same name. Instead of specifying the server login, you may instead associate the user to a certificate or asymmetric key. Finally, specify the schema that you want to associate to the user. If you do not specify the default schema, SQL Server will map the user to the dbo schema.

Note SQL Server 2008 allows you to create a database user without specifying a server login. Most of the reasons that we could think of to use this option would require some double work. At some point, you are going to have to go back and associate those users to server logins. We are not saying that the option is good or bad; we're merely pointing out that the option exists if you want to use it.

See the following code for an example of creating a database user for an existing server principal.

```
USE AdventureWorks2008
GO

CREATE USER apressSecurity
FOR LOGIN apressSecurity
WITH DEFAULT_SCHEMA = dbo
GO
```

Now, test the following code sample to easily combine the creation of a SQL Server login with the mapping of the database user.

```
USE master
GO

CREATE LOGIN apressReader WITH PASSWORD = 'P@ssw0rd!' ,CHECK_POLICY = ON,_
CHECK_EXPIRATION = ON,
DEFAULT_DATABASE = Adventureworks2008;
GO

USE AdventureWorks2008
GO

CREATE USER apressReader
FOR LOGIN apressReader
WITH DEFAULT_SCHEMA = dbo
GO
```

Database Roles

SQL Server 2008 supports two types of database roles: fixed and flexible roles. Fixed roles are the predefined database roles created by Microsoft for SQL Server. These roles cannot be modified. You can add database users to them, but you cannot (nor should you try to) change them.

Flexible roles are the roles you create to group users together, in terms of functionality that they perform, within your database. Generally, grouping database users together within a database role enables you to more easily control their permissions. From an administrative point of view, you should find it easier to define the permissions for the role and then add users to the role accordingly than to repeatedly define the same permissions for each user. That way, you can minimize the amount of time it takes to grant users access to the objects within the database.

Understanding Fixed Roles

Following is a list of the fixed database roles that are currently available:

- DB_Owner: Performs all configuration and maintenance tasks within the database.

- DB_SecurityAdmin: Modifies role membership and manages permissions.

- DB_AccessAdmin: Controls the addition and removal of access to the database for Windows users, Windows groups, and SQL Server logins.

- `DB_BackupOperator`: Possesses the ability to back up the database.

- `DB_DDLAdmin`: Contains the ability to execute data definition commands.

- `DB_DataWriter`: Inserts, updates, and deletes data from the tables in the database.

- `DB_DataReader`: Selects or reads data from the tables in the database.

- `DB_DenyDataWriter`: Restricts insert, update, and delete data from the tables in the database.

- `Public`: The default role database users are granted access to.

It is up to you to decide what fixed roles to grant users access to and what roles you may want to create. Microsoft's goal with fixed roles is to make it easy for you to delegate commonly performed administrative tasks to users.

Creating a Database Role

To create a database role, simply supply the name of the database role that you want to create. Then specify the permissions that you want the role to have. You can specify who owns the role by using the `Authorization` command, but by default, the user who creates the role owns it. The only remaining task comes from assigning database users to the role by using `sp_addrolemember`.

Often times, junior (JR) DBAs have restricted read-only access in your production environment because they are more prone to make costly mistakes than a seasoned DBA. However, you may want JR DBAs to have the ability to query database scoped Dynamic Management Views (DMVs) in order to perform analysis on the production databases, which requires more privileges than the `db_datareader` role permits. In this case, you can create a new database role for the JR DBAs instead of granting them access to the database using a fixed role.

Execute the code in Listing 8-2 to create a `JR_DBA` role and to grant the appropriate permissions to the role. Once you have created the role, you can assign users to it just as if it were a fixed role. Those users will then be able to query data from tables and retrieve data from database state DMVs.

Listing 8-2. *Creating a Role and Granting Execute Permissions*

```
USE AdventureWorks2008
GO


CREATE ROLE JR_DBA
GO


GRANT  VIEW DATABASE STATE,SELECT to JR_DBA
GO
```

Application Roles

An application role is a database principal that allows an application to connect to a database and perform actions according to the permissions of the role. Unlike other database roles, application roles do not allow you to add users to the role, and they are created with passwords. By default, application roles are disabled until an application connects to the database and supplies the application role's password.

Here's an example of creating an application role:

```
Use AdventureWorks2008
GO

CREATE APPLICATION ROLE authorApps
WITH PASSWORD = '@uthOrA@pp5@!'
GO

GRANT SELECT, UPDATE, INSERT , DELETE to AuthorApps
GO
```

Having created this role, you can enable it from an application by having that application execute the following stored procedure call:

```
exec sp_setapprole authorApps, '@uthOrA@pp5@!'
```

Your application supplies the password. The stored procedure checks that password against the one you specified when you created the role. If the password is correct, the stored procedure will enable the role, giving the application all the permissions that you have granted to the role. The permissions remain in effect for the duration of the session.

Securables

Securables are objects governing the control and access of SQL Server's security system. You can grant permissions to principals to access or manage securables.

Managing Server Securables

Server securables are the objects that you govern and manage at a server level. Before granting access to a securable, SQL Server ensures that a principal has the appropriate permission. Server securables also have to be distinctive on the server such that no two server securables have the same name. And only Windows and SQL Server principals can have permission to access server securables. Examples of server securables are as follows:

- Endpoints
- Databases
- SQL Server logins

The following sections will review the steps it takes to grant and deny access to server securables.

Granting Access to Server Securables

As we discussed in the previous section, Windows and SQL Server principals are the only principals that can be granted access to server securables. The following example shows you how to grant access to a database server securable.

```
USE master;
GO

GRANT SHUTDOWN,CREATE ANY DATABASE, ALTER ANY DATABASE,
VIEW ANY DATABASE TO apressSecurity;
```

The syntax for granting access to server securables will vary depending on the securable that you are managing. However, the basic idea is the same. You specify the GRANT clause, the permissions you want to grant, and a server principal in which to grant the permissions.

Denying Access to Server Securables

Denying access to server securables is similar to granting access to server securables. Using the previous example, we will prevent that user from anything besides viewing databases. The following example prevents the user from shutting down, creating, and altering databases:

```
Use master;
GO

DENY SHUTDOWN, CREATE ANY DATABASE, ALTER ANY DATABASE TO APRESSSECURITY;
GO
```

You can see from the preceding example the similarities between granting and denying access to securables. To deny access to server securables, you specify the DENY clause, the permissions you want to deny, and the server principal that you want to deny the permissions on.

Managing Database Securables

Database securables are database-specific objects that are accessed and managed by database principals. Unlike server securables that must be unique on a server instance, database securables can exist multiple times on an instance. However, the database securable must be unique within a database. Some examples of database securables are as follows:

- Application roles
- Database roles
- Assemblies
- Asymmetric keys
- Symmetric keys
- Certificates
- Contracts

- Full-text catalogs
- Message types
- Remote service bindings
- Services
- Schemas
- Database users

The following sections will discuss granting and denying permissions to database securables.

Granting Access to Database Securables

Granting access to database securables closely resembles granting access to server securables. The following example will grant access to database-level securables:

```
USE Apress;
GO

GRANT BACKUP DATABASE, BACKUP LOG TO APRESSSECURITY;
GO
```

After reviewing this example, hopefully you can see the similarities in granting permissions to securables in SQL Server 2008. Once you understand the options that are available to you, then you should be able to get as granular as necessary to control the access to database securables for your database principals.

Denying Access to Database Securables

Denying access to database securables is equally as easy as granting access. The following example will deny database principals access to database securables:

```
USE Apress;
GO

DENY CREATE ASSEMBLY, ALTER ANY ASSEMBLY TO APRESSSECURITY
GO
```

Understanding Schema Securables

With the new role of schemas in SQL Server 2008, schema securables are important to understand. Schema securables are collections of objects owned by a user. Unlike SQL Server 2000, multiple users can be a part of a schema. Multiple schemas can exist within the database, and each schema name must be unique. Within a schema, objects must have distinct names, but a database may have objects with the same name as long as the schemas are different. The following is a list of schema securables:

- Constraint

- Function

- Procedure

- Queue

- Statistic

- Synonym

- Table

- Type

- View

- XML collection

Now that we have shown you the objects that can be stored within schemas, let's talk about some of the usages of schemas.

Defaulting User Schemas

When creating a user, the option exists to set the default schema for the user. The default schema determines the default objects that are accessible by the user when executing queries. The purpose of assigning a user to a schema usually means that the bulk of the objects that user requires access to will be in that schema. That will save the users from having to specify the owner in all of the queries they execute. Granting a user access to a schema by default also ensures all objects created by that user exist in their default schema.

From a security perspective, you can grant access to a user in a schema and prevent the user from accessing any of the other objects in any other schemas in the database. Granted, there are times when users need to have permissions to other schemas and granting those permissions are easily accomplished. However, the new functionality of schemas enables you to keep users within their box or schema without having to force the permissions at the database level. The next couple of examples will provide you with more detail on how schema security works.

The example in Listing 8-3 shows you how to create a SQL Server login, how to create a database user with a default schema, and finally how to add the database user to a role.

Listing 8-3. *Script Used to Create a Login, to Create a User, and to Add the User to the db_datareader Role*

```
USE master
GO

CREATE LOGIN apressWriter WITH PASSWORD = 'P@ssw0rd!' ,
CHECK_POLICY = ON, CHECK_EXPIRATION = ON,
DEFAULT_DATABASE = Adventureworks2008
GO
```

```
USE AdventureWorks2008
GO

CREATE USER apressWriter
FOR LOGIN apressWriter
WITH DEFAULT_SCHEMA = SALES
GO

EXEC sp_addrolemember db_datareader, apressWriter
GO
```

If you log in using the recently created user, you will notice that you can query the tables within the SALES schema without specifying "Sales." Because the user has access to the db_datareader for the database, you can access the other schemas as well. In order to query those tables, you have to specify the schema and then the table or HumanResources.Employee. Now, create our own schema.

Creating Schemas

Creating a schema is simple and only requires a couple of steps. Review the following schema syntax:

```
CREATE SCHEMA schema_clause_name [ schema_element [...n]
```

First, you specify the name that you want to represent the schema in the database, and then you identify the owner of the schema. By default, the owner will be the creator if there is no change on the authorization of the schema. One of the interesting things about creating schemas is that you can create tables and views, as well as grant, deny, and revoke permissions all within the CREATE statement. Even if the table or view does not exist, you can go ahead and grant the schema permissions to it. The script in Listing 8-4 is going to create a schema, make the apressWriter user the owner of the schema, and remove the user from the db_datareader role.

Listing 8-4. *SQL Script That Creates a Schema and a Table, and Then Removes the Previously Created User from the db_datareader Role*

```
USE AdventureWorks2008
GO

CREATE SCHEMA APWriter AUTHORIZATION apressWriter
CREATE TABLE APWriter.books
(bookId int,
 Title varchar(100)
)
GO

EXEC sp_droprolemember db_datareader, apressWriter
GO
```

What do you think will happen when trying to perform actions in the newly created schema? Can you query the newly created table? Can you create objects? Run the following commands to see what your results are.

```
SELECT * FROM APwriter.books
```

```
CREATE TABLE APWriter.books2
(bookId int,
Title varchar(100)
)
GO
```

```
SELECT * FROM APwriter.books2
```

The query results show that you can actually query the table and create objects in the schema that you own even though you do not have explicit database permissions. That is because you explicitly own the schema, which enables you to perform the actions. However, you have no rights to other objects within the database. Run the following:

```
SELECT * FROM Sales.CreditCard
```

You will get an error message that prevents you from accessing the table. Think about the security options that are available to you if you really start playing with schemas and what users can access.

Permissions

Permissions are the rights granted to principals that determine the actions performed with the securables. In SQL Server 2008, there are three basic functions achieved with permissions: You can grant them, revoke them, and deny them. There are so many permissions that we are not going to be able to cover them all; however, we are going to discuss some of the types of permissions and some of the different securables that permissions are applied to. We will also discuss how you can manage permissions.

Types of Permissions

This section provides you with multiple types of permissions and securables. There are multiple types of permissions applied to securables at the server, database, and schema levels. The following list briefly discusses some of the permission types:

- ALTER: Applies to tables, views, procedures, functions, and Service Broker queues. The ALTER permission allows you to modify the object.

- CONTROL: Applies to tables, views, procedures, functions, synonyms, and Service Broker queues. The CONTROL permission provides the principal with all the permissions on the securable.

- DELETE: Applies to tables, views, synonyms, and their columns. The DELETE permission allows you to delete data from the object.

- EXECUTE: Applies to procedures, functions, and synonyms. The EXECUTE permission allows the user to execute the object.

- SELECT: Applies to tables, views, table-valued functions, synonyms, and their associated columns. The SELECT permission enables you to query or read the data from the objects.

- UPDATE: Applies to tables, views, and synonyms. The UPDATE permission enables you to update the data in the objects.

- VIEW DEFINITION: Applies to tables, views, procedures, functions, synonyms, and Service Broker queues. The VIEW DEFINITION permission allows the user to see metadata for the objects.

Make sure you spend some time to understand the various permission types. It does not matter if you are dealing with server, database, or schema securables: You need to understand the available permission types. Once you do, you will be able to apply the appropriate permissions to the principals. Look at SQL Server Books Online for the remaining permission types.

Permission Grouping

Major categories consist of multiple types of permissions. Granting, denying, and revoking permissions are the standard actions that occur to each one of the categories. Those permissions will control all of the objects and its securables within it. The following is a list of some of the major permissions groups:

- *Server*: Controls the permissions that influence the entire server. Server permissions dictate who can create objects within the server, who can access objects within the server, and what can be accessed within the server.

- *Database*: Controls the permissions that apply to objects within the database. The database permissions decide what is accessed, created, and manipulated within the database.

- *Schema*: Controls the objects within a schema within a database. Schema permissions control who views, creates, executes, and manipulates objects within the schema.

- *Assembly*: Controls permission to assemblies to execute, alter, or take control of the assembly.

- *Certificate*: Controls permission to allow control or modification of a certificate.

- *Object*: Controls permissions that reside on schema securables that control the reads, writes, and executes on the schema's objects.

The preceding list does not contain all of the securable groups, so navigate to SQL Server Books Online to finish researching the different groups.

Managing Permissions

Permissions in SQL Server 2008 are similar to those in previous editions in terms of managing permissions. To grant, deny, or revoke permissions, you identify the Windows, SQL Server, or database principal and perform the appropriate action on the securable. In SQL Server 2008, the same rules apply. The most restrictive permissions govern the access and restriction levels for the user. The most important thing to remember about managing permissions in SQL Server 2008 is to spend a little extra time understanding the types of permissions and the different permission groups to accelerate your knowledge of the security system and its various permissions. We have reviewed multiple examples of granting and denying permissions in the previous sections, so we are not going to duplicate those examples.

GUI Security Administration

We have finished discussing SQL Server 2008 and its various principals, securables, and permissions and how to create them using T-SQL. However, at times, you will utilize SQL Server Management Studio to actually create the accounts and assign the appropriate permissions. The purpose of this section is to create a quick reference guide that shows you where to find the various security options within SQL Server Management Studio.

Creating a User

Once you have connected to SQL Server Management Studio, expand the Security folder for your database instance to display the options shown in Figure 8-2. The available security options in SQL Server 2008 are Logins, Server Roles, Credentials, Cryptographic Providers, Audits, and Server Audit Specifications. You may notice that many of the options are new, especially if you are coming straight from SQL Server 2000 where the only available options were Logins and Server Roles.

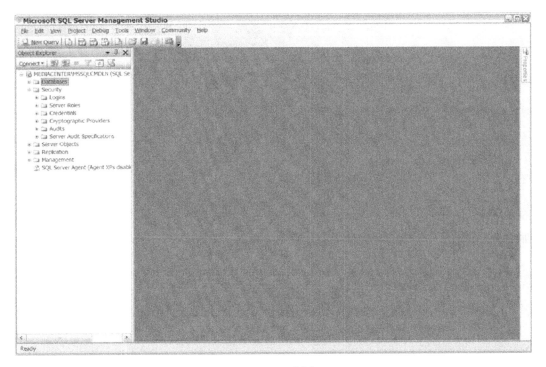

Figure 8-2. *The available options under the Security folder*

As with previous versions of SQL Server, the Logins folder is the category used to view and create SQL Server logins. Expanding the Logins folder will enable you to review the current list of user accounts that have access to that instance of SQL Server. After you have reviewed the user accounts and determined that the user that you intend to create does not exist, you can right-click the Logins folder (or any user contained in the Logins folder) and select New Login from the context menu to create a new user.

Selecting the New Login option will open the Login properties (General page) shown in Figure 8-3, where you can start populating the data for a new user.

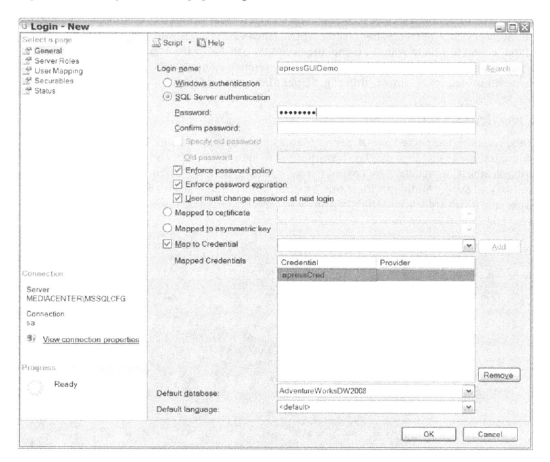

Figure 8-3. *Login properties (General page) dialog box*

Following is a brief discussion of some of the selectable options available to you during the user-creation process:

- *Windows Authentication*: Specifies that the user account will utilize Windows authentication or validation method to validate the password credentials to log in to SQL Server.

- *SQL Server Authentication*: Determines that the user account will use SQL Server to validate password credentials in order to log in to SQL Server.

- *Enforce Password Policy*: Forces user accounts to abide by the strong password policy for SQL authentication only.

- *Enforce Password Expiration*: Requires the passwords of user accounts to expire after a predetermined interval for SQL authentication only.

- *Mapped to Certificate*: Allows you to identify the certificate you want to use to map the user from.

- *Mapped to Asymmetric Key*: Allows you to map to the asymmetric key to associate the user from.

- *Mapped to Credential*: Identifies the credential you want to associate the user to.

- *Default Database*: Identifies the database that the user will connect to upon logging into the SQL Server.

- *Default Language*: Identifies the default schema to associate the user with in the database.

Obviously, the Login Name option is the name that you want to utilize for the user to access SQL Server.

Note If you are creating a Windows authentication account, then you can search for the user with the Search button. The Search button lets you scan the local computer, work group, or domain in order to find the user that you want added.

After creating the login name, type in the password for the user (if you are using SQL authentication) to log in to SQL Server. Decide if you want to enforce a password policy, if you want the password to expire, and if you want users to change their passwords the next time they log in. If you are creating a user for a certificate or asymmetric key, then select the appropriate option on the screen. If the user needs access to resources outside of SQL Server and you want that user associated with a credential, then select the appropriate credential for the available options. Finally, you determine the default database that you want the user to log in to when connecting to SQL Server.

After you have reviewed your selections on the General page, then navigate to the Server Roles page to configure the roles of the user (see Figure 8-4). The fixed roles are available for you to choose from. Select the SQL Server roles that you want the user associated with.

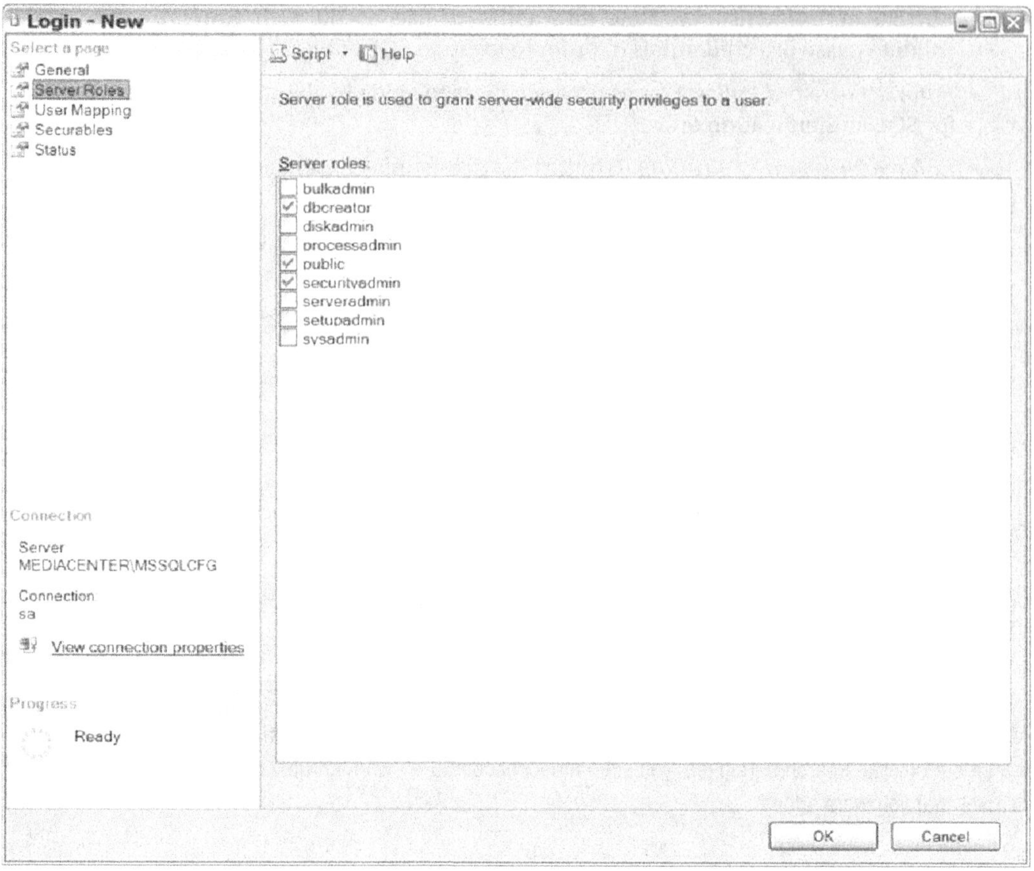

Figure 8-4. *Login properties (Server Roles page)*

Once you have completed assigning the user to appropriate SQL Server roles, then you are ready to give the user access to specific databases. Figure 8-5 displays the sample User Mapping page. First, select the database that you want the user to have access to by selecting the check box in the Map column. After selecting the database, a username is populated and the manipulation of the database role membership options becomes available. The User column contains the username that provides the user with rights and permissions in the database. Options exist to enable you to modify the user to a different name, as long as that name is not already being used within the database. We prefer to leave the usernames the same for the server and the databases. That way, all usernames are consistent among all databases, which minimizes confusion. The database role membership grants the user access to perform actions within the database. Select the check box next to the appropriate role that will provide users with the access you need them to have.

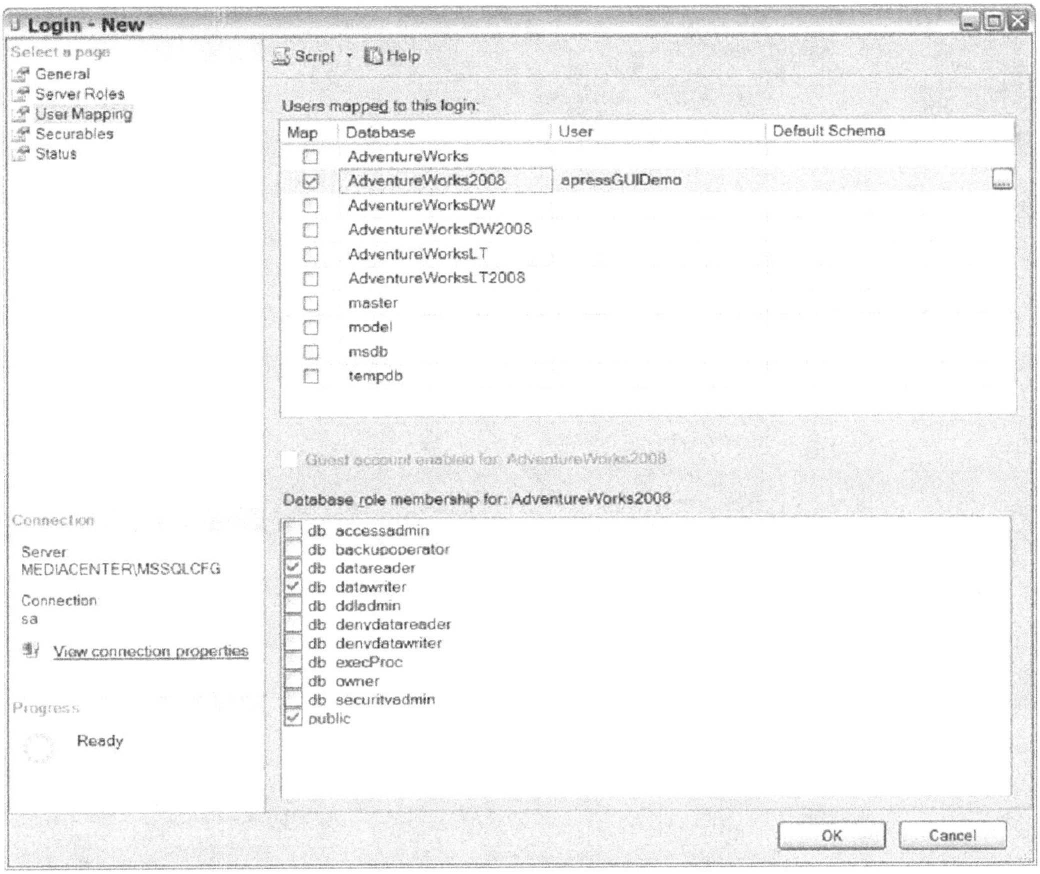

Figure 8-5. *Login properties (User Mapping page)*

Once you have selected all the databases you want the user mapped to, select the Securables page, shown in Figure 8-6. The Securables page enables you to specify grant or deny privileges on server-level securables. Using the Search button, you can look for servers, endpoints, or login accounts. Once you narrow down your search, you have the option to grant permissions to your username principal on the available securables.

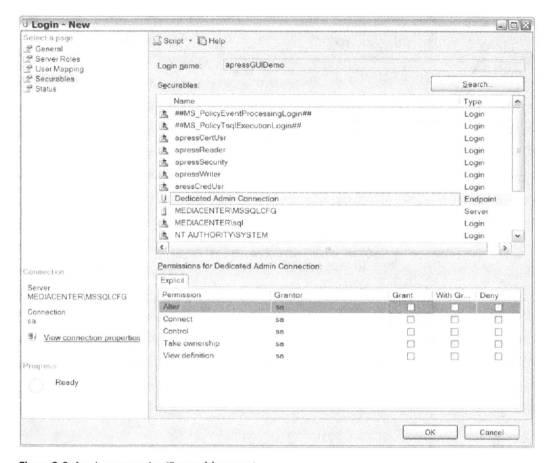

Figure 8-6. *Login properties (Securables page)*

The last option in the Login dialog box is the Status page, shown in Figure 8-7. The Status page provides you with the capability to give the user access to connect to the Database Engine and to enable or disable the login.

One feature of SQL Server 2008 that we really enjoy is the ability to script out the actual code that will perform the tasks accomplished in the GUI. To generate your script, select from the Script drop-down list to determine how you want the script generated for you. So after you have finished selecting the last options Login dialog box, you can script out the code changes and then determine if you want to click OK or run the code in a query window.

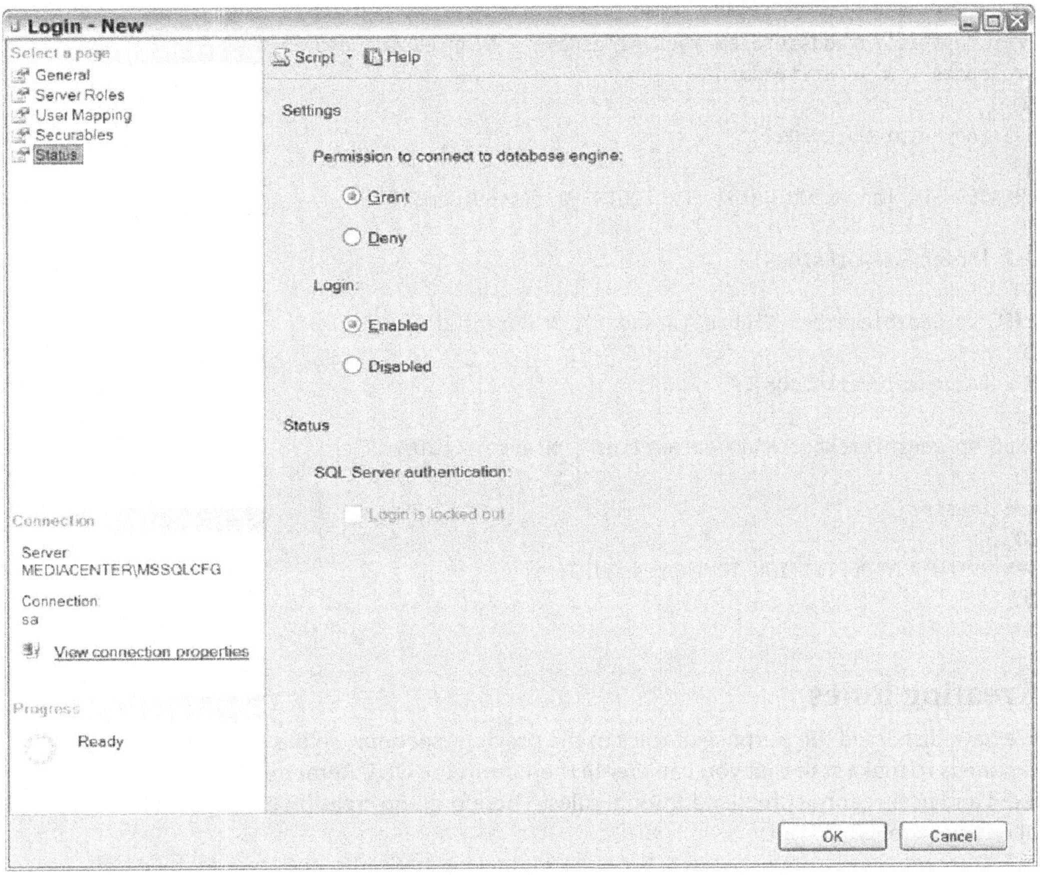

Figure 8-7. *Login properties (Status page)*

Review the sample creation code in Listing 8-5 to see how SQL Server generates a login script. One good tip is to keep the code in case only a portion of the user is created and a failure occurs during the GUI creation. Just execute the script past where the failure occurred, and you are good to go.

Listing 8-5. *SQL Script for Creating a Login*

```
USE [master]
GO
CREATE LOGIN [apressGUIDemo] WITH PASSWORD=N'ABC123#@' _
MUST_CHANGE, DEFAULT_DATABASE=[AdventureWorksDW2008], _
CHECK_EXPIRATION=ON, CHECK_POLICY=ON
GO
ALTER LOGIN [apressGUIDemo] ADD CREDENTIAL [apressCred]
GO
EXEC master..sp_addsrvrolemember @loginame = N'apressGUIDemo',_
 @rolename = N'dbcreator'
```

```
GO
EXEC master..sp_addsrvrolemember @loginame = N'apressGUIDemo', _
@rolename = N'securityadmin'
GO
USE [AdventureWorks2008]
GO
CREATE USER [apressGUIDemo] FOR LOGIN [apressGUIDemo]
GO
USE [AdventureWorks2008]
GO
EXEC sp_addrolemember N'db_datareader', N'apressGUIDemo'
GO
USE [AdventureWorks2008]
GO
EXEC sp_addrolemember N'db_datawriter', N'apressGUIDemo'
GO
use [master]
GO
DENY VIEW ANY DEFINITION TO [apressGUIDemo]
GO
```

Creating Roles

We have discussed the purpose of roles in the previous sections, so the purpose of this section is to make sure that you can create them from the GUI. Remember, Server roles are fixed and users cannot create additional roles. Therefore, the creation examples will consist of database roles.

Once you have connected to SQL Server Management Studio, navigate to the database where you would like to create a role. Keep in mind, database roles are database specific, so you have to create the role in every database you would like that role to exist.

After you expand the database, expand the Security folder. To create a role, you can right-click on the Roles folder, highlight New, and then select Database Role or Application Role (see Figure 8-8). You can also right-click on the Database Role or Application Role folder and select the appropriate new role.

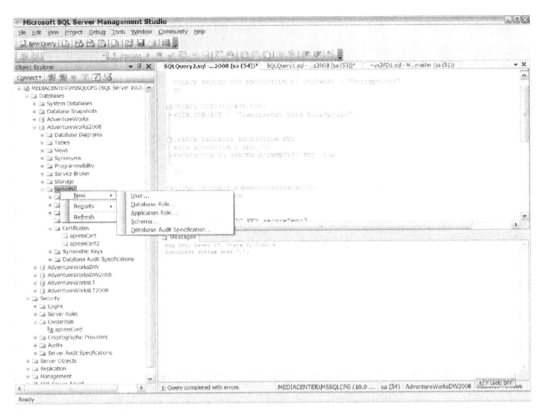

Figure 8-8. *The navigation and creation options for database and application roles*

For this example, we are going to create a database role. So utilize one of the methods just mentioned and select New, Database Role. Figure 8-9 shows the General page of the Database Role – New dialog box.

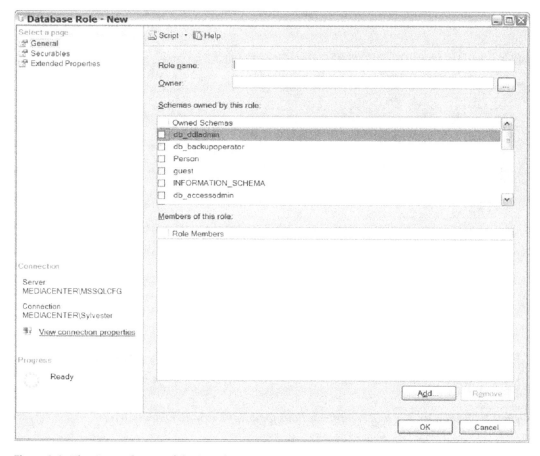

Figure 8-9. *The General page of the Database Role – New dialog box*

First, name your database role in the Role Name field . Next, decide who the owner of the role will be. By default, the owner will be the creator. After the owner specification, decide what schemas are owned by the role. This is a great opportunity to grant total control of the schema to the users of this role. Setting this option is another way of enabling the schema to appear owned by all users of the role from a functionality perspective. Unless permissions are restricted further, each user will have total control within this schema.

The last step on this screen is to add database principals to the role. SQL Server 2008 allows you to search for the users and roles by clicking on the Add button. Once you select the Add button, you have two options: Select Object Types and Browse (not shown in the figures). From the Select Database User or Role screen, click on the Object Types button to see the available object types. Figure 8-10 shows you the object types that are available for you to choose from.

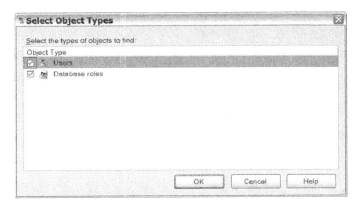

Figure 8-10. *Adding database principals to a role*

After you select the object types, click on the OK Button. Select the Browse button to find all of the specified object types (users and database roles) similar to those shown in Figure 8-11. Check the boxes next to the database principals you want added, click OK, and then OK again on the next screen. You will see the selected objects in the main window.

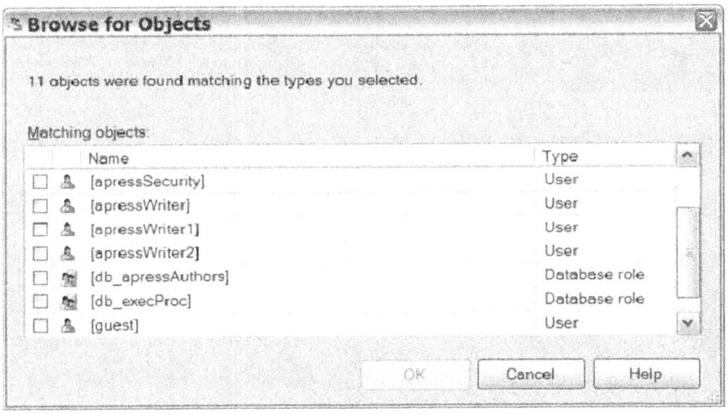

Figure 8-11. *Database principals that can be added to the role*

Once you complete the General page, click on the Securables page. The Securables page will allow you to select the securables or objects that you want to assign permissions to. This page is where you restrict the permissions of the database principals for the role. To manage the permissions for database securables, click on the Search button and pick the objects that you would like to search through. Figure 8-12 shows you the objects options that are available to you that are database securables. You can select specific objects, all the objects of a certain type, or all the objects that belong to a certain schema.

Figure 8-12. *Types of objects that can be searched in the Securables options*

Once you have finished selecting the type of objects you want to choose from, you are directed to a screen that corresponds to the selection shown in Figure 8-12. For this example, we selected specific objects. Figure 8-13 shows the various object types that are available for you to choose from.

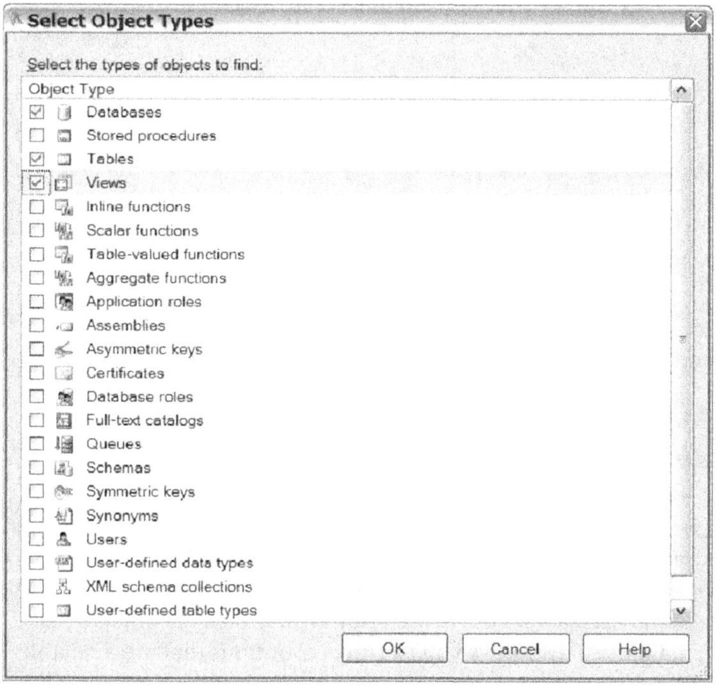

Figure 8-13. *The available database securables that can be searched*

After you have determined the object types that you want to search through, click the Browse button to choose the actual objects that you want to manage. After you select the specific objects, the Securables page will show the available securables on the top half of the page and available permissions for the securable on the bottom half of the page (see

Figure 8-14). To manage permissions, select the securable from the top of the page (say, the books2 table), and the bottom of the page will show all of the available permissions that you can grant or deny at the database level. Continue selecting securables and managing the permissions for the objects. From these screen shots, we hope that you can see how easy it is to control the access each role has within your database. That way, you ensure security is at your pre-determined level.

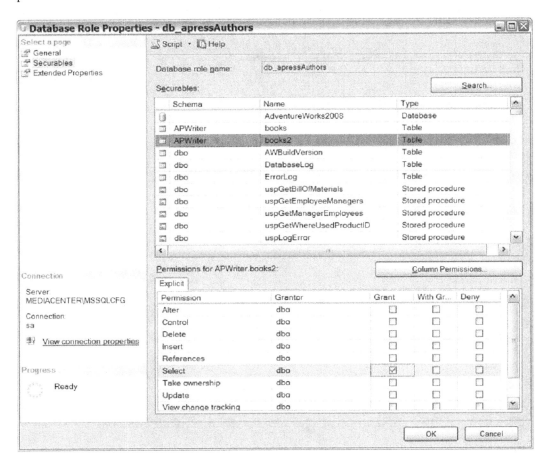

Figure 8-14. *The Securables page with the available securables and associated permissions*

Creating Schemas

With the emergence of schemas in SQL Server, it is important to make sure you know how to locate and create schemas from within SQL Server Management Studio. Remember that schemas are database specific. You will need to create each schema in every database that you want the schema. Schemas are located within the Security folder of the database.

To create schemas, connect to SQL Server Management Studio and navigate to the database where you want to create the schema. Next, expand the Security folder, right-click on the

Schema folder or an existing schema, and select New Schema from the context menu. Review Figure 8-15 to see the General page on the Schema – New dialog box. First, name your schema and then identify its owner. Any database principal (meaning any database user, database role, or application role) can own the schema. Schema owners can also own multiple schemas. The owner of the schema will always have control permissions for the objects within the schema.

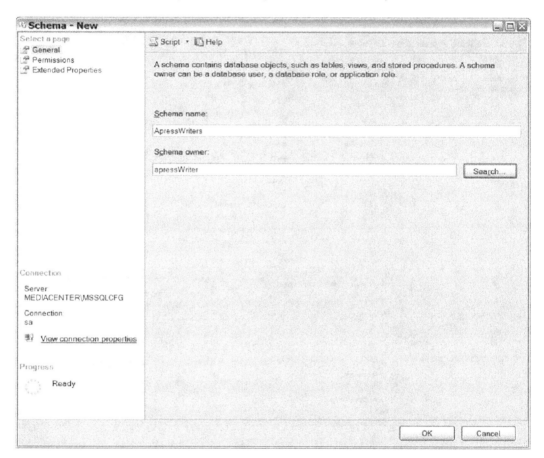

Figure 8-15. *The General page of the schema creation dialog*

After you have completed the available options on the General page, select the Permissions page to complete creating the schema. To grant permissions to the available database principals, click on the Search button. Select the Object Types button, and then you will be directed to the Select Object Types dialog. Figure 8-16 shows you the available database securables that you can grant access to for the schema.

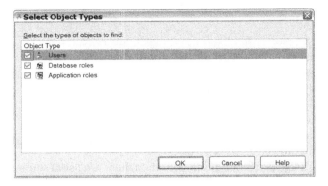

Figure 8-16. *The available principals that can be added to schemas*

Once you are done selecting the object types, click the OK button to return to the screen showing object types and the Browse button. Finally, click on the Browse button to see the available principals. Once you select the principals that you want to apply permissions to, click OK and you will routed back to the Permissions page. The Permission page now contains the selected database principals in the top half of the page with their corresponding available permissions on the bottom half (see Figure 8-17). Select the principal and then add the appropriate permissions to the principal.

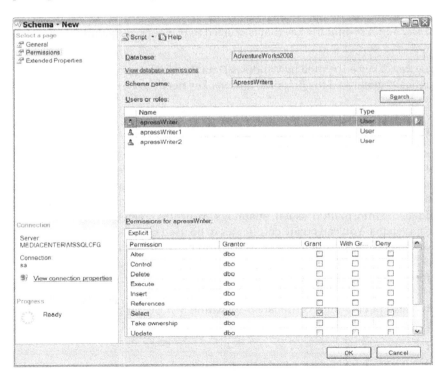

Figure 8-17. *The users and roles and the permissions available to them*

Encryption

Encrypting the physical data utilized by SQL Server has become increasingly popular, with a variety of restrictions placed upon the database administrators by auditing agencies. Surely, you have heard the reports of compromised data, which resulted in the stealing of customer information. A large number of the decision makers within organizations think that securing the physical data via encryption would protect the company's data in the event that your network security is compromised and hackers were able to access SQL Server. Because of that thought process and many other valid reasons for encryption, we have dedicated a section to the various SQL Server 2008 encryption methods.

Before discussing the various methodologies of encrypting your data, here is a list of some frequently used terms:

- *Encryption*: A method of modifying data to a binary string that cannot be easily recognized.

- *Decryption*: The method used to convert the binary string back to the original text data representation.

- *Extensible Key Management (EKM)*: A module that holds symmetric and asymmetric keys outside of SQL Server.

- *Asymmetric keys*: Private and public keys used to encrypt and decrypt data. The private key can encrypt the data, while the public key will decrypt it and vice versa.

- *Symmetric key*: A method used to encrypt and decrypt the data.

- *Database master key*: A symmetric key that is utilized to protect keys within the database.

- *Service master key*: A key encrypted by Windows Data Protection application interface (API) automatically generated the first time another key needs to be encrypted.

Encrypting Data Using Certificate Encryption

Certificate encryption is used to identify people, devices, and organizations. The certificates contain information about the person, organization, or device, the usage period of the certificate (the effective and expire dates), who issued the certificate, the digital signature, and most important the public key that is bound to a private key. Certification authorities (CAs) generate certificates that validate the information issued, enabling certificates created by the authority to be trusted on most systems. You can create certificates to be used on your local network, and they can be successfully implemented as long as you don't want to use the certificate outside of your network. SQL Server 2008 allows you to create your own certificates to secure web service endpoints, forcing applications to use secure connection methods in order to access the endpoints.

Multiple options exist for creating a certificate from within SQL Server 2008. The following code sample provides you with the syntax:

```
CREATE CERTIFICATE certificate_name
    { FROM <existing_keys> | <generate_new_keys> }
    [ ACTIVE FOR BEGIN_DIALOG = { ON | OFF } ]
```

You can create a certificate from scratch by specifying the name, the subject, the expire and effective dates, and finally the encryption key. The encryption key specifies the password for the private key of the certificate. SQL Server will use the database master key if you do not specify an encryption key.

You can also create a certificate from a file, assembly, or executable. If you are using a file to create the certificate, then the file must contain the path to a file with the private key in it. The assembly must already be loaded into the database in order to create a certificate from the assemblies. Then, the CREATE CERTIFICATE statement will just reference the database assembly. When using the executable option, the path to the executable must contain the certificate. Let's review a couple of examples of certificate creation:

```
USE AdventureWorks2008
GO


CREATE CERTIFICATE secureDemo1
ENCRYPTION BY PASSWORD = '53cur3Dem0!'
WITH SUBJECT = 'Certificate Demonstration',
START_DATE = '01/01/2009',
EXPIRY_DATE = '12/31/2009'

GO
```

Remember, if you do not specify the ENCRYPTION BY PASSWORD option, then SQL Server 2008 will use the database master key to create the password. The next script shows you how to create the database master key if one does not exist.

```
USE AdventureWorks2008
GO


CREATE MASTER KEY ENCRYPTION BY PASSWORD = '3ncrypt1on!'
GO



CREATE CERTIFICATE secureDemo2
WITH SUBJECT = 'Certificate Demonstration2',
START_DATE = '01/01/2009',
EXPIRY_DATE = '12/31/2009'
GO
```

Once you have created the certificate, encryption and decryption occurs by using the ENCYRPTBYCERT and DECRYPTBYCERT functions (see the following code example in Listing 8-6).

Listing 8-6. *SQL Script That Encrypts and Decrypts Text Using a Certificate*

```
USE AdventureWorks2008
GO
declare @encryptedAuthor varchar(1000),
@author varchar(50) = 'Sylvester Carstarphen',
@decryptedAuthor varchar(1000),
```

```
@certificatePassword nvarchar(64) = '53cur3Dem0!'
```

```
set @encryptedAuthor = ENCRYPTBYCERT(cert_id('secureDemo1'),@author)
print @encryptedAuthor

set @decryptedAuthor = DECRYPTBYCERT(cert_id('secureDemo1'),@encryptedAuthor,__
@certificatePassword)
print @decryptedAuthor
```

The output of Listing 8-6 is shown in Figure 8-18.

Figure 8-18. *The results of the certificate encryption and decryption script*

Encrypting Data Using Asymmetric Keys

Asymmetric keys consists of two keys: a public key that is transferred over networks and a private key that is not shared with anyone. As a team, the public key encrypts the data prior to sending it to the recipient, and the private key decrypts the message. Only the public and private key pair can encrypt and decrypt each other's data. Think about it this way: When someone wants to communicate with you via an encrypted message, they must have your public key in order to encrypt the message. When you receive their message, you will decrypt the message using your private key to read their response. As you may have guessed, this process has a negative impact on the CPU. Because of this, the process is rarely utilized in large data volumes.

The following code provides the syntax for creating an asymmetric key:

```
CREATE ASYMMETRIC KEY Asym_Key_Name    {
     FROM <Asym_Key_Source>
     |
     WITH ALGORITHM = <key_option>
  [ ENCRYPTION BY PASSWORD = 'password' ]
```

To create an asymmetric key, you must specify an algorithm utilized to encrypt the key or specify a location where to get the key. The three source locations where the asymmetric key can be loaded from are a file system, an executable, or an assembly. The CREATE statement also requires you to specify one of the three types of available encryption algorithms to encrypt the keys. You can also decide if you want to store the key in the EKM, map an existing SQL Server key to another key that exists in the EKM, or specify the key name to use from the EKM. Review the following code samples to see how to create asymmetric keys.

```
USE AdventureWorks2008
GO

CREATE ASYMMETRIC KEY secureDemo3
WITH ALGORITHM = RSA_1024
ENCRYPTION BY PASSWORD = '@5ymm3tr1c';
GO
```

After creating the asymmetric key, you can encrypt and decrypt data by using the ENCRYPT-BYASYMKEY and DECRYPTBYASYMKEY functions (see the following code sample in Listing 8-7).

Listing 8-7. *SQL Script That Encrypts and Decrypts Data Using Asymmetric Keys*

```
declare @encryptedAuthor varchar(1000),
@author varchar(50) = 'Sylvester Carstarphen',
@decryptedAuthor varchar(1000),
@certificatePassword nvarchar(64) = '@5ymm3tr1c'

set @encryptedAuthor = ENCRYPTBYASYMKEY(ASYMKEY_ID('secureDemo3'),@author)
print @encryptedAuthor

set @decryptedAuthor = DECRYPTBYASYMKEY(ASYMKEY_ID('secureDemo3'),_
@encryptedAuthor ,@certificatePassword)
print @decryptedAuthor
```

Take a look at Figure 8-19 to see the output of Listing 8-7.

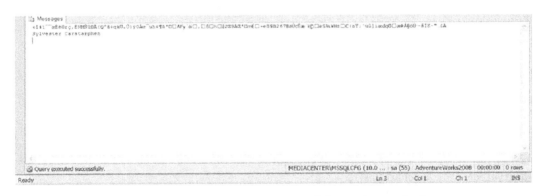

Figure 8-19. *The results of the asymmetric encryption and decryption methods*

Encrypting Data Using Symmetric Keys

Using symmetric keys for data encryption is one of the fastest encryption methods available in SQL Server 2008. Symmetric keys utilize the same key to encrypt and decrypt the data. From a SQL Server perspective, data encryption occurs when SQL Server writes to disk and decryption occurs when data is requested from disk by queries or other methods.

The following code provides you with the syntax for creating symmetric keys:

```
CREATE SYMMETRIC KEY key_name
[ FROM PROVIDER Provider_Name ]
    WITH <key_options> [ , ... n ]
        |
    ENCRYPTION BY <encrypting_mechanism> [ , ... n ]
```

The creation of the symmetric key must consist of an encryption mechanism. Based on the encryption mechanism you would like to use, choose that option within the creation step and populate the requested data accordingly. The possible encryption mechanisms are encrypted by password, certificate, asymmetric, symmetric, or EKM. Lastly, there are two key options: Key Source and Identify Value, which are used to manage temporary keys. The Key Source specifies a pass phrase to derive the key from, while the Identity Value specifies a phrase used to create the globally unique identifiers (GUIDs) that identify data created by the temporary key. The following code creates a symmetric key encrypting the password using the asymmetric key that was created in the preceding section called "Encrypting Data Using Asymmetric Keys."

```
USE AdventureWorks2008
GO


CREATE SYMMETRIC KEY secureDemo5
WITH ALGORITHM = TRIPLE_DES
ENCRYPTION BY ASYMMETRIC KEY secureDemo3
GO
```

The symmetric key allows you to encrypt and decrypt data by using the DECRYPTBYKEY and the ENCRYPTBYKEY functions. The code example in Listing 8-8 shows an example of the encryption and decryption process.

Listing 8-8. *Encrypting and Decrypting Data Using Symmetric Keys*

```
USE AdventureWorks2008
GO

declare @encryptedAuthor varchar(1000),
@author varchar(50) = 'Sylvester Carstarphen',
@decryptedAuthor varchar(1000),
@certificatePassword nvarchar(64) = '@5ymm3tr1c'


OPEN SYMMETRIC KEY secureDemo5
DECRYPTION BY ASYMMETRIC KEY secureDemo3 WITH PASSWORD = '@5ymm3tr1c'
```

```
set @encryptedAuthor = ENCRYPTBYKEY(KEY_GUID('secureDemo5'),@author)

print @encryptedAuthor


set @decryptedAuthor = DECRYPTBYASYMKEY(ASYMKEY_ID('secureDemo3'),@encryptedAuthor,_
@certificatePassword)
set @decryptedAuthor = DECRYPTBYKEY(@encryptedAuthor)
print @decryptedAuthor
```

The output of Listing 8-8 is shown in Figure 8-20.

Figure 8-20. *Results of the symmetric encryption and decryption script*

Extensible Key Management

Extensible Key Management (EKM) is an Enterprise Edition feature that enables encryption keys that guard database files stored in a module outside of the database. Extensible Key Management is used to generate, retrieve, and store the encryption keys external to SQL Server. The Extensible Key Management module is accessed from within SQL Server 2008 using the SQL Server service mapped credentials (review the previous section to refresh your memory on credentials if needed). The Extensible Key Management module is a tool that interfaces with other vendors' encryption software and hardware to provide enhanced encryption and decryption features and functionality.

In order to utilize the Extensible Key Management module, you must enable it using sp_configure. After enabling the EKM module, you simply use the encryption key stored on the EKM to populate the ENCRYPTION BY keyword. Review the following code sample to utilize the EKM module.

```
EXEC sp_configure 'show advanced options', 1
GO
RECONFIGURE
GO


EXEC sp_configure 'EKM provider enabled', 1
GO
RECONFIGURE
```

```
GO
USE AdventureWorks2008
GO

CREATE SYMMETRIC KEY secureDemo6
WITH ALGORITHM = AES_256
ENCRYPTION BY EKM_secureDemo1
GO
```

Transparent Data Encryption

Transparent Data Encryption (TDE) is a SQL Server 2008 feature that allows the encryption of data and log files seamlessly to the application and its users. Because of the methodology utilized for TDE, database securables do not require modification of any sort. In other words, this feature does not force you to modify tables like previous editions of SQL Server. Because the objects remain the same, all data types, indexes, and keys function without data integrity or security risks.

When enabling TDE, a background process runs, encrypting all of the data stored within the data files. There are two types of locks issued during this process: an update lock and a shared lock. As long as user processes do not conflict with the issued lock, then the impact to the application is minimal. Depending on the size of your database, the initial encryption process could take some time and impact the performance of the application. We recommend enabling TDE during a maintenance window to guarantee minimal impact to production. Once the scan completes, all data stored within the data files will be encrypted. One interesting fact is that TDE will not increase the size of your database—your data files prior to the encryption process are the same size as the data files post-encryption.

TDE starts encrypting and decrypting data as data enters and leaves the buffer. When the request by a query for data that currently reside on disk occurs, the decryption process will decrypt that data prior to loading it in memory. Similarly, when data is leaving memory heading to disk, the encryption of the data occurs before reaching its destination. Handling encryption and decryption at memory level is what allows TDE to be seamless to the application and its users. Because the decryption of data occurs in memory, the result set transmitted back to the application is in plain text. Just remember, any process that will write an encrypted database to disk through memory will encrypt the data, including processes like database backups and snapshots.

As a database administrator, you should test TDE within a non-production environment before implementing it in production. Database servers that currently have low CPU and IO should not have a problem implementing TDE. For the servers that have a higher than normal CPU or IO, we would be a little hesitant to blindly turn on TDE. Keep in mind that encrypting and decrypting data is a CPU-intensive process. If you are currently having CPU problems, then do not add the additional processes on your server until the current CPU issues are resolved. Some studies have suggested that environments have experienced a 3% to 5% increase in CPU utilization due to enabling TDE. The best advice we can provide you is to baseline your environment and simulate workloads in a test environment to ensure that your application performs the same with the new encryption method enabled.

Enabling TDE is rather easy—you just enable encryption on the database. However, before enabling encryption, you want to make sure that you create a master database key, create a certificate that uses the master key, and then create a database key using the recently created certificate. Review and execute the following T-SQL example.

```
USE Master
GO

CREATE MASTER KEY ENCRYPTION BY PASSWORD = '3ncrypt1on!'
GO

CREATE CERTIFICATE CertTDE
WITH SUBJECT = 'Transparent Data Encryption'

USE AdventureWorks2008
GO

CREATE DATABASE ENCRYPTION KEY
WITH ALGORITHM = AES_256
ENCRYPTION BY SERVER CERTIFICATE CertTDE

GO

ALTER DATABASE AdventureWorks2008
SET ENCRYPTION ON
GO
```

■**Caution** Make sure you back up your master and database keys and then store them in a location on another server. If you have to restore the database on another server and you do not have the keys used to encrypt your data, then you will not be able to decrypt the data within your database. Discussions on backing up and restoring your encryption keys occurs in Chapters 11 and 12.

Summary

As we conclude this chapter on securing access to SQL Server 2008, the objects within the databases, and the physical data itself, we hope that you have expanded your knowledge about SQL Server 2008 security terms and methods of securing your server. Security is such an important aspect of being a database administrator that you would be cheating yourself by not understanding the verbiage. Spend some extra time experimenting with the various principals, securables, schemas, permissions, and encryption methods to better prepare for making recommendations or implementing security features. Now prepare yourself to learn how to administer the various objects within SQL Server 2008.

CHAPTER 9

■ ■ ■

Administering Database Objects

The purpose for every SQL Server installation is the necessity of a database; however, simply creating a database will not make an application work. Many objects work in concert to provide a positive user experience when interacting with a database. If you look at the Object Explorer in SQL Server Management Studio, you will see there are several objects and features available to aid you in administering the database. SQL Server even has its own set of system databases that manage data within SQL Server itself. This chapter will walk you through many of these objects and features and explain the impact each one has on you as a DBA.

Database 101

Before we talk about administering objects, let's briefly review the database itself. A database is made up of two or more physical files (one data and one log). Here are some key things to keep in mind about those files:

- The data files contain the actual data that is stored in the database and the objects required to support the data.

- The log files contain information needed to recover transactions.

- The data files are stored in logical containers called filegroups.

When you create an object in a database, you can specify the filegroup where the object will be created. If you do not specify a filegroup when creating an object, it will belong to the default filegroup. One filegroup can contain multiple data files, which allows you to spread data processing over multiple disks. For example, if you create a new filegroup and place two data files in the filegroup that are located on separate disks, any object created on that filegroup will be able to take advantage of using multiple disks to service requests. Filegroups are also often used to move indexes or large tables to a separate physical disk in order to increase query performance.

Working with System Databases

The first thing you come across when opening the Databases folder in the Object Explorer (shown in Figure 9-1) is a folder called System Databases. This folder is where you can find the databases that SQL Server uses to store the internal system information necessary for the operation of SQL Server itself. It is important to have an understanding of each system database. I find myself using them often to write queries to help with administration tasks. Actually, one of the questions I always ask when interviewing DBAs is to name all of the system databases and describe each of their functions. Because there is a hidden system database, the interview question even has built-in extra credit points.

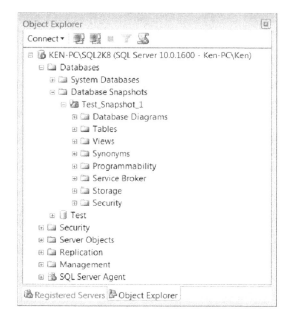

Figure 9-1. *SQL Server Management Studio Object Explorer (Expanded Databases)*

■**Caution** You should not manually alter the system databases, with the exception of adding custom configuration items to the model database. Certain changes to the system databases could cause major issues within SQL Server.

The following list provides a brief description of each of the system databases:

- `master`: The `master` database contains all of the system information that pertains to an instance of SQL Server, such as logins, database names, and file locations.

- `model`: The `model` database is used as a template when creating a new database. Any changes applied to the `model` database will be reflected in any user database that you create after the changes have been made.

- `msdb`: The `msdb` database is used to store configuration and logging information by features, such as SQL Server Agent, Service Broker, Database Mail, log shipping, and backups.

- `tempdb`: The `tempdb` database is used to store temporary objects created by SQL Server when generating result sets. The `tempdb` is recreated every time SQL Server is restarted. If you ever want to find out how long SQL Server has been running, you can just select the `create_date` for the `tempdb` from `sys.databases`, as shown in the following query:

```
Select create_date AS SystemUpSince From sys.databases Where name = 'tempdb'
```

- Resource: This is a read-only database containing system objects that appear in the sys schema of every database. The Resource database is overwritten during the upgrade process to update the system objects.

You cannot see the Resource database from SQL Server Management Studio, but the data files are called mssqlsystemresource.mdf and mssqlsystemresource.ldf and are located in the C:\Program Files\Microsoft SQL Server\MSSQL10.InstanceName\MSSQL\Binn\ folder for a default installation. If you are one of those people who would like to see the data that is stored in the Resource database, just make a copy of the data files, rename them, and restore them with a name like `ResourceTest`.

Working with Database Snapshots

The next folder you see under Databases in the Object Explorer is Database Snapshots. Database snapshots were introduced in SQL Server 2005 and provide you with the ability to create a read-only copy of a database at a given point in time. Any transactions that are uncommitted at the time you create a snapshot will not be included in the database snapshot. You can create multiple snapshots of a source database, but those snapshots must reside on the same instance as the source database.

A database snapshot only contains the data pages that have changed in the source database since the snapshot was created. It contains the original copies of those pages in order to give the effect of a read-only view. The file that is created to hold the changed data pages when the snapshot is created is known as a *sparse file*. A database snapshot sparse file will start out very small and will grow larger as changes are made to the source database.

A database snapshot can never be any bigger than the size of the source database at the time the snapshot was created. Since the snapshot only contains changed pages, it relies on the source database to provide the pages that have not changed; if the source database is unavailable, then so is the snapshot. A source database that contains a snapshot cannot be dropped, detached, or restored until all of the snapshots have been dropped.

You can use database snapshots for things such as reporting solutions and reverting the source database back to the time the snapshot was taken. Using a snapshot as a reporting solution is very helpful when using database mirroring, as stated in the "Database Mirroring" section in Chapter 3. You can create a database snapshot on all the database recovery models, but database snapshots are only available in the Enterprise Edition of SQL Server.

Creating a Database Snapshot

To create a database snapshot, you must issue the CREATE DATABASE command with the AS SNAPSHOT OF clause; you cannot create a database snapshot using the SQL Server Management Studio GUI. Any user who has the right to create a database can create a database snapshot.

Before you create a database snapshot, you need to know the logical files names for every data file in the source database. You can get the logical file name by executing the following query against the source database:

```
SELECT name FROM sys.database_files WHERE type <> 1
```

Listing 9-1 shows the syntax for creating a new database snapshot against the Adventure-Works database. Following are the parameters used in that script:

Test_Snapshot_1 is the name of the new database snapshot.

AdventureWorks_Data is the logical file name of the data file in the AdventureWorks database.

FileName is the name of the snapshot file that will hold the changed data files. You can use any file name, extension, and location that you like for the snapshot file.

AdventureWorks is the source database name following the AS SNAPSHOT OF clause.

Listing 9-1. *Syntax Used to Generate a Database Snapshot*

```
CREATE DATABASE Test_Snapshot_1
 ON
(Name = AdventureWorks_Data,
 FileName = 'C:\Test_Data.ss')
 AS SNAPSHOT OF AdventureWorks
```

To create a database snapshot with multiple filegroups, you need to supply the Name and FileName parameters for each filegroup, as shown in Listing 9-2.

Listing 9-2. *Syntax Used to Generate a Database Snapshot Using Multiple Filegroups*

```
CREATE DATABASE <Snapshot Name>
 ON
(Name = <Logical_FileName_1>,
 FileName =<Snapshot File Location 1>),
(Name =<Logical_FileName_2>,
 FileName =<Snapshot File Location 2>)
 AS SNAPSHOT OF <DatabaseName>
```

Viewing and Querying a Snapshot

Once you have created a snapshot, you can view it in the Database Snapshots folder under the Databases node in the SQL Server Management Studio Object Explorer (refer to Figure 9-1).

You can now query the snapshot as if it were any other database. Notice that if you query `sys.database_files` as shown in Figure 9-2, the physical file names are actually the source database file names and not the snapshot file names created back in Listing 9-1. Querying the snapshot gives the effect of querying an exact copy of the source database at the time you created the snapshot.

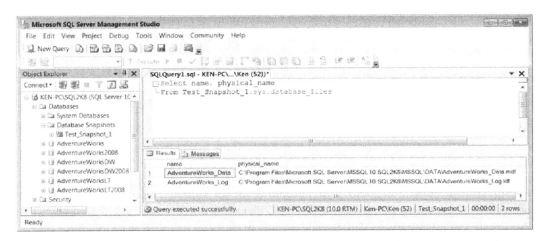

Figure 9-2. *Querying sys.database_files from the snapshot returns the source database's metadata.*

Since querying the snapshot returns metadata about the source database, you have to query the master database (as shown in Listing 9-3) to return the metadata for the snapshot.

Listing 9-3. *Query to View the Snapshot Metadata*

```
SELECT B.name DatabaseName,
            A.name LogicalName,
            B.database_id,
            B.source_database_id,
            A.physical_name
 FROM master.sys.master_files A
         JOIN master.sys.databases B
         ON   A.database_id = B.database_id
```

You can see the result set of Listing 9-3 in Figure 9-3. Notice that the snapshot database name Test_Snapshot_1 has a value of 6 for the source_database_id, which references the database_id of the AdventureWorks database.

	DatabaseName	LogicalName	database_id	source_database_id	physical_name
1	master	master	1	NULL	C:\Program Files\Microsoft SQL Server\MSSQL.10.SQL2K8\MSSQL\DATA\master.mdf
2	master	mastlog	1	NULL	C:\Program Files\Microsoft SQL Server\MSSQL.10.SQL2K8\MSSQL\DATA\mastlog.ldf
3	tempdb	tempdev	2	NULL	C:\Program Files\Microsoft SQL Server\MSSQL.10.SQL2K8\MSSQL\DATA\tempdb.mdf
4	tempdb	templog	2	NULL	C:\Program Files\Microsoft SQL Server\MSSQL.10.SQL2K8\MSSQL\DATA\templog.ldf
5	model	modeldev	3	NULL	C:\Program Files\Microsoft SQL Server\MSSQL.10.SQL2K8\MSSQL\DATA\model.mdf
6	model	modellog	3	NULL	C:\Program Files\Microsoft SQL Server\MSSQL.10.SQL2K8\MSSQL\DATA\modellog.ldf
7	msdb	MSDBData	4	NULL	C:\Program Files\Microsoft SQL Server\MSSQL.10.SQL2K8\MSSQL\DATA\MSDBData.mdf
8	msdb	MSDBLog	4	NULL	C:\Program Files\Microsoft SQL Server\MSSQL.10.SQL2K8\MSSQL\DATA\MSDBLog.ldf
9	Test_Snapshot_1	AdventureWorks_Data	5	6	C:\Test_Data.ss
10	AdventureWorks	AdventureWorks_Data	6	NULL	C:\Program Files\Microsoft SQL Server\MSSQL.10.SQL2K8\MSSQL\DATA\AdventureWorks_Data.mdf
11	AdventureWorks	AdventureWorks_Log	6	NULL	C:\Program Files\Microsoft SQL Server\MSSQL.10.SQL2K8\MSSQL\DATA\AdventureWorks_Log.ldf

Figure 9-3. *The result set from querying metadata for a snapshot database*

To drop a snapshot, all you need to do is issue the DROP DATABASE command using the same syntax you would use to drop any database. Run the following statement to drop the Test_Snapshot_1 database snapshot used in this section:

```
DROP DATABASE  Test_Snapshot_1
```

Reverting a Database to a Database Snapshot

You can revert a source database to the state it was in at the time a snapshot was taken using the RESTORE DATABASE statement with the FROM DATABASE_SNAPSHOT clause. Reverting a database is a quick way to roll back major changes to the source database. For example, you may want to create a database snapshot prior to running vendor-supplied upgrade scripts. Reverting a database due to an error will often be faster than restoring the entire database because only the changed pages will have to be overwritten. Reverting a database does not, however, replace the need for a good database backup. If the source database becomes corrupt, you will not be able to revert it using a snapshot.

When a source database is restored using a snapshot, the updated data files on the source database are overwritten using the data pages from the snapshot sparse file. The log file in the source database is then overwritten and re-created.

Before you revert a database to a snapshot, you should do the following:

- Make sure the source database does not contain read-only or compressed filegroups.

- Make sure all the files are online that were online when the snapshot was created.

- Delete all snapshots of the source database, except the one you are reverting to.

Once you decide to revert a source database to a snapshot, you will need the source database name and the name of the snapshot. You can get the database names by running the query that was shown in Listing 9-3. While you are gathering the database names, you should also verify that the snapshot you are reverting to is the only snapshot with the source_database_id of the database you will be reverting. Then use the syntax shown in Listing 9-4 to revert your database. The listing reverts the AdventureWorks database to a snapshot named Test_Snapshot_1. If you have already dropped the snapshot we created in the previous section, you can re-create it by running the code in Listing 9-1.

Listing 9-4. *Syntax Used to Revert a Database to a Database Snapshot*

```
USE master
GO
RESTORE DATABASE AdventureWorks FROM DATABASE_SNAPSHOT = 'Test_Snapshot_1'
```

■**Note** Reverting a database breaks the log backup chain, so you need take a full backup of a database once it has been reverted. If you do not take a full backup of the database before you try to take a transaction log backup, you will receive an error message stating that the BACKUP LOG cannot be performed because there is no current database backup.

Working with Tables

The remaining objects discussed in this chapter are database objects, and they are located in folder structures under each individual database (with the exception of logon triggers, which we will discuss in the "Working with Triggers" section later in this chapter). As you expand a database, you will encounter the Tables folder. A table is the most important object in the database because it allows you to store data in a logical, structured manner that can be retrieved and processed as needed. You can create up to 2 billion tables per database, and each table can have up to 30,000 columns. The number of rows each table can have is only limited by the available disk space on the server.

Default Constraints

You can define default constraints on columns within a table in order to insert a predefined value into those columns whenever a specific value is not provided. Each column can have only one default constraint. You can create the default when you create a table, or you can add it later using the ALTER TABLE statement. You cannot alter a default. To "change" a default, you must drop the existing constraint and create a new one.

To create a default on a column when you create a table, you can specify the constraint following the column definition. In Listing 9-5, we are creating a table called Orders with an OrderID and an OrderDate column. The OrderDate column has a default named DF_Orders_OrderDate. The column will be given the value of getdate() whenever a value is not otherwise specified.

Listing 9-5. *Syntax to Create a Default on a Column When Creating a Table*

```
USE AdventureWorks2008
GO

CREATE TABLE Orders
(OrderID int identity,
 OrderDate DateTime NOT NULL
    CONSTRAINT [DF_Orders_OrderDate] DEFAULT (getdate()) )
```

If you want to add a default to a column in a table that already exists, you can use the
ALTER TABLE statement, as shown in Listing 9-6. You will end up with the exact same table by
running the code in Listing 9-5 or Listing 9-6.

Listing 9-6. *Syntax to Create a Constraint on a Preexisting Column*

```
USE AdventureWorks2008
GO

--Drop the table if it currently exists
IF OBJECT_ID('dbo.Orders', 'U') IS NOT NULL
  DROP TABLE dbo.Orders;

--Create the Orders table
CREATE TABLE Orders
(OrderID int identity ,
 OrderDate DateTime NOT NULL)

--Alter the Orders table to add the default constraint
 ALTER TABLE dbo.Orders
 ADD CONSTRAINT [DF_Orders_OrderDate]
 DEFAULT (getdate()) FOR OrderDate
```

You can also use the ALTER TABLE statement to add a new column with a default value, as
shown in Listing 9-7. You can use the WITH VALUES clause to apply the default to any existing
row in the table. If the WITH VALUES clause is not used, all of the preexisting rows will contain a
NULL value, and the default will only be applied to new rows.

Listing 9-7. *Syntax to Add a Column to a Table with a Default Using the ADD VALUES Clause*

```
USE AdventureWorks2008
GO

--Drop the table if it currently exists
IF OBJECT_ID('dbo.Orders', 'U') IS NOT NULL
  DROP TABLE dbo.Orders;
```

```
--Create the Orders table
CREATE TABLE Orders
(OrderID int NOT NULL)

--Insert 3 records into the Orders table
INSERT INTO Orders (OrderID)
VALUES(1),(2),(3)

--Alter the table to add the default
 ALTER TABLE dbo.Orders
 ADD OrderDate Datetime  NULL
 CONSTRAINT [DF_Orders_OrderDate]
 DEFAULT (getdate()) WITH VALUES

 --Select to see the default was applied to the existing rows
 SELECT OrderID, OrderDate FROM Orders
```

As you can see in Figure 9-4, the new default was applied to all three existing columns, giving each row the exact same OrderDate. If you remove the WITH VALUES clause from Listing 9-7, all of the order dates would be NULL. If you define the new OrderDate column as NOT NULL, you do not have to specify the WITH VALUES clause as it will be implied.

	OrderID	OrderDate
1	1	2009-04-11 11:57:30.280
2	2	2009-04-11 11:57:30.280
3	3	2009-04-11 11:57:30.280

Figure 9-4. *Result set returned from Listing 9-7*

You can drop a default constraint by using the ALTER TABLE statement with the DROP CONSTRAINT clause, as shown in Listing 9-8.

Listing 9-8. *Code Used to Drop a Default Constraint*

```
ALTER TABLE Orders DROP CONSTRAINT DF_Orders_OrderDate
```

Primary Key Constraints

A primary key is a column or set of columns that can be used to uniquely identify a row in a table. If you use multiple columns to create a primary key, it is referred to as a *composite key*. Data can be repeated in each individual column in the composite key as long as all of the data elements that make up the composite key are unique for each row in the table.

You can create the primary key when you create the table, or create it later using the ALTER TABLE statement. When you create a primary key, SQL Server automatically creates a unique index to enforce that uniqueness. The unique index will be clustered unless you specify nonclustered, or if there is already a clustered index on the table.

To create a primary key on a column when creating a table, you need to specify the PRIMARY KEY keyword following the column definition. Optionally, you can specify CLUSTERED or NONCLUSTERED to determine the type of index that will be generated. You also have the option to specify the name of the constraint that will be created by using the CONSTRAINT keyword followed by the name of the constraint. If you do not name the constraint, you will be at the mercy of SQL Server and will end up with an auto-generated name like PK__Orders__C3905BAF52793849. Listing 9-9 shows the syntax for creating a primary key when creating a table.

Listing 9-9. *Syntax for Creating a Primary Key When Creating a Table*

```
USE AdventureWorks2008
GO

--Drop the table if it currently exists
IF OBJECT_ID('dbo.Orders', 'U') IS NOT NULL
  DROP TABLE dbo.Orders;

--Create the Orders table
CREATE TABLE Orders
(OrderID int NOT NULL CONSTRAINT PK_ORDERS PRIMARY KEY CLUSTERED)
```

To create a primary key after a table has been created, you can use the ALTER TABLE statement. Listing 9-10 shows how to create a composite key on a table after the table has already been created. Since the OrderID will be repeated for each ProductID contained in the Order-Details table for a single order, you can uniquely identify the order using the OrderID and the ProductID combined.

Listing 9-10. *Syntax to Create a Composite Key Using the ALTER TABLE Statement*

```
USE AdventureWorks2008
GO

--Drop the table if it currently exists
IF OBJECT_ID('dbo.OrderDetails', 'U') IS NOT NULL
  DROP TABLE dbo.OrderDetails;

--Create the OrderDetails table
CREATE TABLE OrderDetails
(OrderID int NOT NULL,
 ProductID int NOT NULL)

--Alter the OrderDetails table to add a composite key
ALTER TABLE OrderDetails
ADD  CONSTRAINT PK_Order_Details PRIMARY KEY CLUSTERED
(OrderID,
 ProductID)
```

To remove a primary key from a table, you need to issue the ALTER TABLE statement with the DROP CONSTRAINT keywords followed by the name of the primary key, as shown in Listing 9-11.

Listing 9-11. *Syntax to Remove a Primary Key Constraint*

```
ALTER TABLE OrderDetails DROP CONSTRAINT PK_Order_Details
```

Unique Constraints

You can use a unique constraint to maintain distinct values in a column or set of columns that do not participate in the primary key. As with a primary key, when you create a unique constraint, SQL Server automatically creates a unique index to ensure the column values are distinct. Unlike with a primary key, you can define multiple unique constraints per table. You can also define a unique constraint on one or more columns that accept NULL values; however, if you define a unique constraint on single column, that column can accept only one NULL value.

To create a unique constraint on a column when creating a table, you need to specify the UNIQUE keyword following the column definition. Optionally, you can specify CLUSTERED or NONCLUSTERED to determine the type of index that will be generated; NONCLUSTERED is the default. Remember, you can have only one clustered index per table, so if you are using a clustered index for your primary key, the index on the unique constraint must be nonclustered. You also have the option to specify the name of the constraint by using the CONSTRAINT keyword followed by the name of the constraint. Listing 9-12 shows the syntax for creating a unique constraint when creating a table.

Listing 9-12. *Syntax for Creating a Unique Constraint When Creating a Table*

```
USE AdventureWorks2008
GO

--Drop the table if it currently exists
IF OBJECT_ID('dbo.Orders', 'U') IS NOT NULL
  DROP TABLE dbo.Orders;

--Create the Orders table
CREATE TABLE Orders
(OrderID int NOT NULL CONSTRAINT PK_ORDERS PRIMARY KEY CLUSTERED,
 OrderNumber int NULL CONSTRAINT UQ_ORDER_NUMBER UNIQUE NONCLUSTERED)
```

To create a unique constraint after you have already created a table, you can use the ALTER TABLE statement. Listing 9-13 shows how to create a unique constraint using multiple columns on an existing table.

Listing 9-13. *Syntax to Create a Unique Constraint Using the ALTER TABLE Statement*

```
USE AdventureWorks2008
GO

--Drop the table if it currently exists
IF OBJECT_ID('dbo.OrderDetails', 'U') IS NOT NULL
  DROP TABLE dbo.OrderDetails;
```

```
--Create the OrderDetails table
CREATE TABLE OrderDetails
(OrderID int NOT NULL CONSTRAINT PK_ORDERDETAILS PRIMARY KEY CLUSTERED,
 OrderNumber int NULL,
 CustomerNumber int NOT NULL)

--Alter the OrderDetails table to add the unique constraint
ALTER TABLE OrderDetails
ADD  CONSTRAINT UQ_ORDER_CUSTOMER_NBR UNIQUE
(OrderNumber,
 CustomerNumber)
```

To remove a unique constraint from a table, you need to issue the ALTER TABLE statement with the DROP CONSTRAINT keywords followed by the name of the unique constraint, as shown in Listing 9-14.

Listing 9-14. *Syntax to Remove a Unique Constraint*

```
ALTER TABLE OrderDetails DROP CONSTRAINT UQ_ORDER_CUSTOMER_NBR
```

Foreign Key Constraints

You can create a foreign key to enforce a relationship between the data in two tables. Say that you have an Orders table and an OrderDetails table. When a customer places an order, you insert one record into Orders. Then, for each line item, you place a record into OrderDetails. Naturally you would want each line item in OrderDetails to contain the order number, so that you could refer to the order record for any given line item. That order number in OrderDetails is an example of a foreign key. By defining such a relationship explicitly, you enable SQL Server to ensure that each order number in the child table OrderDetails represents a valid order in the parent table Orders.

▓Note You cannot change a primary key or unique constraint while it is being referenced by a foreign key constraint; you have to remove the foreign key first.

To create a foreign key you can use the ALTER TABLE statement. You can use the NO CHECK option to force the creation of the foreign key, even if the existing data does not meet the foreign key requirements. All data entered after the foreign key is created will then be forced comply with the constraint. Listing 9-15 uses the ALTER TABLE statement to create a foreign key constraint on the OrderID column in the OrderDetails table that references the OrderID column in the Orders table.

You can specify the CASCADE option to apply any updates or deletes made to the Orders table to the OrderDetails table. For example, if an order is deleted from the Orders table, all of the records in the OrderDetails table that reference that OrderID will be deleted as well.

Listing 9-15. *Creating a Foreign Key Constraint Between Two Tables*

```
USE AdventureWorks2008
GO

--Drop the tables if they currently exist
IF OBJECT_ID('dbo.OrderDetails', 'U') IS NOT NULL
  DROP TABLE dbo.OrderDetails;

IF OBJECT_ID('dbo.Orders', 'U') IS NOT NULL
  DROP TABLE dbo.Orders;

--Create the tables
CREATE TABLE Orders
(OrderID int NOT NULL CONSTRAINT PK_ORDERS PRIMARY KEY CLUSTERED,
OrderNumber int NULL CONSTRAINT UQ_ORDER_NUMBER UNIQUE NONCLUSTERED)

CREATE TABLE OrderDetails
(OrderDetailID int IDENTITY (1,1) NOT NULL
CONSTRAINT PK_ORDER_DETAILS PRIMARY KEY CLUSTERED,
OrderID int NOT NULL,
ProductID int NOT NULL)

--Add the foreign key constraint
ALTER TABLE OrderDetails WITH NOCHECK
ADD CONSTRAINT FK_OrderDetails_Orders FOREIGN KEY(OrderID)
REFERENCES Orders (OrderID)
ON UPDATE  CASCADE
ON DELETE  CASCADE
```

The script from Listing 9-15 creates the tables shown in Figure 9-5 with a one-to-many relationship between the Orders and the OrderDetails tables.

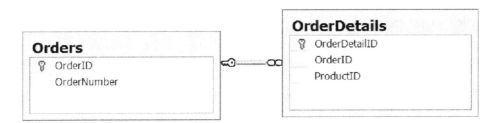

Figure 9-5. *Foreign key relationship between the Orders and OrderDetails tables*

You can disable a foreign key when you want to perform certain operations, such as inserts and deletes that the foreign key would cause to fail. Execute the ALTER TABLE statement with the NOCHECK CONSTRAINT keywords followed by the constraint name. Optionally, you can use the ALL keyword to disable all constraints on a table at once. Re-enable the constraints by changing the NOCHECK keyword to CHECK and reissuing the statement. Listing 9-16 shows the syntax to disable and enable constraints.

■**Note** You can disable only foreign key and check constraints using the NOCHECK keyword. Any other constraints, such as primary key and unique constraints, will still be enabled.

Listing 9-16. *Syntax Used to Disable/Enable Constraints*

```
--Disable the FK_OrderDetails_Orders constraint on the OrderDetails table
ALTER TABLE OrderDetails NOCHECK CONSTRAINT FK_OrderDetails_Orders

--Disable the all constraints on the OrderDetails table
ALTER TABLE OrderDetails NOCHECK CONSTRAINT ALL

--Enable the FK_OrderDetails_Orders constraint on the OrderDetails table
ALTER TABLE OrderDetails CHECK CONSTRAINT FK_OrderDetails_Orders

--Enable the all constraints on the OrderDetails table
ALTER TABLE OrderDetails CHECK CONSTRAINT ALL
```

To remove a foreign key constraint from a table, issue the ALTER TABLE statement with the DROP CONSTRAINT keywords followed by the name of the foreign key constraint, as shown in Listing 9-17.

Listing 9-17. *Code to Remove a Foreign Key Constraint*

```
ALTER TABLE dbo.OrderDetails DROP CONSTRAINT FK_OrderDetails_Orders
```

Check Constraints

You can use a check constraint to help enforce domain integrity by validating or checking the data that is being inserted into a column before accepting the value. For example, you can use a check constraint to verify that a valid range of dates are being inserted into a column. You can use any logical expression that returns True or False to create a check constraint.

The code in Listing 9-18 creates a check constraint on a table named CustInfo on the DateOfBirth column to verify that any date of birth is greater than 1/1/1900 and less than the current date.

Listing 9-18. *Syntax to Create a Check Constraint When Creating a Table*

```
USE AdventureWorks2008
GO

--Drop the table if it currently exists
IF OBJECT_ID('dbo.CustInfo', 'U') IS NOT NULL
  DROP TABLE dbo.CustInfo;

CREATE TABLE CustInfo
(CustID int IDENTITY(1,1) PRIMARY KEY,
 DateOfBirth DATE
 CONSTRAINT ValidDateOfBirth
 CHECK (DateOfBirth > '1/1/1900' AND DateOfBirth < getdate()))
```

Now if you try to run the query INSERT INTO CustInfo (DateOfBirth) VALUES ('1/1/1899') to insert a date that is out of the valid date range defined by the check constraint in Listing 9-18, you will get the error message shown in Figure 9-6.

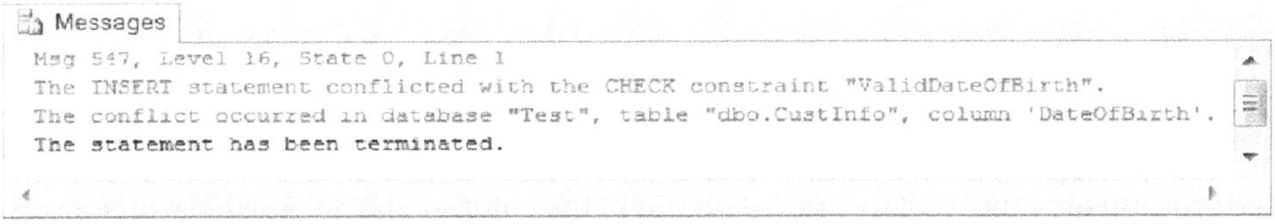

Figure 9-6. *Error message returned when trying to insert an out-of-range date as defined by the check constraint in Listing 9-18*

■**Note** A NULL value evaluates to Unknown instead of True or False, so if you try to insert a NULL value into a column with a check constraint, the insert will succeed.

To create a check constraint on a table that has already been created, use the ALTER TABLE statement, as shown in Listing 9-19. The WITH NOCHECK option will allow the check constraint to be applied even if there are current records in the table that do not meet the requirements of the constraint.

Listing 9-19. *Syntax to Create a Check Constraint Using the ALTER TABLE Statement*

```
USE AdventureWorks2008
GO

--Drop the table if it currently exists
IF OBJECT_ID('dbo.CustInfo', 'U') IS NOT NULL
  DROP TABLE dbo.CustInfo;
```

```
--Create the table
CREATE TABLE CustInfo
(CustID int IDENTITY(1,1) PRIMARY KEY,
 DateOfBirth DATE)

--Alter the table to add the check constraint
ALTER TABLE CustInfo WITH NOCHECK
ADD CONSTRAINT ValidDateOfBirth
CHECK (DateOfBirth > '1/1/1900' AND DateOfBirth < getdate())
```

You also have the ability to disable check constraints to allow you to perform certain operations. You can disable check constraints using the same syntax as disabling foreign key constraints. For the exact syntax, see the previous "Foreign Key Constraints" section. To remove a check constraint from a table, you need to issue the ALTER TABLE statement with the DROP CONSTRAINT keywords followed by the name of the check constraint, as shown in Listing 9-20.

Listing 9-20. *Syntax for Removing a Check Constraint*

```
ALTER TABLE CustInfo DROP CONSTRAINT ValidDateOfBirth
```

Sparse Columns

The sparse column feature is new in SQL Server 2008. You can declare a column using the sparse keyword, and anytime a NULL value is entered in the column, that NULL value will not use any disk space. Sounds good, right? But there is a catch.

Sparse columns require an extra 4 bytes of storage for each non-NULL, fixed-length value in the table. So while they require zero bytes to store a NULL value, they require extra space to store non-NULL values. Therefore, it is very important to have a reasonable ratio of NULL to non-NULL values. Otherwise, use of the sparse columns feature will end up costing you disk space rather than saving it.

The fewer bytes a data type requires, the higher the percentage of NULL values you will need in the column in order to save space via the sparse columns feature. There is a table in SQL Server Books Online you can use to determine the estimated space savings per data type (see "Using Sparse Columns" at http://msdn.microsoft.com/en-us/library/cc280604.aspx).

Sparse columns must allow NULL values and cannot include the following data types:

- Geography
- Geometry
- Image
- ntext
- Text
- Timestamp
- User-defined data types

Let's look at the sample code in Listing 9-21. Address Lines 1 and 2 are required, so you cannot define them as sparse columns. Address Lines 3 and 4 are not required, but they are often used and would not be good candidates for sparse columns. However, Address Lines 5 and 6 are rarely populated, so you can define them as sparse and benefit from the disk savings.

Listing 9-21. *Syntax for Creating a Table Using Sparse Columns*

```
USE AdventureWorks2008
GO

--Drop the table if it currently exists
IF OBJECT_ID('dbo.CustInfo', 'U') IS NOT NULL
  DROP TABLE dbo.CustInfo;

--Create the table
CREATE TABLE CustInfo
(CustID INT PRIMARY KEY,
Addr_Line1 VARCHAR(100) NOT NULL,
Addr_Line2 VARCHAR(100) NOT NULL,
Addr_Line3 VARCHAR(100) NULL,
Addr_Line4 VARCHAR(100) NULL,
Addr_Line5 VARCHAR(100) SPARSE NULL,
Addr_Line6 VARCHAR(100) SPARSE NULL)
```

If you want to add the SPARSE option to a column in a table that already exists, you can use the ALTER TABLE statement. Listing 9-22 shows how to use the ALTER TABLE statement to change the Addr_Line4 column in the CustInfo table to a sparse column. If you want to drop the SPARSE option from a column, all you need to do is change the ADD keyword to DROP, as shown in Listing 9-23.

Listing 9-22. *Syntax for Adding the SPARSE Option to a Column Using the ALTER TABLE Statement*

```
ALTER TABLE CustInfo ALTER COLUMN Addr_Line4 ADD SPARSE
```

Listing 9-23. *Syntax for Dropping the SPARSE Option from a Column Using the ALTER TABLE Statement*

```
ALTER TABLE CustInfo ALTER COLUMN Addr_Line4 DROP SPARSE
```

Compression

You can enable compression on tables and indexes in SQL Server 2008 to reduce the disk space needed to store the data in those tables and indexes. Table and index compression is only available in the Enterprise and Developer Editions of SQL Server. You can implement two different levels of compression: row-level compression and page-level compression.

Row-level compression works by reducing the metadata required to store the data itself. Row-level compression also reduces the amount of storage by using variable length storage for fixed length data types, including numeric data types. For example, a column with a data type int may require 1 byte to store the number 1 and 2 bytes to store the number 1,000 instead of requiring 4 bytes of storage for every single value.

Page-level compression works by implementing row-level compression along with two other techniques called prefix compression and dictionary compression. *Prefix compression* works by identifying a common value for the data in each column that can be used to reduce storage requirements. The value is then replaced by a pointer to the value that is stored in the compression information structure stored immediately after the page header. *Dictionary compression* also replaces values on the page with a pointer to a common value in the compression information structure. The main difference is that dictionary compression is not limited to a single column; it looks for common values on the entire page. Page compression does not occur immediately, as there would be no benefit in compressing a nearly empty page.

There are a few things to keep in mind when using data compression. Data compression requires less input and output (IO) because it requires fewer disk reads to access the data. However, data compression will increase the CPU because SQL Server now has to compress and uncompress the data. Page-level compression provides a higher compression ratio than row-level compression, but you may see higher levels of CPU utilization when using page-level compression. Deciding whether to use row-level, page-level, or no compression at all is entirely dependent on how each option affects your environment. You could see drastic space savings and increased performance by enabling compression; however, if you are already CPU bound, you may hinder performance by enabling compression.

You can use the sp_estimate_data_compression_savings stored procedure to determine the estimated space you will save by enabling row or page compression, as shown in Figure 9-7.

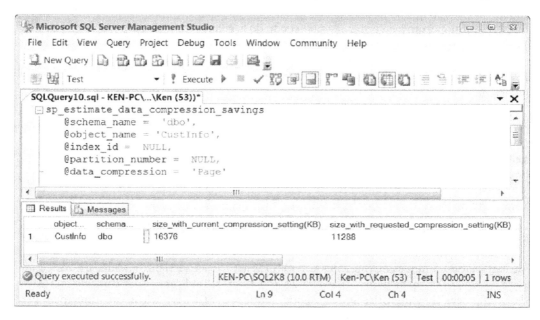

Figure 9-7. *Estimated savings using page compression on the CustInfo table*

To create a compressed table, you need to specify the compression type (row or page) you would like following the table definition. Listing 9-24 shows the correct syntax to create a table with page compression.

Listing 9-24. *Syntax to Enable Page Compression When Creating a Table*

```
USE AdventureWorks2008
GO

--Drop the table if it currently exists
IF OBJECT_ID('dbo.CustInfo', 'U') IS NOT NULL
  DROP TABLE dbo.CustInfo;

--Create the table with page compression
CREATE TABLE Orders
(OrderID int identity,
OrderDate DateTime NOT NULL)
WITH (DATA_COMPRESSION = PAGE)
```

To add compression or change the existing compression on a table, you can use the ALTER TABLE statement to rebuild the current pages with the selected compression type. Listing 9-25 changes the compression to row-level compression for the Orders table. To remove compression, all you need to do is change the value to DATA_COMPRESSION = NONE.

Listing 9-25. *Syntax to Add or Change the Compression on an Existing Table*

```
ALTER TABLE Orders
REBUILD WITH (DATA_COMPRESSION = ROW)
```

Partitions

You can use partitioning to increase query performance and decrease maintenance time on large tables by working with subsets of data without altering the presentation layer. You must be running the Enterprise or Developer Edition of SQL Server in order to take advantage of partitioned tables and indexes. In order to implement table partitioning, you must first create a partition function, then create a partition scheme, and finally create a table that uses the partition scheme.

Listing 9-26 shows the syntax needed in order to create a partitioned table.

Listing 9-26. *Syntax to Create a Partitioned Table*

```
USE AdventureWorks2008
GO

--Create partition function
CREATE PARTITION FUNCTION SamplePartitionFunction (Datetime)
AS RANGE RIGHT FOR VALUES ('1/1/2000');
GO
```

```
--Create partition scheme
CREATE PARTITION SCHEME SamplePartitionScheme
AS PARTITION SamplePartitionFunction
TO ([PRIMARY], [PRIMARY]);
GO

--Create partition table
CREATE TABLE SamplePartitionTable
 (ID INT NOT NULL,
 SomeDateColumn DATETIME)
 ON SamplePartitionScheme (SomeDateColumn);
GO

--Insert sample data
INSERT INTO SamplePartitionTable
VALUES (1,'1/1/1999'), (2,'1/15/1999'), (3,'1/21/1999'),
 (4,'1/1/2000'), (5,'1/20/2006')

--Query the sys.partitions table to show the inserted rows for each partition
SELECT partition_number, rows
FROM sys.partitions
WHERE object_id = OBJECT_ID('SamplePartitionTable')
```

Figure 9-8 shows the results returned from querying the sys.partitions table. Notice that the second partition has two rows. You can use the LEFT or RIGHT keyword when creating the function to determine which filegroup will contain the value specified as the divisor. If no value is specified, the value will reside in the left filegroup. Since we specified RANGE RIGHT for the divisor value 1/1/2000, it was inserted into the second partition.

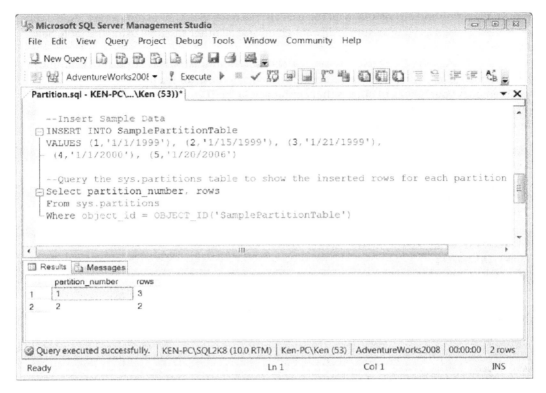

Figure 9-8. *Results of Listing 9-26*

You create a partition function to specify how the rows in the table will be divided or partitioned based upon the values in the partitioning columns. The scheme actually assigns the partitions defined using the partition function to a specific filegroup. You can assign each partition to the same filegroup, but using multiple filegroups gives you the added ability to create a backup of each partition separately by performing a filegroup backup. At the very minimum, you must define enough filegroups in the partition scheme to hold the partitions defined by the partition function, but you can also add extra filegroups that will be marked next for use if the function is altered to create extra partitions. You must have one more filegroup defined in the partition scheme than the number of ranges defined in the partition function. For example, if you define a single range in the partition function, the rows will be divided into two filegroups.

Temporary Tables

Temporary tables are like regular tables, except they are stored in the `tempdb` and automatically dropped after they have been used. There are two types of temporary tables, local and global. Local temporary tables are defined using a pound sign (#) in front of the table name and is visible only to the session that created it. As soon as the session is disconnected, the temporary table is deleted. Global temporary tables are defined using double pound signs (##) in front of the table name and are visible to all the users in the database. Global temporary tables will be deleted as soon as your session is disconnected and all other sessions using the table have disconnected as well.

You will often find DBAs using temporary tables in administrative scripts. For example, you can run the following script to insert the contents of the error log into a temporary table, and then filter your results to entries that contain an error. If you were just using the sp_read-errorlog stored procedure, you would have to scroll through all the results and manually look for entries containing an error.

```
--Create the temp table
CREATE TABLE #Temp
(LogDate DateTime,
 ProcessInfo varchar(255),
 Txt varchar(Max))

--Insert the data from the error log
INSERT INTO #Temp
EXEC sp_readerrorlog

--Select only txt containing err
SELECT * FROM #Temp
WHERE Txt LIKE '%err%'

--Drop temp table
DROP TABLE #Temp
```

Caution Global temporary tables can cause major application issues. For example, if you define a global temporary table in a stored procedure that is called multiple times before the global temporary table has been deleted, it will cause the next CREATE statement to fail.

Working with Views

Views are virtual tables that represent the result set of a select statement from one or more tables or other views. In most cases, that is unless a view is indexed, a view is basically a pre-defined query that is stored and executed whenever the view is referenced in a query.

You can use a view to limit user access to sensitive information in the underlying table. For example, you can create a view that only includes a subset of columns in a table and give the user access to the view instead of the underlying table. You can also use a WHERE clause to limit the rows of data that are returned, ensuring the user can see only specific rows.

There are a few limitations you need to be aware of when creating a view. A SELECT statement in a view cannot include any of the following:

- A COMPUTE or COMPUTE BY clause.

- An ORDER BY clause without also including the TOP clause. The workaround for this is to select the top 100 percent, as in the following query: SELECT TOP 100 PERCENT FROM <table> ORDER BY <columns>.

- The INTO keyword used to create a new table.

- The OPTION clause.

- A reference to a temporary table or table variable.

The example in Listing 9-27 creates a view that shows the name and department description of all the employees in a single department. As you can see in the example, we are able to use the view to hide the employee's social security number. We are also able to provide more user-friendly column names by using an alias. The WITH ENCRYPTION option prevents the view definition from being displayed. You should be careful when using the encryption option because you will not be able to retrieve the definition from the database if you need it.

Listing 9-27. *Sample Code Used to Create an Encrypted View*

```
USE AdventureWorks2008
GO

CREATE TABLE Employee
(EmpID int NOT NULL CONSTRAINT PK_EMP PRIMARY KEY CLUSTERED,
EmpFirstName Varchar(50),
EmpLastName Varchar(50),
EmpSSN Varchar(9),
DepartmentID int)
GO

CREATE TABLE Department
(DepartmentID int NOT NULL CONSTRAINT PK_DEPT PRIMARY KEY CLUSTERED,
DepartmentDscr Varchar(50))
GO

CREATE VIEW vMarketingEmployees
WITH ENCRYPTION
AS
SELECT dbo.Employee.EmpFirstName AS FirstName,
       dbo.Employee.EmpLastName AS LastName,
       dbo.Department.DepartmentDscr AS Department
FROM  dbo.Department INNER JOIN
      dbo.Employee ON dbo.Department.DepartmentID = dbo.Employee.DepartmentID
WHERE dbo.Department.DepartmentID = 1
```

Let's say you found out that the Marketing department is actually DepartmentID 2 instead of 1. You can use the ALTER VIEW statement shown in Listing 9-28 to make the changes. While making the changes, you also decide to remove the encryption option. All you have to do to remove the encryption is not to specify the option when running the ALTER VIEW statement.

Listing 9-28. *Syntax Used to Alter an Existing View*

```
USE AdventureWorks2008
GO

ALTER VIEW vMarketingEmployees
AS
SELECT dbo.Employee.EmpFirstName AS FirstName,
       dbo.Employee.EmpLastName AS LastName,
       dbo.Department.DepartmentDscr AS Department
FROM  dbo.Department INNER JOIN
      dbo.Employee ON dbo.Department.DepartmentID = dbo.Employee.DepartmentID
WHERE dbo.Department.DepartmentID = 2
```

To remove a view from the database, all you have to do is issue the DROP VIEW statement followed by the view name, as shown in Listing 9-29.

Listing 9-29. *Syntax to Remove a View from the Database*

```
DROP VIEW vMarketingEmployees
```

Partitioned Views

Distributed partitioned views are those that reference data across multiple servers and combine the data to the user as a single result set. You can use distributed partitioned views to form a federation of database servers, which are separately managed servers used to spread the processing load for a single application across multiple servers. Listing 9-30 shows an example of a distributed partitioned view.

■Note You can create a local partitioned view by referencing only tables on the same server; however, creating partitioned tables is the preferred method for locally partitioning data.

Listing 9-30. *Common Syntax Used in a Distributed Partitioned View*

```
CREATE VIEW vDistributedSample
AS
SELECT col1, col2, col3 FROM Server1.DBName.dbo.TableName
UNION ALL
SELECT col1, col2, col3 FROM Server2. DBName.dbo.TableName
UNION ALL
SELECT col1, col2, col3 FROM Server3.DBName.dbo.TableName
```

Updateable Views

You can use a view to insert, update, and delete data in the underlying tables as long as certain conditions are met:

- All the columns being modified must be in the same base table.

- The columns must also directly reference the base table; you cannot modify computed columns or columns that are derived from or affected by aggregate functions.

- If the WITH CHECK option is specified, as shown in Listing 9-31, the view cannot be updated in any way that would cause the updated record to disappear from the result set.

For example, given the view created in Listing 9-31, you could not run an UPDATE statement to set the DepartmentID = 2.

Listing 9-31. *Syntax to Create an Updatable View Using the WITH CHECK Option*

```
USE AdventureWorks2008
GO

--Drop the view if it currently exists
IF OBJECT_ID('dbo.vMarketingEmployees', 'V') IS NOT NULL
  DROP VIEW dbo.vMarketingEmployees;

GO

--Create a view using the WITH CHECK option
CREATE VIEW vMarketingEmployees
AS
SELECT dbo.Employee.EmpFirstName AS FirstName,
       dbo.Employee.EmpLastName AS LastName,
       dbo.Department.DepartmentID,
       dbo.Department.DepartmentDscr AS Department
FROM  dbo.Department INNER JOIN
      dbo.Employee ON dbo.Department.DepartmentID = dbo.Employee.DepartmentID
WHERE dbo.Department.DepartmentID = 1
WITH CHECK OPTION
```

If you look at Figure 9-9, you can see that trying to change DepartmentID fails, since it will violate the CHECK OPTION constraint, but changing Department is successful.

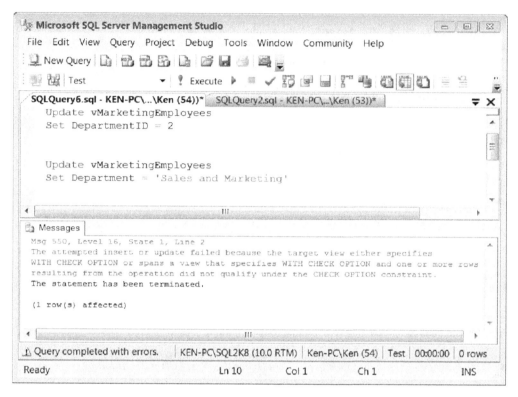

Figure 9-9. *Results of updating a view that uses the WITH CHECK option*

Indexed Views

If you have a process-intensive view that is run often, you can improve performance and reduce the processing time needed to execute the view by creating an index on the view. The first index you create on a view must be a unique clustered index, which causes the result set of the view to be stored in the database. Thereafter, you can create nonclustered indexes.

Listing 9-32 shows an example of creating an indexed view. Notice the WITH SCHEMABINDING clause in the CREATE VIEW statement. If you plan to create an index on a view, then you must first create the view using that clause, which prevents any changes to the underlying tables referenced by the view that would affect the view definition. An indexed view is essentially a stored result set returned by the view, so SQL Server does not have to process the query each time the view is referenced. By creating the view WITH SCHEMABINDING, SQL Server can ensure that no underlying changes to the data will invalidate the stored results.

There are several other requirements that must be met in order to create an indexed view. For the specific requirements, refer to the topic "Creating Indexed Views" in SQL Server Books Online.

Listing 9-32. *Syntax to Create an Indexed View*

```
USE AdventureWorks2008
GO


CREATE VIEW vEmployees
WITH SCHEMABINDING
AS
SELECT dbo.Employee.EmpFirstName AS FirstName,
       dbo.Employee.EmpLastName AS LastName,
       dbo.Department.DepartmentID,
       dbo.Department.DepartmentDscr AS Department
FROM  dbo.Department INNER JOIN
       dbo.Employee ON dbo.Department.DepartmentID = dbo.Employee.DepartmentID
GO
--Create an index on the view
CREATE UNIQUE CLUSTERED INDEX IDX_vEmployee_Dept
 ON vEmployees (DepartmentID);
GO
```

Indexed views are best suited for situations where the underlying data is rarely updated; because as the data is updated in the base tables, the data must also be updated in the indexed view to reflect the changes. If the data is frequently updated, maintaining the index could actually lead to performance issues instead of performance gains. There are many caveats to using indexed views that could lead to an administrative headache, so you shouldn't go around creating indexes on all your views. However, there are certain situations, especially in a data warehouse environment, where indexed views can provide an enormous performance benefit.

You can create an indexed view in any edition of SQL Server 2008, but you receive some extra benefits when you are running the Enterprise Edition. In the Enterprise Edition, the query optimizer can automatically take advantage of an index created on a view, even if the view is not specifically referenced in a query.

Working with Synonyms

You can create a synonym in SQL Server that references a base object, and then reference the synonym to perform operations on the base object. You can use a synonym in place of a three- or four-part naming convention. You can also use a synonym to reference objects on a linked server, thereby masking the server name. If the database on the linked server is moved, all you need to do is change the synonym instead of having to change every object where the linked server is referenced.

Following is a list of rules you need to know when using synonyms:

- You can use a synonym to reference the base object in the following query contexts:

  - SELECT, including subqueries

  - INSERT

  - UPDATE

- DELETE

- EXECUTE

- You cannot reference a synonym that is located on a linked server.

- You cannot use a synonym in a Data Definition Language (DDL) statement, such as an ALTER TABLE command.

- Synonyms are not schema bound; therefore, they cannot be referenced by schema-bound objects such as these:

  - CHECK constraints

  - Computed columns

  - Defaults

  - Rules

  - Schema-bound views and functions

To create a synonym, right-click on the Synonyms folder located under the database where you would like to create the synonym and select New Synonym from the context menu. This will bring up the New Synonym dialog box, as shown in Figure 9-10.

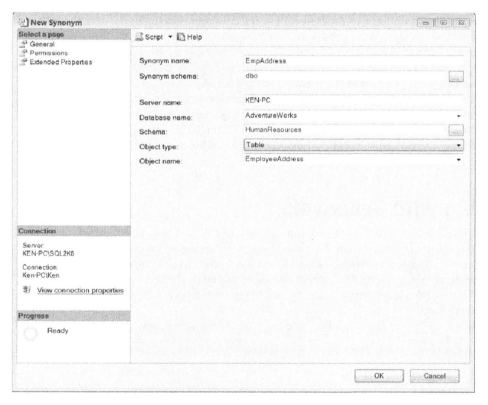

Figure 9-10. *New Synonym dialog box*

Next, fill in the fields and choose an object type from the drop-down list. Following are the components of a synonym definition:

Synonym Name is the name of the synonym that will be created.

Synonym Schema is the name of the schema where the synonym will be created.

Server Name is either the local server name or the name of a linked server containing the base object.

Database Name is the name of the database containing the base object.

Schema is the name of the schema where the base object is located.

Object Type defines the base object type (view, table, stored procedure, or function). Object type is a drop-down selection in Figure 9-10.

Object Name is the name of the base object.

Figure 9-10 creates a synonym called `EmpAddress` that references the HumanResources. EmployeeAddress table in the AdventureWorks database on a linked server called KEN-PC. The results of querying the `EmpAddress` synonym can be seen in Figure 9-11.

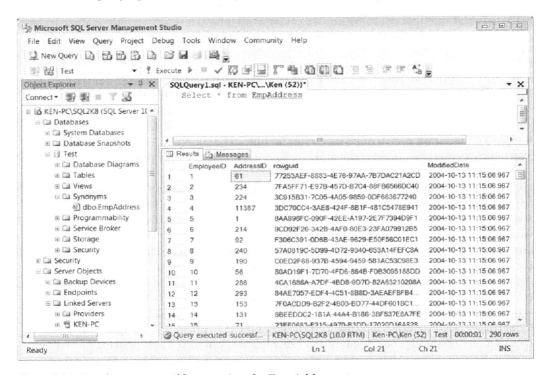

Figure 9-11. *Result set returned by querying the EmpAddress synonym*

You can also use T-SQL to create a synonym. The following statement is the equivalent to the parameters provided to create the `EmpAddress` synonym back in Figure 9-10.

```
CREATE SYNONYM [dbo].[EmpAddress]
FOR [KEN-PC].[AdventureWorks].[HumanResources].[EmployeeAddress]
```

You do not need permissions on the base object in order to create a synonym. For that matter, the base object does not even need to exist to create a synonym; all of the security and existence checks are deferred until runtime. Also, the permissions that you set on a synonym apply only to the synonym and not to the base object. For example, when you grant Select permission to a synonym, you are giving permission to query the synonym itself, and not to query the underlying object. You can query the sys.synonyms catalog view to return the meta-data about the synonym, including the base object name.

To drop a synonym, all you need to do is execute the DROP SYNONYM command followed by the synonym name or right-click the synonym and select Delete from the context menu.

```
DROP SYNONYM [schema].SynonymName
```

You can drop a synonym even if other objects are referencing it. You will not encounter an error until executing the object that references the synonym.

Working with Stored Procedures

You can find stored procedures, along with the rest of the objects discussed in this chapter, under the Programmability folder for each database in Object Explorer. Stored procedures are routines saved in the database that contain business logic used to perform predefined actions and return information about the action that was performed. If you can write a set of code to run in a batch statement, you can most likely encapsulate the code in a stored procedure. A stored procedure can accept input parameters; perform a number of actions using both DDL and Data Manipulation Language (DML) statements, and return output to the client in the form of a scalar value, one or more result sets, or output parameters. A stored procedure can also return an execution status indicating the success or failure of the procedure.

Stored procedures provide many benefits when executing T-SQL including code reus-ability. You can code logic in stored procedures and call the stored procedure from any application that requires the same information. Stored procedures also provide a layer of abstraction from the application. You can easily change the code within the stored procedure without having to make any changes to the application. You also reduce the network traffic that is sent between the client and the database server. Instead of sending an entire query or batch of code over the network, you will only need to send a single line to execute the proce-dure. Stored procedures often lead to a performance increase because the query optimizer compiles a query plan for the stored procedure the first time it is executed, and the query plan is then reused for subsequent executions. The reason I say a compiled query plan often leads to increased performance is because in some cases the query plan that the query optimizer chose when the stored procedure was first executed may not be the best plan for subsequent executions with different parameters and actually causes a performance hit. Stored proce-dures enhance security by allowing you to grant rights to execute the procedure instead of giving access directly to the base tables. Also, by using parameterized queries, you reduce the chances of a SQL injection attack. Keep in mind that just because you use a stored procedure does not mean you are immune to a SQL injection attack. Bad coding techniques, such as dynamic SQL, are prone to a SQL injection no matter where the code is encapsulated.

When you create a stored procedure, you should not use the sp_ naming convention because this prefix is designated for SQL Server system stored procedures. If you create a procedure with the sp_ prefix, it may conflict with a current or future system stored procedure. Listing 9-33 shows how to create a simple stored procedure that accepts a group name as a parameter and returns all the departments in that group.

Listing 9-33. *Syntax to Create and Execute a Stored Procedure That Accepts a Parameter and Returns a Result Set*

```
USE AdventureWorks2008
GO

CREATE PROCEDURE dbo.DepartmentNameByGroup_Select (@GroupName nvarchar(50))
AS
SELECT DepartmentID,
          Name AS DepartmentName
FROM HumanResources.Department
WHERE GroupName = @GroupName

GO
--Execute the stored procedure
EXEC dbo.DepartmentNameByGroup_Select 'Executive General and Administration'
```

You can see the results of Listing 9-33 in Figure 9-12. You would typically create a stored procedure like the one in Listing 9-33 to bind to a drop-down list in an application.

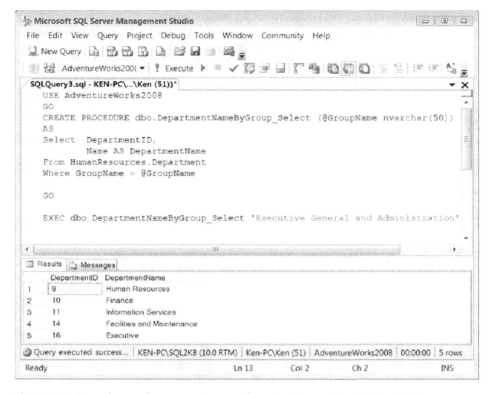

Figure 9-12. *Stored procedure execution results using the code in Listing 9-33*

You can use an output parameter to capture and return a single value to the code that calls the stored procedure. However, you can have multiple output parameters within a single stored procedure. The following example in Listing 9-34 alters the stored procedure that we created in Listing 9-33 to add an output parameter named @DepartmentCount that is used to hold the number of departments for the group being returned. (Notice the OUTPUT clause in the parameter definition.)

When you run a procedure with an output variable, you must define a variable in the calling code to hold the return value. In Listing 9-34, we have defined a variable called @NbrOfDepartments. That is the variable that receives the value from the procedure's output parameter.

You must also use the OUTPUT clause following the variable that will be used to capture the return value, or you will end up with a NULL variable in the calling code. So you must use the keyword OUTPUT in the parameter definition, as well as when actually passing the parameter to the procedure.

Listing 9-34. *Syntax to Alter the Stored Procedure Created in Listing 9-33 to Use an Output Parameter*

```
USE AdventureWorks2008
GO
ALTER PROCEDURE dbo.DepartmentNameByGroup_Select
 (@GroupName nvarchar(50),
  @DepartmentCount int OUTPUT)
AS
SELECT  DepartmentID,
            Name AS DepartmentName
FROM HumanResources.Department
WHERE GroupName = @GroupName
GROUP BY DepartmentID,
         Name;

SELECT @DepartmentCount=COUNT(1)
FROM HumanResources.Department
WHERE GroupName = @GroupName;
GO

--Execute the stored procedure
DECLARE @NbrOfDepartments int

EXEC dbo.DepartmentNameByGroup_Select
     'Executive General and Administration',
     @NbrOfDepartments OUTPUT

SELECT 'There Are ' +
CAST(@NbrOfDepartments as varchar(50)) +
' Departments In This Group.'
```

As you can see in Figure 9-13, the code from Listing 9-34 contains two result sets. The output parameter has no visual effect on the first result set; you can only see the output returned from the stored procedure by specifying the variable used to capture the output in a second query.

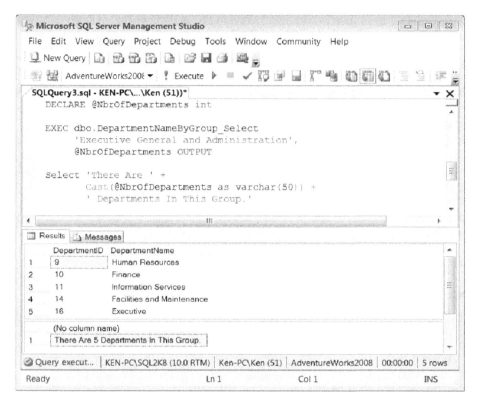

Figure 9-13. *Stored procedure execution results using the code in Listing 9-34*

You can also use the RETURN clause to return information to the code that calls a stored procedure. The RETURN clause is more limited than using output parameters in that you can only have a single RETURN clause per stored procedure that returns an integer value. The RETURN clause also immediately stops the execution of a stored procedure and returns control to the calling code.

Listing 9-35 alters the stored procedure created in Listing 9-33 to use the RETURN clause to return the number of departments for a group. Notice that now we are setting the @NbrOfDepartments variable equal to the results of the stored procedure instead of using it as a parameter as we did with the output parameters. The result set is exactly the same as what was shown in Figure 9-13.

Listing 9-35. *Syntax to Alter the Stored Procedure Created in Listing 9-33 to Use the RETURN Clause*

```
USE AdventureWorks2008
GO
ALTER PROCEDURE dbo.DepartmentNameByGroup_Select
 (@GroupName nvarchar(50))
AS
```

```
SELECT  DepartmentID,
            Name AS DepartmentName
FROM HumanResources.Department
WHERE GroupName = @GroupName
GROUP BY DepartmentID,
         Name;

RETURN (SELECT COUNT(1)
        FROM HumanResources.Department
        WHERE GroupName = @GroupName);

GO


--Execute the stored procedure
DECLARE @NbrOfDepartments int

EXEC @NbrOfDepartments =
     dbo.DepartmentNameByGroup_Select 'Executive General and Administration'

SELECT 'There Are ' +
CAST(@NbrOfDepartments as varchar(50)) +
' Departments In This Group.'
```

Because a stored procedure's query plan is cached, you may find yourself needing to recompile a stored procedure in order to benefit from recent changes to your database, such as an added index. A stored procedure is automatically recompiled the first time it is run after SQL Server is restarted as well as when the structure of an underlying table is changed, but adding an index does not force a recompile.

You can use the sp_recompile system stored procedure to force a stored procedure to produce a new query plan the next time it is executed (see Listing 9-36). The sp_recompile procedure takes an object name as an input parameter. If you pass in the name of a stored procedure, it will be recompiled the next time it runs; if you pass in the name of a table, any stored procedure that runs against that table will be recompiled.

Listing 9-36. *Syntax to Force the dbo.DepartmentNameByGroup_Select Stored Procedure to Generate a New Execution Plan*

```
USE AdventureWorks2008
GO
EXEC sp_recompile 'dbo.DepartmentNameByGroup_Select'
GO
```

To remove a stored procedure from the database, you can issue the DROP PROCEDURE statement followed by the procedure name, as shown in Listing 9-37.

Listing 9-37. *Syntax to Drop a Stored Procedure from the Database*

```
DROP PROCEDURE dbo.DepartmentNameByGroup_Select
```

You also have the option to execute a stored procedure automatically whenever SQL Server starts by using the sp_procoption system stored procedure. In order to enable a stored procedure for auto execution, it must exist in the master database and cannot contain input or output parameters. The code in Listing 9-38 shows the syntax to enable a stored procedure for auto execution. In order to disable auto execution on the stored procedure, change the @OptionValue to off.

Listing 9-38. *Syntax to Enable Stored Procedure Execution on SQL Server Startup*

```
sp_procoption @ProcName = 'uspSystemMaintenance',
                        @OptionName = 'startup',
                        @OptionValue = 'on'
```

Working with Functions

A user-defined function is a saved routine that can accept parameters and return a value based on programming logic. There are two types of user-defined functions in SQL Server, scalar-valued functions and table-valued functions. Table-valued functions are further classified as inline functions or multi-statement functions.

Scalar-Valued Functions

You can create a scalar-valued function to return a single value of the data type that is defined following the RETURNS clause. The RETURNS clause is used in the function definition to mandate the data type used by the RETURN statement in the body of the function. You cannot create a function that returns a value of types text, ntext, image, cursor, or timestamp. The example in Listing 9-39 uses a scalar-valued function to return a running balance of all the orders that were placed for a certain customer.

Listing 9-39. *Sample Scalar-Valued Function to Return a Running Balance*

```
--Create sample tables
CREATE TABLE CustOrders
(OrderID int PRIMARY KEY,
 CustID int,
 InvoiceAmt float)

CREATE TABLE Customers
 (CustID int PRIMARY KEY,
 CustName varchar(50))

--Insert sample data
INSERT INTO Customers
VALUES (1,'Ken Simmons'),(2,'Sylvester Carstarphen')
```

```
INSERT INTO CustOrders
VALUES (1,1,500.25),(2,1,124.73),(3,1,42.86),(4,2,120.80),(5,2,12.74)
GO


--Create function to return running balance
CREATE FUNCTION dbo.udf_RunningSalesBalance
 (@CustID int,
  @OrderID int)
RETURNS float
AS
BEGIN
      RETURN (SELECT SUM(InvoiceAmt)
                        FROM CustOrders
                        WHERE CustID = @CustID AND OrderID <= @OrderID)
END

GO


--Query the new function
SELECT OrderID,
          CustName,
          InvoiceAmt,
          dbo.udf_RunningSalesBalance(Customers.CustID, OrderID) RunningSales
FROM Customers JOIN
          CustOrders ON Customers.CustID = CustOrders.CustID
```

You can see the results returned from querying the scalar function from Listing 9-39 in Figure 9-14. As you can see in the RunningSales column, by passing in the CustID and the OrderID to the scalar function, you can do a SUM on the InvoiceAmt where the CustID equals the CustID, and the OrderID is less than or equal to the OrderID. This calculation is performed for each row in order to return a running balance.

	OrderID	CustName	InvoiceAmt	RunningSales
1	1	Ken Simmons	500.25	500.25
2	2	Ken Simmons	124.73	624.98
3	3	Ken Simmons	42.86	667.84
4	4	Sylvester Carstarphen	120.8	120.8
5	5	Sylvester Carstarphen	12.74	133.54

Figure 9-14. *Result set returned by the scalar function created in Listing 9-39*

Table-Valued Functions

Table-valued functions can be used to provide similar functionality to views and stored procedures, but table-valued functions provide some interesting benefits. Like a view, an inline table-valued function returns a result set based on a single query; but, inline table-valued functions can accept parameters and views cannot. Multi-statement table-valued functions can be used to encapsulate programming logic like stored procedures, but unlike stored procedures, you can reference multi-statement table-valued functions in the FROM clause of a SQL statement.

The following example in Listing 9-40 shows how to create an inline table-valued function that can accept parameters and be used in the FROM clause of a SQL statement. The function uses the Customers and CustOrders tables that were created in Listing 9-39.

Listing 9-40. *Syntax to Create an Inline Table-Valued Function*

```
CREATE FUNCTION dbo.udf_TotalSalesByCustomer (@CustID int)
RETURNS TABLE
AS
RETURN
(
 SELECT Customers.CustID,
           CustName,
           SUM(InvoiceAmt) TotalSales
 FROM Customers JOIN
           CustOrders ON Customers.CustID = CustOrders.CustID
 WHERE Customers.CustID = @CustID
 GROUP BY Customers.CustID,
           CustName
)
GO

--Query the inline table-valued function with CustID 1
SELECT A.CustID,
           A.CustName,
           CustOrders.OrderID,
           CustOrders.InvoiceAmt,
           A.TotalSales
FROM dbo.udf_TotalSalesByCustomer(1) A
      JOIN  CustOrders ON A.CustID = CustOrders.CustID
```

You can see the results of Listing 9-40 in Figure 9-15. By giving the function an alias (in this case A), you can reference the results throughout the query. Being able to reference the output returned by the function gives you the ability to do things such as JOIN the CustOrders table with the function and display the columns returned by the function in the SELECT statement.

	CustID	CustName	OrderID	InvoiceAmt	TotalSales
1	1	Ken Simmons	1	500.25	667.84
2	1	Ken Simmons	2	124.73	667.84
3	1	Ken Simmons	3	42.86	667.84

Figure 9-15. *Result set returned by the inline table-valued function created in Listing 9-40*

The syntax for creating a multi-statement table-valued function is much like creating a scalar function, except you use a table variable to return a result set instead of returning a single value. You need to define the table variable that will be used to return the result set from a multi-statement table-valued function following the RETURNS clause. The function in Listing 9-41 uses logic to check if the customer has ordered more than $500 worth of merchandise. If so, a result set is returned applying a 10% discount to all of the orders for that customer.

Listing 9-41. *Syntax Used to Create a Multi-Statement Table-Valued Function*

```
CREATE FUNCTION dbo.udf_CustomerDiscount (@CustID int)
RETURNS @CustDiscount TABLE
          (OrderID int,
           InvoiceAmt float,
           InvoiceAmtWithDiscount decimal(10,2))
AS
BEGIN
  IF (SELECT SUM(InvoiceAmt)
      FROM CustOrders
      WHERE CustID = @CustID) > 500

      BEGIN
          INSERT INTO @CustDiscount
          SELECT OrderID, InvoiceAmt, InvoiceAmt * .9
          FROM CustOrders
          WHERE CustID = @CustID
      END
  ELSE
    BEGIN
          INSERT INTO @CustDiscount
          SELECT OrderID, InvoiceAmt, InvoiceAmt
          FROM CustOrders
          WHERE CustID = @CustID
    END

  RETURN

END

GO

--Query the multi-statement table-valued function
SELECT * FROM dbo.udf_CustomerDiscount(1)
```

You can view the results of Listing 9-41 in Figure 9-16. You can see that since customer 1 has more than $500 worth of merchandise, the discount is applied to the InvoiceAmtWith Discount column. If you execute the same multi-statement table-valued function for customer 2, the discount will not be reflected in the InvoiceAmtWithDiscount column, since they have ordered less than $500 worth of merchandise.

	OrderID	InvoiceAmt	InvoiceAmtWithDiscount
1	1	500.25	450.23
2	2	124.73	112.26
3	3	42.86	38.57

Figure 9-16. *Result set returned by the multi-statement table-valued function created in Listing 9-41*

To alter a function, you use the same syntax as creating a function, except you will need to change the CREATE keyword to ALTER. To drop an existing function, you need to issue the DROP FUNCTION statement followed by the function name, as shown in Listing 9-42.

Listing 9-42. *Syntax to Drop a User-Defined Function from the Database*

```
DROP FUNCTION dbo.udf_CustomerDiscount
```

Working with Triggers

A *trigger* is a procedure that is stored and executed in response to an event that occurs in SQL Server. There are three different types of triggers you can create: DML triggers, DDL triggers, and logon triggers. You can create multiple triggers of the same type on the same event. For example, you can create multiple triggers that fire on the same INSERT event on a single table. Using triggers is a good way to make sure something always happens automatically whenever a specific event occurs. On the downside, we have seen some strange error messages generated by triggers when trying to perform common DBA tasks. The reason we say strange is that if you are not aware of a trigger and you try to insert data into a table, you can receive a message that was generated by the trigger that has nothing to do with an INSERT statement at all. We have seen DBAs try to track down these messages without even considering that the table in question had a trigger, resulting in a lot of extra work.

DML Triggers

DML triggers are fired when an INSERT, UPDATE, or DELETE statement is executed against a table or view. You can configure DML triggers to fire after or instead of an event, although you can only define an INSTEAD OF trigger on a view. You can create only one INSTEAD OF trigger on a table, but you can create multiple AFTER triggers. You can control which AFTER trigger will execute first and last by using the sp_settriggerorder system stored procedure; the remaining triggers will fire in random order. If you define a DML trigger to execute after an event (which is the default behavior), it will only be fired on the successful completion of the event. Even if you execute a DML statement that does not affect any rows, any associated DML trigger is still fired. You can access rows that are changed in the base table using the inserted and deleted logical tables that are available in every DML trigger. The deleted table holds the rows that are removed from the base table, while the inserted table holds the rows that have been inserted or updated.

The example in Listing 9-43 creates a trigger that will fire when an UPDATE or DELETE statement is executed against the Store table in the AdventureWorks2008 database. The trigger checks the inserted and deleted tables to make sure the statement did not impact more than one record. If more than one record is updated or deleted, the statement is rolled back and the user receives an error message. Thus if you execute the UPDATE statement in Listing 9-43 without the WHERE clause, the trigger will roll back the transaction because you are trying to update every row in the table. If you uncomment the WHERE clause, the UPDATE statement will only affect one row and complete successfully.

Listing 9-43. *Syntax to Create a DML Trigger That Prevents Updating or Deleting More Than One Row in a Table at a Time*

```
USE AdventureWorks2008
GO


CREATE TRIGGER Sales.ModificationCheck
ON Sales.Store
AFTER UPDATE, DELETE
AS
IF (SELECT COUNT(*) FROM inserted ) > 1 OR
    (SELECT COUNT(*) FROM deleted) > 1
    BEGIN
        RAISERROR('You may only modify one row at a time.',10,1);
        ROLLBACK TRANSACTION
    END
GO


--Try to update multiple rows
UPDATE Sales.Store
SET Name = Name + '_1'
--WHERE Sales.Store.BusinessEntityID = 292
```

DDL Triggers

DDL triggers are fired in response to CREATE, ALTER, DROP, GRANT, DENY, REVOKE, or UPDATE STATISTICS statements. You can create DDL triggers in the context of a single database or an entire server instance. You cannot configure a DDL trigger to run instead of the event; they are only fired after the event. DDL triggers are a good way to prevent certain actions, such as a user dropping a table without first disabling the trigger. You can also use a DDL trigger to log alterations to the database or to perform an action, such as sending an email informing you of a change. Instead of using the inserted and deleted tables, you can access data about the changes being made using the EVENTDATA() function. That information is returned in XML form.

The example in Listing 9-44 creates a DDL trigger on the AdventureWorks2008 database that will not allow you to drop a table between the hours of 8:00 AM and 10:00 PM.

Listing 9-44. *Syntax to Create a DDL Trigger That Prevents Dropping a Table Between the Hours of 8:00 AM and 10:00 PM*

```
USE AdventureWorks2008
GO

CREATE TRIGGER DropTableCheck
ON DATABASE
FOR DROP_TABLE
AS
DECLARE @EventData AS Varchar(1000)
SELECT @EventData= EVENTDATA().value
('(/EVENT_INSTANCE/TSQLCommand/CommandText)[1]','nvarchar(max)')

DELCARE @Msg Varchar(1000)

IF (SELECT CAST(GETDATE() AS TIME)) > '08:00' AND
    (SELECT CAST(GETDATE() AS TIME)) < '22:00'
    BEGIN
      SET @Msg = 'The Command - "' + @EventData +
          '" is not allowed. You must drop tables during the maintenance window.'
      RAISERROR (@Msg,10, 1)
      ROLLBACK TRANSACTION
    END
GO

--Create a sample table
CREATE TABLE VeryImportantTable
(ID INT)
GO

--Try to drop the table
DROP TABLE VeryImportantTable
```

Logon Triggers

Logon triggers are fired in response to the LOGON event that occurs after a user is authenticated and before the actual connection is established to SQL Server. When you create a logon trigger, it applies to an entire SQL Server instance and is stored in the master database. Logon triggers are the only objects in this chapter that are not located somewhere under the Databases node in Object Explorer. You can find logon triggers in the Triggers folder under the Server Objects node. As with DDL triggers, logon triggers can only be fired after the event has occurred; however, logon triggers do not fire if a login attempt fails. Because the user is not actually connected when the logon trigger fires, any error messages and print statements that occur in the logon trigger are sent to the error log. As with DDL triggers, logon triggers also use the EVENTDATA() function to return information about the event.

The following sample in Listing 9-45 creates a logon trigger that only allows local logins or logins from a specific host. The Print statement will record the failed login attempt in the SQL Server error log.

Listing 9-45. *Syntax to Create a Logon Trigger*

```
CREATE TRIGGER HostCheck
ON ALL SERVER
FOR LOGON
AS
BEGIN
  DECLARE @ClientHost Varchar(1000)
  SET @ClientHost = EVENTDATA().value
  ('(/EVENT_INSTANCE/ClientHost)[1]', 'varchar(50)')

  IF @ClientHost NOT IN ('<local machine>','192.168.0.101')
     BEGIN
       Print 'Logon blocked for ' + @ClientHost
       ROLLBACK TRANSACTION
   END
END
GO
```

Working with the Common Language Runtime

The common language runtime (CLR) allows you to write stored procedures, triggers, user-defined functions, user-defined types, and user-defined aggregates using a .NET programming language that can be managed and executed from SQL Server. The purpose of this section is not to teach you how to write CLR code, but to discuss the management implications of using CLR in your environment.

Before you can implement CLR, you need to enable CLR integration by using the sp_configure system procedure, as shown in Listing 9-46. To disable CLR, change the value following the 'clr enabled' parameter from 1 to 0.

Listing 9-46. *Syntax to Enable CLR Integration Functionality*

```
sp_configure 'show advanced options', 1;
GO
RECONFIGURE;
GO
sp_configure 'clr enabled', 1;
GO
RECONFIGURE;
GO
```

CLR is not supported with lightweight pooling enabled because certain features will not work while running in fiber mode. To disable lightweight pooling, run the script shown in Listing 9-47.

Listing 9-47. *Syntax to Disable Lightweight Pooling*

```
sp_configure 'show advanced options', 1;
GO
RECONFIGURE;
GO
sp_configure 'lightweight pooling', 0;
GO
RECONFIGURE;
GO
```

CLR is implemented in SQL Server in the form of assemblies. An *assembly* is a compiled DLL file that is hosted within SQL Server. In order to use an assembly, you must first register it in SQL Server using the CREATE ASSEMBLY statement, as shown in Listing 9-48. To load a new version of an assembly, just change the CREATE keyword to ALTER.

Listing 9-48. *Syntax Used to Register an Assembly in SQL Server*

```
CREATE ASSEMBLY CLRProcDemo
FROM 'C:\ CLRProcDemo.dll'
WITH PERMISSION_SET = EXTERNAL_ACCESS
```

You can specify three different security levels when registering an assembly: SAFE, EXTERNAL_ACCESS, and UNSAFE. SAFE is the default setting that will be applied to an assembly if the permission set is not explicitly specified. The SAFE permission set is the most restrictive, allowing only internal computations and local data access. The EXTERNAL_ACCESS permission set has the same local data access as the SAFE permission set, but the EXTERNAL_ACCESS permission set can also access external resources, such as registry keys and files. The UNSAFE permission set gives an assembly unrestricted access to internal and external resources.

If you create an assembly with a permission set other than SAFE, you have to perform one of two actions in order to run the assembly. You can either set the TRUSTWORTHY database property to ON by running the statement ALTER DATABASE DatabaseName SET TRUSTWORTY ON, or sign the assembly with a strong key. Microsoft recommends that you sign the assembly with a strong key instead of setting the TRUSTWORTHY property to ON. To sign the assembly with a strong key, you need to create an asymmetric key from the assembly, create a login from the asymmetric key, and then grant UNSAFE or EXTERNAL_ACCESS to the login, as shown in Listing 9-49.

Listing 9-49. *Syntax Used to Sign an Assembly with a Strong Key*

```
USE master
GO
CREATE ASYMMETRIC KEY CLRProcDemoKey FROM EXECUTABLE FILE = 'C:\ CLRProcDemo.dll'
CREATE LOGIN CLRDemoLogin FROM ASYMMETRIC KEY CLRProcDemoKey
GRANT EXTERNAL ACCESS ASSEMBLY TO CLRDemoLogin
GO
```

Once you have registered the assembly, you can now create an object in SQL Server that references the assembly (see Listing 9-50). The AssemblyName is the name that was used to register the assembly in SQL Server. In this case, the AssemblyName is CLRProcDemo that was created in Listing 9-48. The ClassName and MethodName actually come from the DLL internally and are dependent on the names that were used within the DLL. Once you have created the procedure, you can execute it just as if it were any other stored procedure in SQL Server.

Listing 9-50. *Syntax to Create a Stored Procedure That References an Assembly*

```
CREATE PROCEDURE TestCLRStoredProc
AS
EXTERNAL NAME AssemblyName.ClassName.MethodName
```

To remove an assembly from the database, you can issue the DROP ASSEMBLY statement followed by the assembly name, as shown in Listing 9-51.

Listing 9-51. *Syntax to Remove an Assembly from a Database*

```
DROP ASSEMBLY CLRProcDemo
```

Summary

This chapter has covered creating and managing many of the database objects available in SQL Server 2008. You can perform most of the code listed in the chapter using the SQL Server GUI, but it is important to understand what is actually going on under the hood. Whenever we use the GUI, we always generate the SQL script to a new query window so we can review the code before actually applying it to the database. Now that we have discussed administering database objects, the next chapter will focus on how to create indexes to provide optimal performance and reduce the overhead needed to access the data in the database. Knowing when and how to use database objects and having the proper indexes will provide a better experience for both you and the end users.

CHAPTER 10

■ ■ ■

Indexing for Performance

Effectively creating indexes within your databases will single handedly provide the largest increase in application performance. Unfortunately, creating indexes incorrectly or without regard for the application's behavior can actually hinder performance. A good database administrator will pay close attention to the actions of the application and understand that you may have to be flexible with regard to the index creation tips, recommendations, and guidelines that you have researched. The purpose of this chapter is to enhance your understanding of indexes and help you with the development of your rules for creating indexes.

Index Vocabulary, Structure, and Concepts

Before we start discussing index creation and all the various tips to consider, let's make sure that we are on the same page in terms of the terminology used when discussing indexes. The next several sections on terminology will lay the groundwork for the examples and conversations regarding indexes that come later on in this chapter.

Heaps

When data is stored for a table within your database when no clustered indexes are present, the table is stored in what is called a *heap*. System objects, like `sys.indexes` and `sys.partitions`, with index ID values of zero identify the table as a heap table. In most instances, heaps are not the preferred method of storing your tables because of the access method required for retrieving data. When no indexes exist on a table, then scanning the entire table is the only method for retrieving data from the table. After the execution of a query against the table, SQL Server has to check every row in the table to determine if it meets the conditions of the query. The method of scanning an entire heap table is referred to as a *table scan*. Most of the time, table scans are not the most efficient method of retrieving data from a table; however, there are times when SQL Server optimizer will determine that a table scan is the most efficient method to retrieve the data. (We will review samples of the performance difference of table scans in the "Putting It All Together" section later in this chapter.)

Clustered Indexes

Clustered indexes are one of the two main types of indexes supported in SQL Server. A clustered index stores the rows of its underlying table in the sorted order of the clustered index keys. The clustered index keys are the column(s) you select to represent how you want data ordered on disk. Since the order of the table is determined by the clustered index, only one clustered index can be defined on a table. Clustered indexes are represented in system tables and views, like sys.objects and sys.partitions, by the value 1 in the index ID column.

Queries against tables that contain clustered indexes may perform at extremely fast rates or dreadfully slow rates. When indexes are involved, you can scan an entire index looking for the data that meets your criteria or seek a record based on the supplied criteria. In other words, if you are looking for an employee with an identification number of 100 and the table has a clustered index on the identification number, then SQL Server will seek employee 100, which is very fast. However, if you are looking for every employee who has a first name of Joe and you have a clustered index on an identification number, then SQL Server is going to scan the entire clustered index looking for every Joe. That can take a while if you have a large number of employees in the table. You will see multiple examples of clustered index scan performance later in the "Putting It All Together" section.

Nonclustered Indexes

Nonclustered indexes are the second main type of index supported in SQL Server. A nonclustered index contains the index key value and the row identifier for finding the rest of the data for every row in the table. Nonclustered indexes can be created on clustered index and heap tables. When a nonclustered index is created on a clustered index table, the row identifier holds the clustered index key and that key points to the actual data. If the nonclustered index exists on a heap table, then the row identifier points to the address of the data pages. Regardless of the table type, clustered or heap, retrieving the actual data pages requires additional steps, thus increasing IO. Ideally, you want to decrease IO, not increase it.

SQL Server 2008 allows you to create up to 999 clustered indexes on a given table, and you can specify the list of columns for each of those. But keep this in mind: Just because SQL Server 2008 allows you to perform certain actions does not mean that you are required to do so.

Nonclustered indexes are represented in SQL Server 2008 system tables and views with an index ID greater than 1. SQL Server 2008 will scan or seek on a nonclustered index when the index keys are useful in finding the data based on the criteria of the query being executed. We will cover index selection in more detail later in this chapter, but it is important to understand at this point that SQL Server 2008's query optimizer will determine the most useful index to return the results of the query in the fastest or an acceptable amount of time.

Structure of Indexes and the Heap

Indexes within SQL Server 2008 are stored in B-tree data structure. The B-tree data structure is divided into three basic parts: the root (top-most level of the tree), the leaf level (bottom-most portion of the tree), and the intermediate level (everything in between). The root and intermediate levels contain the keys specified during creation and depending on the index type, clustered or nonclustered index, the row identifier with the clustered index key or the address of the data pages. On the intermediate and leaf level pages, SQL Server uses a double linked list to navigate from page to page. Based on the search criteria of the query, SQL Server will traverse the tree starting at the root heading downward until it reaches the leaf level pages. Let's take a closer look at the structure of both types of indexes.

Clustered Index Structure

Keep in mind that clustered indexes determine the order of the data on disk. The key of a clustered index will be sorted in ascending or descending order. For the next couple of examples, let's assume that you have a table with over 300 employees in it. The employee table has several columns that include employee ID, first name, and last name. If you cluster the employee table on the employee ID, then Figure 10-1 demonstrates the structure of that clustered index on disk. The root level page contains employee ID 100 and 200, with pointers to the pages that are greater than 200 or less than 200. The intermediate level contains the key value of employee IDs 1 and 100 and 200 and 300, along with pointers to the page where that data is stored. The leaf level pages actually contain all the data of each employee ID within the table.

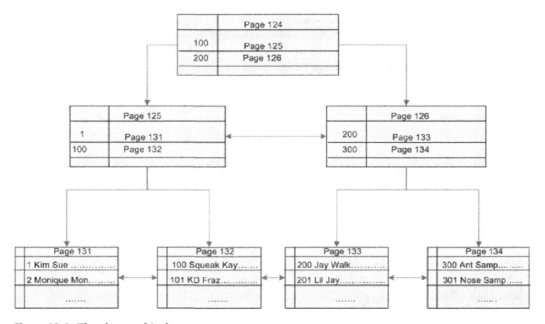

Figure 10-1. *The clustered index structure*

The following steps list the process that SQL Server goes through to retrieve data from clustered index structures.

1. Query the sys.system_internals_allocation_units to identify the root node page address for the index.

2. Compare the value from the query to the values on the root page.

3. Identify the uppermost key value that is less than or equal to the value from the query.

4. Trace the pointer to the page specified key value down to the next level.

5. Repeat steps 3 and 4 until you reach the leaf level pages.

6. Once the leaf level pages are reached, SQL Server searches through data pages looking for the query value. If no data pages are found, the query will return no results.

Nonclustered Index Structure

Nonclustered index structures look highly similar to the clustered index structures. Non-clustered indexes have three main levels as well: the root level, the leaf level, and the intermediate levels. The main difference between the clustered index structure and the nonclustered index structure is the data stored within the leaf level and the data row locator within the structure. Remember that the leaf level pages in a nonclustered index contain references to data pages or to index keys instead of the actual data.

Figure 10-2 shows the structure of the nonclustered index. The example uses a first name for the index key. The root level of the nonclustered index contains the first name along with the pointer to the next page and the data row locator. The intermediate level has the first name ranges divided evenly, as well as the next page and data row locators. The leaf level pages contain the keys, or first names, in this example. If the underlying table is organized by a clustered index, then the leaf level pages of the nonclustered index will contain clustered index keys (also called *data row locators*). If the underlying table is a heap, then the leaf level pages will contain pointers to data pages in the heap.

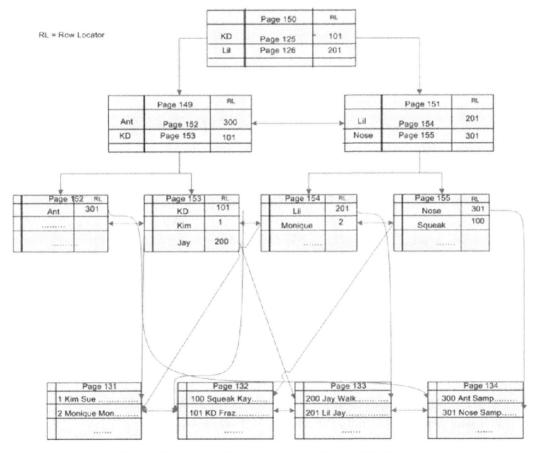

Figure 10-2. *The nonclustered indexes with pointers to the clustered index*

Heap Structure

We would like to briefly mention the structure of heaps in this section. Unlike clustered and nonclustered indexes, the data stored within a heap table has no structure. The data stored within a heap table is linked by the index allocation map (IAM) pages that are allocated for the object. The sys.system_internals_allocation_units systems object points to the first IAM page where the data is stored. Because of the lack of order within the heap, SQL Server has to scan each page of the entire heap to determine what data meets the criteria of any given query. Because of this, table scans on heaps are often times inefficient. You should avoid scans on heaps as much as possible.

Indexes Created by Constraints

In Chapter 9, we discussed constraints and the creation of their corresponding indexes. This section ensures you understand the terminology used when people mention primary and unique indexes.

Primary Indexes

What in the world is a primary index? I really don't know, but I have heard this term used frequently by non-database administrators. (Well, that's my story and I'm sticking to it.) Generally, most people who use the term *primary index* are actually referring to the index created after they specify the primary key for a table. The primary key can create a clustered or nonclustered index that forces uniqueness within the key values and does not allow null values. When someone says that the primary index is the main index used for retrieving data, just smile and say yes; the clustered index will determine the order of the data and will be used frequently. You can correct the person if you want, but we often find it easier to be subtle and slide the correct terms in there when you get the chance.

Unique Indexes

Unique indexes are created on the key columns of an index. A unique index forces distinctness among the data for the specified columns. Tables can have multiple unique indexes. Unique indexes allow nulls to exist in the key columns. From a SQL Server perspective, it does not matter if a unique index or a unique constraint is created first; the validation process of the data is the same, and the result will consist of a unique index. After creating the index, validation of the index keys occur for the data in the table to ensure that the values are unique.

The validation of the key values of a unique index happens before you insert data into the table. If you are attempting to insert multiple records into a table and one record violates the unique index, then none of the data will be inserted and the entire statement will fail unless you set the IGNORE_DUP_KEY option to ON.

In batches where unique indexes are violated, the IGNORE_DUP_KEY option allows insertion of the records that don't violate the unique index, while only the offenders fail. See "Creating Clustered and Nonclustered Indexes" later in this chapter for more information about the IGNORE_DUP_KEY option.

Other Ways to Categorize Indexes

There are many ways to categorize index types. The distinction between clustered and non-clustered is fundamental, and you'll commonly encounter the terms *primary index* and *unique index*. But there are other ways to divide indexes into different types. The following sections describe some of the types you'll encounter in your work as a DBA.

Composite Indexes

Composite indexes are those created on objects that contain multiple columns. Composite indexes may include up to 16 columns that are all from the same table or view. The combined column values of a composite index cannot be greater than 900 bytes. Pay close attention to the structure of your columns while creating your indexes. Make sure the index keys are in the same order as the WHERE clause of your queries. SQL Server is more likely to use the index when the two are in the same order.

Filtered Indexes

Filtered indexes are a new feature of SQL Server 2008 whereby you can create nonclustered indexes on subsets of data from the table. Think about a WHERE clause on a table: If you want to minimize the number of records retrieved from a table, then you specify a condition within the WHERE clause to prevent that data from being returned. Well, the filtered index works in a similar fashion—you specify the rules to exclude data from an index. Remember, nonclustered indexes contain rows for all the data within a table. Filtered indexes will prevent all of the data from being stored within the index.

Filtered indexes provide benefits like improved query performance and data storage. From a performance perspective, looking for data within a smaller subset of records will decrease the seek time and increase query performance. Filtered indexes will also utilize less space on disk because the index does not have to store a record for every row within the table. We will discuss some tips and recommendations in the "Creating Filtered Indexes" section later in this chapter.

XML Indexes

SQL Server 2008 supports indexes on the XML data type. XML indexes support two types: a primary index and a secondary index. The primary XML index must be created first and represents all of the tags, data, and paths for each row in the XML column within the table. To increase performance, you can create secondary XML indexes on the path, value, and properties of the XML column depending on how the XML columns are queried. Once you understand the data that will be retrieved from the XML column, spend some time designing the appropriate index strategy on the column.

Compressed Indexes

In Chapter 9, we discussed compression in great detail. We just want to reiterate that data compression is a configurable option for clustered and nonclustered indexes. The configurable options allow both row and page compression. Please review the "Compression" section in Chapter 9 for additional information.

Other Index Concepts and Terminology

The following sections describe other terms and concepts that you'll encounter when talking about indexes. Understanding and applying these concepts will increase your chances of creating effective and useful indexes.

Include Columns

Include columns are non-key columns stored on the leaf level of nonclustered indexes. Keep in mind that key columns of nonclustered indexes are stored at the intermediate and leaf levels of indexes, while include columns are only stored on the leaf levels. Include columns also allow you to bypass the restrictions set for the composite keys by allowing you to have more than 16 columns of a size larger than 900 bytes. You can have 1023 columns in an INCLUDE statement without a size limit on disk. The primary benefit of include columns and composite keys stem from the usefulness of covering your queries.

Covering Queries

Covering your query generally means having the values needed for the SELECT clause and the WHERE clause available in your nonclustered indexes. Because the data is available in your nonclustered indexes, SQL Server does not have to perform costly lookup operations to gather the remaining information needed for the query. Your first thought may be to cover all queries, but there is a cost associated with that. You have to be careful and determine just which queries you want to cover based on the priority of the queries within your system.

Searchable Arguments

Searchable arguments (SARGs) are mentioned in SQL Server when discussing methods for minimizing or filtering the results of a query. In other words, a searchable argument is used when comparing a constant to columns in WHERE clauses and ON statements in a JOIN clause. Examples of searchable arguments include the following:

- LastName = 'carstarphen'
- income > 50000
- birthMonth between 'January' and 'February'
- jobTitle like '%Administrator%'

Using SARGs are the methods SQL Server uses to identify an index to aid in data retrieval. When creating indexes, you definitely want to think about the frequently accessed searchable arguments used by the application.

Cardinality

When creating indexes in SQL Server, you always want to think about the cardinality of your data. *Cardinality* in SQL Server refers to the uniqueness of the data within the columns. The higher the cardinality, the less the data is duplicated in a given column. The lower the cardinality, the more the data is the same within the column. The query optimizer will utilize the cardinality of the data when determining the most efficient execution plan to use.

Indexes that have a lot of duplication, or low cardinality, will not be nearly as useful as an index with very little duplication, or a high cardinality. Think about a person table that has three columns in it: Social Security Number, Age, and Favorite Color (only basic colors). The Social Security Number column will have a higher cardinality than the Age column, which will have a higher cardinality than Favorite Color. When creating your indexes, you want to create them on Social Security number first, followed by age, and then by color if you absolutely have to. Clearly, looking for someone's Social Security number will be faster than finding a person by their favorite color. You are going to return more rows when searching by colors, requiring some additional filtering after returning the data.

Creating Indexes via T-SQL

The terminology discussed in the previous section is important for understanding the rest of the chapter, as well as for conversation and training sessions that you attend with other database administrators. However, there is more to creating indexes then just knowing the syntax and following tips and recommendations that you find from various sources. As a database administrator, you must ensure that the indexes created on your system do not hinder performance rather than improve it.

Understanding the usage patterns of your applications significantly improves your decision making when determining the indexes you create on your system. Because of the volume of queries executed on a system, covering every query with an exact index is usually not the best thing to do. When you understand the usage patterns of an application, you can make better decisions in terms of prioritizing the importance of frequently executed queries. Determining the indexes to create on your system then becomes an easier task.

Creating Clustered and Nonclustered Indexes

Creating clustered and nonclustered indexes in SQL Server is one of the fundamental tasks of database administrators. The general syntax is the same for creating each type. However, the issues to think about when you're in the planning stage can be different.

Issues When Creating Clustered Indexes

As discussed earlier, clustered indexes determine the order of the data for each table and are accessed frequently. When choosing your clustered indexes, think about the following points:

- *Data accessibility*: Think about how the data within the table is utilized and accessed. Are you going to be adding, updating, and deleting records often? Are you going to be bulk loading data daily or monthly and then retrieving data from the table all day long? Understanding the accessibility of the data will help you determine the key value.

- *Narrow keys*: Remember that every nonclustered index will contain the clustered index key. So large clustered index keys could potentially cause fragmentation problems in nonclustered index pages. Just keep narrow keys in mind while determining the clustered index key.

- *Uniqueness*: Unique values for clustered index keys enable queries that use the clustered index (as well as queries that use the nonclustered index and need to lookup the data associated with the data row locator) more efficient. SQL Server has to force uniqueness when data is inserted into a clustered index, which cost IO and processing time. Creating a unique key yourself is the preferred method.

- *Sequential keys*: Consider choosing a clustered index key that is sequential in terms of time or numbers. If the order of your clustered key is sequential, then inserting data will always occur in a fashion that minimizes page splits. The data is added to the end of pages, minimizing the cost of ordering all of your data.

- *Static keys*: Choose clustered index keys that will not be modified. If the modification of the clustered index key occurs, then all of the nonclustered indexes associated with the key will also require updates. The table will also have to reorder the data if the key value moves to another page. Clearly, you can see how costly this operation would be on your system if updates happened frequently.

- *Order By columns*: Columns that are often used in ORDER BY clauses may be candidates for clustered indexes. Remember, the data will be ordered based on the key values in the clustered index creation.

- JOIN *clauses*: The primary table that contains the column used for joining multiple tables together may prove to be beneficial for clustered indexes. This option really coincides with understanding your data and usage patterns.

Think seriously about these issues when creating a clustered index because the performance of your application depends on your making correct and reasonable choices.

Issues When Creating Nonclustered Indexes

There are a number of items to consider before creating nonclustered indexes. Nonclustered indexes are equally important as the clustered indexes that we just discussed. In fact, you might find that you rely on nonclustered indexes more than on your clustered indexes to fulfill the requests of queries. Following are some things to think about:

- *Data accessibility*: Yes, accessibility is important for nonclustered indexes, too. Think about your data access patterns a step further than you did with the clustered indexes. Clustered indexes focus on the structure of your data. Nonclustered indexes should focus on the various types of questions that the data will answer. For example, how many accounts were opened in the past week?

- *Priority queries*: Make sure you start creating indexes for the highest priority, most frequently accessed queries first. If you focus on the highest priority queries first, you will ensure that the response time of the application is sufficient while you work on the other queries over time.

- *Cover your queries*: When determining the index keys for your high-priority queries, think about covering your queries. Depending on the query, you may want to cover the SELECT and WHERE clauses of those queries. Spend some time analyzing your queries and determining what the best strategy is to cover the queries.

- *Don't cover everything*: Although SQL Server allows you to cover every column in a query, that doesn't mean you should. Just because you increase the performance of one query does not mean you will not impact the other queries that write to that table.

- *Don't over index*: Remember, all the data for the key values that you choose will be stored in the nonclustered index as well as in the table. Every time the table is inserted, updated, or deleted, every nonclustered index whose key columns are modified will be impacted. Be careful not to over index a table such that performance is impacted. Review the "Post-Index Creation" section for more information on determining the cost of writes to indexes.

- *Uniqueness*: Try to create nonclustered indexes on key columns where the cardinality or selectivity is high. The query optimizer will be more likely to use those nonclustered indexes instead of doing a table scan.

- JOIN clauses: Pay attention to columns listed in JOIN clauses. Parent/child joins are common. Parent tables are typically accessed through their primary keys, which often correspond to their clustered indexes. What is often overlooked, though, are the foreign key values in the child tables. Consider indexing those using nonclustered indexes. For example, you might create a nonclustered index on the order_number column in a line_items table.

Nonclustered indexes will be utilized frequently within your application and can provide significant performance improvements. Just keep in mind that adding nonclustered indexes incorrectly could potentially cause performance problems. So plan your indexes before implementation.

Creating an Index

Finally, we will actually create some indexes. The syntax for index creation is fairly straightforward. The following script shows the create index syntax:

```
CREATE [CLUSTERED | NONCLUSTERED] INDEX  index_name
ON <object>(column [ASC | DESC], [,...])
[INCLUDE ( column_name [,...n])
[WITH (relational_index_options [,...n])
```

The preceding code shows you how to build composite indexes, which are indexes with multiple columns. You can also see the syntax for specifying the relational index options that you want to use. Let's go ahead and use the syntax in some examples. The first two examples create a clustered and nonclustered index with the default option values:

```
USE AdventureWorks2008
GO

CREATE CLUSTERED INDEX ix_bookId
ON apWriter.Books(bookId)

CREATE NONCLUSTERED INDEX ix_Title
ON apWriter.Books(Title)
```

As you create more indexes, you should take advantage of relational index options. When you create an index, you can specify the following:

- `ALLOW_ROW_LOCKS`: Allows the Database Engine to use row locks if it deems them necessary.

- `ALLOW_PAGE_LOCKS`: Allows the Database Engine to use page locks if necessary.

- `DATA_COMPRESSION`: Identifies the type of compression you want used for the clustered and nonclustered indexes. The available options are as follows: `NONE` (indicating that you don't want the data compressed), `ROW` (to compress data row by row), and `PAGE` (to compress entire pages at a time).

- `DROP_EXISTING`: Allows the dropping of a named index prior to rebuilding the index. The index names must be identical, even though you can change the definition of the index. We have mixed feelings about using this option. It removes the benefit of online index operations, which allow the index to still be used during the rebuild process. If you need to change the definition of an index, you can create another index and drop the previous one once you are done. On the other hand, this option is helpful if you are recreating an index mentioned in any hints that your application places into its queries. Obviously, you would want your newly rebuilt index to have the same name in that case. Regardless of our opinion, the choice exists for you to use.

- `FILLFACTOR`: Determines how much free space remains on a leaf level page when creating and rebuilding indexes. The default value is 0, or 100% full. We generally specify a lesser `FILLFACTOR` option on indexes that are going to have records inserted within the index instead of at the bottom or end of the page. That's because writes that result in new index entries in the middle of a page can lead to *page splits*. Frequent page splits will influence performance because of the cost of the split and fragmentation created within the index.

- `IGNORE_DUP_KEY`: Prevents records that violate a unique constraint from causing the entire batch inserts or updates to fail. Without enabling this option, one record that violates the unique constraint will cause all the records not to be written to the table.

- `MAXDOP`: Gives you the opportunity to override the server setting for the maximum degree of parallelism used for the index operations. The available options are as follows: 1 (prevents parallel execution), any number greater than 1 (specifies the number of parallel executions allowed up to 64), and 0 (uses the appropriate number of processors based on the current load of the system).

- `ONLINE`: Allows you to create, rebuild, or drop indexes without preventing user access to the data in the underlying table. By default, this option is set to off, which causes the underlying table to be locked, thereby preventing user access. Tables that contain large object (LOB) data types like Varchar(Max), Varchar(Binary), and XML, cannot be rebuilt while online. There are also a couple of other conditions that prevent online index maintenance. Consider using `ONLINE` where possible to limit the impact of index maintenance to your application users. Online index operations are Enterprise Edition features only.

- `PAD_INDEX`: When specified with `FILLFACTOR`, determines the amount of free space stored on the intermediate level pages of an index. The `PAD_INDEX` option will use the same percentage specified in the `FILLFACTOR` option. The intermediate level page has to be large enough to store at least two records, and if the `FILLFACTOR` is not large enough, then the Database Engine will override the `FILLFACTOR` percentage internally.

- `SORT_IN_TEMPDB`: Identifies the location where the temporary sorting of the index will take place. If `tempdb` is stored on a separate physical drive from the data, then the index creation process should complete in a shorter amount of time. Bear in mind, though, that sorting the data in a separate database requires that SQL Server move the data to that target database. For that reason, sorting in `tempdb` increases the amount of disk space needed over the default behavior.

- `STATISTICS_NORECOMPUTE`: Gives you the option not to update statistics after the index is created or rebuilt. The default value is no, which forces the statistics to update automatically. You may want to experiment with this option if `AUTO UPDATE STATISTICS` is giving you a problem, specifically on larger tables.

Now let's create some covering indexes with composite keys and include columns. You can also play with some of the relational index options. The following code example demonstrates the creation of a composite key with the `FILLFACTOR` option set to 75% and online operations turned on. The `FILLFACTOR` for this index is set because you can easily see new people being added and the index having to make room for their last names to fit on the respective pages. The goal is to minimize the page splits every time a new person is added, so we leave some free space on the leaf level pages at creation time.

```
USE AdventureWorks2008
GO

CREATE NONCLUSTERED INDEX ix_peronName
ON person.Person(LastName, FirstName, MiddleName)
WITH (FILLFACTOR = 75, ONLINE = ON, MAXDOP = 2)
```

Now, let's say you have decided that you want the middle name as a key value for the previously created index. Since the middle name is returned in most of the queries, you decide to include the middle name to reduce lookups on the primary key. You also don't want to break the index hints that are in place, so you keep the same name. The following code shows an example of the `DROP_EXISITNG` option with an `INCLUDE` option:

```
USE AdventureWorks2008
GO

CREATE NONCLUSTERED INDEX ix_peronName
ON person.Person(LastName, FirstName)
INCLUDE (MiddleName)
WITH (FILLFACTOR = 75, ONLINE = ON, MAXDOP = 2, DROP_EXISTING = ON)
```

Lastly, we want to show you an example of using data compression with your index creation statement. The following code creates an index with page data compression enabled:

```
USE AdventureWorks2008
GO
CREATE NONCLUSTERED INDEX ix_peronName6
ON person.Person(LastName, FirstName, MiddleName)
INCLUDE (Suffix,Title)
WITH (FILLFACTOR = 75, ONLINE = ON, DATA_COMPRESSION = PAGE)
```

Compression not only saves disk space, but sometimes it can actually increase performance. That's because using compression means more entries can fit on a page, resulting in fewer pages of IO.

Creating Unique and Primary Key Indexes

Creating unique and primary key indexes are methods of ensuring distinctness within key columns. Remember a table can have only one primary key but multiple unique indexes. Unique indexes can exist as both clustered and nonclustered indexes. Frequently, the primary key is the clustered index on a table. Creating unique indexes requires you to understand the data. The following list provides some things you should consider before creating primary keys and unique indexes:

- *Uniqueness within the data*: Make sure the keys of an index will truly be unique within the context of the data. Think through as many scenarios as possible prior to implementing a unique index. When designing a database environment, some things sound like they should be unique when in actuality opportunities for duplication exist. For example, you may decide that every Social Security number will be unique within your environment. That sounds great until you get a duplicated Social Security number. (Trust us, it happens.) Make sure you think through your unique keys so that you don't create a constraint that will come back to haunt you down the road.

- *Nulls in key columns*: Keep in mind that primary keys force uniqueness and don't allow nulls in the key columns, whereas unique indexes do allow nulls.

- *Updates to keys*: You can update the key of a unique index, but not the key of a primary index.

- *Query optimizations*: Don't overlook possible query optimizations that can come about from choices you make at index creation time. For example, when you are creating an index on one or more columns and your data is such that it is valid to create that index as a unique index, then do so. A unique index helps the query optimizer by letting the it know that the data within the key will be unique. Don't miss out on the opportunity to improve the performance of your system by not taking advantage of unique index creation opportunities.

The syntax for creating a unique clustered or nonclustered index is similar to that for creating clustered and nonclustered indexes. The only difference comes from the keyword UNIQUE. By default, primary key constraints create unique clustered indexes, and unique constraints create unique indexes. However, you are the one in control. If you want the primary key represented by a unique nonclustered index, then you can create the index that way. The following code demonstrates how to create unique indexes:

```
CREATE UNIQUE [CLUSTERED | NONCLUSTERED] INDEX  index_name
ON <object>(column [ASC | DESC], [,...])
[INCLUDE ( column_name [,...n])
[WITH (relational_index_options [,...n])
```

Now that you understand the syntax, review the following code and create a unique clustered and nonclustered index:

```
USE AdventureWorks2008
GO


CREATE UNIQUE CLUSTERED INDEX ix_bookId
ON apWriter.Books2(bookId)
WITH(ONLINE = ON, FILLFACTOR = 95, DROP_EXISTING = ON)

USE AdventureWorks2008
GO
CREATE UNIQUE NONCLUSTERED INDEX ix_AuthorTitle
ON apWriter.Books2(Title)
WITH(IGNORE_DUP_KEY = ON, ONLINE = ON, DROP_EXISTING = ON)
```

The first code example re-creates a clustered index on the example database, specifying the FILLFACTOR and an online index operation. The second example re-creates an index, using the same name but removing a key column. The re-creation is done with the index online. The option IGNORE_DUP_KEY is enabled, preventing records that violate unique constraints from causing the entire batch modification to fail.

Creating Filtered Indexes

With the introduction of filtered indexes in SQL Server 2008, you can create indexes for subsets of data. The data stored within a filtered index is restricted only to rows meeting the WHERE clause that you specify. Consider filtered indexes as nonclustered indexes optimized for performance. With a smaller subset of data, retrievals from a filtered index will be faster, storage of the index on disk will be smaller, and maintenance of the index will cost less and happen less frequently because writes only occur when data meeting the filter specification is modified. The following list describes some things that you should consider before creating filtered indexes.

- *Data accessibility*: When creating filtered indexes, understanding your data is even more important. Make sure that your filtered indexes will be for subsets of data that are meaningful for your application. If you frequently query only Ford automobiles by the number of seating positions, then a filtered index on number_of_seats specifying where make="Ford" might make sense. But specifying where make="GM" in that case would be silly.

- *Choose subsets wisely*: When deciding to create a filtered index on a subset of data, make sure the query optimizer will find the filtered index useful. Think about using filtered indexes to help queries that filter through unpopulated key values or useless values that the application does not care about. Have you ever supported an application that stopped using a particular value in a field? The primary type of data queried used to be 1–3, but now the new version of the application only populates and retrieves values 5–7. Filtered indexes are useful in such scenarios because they keep currently unused key values out of your nonclustered indexes.

- *Cover your queries*: Make sure the query optimizer utilizes your filtered indexes by ensuring that they cover the intended queries. Limit the number of includes and key columns that exist in the filtered indexes. If the performance of your queries is fast enough just from creating filtered indexes alone, then you may not even have to add any include columns to those indexes. The bottom line: Make sure unused columns are not added to your indexes.

To create a filtered index, write a WHERE clause into your creation statement. The following syntax shows how and where to do that:

```
CREATE [CLUSTERED | NONCLUSTERED] INDEX  index_name
ON <object>(column [ASC | DESC], [,...])
[INCLUDE ( column_name [,...n])
WHERE <filter_predicate>
[WITH (relational_index_options [,...n])
```

One example to demonstrate the usefulness of filtered indexes comes from an invoice system. Companies often provide goods and services for their customers and bill them later. These companies keep track of the invoices that they mail their customers and often generate reports or retrieve information pertaining to the unpaid invoices. With filtered indexes, you can create an index that only contains unpaid invoices. Such an index might be very useful when created on a table containing all invoices. Imagine a collection group that queries the table a number of times to contact customers for payment. Having a small index specifically covering customers with amounts due will tend to make the collection's groups queries run faster than they would if they each had to slog through an index including all of the older, paid-for orders.

The following code is an example of a script that creates a table and the appropriate indexes for the scenario we've just described:

```
USE AdventureWorks2008
CREATE TABLE dbo.Invoice
(
 InvoiceId INT IDENTITY(1,1),
 CompanyName VARCHAR(200),
 isPaid smallint
)
GO

CREATE CLUSTERED INDEX ix_Invoice
ON dbo.Invoice(InvoiceId)
GO

CREATE NONCLUSTERED INDEX ix_FilterUnPaid
ON dbo.Invoice(inVoiceStatus) include(companyName)
WHERE isPaid = 0
```

Reviewing this code, you can see that it creates an invoice table, a clustered index, and a nonclustered index. The nonclustered index is the filtered index that restricts data to rows where isPaid = 0. If you want to see the indexes work, use the following code to add data to the table:

```
INSERT INTO dbo.Invoice
(CompanyName,isPaid)
VALUES('Apress',0),
('Apress1',0),
('Sylvester123',1)
```

Once you have inserted the data, execute the query in Listing 10-1. Results of the query are shown in Figure 10-3.

Listing 10-1. *SQL Query Used to Retrieve Information from the Invoice Table with isPaid = 1.*

```
SELECT CompanyName
FROM dbo.Invoice
WHERE isPaid = 1
```

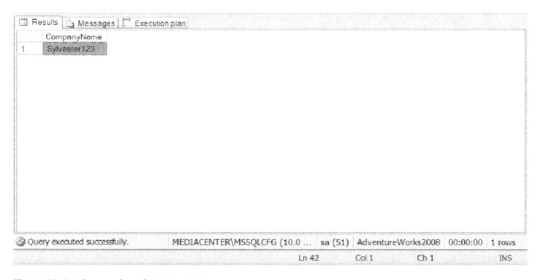

Figure 10-3. *The results of Listing 10-1*

To view the indexes utilized during execution of the query, turn on the option to Include the Actual Execution Plan and re-run the preceding query. Figure 10-4 shows the execution plan used for the query.

Figure 10-4. *The execution plan from Listing 10-1*

The plan in Figure 10-4 shows that the query executed using the clustered index on the invoice table. The filtered index was not used because it only covers the case where isPaid=0, not where isPaid=1.

So the index scan has to be performed on the clustered index. Now let's see what happens when you modify the query to retrieve data that has not been paid. Execute the query in Listing 10-2 and see the results in Figure 10-5.

Listing 10-2. *SQL Statement to Retrieve the Invoices from the Invoice Table Where isPaid = 0*

```
SELECT CompanyName
FROM dbo.Invoice
WHERE isPaid= 0
```

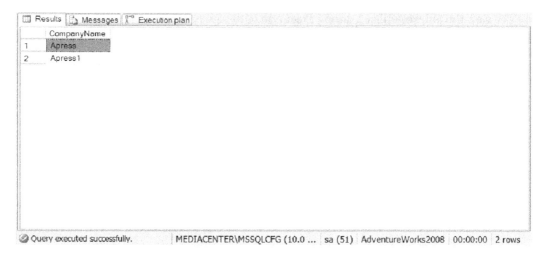

Figure 10-5. *The results of Listing 10-2*

Now, review the execution plan of Listing 10-2, as shown in Figure 10-6. This time it shows that the optimizer was able to use the filtered index.

Figure 10-6. *The execution plan for Listing 10-2*

Filtered indexes can be very powerful. Don't go crazy with them, but it's worth researching to see whether you have opportunity to use them in your own environment.

Creating XML Indexes

SQL Server 2008 allows you to create two types of indexes on your XML data types: a primary XML index and a secondary XML index. Combined, the two index types cover the paths, values, properties, and tags within your XML column. Before creating XML indexes on a table, you must first create a clustered index. The clustered index is required in XML indexes to make sure that XML indexes can fit into existing partition schemas. Keep in mind that XML columns are large, as large as 2 GB, and that they are stored in binary large objects (BLOBs). If your application is utilizing XML columns frequently, you may want to spend some time understanding how XML indexes can benefit your system. The syntax for creating a primary and secondary index is straightforward:

```
CREATE [PRIMARY] XML INDEX index_name
    ON <object> (xml_column_name)
  [USING XML INDEX xml_index_name
   [ FOR { VALUE| PATH |  PROPERTY} ] ]
[ WITH  ( <xml_index_option> [ ,...n]  ]
```

You will notice that an option exists to specify whether you are creating a primary XML index. When creating a secondary XML index, you simply employ the USING XML INDEX option to identify which primary XML index you are associating the index to. Then specify the FOR option to say whether your secondary index will be a value, path, or property index.

Let's create a table that stores XML execution plans. We'll use that table as the basis for creating primary and secondary XML indexes. Remember, we need a clustered, primary key on the table in order to create a primary XML index. Here's the table creation statement:

```
CREATE TABLE execPlans
( execPlanId INT IDENTITY(1,1),
 executionPlan XML

CONSTRAINT [PK_execPlans] PRIMARY KEY CLUSTERED
(
 [execPlanId] ASC
))
GO
```

Primary XML Indexes

You must create a primary XML index before creating any secondary indexes. A primary XML index arranges all tags, paths, and values of the data stored in the XML column. A primary XML index breaks an XML string down into multiple rows that represent the nodes of the XML BLOB. The values of the tags are returned when the XML column is queried. Because primary XML indexes contain the values of the tags, using primary XML indexes increases the performance of your queries when looking for values within the XML column.

The following example shows you how to create a primary XML index on the recently created table:

```
CREATE PRIMARY XML INDEX pindexExecPlan
ON execPlans(executionPlan)

GO
```

Secondary XML Indexes

After you have created a primary XML index on a column, you have the option of creating one or more secondary XML indexes on the same column. There are three types of secondary XML indexes that you can create: path, value, and property. The type of queries executed against the column should drive the secondary index types that you create. For example:

- Creating a path index may increase the performance of application queries searching for paths within an XML document.

- A secondary index on a specific property can help queries that look at specific property values within one or more XML tags.

- Create value indexes to support queries that look at specific values enclosed by XML tags.

Now, let's create a secondary index that is a path index because we frequently look for missing index tags within the XML string. Here is our secondary index creation statement:

```
CREATE XML INDEX sindexExecPlan
ON execPlans(executionPlan)
 USING XML INDEX pindexExecPlan
 FOR PATH
```

Creating Indexes Using the GUI

SQL Server Management Studio (SSMS) allows you to create clustered and nonclustered indexes from a GUI interface. Often times, we utilize SSMS to review the include columns of an index or to modify an index quickly. The purpose of this section is to ensure that you can create and modify clustered and and nonclustered indexes from within SSMS.

Creating an Example Table

First connect to an instance of SQL Server 2008 using SSMS and navigate to the database of your choice. To make sure you have a common starting point, create a table with five columns. Review the GUI creation of the table, shown in Figure 10-7. For simplicity, the name of the table is table1 with column1, column2, and so on. Make one of the columns (say, column1) an integer, and specify it as the identity column. The remaining data types of the other columns are not important, but for demo purposes, make sure the columns are not BLOB data types.

Figure 10-7. *Column creation within the GUI*

Once you have added the columns, save the table, name it, and exit the column creation screen. Next, navigate to the table you just created by expanding the Tables folder. Once you arrive at the table, click on the plus sign next to the table name and select the Indexes folder. That section should be empty.

Creating a Clustered Index via the GUI

To create a new index, right-click on the Indexes folder and select New Index. Figure 10-8 shows the General section of the index creation screen.

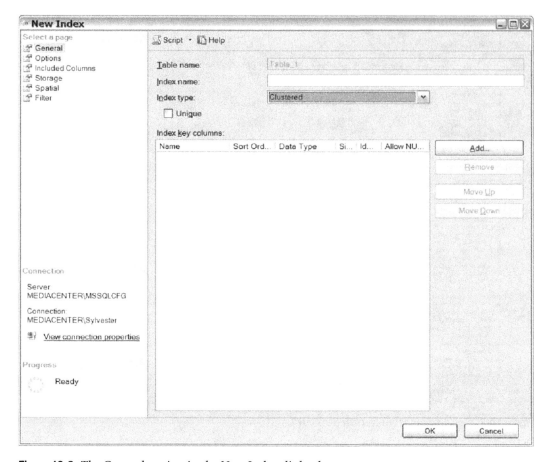

Figure 10-8. *The General section in the New Index dialog box*

In the General section, name your index by populating the Index Name text box. Then, click on the Index Type drop-down list and select the type of index. You can choose from Clustered, Nonclustered, Primary XML, and Spatial. For the current example, select the Clustered index option, and then click on the Add button. You'll be taken to a Select Columns dialog, resembling Figure 10-9. The dialog displays all the columns within the table. Select the identity column that you created for your clustered index and click OK.

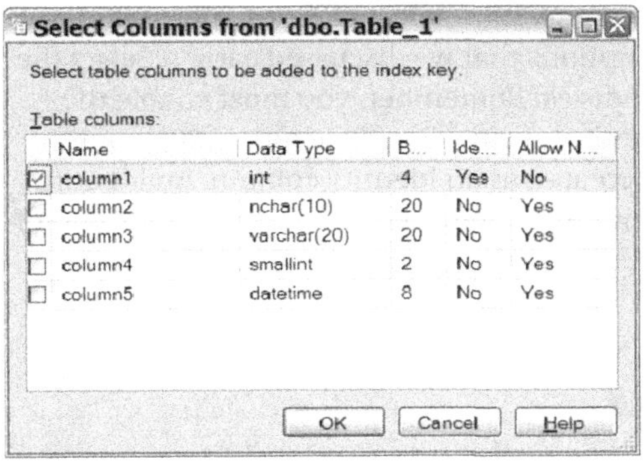

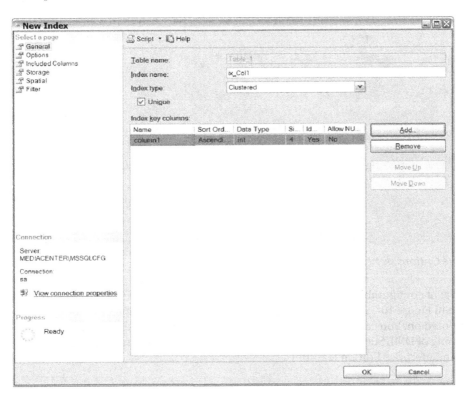

Figure 10-9. *The Select Columns dialog for adding columns to an index*

After you have selected the columns that you want added to the index, there should be information about the column(s) displayed for you under the Index Key Columns area, shown in Figure 10-10. Review that area and determine if additional columns are needed and that you have selected the correct columns. If you want the key columns to be unique, check the box for that option.

Figure 10-10. *The New Index dialog after you have selected the index columns*

Once you reviewed the information in the General section, select Options. The Options section (see Figure 10-11) lists the relational index options that we discussed earlier. Select the relational options that you want enabled on your indexes. Remember, you must enable the Set Fill Factor option in order to select the Pad Index box. Leave the fill factor at 100% for this example because the clustered index key has been created as an identity column. An identity column always increases in value, meaning that new entries will always be added to the end of the index, never into the middle.

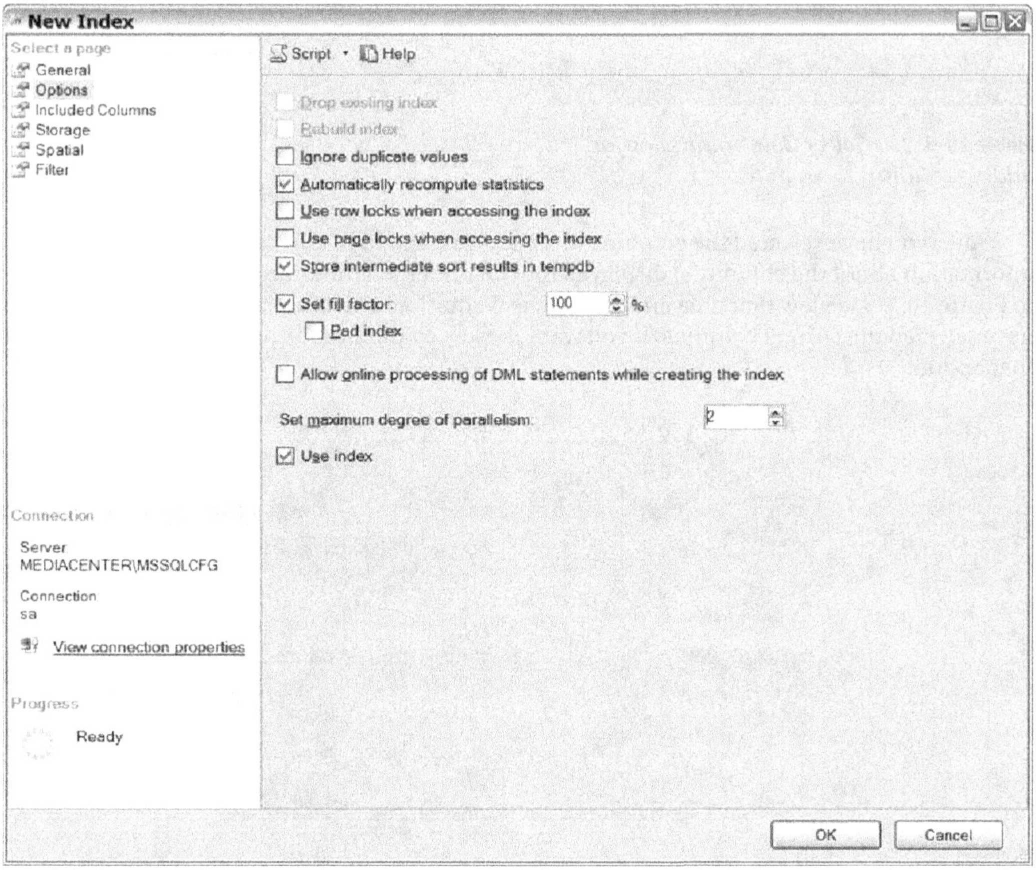

Figure 10-11. *The Options section in the New Index dialog*

The next set of configurable options available for the clustered index is in the Storage section, shown in Figure 10-12. The Storage section allows you to determine what filegroup an index will be stored on. You can also enable online index operations by checking the box Allow Online Processing of DML Statements While Creating the Index. (Remember that online index processing is an Enterprise Edition feature.)

Note As discussed in the Chapter 2, spreading your indexes across multiple physical drives may provide performance improvements. To do this, create separate filegroups and then assign different indexes to different filegroups.

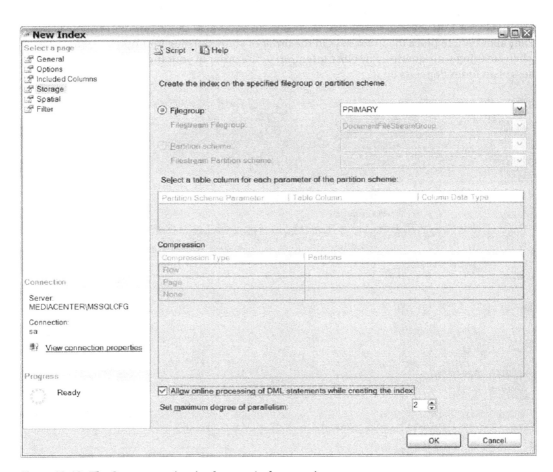

Figure 10-12. *The Storage section in the new index creation process*

There are three remaining sections: Included Columns, Spatial, and Filter, but they don't apply to clustered indexes. Ignore those, and click on OK to create your new index. You should see the created index under the Indexes folder on the left side of your SSMS screen. You may have to refresh the folder before the index shows up.

Creating a Nonclustered Index via the GUI

Now that you have created a clustered index, let's go through the process of creating a non-clustered index. Right-click on the Indexes folder and select New Index. In the General section, shown in Figure 10-13, populate the name of your index and select Nonclustered as the index type from the drop-down list. Click on the Add button, and select the columns that you want for the index key. For this demonstration, select two columns: column2 and column3. Click on the OK button, and you will see the two columns that you added listed in the Index Key Columns area. You will also notice that the Move Up and Move Down buttons are now active. They allow you to place the index keys in the order of your choosing for improved efficiency when covering your queries. Pay close attention to the order of your index keys—the usefulness of an index depends on it.

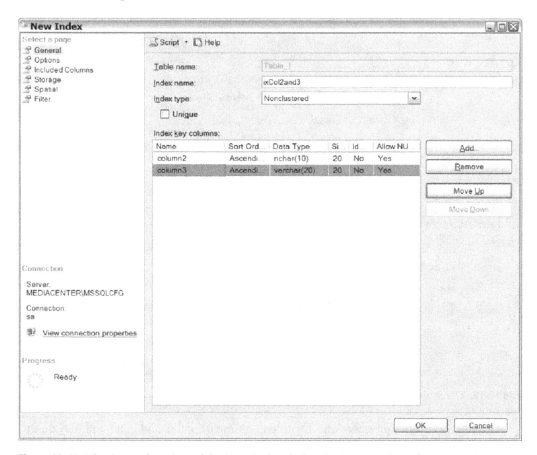

Figure 10-13. *The General section of the New Index dialog during creation of a composite non-clustered index*

The Options section lets you specify relational index options for nonclustered indexes. Because we talked about this section already, we are going to move on to the Included Columns section. Keep in mind, included columns are those that are stored on the leaf level pages of a nonclustered index to aid in covering your queries.

Figure 10-14 displays the Included Columns page. Click on the Add button to specify columns that you want included. Adding nonkey columns to the Included Columns section works the same as adding key columns to the index. Click Add, choose the columns you want, click OK, and the nonkey columns area is populated with the columns you selected. Remember that the clustered index key is stored on all leaf level pages, so there is no need to include the clustered index column.

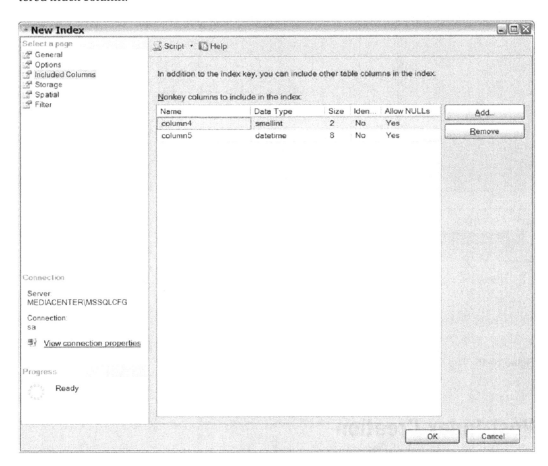

Figure 10-14. *The Included Columns section of the new index creation process*

The last section of the New Index dialog is the Filtered section, shown in Figure 10-15. The Filtered section enables you to designate the FILTER clause to apply to a nonclustered index. The area consists of a big white box for you to add your filter, which is essentially a WHERE clause that you would write in any SQL query. However, do not write the word "where." Simply write one or more conditions, such as the one shown in Figure 10-15. Separate those conditions using keywords like AND and OR.

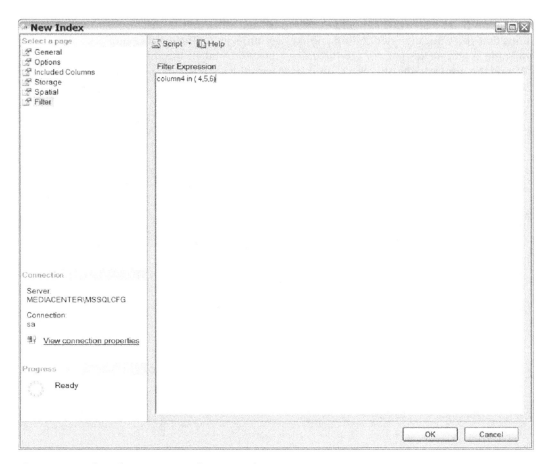

Figure 10-15. *The Filter section in the new index creation process*

Post-Index Creation

Creating indexes within SQL Server is an art, not a science. The tips, tricks and recommendations for creating indexes are useful starting points. If you think you can just follow that information, create the indexes in your environment, and not have to worry about indexes again, then you are mistaken. The more complex the system, the harder it is to apply best practices without your personal modification. As the database administrator, your role is to add your own flavor, the artistic piece to your database system to make sure everything runs as smoothly as possible. We would love to provide you with some gold nuggets, some guaranteed rules that will work in every environment, but the truth is that everything depends on the environment you are supporting. However, we will provide you with some processes that we do before and after creating indexes to ensure that they are helping our environment and not hurting it.

Performance of Insert, Update, and Delete Statements

Keep an eye on the performance of insert, update, and delete statements before and after adding indexes to a table. To that end, be sure to gather statistical data about a table before adding an index to it. Following is some of the information that we gather before adding indexes:

- *The row count and size of the table in bytes*: The number of rows and the table's projected growth in terms of rows and size helps you determine the amount of time that you spend analyzing the creation of the index. If the table is relatively small, and will remain small, but there is just a slow application query running against it, then you should quickly add an index and move on. If the poorly performing query is on a large table with a large number of records, then you should spend more time in the analysis phase.

- *The current list of indexes that exist on the table*: The indexes that exist on the table are important for a couple of different reasons. You want to make sure you know what indexes exists so you don't duplicate an index. Reviewing the current indexes on a table may also lead you down the path that determines that you don't need to create an additional index. You may be able to add an additional clause in your query to take advantage of an existing index or just include a column to an existing index.

- *The average response times of frequent queries against the table*: The response times of the queries that are frequently executed against the object in question are important. With them, you can determine what the performance of those queries is after the index addition. The last thing you want is to speed up one query and dramatically slow down the other queries.

- *The frequency and type of access to the table*: For example, is the table used for a lot of reads, or does it experience heavy write volumes? Understanding the type of access against the table will ultimately help drive your indexing strategy. If the table is heavily used for reads and very little for writes, then you can cover more queries and over index because of the little cost of writes. If the table is heavily used for writes or both reads and writes, then you have to consider the cost of the writes and be careful when covering your queries.

- *The projected growth rate of the table*: The projected growth rate just helps you plan your indexing strategy better. Just because a table is small today, doesn't mean it will be small three, six, or 12 months from now. Make sure the index strategy that you deploy considers those facts.

Determining the speed of the writes on a table is essential prior to index creation. In SQL Server 2008, there are several methods for capturing this information. Those who control data access via stored procedures have it easy. You can query the system catalog for stored procedures that reference the table in question. Then you can capture the statistics on those stored procedures before and after you have created an index on the table and compare the results.

In order to gather the stats on your procedures or capture the queries executed against the objects, you can utilize SQL Server Profiler for access to that table, or you can query SYS.DM_EXEC_QUERY_STATS Dynamic Management View (DMV) and search for the queries that access those tables. Once you find the queries in the DMV, you can use the execution count along with total_elapsed_time and a series of other columns to quickly compute the average runtime of queries against the table. It doesn't matter if you use SYS.DM_EXEC_QUERY_STATS or the Profiler—you should be able capture some statistics to use before and after the index creation on the table. Armed with information, go ahead and create the index that you plan to create, preferably in a test environment. For those who have good QA environments with load testing tools, then your environment may be a good place to verify that the index creation will not negatively affect the application. Set up your load testing tool to simulate a series of application functions, including the one that you plan on fixing with the addition of the new index. Hopefully, your tool will enable you to see the response times of all the queries giving you a good baseline. After you apply the index, re-run the test and compare your results. If the difference in response times is acceptable, then apply the index to your production environment and monitor your system. Monitor the averages of your queries to ensure their durations are acceptable to the application users. Monitor your indexes for as long as you need to make sure the performance is what you expected.

■**Note** One other useful DMV is SYS.DM_DB_INDEX_USAGE_STATS. This view allows you to see how often a newly created index is actually used. We cover useful dynamic management views in the following section.

Useful Dynamic Management Views

When determining the usefulness of your indexes, identifying statistics on the queries that execute against objects, and validating some of the suggestions for index creations, we frequently use DMVs. The DMVs in question are SYS.DM_EXEC_QUERY_STATS, SYS.DM_DB_INDEX_USAGE_STATS, and the series of DMVs associated with the missing index feature in SQL Server 2008.

SYS.DM_EXEC_QUERY_STATS

The SYS.DM_EXEC_QUERY_STATS view captures the queries executed against SQL Server. The view gives information about CPU usage, the physical reads and writes, the execution times in terms of how long a query runs, the number of times it runs, and much more. See Figure 10-16 for some sample output from querying SYS.DM_EXEC_QUERY_STATS.

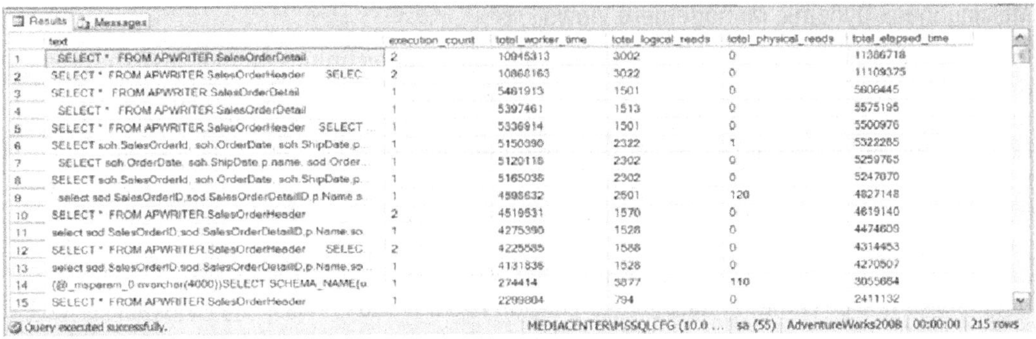

	text	execution_count	total_worker_time	total_logical_reads	total_physical_reads	total_elapsed_time
1	SELECT * FROM APWRITER.SalesOrderDetail	2	10945313	3002	0	11386718
2	SELECT * FROM APWRITER.SalesOrderHeader SELEC	2	10868163	3022	0	11109375
3	SELECT * FROM APWRITER.SalesOrderDetail	1	5481913	1501	0	5806445
4	SELECT * FROM APWRITER.SalesOrderDetail	1	5397461	1513	0	5575195
5	SELECT * FROM APWRITER.SalesOrderHeader SELECT ...	1	5336914	1501	0	5500976
6	SELECT soh.SalesOrderId, soh.OrderDate, soh.ShipDate,p...	1	5150390	2322	1	5322265
7	SELECT soh.OrderDate, soh.ShipDate,p.name, sod.Order...	1	5120118	2302	0	5259765
8	SELECT soh.SalesOrderId, soh.OrderDate, soh.ShipDate,p...	1	5165038	2302	0	5247070
9	select sod.SalesOrderID,sod.SalesOrderDetailID,p.Name,s...	1	4598632	2501	120	4827148
10	SELECT * FROM APWRITER.SalesOrderHeader	2	4519531	1570	0	4619140
11	select sod.SalesOrderID,sod.SalesOrderDetailID,p.Name,so...	1	4275390	1528	0	4474609
12	SELECT * FROM APWRITER.SalesOrderHeader SELEC	2	4225585	1588	0	4314453
13	select sod.SalesOrderID,sod.SalesOrderDetailID,p.Name,so...	1	4131836	1528	0	4270507
14	(@_msparam_0 nvarchar(4000))SELECT SCHEMA_NAME(u...	1	274414	5877	110	3055664
15	SELECT * FROM APWRITER.SalesOrderHeader	1	2299804	794	0	2411132

Query executed successfully. MEDIACENTER\MSSQLCFG (10.0 ... sa (55) AdventureWorks2008 00:00:00 215 rows

Figure 10-16. *The output of the SYS.DM_EXEC_QUERY_STATS DMV*

One of the most useful aspects of SYS.DM_EXEC_QUERY_STATS is that it provides you with the statistical information needed to determine whether write queries are performing in an acceptable time frame before and after index creation. Spend some time with this view to make sure you completely understand its usefulness.

SYS.DM_DB_INDEX_USAGE_STATS

SYS.DM_DB_INDEX_USAGE_STATS is extremely powerful when it comes to determining the usage of the indexes that exist on a table. The view provides the number of index scans, index seeks, lookups, and writes for each of the indexes that are queried in your system.

Using SYS.DM_DB_INDEX_USAGE_STATS, you can determine whether the indexes on a table are heavy on reads, heavy on writes, or both. The view will also show you how an index is performing right after creation. It is rewarding to create a new index, and then watch the number of seeks on that index skyrocket. That leaves you feeling like you are doing your job. See Figure 10-17 for sample output from querying this very useful view.

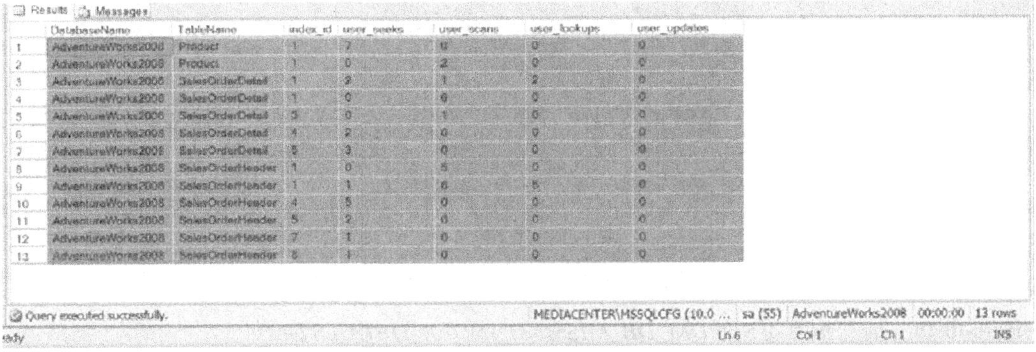

	DatabaseName	TableName	index_id	user_seeks	user_scans	user_lookups	user_updates
1	AdventureWorks2008	Product	1	7	0	0	0
2	AdventureWorks2008	Product	1	0	2	0	0
3	AdventureWorks2008	SalesOrderDetail	1	2	1	2	0
4	AdventureWorks2008	SalesOrderDetail	1	0	6	0	0
5	AdventureWorks2008	SalesOrderDetail	3	0	1	0	0
6	AdventureWorks2008	SalesOrderDetail	4	2	0	0	0
7	AdventureWorks2008	SalesOrderDetail	5	3	0	0	0
8	AdventureWorks2008	SalesOrderHeader	1	0	5	0	0
9	AdventureWorks2008	SalesOrderHeader	1	1	6	5	0
10	AdventureWorks2008	SalesOrderHeader	4	5	0	0	0
11	AdventureWorks2008	SalesOrderHeader	5	2	0	0	0
12	AdventureWorks2008	SalesOrderHeader	7	1	0	0	0
13	AdventureWorks2008	SalesOrderHeader	8	1	0	0	0

Query executed successfully. MEDIACENTER\MSSQLCFG (10.0 ... sa (55) AdventureWorks2008 00:00:00 13 rows

Figure 10-17. *The output of the SYS.DM_DB_INDEX_USAGE_STATS DMV*

Missing Index Dynamic Management Views

In SQL Server 2008, the missing index feature identifies opportunities for indexes to be created on your system. The query optimizer determines that an index would be utilized if an index that met certain criteria existed. The missing index views provide the recommended index key, include columns, and some usage statistics that indicate the index should be created.

Hopefully, you can see the performance implications of using the missing index DMVs, but for this section we would like to discuss another purpose. You can use the missing index views to help validate if the system agrees with an index that you want to create on your database. Granted, what the system thinks and what you think will be different from time to time, but there should be some similarities as well. Don't go out and create every index suggested by the missing index views. Use the missing index views as a method by which you can validate your index creation ideas against what the system thinks prior to creation.

Using the `SYS.DM_DB_MISSING_INDEX_DETAILS` DMV, you can query the view to see all of the identified missing indexes for the instance or for a particular object. When you are evaluating the index that you want to create, take a quick peek at the results of the DMV to see if the system has identified that index as well. The following query retrieves the table name and columns that the system has identified as useful for queries.

```
SELECT OBJECT_NAME(object_id,database_id) TableName,
equality_columns,inequality_columns,included_columns
FROM   SYS.DM_DB_MISSING_INDEX_DETAILS
```

Figure 10-18 shows the sample output of the preceding query. The equality_columns are column names that are used in queries with an equals sign, like `title ='Pro SQL Server Administration'`. The inequality_columns are column names that are utilized in queries with an inequality, like `date < '2009-01-01'`. The included_columns are columns that should be included in the index.

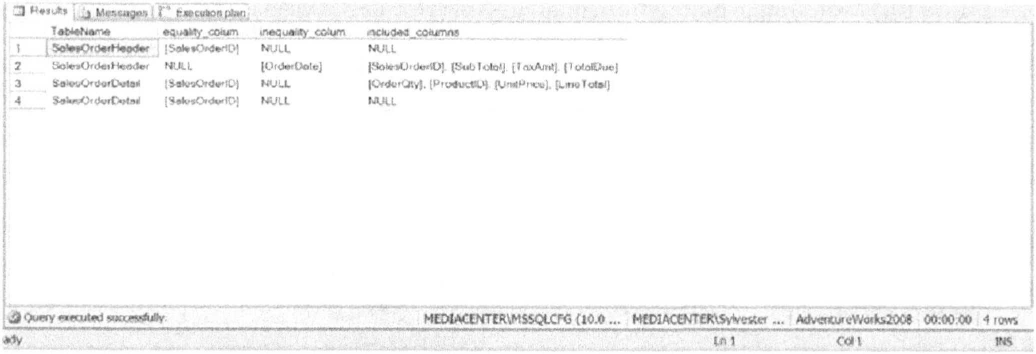

	TableName	equality_colum	inequality_colum	included_columns
1	SalesOrderHeader	[SalesOrderID]	NULL	NULL
2	SalesOrderHeader	NULL	[OrderDate]	[SalesOrderID], [SubTotal], [TaxAmt], [TotalDue]
3	SalesOrderDetail	[SalesOrderID]	NULL	[OrderQty], [ProductID], [UnitPrice], [LineTotal]
4	SalesOrderDetail	[SalesOrderID]	NULL	NULL

Figure 10-18. *The results of SYS.DM_DB_MISSING_INDEX_DETAILS DMV*

Putting It All Together

Throughout this chapter, we have covered numerous terms, strategies, and best practices for creating indexes. Understanding the tips and recommendations are important for creating an index strategy that increases the performance of your system. Reading words are helpful, but in our opinion, working with and seeing the examples are more beneficial.

This section demonstrates the terms and strategies discussed throughout this chapter. For each example, we show you the queries and their execution plans. The goal of this section is not to show you how to read execution plans, but to show you the performance difference displayed within execution plans for the various indexing options. There are entire books dedicated to nothing but indexing, so we won't show you every indexing method example. However, this glimpse into the performance improvements for the various types of indexing should enable you to play with the different strategies within your environment.

Setting Up the Scenario

For the demonstrations in this section, we use a series of sales tables within the Adventure-Works2008 database. We would like you to create copies of those tables, move data into those copies, and create some indexes on them. We are going to use three tables: the sales header table, sales details table, and the product table. The following code sample creates the tables in a separate schema and moves data into them:

```
USE AdventureWorks2008
GO

SELECT *
INTO AdventureWorks2008.APWRITER.Product
FROM AdventureWorks2008.Production.Product

SELECT *
INTO AdventureWorks2008.APWRITER.SalesOrderDetail
FROM AdventureWorks2008.Sales.SalesOrderDetail

SELECT *
INTO AdventureWorks2008.APWRITER.SalesOrderHeader
FROM AdventureWorks2008.Sales.SalesOrderHeader
```

If you do not have the APWRITER schema created, then use a schema that exists on your system or create a separate schema just for the tables. Before we begin, let's make sure you understand the relationship between the tables. The SalesOrderHeader table contains the information about when a sale was created. The SalesOrderDetail table contains a list of all of the details related to the sale. The Product table has the products that exist within each sale detail. In other words, SalesOrderHeader tables have order details and the order details have products. Enable the Include Actual Execution Plan option before you execute the following queries.

Table Scans

The first thing you notice if you query the three newly created tables is that the query optimizer does a table scan. As you can see, to retrieve all the data from a table, the table scan is not necessarily a bad option; however, retrieving specific records from within a heap table may prove costly. Enable execution plans in your query window, and execute the following queries. You'll see their execution plans displayed in Figure 10-19.

```
USE AdventureWorks2008
GO

SELECT *
FROM APWRITER.SalesOrderHeader

SELECT *
FROM APWRITER.SalesOrderDetail

SELECT *
FROM APWRITER.Product
```

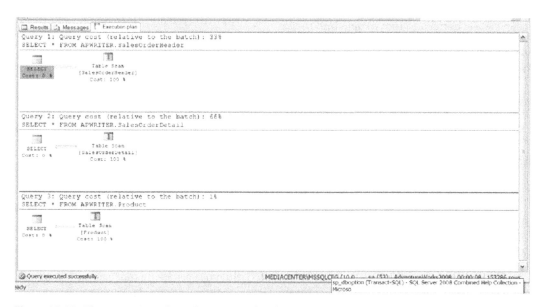

Figure 10-19. *The execution plan of querying the three tables*

Now instead of just retrieving all the data from the tables, you may want to retrieve specific results from each one of the tables. The following code retrieves specific information from joining the newly created tables. Figure 10-20 shows the resulting execution plan.

```
SELECT soh.SalesOrderId, soh.OrderDate, soh.ShipDate,p.Name, sod.OrderQty,
 sod.UnitPrice, sod.LineTotal
FROM apWriter.SalesOrderHeader soh JOIN apWriter.SalesOrderDetail sod
ON  soh.SalesOrderId = sod.SalesOrderId
 JOIN apWriter.Product p on sod.ProductId = p.ProductId
WHERE soh.SalesOrderId = 60941
```

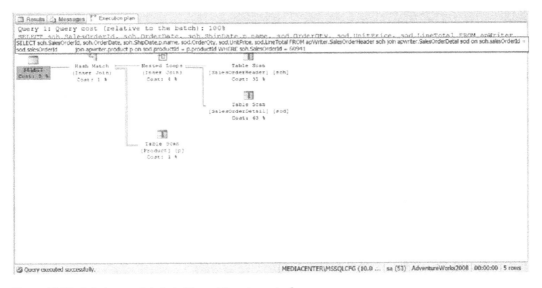

Figure 10-20. *Joining multiple tables without any indexes*

The execution plan and the response time suggest that joining multiple tables together via table scan is not the most efficient way to retrieve data. So the first rule that we would like to demonstrate is the benefit of creating clustered indexes on tables.

Clustered Index Seeks

The first two index creations in Listing 10-3 create clustered indexes on the SalesOrderHeader and Product tables. Then comes a query. Then the listing creates a clustered index on the SalesOrderDetail table. Finally, the query is executed again, showing the improvement from using a clustered index over the table scan.

Listing 10-3. *SQL Script to Create Clustered Indexes and Retrieve Data from the Newly Created Tables*

```
CREATE CLUSTERED INDEX ix_SalesOrderId ON
apWriter.SalesOrderHeader(SalesOrderId)

CREATE CLUSTERED INDEX ix_ProductId ON apWriter.Product(ProductId)
```

```
SELECT *
FROM apWriter.SalesOrderDetail
WHERE SalesOrderId = 74853

CREATE CLUSTERED INDEX ix_SalesOrderIdDetailId
ON apWriter.SalesOrderDetail(SalesOrderId,SalesOrderDetailId)

SELECT *
FROM apWriter.SalesOrderDetail
WHERE SalesOrderId = 74853
```

Figure 10-21 shows the execution plans from executing Listing 10-3. Notice the missing index message. You are notified of missing indexes by default in SQL Server 2008. The information in that message is the same that you could get manually by querying the missing index views described earlier.

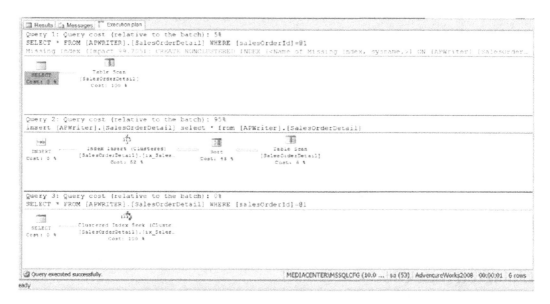

Figure 10-21. *The execution plan of a table scan versus a clustered index seek*

Also notice the cost difference between the table scan and the clustered index seek. If you run your multiple table query for a sales order, you will see that clustered index seeks are used instead of table scans. For example, execute the following query. You should see an execution plan like that shown in Figure 10-22.

```
SELECT soh.SalesOrderId, soh.OrderDate, soh.ShipDate,p.Name, sod.OrderQty,
 sod.UnitPrice, sod.LineTotal
FROM apWriter.SalesOrderHeader soh
 JOIN apWriter.SalesOrderDetail sod ON soh.SalesOrderId = sod.salesOrderId
 JOIN apWriter.Product p ON sod.ProductId = p.ProductId
WHERE soh.SalesOrderId = 74853
```

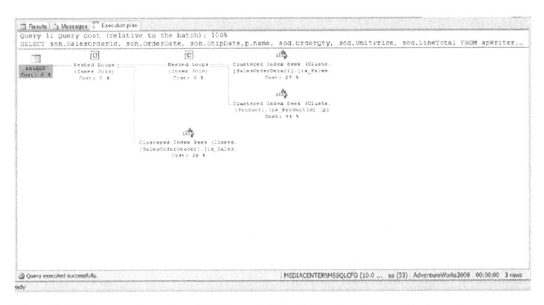

Figure 10-22. *The execution plan of joining multiple tables using clustered index seeks*

Covering Your Queries

Now that you have your clustered indexes created, think about what will happen if you want to retrieve all of the orders in a given time frame. Let's run the following query. Figure 10-23 shows the execution plan.

```
SELECT soh.SalesOrderID,soh.SubTotal, soh.TaxAmt, soh.TotalDue
FROM apWriter.SalesOrderHeader soh
WHERE soh.OrderDate > '2003-12-31'
```

Figure 10-23. *The execution plan of a query that retrieves a date range of orders*

From looking at the execution plan in Figure 10-23, you can see that the query optimizer decided to do a clustered index scan to retrieve the data. That's the same as scanning the entire table. The query optimizer decided that it was faster to scan the entire table than to use any of the indexes defined on the table. Of course, the only index that we've defined so far is not useful for the query we've just executed.

We can improve things by helping the query optimizer out. Execute the code example in Listing 10-4 to create a nonclustered index on the OrderDate column. Then the listing executes the query that was ran previously. Listing 10-4 adds an additional query to the listing to prove another point. You should see the same execution plan as shown in Figure 10-24.

Listing 10-4. *SQL Script to Create Nonclustered Index and Query the Data for a Given Date Range*

```
CREATE NONCLUSTERED INDEX ix_OrderDate ON  apWriter.SalesOrderHeader(OrderDate)

SELECT soh.SalesOrderID,soh.SubTotal, soh.TaxAmt, soh.TotalDue
FROM apWriter.SalesOrderHeader soh
WHERE soh.OrderDate > '2003-12-31'

SELECT OrderDate,soh.SalesOrderID,soh.SubTotal, soh.TaxAmt, soh.TotalDue
FROM AdventureWorks2008.apWriter.SalesOrderHeader soh
WHERE soh.OrderDate = '2004-01-01'
```

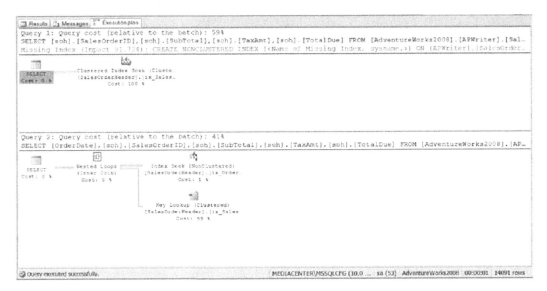

Figure 10-24. *The execution plan from the same query on which Figure 10-23 was based, but this time with a supporting index in place*

After running the first query, you should have noticed that the query optimizer still uses the clustered index to retrieve the data in the date range and the nonclustered index for an equal query. Why is that? To help answer that question, let's examine the execution plan of the second query in Listing 10-5. The query optimizer determines that it is faster to use the nonclustered index to find the specific order date and then do a lookup for the additional information required to fulfill the query results. Remember, the nonclustered index only contains the nonclustered index key and a row locator for the remainder of the data. The queries are looking for the subtotal, the tax amount, and the total due for an order. So when the query is looking for specific indexed data, like the second query, the query optimizer can quickly find that information using the nonclustered index.

On the other hand, the first query is looking for a range of data. The query optimizer decided that with the number of records that will be retrieved, it's faster to scan the clustered index for the date range since no lookup is required. To prove the cost difference between the two indexes, the query in Listing 10-5 forces the query optimizer to use the nonclustered index on the order date for the first query. Figure 10-25 shows the resulting execution plan.

Listing 10-5. *SQL Script That Forces SQL Server to Use the Nonclustered Index for the Date Range Scan*

```
SELECT soh.SalesOrderID,soh.SubTotal, soh.TaxAmt, soh.TotalDue
FROM apWriter.SalesOrderHeader soh with(index(ix_OrderDate))
WHERE soh.OrderDate > '2003-12-31'

SELECT soh.SalesOrderID,soh.SubTotal, soh.TaxAmt, soh.TotalDue
FROM apWriter.SalesOrderHeader soh
WHERE soh.OrderDate > '2003-12-31'
```

Figure 10-25. *The difference between using the nonclustered index versus the clustered index for querying the OrderDate range*

As you can see, the use of the nonclustered index included the bookmark lookups, and that plan is more costly than just scanning the clustered index. One thing you can do to increase the performance impact of the nonclustered index is to cover the query completely. Listing 10-6 shows an example of a nonclustered index created on OrderDate that includes the subtotal, the tax amount, and the total due columns.

To show the cost difference between using each index, the code forces the use of each of the different indexes that we've created. That way, you can see the difference between using a clustered index, the nonclustered index on order date, and the nonclustered index on order date with the include columns. Figure 10-26 shows the resulting execution plans. Clearly, you can see that the nonclustered index with include columns covering the query provides the most efficient method for accessing the data.

Listing 10-6. *SQL Script That Creates a Nonclustered Index and Uses the Different Indexes That Exist on the Table*

```
CREATE NONCLUSTERED INDEX ix_OrderDatewInclude
ON apWriter.SalesOrderHeader(OrderDate) INCLUDE (SubTotal, TaxAmt, TotalDue)

SELECT soh.SalesOrderID,soh.SubTotal, soh.TaxAmt, soh.TotalDue
FROM apWriter.SalesOrderHeader soh WITH (index(ix_OrderDate))
WHERE soh.OrderDate > '2003-12-31'
```

```
SELECT soh.SalesOrderID,soh.SubTotal, soh.TaxAmt, soh.TotalDue
FROM apWriter.SalesOrderHeader soh WITH(index(ix_OrderDatewInclude))
WHERE soh.OrderDate > '2003-12-31'

SELECT soh.SalesOrderID,soh.SubTotal, soh.TaxAmt, soh.TotalDue
FROM apWriter.SalesOrderHeader soh WITH(index(ix_SalesOrderId))
WHERE soh.OrderDate > '2003-12-31'
```

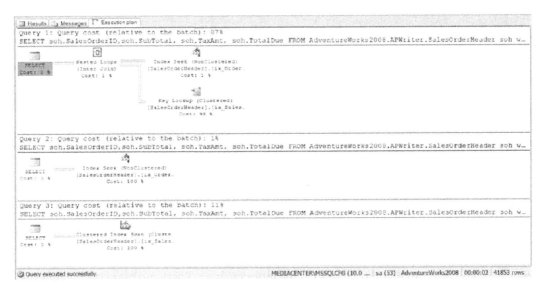

Figure 10-26. *The comparison of the clustered index, the nonclustered index, and the nonclustered index with include columns*

Indexing JOIN Criteria

Next, you want to retrieve all the orders that contain a certain product. Let's query the SalesOrderDetail table to identify the records. Execute the following code sample. The resulting plan is shown in Figure 10-27.

```
SELECT sod.SalesOrderID,sod.SalesOrderDetailID,p.Name,sod.OrderQty
FROM apWriter.SalesOrderDetail sod JOIN apWriter.Product p
 ON sod.ProductId = p.ProductId
WHERE p.ProductId = 843
```

Figure 10-27. *The execution plan of joining the SalesOrderDetail and Product tables*

As you review the execution plan, you should see that the bulk of the cost of the query comes from the clustered index scan on the SalesOrderDetail table. If you follow some of the tips discussed in this chapter, then you need to create a nonclustered index on the foreign key within the SalesOrderDetail table.

Since you are also querying the data for the order quantity, you may want to cover the query and include the OrderQty column in the index creation. For demo purposes, Listing 10-7 creates two indexes: a nonclustered index on just the product ID and a nonclustered index on the product ID that includes the OrderQty column as well.

Listing 10-7. *SQL Code That Creates Nonclustered Indexes and Queries Multiple Tables*

```
CREATE NONCLUSTERED INDEX ix_ProductId
ON apWriter.SalesOrderDetail(ProductId)

CREATE NONCLUSTERED INDEX ix_ProductIdInclude
ON apWriter.SalesOrderDetail(ProductId) INCLUDE (OrderQty)

SELECT sod.SalesOrderID,sod.SalesOrderDetailID,p.Name,sod.OrderQty
FROM AdventureWorks2008.apWriter.SalesOrderDetail sod
WITH (index(ix_ProductIdInclude)) JOIN AdventureWorks2008.apWriter.Product p
 ON sod.ProductId = p.ProductId
WHERE p.ProductId = 843

SELECT sod.SalesOrderID,sod.SalesOrderDetailID,p.Name,sod.OrderQty
FROM apWriter.SalesOrderDetail sod with(index(ix_ProductId))
JOIN apWriter.Product p on sod.ProductId = p.ProductId
WHERE  p.ProductId = 843
```

After creating the indexes, Listing 10-7 executes two queries to demonstrate the impact of those indexes. Figure 10-28 shows the resulting execution plans.

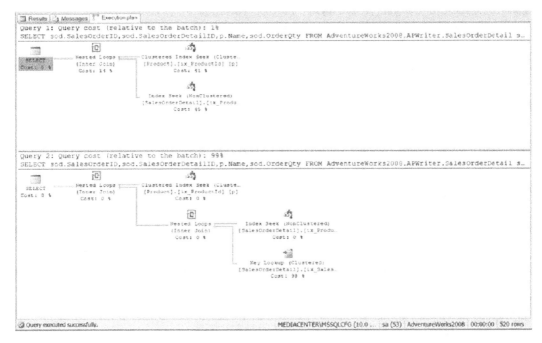

Figure 10-28. *The execution plan of Listing 10-7 using the nonclustered index compared to the nonclustered index with include column*

The execution plan in Figure 10-28 shows the nonclustered index with the include columns, or the first query in the execution plan. The query cost is less because the index covers the query. Pop quiz: Why don't you have to include the SalesOrderId in the index in order to cover the query? Keep in mind that nonclustered indexes contain the clustered index key on the intermediate and leaf level pages. So the query optimizers already have those values and no lookup is required.

Filtered Indexes

For the last example, we would like to create a filtered index. Assume that the corporate office exists in territory 4, and you want all of your queries for the VIPs of the company to be extremely fast. For demonstration purposes, assume that the director of sales runs a daily report to see the number of sales and the Totaldue of sales for his region, and every time that query runs slowly, your boss gets a phone call. So instead of creating a nonclustered index on the Territory column, you're going to create a filtered index on the Territory column just for his area. The code in Listing 10-8 creates a nonclustered index on TerritoryID and a filtered nonclustered index for territory 4.

Listing 10-8. *SQL Script That Creates a Filtered Index*

```
CREATE NONCLUSTERED INDEX ix_Territory ON
apWriter.SalesOrderHeader(TerritoryID) INCLUDE (OrderDate,TotalDue)

CREATE NONCLUSTERED INDEX ix_TerritoryFiltered
ON apWriter.SalesOrderHeader(TerritoryID) INCLUDE (OrderDate,TotalDue)
WHERE TerritoryID = 4

GO

SELECT SalesOrderId, OrderDate,TotalDue
FROM apWriter.SalesOrderHeader soh WITH(index(ix_Territory))
WHERE TerritoryID = 4

SELECT SalesOrderId, OrderDate,TotalDue
FROM apWriter.SalesOrderHeader soh WITH (index(ix_TerritoryFiltered))
WHERE TerritoryID = 4
```

The listing queries the SalesOrderHeader table for a particular territory. The execution plan will show the difference between a filtered index and a nonclustered index. The execution plan of Listing 10-8 is shown in Figure 10-29. After reviewing the execution plan, you can easily see the benefit of using filtered indexes instead of just nonclustered indexes.

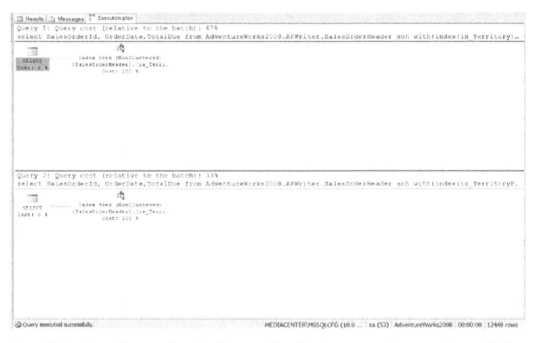

Figure 10-29. *The performance benefit of using a filtered index compared to a nonclustered index*

Summary

As we conclude this chapter, we hope you spend some time playing with some of the indexing tips and recommendations within your environment. Obviously, we cannot demonstrate every tip or recommendation discussed throughout this chapter. The goal was to show you how to determine the best or most efficient method for creating indexes within your environment. Test, test, and test a little more using the methods discussed in this chapter to make sure that the indexes won't negatively impact performance. Granted, you are going to make mistakes, and you won't be perfect the first time, but taking time with the various options will help you with index creation.

As important as indexes are for maintaining the performance of the application, backing up the data is even more important. As a database administrator, one of your most important roles is to make sure you don't lose data. In the next chapter, we will discuss the various backup solutions that exist within SQL Server 2008.

CHAPTER 11

■ ■ ■

Managing Backups

Understanding backups is extremely important for every database administrator (DBA)—it can make or break your career. If you need to restore a database, you can be a hero in a matter of minutes. On the other hand, if you don't have a good backup to restore, you may end up looking for a new job. In our opinion, having the knowledge to properly back up and restore a database is the most important skill a DBA can possess. That being said, we think backing up a database is often the most easily overlooked skill. It's easy to set up a maintenance plan or backup job and think you are covered—a kind of set-it-and-forget-it mentality. The problem with this attitude is that a backup is something you do not know is being performed incorrectly until you need to use it, which is not the best time to find out. There are several backup options available in SQL Server 2008 that you should master in order to make sure you don't find yourself trying to explain why you can't restore a database everyone thought was being backed up.

Recovery Models

The first thing you need to be aware of when determining a backup strategy is the database recovery model. A database recovery model determines how transactions are logged and therefore impacts the type of backup operations that can be performed on a database. You can set a database to use one of three different recovery models that provide different levels of transaction protection.

- *Full*: The full recovery model provides the highest level of data protection by logging all transactions. It is usually the preferred recovery model for all production databases. The full recovery model also gives you the most flexibility in your backup strategy by allowing you to perform any type of backup available in SQL Server.

- *Bulk-logged*: The bulk-logged recovery model is much like the full recovery model except that certain operations are minimally logged, reducing the space that would be required to store the entire transaction in the log file. You will also receive performance gains on bulk operations, since only the end result is logged and not the entire operation. As with the full recovery model, you can also perform any type of backup for a database that is bulk-logged. The limitation is that you may not be able to do a point-in-time recovery (which you will see in the next chapter) if a bulk operation has been performed. The following are considered bulk operations and are minimally logged when using the bulk-logged recovery model.

- SELECT INTO

- BCP

- BULK INSERT

- OPENROWSET with the BULK rowset provider

- CREATE INDEX

- ALTER INDEX REBUILD

- DROP INDEX (The page deallocation is fully logged, but if a heap rebuild is necessary, it will be minimally logged.)

- Partial updates to large data types using the .WRITE clause

- *Simple*: The simple recovery model does not offer any form of logged data protection and is generally not used in production environments that require point-in-time recovery since the last full backup. The transaction log only holds the data until a checkpoint has occurred and the data is written to disk. For this reason, you cannot perform transaction log backups on a database that is using the simple recovery model. As with the bulk-logged recovery model, bulk operations are also minimally logged using the simple recovery model.

You can also use sort of a hybrid method between the full and bulk-logged recovery models. You can set the database to use the full recovery model, and then change it to use bulk-logged when performing specific bulk operations that may not perform well using the full recovery model. You should back up the log before switching to the bulk-logged recovery model, and then back up once again after switching back to the full recovery model. This will minimize the logs that cannot be restored using the point-in-time recovery option.

To check the current recovery model, you can use the DATABASEPROPERTYEX system function using the RECOVERY parameter, as shown in Listing 11-1. To change a database recovery model, you can use the ALTER DATABASE statement specifying FULL, BULK_LOGGED, or SIMPLE, also shown in Listing 11-1.

Listing 11-1. *Code to View and Change the Database Recovery Model*

```
USE master
GO

--Select the database recovery model
SELECT DATABASEPROPERTYEX('AdventureWorks2008','RECOVERY');

--Change the database recovery model
ALTER DATABASE AdventureWorks2008 SET RECOVERY FULL;
```

Backup Architecture

Backups are grouped into logical containers known as media sets. A *media set* is one or more tapes or disk files that contain an ordered collection of backups. A media set must be either completely on tape or completely on disk. You can't create a media set that spans multiple

device types. A new media set is created the first time a backup is performed or by using the
FORMAT option in the BACKUP statement. The FORMAT option deletes the old media header and
creates a new header for the media set. The header contains information about the media type
and media family.

   Media family refers to the type of device that was used to create the media set. If you use
multiple backup devices in a media set, your backup set will contain multiple media families.
For example, if you back up your database to two disk files, the media set will contain two
media families that are both marked as disk devices.

   Media sets are made up of one or more backup sets. A backup set consists of all the
information gathered during an individual backup process. Each time a successful backup is
performed, a backup set is added to the media set. The backup set is evenly distributed across
all the devices that make up the media set.

   Look at the sample code in Listing 11-2. The BACKUP command creates a media set named
AdventureWorks2008_MediaSet that contains two disk devices, meaning the media set contains
two media families. Each time the BACKUP command is executed, a backup set is evenly written
across the two devices. The illustration shown in Figure 11-1 assumes you have executed the
BACKUP command three times to create three backup sets.

Listing 11-2. *Code to Create a Media Set with Multiple Devices*

```
USE master
GO
BACKUP DATABASE [AdventureWorks2008] TO
DISK = 'C:\Backup\AdventureWorks2008_1.bak',
DISK = 'D:\Backup\AdventureWorks2008_2.bak'
WITH MEDIANAME = 'AdventureWorks2008_MediaSet'
GO
```

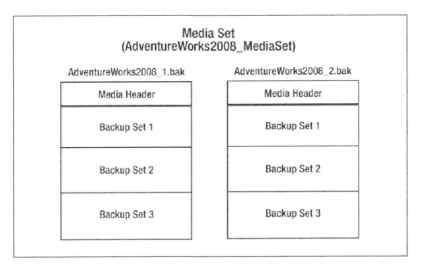

Figure 11-1. *AdventureWorks2008 backup media set created by the code in Listing 11-2*

Most of the time this architecture goes unnoticed because a database is backed up to a media set on a single disk to a single file; so we tend to think of it as just a backup file. If you think of backups in terms of backup sets, media sets, and media families, it will make a lot more sense when reviewing many of the backup options available in SQL Server.

Backup Types

Not every backup must be of your entire database. SQL Server supports numerous options for backing up all or part of your database. Most backup strategies begin with what is termed a *full backup*. Other backup types, such as the differential backup and the transaction log backup, meet specific needs and help keep your backups manageable.

Full Backups

A full backup captures the entire database, including part of the transaction log, so the database may be completely restored to a consistent state at the point in time when the full backup completed. Any uncommitted transactions that were open at the time the backup completed will be rolled back in the event of a restore. The full backup also serves as a base for subsequent differential and log backups. You can't take differential or log backups on a database if you have never taken a full backup. Typically, you will take a full backup once a day if the database size is within reason, and then supplement with transaction log backups throughout the day. If the database is too large to create daily backups in a timely fashion, you can take less frequent full backups, perhaps on a weekly basis, and then supplement with differential backups throughout the week. No matter what strategy you choose, it all begins with a full backup of the database.

SQL Server only backs up the data pages in the database that have currently been used, so the full backup will generally be smaller than the size of the database. You can use the `sp_spaceused` system stored procedure to estimate the size of a full backup by subtracting the unallocated space from the database size. For example, the size of the full backup for `AdventureWorks2008` (as shown in Figure 11-2) would be roughly 183 MB (198.00 MB – 15.45 MB = 182.55 MB).

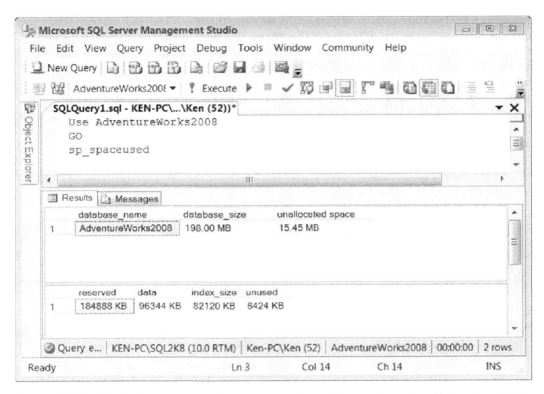

Figure 11-2. *Results of the sp_spaceused system stored procedure used to estimate the size of a full backup*

The basic syntax to create a full database backup is shown in Listing 11-3. There are several other options you can specify when creating a full backup. We will discuss the individual options later in this chapter in the "GUI Backup Interface" section.

Listing 11-3. *Basic Syntax to Create a Full Database Backup*

```
BACKUP DATABASE AdventureWorks2008
TO  DISK = 'C:\Backups\AdventureWorks2008.bak'
```

Differential Backups

A differential backup captures all changes that have occurred in the database since the last full backup. The differential backup uses a bitmap page that contains a bit for every extent to keep track of the changes. The bit is set to 1 in the bitmap page for each changed extent since the last full backup referred to as the differential base. Each subsequent differential backup following a full backup contains all changes made since the last full backup, not just the changes made since the last differential. This means that over time, the differential backup can become as large as the full backup itself. In order to benefit from the speed advantage and space savings of differential backups, you should make sure to schedule your full backups in short enough intervals to serve as a new differential base, so the differential backup remains significantly smaller than the full backup. Figure 11-3 uses the backup history tables to show the relationship between a differential backup and its base full backup. Notice that the differential_base_guid for backup_set_id 38 and 41 are the same as the backup_set_uuid for backup_set_id 35, which is the full database backup that serves as the differential base.

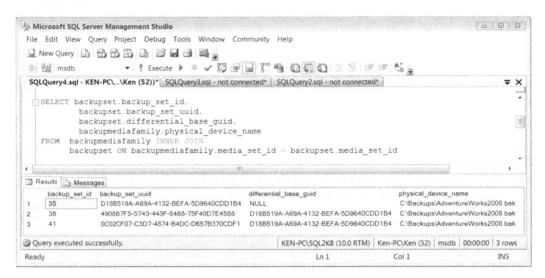

Figure 11-3. *Relationship between a differential backup set and its base full backup*

Differential backups work well when creating a backup plan for a large database with infrequent changes. Instead of having to create a full daily backup that would capture mostly the same data, you can create a full weekly backup and supplement with daily differential backups while using transaction log backups throughout the day. Listing 11-4 shows the basic syntax used to create a differential backup.

Listing 11-4. *Basic Syntax to Create a Differential Database Backup*

```
BACKUP DATABASE AdventureWorks2008
TO  DISK = 'C:\Backups\AdventureWorks2008_diff.bak'
WITH  DIFFERENTIAL
GO
```

Transaction Log Backups

If you are using the full or the bulk-logged recovery model you must schedule regular transaction log backups. Routine transaction log backups not only provide the highest level of data protection, they also truncate the inactive portions of the log and enable you to reuse the log space for new transactions. If you never back up your transaction logs, the logs will never be truncated and will ultimately grow out of control. Beginning with SQL Server 2005, you can now make concurrent full database backups and transaction log backups. In previous versions, the transaction log backup would wait for the full backup to complete before proceeding. You cannot make transaction log backups using the simple recovery model because SQL Server automatically truncates the log on checkpoint.

Each transaction log backup only contains the new log records that were not backed up in the previous transaction log backup. A succession of uninterrupted transaction log backups forms a log chain that allows you to restore to a point in time within the log chain. SQL Server assigns each transaction log backup a log sequence number (LSN) that it uses to maintain the log chain. Once the log chain is broken for any reason, such as a missing backup file or data corruption, you cannot restore any further transactions in the chain until you take a full or differential database backup to serve as a new base for the chain. The code in Listing 11-5 shows the basic syntax used to back up the AdventureWorks2008 transaction log. Typically, transaction log backups use the file extension .trn, but this is not required.

Listing 11-5. *Basic Syntax Used to Back Up a Transaction Log*

```
BACKUP LOG AdventrueWorks2008
TO DISK = 'C:\Backups\AdventureWorks2008.trn'
```

SQL Server records every successful backup in the SQL Server error log and the system event log. If you are taking many recurring transaction log backups, this can add a lot of extra information in the error log files, making them harder to manage and to find useful information. You can disable SQL Server logging successful backup messages by adding the -T3226 trace flag to the SQL Server startup parameters. To add the trace flag, open the SQL Server Configuration Manager, right-click the SQL Server service for the appropriate instance, and select Properties from the context menu. Select the Advanced tab and enter the trace flag in the startup parameters text box using a semicolon as a separator (see Figure 11-4).

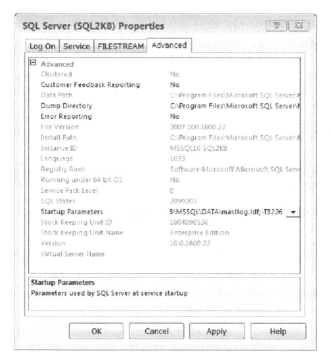

Figure 11-4. *SQL Server Properties dialog Advanced tab*

Partial Backups

Partial backups were introduced in SQL Server 2005 to provide an alternative way to back up large databases that contain read-only filegroups. Partial backups are similar to full backups except that they are designed to back up only the primary filegroup, any read/write filegroups, and any read-only filegroups that are optionally specified. If you create a partial backup of a read-only database, only the primary filegroup will be included in the backup.

Just as with full backups, you can also create a differential partial backup that uses a partial backup as a differential base. The differential partial backup will then only contain the changed extents since the last partial backup. If your last partial backup included any optional read/write filegroups, you must also include them in the differential partial backup. You cannot create a differential partial backup that uses a full backup as a differential base.

SQL Server does not support partial backups using the SQL Server Management Studio GUI. You must use T-SQL in order to create a partial backup. Listing 11-6 shows the syntax used to create a partial backup and a differential partial backup of the AdventureWorks2008 database.

Listing 11-6. *Syntax Used to Create a Partial Backup and a Differential Partial Backup*

```
--Partial backup
BACKUP DATABASE AdventureWorks2008
READ_WRITE_FILEGROUPS -- [ , <optional_filegroups> ]
TO DISK = 'C:\Backups\AdventureWorks2008_part.bak'

--Differential partial backup
BACKUP DATABASE AdventureWorks2008
READ_WRITE_FILEGROUPS -- [ , < optional_filegroups> ]
TO DISK = 'C:\Backups\AdventureWorks2008_part_diff.bak'
WITH DIFFERENTIAL
```

File Backups

File backups allow you to create a backup that contains individual files or filegroups. File backups give you the flexibility to take backups of large databases based on usage patterns. For example, you may have a set of tables that is only updated once a month in one filegroup and frequently updated tables in another. You may also want to use file backups if you have multiple filegroups on separate disks. If a single disk fails, you will only need to restore the file backup for files contained on a single disk instead of the entire database.

Unless your database is in Simple mode, you also need to make sure you are backing up the transaction log when working with file backups. In order to completely restore a database using file backups, you must have the appropriate transaction log backups as well. All of the file backups plus the transaction log backups taken since the first file backup are equivalent to a full backup. You can also create a differential file backup to increase recovery time that will only contain the changed extents since the last full file backup. Listing 11-7 shows the syntax to create a full and differential file backup using both files and filegroups.

■**Note** You can create a file backup on a database using the simple recovery model; however, you must back up all the read/write filegroups at the same time so that you can restore the database to a consistent point in time. The easiest way to back up all the read/write filegroups at the same time is by using the READ_WRITE_FILEGROUPS option in the BACKUP statement, which creates a partial backup as discussed in the previous section. Basically, the simplest way to perform a file backup of a database that is in Simple mode is not to perform a file backup (which would require you to list out each individual filegroup), but rather to perform a partial backup instead.

Listing 11-7. *Syntax Used to Create a File Backup and a Differential File Backup Using Files and Filegroups*

```
--Backup the AdventureWorks2008_data file in the PRIMARY filegroup
BACKUP DATABASE AdventureWorks2008
FILE = 'AdventureWorks2008_Data'
TO DISK = 'C:\Backups\AdventureWorks2008_Data.bak'
GO

--Backup the PRIMARY filegroup
BACKUP DATABASE AdventureWorks2008
FILEGROUP = 'PRIMARY'
TO DISK = 'C:\Backups\AW2008_PRIMARY.bak'
GO

--Create a differential backup of the PRIMARY filegroup
BACKUP DATABASE AdventureWorks2008
FILEGROUP = 'PRIMARY'
TO DISK = 'C:\Backups\AW2008_PRIMARY_diff.bak'
WITH DIFFERENTIAL
```

Copy-Only Backups

You can create a copy-only backup to perform a full or transaction log backup; this is independent of the normal backup sequence that is maintained using standard backup operations. Copy-only backups were introduced in SQL Server 2005 to enable you to backup a database without interfering with the normal backup and restore routine. For example, you cannot use a copy-only full backup as a differential base because the differential backup ignores the fact that the copy-only backup was made, and the differential is based on the last full backup that was made without using the copy-only option. A transaction log copy-only backup allows you to create a backup of the transaction log without breaking the log sequence number or truncating the transaction log. As with any other transaction log backup, you cannot create a copy-only log backup of a database using the simple recovery model. The code in Listing 11-8 shows the syntax for creating a full and transaction log copy-only backup of the AdventureWorks2008 database. As you can see, creating a copy-only backup is just a matter of adding the COPY_ONLY option to the WITH clause of the BACKUP statement.

Listing 11-8. *Syntax Used to Create Copy-Only Backups*

```
USE master
GO

--Create a copy-only full backup
BACKUP DATABASE AdventureWorks2008
TO  DISK = 'C:\AdventureWorks2008.bak'
WITH  COPY_ONLY
GO
```

```
--Create a copy-only log backup
BACKUP LOG AdventureWorks2008
TO  DISK = 'C:\AdventureWorks2008.trn'
WITH  COPY_ONLY
GO
```

Note SQL Server 2008 introduces the ability to create a copy-only database backup using the GUI. In SQL Server 2005, the only way to create a copy-only backup is by using T-SQL.

Backup Compression

Backup compression is a long-awaited feature that was added in SQL Server 2008. Prior to SQL Server 2008, you had to purchase third-party tools in order to achieve backup compression. You can only create a compressed backup using the Enterprise Edition of SQL Server 2008; however, restoring a compressed backup is supported in all editions of SQL Server 2008.

By default, backup compression is turned off at the server level. To change the default configuration for backup compression, you can use the sp_configure stored procedure with the 'backup compression default' parameter. You can specify value of '1' to enable the default behavior for all backups to be compressed and specify '0' to disable default compression. You can run the code in Listing 11-9 to enable default compression.

Listing 11-9. *Code to Enable Default Compression*

```
USE master
GO

EXEC sp_configure 'backup compression default', '1';
RECONFIGURE WITH OVERRIDE;
```

You can override the default behavior for backup compression by specifying WITH COMPRESSION or WITH NO_COMPRESSION when issuing the backup statement. Listing 11-10 shows the syntax to create a backup on the AdventureWorks2008 database both with and without compression.

Listing 11-10. *Syntax to Create a Backup with and Without Compression*

```
USE master
GO

PRINT '----------AdventureWorks2008 With Compression----------'
```

```
--Create a full backup with compression
BACKUP DATABASE AdventureWorks2008
TO  DISK = 'C:\Backups\AdventureWorks2008_C.bak'
WITH  COMPRESSION

GO

PRINT Char(13) + '----------AdventureWorks2008 No Compression----------'

--Create a full backup with no compression
BACKUP DATABASE AdventureWorks2008
TO  DISK = 'C:\Backups\AdventureWorks2008_NC.bak'
WITH  NO_COMPRESSION

GO
```

As you can see in Figure 11-5, a backup using compression completes more quickly because the backup file is smaller and requires less IO. The compressed backup completed in 8.192 seconds averaging 22.045 MB per second, while the non-compressed backup completed in 13.209 seconds averaging only 13.672 MB per second.

```
Messages
----------AdventureWorks2008 With Compression----------
Processed 23080 pages for database 'AdventureWorks2008', file 'AdventureWorks2008_Data' on file 1.
Processed 36 pages for database 'AdventureWorks2008', file 'FileStreamDocuments' on file 1.
Processed 1 pages for database 'AdventureWorks2008', file 'AdventureWorks2008_Log' on file 1.
BACKUP DATABASE successfully processed 23117 pages in 8.192 seconds (22.045 MB/sec).

----------AdventureWorks2008 No Compression----------
Processed 23080 pages for database 'AdventureWorks2008', file 'AdventureWorks2008_Data' on file 1.
Processed 36 pages for database 'AdventureWorks2008', file 'FileStreamDocuments' on file 1.
Processed 1 pages for database 'AdventureWorks2008', file 'AdventureWorks2008_Log' on file 1.
BACKUP DATABASE successfully processed 23117 pages in 13.209 seconds (13.672 MB/sec).
```

Figure 11-5. *Backup results using compression vs. no compression*

The increased backup speed also increases the CPU required to process the backup, which could impact other operations on the server while the backup is being performed. If a compressed backup has a negative impact on concurrent processes, you can use the Resource Governor to limit the CPU used by the backup process. (We will cover the Resource Governor in Chapter 16.)

There are a couple of factors that determine the amount of space you will save by using backup compression. For example, text data compresses a lot more than the other data types, and encrypted data hardly compresses at all. Also, if you are using compressed tables, you will not benefit much by using backup compression. The backupset table in the msdb holds the backup size and the compressed backup size, so you can determine the amount of space you are actually saving by using backup compression. Listing 11-11 shows a sample query you can use to determine the amount of compression you are achieving by using backup compression.

Listing 11-11. *Code to Determine the Compression Percentage per Backup*

```
SELECT database_name,
       backup_finish_date,
       1 - (compressed_backup_size/backup_size) PercentCompressed
FROM msdb.dbo.backupset
WHERE backup_size > compressed_backup_size
```

Logical Backup Devices

You can create a logical backup device that points to a physical backup device, which enables you to back up and restore using the logical name instead of the actual physical device. This is useful for providing an abstraction layer between backup scripts and the actual physical backup devices. For example, if you need to change the location for your backups, instead of changing every script, all you need to do is delete the old logical backup device and create a new one that points to the appropriate location.

To create a logical backup device, you can use the sp_addumpdevice system stored procedure. The code in Listing 11-12 creates a logical backup device named AdventureWorks BackupDevice that points to the physical backup device C:\Backup\AdventureWorks2008.bak. To drop a logical backup device, you can execute the sp_dropdevice system stored procedure followed by the name of the device (also shown in Listing 11-12).

Listing 11-12. *Code to Add and Remove a Logical Backup Device Using T-SQL*

```
USE master
GO
--Add logical backup device
EXEC sp_addumpdevice
        @devtype ='disk',
        @logicalname ='AdventureWorksBackupDevice' ,
        @physicalname ='C:\Backup\AdventureWorks2008.bak'
GO

--Remove logical backup device
EXEC sp_dropdevice 'AdventureWorksBackupDevice'
GO
```

You can also add a logical backup device using the SQL Server Management Studio GUI. Expand the Server Objects node in the Object Explorer, right-click on the Backup Devices folder, and select New Backup Device from the context menu. This will bring you to the Backup Device dialog box, as shown in Figure 11-6. Enter the logical device name, device type, and physical location, and then select OK to create the device.

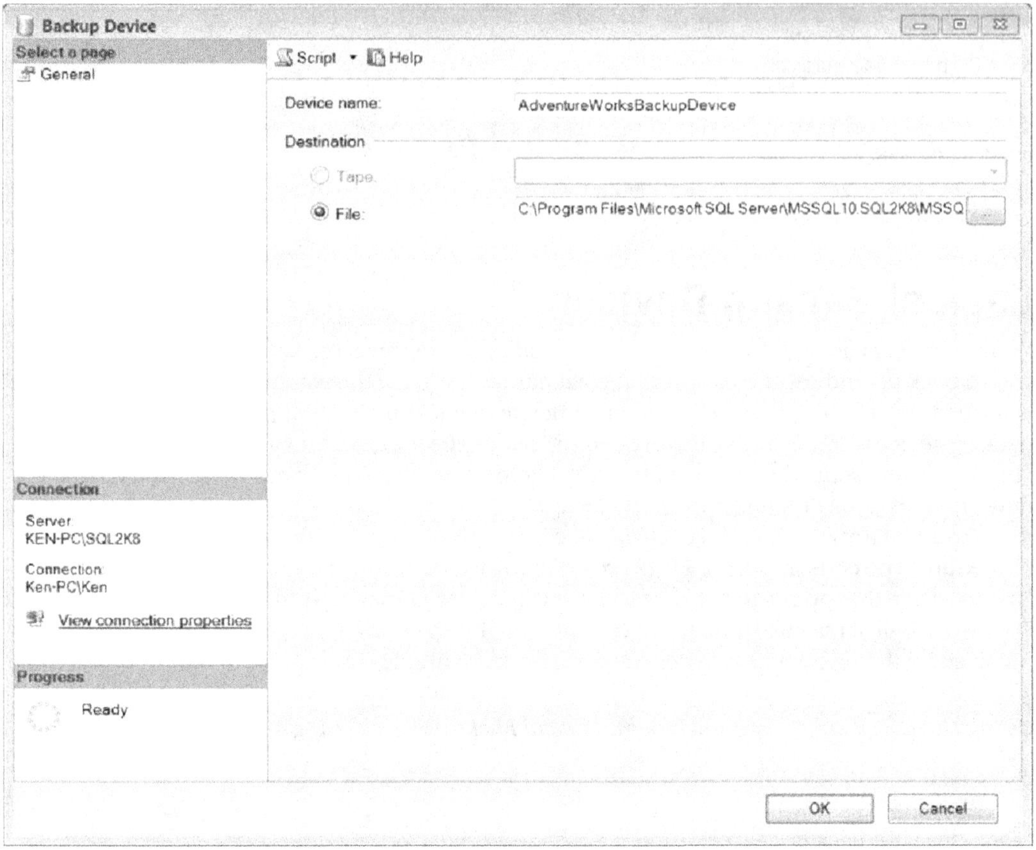

Figure 11-6. *Backup Device dialog General section*

Once you create the backup device, the next time you open the Backup Device dialog box, you will see a Media Contents page. You can open the Backup Device dialog box again by double-clicking the appropriate device in the Backup Devices folder. The Media Contents page displays all of the backup sets that are contained in the logical backup device, as shown in Figure 11-7. We have taken two full backups before opening the dialog box again for demonstration purposes.

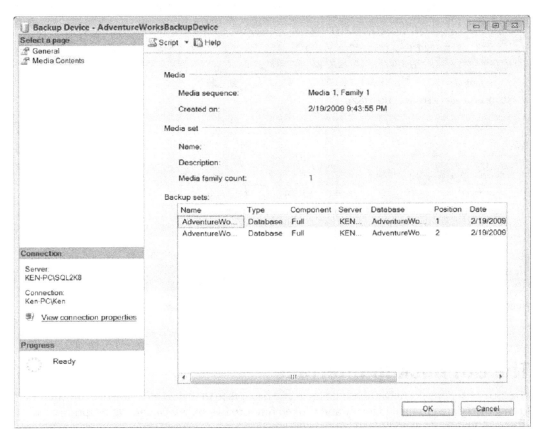

Figure 11-7. *Backup Device dialog Media Contents section*

You can query the `sys.backup_devices` catalog view to display a list all of the current logical backup devices, along with the physical device type and location. Figure 11-8 shows the results for the backup device we created in this section.

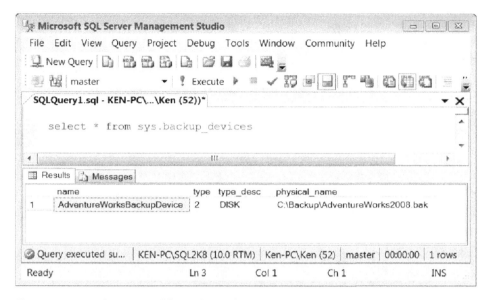

Figure 11-8. *Results returned from the sys.backup_devices catalog view*

The GUI Backup Interface

The GUI-based, Back Up Database dialog is the best place to review all of the backup choices because they are grouped logically and broken out into two pages: General and Options, as shown in Figures 11-9 and 11-10.

If you are unsure how certain configuration changes affect the BACKUP command, you can generate a script with the selected configuration and analyze the output. Using the GUI interface will also prevent you from creating a BACKUP command that contains certain logical errors. For example, you are not given the option to create a transaction log backup on a database that is using the simple recovery model.

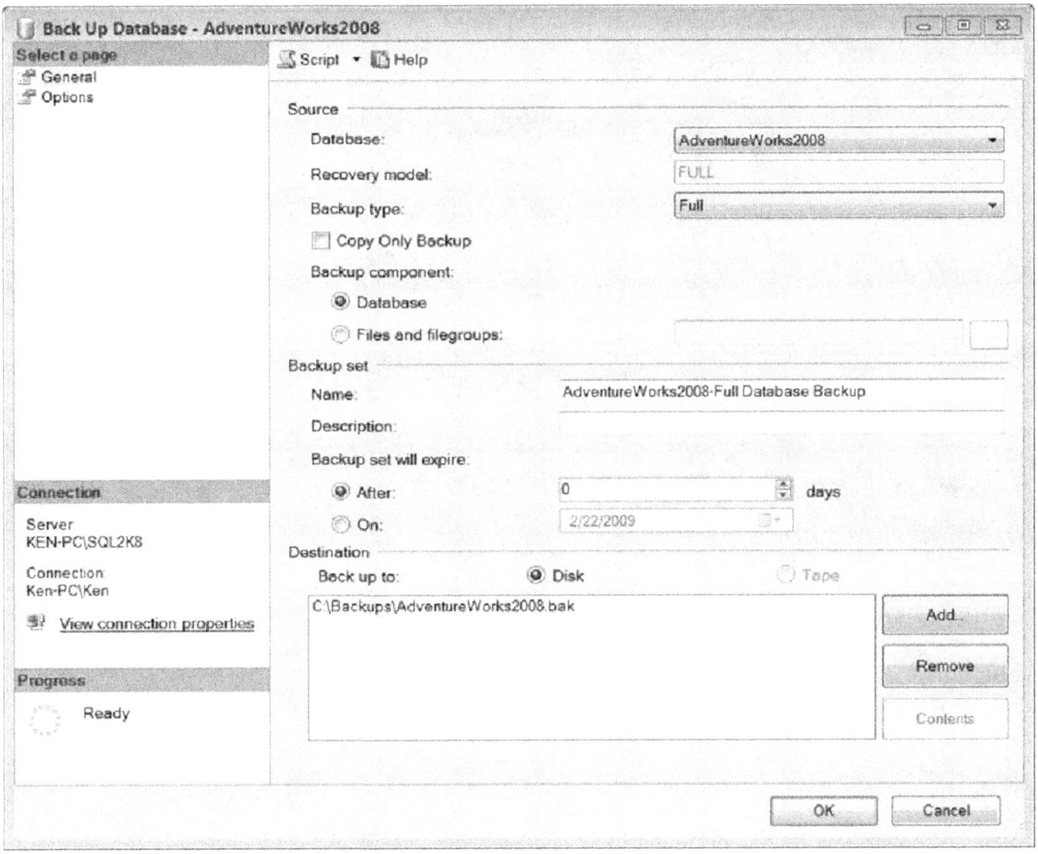

Figure 11-9. *Back Up Database dialog box General section*

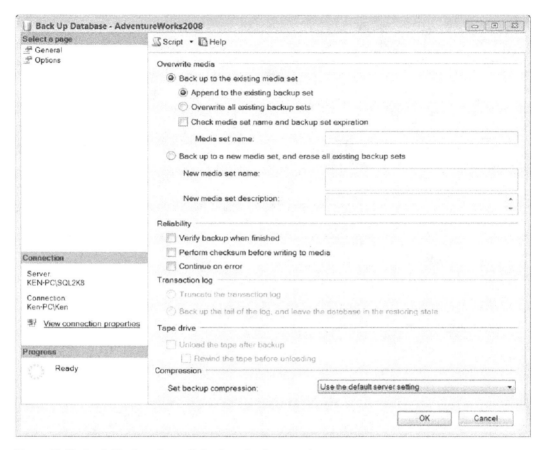

Figure 11-10. *Back Up Database dialog box Options section*

The General page, shown in Figure 11-9, consists of three areas: Source, Backup Set, and Destination. Let's take a look at the specific configurations available in each:

- *Database*: Drop-down list containing the databases available to back up.

- *Recovery Model*: Read-only text box that displays the recovery model for the selected database. This will affect the type of backups that can be performed.

- *Backup Type*: Drop-down that lists the available backup types based on the recovery model for the selected database.

- *Copy Only Backup*: Check box used to create a copy-only backup. Selecting this option will add the WITH COPY_ONLY clause to the BACKUP command.

- *Backup Component*: Option buttons that determine whether you will back up the entire database or only a specific file or filegroup.

- *Name*: The logical name given to the backup set. SQL Server will automatically suggest a name based on the options selected in the Source area.

- *Description*: Logical description that can be given to the backup set.

- *Backup Set Will Expire*: Option that determines when the backup set can be over-written using the INIT option. You can specify a date the backup set will expire or enter a number of days to retain the backup set. A backup set will never expire if you enter a value of 0 in the number of days.

- *Back Up To*: Option that determines if you will back up to disk or tape.

- *Add button*: Displays the Select Backup Destination dialog box shown in Figure 11-11 that allows you to add a backup file or device to the backup set. You can add up to 64 devices for a single backup set.

Figure 11-11. *Select Backup Destination dialog box*

- *Remove button*: Removes the highlighted backup device from the backup set.

- *Contents button*: Displays the Device Contents dialog box shown in Figure 11-12, which contains information about the media content for the highlighted backup device.

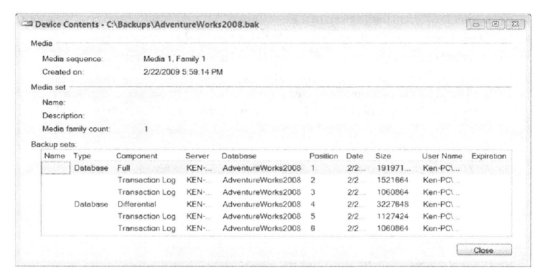

Figure 11-12. *Device Contents dialog box*

The Options page (shown earlier in Figure 11-10) consists of five areas: Overwrite Media, Reliability, Transaction Log, Tape Drive, and Compression. Let's take a look at the specific configurations available in each:

- *Back Up to the Existing Media Set*: This option adds the NOFORMAT clause to the BACKUP statement to ensure that the media header is not overwritten.

- *Append to the Existing Backup Set*: This option adds the NOINIT clause to the BACKUP statement to instruct the backup to append the backup set to the existing media set.

- *Overwrite All Existing Backup Sets*: This option adds the INIT clause to the BACKUP statement that instructs the backup to overwrite the existing backup sets.

- *Check Media Set Name and Backup Set Expiration*: This option adds the NOSKIP clause to the BACKUP statement that forces the backup to check the expiration date for the backup set before it is allowed to be overwritten. You can optionally add a media set name when this option is checked. This will add the MEDIANAME clause to the BACKUP statement that forces the existing media set name to match the entered media set name before the backup will successfully complete.

- *Back Up to a New Media Set, and Erase All Existing Backup Sets*: This option adds the FORMAT clause to the BACKUP statement in order to overwrite the media header and the INIT clause to overwrite the backup sets. The SKIP option will also be added to the BACKUP statement when this option is selected to bypass the validation checks for media name and expiration. The SKIP option is not required because it is always the default behavior whenever the FORMAT clause is used.

- *New Media Set Name*: This option adds the MEDIANAME clause to the BACKUP statement that will be used for the new media set.

- *New Media Set Description*: This option adds the MEDIADESCRIPTION clause to the BACKUP statement to provide a description for the media set.

- *Verify Backup When Finished*: This option will actually create a RESTORE VERIFYONLY statement following the BACKUP command that verifies the backup contents are readable.

- *Perform Checksum Before Writing to Media*: This option adds the CHECKSUM clause to the BACKUP statement that will verify the checksum and torn page information before writing each page to disk. A checksum will also be created for the entire backup. This option will add additional overhead to the backup operation.

- *Continue on Error*: This option adds the CONTINUE_AFTER_ERROR clause to the BACKUP statement that instructs the backup to continue if checksum or torn page errors are detected. The default option is STOP_ON_ERROR.

- *Truncate the Transaction Log*: This option is only available for transaction log backups. This instructs the backup to truncate the transaction log after the backup has completed. Selecting this option does not add anything to the BACKUP statement because this is the default behavior for transaction log backups.

- *Backup the Tail of the Log, and Leave the Database in the Restoring State*: This option is only available for transaction log backups. This option will add the NO_TRUNCATE clause to the BACKUP statement that causes the BACKUP statement to back up the log regardless of the state of the database and does not truncate the log. This will also add the NORECOVERY clause to the BACKUP statement that leaves the database in a restoring state after the backup has completed. This option is generally used to back up the tail of the transaction log on a damaged database before performing a restore.

- *Unload the Tape After Backup*: This option adds the UNLOAD clause to the BACKUP statement that is used automatically to unload a tape after a backup completes.

- *Rewind the Tape Before Unloading*: This option adds the REWIND clause to the BACKUP statement that is used automatically to rewind a tape before unloading after a backup completes.

- *Set Backup Compression*: This option allows you to accept the default server setting for compressed backups or to override the default setting by specifically choosing to compress or not compress the backup. If the default setting is chosen, nothing will be added to the BACKUP statement. If you choose the Compress Backup option, the COMPRESSION clause will be added to the BACKUP statement. If you choose the Do Not Compress Backup option, the NO_COMPRESSION clause will be added to the BACKUP statement.

Another option that is always added by default when using the GUI is the STATS option. The STATS option is used to show backup progress. You can specify a percentage to report. For example STATS = 20 will display a message for roughly every 20% of the backup that has completed. If you specify the STATS option without an assigned percentage, you will receive messages at 10% intervals.

Backups from T-SQL

Anything you can do in the GUI, you can do using T-SQL. Actually, the only way to specify certain options and perform certain types of backups is by using T-SQL. Using the GUI is a good way to perform a quick backup or script out a BACKUP command that you can tweak a little using T-SQL to get exactly what you are looking for. I always script out my BACKUP statements that are generated by the GUI and review them before actually executing the command in order to make sure the statement is doing exactly what I am expecting. The complete syntax for creating a database backup is shown in Listing 11-13.

Listing 11-13. *Complete Syntax Used for Creating Database Backups*

```
--BACKUP STATEMENTS

--Backup database
BACKUP DATABASE { database_name | @database_name_var }
 TO <backup_device> [ ,...n ]
 [ <MIRROR TO clause> ] [ next-mirror-to ]
 [ WITH { DIFFERENTIAL | <general_WITH_options> [ ,...n ] } ]
[;]

--Backup files or filegroups
BACKUP DATABASE { database_name | @database_name_var }
 <file_or_filegroup> [ ,...n ]
 TO <backup_device> [ ,...n ]
 [ <MIRROR TO clause> ] [ next-mirror-to ]
 [ WITH { DIFFERENTIAL | <general_WITH_options> [ ,...n ] } ]
[;]

--Partial backup
BACKUP DATABASE { database_name | @database_name_var }
 READ_WRITE_FILEGROUPS [ , <read_only_filegroup> [ ,...n ] ]
 TO <backup_device> [ ,...n ]
 [ <MIRROR TO clause> ] [ next-mirror-to ]
 [ WITH { DIFFERENTIAL | <general_WITH_options> [ ,...n ] } ]
[;]

--Transaction log backup
BACKUP LOG { database_name | @database_name_var }
 TO <backup_device> [ ,...n ]
 [ <MIRROR TO clause> ] [ next-mirror-to ]
 [ WITH { <general_WITH_options> | <log-specific_optionspec> } [ ,...n ] ]
[;]


--BACKUP DESTINATION OPTIONS
```

```
<backup_device>::=
 {
 { logical_device_name | @logical_device_name_var }
 | { DISK | TAPE } =
 { 'physical_device_name' | @physical_device_name_var }
 }

<MIRROR TO clause>::=
 MIRROR TO <backup_device> [ ,...n ]

<file_or_filegroup>::=
 {
 FILE = { logical_file_name | @logical_file_name_var }
 | FILEGROUP = { logical_filegroup_name | @logical_filegroup_name_var }
 }

<read_only_filegroup>::=
 FILEGROUP = { logical_filegroup_name | @logical_filegroup_name_var }

--WITH OPTIONS

--Backup set options
 COPY_ONLY
 | { COMPRESSION | NO_COMPRESSION }
 | DESCRIPTION = { 'text' | @text_variable }
 | NAME = { backup_set_name | @backup_set_name_var }
 | PASSWORD = { password | @password_variable }
 | { EXPIREDATE = { 'date' | @date_var }
 | RETAINDAYS = { days | @days_var } }

--Media set options
 { NOINIT | INIT }
 | { NOSKIP | SKIP }
 | { NOFORMAT | FORMAT }
 | MEDIADESCRIPTION = { 'text' | @text_variable }
 | MEDIANAME = { media_name | @media_name_variable }
 | MEDIAPASSWORD = { mediapassword | @mediapassword_variable }
 | BLOCKSIZE = { blocksize | @blocksize_variable }

--Data transfer options
 BUFFERCOUNT = { buffercount | @buffercount_variable }
 | MAXTRANSFERSIZE = { maxtransfersize | @maxtransfersize_variable }

--Error management options
 { NO_CHECKSUM | CHECKSUM }
 | { STOP_ON_ERROR | CONTINUE_AFTER_ERROR }
```

```
--Compatibility options
 RESTART

--Monitoring options
 STATS [ = percentage ]

--Tape options
 { REWIND | NOREWIND }
 | { UNLOAD | NOUNLOAD }

--Log-specific options
 { NORECOVERY | STANDBY = undo_file_name }
 | NO_TRUNCATE
```

Using Encryption

When you are using encryption in SQL Server, it is extremely important to back up any encryption keys and certificates and store them in a secure offsite location. For example, if you are using transparent data encryption, you cannot restore the encrypted database on a new system without having the encryption key. There is no back door. You can't attach the data files or restore the database, period. There are three objects you should back up when using encryption in SQL Server: the service master key, the database master key, and any certificates used for encryption.

The service master key is the root encryption key for the entire instance of SQL Server. SQL Server automatically creates the service master key the first time it is needed to encrypt another key. You should back up the service master key and keep it and the encryption password in a secure offsite location. The code to back up the service master key is shown in Listing 11-14.

Listing 11-14. *Code to Backup the Service Master Key*

```
BACKUP SERVICE MASTER KEY
TO FILE = 'c:\service_master_key'
ENCRYPTION BY PASSWORD = '3ncryptiOnP@$$wOrd'
GO
```

The next thing you need to back up is the database master key. SQL Server uses the database master key to encrypt other keys and certificates within the database. If the key is accidently deleted, SQL Server will not be able to decrypt any objects created using that key. Therefore, you should back up the database master key and store it in a secure offsite location. You should also keep a local copy for immediate use. If you encrypted the database master key using a password, you will first have to open the key before backing it up. If you encrypted the database master key using the service master key, you do not have to open the key prior to backing it up. The code to back up the database master key for the master database is shown in Listing 11-15.

Listing 11-15. *Code to Back Up the Database Master Key*

```
USE master
GO
--Open the master key (This is not required if the master key
-- is encrypted using the service master key.)
OPEN MASTER KEY DECRYPTION BY PASSWORD = 'M@$t3r_K3y_3ncryptiOnP@$$wOrd '

--Back up the database master key
BACKUP MASTER KEY
TO FILE = 'c:\database_master_key'
ENCRYPTION BY PASSWORD = '3ncryptiOnP@$$wOrd'
GO
```

Finally, you need to back up any certificates and store them in a secure offsite location. The code in Listing 11-16 shows the syntax used to back up a certificate along with the private key.

Listing 11-16. *Code to Back Up a Certificate and the Private Key*

```
USE master
GO

BACKUP CERTIFICATE TestCert
TO FILE = 'C:\TestCert.cer'
WITH PRIVATE KEY
        (FILE = 'C:\TestCertKey.pvk',
        ENCRYPTION BY PASSWORD = '3ncryptiOnP@$$wOrd');
GO
```

Backing Up the System Databases

You need to make sure you include the system databases as a part of your backup strategy. If you have to rebuild a server, you will be able to use the system database backups to restore any custom configurations, including jobs, logins, and so on. We generally include the system databases in a full daily backup routine and take special one-off backups after certain information in the database changes.

Following are the system databases and some things that you need to know about backing them up:

- master: The master database uses the simple recovery model, and you can only perform full database backups of the master database. You should back up this database whenever certain operations cause it to be updated, including the following:

  - Adding and removing user databases

  - Adding and removing logins

- Adding and removing a backup device

- Adding and removing linked servers and remote logins

- Modifying metadata for user databases, such as file locations or adding and removing filegroups

- msdb: The msdb database uses the simple recovery model by default, but it can be configured to use any recovery model. For example, you can change the recovery model of the msdb to full and take advantage of transaction log backups if you are highly dependent on information that is stored in this database. The information in the msdb database changes often because it logs historical information for items like backups, SQL Agent jobs, and database mail. At minimum, you should take a full backup of the msdb after making configuration changes, including the following:

  - Adding and removing SQL Agent jobs

  - Adding and removing maintenance plans

  - Importing SSIS packages

  - Adding and removing Policies and central management servers

  - Configuring log shipping

  - Configuring database mail

  - Configuring operators and alerts

- model: This database uses the full recovery model by default, but it can be configured to use any recovery model. Remember, since the model database serves as a template for all new user databases, if you change the recovery model in the model database, any newly created databases will be created with this recovery model as well. You only need to perform full database backups of the model database whenever you make custom configuration changes. Even though the recovery model is set to full, there is no activity in the model database to warrant transaction log backups.

- tempdb: The recovery model for the tempdb is simple and cannot be changed. Every time you restart SQL Server, the tempdb is recreated, and any data stored in it is lost. Since the tempdb is recreated every time SQL Server is restarted, you are not allowed to perform any type of backup operations on it.

- Resource: This is a read-only database and is not visible in SQL Server Management Studio. The Resource database is only updated whenever service packs are applied to SQL Server. You cannot back up the Resource database using a SQL Server backup operation. To backup this database, you must perform a file-based backup operation by copying the mssqlsystemresource.mdf file to your backup location. Unlike other data files, you do not have to stop the SQL Server service in order to copy the Resource data files.

Backup History

SQL Server maintains a set of tables that hold the backup history that is performed on each server instance in the msdb database. You can use these tables to gather useful information, such as the last time a backup was performed on each database. The backup history tables include the following:

- *backupfile*: Contains information about the data and log files for a database backup.

- *backupfilegroup*: Contains information about every filegroup in a database when the backup was performed.

- *backupmediafamily*: Holds one row for each media family, including the logical device name, physical device name, and device type.

- *backupmediaset*: Holds one row for each backup media set. Each media set can have multiple media families.

- *backupset*: Holds a single row for each backup set created by a successful backup operation. The backupset table holds information like the database name, the backup start and end times, and log sequence numbers at the time of backup.

After a while of capturing backup information, the backup history tables can become rather large depending on the number and frequency of backups performed. We have seen the msdb grow to a fairly substantial size because of the amount of data stored in the backup history tables. Microsoft provides the sp_delete_backuphistory system stored procedure that you can use to limit the amount of history stored in these tables. The sp_delete_backuphistory procedure enables you to enter a date/time parameter that will remove all data created before a certain date or time. For example, the statement Exec msdb.dbo.sp_delete_backuphistory '1/1/2009' will remove all the records from the backup history tables in the mdsb that were created before January 1, 2009.

Caution If your msdb database already contains a lot of data in the history tables, it is best to delete the data for smaller date ranges and test the impact on the server instead of trying to remove several months or years all at once.

Listing 11-17 shows a script you can use to keep a specified amount of history in the database without deleting all of the history at once. If you have a lot of history in your backup tables, you should start deleting the data in smaller chunks until you see the impact that removing the data has on your server. We maintain six months of history and never delete more than three months of history each time the script is executed. Let's say you schedule this script to run once a week. Every week you will delete three months of history until you eventually delete all the backup data you have built up prior to implementing this script and only have to delete a single week of backup history.

Listing 11-17. *Script to Remove Backup History in the msdb in Three-Month Intervals While Maintaining Six Months of History*

```
USE msdb
GO

--Keep 6 months of history, but never delete more than 3 months at a time.
Declare @dte Datetime
SET @dte = (SELECT MIN(backup_start_date) FROM backupset WITH (nolock))
SET @dte = (SELECT dateadd(mm,3,@dte))

IF (dateadd(mm,-6,getdate()) < @dte )
 SET @dte = dateadd(mm,-6,getdate())

PRINT @dte

EXEC sp_delete_backuphistory @dte
```

If you want to remove all the backup history for a specific database, you can execute the sp_delete_database_backuphistory system stored procedure followed by the database name. For example, the statement Exec msdb.dbo.sp_delete_database_backuphistory 'AdventureWorks2008' will remove all the records from the backup history tables in the msdb for the AdventureWorks2008 database.

Summary

Okay, we have gone over several backup options available in SQL Server 2008, but that is only the half of it. The next chapter will tie it all together when we discuss the restore options and other restore considerations. While knowing all the restore options so that you can quickly recover a database is important, making sure you have a good backup is even more important. You can memorize every restore command there is, but if you don't have a good backup then they won't do you any good.

CHAPTER 12

Restore and Recovery Strategies

The ability to restore databases in SQL Server 2008 is essential to recovering a system when catastrophes arise. In order to restore your databases, you need a backup strategy that fulfills the requirements set forth by your business requirements. If your backup strategy is inadequate, then you will not be able to recover to the predetermined interval required to fulfill the requirements of your application. Ultimately, your application will lose data, and the users and your management will be very unhappy. In the last chapter, we covered the details of creating effective and efficient backup strategies. This chapter will focus on the skills needed to restore a database when the time arises.

Restore Vocabulary

Before we can really get into the details of restoring databases, you need to understand the basic vocabulary used by database administrators when discussing recovery options. The f ollowing list contains some of these frequently used terms:

- *Recovery model*: Determines the available backup options for your system. Three basic options exist—simple, full, and bulk-logged.

- *Point-in-time recovery*: Method used to restore your database to a specific time before a catastrophe or disaster occurred. SQL Server 2008 provides you with multiple methods to restore your database to a specific time.

- *Transaction log restore*: Allows you to retrieve or apply the changes within the transaction log to your database. These allow you to restore the database to a specific point in time.

- *Differential restore*: Allows you to restore all the changes that have occurred since the last full backup was applied.

- *Full database restore*: Restores the database to what it looked liked exactly when the backup occurred.

- RESTORE HEADERONLY: Displays the header information for all of the backup sets contained in a given backup device. In other words, the RESTORE HEADERONLY option lists all of the files and the times at which the backup occurred, along with other information about the files within the backup set.

- RESTORE FILELISTONLY: Allows you to view the file names along with other information about the files themselves stored within the backup set.

- *File restore*: Allows you to restore multiple files or filegroups that exist in a multiple filegroup database.

- *Page restore*: Replaces corrupt pages without having to restore the entire database.

- *Piecemeal restore*: Restores multiple files or filegroups after the primary filegroup has already been brought online.

- *Snapshot restore*: Restores a database snapshot instead of a full database backup to get the database to what it looked like at the time of the backup.

- *Logical sequence number (LSN)*: The sequence number that tracks the order in which backups occur on a database. LSNs are important for understanding the order in which events occurred.

- RECOVERY: The option utilized in scripts for bringing your database online.

- NORECOVERY: The option utilized in scripts to enable your database to have additional transaction logs or differential backups applied to it.

- *Online restore*: Describes the database state when restoring parts or pieces of your database while the database is accepting transactions.

- *Offline restore*: Describes the database state when a restore is occurring, and the database is not accepting transactions.

Now that you understand some common vocabulary used when discussing restores, let's just dive into some of the detail of recovering or restoring your system.

The Importance of Recovery Models

In Chapter 11, we discussed in detail the various recovery models available in SQL Server. Remember, the recovery model chosen will determine your available options when the time comes to restore your database. Obviously, since you can't take a transaction log backup if your database is using the simple recovery model, you are limited to restoring your database with the last full backup; but there are some less obvious nuances with database recovery models. For example, if you select the bulk-logged recovery model, you may or may not be able to use your transaction log backups to perform a point-in-time recovery. If no bulk transactions have occurred within your transaction log backup, you can perform a point-in-time recovery; but if there is a bulk transaction, you have to restore the entire transaction log.

Make sure the recovery model you choose allows you to fulfill the business requirements set forth by your organization to meet the recovery needs for your applications. For example, if the requirements specify that you need to be able to recover your data to a specific point in time, then the simple recovery model may not be the best one to utilize on your database.

The best advice we can give you is to make sure you understand the limitations of the recovery model that you select. Do not wait until your system is down or you need to restore your database to realize that you have chosen the wrong recovery model. Trust us—reporting to management that you are unable to recover the data because you used the wrong recovery model is not a fun situation. Spend the time up front; review the recovery models of all your databases, including the ones that you are *almost sure* are set to the appropriate recovery model, and then make sure the recovery models are set correctly to fulfill the business requirements.

Practicing Your Recovery Strategy

Throughout this chapter, we are going to cover the various recovery options available to you in SQL Server 2008. Depending on the backup strategy chosen, the complexity and the amount of time of your recovery strategy will vary. Regardless of your chosen recovery strategy, please make sure you spend some time testing that strategy. The following list provides some benefits of practicing your recovery strategy. Practice is

A verification process that enables you to ensure your recovery strategy meets your business requirements. Once you have simulated the various scenarios that would require you to restore your database and validated that you were able to recover correctly, you can document that your recovery strategy is able to meet your requirements.

A method for verifying that you have good backups to recover from. On a predetermined cycle, you should restore your backups to ensure that they are not corrupt and are usable. Do not wait until you need your backups to validate that you have good backups. Remember, your job is to make sure you don't lose data. Frequent validation of your backups increases the chances that you will be able to recover successfully. So spend a little time validating your database backups; document the day and time in which your validation occurred. That way, management may be a little more forgiving in the event that your database backups are not usable.

An opportunity to practice when you're not under pressure. When systems go down, there is a lot of management and user pressure to get the system back up and available quickly. Being comfortable with your recovery strategy will help ease some of that pressure. Think about it: When you know the restore options that are available to you, that your backups are good because you verified them by restoring them, that you can meet the business requirements, and that you have practiced and restored the database hundreds of times, then you should be comfortable restoring the database under pressure. On the other hand, if you don't know if you have transaction logs or differential backups, or you haven't verified any backups from that server in over a year, then the pressure of the system being down can add some unneeded stress to the situation. So we would encourage you to practice your recovery strategy to make sure you're ready when the time comes.

A good baseline for determining the amount of time it will take to recover your database(s). The first question you will be asked when the user deletes data and you have to go to a backup, or when a server has gone down and you have to move the database to another server, is this: How long is it going to take before the system is available? Practicing your recovery strategy will enable you to provide better estimates during a crisis. Providing an inaccurate estimate for the amount of time that it will take to recover your system only adds to your headache, especially if the process takes longer than you estimate. Document the amount of time it takes to restore each database on a server along with the amount of time it takes to transfer that database from your off-site storage. Having those times available helps prepare all parties involved when recovering your system.

Peace of mind. When you practice, practice, and practice your recovery strategy, then that should increase your confidence when it comes to your ability to recover when bad things happen to your system. Knowing that you can recover from any situation will help you sleep at night. It also helps you prepare management for potential failure points and aids in discussions for other high-availability solutions. Since part of your responsibility as a database administrator requires you to minimize data loss, practicing and ensuring the validity of your recovery strategy helps you stay employed when disk drives fail, servers crash, or when other types of disasters strike.

We hope that after reading some of the preceding benefits of practicing your recovery strategy, you will make time to practice recovering your system. As a DBA, you should take pride in making sure that the recovery strategies meet and exceed the expectations of the business.

Types of Restores

SQL Server 2008 offers various methods for recovering or restoring your databases. The next couple of sections will cover in detail the commands and syntax used to restore your databases.

Let's review the basic syntax for restoring full database backups, as shown in the following code:

```
RESTORE DATABASE { database_name | @database_name_var }
 [ FROM <backup_device> [ ,...n ] ]
 [ WITH
  [ { STOP_ON_ERROR | CONTINUE_AFTER_ERROR}],
  [{ FILE= {File_number}}],
  [ MOVE 'logical_file_name' to 'operating_system_file_name' ][,...n],
  [NORECOVERY |RECOVERY | STANDBY =
        {standby_file_name | @standby_file_name_var } ],
  [PARTIAL],
  [REPLACE],
  [RESTART],
  [STATS],
  [{STOP AT = {date_time} |
     STOPATMARK = {'mark_name'}
     STOPBEFOREMAKR = {'mark_name'}]
]
```

Before we discuss each type of the RESTORE statements, let's discuss some of the options available to you within T-SQL, as shown in the following list:

- *Backup device*: The device type where you will retrieve your backup file from. Available device types are disk and tape or a logical device name.

- DATABASE_SNAPSHOT: Enables you to restore the database back to what it looked like at the time the snapshot was taken. The snapshot serves as the full database backup file in this instance.

- FILE *or* FILEGROUP: Specifies the files or groups of files that you are attempting to restore.

- MOVE: An option that allows you to relocate your logical file name to another physical location during the restore process. In other words, if the original data files were stored in a location that does not exist on the server where you are attempting to restore the file, then you can move or change the location during the restore process to place the file on drives that are available on the server.

- NORECOVERY: An option available to specify that you wish to add additional files to the database. When this option is specified, the database is still allowed to roll forward additional files.

- PARTIAL: The option that starts the first stage of a piecemeal restore where you restore the primary filegroup.

- RECOVERY: The default action when executing the RESTORE command. The RECOVERY option informs SQL Server that you do not wish to apply any additional files and that database should be available for user transactions.

- REPLACE: An option created to prevent the database administrator from accidentally overwriting the wrong database. If the database names do not match the name in the backup set, the REPLACE option must be used to restore the database backup file.

- RESTART: An option that allows you to restart a failed restore process from the point where the failure occurred. Make sure you keep this option in mind because it can save you a lot of time after a failure within the restoration process. There is nothing worse than starting a restore process from the beginning when it has almost finished.

- STANDBY: An option similar to the NORECOVERY option that allows you to apply additional logs and differential databases to your database; however, the STANDBY option allows you to actually read the database between transaction log restores. Without specifying the STANDBY option, in order to bring the database to a readable state, SQL Server has to roll back any uncommitted transactions, which will break the restore process. With the STANDBY option, SQL Server still has to roll back the uncommitted transactions, but you must specify a standby file (previously known as an *undo* file) that will store the information needed to "undo" the process of rolling back the transactions, which will allow for further restores.

- STATS: The option that reports to you the completion percentage of the restore operation. This option is very handy when restoring backup files and you need to know how fast or slow the restore process is going.

- STOPAT: Specifies where you want the restore process to stop. This option is very useful when performing point-in-time recoveries.

- STOPATMARK: An option used to identify the location where to stop the restore process. Assume you are getting ready to perform a series of steps and you want to mark the point in time before you start the process. You can mark your transaction by giving it a name, and then you can restore back to that point by using the STOPATMARK option and specifying the transaction name. The restore point will include the named transaction only if the transaction was originally committed to the database.

- STOPBEFOREMARK: Allows you to restore the database to exactly what the system looked like right before you marked the transaction log.

Now that you understand some of the options that are available during the restore process, let's get into the RESTORE statements.

Restoring Full Backups

Restoring a full backup brings a database back to the state when the full database backup occurred. Unlike differential and transaction log restores, full database restores can stand alone and are not required to run with the other restore methods. However, a full backup restore is required as the first step of the recovery process for differential and/or transaction log backups. Full database backup restores are offline restores.

The syntax for full backup restores may seem a little overwhelming, but the basic RESTORE statements are very simple. You just need to understand the various restore options so you know what's available in the event that you need to perform additional non-routine operations during a restore. Do not feel that you have to use all of the restore options just because they exist. The following code shows a much simpler statement to restore the Aventureworks2008 database:

```
USE master
GO
RESTORE DATABASE AdventureWorks2008
FROM DISK = 'C:\Backup\AdventureWorks2008.bak'
WITH RECOVERY,
STATS
```

Restoring Transaction Logs

You can use transaction log restores to recover a database to any point in time. You must use transaction log restores in conjunction with full and/or differential database restores. As long as you have a full backup, you can restore as many contiguous transaction log backups that you have as long as the LSNs are in order. The following list contains some tips for restoring transaction logs:

- Make sure you leave the database in a STANDBY or a NORECOVERY state when you restore the full and differential database backups.

- You must restore the transaction logs in the order in which they were taken based on the LSN.

- If you want to apply multiple transaction logs, make sure you specify STANDBY or NORECOVERY for each restore until you apply the last transaction log.

As long as you remember those simple rules, you will not run into problems restoring transaction log backups. Now, it may be a good idea to build a script that enables you to restore multiple logs without having to manually restore each one. Such a script definitely saves us time when we need to restore multiple transaction logs. The article at the following link presents a script you can incorporate into your backups that will always allow you to have the most recent restore scripts on hand (www.mssqltips.com/tip.asp?tip=1611).

The syntax for restoring transaction logs is fairly simple and straightforward, as illustrated in Listing 12-1. Specify the database name that you restore the logs against, the location where you would get the logs from, and whether or not additional logs are going to be applied during the restore process.

As always, multiple usable options exist for restoring transaction logs. Make sure you know what the available options are just in case you need them; however, there is no reason to use the available options if they aren't needed.

Listing 12-1. *SQL Code to Restore Transaction Logs*

```
USE master
GO

RESTORE LOG AdventureWorks2008
FROM DISK = 'c:\backups\AdventureWorks_log.bak'
WITH FILE =1,
STANDBY = 'C:\backups\UNDO.BAK',
STATS

RESTORE LOG AdventureWorks2008
FROM DISK = 'c:\backups\AdventureWorks_log.bak'
WITH FILE =2,
RECOVERY,
STATS
```

Restoring Differential Backups

Remember that differential backups capture all the changes that have occurred within the database since the last full backup. Your backup strategy may require you to have multiple differential backups available for use during a recovery. The point that you would like to recover your database to will determine which differential backup you should use.

When it comes to restoring differential backups, you do not have to restore multiple differential backups in order to restore your database. For example, let's say that your backup strategy takes a full backup on Sunday nights followed by differential backups every other night of the week. If you want to recover your database to what it looked like on Wednesday, you do not have to restore Monday's, Tuesday's, and then Wednesday's differential backups. You would only have to restore the full backup from Sunday, and then the differential backup from Wednesday in order to recover your database.

■Note Remember, in order to apply a differential backup, the database has to be in NORECOVERY or STANDBY mode and that transaction logs can be applied after a differential backup has been restored.

The syntax for a differential backup restore is identical to the syntax for restoring a full database backup. Outside of a few options, which you will not likely use for the differential restore, the only differentiating factor between a full database restore and a differential database restore is the type of file you reference in the FROM DISK clause of the RESTORE statement. For example:

```
USE master
GO
RESTORE DATABASE AdventureWorks2008
FROM DISK = 'c:\backups\AdventureWorksDif.bak'
WITH RECOVERY,
STATS
```

In this example, the .bak file is one that has been generated by a differential backup. Hence, the statement in this example initiates a differential recovery.

Restoring Files and Filegroups

File or filegroup restores enable you to restore a damaged file instead of restoring an entire database. If you have multiple files or filegroups within a database and only one of those files or filegroups is damaged, then you can restore only the damaged file or filegroup, minimizing the amount of recovery time needed. If the damaged filegroup is not your primary filegroup, then you can even restore the damaged filegroup while the other files or filegroups are online. When restoring a particular file or filegroup, then that file or filegroup will be offline until the restoration process completes. By default, when a database is online, then a filegroup restore will be an online operation, leaving the remainder of the filegroups online. If a database is offline, then a filegroup restore performs the restoration process offline. Discussions of online and offline operations occur in more detail in the "Online Recoveries" section later in this chapter.

The syntax for file or filegroup restores, shown in Listing 12-2, is pretty straightforward and easy to follow. Assuming that you have multiple filegroups within your database, then specify the name of the database to restore, the location from which to retrieve a file from, the file to restore, and the name of the filegroup, including the appropriate recovery action.

Listing 12-2. *SQL Code to Restore a File and Filegroup of a Full Database Backup*

```
RESTORE DATABASE AdventureWorks2008
 FILE = 'AdventureWorksIndex.ndf',
 FILEGROUP = 'Indexes'
FROM DISK = 'c:\backups\AdventureWorksFileGroup.bak'
WITH RECOVERY,
STATS
```

Listing 12-2 restores a file within a filegroup and attempts to make the database active. As you can see in Figure 12-1, we received an error message because we have not applied all the necessary transaction logs.

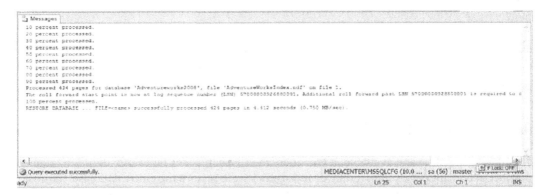

Figure 12-1. *The results of a file and filegroup restore without applying all the necessary transaction logs*

Why did we receive this error? When restoring files and/or filegroups for a database, you have to make sure that all files and filegroups are in a consistent state with the primary filegroup. In order to make sure all the filegroups are consistent, you have to restore any transaction log backups created after the last restored full or differential database backup. In other words, if you created three transaction log backups after your nightly backup, then you would have to restore all three transaction log backups to the filegroups before you could bring the database online. Luckily, SQL Server will only apply the transaction logs that you are restoring to the recovering filegroup, so you don't have to worry about modifying data within other filegroups unintentionally. If you have not created any transaction log backups or if the database is in a recovery model that does not support transaction log backups, then you don't have to worry about the filegroups being in a consistent state. Restoring the database backup takes care of that issue for you.

In Listing 12-3, a script brings the Indexes filegroup to a consistent state as the Primary filegroup. The script restores the file and filegroup from a full database backup, and then restores a transaction log backup created after the full backup.

Listing 12-3. *T-SQL Code to Restore File and Filegroups and Apply a Transaction Log to That Filegroup*

```
RESTORE DATABASE AdventureWorks2008
 FILE = 'AdventureWorksIndex.ndf',
 FILEGROUP = 'Indexes'
FROM DISK = 'c:\backups\AdventureWorksFileGroup.bak'
WITH NORECOVERY,
STATS
```

```
RESTORE LOG AdventureWorks2008
FROM DISK  = 'c:\backups\AdventureWorks_log.bak'
RECOVERY,
STATS
```

Restoring Pages

You can use page restores to restore specific pages that exist within your database without having to restore an entire database backup. Generally, you utilize this restore option to replace corrupt pages in your database. In SQL Server, you can identify suspected corrupt pages in the `suspect_pages` table in the `msdb` database. If a small number of pages are corrupt, then it may be more efficient to restore the pages within the file instead of the entire file itself. The ability to restore a handful of pages instead of an entire file will help you to keep more of your database online and available. If you query the `suspect_pages` table and identify a large number of corrupt pages, then it may be more efficient to restore the entire database. In most cases, when the database is online, then the page restores as an online operation. Unfortunately, controlling whether or not the page restore remains online is left in the hands of SQL Server and is out of your control.

When restoring the pages, you can use differential and transaction log backups. Applying these will only impact the pages specified within your `RESTORE` statement. Rolling forward, the logs will ensure that the pages are in line with the other data in terms of referential integrity at the end of the restore process.

The syntax for page restores, displayed in Listing 12-4, resembles the restore statements discussed earlier in this chapter. You simply specify the name of the database that you want to restore, the locations of the restore files, the pages that you would like to restore, and the appropriate recovery model.

Listing 12-4. *SQL Code to Restore a Page of a Full Database Backup*

```
USE master
GO

RESTORE DATABASE AdventureWorks2008
PAGE = '4:300'
FROM DISK = 'c:\backups\AdventureWorksFileGroup3.bak'
WITH RECOVERY
```

Piecemeal Restores

The piecemeal restore is an option to restore your primary filegroup and indicate that you will restore your other filegroups at a later time. The main idea is that you want to get up and running as soon as possible. To that end, you restore your main filegroup, and as time permits, restore additional filegroups to get the remaining data.

During a piecemeal restore, once the primary filegroup finishes restoring, it will be online and able to take transactions. The remaining filegroups will remain in an offline state until you bring them online.

Listing 12-5 shows an example command for performing a piecemeal restore. Just specify the database name that you would like to restore, the location of the restore file, the PARTIAL option, and any other filegroup that you would like restored with the appropriate recovery options.

The main difference in Listing 12-5 from earlier commands comes from the need to specify a PARTIAL option in the first restore sequence. The PARTIAL option lets SQL Server know that you will be restoring the primary filegroup and any other filegroup specified in the initial statement only. After you specify the PARTIAL option in the initial statement, you do not have to specify it anymore when restoring the remaining filegroups.

Listing 12-5. *SQL Code to Perform a Piecemeal Restore*

```
USE master
GO


RESTORE DATABASE AdventureWorks2008
FILEGROUP = 'Primary'
FROM DISK = 'c:\backups\AdventureWorksFileGroup3.bak'
WITH PARTIAL,
RECOVERY,
STATS
```

Restoring Snapshots

Options exist in SQL Server 2008 to restore a database from an existing snapshot. Once you restore the database from a snapshot, you are unable to roll forward any transactions that have occurred since capturing the snapshot. So make sure the snapshot contains *all* the data that you would like to restore prior to overwriting your database.

Do realize that you cannot depend on a database snapshot as your source for restoring damaged database files. That's because whatever file is damaged might be one of the files holding your snapshot data. It's also because a database snapshot is an incomplete copy of the data in a database.

Snapshot restores cannot be used on databases that contain FILESTREAM BLOBs, so make sure your database does not contain any of these before relying on database snapshots in the event of a problem. So prior to restoring the database from a snapshot, spend some time analyzing the restrictions of this option and make sure it will accomplish all of your goals.

The syntax for restoring a database from a database snapshot is straightforward (see Listing 12-6). Modify the FROM clause to specify that you want to restore from a database snapshot, and then supply the name of the snapshot. Using the snapshot restore minimizes the need to focus on any of the other options because the WITH option is not utilized with snapshot restores.

Listing 12-6. *SQL Code to Restore from a Database Snapshot*

```
USE master
GO

RESTORE DATABASE Adventureworks
FROM DATABASE_SNAPSHOT = 'AdventureWorks_ss'
```

RESTORE HEADERONLY

SQL Server allows you to review all of the backup header information stored within a backup device. To view that information, execute the command RESTORE HEADERONLY on the database file in question. The information will consist of the backed up database name, server name that the database exists on, when the backup was taken, and a lot more information about each backup header stored on the device.

The HEADERONLY option is very useful when reviewing transaction log backups and determining what file to restore in order to get to a particular point in time. The RESTORE HEADERONLY option will list all the files stored within the backup set, the start time in which the transaction logs took place, the LSN numbers (which are useful if you are trying to determine which file is next in the restore sequence), and a lot more. Make sure you understand how to use this restore option in the event that you need to restore to a point in time without the GUI.

The syntax for the RESTORE HEADERONLY option is extremely simple. The most important option you have to specify outside of the command name is the name of the backup device you want to review the header information. Once you populate the file name, then execute the command to review all the information provided. For example:

```
USE master
GO


RESTORE HEADERONLY
FROM DISK  = 'c:\backups\AdventureWorks_log.bak'
```

RESTORE FILELISTONLY

As the name FILELISTONLY indicates, this restore option only displays the information about the file or filegroup stored within a backup set. The FILELISTONLY option displays the entire filegroup's contents within the file, its logical and physical names, and various other informational columns about the files. This option is extremely useful when you are attempting to restore a database and you need to move the logical file names to a different physical drive. Store this option in your knowledge bank to use when referring to the file stored within the backup set.

The syntax for RESTORE FILELISTONLY is similar to the RESTORE HEADERONLY option. Outside of the FILELISTONLY option, the other thing you specify is the backup media that you want to review the information on and execute the command. See the following code example:

```
USE master
GO

RESTORE FILELISTONLY
FROM DISK  = 'c:\backups\AdventureWorks_log.bak'
```

RESTORE VERIFYONLY

The RESTORE VERIFYONLY option within SQL Server allows you to validate your database backups without actually performing the restore operation. The VERIFYONLY option does additional checking to ensure that the backup file is complete and the entire data set is readable, but it does not check the actual data structures of the backup set. SQL Server does its best to increase the probability that a good backup exists after a check against the file. Although RESTORE VERIFYONLY does not guarantee that you have a good backup, running this option against your data file gives you some protection in that SQL Server thinks it can restore that file in the event it has to utilize that file.

The RESTORE VERIFYONLY option syntax allows you to specify the backup device. Once you have specified the option, execute the command to determine if SQL Server thinks the backup file is comparable. Following is an example:

```
USE master
GO

RESTORE VERIFYONLY
FROM DISK  = 'c:\backups\AdventureWorks_log.bak'
```

Online Recoveries

The type of restore that you are going to perform will determine if portions of the database will remain online. If the database is in an offline state, then all of the restore options performed occur in the offline state until you bring the database back online. When the database is in an online state, then the type of restore will determine if the entire database is brought offline or only the impacted portion of the database. Whenever you restore any part of the database, that piece of the database will be offline during the restore process. The following list shows which restore options support online recoveries:

- File and filegroup restores

- Page restores

- Piecemeal restores

- Manually loading data

Restore Considerations

Before we start demonstrating examples of restoring the various database types, we would like to cover some additional options to consider. If you do not spend enough time thinking about how you will deal with the options listed in the following section, you could drastically increase your recovery time or, in the worst-case scenario, you may not be able to recover your database at all.

Utilizing Filegroups for Faster Restores

In SQL Server 2008, restoration processes exist to restore parts of filegroups of a database, while other filegroups are online and receiving transactions. When you understand the data within your database, opportunities may exist to separate your database into multiple file-groups. Once you have multiple filegroups, when restoring your database, an application does not have to wait until the entire database is restored before it can connect to the database.

For example, imagine your database contains archive tables used for viewing historical information. Since the application does not require the archive tables for basic functionality, you separate those tables into a different filegroup from the primary filegroup. When the time comes to restore your database, you can simply restore the primary filegroup, and then allow the application to connect to your database while you restore the other filegroups at your leisure. Think about it: The archive tables are generally large, but ideally, it would be nice if you could have your application up and running while you were restoring the archive tables that exist in another filegroup. If archive tables exist within your database, then consider moving those objects into another filegroup to decrease the amount of time recoveries take. We cannot determine how to utilize filegroups within your environment, but we hope you consider separating objects into multiple filegroups to decrease the amount of time it takes for restores.

Preparing for Hardware Failures

In many instances, hardware failures will occur on your database server without a warning. Making time to plan the recovery of your databases prior to the failure is definitely a worthwhile exercise.

Assume for discussion purposes that you do not have a redundant server available for the database server in question. In other words, the organization decided that it didn't want to purchase the high-availability option you presented to them. You and your system administrator should then work together to document the amount of time it will take for the delivery of hardware replacement parts in the event of a hardware failure. That way you can start to answer the questions that arise regarding the amount of time the server might be unavailable, such as the following:

- Is your organization prepared to deal with that amount of downtime?

- What options do you have available to you to get the database or multiple databases back up in a minimal amount of time?

- Can a secondary server handle the additional data and workload of the existing server?

- How will the application code handle running as a separate instance?

All of these questions and more need to be considered because we know hours of downtime agreed upon prior to the failure will be thrown out the window when the application is down. Executives who are agreeable to the risk of downtime when everything is up and running have a way of developing amnesia on that point when a database goes down. Spend some time thinking through your available options with the hope of minimizing the amount of time needed to recover your database during a crisis.

Recovering from Scratch

When discussing the mean time to failure of hardware and the other major problems that could occur on your database server, document processes to enable you to recover your system from scratch. What does this mean? Depending on the scenario, you may have to reinstall SQL Server, set up all of your databases, and re-create all of the processes that exist outside of SQL Server, like batch file processes or VB script apps, in order to get your system back up and running. The ability to restore your databases is just one small part of the equation. Recovering server-specific settings that only exist on the old server is what will likely create all the challenges. If you follow some of our advice from Chapter 2 and set up all of your servers similarly, then starting from scratch will not be as painful. If you do not configure all your servers the same, then be sure to document the following for each one of them:

- *Drive letters*: If you re-create the drives in the same manor they were created on the previous server, then less work will be required to change existing processes that refer to specific drive letters.

- *Folder structure*: The ability to re-create your folders for processes that reference them minimizes the time it will take troubleshooting process failures.

- *Installation path*: The installation path of your SQL Server instances.

- *Shared folders*: Any shared folders, the users, and their permissions.

- *Service accounts*: The accounts used to run your SQL Server services.

- *File transfer process*: Any applications that are responsible for moving files to or from the server may need to change as a result of the new server location. Knowing all of the external process that touch your server will save you an enormous amount of time.

- *Passwords*: Having copies of passwords handy will minimize the amount of time and effort needed to restore the database, such as linked server passwords, service passwords that may be used in SSIS packages, or any other passwords needed for existing processes to run without forcing a password reset.

- *Exact version of SQL Server*: You need to know the exact version of SQL Server you are running.

- *Server settings*: In all scenarios, you may not be able to restore the master database from your existing server, so you want to document the settings on the existing server that enable your application to run optimally.

The ability to recover quickly when disasters occur is a characteristic that separates good database administrators from great database administrators. Having the preceding information available for any of the servers that you support will definitely minimize the amount of time it takes to restore your application to its full capabilities. Be smart—make sure the documented information is not stored on the same database server. Store the documentation in a location that will be available when you have to start recovering your database server. In a perfect world, options would always exist to prevent you from having to start from scratch and re-create your environment. Unfortunately, the unexpected happens without warning, so you must have the capability to deal with such occurrences. Documenting server information will ultimately help you and any other database administrator recovering your system minimize the downtime.

Recovery Examples

In order to complete the topics discussed throughout this chapter, we would like to demonstrate some of the recovery strategies that we implement in our own environments. We cannot show every possible recovery strategy. However, we will provide examples that show the use of multiple recovery options.

Example 1: The Piecemeal Restore

Earlier in this chapter, we talked about piecemeal restores. Piecemeal restores are one of the recovery options that will allow you to make your database available faster by initially restoring the important filegroups and then restoring secondary filegroups later. This recovery option sounds great, but quickly introduces a question: What happens to transactions normally written to a filegroup that is currently offline?

In this example, we demonstrate the piecemeal restore of a multiple filegroup database that has clustered and nonclustered indexes separated into multiple filegroups. We will show you what happens when you attempt to insert records into a clustered index while the nonclustered indexes are offline.

Creating the Example Database

Using the script in Listing 12-7, create a new database with two additional filegroups, create three new tables using the data from the AdventureWorks2008 database, create the clustered indexes on the clustered index filegroup, and create the nonclustered indexes on the nonclustered indexes filegroup. Review and execute the script on your instance.

Listing 12-7. *SQL Script That Creates a Database for Example 1*

```
USE master
GO


-- Create the PiecemealRestore database

CREATE DATABASE PiecemealRestore
ON PRIMARY
( NAME = CLUSTEREDINDEX, FILENAME = 'c:\PiecemealRestore_Clus_data.mdf'),
FILEGROUP NONCLUSTINDEXES
( NAME = NONCLUSTEREDINDEX, FILENAME = 'c:\PiecemealRestore_NonClus_data.ndf')

GO


-- Review the files and filegroups post-creation
USE PiecemealRestore
GO


EXEC sp_helpfile
GO


-- Back up the database so you can always get back to a clean database
BACKUP DATABASE PiecemealRestore
TO DISK = 'c:\PiecemealRestoreCLean.bak'

--  Add the three tables to the PiecemealRestore
```

```
SELECT *
INTO Product
FROM AdventureWorks2008.Production.Product

SELECT *
INTO SalesOrderDetail
FROM AdventureWorks2008.Sales.SalesOrderDetail

SELECT *
INTO SalesOrderHeader
FROM AdventureWorks2008.Sales.SalesOrderHeader


--Validate that the tables have data in them

SELECT TOP 10 *
FROM Product

SELECT TOP 10 *
FROM SalesOrderDetail

SELECT TOP 10 *
FROM SalesOrderHeader

-- Create clustered index
CREATE CLUSTERED INDEX ix_SalesOrderId
ON SalesOrderHeader(SalesOrderId)
ON [Primary]

CREATE CLUSTERED INDEX ix_ProductId ON Product(ProductId)
ON [Primary]

CREATE CLUSTERED INDEX ix_SalesOrderIdDetailId
ON SalesOrderDetail(SalesOrderId,SalesOrderDetailId)
ON [Primary]

-- Create nonclustered indexes
CREATE NONCLUSTERED INDEX ix_OrderDatewInclude2 ON
SalesOrderHeader(orderDate)
INCLUDE(subTotal, TaxAmt, TotalDue)ON NONCLUSTINDEXES

CREATE NONCLUSTERED INDEX ix_ProductIdInclude
ON SalesOrderDetail(ProductId) INCLUDE(OrderQty)
ON NONCLUSTINDEXES
GO

BACKUP LOG PiecemealRestore
TO DISK = 'C:\PiecemealRestore_tlog.bak'
```

Reviewing Execution Plans

After you have successfully executed Listing 12-7, enable execution plans within SQL Server Management Studio. Then execute the query in Listing 12-8, making sure you review the execution plan.

Listing 12-8. *SQL Script That Returns the Sales Order Information for a Particular Date Range*

```
USE PiecemealRestore
GO

SELECT soh.SalesOrderID,soh.SubTotal, soh.TaxAmt, soh.TotalDue
FROM SalesOrderHeader soh
WHERE soh.OrderDate > '2003-12-31'

SELECT sod.SalesOrderID,sod.SalesOrderDetailID,p.Name,sod.OrderQty
FROM SalesOrderDetail sod    join Product p
 on sod.ProductID = p.ProductID
WHERE p.ProductID = 843
```

Figure 12-2 is an example of the execution plan generated. You will notice that the queries are using clustered and nonclustered indexes to process the query requests.

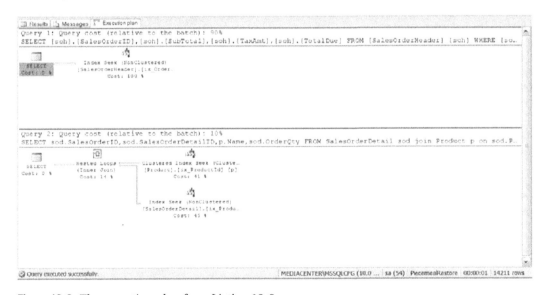

Figure 12-2. *The execution plan from Listing 12-8*

Backing Up the Tail End of the Transaction Log

Earlier, you backed up the database before you added the tables and indexes. You backed up a transaction log after you added the table and indexes. (That backup operation was the very last step in Listing 12-7.) Now you are going to back up the transaction log to capture any changes that have occurred since the last backup before we restore over the database. Execute the following code:

```
USE master
GO
BACKUP LOG PiecemealRestore
TO DISK = 'C:\PiecemealRestore_tlog.bak'
WITH NORECOVERY
```

Restoring the Database

Now that you have the transaction logs backed up, you are ready to restore the database. Pretend that all is now lost. You will be using a piecemeal recovery strategy to get your database back up and running.

Note SQL Server 2008 requires you to back up the tail end of the log prior to restoring a database over it. The tail end of the log refers to the transaction log backed up right before you restore over the database. It contains the transactions committed to the database since the last transaction log backup.

Your first task is to restore the primary filegroup. To that end, execute the code in Listing 12-9. This code restores your database, giving it the new name PiecemealRestore.

Once the primary filegroup is restored, query the master files system object to review the status of the database files in the newly-restored database. Listing 12-9 provides these queries for you.

Listing 12-9. *SQL Script That Restores the Database and Retrieves Data from the Newly Created Tables*

```
USE master
GO

RESTORE DATABASE PiecemealRestore
FILEGROUP = 'PRIMARY'
FROM DISK = 'c:\PiecemealRestoreCLean.bak'
WITH PARTIAL,
STANDBY = 'undoRestore.bak',
STATS

GO
USE PiecemealRestore
GO
```

```
-- Failures will occur when querying the following three tables
SELECT TOP 10 *
FROM Product

SELECT TOP 10 *
FROM SalesOrderDetail

SELECT TOP 10 *
FROM SalesOrderHeader


SELECT name,state_desc,create_lsn,redo_start_lsn
FROM sys.master_files
WHERE database_id = DB_ID('PiecemealRestore')
```

Figure 12-3 displays the status of the filegroups. Notice that the state description of the NONCLUSTEREDINDEX filegroup is in a RECOVERY_PENDING state. This means that the filegroup has not been fully restored. The primary filegroup is restored. The database is up and running. You may now restore any RECOVERY_PENDING filegroups at your leisure.

	name	state_desc	create_lsn	redo_start_lsn
1	CLUSTEREDINDEX	ONLINE	NULL	22000000015200001
2	PiecemealRestore_log	ONLINE	NULL	NULL
3	NONCLUSTEREDINDEX	RECOVERY_PENDING	22000000005800002	121000000176800001

Figure 12-3. *The status of the PiecemealRestore files after a partial restore*

If you execute some queries, you will notice there is no data or tables within the database at this time. That's because you backed up the database right after creation, before the tables were copied into the database.

Since you backed up the transaction log after inserting of the data into the database and creating the indexes, then you have to restore the database to the point in the time where that data exist. Restoring the transaction log to the time after the addition of the data will enable you to accomplish this task.

To figure out which files you want to restore, execute the RESTORE HEADERONLY command, as shown in the following query:

```
USE master
GO

RESTORE HEADERONLY
FROM DISK = 'C:\PiecemealRestore_tlog.bak'
```

The output of the RESTORE HEADERONLY command is displayed in Figure 12-4.

Figure 12-4. *Output of the RESTORE HEADERONLY option*

Once you know which files you want to restore, execute the script in Listing 12-10. Modify the file numbers if there is a difference between the file numbers in the script and the file numbers displayed in your output from Listing 12-10. However, if you have followed this section's example exactly as shown, then you should not have to modify Listing 12-10.

Listing 12-10. *SQL Script to RESTORE HEADERONLY and Transaction Logs Query for the Restore Header Information*

```
USE master
GO

RESTORE LOG PiecemealRestore
FROM DISK = 'C:\PiecemealRestore_tlog.bak'
WITH FILE  = 1,
STANDBY = 'c:\undoRestore.bak',
STATS
GO

-- Query the tables
USE PiecemealRestore
GO
```

```
-- Validate that you have data within the tables
SELECT TOP 10 *
FROM Product

SELECT TOP 10 *
FROM SalesOrderDetail

SELECT TOP 10 *
FROM SalesOrderHeader

-- Ensure that the database is still pending restore status
SELECT name,state_desc,create_lsn,redo_start_lsn
FROM sys.master_files
WHERE database_id = DB_ID('PiecemealRestore')
```

After executing Listing 12-10, specifically the last script, you will notice after the transaction log restore, the NONCLUSTEREDINDEX filegroup is still in a RECOVERY_PENDING state while the other filegroups are online (see Figure 12-5).

Figure 12-5. *The status of the database files after the transaction log has been applied to the database*

Reviewing Execution Plans Without Nonclustered Indexes

The previous steps should have restored the data and clustered indexes. However, re-run the following two queries from Listing 12-8 and compare your results to those from your earlier run:

```
USE PiecemealRestore
GO

SELECT soh.SalesOrderID,soh.SubTotal, soh.TaxAmt, soh.TotalDue
FROM SalesOrderHeader soh
WHERE soh.OrderDate > '2003-12-31'

SELECT sod.SalesOrderID,sod.SalesOrderDetailID,p.Name,sod.OrderQty
FROM SalesOrderDetail sod   join Product p
 ON sod.ProductID = p.ProductID
WHERE p.ProductID = 843
```

Figure 12-6 shows the new execution plan. Pay close attention to it and the indexes used to process the query. If you refer back to Figure 12-2, when both filegroups were online, and compare that plan to the one in Figure 12-6, you can easily see that the query optimizer uses the clustered indexes to process the requests. That's because only the primary filegroup is online, and the nonclustered indexes are not in that filegroup. If you further compare the execution time of the queries with both filegroups online versus just the one, you will see that the clustered indexes do not represent the optimal path to the data. However, the database is online, and it is accepting queries. Depending on the environment that you support, slower performance may be acceptable compared to downtime.

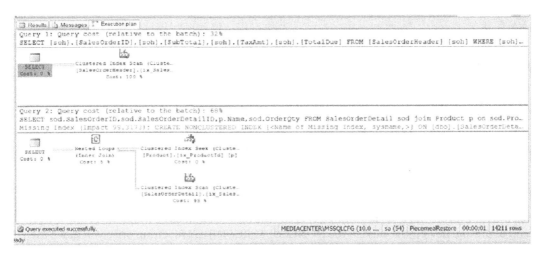

Figure 12-6. *The execution plan when the primary filegroup is the only available filegroup online*

During your pre-restoration process planning, determine how you want to deal with processes that are required to utilize the offline filegroup. In this example, figure out how you want to deal with index hints that force the queries to use specific nonclustered indexes. The following code sample uses an index hint that forces the query to use a nonclustered index.

```
-- Run complex query forcing usage of a nonclustered index
SELECT sod.SalesOrderID,sod.SalesOrderDetailID,p.Name,sod.OrderQty
FROM SalesOrderDetail sod  with (index (ix_ProductIdInclude))
join Product p
 ON sod.ProductID = p.ProductID
WHERE p.ProductID = 843
```

Review the error message (shown in Figure 12-7) that your application will receive when trying to execute a query like this, which depends upon an offline filegroup.

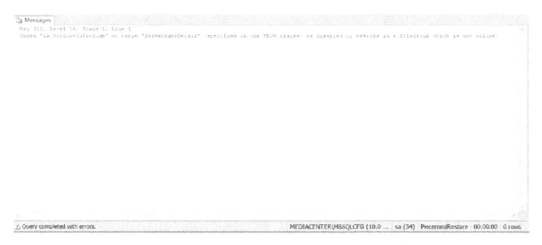

Figure 12-7. *Error message received when trying to access data from an offline filegroup*

Obviously, SQL Server does not respond well to attempts to retrieve data from offline file-groups. During a piecemeal restore, make sure you spend enough time figuring out how you will deal with errors like the one in Figure 12-7. Filegroups will be offline, and there will be a reduction in features or functionality of the applications using the database.

Attempting to Bring the Database Online

Now that you have executed a series of queries and know that the data within your database is current, execute the code in Listing 12-11 to recover the database without restoring the tail end of the log. Review the state of the NONCLUSTEREDINDEX filegroup once you make the database available and ready for transactions.

Listing 12-11. *SQL Code to Bring the Database Online and Review the Status of the Filegroups*

```
USE master
GO

-- Bring the primary filegroup back online
RESTORE DATABASE PiecemealRestore
WITH RECOVERY
```

```
-- Verify the status of the other filegroup
SELECT name,state_desc,create_lsn,redo_start_lsn
FROM sys.master_files
WHERE database_id = DB_ID('PiecemealRestore')
```

After you have restored the database and made it available for transactions, you will notice that the state of the NONCLUSTEREDINDEX filegroup is still in a RECOVERY_PENDING status, as shown in Figure 12-8.

Figure 12-8. *State description of filegroups after primary filegroup is no longer read-only*

Try to write to the database to validate that it is accepting transactions. Make sure you insert a record into one of the tables that has a nonclustered index on it. The following code provides you with an INSERT statement to add the record into the SalesOrderDetail table:

```
-- Add a record into one of the tables
USE PiecemealRestore
GO

INSERT INTO SalesOrderDetail
(SalesOrderID,ProductID,OrderQty,SpecialOfferID,UnitPrice,
UnitPriceDiscount,LineTotal,rowguid,ModifiedDate)
VALUES( 46608,843, 10, 2,15.00, .00, 150.00, NEWID(), GETDATE())
```

Figure 12-9 provides you with the results of executing this query. The error message confirms that attempting to write transactions to the database to an offline filegroup will cause errors. Remember, every record in a clustered index will reside in the nonclustered index. Therefore, when you add a record in the clustered index, a failure occurs when writing that record to the nonclustered index. Piecemeal restores do allow you to restore filegroups at a later point, but the tradeoff is reduced application functionality in the meantime. Piecemeal restores work best on databases that have read-only filegroups or filegroups that will likely not receive writes before everything is fully restored.

Figure 12-9. *The error message that occurs when trying to add data to a table that has non-clustered indexes in an offline state*

Completing the Recovery

In order to get this database back up and fully functional, you need to restore the NONCLUS-TEREDINDEX filegroup back to the same point as the primary filegroup (see Listing 12-12).

Listing 12-12. *SQL Code to Restore the NONCLUSTEREDINDEXES filegroup*

```
--Restore the other filegroup
USE master
GO

RESTORE DATABASE PiecemealRestore
FILEGROUP = 'NONCLUSTINDEXES'
FROM DISK = 'c:\PiecemealRestoreCLean.bak'
WITH NORECOVERY,
STATS
GO
-- Verify the status of the filegroup
SELECT name,state_desc,create_lsn,redo_start_lsn
FROM sys.master_files
WHERE database_id = DB_ID('PiecemealRestore')
```

Figure 12-10 shows you the status of the NONCLUSTEREDINDEX filegroup during the restore process. The output is from the final query in Listing 12-12. When you use the NORECOVERY option to restore files, the state of the file shows as RESTORING.

Figure 12-10. *Status of the NONCLUSTEREDINDEX filegroup after restoring it with NORECOVERY*

Notice in Figure 12-10 that the NONCLUSTEREDINDEX filegroup is currently in a RESTORING state, waiting for the restoration of additional files to that filegroup. The primary filegroup is still online during this time and servicing requests. Feel free to execute some queries against the primary filegroup for verification purposes. Once you are assured that the primary filegroup is online, execute the following script:

```
USE master
GO

RESTORE LOG PiecemealRestore
FROM DISK = 'C:\PiecemealRestore_tlog.bak'
WITH FILE  = 1,
RECOVERY,
STATS
GO

-- Verify the status of the filegroup
SELECT name,state_desc,create_lsn,redo_start_lsn
FROM sys.master_files
WHERE database_id = DB_ID('PiecemealRestore')
```

Figure 12-11 shows the status of the filegroups now that the log has been fully restored.

Figure 12-11. *Status of the NONCLUSTEREDINDEX filegroup after restoring all applicable files*

Verifying Correct Execution Plans

Now that all of the filegroups are online and accepting transactions, execute Listing 12-13 to see the execution plan of the queries shown earlier in Listing 12-8. Also validate that the insert of a record into a nonclustered index completes successfully.

Listing 12-13. *SQL Code to Query Multiple Tables and Insert Data into a Table*

```
-- Run query and review the current execution plan
USE PiecemealRestore
GO

SELECT soh.SalesOrderID,soh.SubTotal, soh.TaxAmt, soh.TotalDue
FROM SalesOrderHeader soh
WHERE soh.OrderDate > '2003-12-31'

SELECT sod.SalesOrderID,sod.SalesOrderDetailID,p.Name,sod.OrderQty
FROM SalesOrderDetail sod    join Product p
 on sod.ProductID = p.ProductID
WHERE p.ProductID = 843

INSERT INTO SalesOrderDetail
(SalesOrderID,ProductID,OrderQty,SpecialOfferID,UnitPrice,UnitPriceDiscount,_
LineTotal,rowguid,ModifiedDate)
VALUES( 46608,843, 10, 2,15.00, .00, 150.00, NEWID(), GETDATE())
```

Figure 12-12 shows the execution plans from Listing 12-13. They should be the same as Figure 12-2.

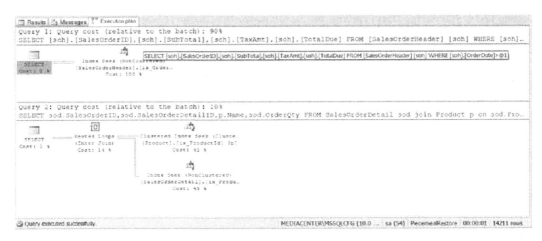

Figure 12-12. *The execution plan of joining multiple tables with all the filegroups restored*

Example 2: Restoring a Compressed and Encrypted Database

Continuing with useful recovery strategies, the next example will demonstrate restoring a compressed, encrypted database to a specific mark within a transaction log to a database on another server, and then copy the data back into the table in the primary database. The example will also use SQL Server Management Studio as much as possible. At the end, we hope you understand what it takes to restore a database encrypted using Transparent Data Encryption (TDE) to another server. We also discovered a useful thing that you should be aware when restoring to a mark that we want to share.

To make this example more realistic, let's paint a picture of a real-life scenario. In your production environment, assume that you have TDE enabled with backup compression for all of your backup commands. At some random time during the day, someone who should not have write access to production forgets to add the WHERE clause to their query and deletes all of the data from a table. Fortunately, the table that contains the deleted data still allows the application to function somewhat, but you need to get the data back as soon as possible while continuing to allow the application to write to the database. Luckily, the user remembered to mark the transaction log before they executed the command. To add a little more spice to the scenario, the server in question does not have enough space on it to hold another copy of the database. Therefore, you are going to have to restore the database on a separate server (or computer/server) in order to restore the data.

Setting Up the Example

Because this chapter focuses on recovery strategies, the example is going to prepare the databases using T-SQL. The code in Listing 12-14 creates a master encryption key, a certificate, and database encryption key. The listing then enables TDE and database compression for backups. Then comes a standard backup of the database, transaction log, and the encryption keys.

Listing 12-14. *SQL Script That Prepares the Database for the Current Code Demonstration*

```
USE master
GO

CREATE MASTER KEY ENCRYPTION BY PASSWORD = '3ncrypt1on!'
GO

BACKUP MASTER KEY TO FILE = 'c:\databaseKeyFile'
encryption by password = '3ncryption'
GO

CREATE CERTIFICATE DataEnc
WITH SUBJECT = 'Transparent Data Encryption'
GO

CREATE DATABASE apressReader
GO


BACKUP CERTIFICATE DataEnc
TO FILE = 'c:\certDataEncrypt'
WITH PRIVATE KEY (FILE = 'c:\certDataEncrypt_key',
encryption by password = '3ncryption')
GO

USE apressReader
GO

CREATE DATABASE ENCRYPTION KEY
WITH ALGORITHM = AES_256
ENCRYPTION BY SERVER CERTIFICATE DataEnc
GO

ALTER DATABASE apressReader
SET ENCRYPTION ON
GO

EXEC sp_configure 'backup compression default',1
GO
RECONFIGURE
GO

CREATE TABLE tblReader
(
 ReaderId int identity(1,1),
 fName varchar(25),
 lName varchar(50),
```

```
 jobTitle varchar(100),
 companyName varchar(50)
)
GO


BACKUP DATABASE apressReader
TO DISK = 'c:\apressReader.bak'
GO


INSERT INTO tblReader
VALUES ('Kim', 'Sue' , 'DBA', 'Top IT Consult'),
 ('Monique', 'Cee','DBA Developer','MC Prof'),
 ('Ant', 'Sams', 'DBA', 'Refer Academy'),
 ('Kend','Squeak','DBA', 'ABCComp')

GO


BACKUP LOG apressReader
TO DISK = 'c:\apressReader_log.bak'

GO


INSERT INTO tblReader
VALUES ('Lil', 'Jay' , 'JR DBA', 'Junior Techs'),
 ('Kd', 'Fra','JR DBA' ,'Junior Techs'),
 ('Nose', 'Samps', 'Lead DBA', 'Junior Techs')

BEGIN TRANSACTION lastInsert
INSERT INTO tblReader
VALUES ('JW', 'Walk' , 'DBA Dev', 'Top Balla'),
 ('Sammy', 'Walk','DBA Dev' ,'Top Balla'),
 ('Rome', 'Southern', 'DBA Dev', 'Top Balla')

COMMIT TRANSACTION lastInsert


SELECT * FROM apressReader.dbo.tblReader


BEGIN TRANSACTION DeleteRows WITH mark 'Delete Last Rows'
DELETE FROM tblReader

COMMIT
```

```
BACKUP LOG apressReader
TO DISK = 'c:\apressreader_log.bak'

-- Backing up tail end of the log.  Always a good practice.
BACKUP LOG apressReader
TO DISK = 'c:\apressreader_log.bak'
```

Using SQL Server Management Studio, restore the full database created in Listing 12-14 from its backup. To maximize this example, connect to another instance of SQL Server. Once connected, right-click on the Database folder and select Restore Database. Figure 12-13 shows the General page of the Restore Database dialog box. To restore the database, populate the To Database field with the name of the database you are creating or restoring over, select From Device, and then navigate to the file name created by Listing 12-14. After choosing the file, select the Options page.

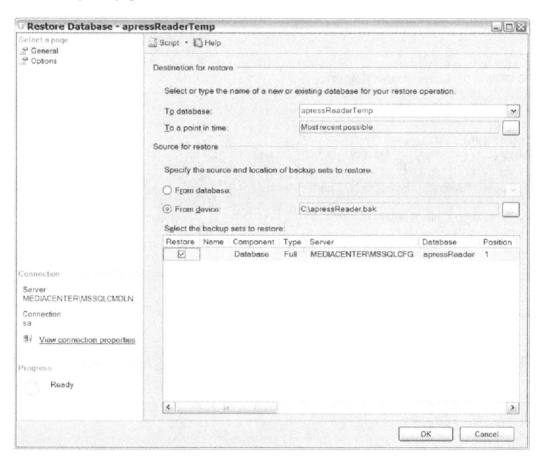

Figure 12-13. *Screenshot of the General tab on the Database screen*

You should get an error like the one shown in Figure 12-14, which prevents you from seeing the file header of the backup file. Remember Chapter 11 discussed how you are unable to attach to a database without copies of the encryption keys used when enabling TDE. This example shows you how far anyone would get if trying to restore your encrypted database without the encryption keys—nowhere.

Figure 12-14. *The error message received when attempting to restore an encrypted database without the encryption keys in place*

Restoring Certificates

In order to restore the database, you need to restore the certificate created in Listing 12-14. If the server has a master key, then simply restore the certificate. If the server does not have a master key, then create a master key and restore the certificate. The following code will restore the certificate created in Listing 12-14.

```
USE master
GO

CREATE CERTIFICATE DataEnc
FROM FILE = 'c:\certDataEncrypt'
WITH PRIVATE KEY (FILE = 'c:\certDataEncrypt_key',
DECRYPTION BY PASSWORD = '3ncryption')
```

After restoring the certificate, continue through the restore database process, making sure you leave the database in NORECOVERY or STANDBY mode.

Restoring Transaction Logs Using SQL Server Management Studio

After recovering the database, navigate to the Restore Transaction Log selection within the GUI (see Figure 12-15).

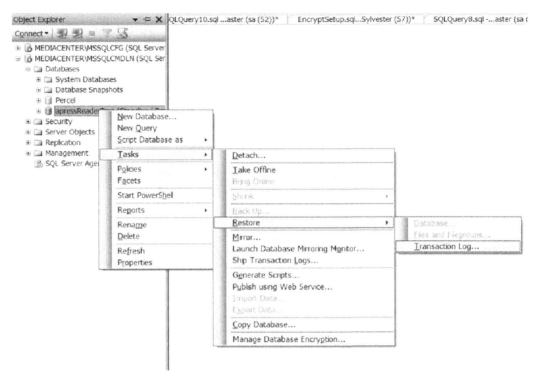

Figure 12-15. *Navigation to the Restore Transaction Log selection*

After you populate the transaction log file name, check the first two files and select the Marked Transaction option button, as shown in Figure 12-16. Click OK.

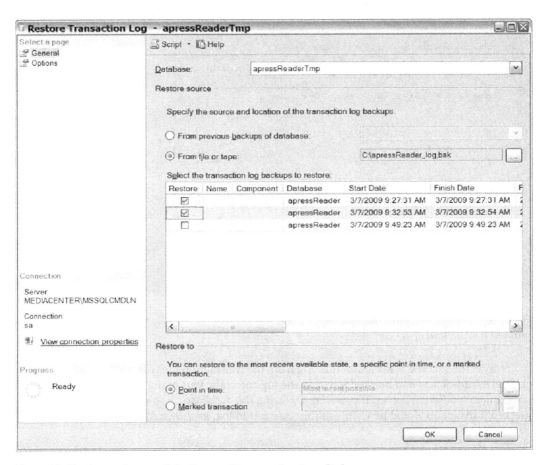

Figure 12-16. *General page of the Restore Transaction Log dialog*

You will be taken to the Select Marked Transaction dialog, shown in Figure 12-17. Probably the first thing you'll notice is that your marked transaction is not in the list. In fact, if you've followed the example here closely, the list will be empty!

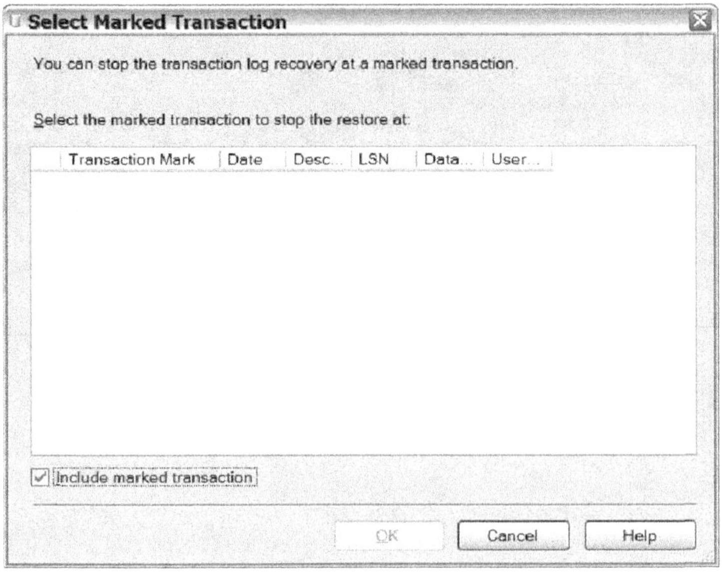

Figure 12-17. *Select Marked Transaction dialog with missing marked transaction*

Why is the marked transaction missing from the transaction log? Clearly, Listing 12-14 created a transaction and marked it within the log correctly. Part of the issue is that you are restoring to a different server. If you were restoring the database on the same server, then the marked transaction would be visible in the transaction log, as shown in Figure 12-18.

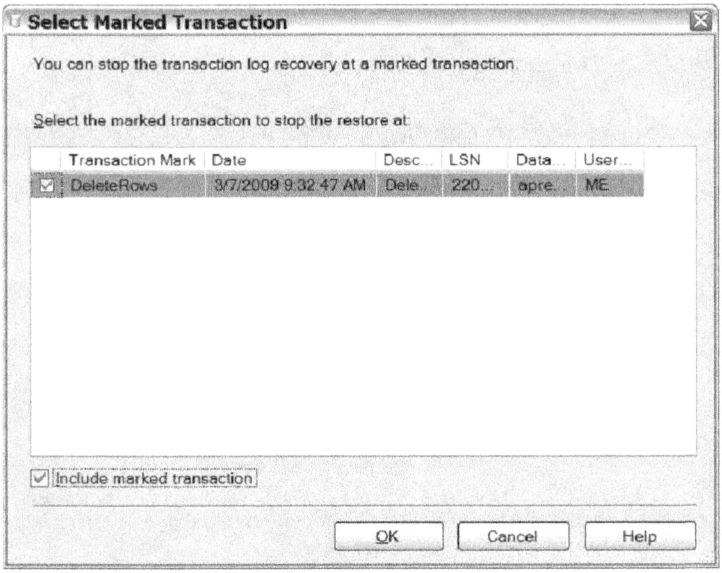

Figure 12-18. *Marked transaction visible in the transaction log*

Clearly, you can see that the script created the marked transaction correctly. It is just not viewable in the Select Marked Transaction dialog when you attempt to restore a transaction log on another server. To utilize the GUI to perform the restoration, you will have to restore to a time instead of to a mark. However, the real question is, can you restore to a mark in T-SQL even though you cannot restore to a mark in SQL Server Management Studio? Thankfully, the answer to that question is yes. This scenario is one in which it truly helps to have some T-SQL knowledge. The code in Listing 12-15 will restore the transaction log to a mark.

Listing 12-15. *SQL Code to Restore a Log to a Mark*

```
RESTORE LOG apressReaderTmp
FROM DISK = 'c:\apressReader_log.bak'
WITH FILE = 1,
STANDBY = 'c:\apressReader_undo.bak'

SELECT * FROM apressReaderTmp.dbo.tblReader


RESTORE LOG apressReaderTmp
FROM DISK = 'c:\apressReader_log.bak'
WITH FILE = 2,
STOPBEFOREMARK = 'DeleteRows',
STANDBY = 'c:\apressReader_undo.bak'

SELECT * FROM apressReaderTmp.dbo.tblReader
```

After restoring the logs, you can query the data to make sure the data exist within the table. You can restore the database back to recovery if you would like, just in case you want proof that the log would have deleted all of the data from the table. Restore the three transaction log files, as shown in Figure 12-19, using the GUI, and then query the table afterward.

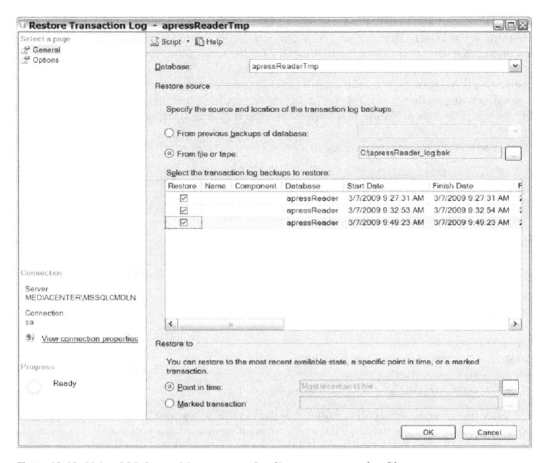

Figure 12-19. *Using SQL Server Management Studio to restore two log files*

Figure 12-20 shows the number of records stored within the tblReader table after you have restored all three logs.

Figure 12-20. *Data within the tblReader table after the restoration of the two transaction logs*

Using whatever method you see fit, copy the data back onto the primary server, the primary database, and the primary table. You should not have any problems, even though both instances and databases have their data encrypted.

You may have noticed that we didn't discuss modifying your recovery procedures because of the database compression. Recovering from a compressed database does not require you to do anything special. Just recover your databases as you would for a decompressed database.

Example 3: Restoring System Databases

SQL Server 2008 has four main system databases that are restorable: master, model, msdb, and distribution (when replication is enabled.) When restoring a system database, the SQL Server version must be the same as the version of the backup file that you are restoring. In other words, you cannot restore an msdb database for SQL Server 2008 onto a SQL Server 2008 instance that is currently running SQL Server 2008 SP 1. That is the main reason why the earlier "Recovering from Scratch" section suggests documenting the exact version of SQL Server that you are running.

You may think documenting the version is an unnecessary task because you can remember the service pack that you are currently running. However, the version also includes any hot fixes that you may have applied to the server after installing the service pack. Remembering those details often times get a little tougher. If you can remember to document the version of SQL Server, then restoring system databases should not be a problem.

If you're restoring the model, msdb, or distribution database, just follow the recovery processes described so far in this chapter. However, restoring the master database requires some additional steps worth covering in detail.

Restoring the master Database from Single User Mode

There are two main methods of restoring or re-creating the master database: restoring it over the currently running master database or rebuilding the master database because SQL Server 2008 will not start.

In order to restore over the master database, SQL Server must be in single user mode. That means only one user can be connected to SQL Server during the restore. To place the server in single user mode, start a command prompt window, navigate to the folder where the executable resides, and then execute the following:

```
Sqlservr.exe -m
```

After you have executed the preceding command, leave the command prompt window open. If you close the window, then you will stop the SQL Server instance from running. Navigate to a query window or the Object Explorer and restore the database as previously discussed. After restoring the master database, your connection to the instance will be broken, and you will have to start the instance again. After reviewing the contents of the master database, you should notice that it is back to the point when the database backup occurred.

Rebuilding the master Database Using REBUILDDATABASE

When the instance of your database will not start and you have exhausted all other possibilities, an option exists to rebuild all of the system databases for that particular instance. This will make your databases look the way they did when you first installed SQL Server and stored them in their original locations. Fortunately, you can restore the system database backups over the newly created databases once the creation completes. You can also move the system database files back to where you want them by following the same steps you used to move the database in the first place. In other words, rebuilding the system databases will require some work to get your environment back to the way that it was, but the obstacles can easily be overcome with a little work.

To rebuild all of the system databases, you are going to execute process like a command-line install. (We discussed command-line installs in detail in Chapter 4, so feel free to review that chapter if you need additional information.) Rebuilding system databases also requires you to have access to the media or network location used for the SQL Server 2008 install. The setup executable requires passing the following parameters to rebuild the databases:

- /Q or /Quiet
- /Action=REBUILDDATABASE
- /INSTANCENAME="InstanceName"
- /SQLSYSADMINACCOUNTS="account"
- /SAPWD="StrongPassword"
- /SQLCOLLATION="CollationName"

Now that you understand the parameters, follow these steps to re-create your system databases:

1. Insert the SQL Server 2008 media into your hard drive.

2. Open the command prompt and navigate to the setup.exe file. If you installed SQL Server remotely or without a disk, navigate to the network or location that contains the setup file.

3. Execute the following:

```
Setup /Q /action=REBUILDDATABASE /INSTANCENAME="InstanceName"
 /SQLSYSAdminAccounts="accounts" /sapwd="StrongPassword"
/SQLCollation="CollationName"
```

Once the process completes, the command-line cursor will return and you can exit the command prompt window. You can start your instance of SQL Server and start restoring any system databases that you want. Remember, since you completely wiped out your system databases, all of your users, jobs, user databases, and other database information will not be available until you restore the previous system databases or recreate the jobs, users, and databases. Either way, your server is back up and running; now you have a little work to do in order to get your environment back to where it was.

Summary

We hope that these last two chapters have reiterated the importance of backups and restores, along with adding some additional things for you to think about. What we present in the sections on practicing your recovery strategies and restore considerations are things that we have learned from experience. We hope that you apply some of those considerations in your environment. At a minimum, practice your recovery strategy multiple times to ensure that you are comfortable recovering your system. As discussed throughout this chapter, understanding available recovery options can potentially have your system available more quickly. Remember, you cannot restore a database if you don't have available backup files. Spending the time planning and testing your backup and recovery strategies will ultimately save you time and data loss in the future. Now get ready to save yourself more time by learning some tips and tricks for automating your system.

CHAPTER 13

■ ■ ■

Automating Routine Maintenance

One of the biggest responsibilities you have as a DBA is proactively making sure that all the servers in your environment are running smoothly. You should not wait for a user to call and complain about slow response times before rebuilding indexes or updating statistics. Also, if you encounter an issue, such as a torn page in a database, it is better to find out sooner than later. If an issue goes undetected long enough, you may not have the backups needed in order to correct it, and your only option may be to accept data loss. In order to sustain a SQL Server instance that provides optimum performance, it requires constant maintenance. Luckily, you can use the same tools within SQL Server to automate maintenance tasks that you use to meet the business needs of the organization. By taking advantage of features like Database Mail, SQL Server Agent, and maintenance plans to automatically maintain your servers and notify you of failures, you will have more free time to work on all of those past due projects you haven't gotten around to.

Database Mail

The first thing you should do when automating maintenance tasks is to set up Database Mail. This will allow you to receive automatic notifications for things like job failures and alerts. After all, what good is automating tasks if you constantly have to go out to each server and make sure everything looks okay?

There are a couple of ways to configure Database Mail. One is using the Database Mail Configuration Wizard and the other is good old T-SQL. First, we will walk you through the wizard and explain the options available when setting up Database Mail, and then we will provide a script using T-SQL that you can use to perform the same actions.

Database Mail Configuration Wizard

Start the Database Mail Configuration Wizard by expanding the Management folder in the SQL Server Management Studio Object Explorer, right-click Database Mail, and then select Configure Database Mail from the context menu. This will bring you to the Welcome screen shown in Figure 13-1.

Figure 13-1. *Database Mail Configuration Wizard Welcome screen*

Select Next to proceed to the Select Configuration Task screen, as shown in Figure 13-2. (You may also choose the option to skip the Welcome screen in the future.)

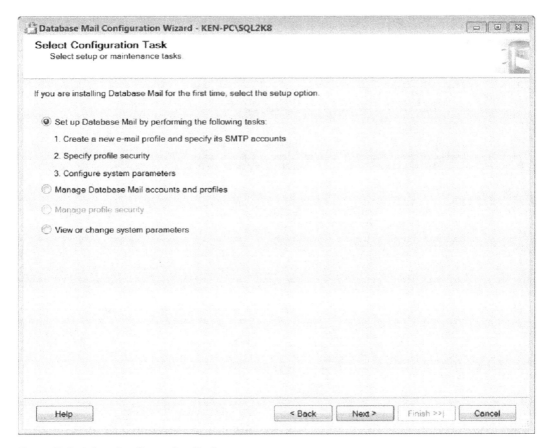

Figure 13-2. *Select Configuration Task screen*

Since this is the first time we are setting up Database Mail, we will select the first option that will perform all the tasks required to initially set up Database Mail. Select Next to continue. If you have not enabled Database Mail on the server, you will be prompted to do so before continuing to the New Profile screen shown in Figure 13-3.

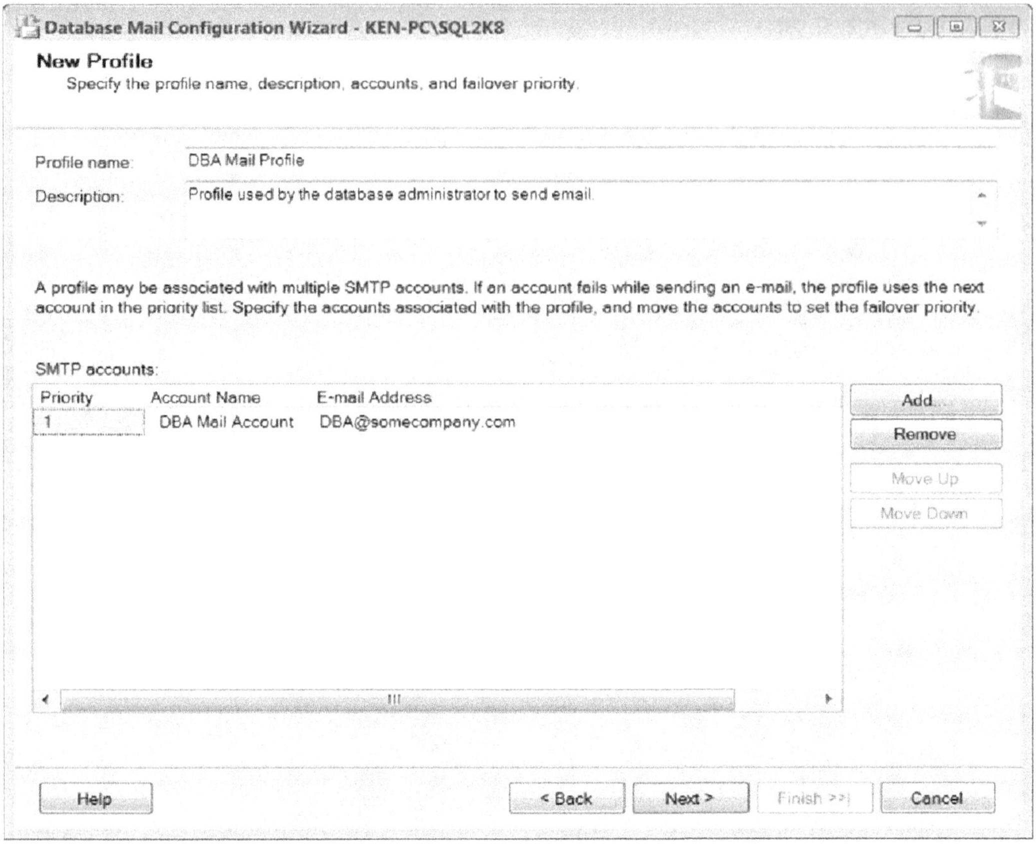

Figure 13-3. *New Profile screen*

Enter the name and an optional description for the new profile you are creating. A profile is a group of database mail accounts you can prioritize to increase the chances of receiving an email if one of the email servers is unavailable. To add an account to the mail profile, select the Add button to display the New Database Mail Account dialog box, shown in Figure 13-4.

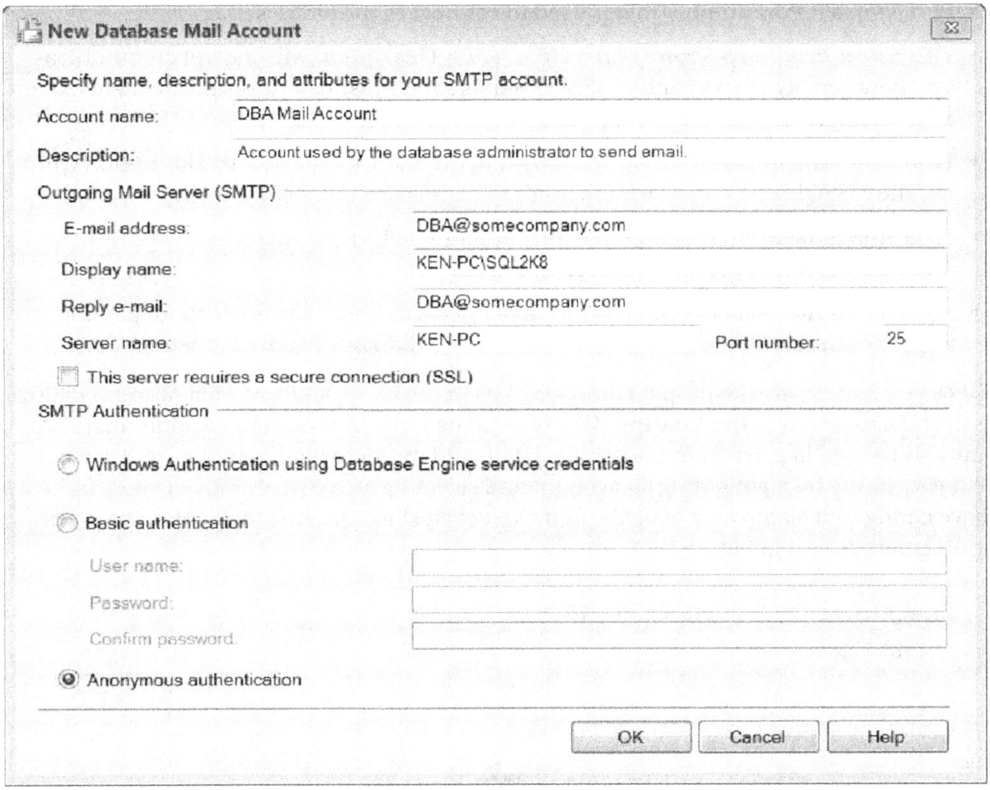

Figure 13-4. *New Database Mail Account dialog*

The New Database Mail Account dialog contains all the information needed for SQL Server to send an email to a Simple Mail Transfer Protocol (SMTP) server. You must create a separate mail account for each SMTP server you would like to use. Enter the appropriate information for your organization. The following list describes the available options when creating a new mail account.

- *Account Name*: Name that will be used to identify the database mail account.

- *Description*: Optional description used to identify the database mail account.

- *E-mail Address*: Email address that the mail is being sent from. This does not have to be an actual email account. You could use something like Severname@company.com, just to indicate the email came from a specific server.

- *Display Name*: Optional name that is displayed on email messages to indicate who the email is from.

- *Reply E-mail*: Optional email address that will be used when someone replies to an email sent by this account.

- *Server Name*: Server name or IP address of the SMTP server that is used to send emails for this account.

- *Port Number*: Port number that is used to connect to the SMTP server.

- *This Server Requires a Secure Connection (SSL)*: This option will encrypt communication between SQL Server and the SMTP server. You must have a certificate installed for SQL Server in order to use this option.

- *Windows Authentication Using Database Engine Service Credentials*: This option will use the MSSQLServer service credentials to connect to the SMTP server.

- *Basic Authentication*: This option allows you to specify a username and password in order to connect to the SMTP server.

- *Anonymous Authentication*: This option connects to SMTP servers without passing any login credentials and is used for SMTP servers that do not require authentication.

Once you have made the proper configurations in the New Database Mail Account dialog box, select OK to return to the New Profile screen. Repeat the process for any additional mail accounts you would like to add to the profile. If you add multiple mail accounts, you can configure their priority by highlighting an account and selecting Move Up or Move Down. Once you have configured all the new mail accounts, select Next to continue to the Manage Profile Security screen, shown in Figure 13-5.

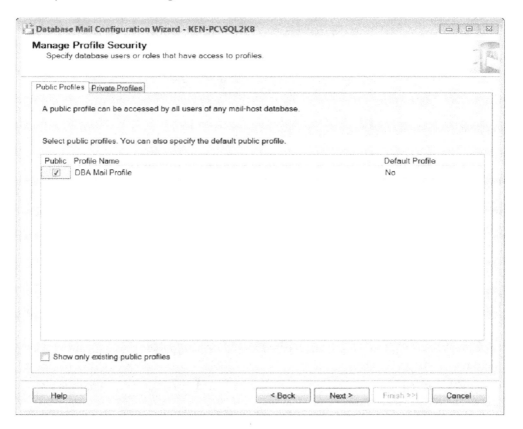

Figure 13-5. *Public Profiles tab of the Manage Profile Security screen*

You can configure Database Mail profiles as public profiles or private profiles. If you configure the profile as public, anyone who can access the msdb is allowed to use the profile to send mail. If you configure the profile as private, the profile will be limited to only specific users. You can also have one default public profile and one default private profile. A default profile allows you to send mail without specifying a profile name. When an account has access to both a default private profile and a default public profile, the default private profile will be used. If you would like to make the profile public, select the Public check box next to the profile name; if you would like to make the profile private, select the Private Profiles tab, as shown in Figure 13-6.

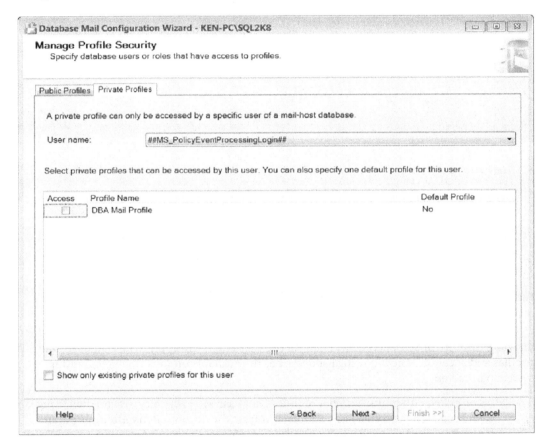

Figure 13-6. *Private Profiles tab of the Manage Profile Security screen*

The key difference between these two tabs is that the Private Profiles tab provides you with a User Name drop-down list that will allow you to grant access to a profile for a specific user. To grant profile access to multiple users, select each username from the list, and then select the Access check box next to the profile name. Once you have configured the profile security, select Next to continue to the Configure System Parameters screen, shown in Figure 13-7.

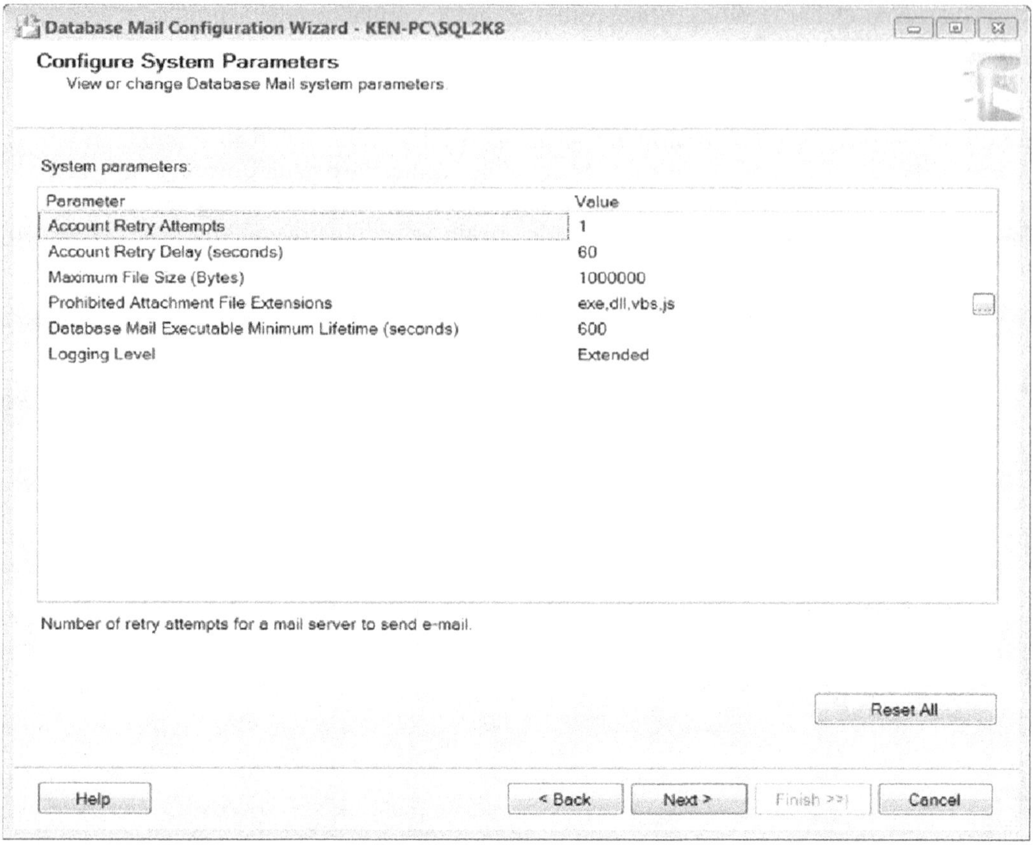

Figure 13-7. *Configure System Parameters screen*

You can use the Configure System Parameters screen to define the system parameters for an entire instance of SQL Server; any changes you make here will apply to all Database Mail profiles and accounts. The following list describes the available options when configuring system parameters.

- *Account Retry Attempts*: Number of times Database Mail will retry to send mail using each account in a profile. For example, if you set the Account Retry Attempts parameter to three and you have two accounts in a profile, each account will retry to send mail three times.

- *Account Retry Delay (Seconds)*: Number of seconds Database Mail will wait between retries. This delay is not the delay between each account in a profile. Database Mail will attempt to use all accounts in a profile, and then wait the defined number of seconds before trying all accounts again.

- *Maximum File Size (Bytes)*: Limits the size of an attachment.

- *Prohibited Attachment File Extensions*: Comma-delimited list of file extensions that are not permitted as attachments when sending Database Mail.

- *Database Mail Executable Minimum Lifetime (Seconds)*: The minimum time the external mail process will remain active even if there are no items in the mail queue. If items are in the queue, the external mail process will remain active until all items are processed.

- *Logging Level*: There are three logging levels you can use to send events to the Database Mail log: Normal, Extended, and Verbose. The Normal logging level will log errors. The Extended logging level will log errors, warnings, and informational messages. (Extended is the default logging level.) The Verbose logging level will log errors, warnings, informational messages, success messages, and internal messages. You should generally only use the Verbose logging level for troubleshooting purposes.

Once you have the system parameters configured, select Next to continue to the Complete the Wizard screen, shown in Figure 13-8. Review the configuration options and select Finish to complete the wizard.

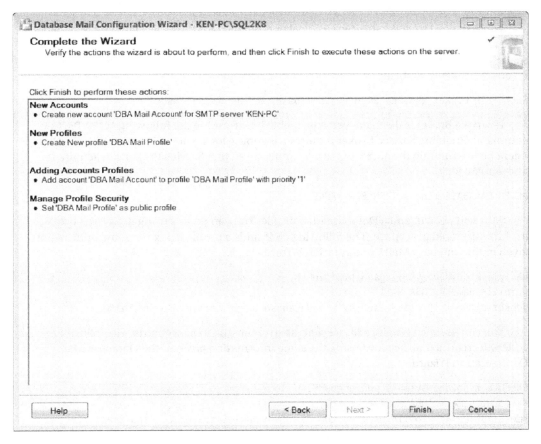

Figure 13-8. *Complete the Wizard screen*

Configuring Database Mail Using T-SQL

I personally prefer using a T-SQL script to set up Database Mail. Not only is it faster when setting up a new server, you can also be sure that you have the same Database Mail configuration on all of your servers. The first thing you need to do is make sure you have Database Mail enabled. You can do this by using the `sp_configure` stored procedure as follows:

```
sp_configure 'show advanced options', 1;
GO
RECONFIGURE;
GO
sp_configure 'Database Mail XPs', 1;
GO
RECONFIGURE
GO
```

You also need to make sure Service Broker is enabled for the `msdb`. Database Mail depends on Service Broker to deliver email messages. If Service Broker is not enabled, your mail messages will queue, but they will not be delivered. You can run the following query to determine if Service Broker is enabled.

```
SELECT is_broker_enabled FROM sys.databases WHERE name = 'msdb'
```

If Service Broker is disabled, you can enable it by running the following `ALTER DATABASE` command. Enabling Service Broker requires a database lock. You will need to stop SQL Server Agent before running the `ALTER DATABASE` command so that Service Broker can acquire the appropriate lock.

```
ALTER DATABASE msdb SET ENABLE_BROKER
```

Now you need to add a Database Mail profile. You can do this using the `sysmail_add_profile_sp` stored procedure. The following code adds a profile using the same information given in the Database Mail Configuration Wizard.

```
EXECUTE msdb.dbo.sysmail_add_profile_sp
@profile_name = 'DBA Mail Profile',
@description = 'Profile used by the database administrator to send email.'
```

You can use the `sysmail_add_account_sp` to create the mail accounts. The following code will create a mail account using the same information given in the Database Mail Configuration Wizard.

```
EXECUTE msdb.dbo.sysmail_add_account_sp
@account_name = 'DBA Mail Account',
@description = 'Profile used by the database administrator to send email.',
@email_address = 'DBA@somecompany.com',
@display_name =  'KEN-PC\SQL2K8',
@mailserver_name =  'KEN-PC'
```

Once you have created a profile and an account, you need to associate the account with the profile by using the `sysmail_add_profileaccount_sp` stored procedure. The following code binds the DBA Mail Account to the DBA Mail Profile with a priority (sequence number) of 1.

If you add multiple accounts with the same priority, Database Mail will randomly choose the account that sends the mail.

```
EXECUTE msdb.dbo.sysmail_add_profileaccount_sp
@profile_name = 'DBA Mail Profile',
@account_name = 'DBA Mail Account',
@sequence_number = 1
```

The final script is shown in Listing 13-1. You can change the script to fit your organization by adding multiple accounts or changing parameters to the correct values. By using the @@ServerName function in the display name, each server will be able to send email using its own name. As you can see, creating a Database Mail script is a far more efficient way to set up Database Mail across multiple servers. In fact, you could even take advantage of multi-server queries discussed in Chapter 7 to deploy Database Mail to all of your servers with a single statement.

Listing 13-1. *Database Mail Setup Script*

```
--MAKE SURE TO STOP SQL SERVER AGENT BEFORE RUNNING THIS SCRIPT!
USE msdb
GO

--Enable Database Mail
sp_configure 'show advanced options', 1;
GO
RECONFIGURE;
GO
sp_configure 'Database Mail XPs', 1;
GO
RECONFIGURE
GO

--Enable Service Broker
ALTER DATABASE msdb SET ENABLE_BROKER

--Add the profile
EXECUTE msdb.dbo.sysmail_add_profile_sp
@profile_name = 'DBA Mail Profile',
@description = 'Profile used by the database administrator to send email.'

--Add the account
EXECUTE msdb.dbo.sysmail_add_account_sp
@account_name = 'DBA Mail Account',
@description = 'Profile used by the database administrator to send email.',
@email_address = 'DBA@somecompany.com',
@display_name = (Select @@ServerName),
@mailserver_name = 'KEN-PC'
```

```
--Associate the account with the profile
EXECUTE msdb.dbo.sysmail_add_profileaccount_sp
@profile_name = 'DBA Mail Profile',
@account_name = 'DBA Mail Account',
@sequence_number = 1

Print 'Don't Forget To Restart SQL Server Agent!'
```

Sending Database Mail

Now that you have configured Database Mail, you are ready to start sending email. You can send mail by using the sp_send_dbmail stored procedure, but you must be a member of the DatabaseMailUser role in the msdb in order to execute it. You can use the sp_send_dbmail stored procedure to send everything from a basic email message to email messages that contain file attachments and query results that are formatted using HTML. Now you can schedule a job to send out that weekly report you have been running manually. Let's look at a few examples.

The following statement will send a basic email with a subject and a body. You can add multiple recipients by using a semicolon as a separator. If the statement is executed successfully, you will see the output "Mail queued" in the Messages pane.

```
--Basic email
EXEC msdb.dbo.sp_send_dbmail
@recipients='Somebody@SomeCompany.com', --[ ; ...n ]
@subject = 'Basic Database Mail Sample',
@body= 'This is a test email.',
@profile_name = 'DBA Email Profile'
```

All you have to do to attach a file is use the same basic syntax previously listed and add the @file_attachements parameter along with the file location. To add multiple file attachments, you can separate each file using a semicolon, just as you can with multiple recipients.

```
--Code to send an email attachment
EXEC msdb.dbo.sp_send_dbmail
@recipients='Somebody@SomeCompany.com', --[ ; ...n ]
@subject ='Database Mail Sample With File Attached',
@body='This is a test email.',
@profile_name ='DBMailProfile',
@file_attachments ='C:\SomeFile.txt'; --[ ; ...n ]
```

You can use the following sample to send an email with an attachment that contains all the databases on the server. Be sure to specify the database that the query in the @query parameter should be executed against by using the @execute_query_database parameter, or you could experience unexpected results or errors by executing the query against the wrong database. If you leave off the @attach_query_result_as_file and @query_attachment_filename parameters, the query results will be displayed in the email following the body text.

```
--Code to send query results
EXEC msdb.dbo.sp_send_dbmail
@recipients='Somebody@SomeCompany.com', --[ ; ...n ]
```

```
@subject ='Query Results As File Sample',
@body='This is a test email.',
@profile_name ='DBA Email Profile',
@query ='SELECT Name FROM sys.sysdatabases',
@execute_query_database = 'master',
@attach_query_result_as_file = 1,
@query_attachment_filename ='Databases.txt'
```

You can also send an email that uses HTML formatting. All you have to do is take advantage of the For XML Path clause to form the body of the email and use some basic HTML tags. By giving the name column an alias of 'td', each name in the result set will be wrapped in <td> tags, which represent a table cell in HTML. The 'tr' following the For XML Path clause will wrap each row in <tr> tags, which represent a table row in HTML. The result set is then given a header using the <th> tags and wrapped in a <table> tag to form a perfectly formatted HTML table using query results.

```
--Code to send an HTML email message
DECLARE @HTML NVARCHAR(MAX) ;

SET @HTML =
 '<table border="1">' +
 '<tr><th>Name</th></tr>' +
 Cast((SELECT name as "td"
        FROM master.sys.sysdatabases
        FOR XML PATH('tr')) as NVARCHAR(MAX)) +
 '</table>' ;

EXEC msdb.dbo.sp_send_dbmail
@recipients='Somebody@SomeCompany.com', --[ ; ...n ]
@subject ='HTML Sample',
@body= @HTML,
@body_format = 'HTML' ,
@profile_name ='DBA Email Profile'
```

Once you have sent an email, you can use the sysmail_allitems view to see all the items that have been processed using Database Mail, as shown in the following query. There are a few other views that may be useful as well. For example, the sysmail_faileditems view shows only failed messages, sysmail_usentitems shows only unsent messages, and sysmail_sentitems shows only sent messages.

```
SELECT * FROM msdb.dbo.sysmail_allitems
```

Database Mail Cleanup Procedures

Database Mail keeps a copy of every email that is sent along with several event log entries in the msdb. Over time, this buildup of sent mail can cause excessive growth in the msdb database. There are two stored procedures you can use to purge mail history in order to keep the msdb database at a manageable size.

You can use the sysmail_delete_mailitems_sp stored procedure to delete email messages older than a specified date or all emails with a certain status. If you execute the sysmail_ delete_mailitems_sp stored procedure without supplying any parameters, all email messages will be deleted. Following is the complete syntax:

```
sysmail_delete_mailitems_sp
  [ [ @sent_before = ] 'sent_before' ] -- '1/1/2009'
  [ , [ @sent_status = ] 'sent_status' ] -- sent, unsent, retrying, failed
```

You can use the sysmail_delete_log_sp stored procedure to delete Database Mail logs older than a specified date or all Database Mail logs for a certain event type. If you execute the sysmail_delete_log_sp stored procedure without supplying any parameters, all Database Mail log entries will be deleted. The complete syntax is as follows:

```
sysmail_delete_log_sp
  [ [ @logged_before = ] 'logged_before' ] --'1/1/2009'
  [, [ @event_type = ] 'event_type' ] --success, warning, error, informational
```

You should incorporate both of these cleanup stored procedures into your regular maintenance routines. (You will see an example of how to automate these Database Mail cleanup procedures in the "Jobs" section later in the chapter.) Come up with an acceptable retention policy for Database Mail, and then execute the cleanup stored procedures accordingly.

SQL Server Agent

SQL Server Agent is at the heart of automating maintenance tasks. There are several things available in SQL Server Agent that can assist you with routine automation and preventative maintenance. You can create operators that will receive notification for certain events. You can define alerts that will capture certain events, and SQL Server Agent can then perform predefined actions in response to those events. You can create jobs that SQL Server Agent can run on a predefined schedule to perform routine preventative maintenance tasks. You can even create a master server in SQL Server Agent so you can manage jobs on multiple target servers from a single server.

Operators

The first thing you need to do is define an operator so you can receive automatic notifications through SQL Server Agent. An operator consists of two basic pieces of information: a name used to identify the operator and the contact information used to notify the operator. To add an operator using SQL Server Management Studio, expand SQL Server Agent in the Object Explorer, right-click the Operators folder, and select New Operator from the context menu. This will open the New Operator dialog box shown in Figure 13-9.

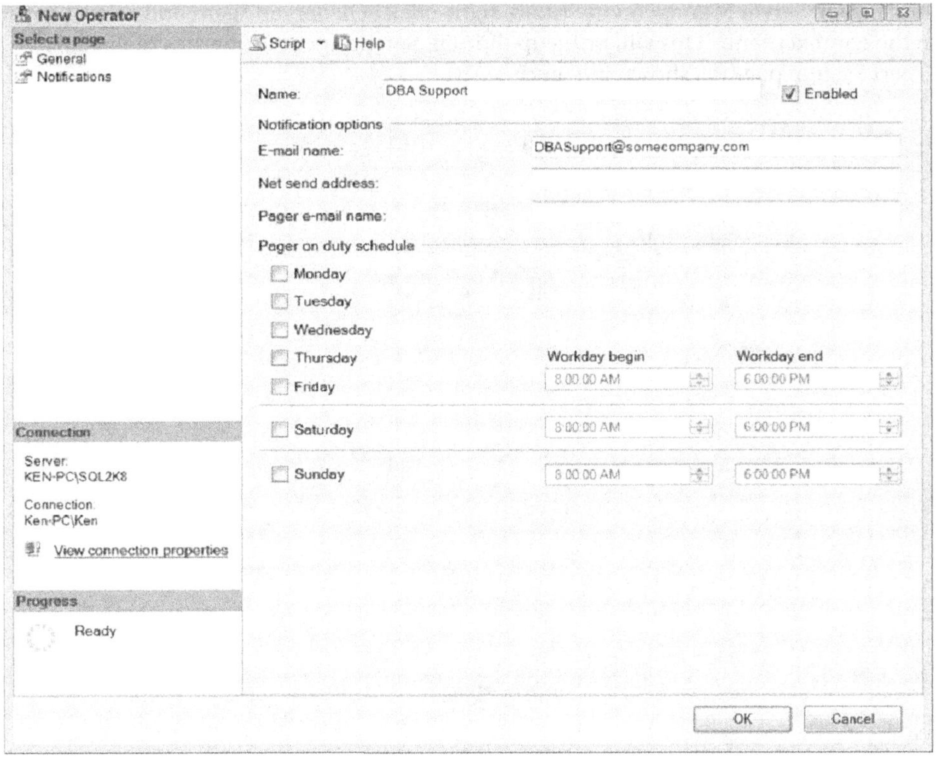

Figure 13-9. *New Operator dialog box*

Enter an operator name and email address, and click OK. Although you can configure net send and pager information, these options are deprecated and will be removed in a future version of SQL Server, so you should avoid using them. The only information you should enter here is the name of the operator and the email address that you will use to receive event notifications.

You can also add an operator using the sp_add_operator procedure located in the msdb. The following statement adds an operator named DBA Support and supplies an email address as the contact information.

```
EXEC msdb.dbo.sp_add_operator
    @name='DBA Support',
    @email_address='DBASupport@somecompany.com'
```

Enabling SQL Server Agent Notifications

You have to enable the alert system in SQL Server Agent before you can start receiving notifications. Once you have configured Database Mail and added an operator, the next thing you should do is enable the alert system and designate a fail-safe operator. This is a designated operator that will receive notifications in the event that the primary operator is unreachable. In SQL Server Management Studio, right-click SQL Server Agent and select prop-erties from the context menu. This will bring up the SQL Server Agent Properties dialog box. Select the Alert System page, as shown in Figure 13-10.

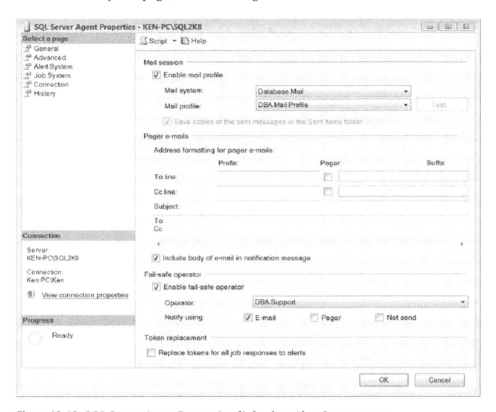

Figure 13-10. *SQL Server Agent Properties dialog box Alert System page*

There are only a few settings on this page you need to configure. Under the Mail Session section, select Enable Mail Profile. This will allow you to select the mail system and profile that SQL Server Agent will use to send notifications. You should select Database Mail from the Mail System drop-down list. SQL Mail is the other available mail system option; however, you should avoid SQL Mail because it will be removed in a future release. Now select the profile SQL Server Agent will use to send alert notifications from the Mail Profile drop-down list. We are using the DBA Mail Profile option created earlier in the chapter in the "Database Mail" section.

The next thing you need to do is select Enable Fail-Safe Operator under the Fail-Safe Operator section. Now you can select the operator from the drop-down list that you want to receive notifications in case the designated operator is unreachable. SQL Server stores the fail-safe operator information in the registry in case the operator tables in the msdb are unavail-able. We are using an operator called DBA Support, as shown in Figure 13-10. You should then select the E-mail check box to specify that the fail-safe operator will receive notifications using email. Remember, you should avoid the Pager and Net Send options, since they will no longer be supported in a future release.

Select OK to close the SQL Server Agent Properties dialog box. *You must restart SQL Server Agent before the new settings will take effect.* You are now ready to start receiving automatic notifications from SQL Server Agent alerts and jobs.

Alerts

A SQL Server Agent alert is an automatic response to a predefined event. You can configure SQL Server Agent alerts to fire in response to SQL Server events, SQL Server performance counters, and Windows Management Instrumentation (WMI) events. Once an event has caused an alert to fire, you can respond to the alert by notifying operators of the event or even running a job after the event has occurred.

So, what kind of alerts should you have in place that will lead to proactive maintenance? At the very minimum, you should have a separate alert configured for fatal errors, which are indicated by severity codes 19 through 25. Let's walk through an example of creating an alert that will notify you of any fatal errors encountered with the severity of 19 called "Fatal Error in Resource." To add an alert using SQL Server Management Studio, expand SQL Server Agent in the Object Explorer, right-click the Alerts folder, and select New Alert from the context menu. This will open the New Alert dialog box shown in Figure 13-11.

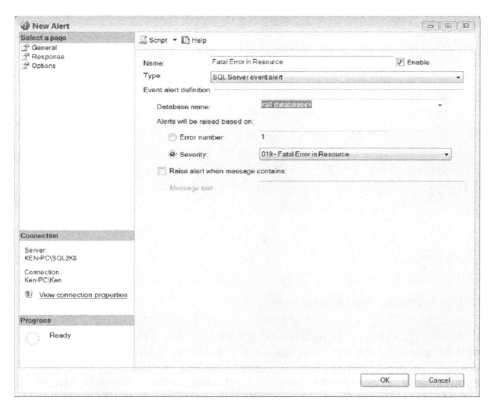

Figure 13-11. *New Alert dialog box General page*

Give the alert a descriptive name and make sure the Enable check box is selected. We will call this alert "Fatal Error in Resource." Select SQL Server Event Alert from the Type drop-down list. The Event Alert Definition section will change depending on the type of alert you have selected. You can limit the alert to a specific database by selecting it from the Database name drop-down list; for this example, you should select <all databases>. We want to monitor errors with a severity of 19, so select the Severity option to enable the drop-down list, and then select 019 - Fatal Error in Resource. Select the Response page, as shown in Figure 13-12, to define the action that SQL Server Agent will perform when the event occurs.

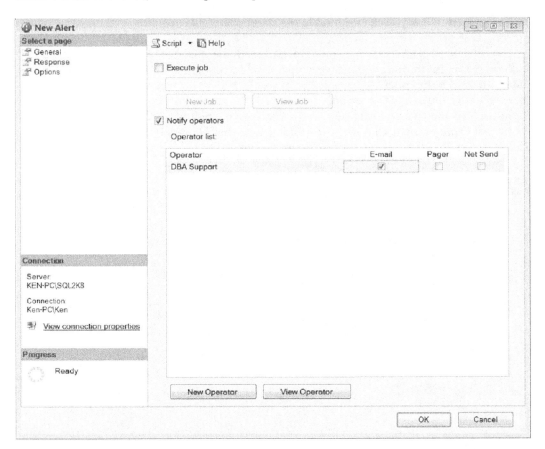

Figure 13-12. *New Alert dialog box Response page*

The Response page allows you to perform two actions in response to an event: execute a job and notify an operator of the event. You can select an existing job to run from the Execute Job drop-down list, or select the New Job button to open the New Job dialog box and create a new job. If you choose a job from the drop-down list and select the View Job button, SQL Server will display the Job Properties dialog box that will allow you to view and edit an existing job.

All of the existing operators are displayed in the Operator List area. Check the E-mail column for each operator you would like to receive a notification email when the alert is triggered. Remember, the Pager and Net Send options are deprecated, so you should avoid these two options. You can select the New Operator button to open the New Operator dialog box, or select the View Operator button to open the Operator Properties dialog box for the selected operator. We have chosen to notify the DBA Support operator we created in the previous "Operators" section. Select the Options page, as shown in Figure 13-13, to make the final configurations to the new alert.

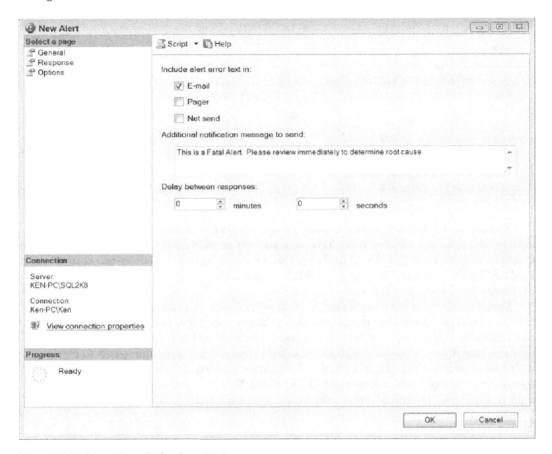

Figure 13-13. *New Alert dialog box Options page*

Select the E-mail check box at the top of the Options page so the error text for the event will be included in the email that the operator receives. The Additional Notification Message to Send text box will allow you to send further information or instructions along with the error text to the operator. You can use the Delay Between Responses section to suspend additional responses for the alert for a specified amount of time. Adding a delay between responses is useful for error messages that may occur in rapid succession; nobody wants to receive a hundred emails in five minutes. Click OK to close the New Alert dialog box and create the alert.

You can repeat this process for each alert you want to create on every SQL Server instance, or you can create a T-SQL script you can quickly run on all of your SQL Server instances. The code in Listing 13-2 will generate the same alert we just created for severity 19 using SQL Server Management Studio.

Listing 13-2. *Code to Create an Alert for Severity 19 Messages*

```
USE msdb
GO
EXEC msdb.dbo.sp_add_alert
    @name=N'Fatal Error in Resource',
    @message_id=0,
    @severity=19,
    @enabled=1,
    @delay_between_responses=0,
    @include_event_description_in=1,
    @notification_message=N'This is a Fatal Alert.  Please review immediately.'
GO

EXEC msdb.dbo.sp_add_notification
    @alert_name=N'Fatal Error in Resource',
    @operator_name=N'DBA Support',
    @notification_method = 1
GO
```

You can also define an alert for a specific error number, regardless of the severity, by entering the exact error number. We have seen some specific blog entries around the need to create an alert for error 825, which deals with an IO issue. You can read more on error 825 on Paul Randal's blog located at http://sqlskills.com/BLOGS/PAUL/post/A-little-known-sign-of-impending-doom-error-825.aspx.

For a complete list of messages and their severity codes, you can query the sys.messages catalog view. There are far too many messages in the sys.messages catalog view to review each one manually. You can narrow down the messages by limiting the results by language and only showing the messages that SQL Server will log. You can also limit the results to messages with a severity of less than 19, as shown in the following query, since you should already be monitoring messages with a severity of 19 and above. You can review the list returned by the following query to determine if you want to add additional alerts for specific errors.

```
SELECT *
FROM sys.messages
WHERE language_id = 1033 and
            is_event_logged = 1 and
            severity < 19
```

Jobs

SQL Server Agent jobs make it possible for you to perform routine scheduled maintenance on your SQL Server instances. A job is made up of a series of steps or actions that work together to perform a task. You can place each job in a category to group tasks that are similar in nature. For example, you can use the Database Maintenance category to group all of your mainte-nance jobs. You can execute a job using a predefined schedule or by using the sp_start_job stored procedure in the msdb. SQL Server Agent can notify an operator when a job fails, when a job succeeds, or any time a job completes. Let's walk through the process of creating a job that you can use to clean up the Database Mail history we described in the "Database Mail Cleanup Procedures" section earlier in the chapter.

Right-click the Jobs folder under SQL Server Agent and select New Job from the context menu to open the New Job dialog box, as shown in Figure 13-14.

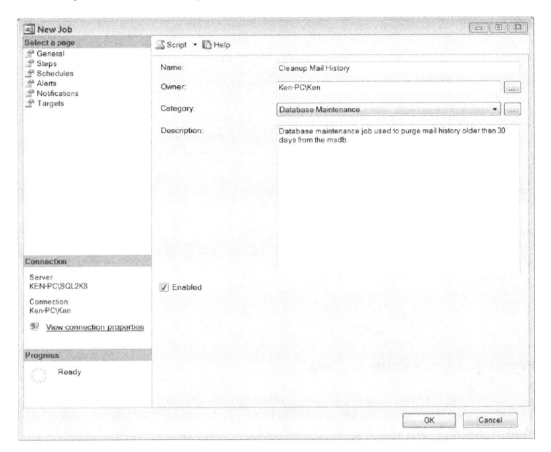

Figure 13-14. *New Job dialog box General page*

Give the job a descriptive name, such as **Cleanup Mail History**. Select Database Mainte-nance from the Category drop-down list. If you do not have a Database Maintenance category or you want to create a new category, you can right-click the Jobs folder and select Manage Job Categories from the context menu. Provide a brief description, such as **Database maintenance job used to purge mail history older than 30 days from the msdb**. If Enabled is unchecked, the job will not run during the scheduled time; however, you can still execute the job using the sp_start_job stored procedure. A disabled job will also run if it is executed in response to an alert. Select the Steps page, as shown in Figure 13-15, to define the steps the job will perform.

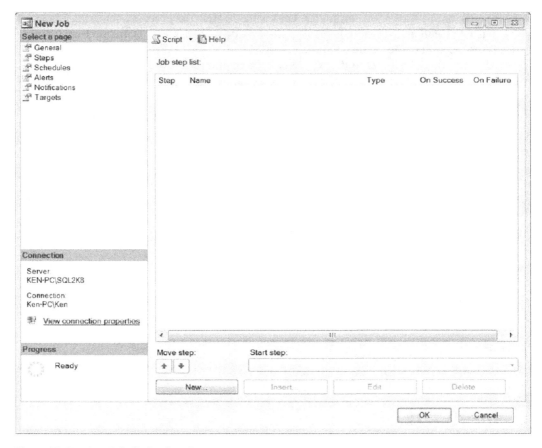

Figure 13-15. *New Job dialog box Steps page*

You can use the Steps page to add, edit, and delete job steps, move the order of the steps, and set the start step for the job. Select the New button to display the New Job Step dialog box shown in Figure 13-16.

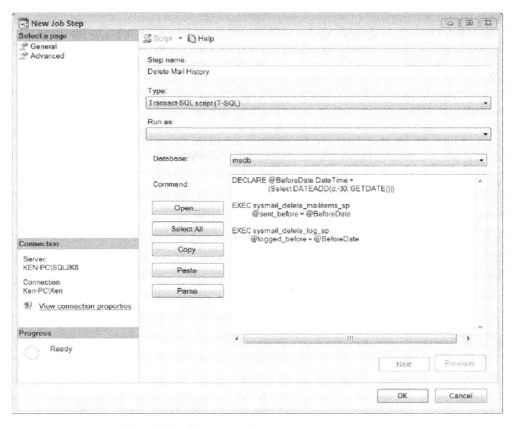

Figure 13-16. *New Job Step dialog box General page*

Give the job step a descriptive name, such as **Delete Mail History**. You can create job steps to execute many different actions, such as the following:

- Operating system commands
- Transact-SQL scripts
- PowerShell scripts
- ActiveX scripts
- Replication tasks
- Analysis Services tasks
- Integration Services packages

■**Caution** ActiveX scripts will be removed from SQL Server Agent in a future version of SQL Server. There-fore, you should avoid using ActiveX scripts in any new jobs.

Since we are executing a SQL script, select Transact-SQL Script (T-SQL) from the Type drop-down list. The Run As drop-down list in the General page does not apply to T-SQL scripts; it only applies to other step types that interact with the OS, such as PowerShell scripts and CmdExec. The Run As option here is for designating a proxy account to run the job step. (We will discuss proxy accounts more in the next section.) Actually, if you change Type selection to something other than T-SQL, and then change it back to T-SQL, the Run As option will be disabled.

Change the Database option to msdb, since that is where the Database Mail cleanup stored procedures are located. Enter the following script in the Command text box. Select the Advanced page, as shown in Figure 13-17, to configure the remaining options for the job step.

```
DECLARE @BeforeDate DateTime =
                    (Select DATEADD(d,-30, GETDATE()))

EXEC sysmail_delete_mailitems_sp
          @sent_before = @BeforeDate

EXEC sysmail_delete_log_sp
          @logged_before = @BeforeDate
```

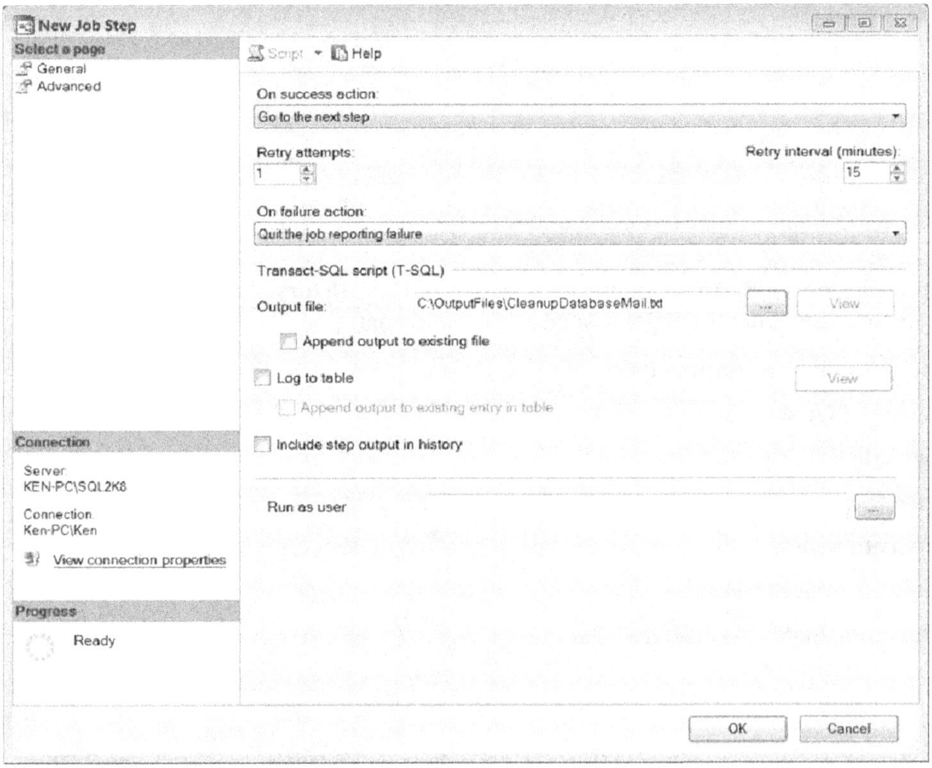

Figure 13-17. *New Job Step dialog box Advanced page*

You can use the Advanced page to define options for the job step, such as completion actions and logging. You can use the On Success Action and On Failure Action lists to quit the job reporting success, quit the job reporting failure, go to the next step, or to select a specific step that you would like to run next as a result of the action. You can use the Retry Attempts and Retry Interval options to set the number of times SQL Server Agent will try to run the steps and how long it will wait between retry attempts before it considers the step a failure. We have set our job step to retry one time 15 minutes after the initial failure. It is important to specify an output file to log the messages returned by the job step. Output files are a tremendous help when troubleshooting issues related to the job failures. The Run As User option in the Advanced page is only applicable for T-SQL scripts. If you create a step that is anything other than T-SQL, the option will not be displayed. The account specified here is the SQL Server account used by SQL Server Agent to execute the job step. Only users with sysadmin rights can set the Run As User option and create output files. Click OK to add the new step to the job.

You can use the Schedules page of the New Job dialog to pick an existing schedule or create a new schedule for the job. Click the Schedules page and select New to open the New Job Schedule dialog box shown in Figure 13-18.

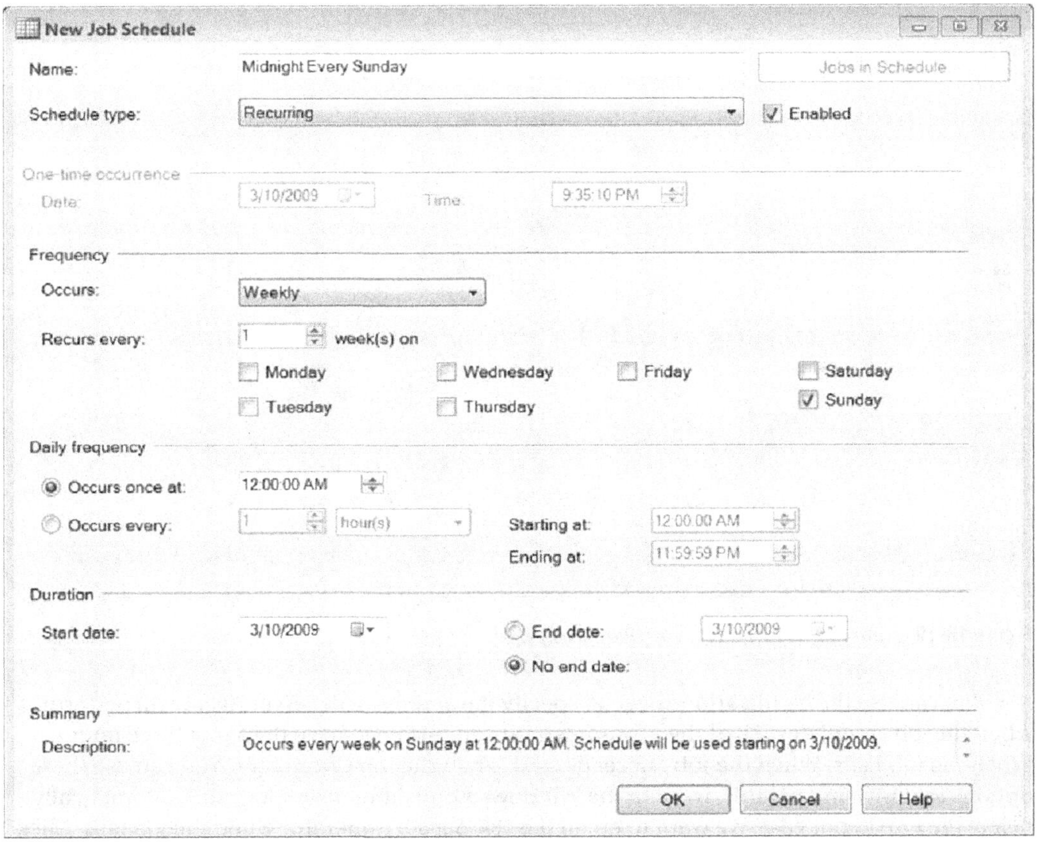

Figure 13-18. *New Job Schedule dialog box*

Give the new schedule a descriptive name, such as **Midnight Every Sunday**. The options are pretty self-explanatory. Select the appropriate schedule for the new job. You will see a Summary area at the bottom that you can use to validate the choices you have made. As indicated by the name, we have created a schedule to run every Sunday at 12:00 AM. Select OK to add the job to the new schedule.

You can use the Alerts page to create a new alert that will execute the job in response to an event. Since we do not need to clean up Database Mail for an alert, skip this page and select Notifications, as shown in Figure 13-19.

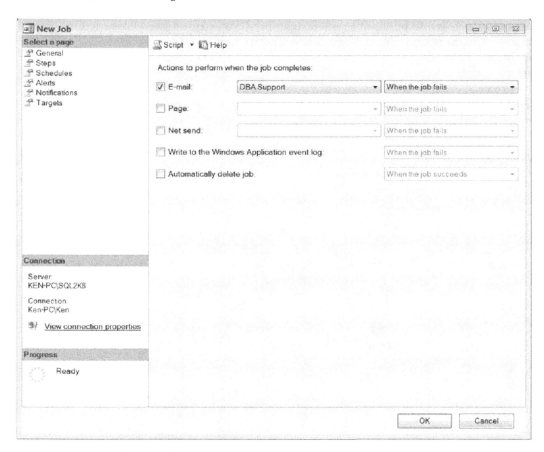

Figure 13-19. *New Job dialog box Notifications page*

You can use the Notifications page to specify the actions SQL Server Agent will perform when the job completes. All of the drop-down lists on this page have the same three options: When the Job Fails, When the Job Succeeds, and When the Job Completes. You can use these options to notify an operator, write to the Windows Application event log, and automatically delete the job. In our case, we want to email the DBA Support operator when the job fails. Click OK to create the new Job.

You only need to worry about the Targets page if you are using master and target servers within SQL Server Agent. SQL Server Agent allows you to designate a SQL Server instance as a master (MSX) server and push jobs to target (TSX) servers. The Targets page allows you to define whether the job will be defined locally or if you will be targeting multiple servers. The jobs on the target servers are read-only and cannot be deleted. In order to set up a MSX server and enlist TSX servers, you can right click on SQL Server Agent, select Multi-Server Administration, and then select Make This a Master. This will start the Master Sever Wizard that will guide you through the process. For more information on master and target servers, search for "Creating a Multiserver Environment" in SQL Server Books Online.

Proxies

You can create a proxy account that allows SQL Server Agent to execute a job step that runs under the credentials of a specified Windows user account. You can use a proxy account to access subsystems external to SQL Server using Windows credentials; therefore, you cannot use a proxy account for a T-SQL job step, since T-SQL is an internal operation. In order to create a proxy account, you must first create a credential that maps to a Windows user account. To open the New Credential dialog box shown in Figure 13-20, expand the Security node in SQL Server Management Studio, right-click the Credentials folder, and select New Credential from the context menu.

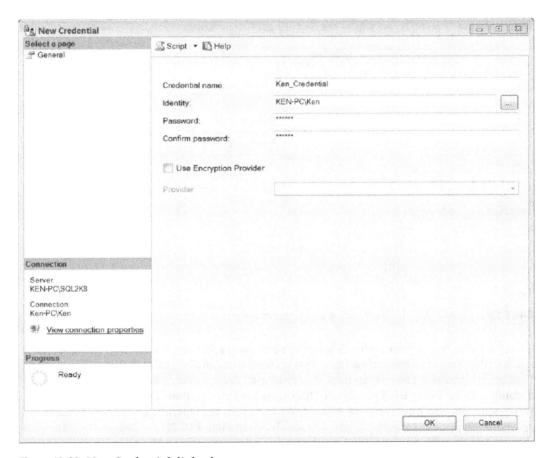

Figure 13-20. *New Credential dialog box*

Enter a descriptive name for the credential. We named ours Ken_Credential, since that is the Windows account we are using. Enter a valid Windows user account in the Identity field. You can select the ellipsis next to the Identity field to display the Select User or Group dialog box, which will allow you to search for and verify Windows user accounts. Enter the password for the Windows user account and select OK to create the new credential. You may also choose to verify the Windows user account by an Extensible Key Management provider if you have one installed on the server.

Now that you have created a credential, you are ready to create a new proxy. Expand SQL Server Agent, right-click the Proxies folder, and select New Proxy from the context menu. This will display the New Proxy Account dialog box shown in Figure 13-21.

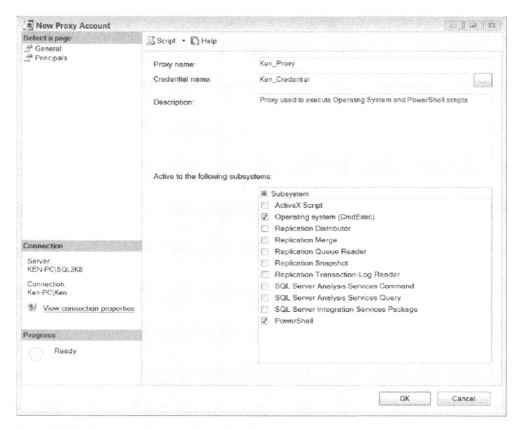

Figure 13-21. *New Proxy Account dialog box General page*

Give the new proxy account a descriptive name; we called ours Ken_Proxy. Now, enter the name of the credential created earlier in this section. You can also select the ellipsis next to the Credential Name text box to search for the credential. Enter a description for the new proxy account, such as **Proxy used to execute Operating System and PowerShell scripts**. Select the subsystems the new proxy account will use. We have selected Operating System (CmdExec) and PowerShell. Select the Principals page, as shown in Figure 13-22, to manage the principals that can use the new proxy account in job steps.

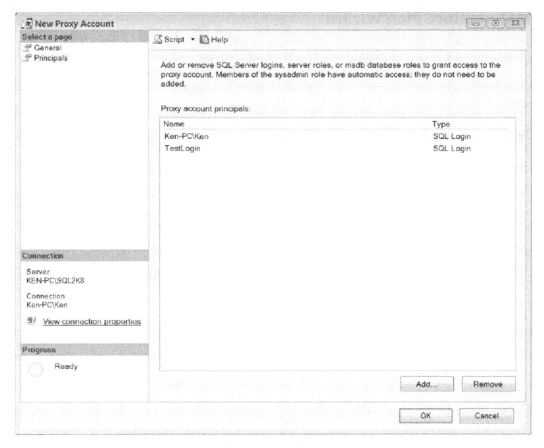

Figure 13-22. *New Proxy Account dialog box Principals page*

Select the Add button to assign SQL Server logins or roles to the proxy account. Members of the sysadmin role have access to all proxy accounts, so you do not need to add them on the Principals page. Click OK to create the new proxy account.

The proxy account is now an available option in the Run As drop-down list on the General page of the New Job Step dialog box. The proxy account is only available in the Run As list if you select Operating System (CmdExec) or PowerShell as the step type, since they are the only two subsystems we allowed the proxy account to use.

Maintenance Plans

Maintenance plans enable you to set up a predefined set of routine maintenance tasks on your SQL Server instances. You can create a maintenance plan by using the Maintenance Plan Wizard or going straight to the Maintenance Plan Design tab. Just like all wizards in SQL Server, the Maintenance Plan Wizard is a pretty straightforward point-and-click operation. The Maintenance Plan Design tab however, gives you a few extra options and provides a little more control over the maintenance tasks. Maintenance plans are nothing more than SQL Server Agent jobs that execute SQL Server Integration Services packages.

Maintenance Plan Wizard

The Maintenance Plan Wizard provides a simple interface for you to define and schedule tasks that perform routine maintenance. Right-click the Maintenance Plans folder located under the Management node and select Maintenance Plan Wizard from the context menu. Click Next when the Welcome screen appears to display the Select Plan Properties page, as shown in Figure 13-23.

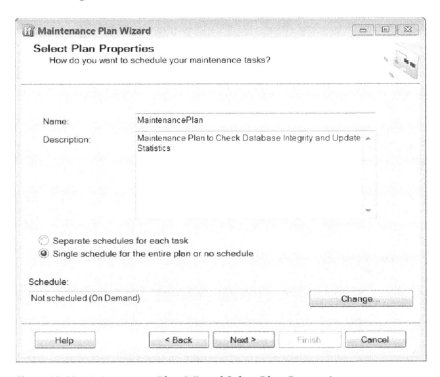

Figure 13-23. *Maintenance Plan Wizard Select Plan Properties page*

Name the maintenance plan and provide a brief description. The main thing to point out on this page is the scheduling options. If you select Separate Schedules for Each Task, a separate SQL Server Agent job will be created for each task, and each will be located in its own subplan. The scheduling option is disabled on this page, and you will need to provide a separate schedule when configuring each individual task. If you select Single Schedule for the Entire Plan or No Schedule, each task will be included in a single subplan using a single SQL Server Agent job, and the individual scheduling options for each task will be disabled. Click Next to display the Select Maintenance Tasks page, shown in Figure 13-24.

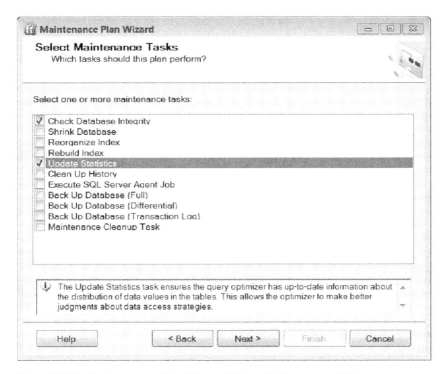

Figure 13-24. *Maintenance Plan Wizard Select Maintenance Tasks page*

You can view a brief description of each task by highlighting it. For example, you can see a description of the Update Statistics task that is highlighted in Figure 13-23. Select the tasks you want to include in the maintenance plan and continue through the wizard to configure each task.

Maintenance Plan Design Tab

You can use the Maintenance Plan Design tab to build a maintenance plan from scratch or use it to tweak plans created by the Maintenance Plan Wizard. One of the things that bothers us about the Maintenance Plan Wizard is the inability to rename the subplans during the setup process. As a result, you end up with SQL Agent jobs named MaintencePlanName.SubPlan_1, MaintencePlanName.SubPlan_2, and so on, for each task that requires a separate job schedule. This naming convention tells you nothing about a given job. For example, does it rebuild indexes, update statistics, back up a database, or what? So the first thing you should do after using the Maintenance Plan Wizard is open the Design tab and rename the subplans to something more descriptive.

To open a plan that has been created using the wizard, just double-click Maintenance Plan located in the Maintenance Plans folder under the Management node in the SQL Server Management Studio Object Explorer. To create a new maintenance plan using the Design tab, right-click the Maintenance Plans folder located under the Management node and select New Maintenance Plan. Enter a name for the new plan when prompted, and click OK. (The Maintenance Plan Design tab is shown in Figure 13-25.)

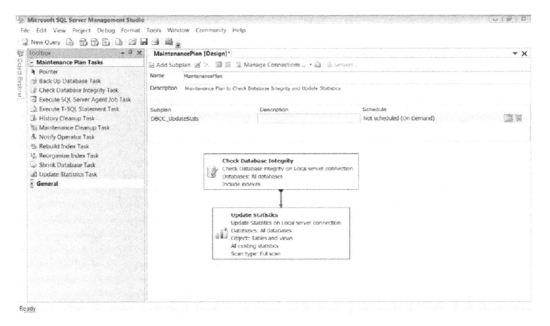

Figure 13-25. *Maintenance Plan Design tab*

If you have ever created a SQL Server Integration Services package, the Design tab should look extremely familiar. From here you can add, remove, and configure subplans (including giving them a descriptive name). Once you have configured the subplans to perform the appropriate maintenance tasks, save the maintenance plan to create or update the SQL Server Agent jobs that run them.

Maintenance Plan Tasks

Now that we have discussed how to create and edit maintenance plans, let's review the available maintenance tasks. There are two maintenance tasks available in the Design tab that are not available in the wizard: Execute T-SQL Statement Task and Notify Operator Task. You may find these two extra tasks useful if you want to perform more customized operations in your maintenance plans. The following is a list of tasks you can perform with maintenance plans.

- *Backup Database Task*: You can use this task to perform a full, differential, or transaction log backup for one or more databases.

- *Check Database Integrity Task*: You can use this task to execute the DBCC CHECKDB command against one or more databases.

- *Execute SQL Server Agent Job Task*: You can use this task to select an existing SQL Server Agent job to run as part of the maintenance plan.

- *Execute T-SQL Statement Task*: You can use this task to execute a custom T-SQL statement as part of the maintenance plan.

- *History Cleanup Task*: You can use this task to clean up backup and restore history, SQL Server Agent job history, and maintenance plan history from the msdb that is older than a specified date.

- *Maintenance Cleanup Task*: You can use this task to delete files such as database backups and maintenance plan text files that are older than a specified date.

- *Notify Operator Task*: You can use this task to send a notification to an existing operator as part of the maintenance plan.

- *Rebuild Index Task*: You can use this task to rebuild all indexes in one or more databases, or you can target specific objects for index rebuilds.

- *Reorganize Index Task*: You can use this task to reorganize all indexes in one or more databases or you can target specific objects for index reorganization.

- *Shrink Database Task*: You can use this task to shrink one or more databases, though you really should not have to shrink databases as a part of your maintenance plan. Constantly shrinking and growing your databases will greatly reduce performance.

- *Update Statistics Task*: You can use this task to update statistics in one or more databases.

You can reproduce every maintenance task using T-SQL. There is no magic going on in the background. We are not against maintenance plans, but we tend to create our own maintenance jobs using T-SQL scripts. We like a little more control than the maintenance plan will allow. For example, instead of blindly rebuilding an index, we check the fragmentation level first. If the fragmentation level is between 5% and 30%, we reorganize the index. If the fragmentation level is greater than 30%, we rebuild the index. For more information on finding index fragmentation levels, search for "Reorganizing and Rebuilding Indexes" in SQL Server Books Online.

Exporting and Importing Maintenance Plans

The whole point of this chapter is automating tasks. We don't know about you, but we don't want to go out to each of our servers and create a new maintenance plan if we have already done it once. An easy way to avoid creating a maintenance plan on each server is by exporting a preexisting plan.

Connect to Integration Services on the SQL Server instance that contains the maintenance plan you would like to export, expand the Maintenance Plans folder, right-click the maintenance plan and select Export Package, as shown in Figure 13-26.

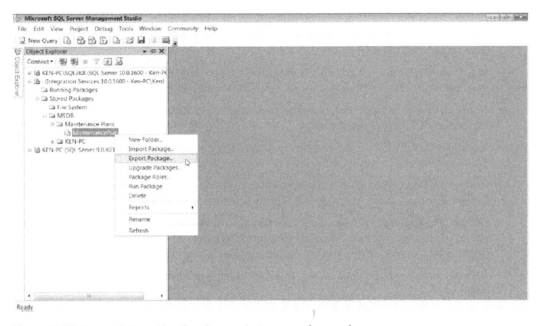

Figure 13-26. *Export Integration Services maintenance plan package*

This will open the Export Package dialog box shown in Figure 13-27. You can use this dialog box to save the maintenance plan to another instance of SQL Server, or save it to the file system so you can import the maintenance plan on the new SQL Server instance later.

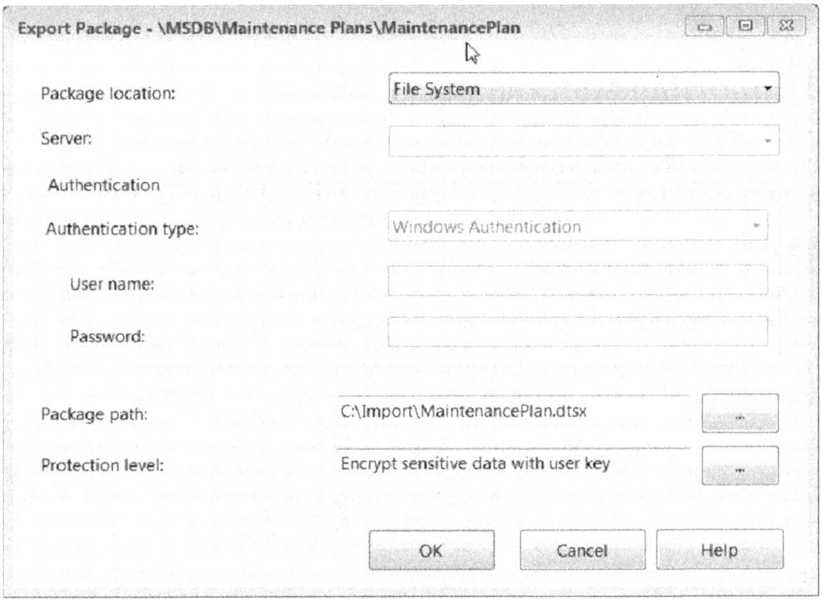

Figure 13-27. *Export Package dialog box*

If you are importing the maintenance plan from the file system, you will need to connect to Integration Services on the new SQL Server instance and right-click the Maintenance Plans folder and select Import Package to open the Import Package dialog box shown in Figure 13-28.

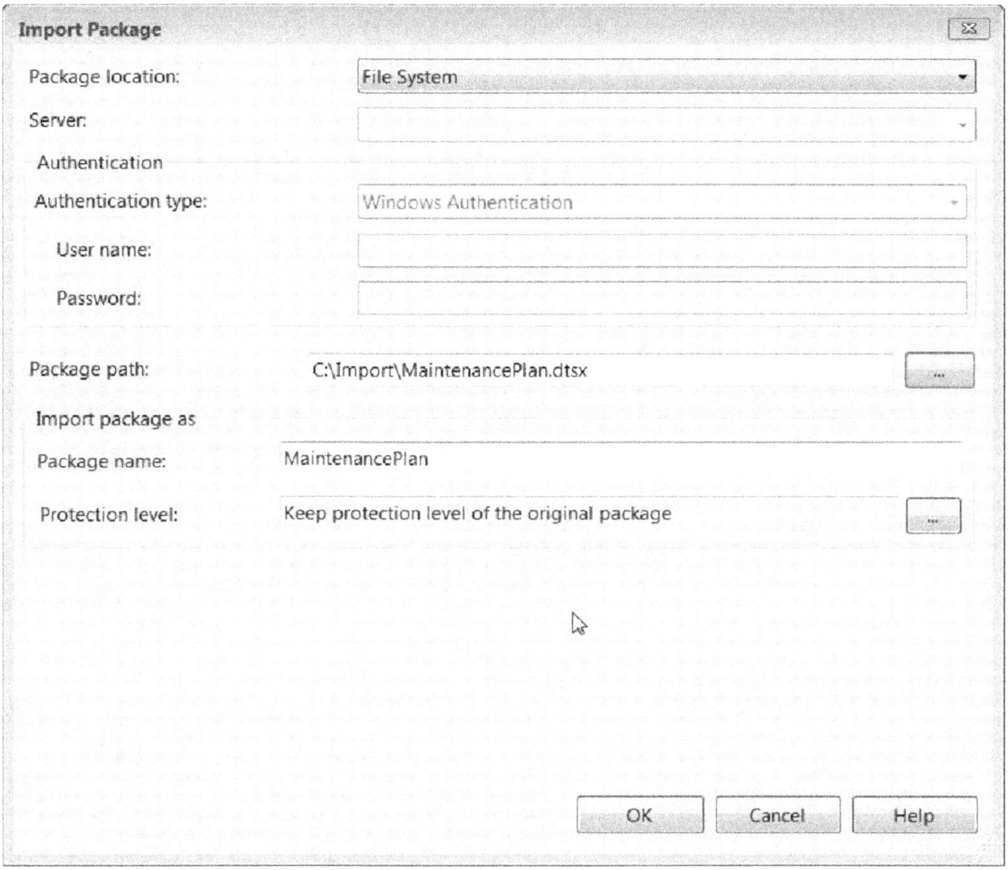

Figure 13-28. *Import Package dialog box*

Once you have imported the maintenance plan on the new instance of SQL Server, you will need to open it using the Design tab and click the Save button in order to create the jobs associated with the plan.

Summary

This chapter has gone over several techniques you can use to automate database maintenance. We have covered everything from setting up Database Mail, creating alerts, defining operators to receive those alerts, creating custom maintenance jobs, and creating maintenance plans. If you take a little time up front to properly configure your SQL Server instances, you will find that being proactive makes for a far better day than being reactive.

Troubleshooting and Tuning

CHAPTER 14

Monitoring Your Server

As a database administrator, you are required to monitor the performance of SQL Server, the users who are logging in to your server, and to identify changes to objects within your environment. When you are effectively monitoring SQL Server, then you can proactively make informed decisions about changes made in your environment. The alternative is that you make reactive decisions, which are often times not thought out completely.

Fortunately, SQL Server 2008 and Windows Server provide useful tools to help you monitor both of them. The three primary tools that you'll use are as follows:

- The performance monitor (PerfMon)

- The Dynamic Management Views (DMVs)

- The profiling and tracing features

Baseline Your Server

The techniques discussed later on in this chapter will demonstrate methods for identifying problems on SQL Server. However, in order to proactively monitor your server and recognize when things are changing, you have to *baseline* your server. This captures statistical information regarding your server over time, and then declares those measurements as the baseline performance measurements. Your monitoring then, involves comparing new measurements against that baseline in order to detect changes.

When you collect baseline metrics, there are a number of areas to consider. Your server uses CPU, memory and disk, and there are other aspects of SQL Server to consider as well. You should try to capture a baseline of statistics for the following items:

- CPU
- Memory
- Physical disk
- SQL server activity
  - Buffer manager
  - General statistics
  - SQL statistics

Creating baseline statistics for your server not only helps you determine what is normal for your environment, but you also document the norm for other members of your team. That definitely helps new employees when their responsibilities consist of supporting existing applications on servers that have baselines documented.

Even if your application has been running on the current server for years, it is still not too late to baseline your server. You need to have some method to determine if your server is gradually performing worse. Having that information will help you justify server replacement and provide better support for your application.

Familiarizing Yourself with the Performance Monitor

Performance monitor is a graphical tool that comes with Microsoft operating systems to monitor different activity of the system. Performance monitor is divided into two basic parts: the system monitor and performance logs and alerts. The System Monitor section provides real-time statistics on system activity in a graph, histogram, or report format. The Performance Logs and Alerts section allows you to store information about the activity on your system and set alerts to fire after surpassing your defined thresholds.

There are multiple methods of launching the performance monitor. You can navigate to the Administrative Tools folder from the Control Panel or Start menu, and then select Performance. Or you can go to the Start menu, select Run, and then type **perfmon**. Once the application launches, you will see a graph with the default counters displayed, as shown in Figure 14-1.

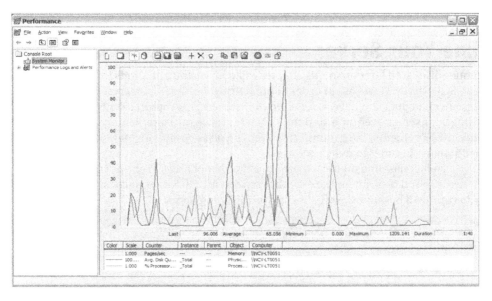

Figure 14-1. *The default counters displayed within the performance monitor*

After you launch the application, there are two options that you need to be familiar with: Add (represented by a plus sign on the toolbar) and Highlight (represented by a yellow light bulb on the toolbar).

The Add option is important because it allows you to increase the number of counters that you can monitor. Once you click on the plus sign or Add option, the Add Counters dialog box will launch (see Figure 14-2).

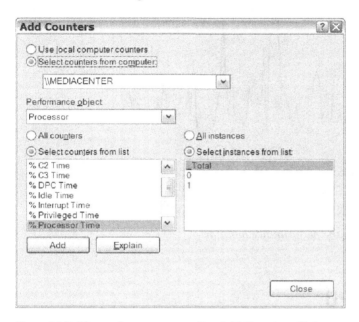

Figure 14-2. *The performance monitor Add Counters dialog*

After reviewing Figure 14-2, you should notice that you have multiple options to choose from when adding counters. You can determine the source of the counters that you want to add. Next, you have to decide which object you want to add counters from. After you select an object, you can determine if you want all counters for the object or if you want to select specific objects from the list. Lastly, where it applies, you can select the instance of the counter that you want to capture. Whatever you do, don't forget about the Explain button, which gives you a brief description of the selected counter. That will definitely help you sort out the meaning of the numerous counters that exist. Once you decide on the counter you want, click on the Add button, and it will populate the graph, histogram, or report.

As you familiarize yourself with the performance monitor, you will add a large number of counters to your graph simultaneously. When you reach that point, it will become increasingly challenging to identify the values of each counter. That's where the Highlight option comes into play. The Highlight option lets you to quickly determine the values of the counters by highlighting them on the display (see Figure 14-3).

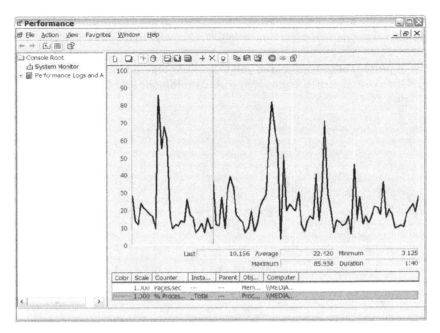

Figure 14-3. *A highlighted counter in the performance monitor*

Monitoring Your CPU

The CPU of the server that SQL Server resides on will do the processing for your applications running SQL Server. Any CPU bottlenecks will thus impact the performance of your server. Monitoring your CPU and the counters that reflect current CPU activity over a given period enables you to identify gradual changes within your environment. Identifying those changes before the situation becomes unmanageable is the key to keeping management and your customers happy.

Using multiple performance monitor counters to identify CPU problems is the best way to determine when you have a CPU bottleneck. Table 14-1 lists some performance counters and recommended values for those counters. You can refer to these recommended values when trying to determine whether you have potential CPU issues.

Table 14-1. *CPU Counters and Their Recommended Values*

Counter Name	Description	Recommended Values
Processor: % Processor Time (Total)	The percentage of time the processor spent executing a non-idle thread	> 80% longer than 15 mins
Processor: % Privilege Time	The amount of time spent executing system processes	< 30%
System: Context Switches	The rate that processors switch among the threads	~5000 per CPU
System: Processor Queue Length	The number of ready threads in a queue	< 2 per Processor
SQL Statistics: Batch Requests/Sec	The batch requests received by SQL Server	Use baseline
SQL Statistics: SQL Compilations/Sec	The number of SQL Server compilations	> 10% of batch requests/sec
SQL Statistics: SQL Recompilations/Sec	The number of SQL Server recompiles	> 10% of SQL compilations/sec

MONITORING CPU WITH TASK MANAGER

This section primarily focuses on the performance monitor and DMVs, but don't forget about tools like the Task Manager. Using Task Manager to monitor CPU is a quick-and-easy method of determining if your CPU is high and the application that is using the bulk of it. When you know what is consuming your CPU, you can better determine the best course of action for further investigation. Figure 14-4 shows an example of Windows Task Manager Processes tab.

Figure 14-4. *The Processes tab within Windows Task Manager*

The thresholds may vary from environment to environment and may need tweaking to identify problems in your environment. Use the thresholds from Table 14-1 as a starting point for monitoring your environment, not as absolute values that you are bound to stay within.

Once the performance monitor is launched, the first thing we do is remove the default counters and add the counters for the resource that we are monitoring. For this example, we added the counters listed in Table 14-1 and any other counters that we have found useful for monitoring CPU. After adding the counters to the display, you should go through them and remove the counters that are in line with your baseline or the thresholds listed in Table 14-1. That way, you remove some of the "busyness" on the screen, and the only counters that remain will be the counters that you really need to evaluate and analyze. Figure 14-5 shows an example of the performance monitor with the counters listed in Table 14-1.

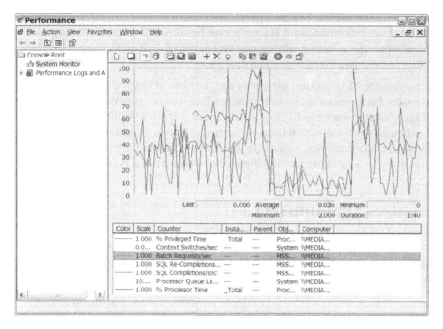

Figure 14-5. *Sample PerfMon counters listed in Table 14-1*

Windows Counters That Indicate CPU Utilization

This section provides additional information about the Windows counters listed in Table 14-1. The `Processor` object lists two counters that we want to discuss: % Processor Time and the % Privilege Time. The `System` object lists the other two counters that we care about: Context Switches and Processor Queue Length. Following are our thoughts on these four key counters:

- *% Processor Time*: The percentage of CPU used on your server. Ideally, we like to keep our servers running in the 20% to 50% range. Spikes above this range will occur, so don't be alarmed when your server temporarily runs high. You should try to identify the process or processes causing the increase in your CPU when it sustains above 80% for a given period. That threshold is one indicator that you may be headed toward a CPU bottleneck.

- *% Privilege Time*: A counter that helps you identify the impact of kernel or system processes on your server. The execution of system processes should consume less than 30% of your total CPU. When this value is consistently greater than 30%, it probably indicates that a Windows service is having a problem.

- *Context Switches/Sec*: These counters list the number of SQL Server threads switching among processors. A high number of context switches can prove costly to your CPU. Numbers higher than 5000 per second could indicate problems, but review the other counters in this section before making that determination. If counters like Processor

Queue Length and Compilations/Sec look good, then chances are your context switches are okay. Another good reference point is your server baseline, which will contain the context switches when the system performance was acceptable. Track changes in the baseline number to help you identify gradual changes.

- *Processor Queue Length*: This counter identifies the number of ready threads waiting on processor resources for processing. Numbers exceeding two per processor should definitely encourage you to investigate CPU. Threads in a ready state waiting on processing indicate that processes are waiting on their opportunity to run. When threads are waiting to run, the applications are not processing requests as fast as they would like to. That could definitely be a problem for the applications using the server.

SQL Server Counters That Impact CPU

This section discusses the SQL Server counters that track CPU-intensive processes that influence your CPU. The counters do not necessarily indicate that you will have performance problems because of the values of the counters. However, CPU utilization should be lower on your system as the following counters values decrease.

- *Batch Requests/Sec*: Measures the number of batch requests received by the SQL Server instance. This number generally represents the activity on SQL Server. Unfortunately, this counter does not capture every statement executed in a stored procedure, but it is the best counter to use to gauge the activity on SQL Server.

  Servers with more than 1000 batch requests/sec generally carry a heavy transactional load. Busy database servers are not a bad thing, but they could cause CPU problems. So baseline your servers and keep an eye on the number of batch requests/sec against your server.

- *SQL Compilations/Sec*: Represents the number of compiles that occur on your SQL Server instance. The first execution of a query on SQL Server generates a compilation and stores the execution plan in the procedure cache. When the query executes again, SQL Server checks to see if that execution plan exists in the procedure cache. Reusing an execution plan found in the procedure cache ultimately saves SQL Server the CPU time needed to compile a plan. Applications that execute ad hoc queries don't take advantage of execution plan reuse, causing increased CPU as plans must be generated often.

  SQL Server compilations should be less than 10% of your batch requests/sec. Results greater than that threshold probably indicate that an application running against that instance of SQL Server is not taking advantage of execution plan reuse. Using Dynamic SQL and stored procedures increases the chances of execution plan reuse, minimizing the number of compiles.

- *SQL Recompilations/Sec*: Represents the number of recompiles that occur on your SQL Server instance. SQL Server decides to recompile for a number of reasons, but some of the most common are statistics updates, schema changes, changes to an index used by an execution plan, and your specifying the recompile option. Once a plan is marked for recompile, the next batch that executes the query will cause the recompile to occur. Recompiles are CPU intensive, especially on complex queries.

SQL Server recompilations should be less than 10% of the number of SQL Server compilations that occur on your instance of SQL Server. When your system exceeds that threshold, you should spend some time identifying the cause of the recompiles. Pay close attention to recompiles after application upgrades. Recompiles after an upgrade generally indicate new changes in the application that are causing the recompiles to occur, and those changes may end up affecting performance. Your baseline can be useful when comparing change in the number of recompiles on your system. Recompiles will happen, but minimize them on your system if you can.

While using the Windows counters, try to combine the results of counters to help identify CPU bottlenecks. When the CPU is sustaining above 80% and the processor queue is above its thresholds, then that combination should force you to investigate the CPU further to ensure SQL Server is not causing a CPU bottleneck. Before making recommendations for purchasing additional CPU, use some of the tips in Chapter 15 to identify queries that consume a lot of CPU and attempt to improve the performance of those queries.

DMVs for Monitoring CPU

SQL Server provides a number of Dynamic Management Views (DMVs) for monitoring CPU. Understanding the relationship between threads, workers, schedulers, and tasks is crucial to understanding the relationship between the CPU DMVs. Here's what you need to know:

1. SQL Server starts, spawns a number of threads, and associates workers to them.

2. A query or batch is broken into one or multiple tasks.

3. The task is assigned to a worker for the duration of the query or batch.

4. Workers are assigned to a scheduler and each scheduler maps to a processor to run.

Let's take a closer look at these DMVs to get a better understanding of the output that they provide. The following list describes some of the data returned by these views:

- `sys.dm_os_threads`: Lists information about the threads created when SQL Server started. These are operating system threads that currently run under the instance of the SQL Server executable. This view is useful for monitoring CPU because it can provide information about runaway threads within the executable along with linking information for the other CPU DMVs.

- `sys.dm_os_workers`: Provides information about the workers assigned to threads within SQL Server. When a worker is ready to run, the worker moves to the front of the runnable queue and tries to run up to 1000 times. After the 1000 tries, the worker moves to the back of the queue. This DMV also returns information about the worker (such as the number of tasks the worker executed), the state of the worker, IO used by the worker, the number of ms_ticks that the worker spent in a suspended and runnable state along with many more columns. Besides important information about the workers, this DMV returns important information for linking to threads, schedulers, and tasks. Spend some time understanding this DMV; it should prove useful when monitoring your CPU.

The query in Listing 14-1 is one that we frequently use and is found in SQL Server Books Online. This listing shows you how long worker threads have been active compared to suspended. The results of Listing 14-1 are shown in Figure 14-6.

Listing 14-1. *SQL Code That Identifies the Amount of Time a Worker Has Been Running Compared to Being Suspended*

```
SELECT t1.session_id,t1.status,t1.command AS command,
t2.state AS worker_state,
w_suspended = CASE t2.wait_started_ms_ticks
 WHEN 0 THEN 0 ELSE t3.ms_ticks - t2.wait_started_ms_ticks
END,
w_runnable = CASE t2.wait_resumed_ms_ticks
WHEN 0 THEN 0 ELSE  t3.ms_ticks - t2.wait_resumed_ms_ticks
END
FROM sys.dm_exec_requests AS t1 INNER JOIN sys.dm_os_workers AS t2
 ON t2.task_address = t1.task_address
CROSS JOIN sys.dm_os_sys_info AS t3
WHERE t1.scheduler_id IS NOT NULL and session_id> 50
```

	session_id	status	command	worker_state	w_suspend	w_runnable
1	51	runnable	ALTER INDEX	RUNNABLE	4	4
2	60	suspended	SELECT	SUSPENDED	74575	74575
3	63	suspended	SELECT	SUSPENDED	74556	74556
4	54	running	DBCC TABLE CHECK	RUNNING	0	17
5	62	runnable	SELECT	RUNNABLE	15	4
6	76	suspended	SELECT	SUSPENDED	74564	74564
7	72	suspended	SELECT	SUSPENDED	74558	74558
8	81	suspended	SELECT	SUSPENDED	86226	86226
9	71	suspended	SELECT	SUSPENDED	86278	86278
10	64	suspended	SELECT	SUSPENDED	74572	74572
11	73	suspended	SELECT	SUSPENDED	74555	74555
12	75	suspended	SELECT	SUSPENDED	74561	74561
13	77	suspended	SELECT	SUSPENDED	74559	74559
14	78	suspended	SELECT	SUSPENDED	74569	74569
15	84	running	SELECT	RUNNING	0	0

Figure 14-6. *The results of Listing 14-1*

- `sys.dm_os_schedulers`: Lists information about the schedulers and the workers assigned to them. This DMV has several interesting columns, including columns that let you know how many workers are associated with each scheduler, how many workers with tasks associated to them are waiting on the scheduler, and the number of active workers each scheduler currently has. Monitoring this view is important because you need to know when the schedulers start to deviate from your baseline. The more workers waiting on scheduler time increases the likelihood of CPU bottlenecks. Make sure you proactively monitor this view in your environment and identify causes for change in this view.

Listing 14-2 contains a query that we frequently run to identify the workload of our schedulers. We pay close attention to the amount of workers that are queuing, specifically the count in the work_queue_count column. Figure 14-7 contains the results of Listing 14-2.

Listing 14-2. *SQL Script That Gathers Statistics on Your Schedulers*

```
SELECT scheduler_id,parent_node_id,current_tasks_count,
runnable_tasks_count, current_workers_count, active_workers_count,
work_queue_count, load_factor
FROM sys.dm_os_schedulers
WHERE  scheduler_id < 255
```

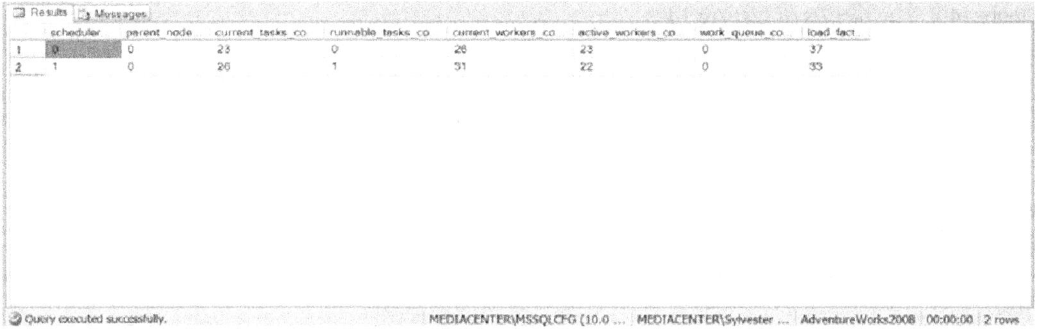

Figure 14-7. *The results of Listing 14-2*

- `sys.dm_os_tasks`: Gives you information about each active task within your SQL Server instance. This DMV has columns that provide you with the physical IO performed by the task, the state of the task, and the scheduler the task is running on, along with several other columns. This DMV also contains columns about the request that caused the creation of the task. That's really important when you want to figure out the query or batch that the task is executing. Listing 14-3 contains a sample script that shows you how to identify the query that caused the creation of the task. The results are shown in Figure 14-8.

Listing 14-3. *SQL Script That Shows the Number of Tasks in a Particular task_state*

```
SELECT r.session_id,task_state,pending_io_count,
r.scheduler_id,command,cpu_time,
total_elapsed_time,sql_handle
FROM sys.dm_os_tasks t
 join sys.dm_exec_requests r on t.request_id =
r.request_id and t.session_id = r.session_id
WHERE r.session_id > 50
```

	session_id	task_state	pending_io_co	scheduler	command	cpu_time	total_elapsed_t	sql_handle
9	74	SUSPENDED	0	0	SELECT	0	155220	0x03000800023007500004A52019B9B50000100000000000000
10	79	SUSPENDED	0	0	SELECT	0	153478	0x03000800023007500004A52019B9B90000100000000000000
11	87	SUSPENDED	0	0	SELECT	0	153471	0x03000800023007500004A52019B9B90000100000000000000
12	54	RUNNING	744	1	DBCC	217883	8213725	0x010008006807CE0C70FB1A0A000000000000000000000000
13	54	SUSPENDED	917	1	DBCC	217883	8213725	0x010008006807CE0C70FB1A0A000000000000000000000000
14	54	RUNNING	747	1	DBCC	217883	8213725	0x010008006807CE0C70FB1A0A000000000000000000000000
15	54	SUSPENDED	693	1	DBCC	217883	8213725	0x010008006807CE0C70FB1A0A000000000000000000000000
16	54	RUNNING	832	1	DBCC	217883	8213725	0x010008006807CE0C70FB1A0A000000000000000000000000
17	54	SUSPENDED	831	1	DBCC	217883	8213725	0x010008006807CE0C70FB1A0A000000000000000000000000
18	54	RUNNING	794	1	DBCC	217883	8213725	0x010008006807CE0C70FB1A0A000000000000000000000000
19	54	RUNNING	791	1	DBCC	217883	8213725	0x010008006807CE0C70FB1A0A000000000000000000000000
20	54	SUSPENDED	688	1	DBCC	217883	8213725	0x010008006807CE0C70FB1A0A000000000000000000000000
21	51	RUNNING	76807	1	ALTER	919006	3218901	0x02000000E281321C2E36131F8FFFD1FC522466A1C95E68
22	54	SUSPENDED	97159	1	DBCC	217883	8213725	0x010008006807CE0C70FB1A0A000000000000000000000000
23	62	RUNNING	3	1	SELECT	7516	717293	0x0200000021444504992EB5559E6ADEE62675C9AE2F42F0
24	73	SUSPENDED	0	1	SELECT	0	161947	0x03000800023007500004A52019B9B50000100000000000000
25	81	SUSPENDED	0	1	SELECT	0	158594	0x03000800E AE8807FFB4952019B9B90000100000000000000
26	76	SUSPENDED	0	1	SELECT	0	155219	0x03000800023007E00004A52019B9B00000100000000000000

Figure 14-8. *The results of Listing 14-3*

When monitoring your CPU, we also discussed the impact of the number of compiles on your system. SQL Server provides you with the sys.dm_exec_query_optimizer_info DMV, which captures information about the SQL Server optimizer. This view contains information about the total number of optimizations, the average elapsed time for the number of optimizations, the cost of the optimizations, and several other columns. With this information, you can determine the cost of the compiles against your system. That may help you convince your developers to use stored procedures over the ad hoc queries that they run in your environment.

Monitoring Your Memory

Memory plays an important role in the performance of SQL Server. When SQL Server does not have enough memory, other resources, such as CPU and disk IO, are often impacted. Understanding the role of memory in SQL Server is important when monitoring your system. In our opinion, that understanding helps you make more sense of the monitors that you use. This section will provide a couple examples of memory usage in SQL Server, and will show methods for determining whether you have memory bottlenecks on your system.

Memory Usage in SQL Server

SQL Server uses memory to process every query. If the data pages requested do not reside in memory or the buffer pool, then SQL Server retrieves the pages from physical disk and loads them. SQL Server tries to keep pages frequently accessed in memory to minimize physical disk IO. SQL Server uses a least-recently-used algorithm to determine the memory pages that should be removed from memory. If you do not have enough memory to process the requests against your system, then SQL Server will remove the frequently accessed pages to make room to process the queries. Because of the constant trips to physical disk, a shortage of memory will cause increased disk IO and an increased duration for queries.

SQL Server also uses memory for its internal structures, such as connections, execution plans, and various SQL Server internal processes. When SQL Server is experiencing memory problems, then there is an impact to its internal structures, which ultimately impacts resources and SQL Server performance. Remember that under the previous section, "SQL

Server Counters That Impact CPU," we discussed the number of compiles in your system. Memory problems can cause an increase in the number of compiles in SQL Server. When there is a shortage of memory, SQL Server may decide to remove execution plans from memory. Later, when queries that usually have compiled plans execute, they have be recompiled, which is a CPU-intensive process.

Counters to Watch

Hopefully, the brief preceding examples helped you understand how memory can impact CPU and disk IO. This is another example of why it is important to use multiple counters to determine what is affecting your server. If you only look at CPU or disk IO counters, you can easily conclude that you need more CPU or disk space when the real problem might be that you are low on memory. Table 14-2 lists some of the counters that you should watch in order to keep tabs on memory utilization.

Table 14-2. *Memory Counters and Their Recommended Values*

Counter Name	Description	Recommended Values
Memory: Pages Input/Sec	The rate pages are read from disk to resolve hard page faults	< 10 Pages
Memory: Available MBytes	The available memory on the server	> 100 MB
Memory: Pages/Sec	The number of pages written to or read from disk	< 100
Memory: Page Faults/Sec	The average number of hard and soft pages faulted per second	Use your baseline
Memory: Page Reads/Sec	The rate at which pages are read from disk to resolve page faults	< 5
SQL Server Buffer Manager: Buffer Cache Hit Ratio	The percentage of pages found in the buffer pool without having to go to disk	> 90 (closer to 99%)
SQL Server Buffer Manager: Checkpoint Pages/Sec	The number of pages per second flushed to the disk by check pointing or other methods	Use your baseline for the recommended value.
SQL Server Buffer Manager: Page Life Expectancy	The amount of time in seconds that pages are allowed to live in the buffer	> 300
SQL Server Buffer Manager: Lazy Writes/Sec	The number of times per second that the lazy writer process moves dirty pages from buffer to disk	> 30
SQL Server Memory Manager: Memory Grants Pending	The number of processes waiting for workspace memory	Should be close to zero
SQL Server Memory Manager: Target Server Memory	The amount of memory that SQL Server would like to have	High or rising values indicate memory pressure
SQL Server Memory Manager: Total Server Memory	The approximate server memory	Server RAM

MONITORING MEMORY WITH TASK MANAGER

Remember that you can use the Task Manager to monitor memory. You can quickly determine how much memory is available by reviewing the Physical Memory section on the Performance tab (see Figure 14-9). If your available memory is less than 100 MB, then you probably should start evaluating what is consuming your memory. In order to see what applications are doing this, click on the Processes tab and sort the data by the Memory Usage column. That method is useful for identifying memory-intensive applications on your server.

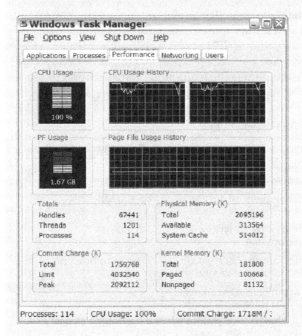

Figure 14-9. *The Performance tab of Windows Task Manager*

Just as with CPU counters, we like to add the counters in Table 14-2 to PerfMon. After adding the memory counters, we like to remove the counters that are in line with our baseline to get rid of some of the congestion to help us focus in on the problem areas. Figure 14-10 shows PerfMon with all the counters listed in Table 14-2.

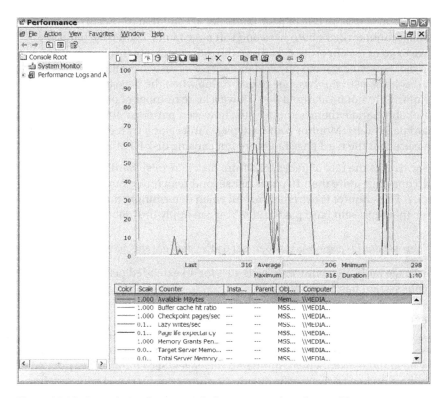

Figure 14-10. *Sample PerfMon graph for counters listed in Table 14-2*

Memory with Windows Counters

The following list explains the Memory object Windows counters listed in Table 14-2. Monitoring memory counters can sometimes be a little tricky, but familiarizing yourself with the counters you will use should help you understand the data presented by the counters. Remember, you have your baseline also to help you determine when performance changes within your system.

- *Available MBytes*: Represents the available memory in megabytes remaining on your server. This counter sums the amount of space on the zeroed, free, and standby memory lists. The zeroed memory is the memory that is filled with zeros to prevent other processes from viewing it. Free memory is the memory ready for use by a process. Standby memory is the memory that was removed from the processes and is waiting to go to disk. This counter represents the last observed value, not an average value, so monitor this value over time to ensure that you don't have minimal memory remaining. If the server that runs SQL Server has multiple applications running on it, you may want to consider moving those applications if your memory is consistently less than the threshold you would like it to be. Monitor this threshold closely because SQL Server does not perform well when it does not have enough memory.

- *Page Faults/Sec*: Represents the rate of page faults per second that are occurring on your system. This counter tracks both hard and soft page faults. Hard page faults are faults that have to go to disk in order to retrieve the requested data, while soft page faults retrieve the requested data in physical memory. Because this value changes from system to system, use your baseline to determine when the page faults rate deviates from the norm. Do not be alarmed if you have a large number of page faults. Your system can probably handle them without issue; however, pay close attention to the number of hard page faults. Monitor your hard page faults along with the physical IO counters to ensure that the hard page faults are not causing disk IO problems.

- *Pages Input/Sec*: Tracks the rate of pages read from disk to resolve hard page faults. Ideally, you do not want more than 10 pages per second read into memory to resolve hard page faults. This counter is extremely useful when determining the number of page faults/sec that represent hard page faults. You can apply the following formula:

```
Pages input per second / page faults per second = percentage hard page faults
```

When the hard page faults percentage exceeds 40% for an extended period of time, the chances are your system has memory issues.

- *Pages/Sec*: Identifies the rate of pages read from and written to disk for resolving memory requests for pages that are not in memory. In other words, Pages/Sec represents pages input/sec and pages output/sec. (Pages output represents the pages removed from memory heading to disk.) A high number in the Pages/Sec counter does not necessarily mean that you have a memory problem. Use other counters and your baseline to help you determine when the Pages/Sec counter is indicating a problem.

- *Page Reads/Sec*: Represents the rate of reads against physical disks that occurred to resolve hard page faults. This counter captures the number of reads per second, not the number of pages read into memory per second. Thus you can use this counter in conjunction with the Pages Input/Sec counter to determine the number of times the disk was read along with the number of pages that were inserted into memory to resolve the hard page faults. You don't want more than five pages read per second into memory. Consider values greater than five as indicative of excessive paging.

Memory with SQL Server Counters

SQL Server provides a number of performance monitor counters to help you monitor memory utilization within SQL Server. These counters are as follows:

- *SQL Server Buffer Manager: Buffer Cache Hit Ratio*: Represents the number of pages found in the buffer pool without having to read from disk. Generally, this percentage should be above 90% and closer to 99%.

- *SQL Server Buffer Manager: Checkpoint Pages/Sec*: The number of pages flushed to disks by checkpoints or other methods that require the flushing of all dirty pages. Dirty pages are data pages entered into the buffer cache, modified, and waiting for changes to write to disk. An increasing number of checkpoints from your baseline indicate increased activity in the buffer pool.

- *SQL Server Buffer Manager: Page Life Expectancy*: Identifies the amount of time in seconds that pages are remaining in memory without reference. The longer pages stay in memory, the greater the benefit for SQL Server. If pages can stay in memory for a long time without reference, then SQL Server will have to go to the physical disk less often to retrieve that data. The industry-recognized time for this counter is 300 seconds, or 5 minutes. Consistently having pages that stay in memory for less than that amount of time may indicate the need for more memory.

- *SQL Server Buffer Manager: Lazy Writes/Sec*: The number of pages written to the buffer manager's lazy writer. Frequent or an increased number of lazy writes can indicate that you don't have enough memory.

- *SQL Server Memory Manager: Memory Grants Pending*: Represents the current number of processes waiting for a workspace memory grant. The workspace memory grant is the total amount of memory dedicated to executing processes. This counter keeps track of the number of processes that are waiting for memory before they can execute. This counter should be as close to zero as possible.

- *SQL Server Memory Manager: Target Server Memory*: Identifies the total amount of dynamic memory the server is willing to consume. This number should be steady. Increasing values indicate the need for more memory.

- *SQL Server Memory Manager: Total Server Memory*: Represents the amount of dynamic memory that SQL Server is currently consuming. This number should be relatively close to the maximum memory setting for the instance.

Remember, monitoring memory using the Windows and SQL counters may be a little tricky at times. Some counters may exceed the recommended thresholds, while others fit well within the ranges. Use your better judgment and your baseline to determine when things are going wrong on your system.

Memory with DMVs and DBCC Commands

SQL Server also provides a number of Dynamic Management Views and Database Consistency Checks (DBCC) commands that you can use to monitor memory. The memory DMVs can be a little overwhelming because there is a lot of data regarding memory and how it's allocated within SQL Server. We are not going to talk about all of the memory DMVs, but we will discuss some of our favorite ones. The following list describes our most frequently used DMVs to monitor memory:

- `sys.dm_os_sys_memory`: Returns information regarding operating system memory. Some of the columns include the system's total memory, the available memory, and the total amount of page files being used.

  One interesting column is system_memory_state_desc, which describes the current state of the memory. Values returned in that column are Available Physical Memory Is High, Available Physical Memory Is Low, Physical Memory Is Steady, and Physical Memory Is Transitioning. You can use the `sys.dm_os_sys_memory` view when you are switching from one server to another, or from one instance to another, to quickly see the available memory and SQL Server's "opinion" on the amount of memory that you have available in your system.

The following query retrieves information from sys.dm_os_sys_memory.

```
SELECT total_physical_memory_kb,available_physical_memory_kb,
system_memory_state_desc
FROM sys.dm_os_sys_memory
```

The results of the preceding query are shown in Figure 14-11.

Figure 14-11. *Sample results of sys.dm_os_sys_memory DMV*

- sys.dm_os_process_memory: Lists information about the memory used within your SQL Server instance. Some of the columns are physical memory in use, available commit limit, total virtual address size, and some others. This view also has two indicators, Process Physical Memory Low and Process Virtual Memory Low, which let you know if the virtual or physical memory is considered low by SQL Server. Once again, this view allows you to quickly see how memory is being used within your SQL Server instance.

- sys.dm_exec_query_memory_grants: Captures information regarding the queries that are waiting or have been given a memory grant. This DMV includes columns that tell you the amount of requested, granted, required, maxed used, and the ideal memory for each query running on your system. As if that information isn't helpful enough, the DMV also returns information about the SQL handles and plan handles so that you can see queries and their execution plans. This view is extremely useful for identifying the memory hog queries running on your system, analyzing their execution plans to see why they are consuming so much memory, and fixing or providing recommendations for fixing the queries.

The following query is one we frequently run to identify memory usage for the queries running on our systems. The results of the query are shown in Figure 14-12.

```
SELECT session_id, request_id,requested_memory_kb,required_memory_kb,
used_memory_kb,ideal_memory_kb,sql_handle, plan_handle
FROM sys.dm_exec_query_memory_grants
```

Figure 14-12. *Sample results of the sys.dm_exec_query_memory_grants DMV*

You also have the ability to monitor the memory of your system by executing the DBCC memorystatus command. This DBCC command lists memory usage for the buffer manager, memory clerks, and a number of other processes that can consume memory within SQL Server. Some of the information provided by the DBCC command can be found in multiple DMVs, but the DBCC command gives you a one-stop shop for the information you are looking for. DBCC memorystatus is also backward compatible with SQL Server 2000.

Monitoring Disk IO

Unless your entire database fits in memory, then the performance of your SQL Server is heavily dependent upon your disk IO. Disk bottlenecks will impact the speed at which pages are moved in and out of memory. Delays in moving pages in and out of memory ultimately affect the performance of the application.

Monitoring disk IO can also be a little tricky. Depending on the counters that you use, you have to evaluate the results based on the number of disk spindles available on the monitored physical disk. Table 14-3 lists some of the counters and thresholds used when monitoring disk IO; it also lists if the number of spindles needs to be considered when using the counter.

Table 14-3. *Disk Counters and Their Recommended Values*

Counter Name	Description	Recommended Values
Physical Disk: Avg Disk Queue Length	The average number of reads and writes queued on the disk	> 2 per spindle
Physical Disk: Avg Disk Reads/Sec or Writes/Sec	The average number of reads/writes from/to disk per second	<=10 ms outstanding (between 10 and 20 okay); > 20 ms (needs attention)
Physical Disk: Disk Reads/Sec or Writes/Sec	The rate of read/write operations on the disk	> 85% of disk capacity
Physical Disk: % Disk Time	Show the busyness of the disk array	> 55% over continuous time
Physical Disk: Current Disk Queue	The number of processes waiting to be executed	
SQL Server Access Methods: Full Scans/Sec	The number of table and index scans that occur on your system	Baseline number should be as low as possible
SQL Server Access Methods: Page Splits/Sec	The number of page splits per second on your system	< 20 per 100 batches/sec

Figure 14-13 shows PerfMon with the counters listed in Table 14-3.

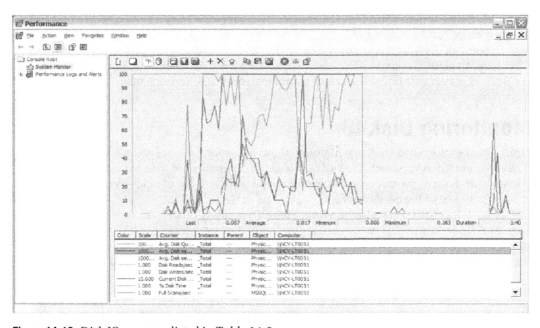

Figure 14-13. *Disk IO counters listed in Table 14-3*

Disk IO with Windows Counters

The following list explains the `Physical Disk` object Windows counters listed in Table 14-3. As you use those counters, remember that the results from some counters must be interpreted in light of the number of spindles within the disk array. For example, if disk D consists of 6 spindles and you are monitoring the Avg Disk Queue length, the counter would have to be greater than 12 before you have reason for concern.

- *Avg Disk Queue Length*: Represents the number of physical reads and writes queued on the selected disk. When your disk IO subsystem is overwhelmed, physical disk reads or writes have to wait before performing their actions. Keep in mind, sustained values greater than two for each spindle requires attention.

- *Avg Disk Reads/Sec or Writes/Sec*: Captures the average amount of time it takes to read/write data to disk. One benefit of this counter is that it measures disk latency. The measurement of disk latency does not care about the number of spindles within the array. The measurement of Avg Disk Reads/Sec or Writes/Sec counter represents the amount of time in milliseconds it takes for the actions to happen. When the counter exceeds 20 ms for a given disk, research the cause of the increased read/write from/to the disk.

- *Reads/Sec or Writes/Sec*: Measures the number of reads or writes per second from/to disk. These numbers need to be less than 85% of the disk capacity. The specifications of your disk drives should identify the number of reads and writes per second the drives support. Make sure the Reads/Sec and Writes/Sec counters do not exceed 85% because the access time increases exponentially beyond 85% capacity.

- *% Disk Time*: Represents the busyness of your disk drives. Drives that sustain more than 55% over time indicate that your disks are overworked and that you likely have a disk IO problem. Figuring out why your disks are so busy will go a long way toward reducing IO problems.

- *Current Disk Queue*: Measures the current processes waiting for IO. Using this counter along with % Disk Time may help you understand what is going on with your disks. If your current disk queue is high and % Disk Time is above your baseline, then that probably is an indicator that application processes are delayed and your disks are bottlenecked.

Disk IO with SQL Server Counters

SQL Server also provides some counters to monitor factors that negatively affect the disk IO on your server. Table 14-3 mentioned the two SQL Server counters that we use the most to determine how factors of SQL Server are impacting disk IO. These counters are located in the SQL Server `Access Methods` object and are further described in the following list:

- *Full Scans/Sec*: Identifies the number of table and index scans occurring on your system per second. Scans are IO-intensive and should run within your databases minimally. If your scan counters are high, then identify the tables that have a large number of scans against them. Use the tips in Chapter 16 to help you identify IO-intensive queries and the tables that account for the scans within your database.

- *Page Splits/Sec*: Represents the number of page splits per second that occur on your system. Page splits occur when there is not enough space on a page to add the data on an existing page. When the page splits, that causes fragmentation and results in IO-intensive processes. Try to keep page splits under 20 per 100 batches/sec. If the number of page splits is greater than that, then review the fill factor you have set up on your indexes and minimize it where appropriate.

Monitoring disk IO is slightly more complex because you have to remember to keep the number of spindles in mind when interpreting the results. Once you get familiar with counters, then monitoring disk IO will be easier. Always use multiple counters to identify disk IO problems, not just the results of one counter. Using that method is more likely to save you time and effort from venturing down the wrong path.

Monitoring Miscellaneous Counters and DMVs

Two general counters may prove useful when monitoring SQL Server: Logins/Sec and User Connections. Both of these counters should be part of your baseline so you have something to compare against over time. They may be helpful when trying to figure out gradual changes in the hardware resources within your environment. These counters may also be useful when you are trying to determine the reason database server resources are being taxed. For example, if you have information showing that the number of users within your environment just doubled, then that may save you a lot of troubleshooting time.

Capturing SQL Server PerfMon Counters Using DMVs

Throughout this chapter, we have discussed a number of SQL Server counters and how to monitor your system using those counters in PerfMon. In SQL Server 2008, the DMV `sys.dm_os_performance_counters` contains the same performance counters stored within SQL Server. So instead of connecting the server and running the performance monitor, you can query the `sys.dm_os_performance_counters` DMV and track the results of the monitor in the database.

Leveraging the SQL Server Profiler

SQL Server Profiler is a graphical tool used to trace the events occurring within SQL Server. SQL Server Profiler uses a large number of events and filters to capture the data and information that interest you. From a monitoring perspective, SQL Server Profiler is an awesome tool to help you quickly identify what's running against your system or to monitor what's running on your system for a period of time. Using SQL Server Profiler, you can identify long-running queries, CPU-intensive queries, queries that utilize a large number of IO, and many more events. Now let's take a look at SQL Server Profiler and how to monitor events.

There are multiple ways to launch SQL Server Profiler. Within SQL Server Management Studio, click on Tools and the select SQL Server Profiler. You can also go to Start, All Programs ➤ Microsoft SQL Server 2008 ➤Performance Tools, and finally select SQL Server

Profiler. For this example, let's assume you connected to SQL Server Profiler from SQL Server Management Studio. Once SQL Server Profiler launches, connect to the server and instance that you want to capture events on. After you connect to the SQL Server instance, you will be directed to the Trace Properties dialog box, shown in Figure 14-14.

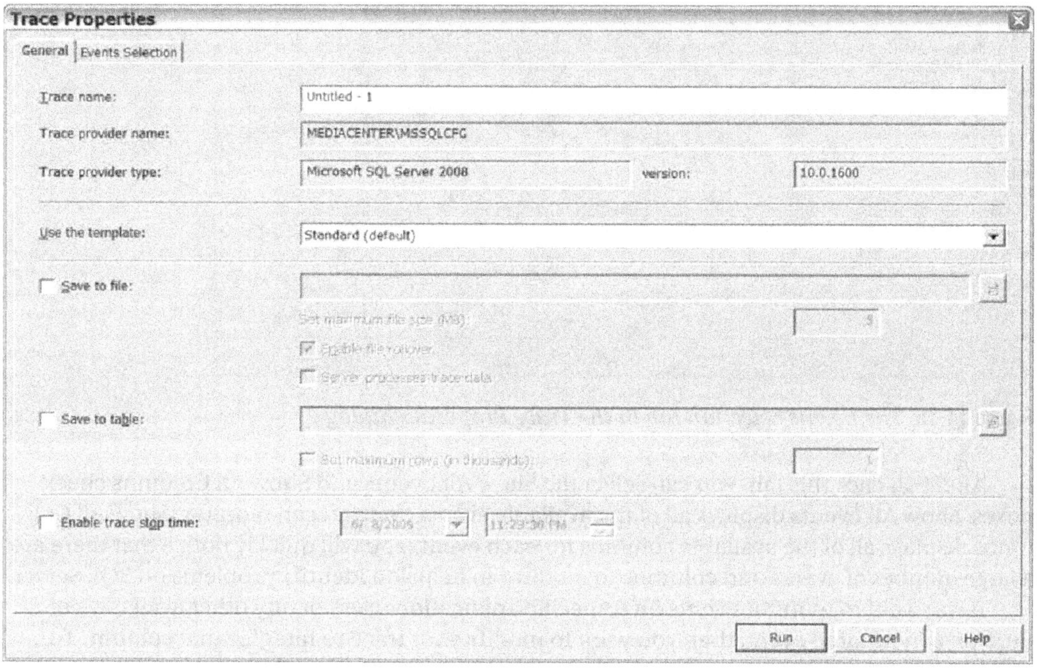

Figure 14-14. *The General tab in the Trace Properties dialog box*

Reviewing Figure 14-14, you will notice there are three decisions to make: which template you want to use, where you want to save the file, and if you want to enable a time for the trace to stop. You can decide if you want to store the data within a table or a file. If you are tracing events on a busy server, then you definitely don't want to write to table. You don't want to increase writes to the databases on your server.

The Enable Trace Stop Time option allows you to pick the date and time when you want the trace to stop. So if you want the trace to stop after a given time, then you can utilize this option so you don't have remember to manually stop the trace.

Microsoft has eight templates to help you trace events on your server. If none of the templates meets your needs, then don't hesitate to use the Standard template. Once you select the template that you want to use, click on the Events Selection tab. Figure 14-15 shows the default events in the Standard template on the Events Selection tab.

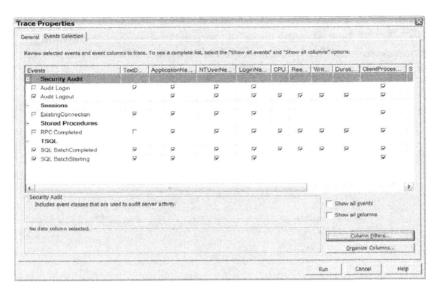

Figure 14-15. *The Events Selection tab in the Trace Properties dialog*

After you click this tab, you can select the Show All Events and Show All Columns check boxes. Show All Events displays all of the available events that you can monitor. Show All Columns displays all of the available columns for each event. You will quickly notice that there are a large number of events and columns to monitor to help you identify problems on SQL Server.

If you want to monitor events for a specific application, user, or any other available column on a monitored event, then you want to modify your trace to filter for that column. To add a filter to your trace, click on the Column Filters button, and the Edit Filter dialog box will load (see Figure 14-16).

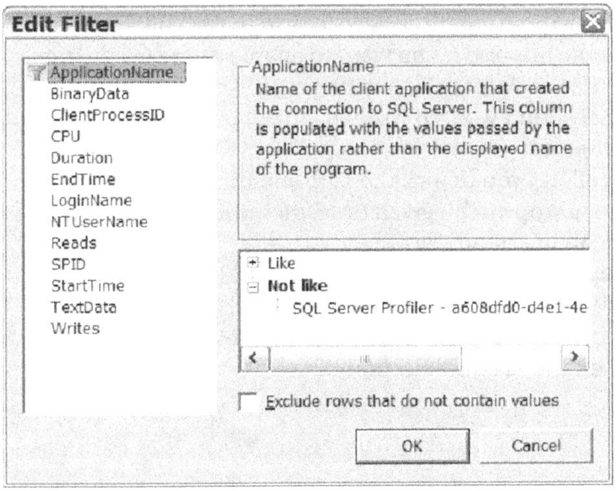

Figure 14-16. *The Edit Filter dialog within SQL Server Profiler*

Once you are on the Edit Filter dialog, select the column that you want to apply the filter to, and then add the text to the appropriate option on the right side of the dialog. Once you add all the filters that you want to apply and land back on the Events Selection tab, then go ahead and click on the Run button to start the trace.

One thing to keep in mind: Running SQL Serve Profiler on the server itself can cause an increase in CPU when you are capturing a large number of events. To prevent the increase in resource utilization caused by SQL Server Profiler you can run server side traces, which provide a minimal impact to your server.

Using Server-Side Tracing

Server-side tracing is a method used to trace events occurring within your system without the GUI interface. You specify events to trace, and filters to narrow your results, using the following stored procedures:

- `sp_trace_create`: Creates the trace definition
- `sp_trace_event`: Adds events and event columns to the trace definition
- `sp_trace_setFilter`: Defines event filters to a trace

Use SQL Server Books Online to identify which parameters to supply to the `sp_trace_event` stored procedure in order to add specific events and columns to a trace. Once you create the trace, you can manage the trace (turn it on and off) by running the `sp_trace_setstatus` stored procedure. You can also view a list all the traces, including SQL Server Profiler traces, as well as the filters, events, and columns for those traces, by invoking the following set of trace functions:

- `fn_trace_getinfo(trace id)`: Retrieves the trace definition for a particular trace ID or all traces if you supply NULL as the parameter.
- `fn_trace_geteventinfo(trace id)`: Identifies the events and columns specified for a trace.
- `fn_trace_getfilterinfo(trace id)`: Displays the filters in place for the trace.

Now that you understand the stored procedures available to create a trace and the functions that allow you to review your trace definition, let's create a trace. Using SQL Server Profiler is the easiest way to do this. Within SQL Server Profiler, you can define the trace using the GUI, checking all of the appropriate boxes, and then script out the T-SQL to create the trace.

Note We use the GUI of SQL Server Profiler to script out our trace files because it is easier than creating these scripts without assistance.

To generate the T-SQL script from SQL Server Profiler, select the events, filters, and columns that you want in your trace, then start your trace and stop it immediately. After the trace stops, navigate to the File option, select Export ➤ Script Trace Definition ➤ For SQL Server 2005-2008. Specify a file name and then click on OK. You will get a file with a trace definition, such as the one in Listing 14-4. Once you have the trace scripted, you can execute that script to create the trace. You can also add new events, columns, and filters as you see fit.

Listing 14-4. *T-SQL Script for Creating a Server-Side Trace*

```
/****************************************************/
/* Created by: SQL Server 2008 Profiler           */
/* Date: 03/25/2009  11:43:51 PM        */
/****************************************************/


-- Create a queue
DECLARE @rc int
DECLARE @TraceID int
DECLARE @maxfilesize bigint
SET @maxfilesize = 5

-- Please replace the text InsertFileNameHere, with an appropriate
-- file name prefixed by a path, e.g., c:\MyFolder\MyTrace. The .trc extension
-- will be appended to the file name automatically. If you are writing from
-- remote server to local drive, please use UNC path and make sure server has
-- write access to your network share.

EXEC @rc = sp_trace_create @TraceID output, 0,
N'InsertFileNameHere', @maxfilesize, NULL
if (@rc != 0) goto error
-- Client-side file and table cannot be scripted

-- Set the events
DECLARE @on bit
SET @on = 1
EXEC sp_trace_setevent @TraceID, 10, 15, @on
exec sp_trace_setevent @TraceID, 10, 16, @on
EXEC sp_trace_setevent @TraceID, 10, 9, @on
EXEC sp_trace_setevent @TraceID, 10, 17, @on
EXEC sp_trace_setevent @TraceID, 10, 2, @on
EXEC sp_trace_setevent @TraceID, 10, 10, @on
EXEC sp_trace_setevent @TraceID, 10, 18, @on
EXEC sp_trace_setevent @TraceID, 10, 11, @on
EXEC sp_trace_setevent @TraceID, 10, 12, @on
EXEC sp_trace_setevent @TraceID, 10, 13, @on
EXEC sp_trace_setevent @TraceID, 10, 6, @on
EXEC sp_trace_setevent @TraceID, 10, 14, @on
EXEC sp_trace_setevent @TraceID, 12, 15, @on
```

```
EXEC sp_trace_setevent @TraceID, 12, 16, @on
EXEC sp_trace_setevent @TraceID, 12, 1, @on
EXEC sp_trace_setevent @TraceID, 12, 9, @on
EXEC sp_trace_setevent @TraceID, 12, 17, @on
EXEC sp_trace_setevent @TraceID, 12, 6, @on
EXEC sp_trace_setevent @TraceID, 12, 10, @on
EXEC sp_trace_setevent @TraceID, 12, 14, @on
EXEC sp_trace_setevent @TraceID, 12, 18, @on
EXEC sp_trace_setevent @TraceID, 12, 11, @on
EXEC sp_trace_setevent @TraceID, 12, 12, @on
EXEC sp_trace_setevent @TraceID, 12, 13, @on


-- Set the filters
DECLARE @intfilter int
DECLARE @bigintfilter bigint

EXEC sp_trace_setfilter @TraceID, 10, 0, 7,
N'SQL Server Profiler - c97955a1-dbf3-4cc8-acc0-4606f7800ab7'
-- Set the trace status to start
EXEC sp_trace_setstatus @TraceID, 1

-- display trace ID for future references
SELECT TraceID=@TraceID
GOTO finish

error:
SELECT ErrorCode=@rc

finish:
GO
```

Automating Your Monitoring

Sometimes starting SQL Server Profiler, reviewing DMVs, or adding counters to the performance monitor after a reported issue is too late to identify what caused the issue. Often times, when you are periodically having problems or want to baseline your server, it is a good idea to automate the monitoring of your server. By automating, we mean automatically taking a snapshot of your DMVs on a routine basis so you can accurately identify the changes over time, start a trace on your server without you or someone on your team having to do it, and capturing predetermined counters without having to start the performance monitor. The idea is that your system will capture the different things you want monitored so you can review them when issues arrive. The following list provides you with some methods for automating the monitoring of DMVs, the performance monitor, and tracing.

- *DMVs*: Store the results of the DMVs into a permanent table by creating a job that retrieves the data from the views. That way, you do not lose the information stored within those DMVs when SQL Server shuts down.

- *Tracing*: Set up a job or other automated process to execute a trace script created using the methods discussed in the "Using Server-Side Tracing" section whenever SQL Server starts. Setting up a process that automatically creates a trace does not cause issues unless you forget to set the option that minimizes the size of your files before a rollover occurs. You should also clean up your trace files before you fill up your drives and make sure the file name you specify during the creation of a new trace does not refer to an already existing file that you want to keep. We generally append a date and time to the file name to get by that last issue.

- *Performance monitor*: Determine the counters that you want to monitor and add them to the Trace section of the performance monitor. Make sure you set a file rollover size to prevent the file from taking up all the space on your server. Create a shortcut to reside in a location that starts and stops performance monitor traces. Implement a process that says when the server starts, then run a batch file or a similar process that executes the shortcut to start the trace. That way, when the server starts, your performance monitor data will start capturing as well.

Now you can automatically capture information about the performance of your system, and you should have the information needed to compare against your baseline. Once you have identified a change in performance from your baseline—whether in CPU, memory, or disk IO—then you want to identify the queries that are causing the change. (Chapter 16 discusses methods for determining what queries are the troublemakers.)

Summary

As we conclude this chapter, we hope that you have learned useful information to assist you while monitoring your server(s). As a database administrator, it is important to proactively monitor your environments to make sure you know what's going on prior to being notified by customers. Being aware of your resource utilization is crucial to ensuring that the application continues to perform as expected. Once you know that you have a resource problem (with CPU, memory, or disk IO), you should attempt to improve the queries impacting those resources before purchasing additional hardware. (Chapter 15 discusses methods for monitoring your server from a security perspective.)

CHAPTER 15

■ ■ ■

Auditing SQL Server

Auditing your SQL Server is an important aspect of protecting your data. As a database administrator, you need to know the users who are logged into your system or attempting to log into your system, and what they are doing once they have gained access.

Auditing what users are doing in your system is less important when you have total control over their access within SQL Server. In other words, if you get to determine all users' access and their permissions, then auditing your users is not as critical because you can restrict their permissions and ensure they perform only the actions that you trust them to perform. Unfortunately, most DBAs do not have total control; you have to give users the access the organization wants them to have, which makes tracking down who is doing what in your system important.

Historically, DBAs have had the ability to audit logon success or failures and enable C2 audit tracing, as well as use SQL Server Profiler or tracing to determine which users are logged in and what they are doing in your system. As helpful as those options are, with the exception of SQL Server Profiler and tracing, DBAs lacked the control to determine the captured events. Even with the default trace running, we often still lacked the exact information needed because no additional filters were added to the default trace. Fortunately, the Enterprise Edition of SQL Server 2008 added a feature named SQL Server Audit that lets you determine the events that are important to you and log them accordingly.

Choosing Your Audit Type

SQL Server Audit allows you to monitor your server from two different aspects: at the server level and the database level. When trying to determine what kind of audit you want to create, there are a several things to think about. Use the following list to help you decide which type of audit to create.

Choose a server audit if you want to monitor the following:

- Actions that impact the entire server
- Actions that monitor changes across all databases
- Actions that monitor changes to schemas to all databases

Choose database audit specifications if you want tomonitor

- Actions specific to a database, object, or schema

- Specific actions of a principal within a database

- Specific actions (SELECT, DELETE, UPDATE, and other Data Manipulation Language [DML] statements) within a database

Once you figure out the type of auditing you want to capture the required information, follow the steps in the next couple of sections to create your audit and store that information.

Creating SQL Server Audits with T-SQL

Before you can define server-level or database-level actions to audit, you must create a SQL Server audit, which is shown in Listing 15-1.

Listing 15-1. *Syntax for Creating a SQL Server Audit*

```
CREATE SERVER AUDIT audit_name

TO { [ FILE (<file_options> [, ...n]) ] | APPLICATION_LOG | SECURITY_LOG }
[ WITH ( <audit_options> [, ...n] ) ]
```

As you can see from the syntax, creating a SQL Server audit defines the setup information for an audit. The audit does not contain any information about the actions either at the database level or the server level within its definition. Actually, server-level and database-level audits must be added to a SQL Server audit to define how and where the information is captured and stored. Now, let's take a closer look at the syntax for creating a SQL Server audit.

After you name the audit, determine if you want it written to a file, application log, or security log. If you decide to write the data to a file, then you need to specify the file path and name, the maximum size of the file, the number of rollover files, and if you want to reserve the maximum file size on disk.

The configurable audit options consist of a QUEUE_DELAY, ON_FAILURE, and AUDIT_GUID. The QUEUE_DELAY option sets the time that can pass before an audit action processes. The representation of time is in milliseconds with the minimal and default value of 1000 milliseconds or 1 second. The ON_FAILURE option decides what to do if the target (location of the audit files) is unreachable. The two configurable options are CONTINUE and SHUTDOWN. The default value is CONTINUE. The AUDIT_GUID option allows you to specify the globally unique identifier (GUID) of an existing audit for purposes where the GUID needs to be the same from environment to environment.

Once you have determined the settings for your SQL Server audit, then creating an audit is fairly simple and straightforward, as shown in Listing 15-2.

Listing 15-2. *SQL Script That Creates a SQL Server Audit*

```
USE master;
GO

CREATE SERVER AUDIT exampleAudit
TO FILE
( FILEPATH = 'C:\', MAXSIZE = 1 GB
)
WITH( ON_FAILURE = CONTINUE)

GO
```

Creating Server Audit Specifications

In order to audit server-level information, then you have to create a server audit specification. A server audit specification consists of server-level action groups. We will discuss server-level action groups in more detail in the next section. For now, just understand that the server-level action groups identify what you are auditing from a server level. The server audit specifications are tracked across the entire instance of SQL Server. There are not any boundaries within the SQL Server instance. Because of this lack of boundaries, you cannot filter down to specific databases within server audits. To create a server audit specification, use the syntax in Listing 15-3.

Listing 15-3. *Syntax for Creating a Server Audit Specification*

```
CREATE SERVER AUDIT SPECIFICATION audit_specification_name
FOR SERVER AUDIT audit_name
  ADD (audit_action_group_name ), ...n,
  WITH ( STATE= ON|OFF)
```

To create the server audit specification, you have to specify which SQL Server audit to associate the server audit specification to. Once you assign the server specification to the server audit, then you add the server-level `audit_action_group` name to the server audit specification. Once you have added all of the server-level `audit_action_group` names that you want to monitor, determine if you want to enable the audit during creation. If you don't, then you must enable it when you are ready to capture the actions in the audit.

Server-Level Action Groups

Server-level action groups are the predefined groups used to audit your server from a server perspective. Since server-level action groups are predefined, then you can't customize the actions that each group captures. The only level of customization you have for a server-level audit comes from deciding which server-level action groups you add to an audit.

There are a large number of server-level actions groups, so we won't be able to discuss them all here. However, we list some of the server-level action groups that we frequently like to use for our server audits.

- `Successful_Login_Group`: Tracks successful principal logins into the instance of SQL Server.

- `Failed_Login_Group`: Identifies unsuccessful principal failures against the instance of SQL Server.

- `Server_Role_Member_Change_Group`: Captures the addition and removal of logins from fixed server roles.

- `Database_Role_Member_Change_Group`: Tracks the addition and removal of logins to database roles.

- `Server_Object_Change_Group`: Captures create, alter, or drop permissions on server objects.

- `Server_Principal_Change_Group`: Tracks the creation, deletion, or alteration of server principals.

- `Database_Change_Group`: Identifies the creation, alteration, or deletion of databases.

- `Database_Object_Change_Group`: Captures create, alter, or delete actions against objects within a database.

- `Database_Principal_Change_Group`: Tracks the creation, modification, or deletion of database principals.

- `Server_Permission_Change_Group`: Identifies when principals grant, revoke, or deny permissions to server objects.

- `Database_Object_Permission_Change_Group`: Captures grant, revoke, or deny permission changes to database objects.

As you can see, server-level audit action groups of SQL Server Audit allow you to monitor a number of actions that occur from a server level. Please review SQL Server Books Online and search for "SQL Server Audit Action Groups and Actions" for a complete list of the groups. Understanding the available options enables you to capture the relevant actions in your environment. If you do not know what is available to monitor, then chances are good you will miss something that could have saved you time when trying to identify the cause of a problem.

Listing 15-4 shows an example of creating a server audit specification with server-level audit action groups.

Listing 15-4. *SQL Code That Creates a Server Audit Specification*

```
CREATE SERVER AUDIT SPECIFICATION serverSpec
FOR SERVER AUDIT exampleAudit
ADD (SERVER_ROLE_MEMBER_CHANGE_GROUP)

GO
```

Testing Your Server Audit Specification

Now that you understand how to create a SQL Server audit and add server audit specifications, let's create an example to demonstrate how the server audit specification works with SQL Server audits. Listing 15-5 creates a SQL Server audit and adds a server audit specification; it also contains code that causes the audit to fire.

Listing 15-5. *SQL Script That Creates a SQL Server Audit and Server Audit Specification*

```
USE master;
GO

-- Create the server audit
CREATE SERVER AUDIT permissionChanges
TO FILE ( FILEPATH = 'C:\',MAXSIZE = 1 GB)
WITH( ON_FAILURE = CONTINUE)

GO

-- Create the server audit specification

CREATE SERVER AUDIT SPECIFICATION serverPermissionChanges
FOR SERVER AUDIT permissionChanges
ADD (SERVER_ROLE_MEMBER_CHANGE_GROUP),
ADD (DATABASE_ROLE_MEMBER_CHANGE_GROUP),
ADD (SERVER_PERMISSION_CHANGE_GROUP),
ADD (SERVER_OBJECT_PERMISSION_CHANGE_GROUP),
ADD (DATABASE_PERMISSION_CHANGE_GROUP),
ADD (DATABASE_OBJECT_PERMISSION_CHANGE_GROUP)

GO


-- Turn the audit and server audit specification ON
ALTER SERVER AUDIT permissionChanges
WITH (STATE = ON)
GO

ALTER SERVER AUDIT SPECIFICATION serverPermissionChanges
WITH (STATE = ON)
GO
-- Creates actions that the audit will pick up

CREATE LOGIN auditTest
WITH PASSWORD = 'Test123!'
GO
EXEC sp_addsrvrolemember auditTest, sysadmin
GO
EXEC sp_dropsrvrolemember auditTest,sysadmin
GO
EXEC sp_addsrvrolemember auditTest, serveradmin
GO
```

```
EXEC sp_addsrvrolemember auditTest, processAdmin
```

To review the contents of the audit, use the fn_get_audit_file function. The following code allows you to see the results of Listing 15-5. The results of the preceding query are shown in Figure 15-1.

```
USE master;
GO

SELECT event_time,server_principal_name, object_name, statement,*
FROM fn_get_audit_file ('C:\perm*',NULL, NULL)
```

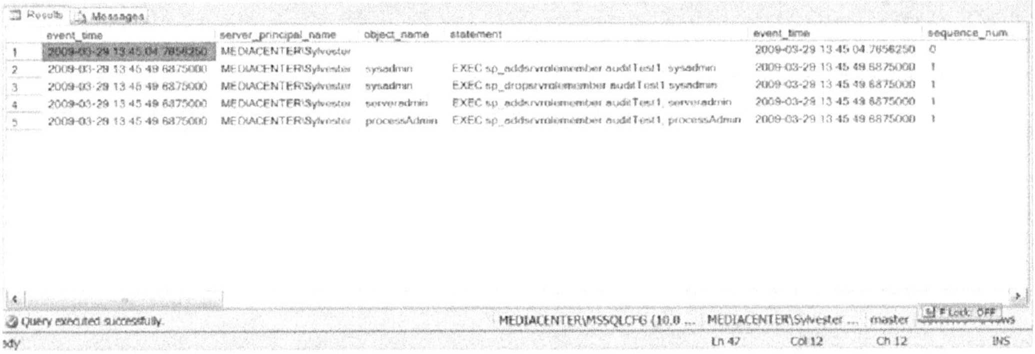

Figure 15-1. *Results of the audit from Listing 15-5*

Creating Database Audit Specifications

If you've determined that you need to audit database-level information, then you need to create a database audit specification to capture that information. Database audit specifications consist of database-level audit action groups and/or database-level audit actions. We will discuss database-level audit action groups and database-level actions in the next couple of sections. For right now, just think of database-level actions and audit action groups as the actions that are defined in order to audit database-level activity.

The syntax for creating a database audit specification is shown in Listing 15-6.

Listing 15-6. *Syntax to Create a Database Audit Specification*

```
CREATE DATABASE AUDIT SPECIFICATION audit_specification_name
FOR SERVER AUDIT audit_name
  ADD ( <audit_action_specification> | audit_action_group_name ) , ...n
```

```
  WITH ( STATE= ON|OFF)
audit_action_specification =
 action [ ,...n ]ON [class ::]securable BY principal [ ,...n ]
```

Similar to creating a server audit specification, the database audit specification must be associated with a server audit. Once you specify the server audit, then add the database-level audit action group or an audit_action_specification. Adding database-level audit action groups is similar to adding server-level audit action groups. Adding the audit_action_specification requires a different syntax. We will discuss adding the database-level audit action groups and database-level audit actions further in the next couple of sections.

Database-Level Audit Action Groups

Database-level audit action groups consist of actions against a specific database. Database-level audit actions enable you to monitor actions on database, schemas, and schema objects within the database. The database-level audit action groups are predefined actions that don't allow customization.

Because there are so many database-level audit action groups, we will not cover them all here. However, following are the database-level audit action groups that we frequently use to audit our systems.

- Database_Role_Member_Change_Group: Tracks the addition and removal of logins to database roles.

- Database_Object_Change_Group: Identifies when CREATE, ALTER, or DROP statements occur against database objects.

- Database_Principal_Change_Group: Tracks creation, alteration, and deletion of database principals.

- Database_Permission_Change_Group: Tracks when permissions change for a database user.

- Database_Object_Permission_Change_Group: Identifies the issuing of grant, deny, or revoke permissions to database objects.

- Schema_Object_Change_Group: Tracks the CREATE, ALTER, and DELETE statements performed on schema objects.

We encourage you to go to SQL Server Books Online and search for "SQL Server Audit Action Groups and Actions" to get a complete list of all the database-level audit action groups. The more aware you are of the available database-level audit action groups, the better you can plan audits on your system.

The following code provides an example of adding database-level audit action groups to a database audit specification. This code sample also creates a SQL Server audit to associate the database-level audit action groups to.

```
USE master;
GO

CREATE SERVER AUDIT exampleAudit2
TO FILE ( FILEPATH = 'C:\',MAXSIZE = 1 GB)
WITH( ON_FAILURE = CONTINUE)

GO

USE AdventureWorks2008
GO

CREATE DATABASE AUDIT SPECIFICATION databaseActionGroup
FOR SERVER AUDIT exampleAudit2
ADD (DATABASE_PERMISSION_CHANGE_GROUP)
GO
```

Database-Level Audit Actions

Database-level audit actions allow you to audit specific, customizable actions within the database. In other words, database-level audit actions against a database, schema, or schema object of your choosing will trigger an audit event. The following list contains the database-level audit actions with brief descriptions:

- Select: Tracks execution of SELECT statements.

- Insert: Determines when the execution of INSERT statements occur.

- Delete: Identifies when DELETE statements execute.

- Update: Tracks UPDATE statements executed against the database.

- Execute: Determines when EXECUTE statements run against the database.

- Receive: Tracks when RECEIVE statements are issued.

- References: Identifies when the references of permissions are checked.

Referring to the syntax in Listing 15-6, you can see that adding the database-level audit action consists of an *action on a securable by a principal*. What does all that mean? An *action* is a database-level auditable action like the items listed in the preceding list—statements like SELECT, INSERT, UPDATE, DELETE. Securables, as discussed in Chapter 8, are the objects within a database that you want to audit. Examples of securables are tables, views, stored procedures, and other database objects. The principal is the SQL Server principal that you want to apply the audit to. In other words, when you define a database-level audit action, you are defining the type of statement you want audited against a table or view, or done by a user.

The following code provides an example of adding database-level audit actions to a database audit specification.

```
USE AdventureWorks2008
GO


CREATE DATABASE AUDIT SPECIFICATION databaseActionGroup
FOR SERVER AUDIT exampleAudit2
ADD (INSERT,UPDATE,DELEETE ON Person.Person by dbo),
```

Testing Your Database Audit Specification

Since you understand the syntax of the CREATE database audit specification, let's construct one. Listing 15-7 creates a database audit specification along with some statements that will force the events to fire causing writes to your audit. For this example, we want to audit who is querying a specific production table. Since we cannot prevent non-application users from having access to the database, we can track if they are viewing tables unrelated to their jobs, such as the salary table for all the employees. Sometimes the best way to prove to management that not everyone needs access to production is to show them examples of abusing the privileges. Capturing users running bad queries or looking at information that they shouldn't helps with that argument. We also monitor the DATABASE_PRINCIPAL_CHANGE_GROUP just in case the user is smart and creates another user to query the table.

Listing 15-7. *SQL Script to Create a Database Audit Specification*

```
USE master;
GO


-- Create the server audit
CREATE SERVER AUDIT salaryViewing
TO FILE ( FILEPATH = 'C:\'',MAXSIZE = 1 GB)


GO


-- Create the database audit specification in the database you want audited
USE AdventureWorks2008
GO


CREATE DATABASE AUDIT SPECIFICATION salaryQueries
FOR SERVER AUDIT salaryViewing
ADD (SELECT,UPDATE ON humanresources.EmployeePayHistory by dbo),
ADD (DATABASE_PRINCIPAL_CHANGE_GROUP)


GO

USE master;
GO

ALTER SERVER AUDIT salaryViewing
WITH (STATE = ON)
GO
```

```
USE AdventureWorks2008
GO

ALTER DATABASE AUDIT SPECIFICATION salaryQueries
WITH (STATE = ON)
GO

SELECT TOP 10 *
FROM AdventureWorks2008.HumanResources.EmployeePayHistory

SELECT JobTitle, Rate,RateChangeDate
FROM AdventureWorks2008.HumanResources.Employee e
 JOIN AdventureWorks2008.HumanResources.EmployeePayHistory eh
 ON e.BusinessEntityID = eh.BusinessEntityId
ORDER BY jobTitle, RateChangeDate DESC


SELECT JobTitle, Rate,RateChangeDate
FROM AdventureWorks2008.HumanResources.Employee e
 JOIN AdventureWorks2008.HumanResources.EmployeePayHistory eh
 ON e.BusinessEntityID = eh.BusinessEntityId
WHERE rate > 50.
ORDER BY jobTitle, RateChangeDate DESC

USE Adventureworks2008
GO

CREATE USER  sneakyUser FOR LOGIN auditTest
GO
```

To view the results of the database specification audit, use the following query. The results of the query are shown in Figure 15-2.

```
SELECT event_time,server_principal_name,database_principal_name,
object_name, statement,*
FROM fn_get_audit_file ('C:\sal*',NULL, NULL)
```

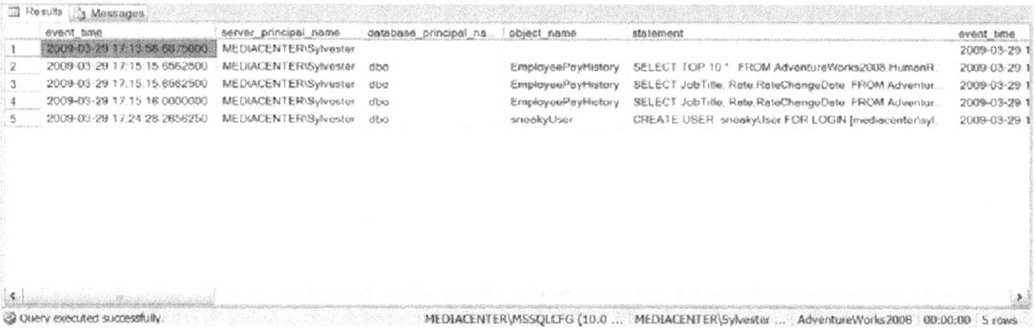

Figure 15-2. *Results of the audit from Listing 15-7*

Creating SQL Server Audits Using the GUI

Since you know how to create SQL Server audits and add server and database audit specifications using T-SQL, we would like to spend a brief moment on the creation of SQL Server audits from SQL Server Management Studio. We are going to create a database audit specification, since you can include database-level audit action groups and a database-level audit action. Remember that database-level audit action groups are the predefined action groups created for you by SQL Server, while you get to define the database-level audit actions. As you know, server audit specifications only use server-level audit action groups, which are similar to the database-level audit action groups.

We are going to follow the same steps used in T-SQL: create an SQL Server audit, create a database specification, add database-level audit action groups, and then database-level audit actions to the database specification. To create a SQL Server audit, connect to an instance of SQL Server using SQL Server Management Studio. Once connected, navigate to the Security folder, expand the folder, then right-click on the Audits folder, and select New Audit. Figure 15-3 shows the options available in the GUI.

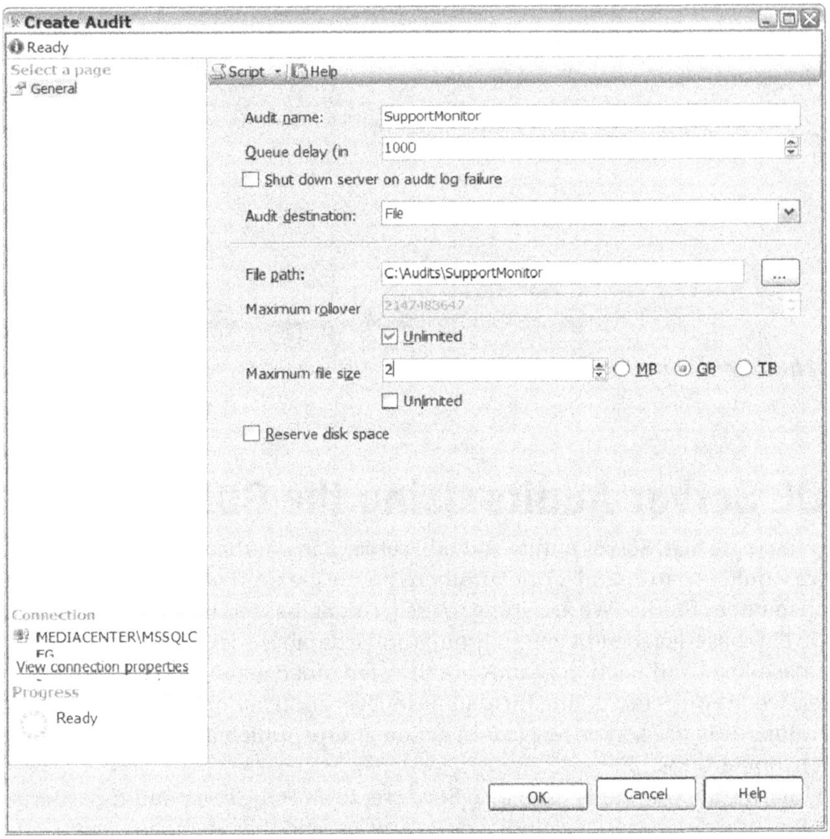

Figure 15-3. *General page of the Create Audit dialog box*

First, name your audit. Then set the queue delay—remember, the measurement is in milliseconds. Select the check box next to Shut Down Server on Audit Log Failure if you want to shut down the SQL Server instance when the audit is unable to log data to the target. After that, determine the audit destination. If you choose File, then you have decide the file path, maximum file size, maximum rollover, and if you want to reserve disk space. Once you populate all of the values, click OK to create the audit.

Creating a Database Audit Specification Using the GUI

After creating the audit, navigate to the database where you want to create the database audit specification, drill down to the Security folder, right-click on the database audit specification, and then select New Database Audit Specification. See Figure 15-4 to review the available options in the Create Database Audit Specification dialog box.

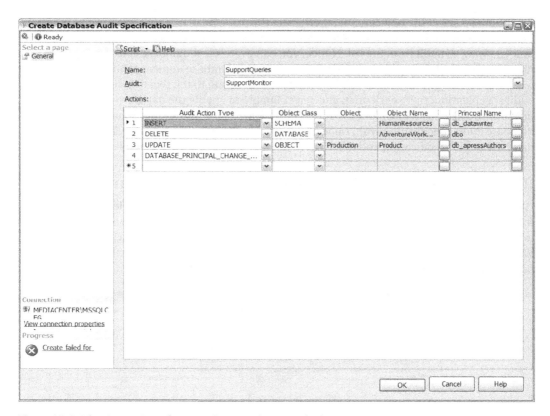

Figure 15-4. *The Create Database Audit Specification dialog*

First, name the database audit specification and select the audit that you want to associate the database specification to. After that, notice that you have four selectable options to create actions for the database specification: Audit Action type, Object Class, Object Name, and Principal Name.

In the first column, the Audit Action Type drop-down list contains the database-level audit action groups and the database-level audit actions. If you select a database-level audit action group, then you do not have any other selectable options to choose from. The action groups we previously discussed already have their actions defined. Choosing a database-level audit action gives you the flexibility to define exactly what you want audited.

The Object Class drop-down list contains three options: Schema, Database, and Object. In other words, do you want to audit the audit action for a database, a particular schema, or for a particular object? The object class you select will determine the types of object names that are available. Choose the object class that you want audited for the audit action type you selected.

The Object Names ellipses will contain all of the object names for the object class selected. For example, if you select Database, then the Object Name drop-down will list all of the available databases. Schemas and objects work similarly. Identify the object name that you want audited and select the name from the list.

After you select the object name, then select the principal name that you want to monitor. When you click on the ellipses, the list displays available principals. Choose the principal name that you want to audit from the list. Notice, you can even select database roles from the list. After you populate the options, click OK and create the database audit specification.

After creating the database audit specification, navigate to the recently created database audit specification, right-click on it, and select Enable to enable the database audit specification. You also need to enable the audit. So navigate to the audit that you associated the database audit specification with, right-click on the audit, and select Enable. Now both the database audit specification and the audit that it is associated with are enabled.

Reviewing Audit Files Using SQL Server Management Studio

We have demonstrated querying a file to review the audit information in a file, but we want to show you how to review the audit information from the GUI. Navigate to the Audits folder under the Server Security folder. Right-click on the audit that you want to review and select View Audit Logs. As shown in Figure 15-5, you can select multiple audits. That can prove helpful if you are trying to correlate when events occurred from multiple audits.

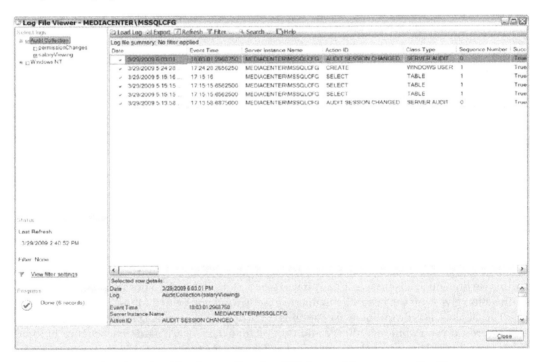

Figure 15-5. *Results of a salaryViewing audit using SQL Server Management Studio*

Audit-Related Startup and Shutdown Problems

Before setting up SQL Server audits, you should be aware that audit problems can lead to trouble in starting or stopping your SQL Server instance.

Failure to Start

When either the ON_Failure = On or Shutdown Server on Audit Log Failure option is checked, SQL Server will not start if it cannot initialize the target for an audit or if it cannot write to the target of an audit. When SQL Server starts, it will attempt to start any enabled audits. If failures occur, you will receive an unfriendly error message like the one in Figure 15-6.

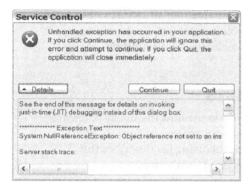

Figure 15-6. *Error message received when attempting to start SQL Server but unable to initialize the target file*

An audit target may not initialize for a number of reasons. The drive might not allow you to allocate all the space required when `Reserve_Disk_Space` is set to on, the problem might be from changes in the file structure where the audit files are stored, and so forth. Whatever the problem, the result is that SQL Server does not start.

If you are like us, then you probably don't want your server not starting because of an audit not initializing. If that happens, then start SQL Server from the command line using the following:

```
sqlservr.exe -f -s < instance name>
```

The instance name is optional, and defaults to MSSQLServer. The -f option will start SQL Server in minimal configuration mode, which allows you to disable or fix the troublesome audit target.

Forced Shutdowns

If SQL Server shuts down because of a failure to write to the log, then it will write an event to the error log stating `MSG_AUDIT_FORCED_SHUTDOWN`. When this occurs, SQL Server still will not start until the problem that caused the shutdown is resolved. To bypass this issue, you can start SQL Server from the command line using the following:

```
sqlservr.exe -m -s<instance name>
```

As before, the instance name is optional. Using `-m` starts SQL Server in single user mode and allows you to disable the audit or change the shutdown option in order to continue.

You may be thinking that that this situation can easily be avoided by setting your audit to `CONTINUE` instead of `SHUTDOWN`. On the other hand, you may have a very good reason for shutting down SQL Server when you cannot log audit information. In either situation, rather intentionally or unintentionally, you may find yourself unable to start SQL Server after an audit shutdown, and you need to know how to get your server back up and running.

Useful SQL Server Audit Objects

Before you finish this chapter, we want to make sure you know how to quickly determine the active audits within your SQL Server instance. We also want you to know how to read data from an audit file without using the GUI. The following list describes the `sys.dm_server_audit_status` DMV and the `fn_get_audit_file` function.

- `sys.dm_server_audit_status`: Lists information for all the SQL Server audits. The DMV contains the current status of the audits, the UTC time of the status change, and for file audits, the location and size of the files.

- `fn_get_audit_file`: Enables you to read the file of an audit. The function expects three parameters: the path and file name (which can include a wildcard), the initial file name to start reading from, and the audit file offset (which tells the function where to start reading from). You can specify `default` or `null` for the last two parameters. The output of the function is a list of audit records ordered by the time that the actions occurred.

Having the ability to review audit files and determine which audits are running proves useful in our environments. We hope these two commands are useful to you as well.

Summary

As we conclude this chapter, we hope you have learned some valuable information to aid you in auditing the activity of your server. SQL Server Audit is a new Enterprise Edition feature that definitely gives database administrators another tool to aid in monitoring servers. Take advantage of this new feature, use it to track activity on your server, and minimize the amount of time it takes to track down user activity on your server.

CHAPTER 16

∎∎∎

Managing Query Performance

Managing query performance is another one of those subjects that requires an entire book to provide the coverage it deserves, especially when you dive into the execution plans. However, dealing with problem queries is an integral part of every DBA's skill set. Luckily, Grant Fritchey and Sajal Dam have written *SQL Server 2008 Query Performance Tuning Distilled* (Apress, 2009), so this doesn't have to be a 500-page chapter.

This chapter will cover many of the new features that will help you deal with problematic queries. First, we will go over a few techniques to help you find these types of queries, and then we will discuss some of the options that give you a little more control over them (even if you can't directly edit the queries themselves). If you are a production DBA, I highly recommend using this chapter as a starting point, and then adding a dedicated book on query tuning to your collection.

Correlating Profiler and the Performance Monitor

One interesting feature added in SQL Server 2005 is the ability to import performance logs into SQL Server Profiler so that you can correlate activity on the system to specific queries. Correlating performance monitor (PerfMon) logs with SQL Server Profiler traces drastically improves your ability to track down the exact queries casing performance issues. Let's walk through a simple example.

Open SQL Server Profiler, then open PerfMon by selecting Performance Monitor from the Tools menu. (These first few steps are in no particular order; you just need to make sure you have PerfMon and Profiler running concurrently so you can correlate the results.)

Now you need to create a new counter log in PerfMon. Expand Performance Logs and Alerts, right-click Counter Logs, and select New Log Settings from the context menu. Give the log a name, such as **Perfmon_Profiler_Demo** and select OK.

Now you can add counters to the new log. Select the Add Counters button and make sure % Processor Time is highlighted in the Counters list and click Add. Click Close to return to the New Log dialog box. Take note of where the log file is located. You will need this later when you import the log into Profiler.

The next thing you need to do is start a new Profiler trace by selecting New Trace from the File menu. Connect to a SQL instance, select the Standard (default) template, and click Run to start the trace. Now that you have both traces running, you need to generate some load on the server. Execute the script in Listing 16-1 to simulate a bad query.

Listing 16-1. *Query to Cause Performance Spike*

```
SELECT * FROM sys.messages
CROSS JOIN sys.messages B
WHERE B.language_id = 1033 AND
 B.text like '%Warning%' AND
 B.text like '%instance%'
```

Before you can correlate the two traces, you have to stop, save, and reopen your Profiler trace, and then stop your PerfMon counter log. Stop the Profiler trace and select Save As ➤ Trace File from the File menu to save the trace. Now reopen the trace by selecting Open ➤ Trace File from the File menu. This is a good time to stop your PerfMon trace as well. Return to PerfMon, highlight the new log you created, and select Stop from the menu.

Now you have a new option available in SQL Server Profiler under the File menu called Import Performance Data. Select Import Performance Data and browse to the location of your PerfMon log file to import it into Profiler. This will open the Performance Counters Limit dialog box so you can select which counters you would like to import into Profiler. Make sure % Processor Time is selected, and click OK. You can now select a point on the PerfMon trace, and Profiler will take you to the query that was executing at that point. As you can see in Figure 16-1, the query in Listing 16-1 was the cause of the spike in PerfMon.

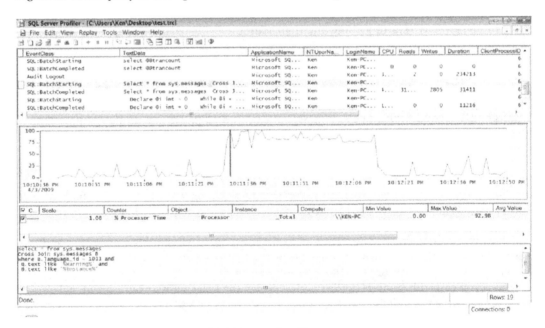

Figure 16-1. *Correlating PerfMon and SQL Server Profiler*

Finding Similar Queries

Prior to SQL Server 2008, finding and tuning similar queries was a daunting task. Prior to SQL Server 2008, you would have to capture a set of queries using a trace or Dynamic Management View (DMV), perform some logic to replace literal values within those queries, and then group by some or all of the query text. The concept is to try to replace literal values with something, such as a pound sign (for example, SELECT col1 FROM Table1 WHERE col1 = # AND col2 = #), so you can group the queries such that the only difference is the parameter values. This approach is very time consuming and in many cases less than accurate. Microsoft has added the query_hash and query_plan_hash columns to the sys.dm_exec_query_stats and the sys.dm_exec_requests DMVs to provide a far more accurate way of finding similar queries.

The sys.dm_exec_query_stats DMV returns aggregate performance statistics about query plans that are currently in cache, and the sys.dm_exec_requests DMV returns information about queries that are currently executing. A *query hash* is a binary hash value that is calculated on a query based on the query text prior to being sent to the optimizer. A *query plan hash* is a binary hash value that is calculated based on a compiled query plan. Two queries may have the same query hash values and different plan hash values. For example, if you execute two queries that are identical except for the literal values, the query hash value will be the same. However, one query may produce an index scan, while the other may produce an index seek in the query plan (depending on the range of values being requested), resulting in different query plan hash values.

Now that you understand the mechanics of using hash values, let's take a look at a few examples. Run the script in Listing 16-2 to clear the plan cache and execute some similar queries.

Listing 16-2. *Sample Queries to Create Similar Hash Values*

```
DBCC FREEPROCCACHE
GO
SELECT * FROM sys.messages WHERE severity = 23
GO
SELECT * FROM sys.messages WHERE severity = 23
GO
SELECT * FROM sys.messages WHERE severity = 23;
GO
SELECT * FROM sys.messages WHERE severity=23
GO
SELECT * FROM sys.messages WHERE severity = 24
GO
SELECT * FROM sys.messages WHERE severity IN (24)
GO
SELECT * FROM sys.messages WHERE severity in (23,24)
GO
```

Now that you have executed a few similar queries, you can review the output from the sys.dm_exec_query_stats DMV. You will also use the sys.dm_exec_sql_text function to return the query text by passing in the plan handle used for the query. Run the query in Listing 16-3 to review the hash values generated by the queries in Listing 16-2.

Listing 16-3. *Query to Analyze the Hash Values Generated by Listing 16-2*

```
SELECT qs.query_hash,
       qs.query_plan_hash,
       st.text ,
       qs.execution_count,
       qs.total_worker_time
FROM sys.dm_exec_query_stats qs
CROSS APPLY sys.dm_exec_sql_text (plan_handle) st
WHERE st.text like 'Select * From sys.messages%'
ORDER BY qs.total_worker_time desc
```

The results from Listing 16-3 are displayed in Figure 16-2. As you can see by the execution count, out of the seven queries we ran, only two of them used the same cached execution plan. The query text must be exactly the same in order for SQL Server to reuse the execution plan. There are only minor differences in the queries we are limiting on severity 23, but even an extra space or a semicolon causes SQL Server to compile a separate execution plan. It would be much more efficient to parameterize these queries so that SQL Server could make use of the same cached execution plan for each one. If you look at the hash values in the first two columns, you will see they all match except for the query in the second row. The query text and query plan were both slightly different enough to produce different hash values.

	query_hash	query_plan_hash	text	execution_count	total_worker_time
1	0xB84F75F41D5F6CD1	0x4FEE97722923BF72	Select * From sys.messages Where severity = 23	2	1570089
2	0x8E8DEF26EA5BA8BE	0x8DAEB35CE07F0FDE	Select * From sys.messages Where severity in (23,24)	1	787045
3	0xB84F75F41D5F6CD1	0x4FEE97722923BF72	Select * From sys.messages Where severity IN (24)	1	784044
4	0xB84F75F41D5F6CD1	0x4FEE97722923BF72	Select * From sys.messages Where severity=23	1	776044
5	0xB84F75F41D5F6CD1	0x4FEE97722923BF72	Select * From sys.messages Where severity = 24	1	776044
6	0xB84F75F41D5F6CD1	0x4FEE97722923BF72	Select * From sys.messages Where severity = 23;	1	774044

Figure 16-2. *Results returned from running the query in Listing 16-3*

Now let's run the query in Listing 16-4 to aggregate the data based on the hash values to get a more accurate view of the execution count and total worker time for the queries run in Listing 16-2.

Listing 16-4. *Query to Aggregate Execution Count and Total Worker Time Using Hash Values*

```
SELECT qs.query_hash,
       qs.query_plan_hash,
       MIN(st.text) QueryTextLike,
       SUM(qs.execution_count) ExecutionCount,
       SUM(qs.total_worker_time)TotalWorkerTime
FROM sys.dm_exec_query_stats qs
CROSS APPLY sys.dm_exec_sql_text (plan_handle) st
WHERE st.text LIKE 'SELECT * FROM sys.messages%'
GROUP BY qs.query_hash, qs.query_plan_hash
ORDER BY TotalWorkerTime DESC
```

Now look at the aggregated results in Figure 16-3. This shows an execution count of six for the queries that share the same hash values. This level of aggregation could raise queries to the top of your result set that may otherwise go unnoticed. For example, if you are looking for the top ten queries with the highest total worker time, and if several like queries were run hundreds of times generating different execution plans, they may not even make the list. Using the new plan hash feature will allow you to focus on tuning the queries actually using the most resources on your system instead of just those heavy hitters that are easy to find.

	query_hash	query_plan_hash	QueryTextLike	ExecutionCount	TotalWorkerTime
1	0xB84F75F41D5F6CD1	0x4FEE97722923BF72	Select * From sys.messages Where severity = 23	6	4680265
2	0x8E8DEF26EA5BA8BE	0x8DAEB35CE07F0FDE	Select * From sys.messages Where severity in (23,24)	1	787045

Figure 16-3. *Results returned from running the query in Listing 16-4*

Running the Standard Performance Reports

Microsoft has written some out-of-the-box reports that offer some useful information when looking for problematic queries. You can write many of the same kinds of reports using DMVs, but the canned reports are a quick and easy way to find some of your worst performing queries.

You can view a list of reports that apply to the entire instance or to a specific database. To display the list of reports shown in Figure 16-4, right-click on the SQL Server instance in SQL Server Management Studio, select Reports ➤ Standard Reports. To display a list of reports for a specific database, right-click on the database instead of the Server Instance.

Server Dashboard
Configuration Changes History
Schema Changes History
Scheduler Health
Memory Consumption
Activity - All Blocking Transactions
Activity - All Cursors
Activity - Top Cursors
Activity - All Sessions
Activity - Top Sessions
Activity - Dormant Sessions
Activity - Top Connections
Top Transactions by Age
Top Transactions by Blocked Transactions Count
Top Transactions by Locks Count
Performance - Batch Execution Statistics
Performance - Object Execution Statistics
Performance - Top Queries by Average CPU Time
Performance - Top Queries by Average IO
Performance - Top Queries by Total CPU Time
Performance - Top Queries by Total IO
Service Broker Statistics
Transaction Log Shipping Status

Figure 16-4. *List of standard reports in SQL Server Management Studio*

You can see a sample of the Performance – Top Queries by Average CPU Time report in Figure 16-5. If you look at the worst performing query, you may notice it was the query we executed in Listing 16-1 to cause the PerfMon spike.

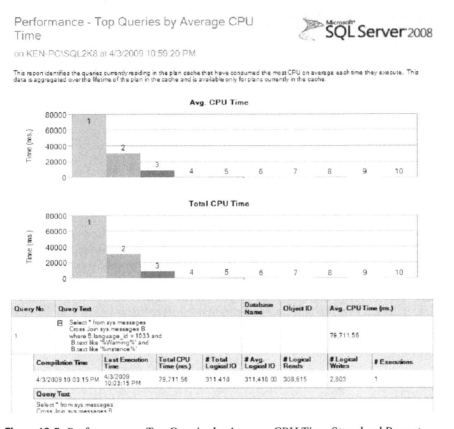

Figure 16-5. *Performance – Top Queries by Average CPU Time Standard Report*

Alternatively, you can use DMVs and execute the query in Listing 16-5 to display the same information. But not only is the standard report in a format that is easier to read, it is also a lot easier to execute. We don't know about you, but unless we have the script handy, we wouldn't want to have to remember the syntax required to write the query in Listing 16-5. If you do want to have the scripts on hand, you can start a trace in Profiler, run a report, and capture the query that the report executed.

Listing 16-5. *Top Ten Queries by Average CPU Time*

```
SELECT TOP 10
    creation_time,
    last_execution_time,
    (total_worker_time+0.0)/1000 as total_worker_time,
    (total_worker_time+0.0)/(execution_count*1000) as [AvgCPUTime],
    total_logical_reads as [LogicalReads],
```

```
        total_logical_writes as [LogicalWrites],
        execution_count,
        total_logical_reads+total_logical_writes as [AggIO],
        (total_logical_reads+total_logical_writes)/(execution_count+0.0) as [AvgIO],
        case when sql_handle IS NULL
            then ' '
            else ( substring(st.text,(qs.statement_start_offset+2)/2,
                (case when qs.statement_end_offset = -1
                    then len(convert(nvarchar(MAX),st.text))*2
                    else qs.statement_end_offset
                    end - qs.statement_start_offset) /2  ) )
        end as query_text,
            db_name(st.dbid) as db_name,
            st.objectid as object_id
FROM sys.dm_exec_query_stats  qs
CROSS apply sys.dm_exec_sql_text(sql_handle) st
WHERE total_worker_time  > 0
ORDER BY [AvgCPUTime] desc
```

One advantage that DMVs have over the reports is that you can run the DMVs from a scheduled job and insert the output in a table. Every time SQL Server is restarted, you lose all of the useful information provided by the DMVs. Storing the output from DMVs in a table allows you to take snapshots of the DMVs so you can analyze the data over a long period of time without worrying about losing all of your information if SQL Server is restarted.

Optimizing for Specific Parameter Values

The OPTIMIZE FOR query hint was introduced in SQL Server 2005 to allow you to specify a value the query optimizer will use when creating an execution plan for parameterized queries. SQL Server 2008 has enhanced this query hint by adding the UNKNOWN option, which instructs the query optimizer to use statistical information when creating the execution plan instead of the supplied value. The OPTIMIZE FOR query hint is useful when different parameter values create different execution plans. If you create a stored procedure, and the execution plan is cached based on infrequently used values, you could suffer from a poorly cached execution plan.

Let's look at a couple of queries where the execution plan changes based on the search value. The query in Listing 16-6 performs a basic join on the SalesOrderDetail and the SalesOrderHeader tables and limits the results to only orders with a quantity of one.

Listing 16-6. *Query That Will Generate an Execution Plan That Uses a Merge Join*

```
USE AdventureWorks2008
GO

SELECT B.CustomerID
FROM Sales.SalesOrderDetail A
    JOIN Sales.SalesOrderHeader B
    ON A.SalesOrderID = B.SalesOrderID
WHERE A.OrderQty = 1
```

The query optimizer chooses a merge join for the query in Listing 16-6 because there are almost 75,000 rows with an order quantity of one. You can view the execution plan for Listing 16-6 in Figure 16-6.

Figure 16-6. *Execution plan generated for the query in Listing 16-6*

Let's execute the same query with one minor change, as shown in Listing 16-7. If you look closely, you will see the only difference between the queries in Listing 16-6 and Listing 16-7 is that we changed the value in the WHERE clause to limit the results to only include orders with an order quantity of ten.

Listing 16-7. *Query That Will Generate an Execution Plan That Uses a Hash Join*

```
USE AdventureWorks2008
GO

SELECT B.CustomerID
FROM Sales.SalesOrderDetail A
    JOIN Sales.SalesOrderHeader B
    ON A.SalesOrderID = B.SalesOrderID
WHERE A.OrderQty = 10
```

As you can see in Figure 16-7, making a simple change in the WHERE clause causes the query optimizer to use a hash match to join the records, since there are only 768 rows with an order quantity of ten.

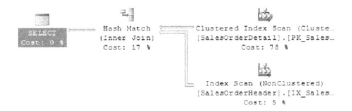

Figure 16-7. *Execution plan generated for the query in Listing 16-7*

Now let's execute the same query using a variable with a value of ten instead of hard coding the value. Let's also optimize the query as if the variable being used contained the number one, as shown in Listing 16-8.

Listing 16-8. *Using the OPTIMIZE FOR Query Hint to Optimize the Execution Plan for a Value of One*

```
USE AdventureWorks2008
GO

DECLARE @ID int =10

SELECT B.CustomerID
FROM Sales.SalesOrderDetail A
     JOIN Sales.SalesOrderHeader B
     ON A.SalesOrderID = B.SalesOrderID
WHERE A.OrderQty = @ID
OPTION (OPTIMIZE FOR (@ID = 1))
```

As you can see in Figure 16-8, the execution plan now contains a merge join instead of the hash join that the query optimizer would have normally chosen for the value of ten.

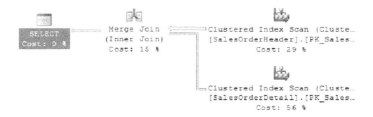

Figure 16-8. *Execution plan generated for the query in Listing 16-8*

Let's execute the query once again using a variable of one, which should cause the query optimizer to choose a merge join. Let's also change the query hint to optimize for UNKNOWN to instruct the query optimizer to use statistical information to create the query plan, as shown in Listing 16-9.

Listing 16-9. *Using the OPTIMIZE FOR query hint to Optimize the Execution Plan for an Unknown Value*

```
USE AdventureWorks2008
GO

DECLARE @ID2 int =1

SELECT B.CustomerID
FROM Sales.SalesOrderDetail A
     JOIN Sales.SalesOrderHeader B
     ON A.SalesOrderID = B.SalesOrderID
WHERE A.OrderQty = @ID2
OPTION (OPTIMIZE FOR (@ID2 UNKNOWN))
```

As you can see in Figure 16-9, the statistical information causes the query optimizer to use a hash join instead of a merge join that the optimizer would have normally chosen for the value of one. It chooses the hash join because, based on the statistical information, you are more likely to pass in a variable that will perform better using the hash join.

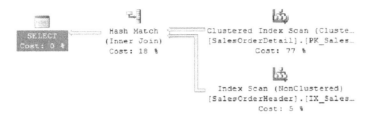

Figure 16-9. *Execution plan generated for the query in Listing 16-9*

Make sure you know the usage patterns of the application when using the OPTIMIZE FOR query hint. You may need to modify the optimization values from time to time. Optimal parameters today may not be the optimal parameters a year from now.

Forcing Index Seeks

The FORCESEEK table hint was introduced in SQL Server 2008 to force an index seek in an execution plan in place of an index scan. The query optimizer does a really good job deciding whether a seek or scan is more efficient, but in certain scenarios you may want to override the execution plan's decision. For example, poor cardinality estimation using the LIKE and IN operators may cause the query optimizer to choose an index scan when an index seek may be more efficient. Another reason for a poor execution plan could be due to plan reuse. For example, an execution plan could be initially generated using parameters that were more efficient using a scan, and now the plan is reused several times for parameters that would be more efficient using a seek. Take a look at the query in Listing 16-10.

Listing 16-10. *Query to Create a Clustered Index Scan*

```
USE AdventureWorks2008
GO

SELECT *
FROM HumanResources.Employee A
     JOIN HumanResources.EmployeeDepartmentHistory B
     ON A.BusinessEntityID = B.BusinessEntityID
WHERE A.BusinessEntityID > 270 OR
        (A.BusinessEntityID < 10 and B.DepartmentID =1)
```

As you can see in Figure 16-10, the query in Listing 16-10 used a clustered index scan on the EmployeeDepartmentHistory table, and then used a merge join to combine the results with the Employee table.

Figure 16-10. *Execution plan created by running the query in Listing 16-10*

Now let's see what happens when we execute the same query using the FORCESEEK table hint by running the query in Listing 16-11.

Listing 16-11. *Query to Force a Clustered Index Seek*

```
USE AdventureWorks2008
GO

SELECT *
FROM HumanResources.Employee A
    JOIN HumanResources.EmployeeDepartmentHistory B WITH (FORCESEEK)
    ON A.BusinessEntityID = B.BusinessEntityID
WHERE A.BusinessEntityID > 270 OR
        (A.BusinessEntityID < 10 and B.DepartmentID =1)
```

As you can see in Figure 16-11, using the FORCESEEK table hint caused the same query to use a clustered index seek on the EmployeeDepartmentHistory table, and the results are now joined with the Employee table using nested loops.

Figure 16-11. *Execution plan created by running the query in Listing 16-11*

Both of these execution plans provide almost identical performance metrics because the result set is so small. However, as the parameters change and the result set gets larger, the execution plan originally chosen by the query optimizer will outperform the execution plan generated using the FORCESEEK option.

Before considering using the FORCESEEK table hint, you should make sure the statistics for the database are up to date. In most cases, the query optimizer will choose the best execution plan for a query, but in rare cases, the FORCESEEK table hint could prove to be a very useful new feature.

Forcing a Specific Execution Plan

Plan forcing was introduced in SQL Server 2005 to provide a way for you to supply an entire execution plan that SQL Server will use to execute a query. Plan forcing is useful when the query optimizer will not produce an optimal execution plan for a query, even though you know a better execution plan is available. If you have a query that performed better prior to an upgrade, you may be able to capture the old execution plan and force the optimizer to use it. You can supply the execution plan in XML format following a query by supplying the USE PLAN option, as shown in Listing 16-12.

Listing 16-12. *Syntax Used to Specify an Execution Plan by Supplying the USE PLAN Query Hint*

```
SELECT *
FROM Table1
    JOIN Table2
    ON Table1.Column = Table2.Column
OPTION (USE PLAN 'N
<ShowPlanXML xmlns="http://schemas.microsoft.com/sqlserver/2004/07/showplan">
  ...
</ShowPlanXML>')
```

In order to supply the execution plan, you must first capture it in XML format. There are a few ways you can capture the XML execution plan to supply the query.

- You can use the SHOWPLAN_XML SET statement to return the XML execution plan instead of running the query, as shown in the following code:

    ```
    SET SHOWPLAN_XML ON
    GO

    SELECT * FROM Table
    SET SHOWPLAN_XML OFF
    GO
    ```

- You can use the STATISTICS XML SET statement to return the XML execution plan following the query result set, as shown in the following code:

    ```
    SET STATISTICS XML ON
    GO

    SELECT * FROM Table
    SET STATISTICS XML OFF
    GO
    ```

- You can use the query_plan column in the `sys.dm_exec_query_plan` Dynamic Management Function, as shown in the following query:

```
SELECT est.text, eqp.query_plan
FROM sys.dm_exec_cached_plans ecp
    CROSS APPLY sys.dm_exec_query_plan(ecp.plan_handle) eqp
    CROSS APPLY sys.dm_exec_sql_text(ecp.plan_handle) est
```

- You can use the `Showplan XML`, `Showplan XML Statistics Profile`, and `Showplan XML For Query Compile` event classes in SQL Server Profiler.

- You can use the `Display Estimated Execution Plan` and `Include Actual Execution Plan` options in SQL Server Management Studio; right-click the execution plan, and select Show Execution Plan XML from the context menu.

If the XML execution plan is invalid in any way, the query will fail. Certain underlying database schema changes may cause the execution plan to become invalid. Therefore, it is extremely important to test any queries that have the USE PLAN query hint after making database changes. Just as with any option you use to override the query optimizer, you should apply the USE PLAN query hint with extreme caution, and then only after you have exhausted your other options, such as creating proper indexes and updating statistics. Since the USE PLAN query hint forces a query to utilize a specified execution plan, the query optimizer will no longer be able to dynamically adjust to changes within the database.

Adding Hints Through Plan Guides

Plan guides were introduced in SQL Server 2005 to provide the ability to add a hint to a query without having to manually alter the query. Many times, you are at the mercy of the queries thrown at your database by certain applications. Plan guides let you supply a hint to those incoming application queries in order to produce a more efficient query plan.

SQL Server 2008 has actually taken plan guides a step further so that you can provide an entire XML query plan as a query hint. Unlike the USE PLAN query hint, an invalid XML query plan supplied as a query hint using plan guides will not cause the query to fail.

Creating a Plan Guide

To create a new plan guide, expand the Programmability node under the database where you would like the plan guide, right-click the Plan Guides folder, and select New Plan Guide from the context menu to display the New Plan Guide dialog box, as shown in Figure 16-12.

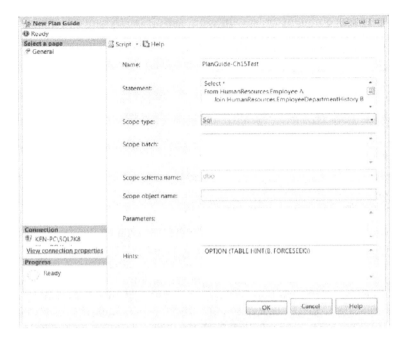

Figure 16-12. *New Plan Guide dialog box*

Let's create a plan guide for the same query used in Listing 16-10 to force the execution plan to use an index seek instead of an index scan. The options available when creating a new plan guide include the following:

- *Name*: Enter a descriptive name for the plan guide. We named ours PlanGuide-Ch15Test.

- *Statement*: Enter the T-SQL statement for which you would like to apply the plan guide. We entered the T-SQL statement from Listing 16-10.

■**Caution** Make sure you enter the T-SQL statement exactly as it will be sent to SQL Server. Even extra spaces will cause the query optimizer to ignore the plan guide.

- *Scope Type*: The scope type specifies the context for matching the T-SQL statement to the plan guide. Valid values are Object, Sql, and Template. Object is the stored procedure, scalar function, multi-statement table-valued function, or T-SQL Data Manipulation Language (DML) trigger that contains the T-SQL statement. Sql indicates that the T-SQL statement is in the context of a stand-alone statement or batch. Template is used to change the default query parameterization behavior. If Template is selected, you can only use the PARAMETERIZATION {FORCED | SIMPLE} query hint. We will be using the Sql scope type in this example.

- *Scope Batch*: Enter the T-SQL batch that contains the statement for which you would like to apply the plan guide. If you leave the Scope Batch box blank, the Statement text will be used.

- *Scope Schema Name*: If the scope type is Object, enter the name of the schema that contains the object.

- *Scope Object Name*: If the scope type is Object, enter the name of the object that contains the T-SQL statement for which you would like to apply the plan guide.

- *Parameters*: Enter the parameter name and data type for the T-SQL statement. The parameters must be submitted exactly as they appear using the sp_executesql statement. If the scope type is Template, parameters are required.

- *Hints*: Enter the query hint or XML execution plan that will be applied to the T-SQL statement. SQL Server 2008 allows you to use the FORCESEEK table hint as a query hint by entering the following statement. (You should also notice that we are referencing the alias B for the table name we used in the query instead of the actual table name.)

```
OPTION (TABLE HINT (B, FORCESEEK))
```

The final T-SQL command to create the plan guide is shown in Listing 16-13. You can query the sys.plan_guides catalog view to return information for each plan guide you have created in the current database.

Listing 16-13. *T-SQL Code to Create the Plan Guide Shown in Figure 16-12*

```
USE AdventureWorks2008
GO

EXEC sp_create_plan_guide
    @name = N'[PlanGuide-Ch15Test]',
    @stmt = N'Select *
FROM HumanResources.Employee A
    JOIN HumanResources.EmployeeDepartmentHistory B
    ON A.BusinessEntityID = B.BusinessEntityID
WHERE A.BusinessEntityID > 270 OR
        (A.BusinessEntityID < 10 and B.DepartmentID =1)',
    @type = N'SQL',
    @hints = N'OPTION (TABLE HINT(B, FORCESEEK))'
GO
```

Validating a Plan Guide

Because a plan guide will not cause a query to fail, it is important to validate the plan guides. This is primarily necessary after you perform an upgrade to SQL Server or change the underlying data structure in the database. If the plan guide is invalid, the query optimizer will ignore it and generate a new execution plan for the query. You can use the sys.fn_validate_plan_guide function to validate a plan guide by passing the plan_guide_id function from the sys.plan_guides catalog view. The sys.fn_validate_plan_guide function will return the first error message encountered when the plan guide is applied to the query. If you receive an empty result set, the plan guide does not contain any errors. The following script will check the validity of all the plan guides in the AdventureWorks2008 database.

```
USE AdventureWorks2008
GO

SELECT plan_guide_id, msgnum, severity, state, message
FROM sys.plan_guides
CROSS APPLY sys.fn_validate_plan_guide(plan_guide_id)
```

You can use the Plan Guide Successful and Plan Guide Unsuccessful events in SQL Server Profiler located under the Performance node to capture valid and invalid attempts of the query optimizer using plan guides. Start a new Profiler trace and select Show All Events, expand the Performance node, and select Plan Guide Successful and Plan Guide Unsuccessful, as shown in Figure 16-13. Select Run to start the trace.

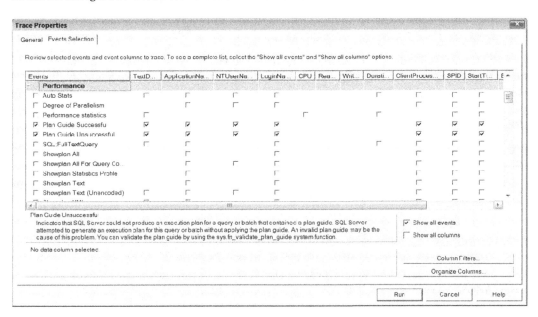

Figure 16-13. *Plan guide events in SQL Server Profiler*

Now, execute the query from Listing 16-10 that we used to create the plan guide. As you can see in Figure 16-14, the query optimizer successfully applied the plan guide to the query, and then the query was executed using the hint provided in the plan guide.

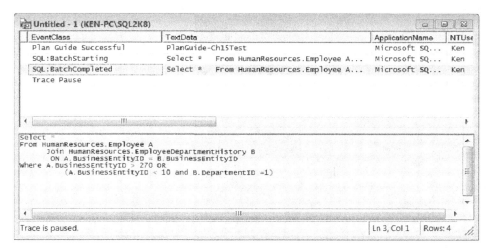

Figure 16-14. *Successful plan guide execution captured using SQL Server Profiler*

Managing Resources with the Resource Governor

In some cases, your queries may be running as efficiently as possible; they may just be running slow due to limited resources. For example, you may have a backup job or a long-running report consuming all of the system resources and slowing down your production queries. Luckily, in SQL Server 2008 you can use the Resource Governor to limit these resource-intensive operations so they have minimal impact on your environment.

The Resource Governor was introduced in SQL Server 2008 as an Enterprise Edition feature. You can use the Resource Governor to limit resource consumption of inbound requests and prioritize workloads in order to maintain a more predictable environment. Currently, you can only limit CPU and memory, but not IO. The Resource Governor only applies to the Database Engine, which means you cannot use the Resource Governor to manage external SQL Server processes, such as Analysis Services, Integration Services, and Reporting Services. Also, the Resource Governor is confined to a single SQL Server instance, limiting your ability to manage resources between instances.

The Resource Governor consists of three main components: a resource pool, a workload group, and a classifier function. A *resource pool* is used to carve up physical system resources available within an instance of SQL Server. A *workload group* is assigned to a resource pool and used to group similar queries so they can be treated as a single unit. Finally, the *classifier function* is used to assign an incoming request to the appropriate workload group. Figure 16-15 shows how an incoming request is routed to the appropriate resource pool. We will use the samples throughout this section to emulate the environment displayed in Figure 16-15.

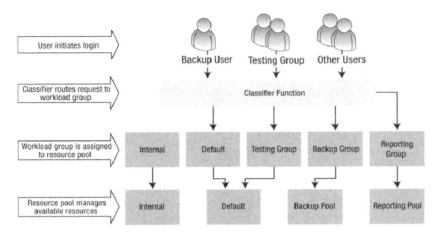

Figure 16-15. *Resource Governor workflow*

Resource Pools

Resource pools are based on the memory and CPU that is available to the SQL Server instance where you are configuring the Resource Governor, not the total resources available to the OS. Resource pools are like mini SQL Server instances inside of an instance. The OS shares memory and CPU between SQL Server instances in the same way a SQL Server instance shares memory and CPU between resource pools.

There are two resource pools created when you install SQL Server 2008 (called *internal* and *default*). The internal resource pool is designated for all of the internal Database Engine processing. You cannot modify the internal resource pool, and it cannot be accessed by any workload groups other than the internal workload group. Also, the CPU and memory are never limited in an internal resource pool. The internal resource pool takes whatever it needs at the time, and the rest of the resource pools divide the remaining CPU and memory appropriately. The default resource pool is where all processes run that have not been assigned to a specific resource pool.

You can create a user-defined resource pool and set the Min and Max properties for CPU and memory. You can change the properties for a resource pool on the fly, and the new settings will apply to any new incoming requests.

▓Tip The Resource Governor does not apply to incoming requests initiated by the dedicated administrator connection (DAC). You should enable the DAC on the SQL Server instances where you are running the Resource Governor for troubleshooting purposes.

The combined minimum totals for CPU and memory cannot exceed 100, while the valid values for the maximum setting for each resource pool are anything greater than the minimum setting and not greater than 100. When you define a minimum setting for a resource pool, you are guaranteeing that resource pool will always have at least the minimum amount of CPU and memory specified, which explains why the total amount cannot exceed 100% of the available resources. The maximum settings for resource pools can overlap, and the available memory will be shared accordingly. The maximum settings are also only enforced during times of CPU and memory pressure. For example, if you define a resource pool with a maximum CPU of 20%, the resource pool may actually use 80% of the CPU if the resources are available. The script in Listing 16-14 will create the Backup and Reporting resource pools shown in Figure 16-15.

Listing 16-14. *Script to Create the Backup and Reporting Resource Pools and Enable Resource Governor*

```
--Create the Backup pool
CREATE RESOURCE POOL BackupPool
 WITH
( MIN_CPU_PERCENT = 0,
 MAX_CPU_PERCENT = 20,
 MIN_MEMORY_PERCENT = 0,
 MAX_MEMORY_PERCENT = 20)
GO

--Create the Reporting pool
CREATE RESOURCE POOL ReportingPool
 WITH
( MIN_CPU_PERCENT = 0,
 MAX_CPU_PERCENT = 25,
 MIN_MEMORY_PERCENT = 0,
 MAX_MEMORY_PERCENT = 25)
GO

--Enable Resource Governor
ALTER RESOURCE GOVERNOR RECONFIGURE
GO
```

We have set the maximum CPU and memory for the Backup pool to 20% and the Reporting pool to 25%. This means that whenever there is resource pressure, the Backup and Reporting pools will only take an average of 45% of the available resources, leaving 55% for all the other requests in the default resource pool. Remember, the internal resource pool will take all the resources it needs, and the rest is considered available to split among the remaining resource pools. The first time you run the ALTER RESOURCE GOVERNOR RECONFIGURE statement, you are enabling the Resource Governor. To disable the Resource Governor, run the ALTER RESOURCE GOVERNOR DISABLE statement.

Workload Groups

The Resource Governor uses workload groups as a way to segregate all incoming requests that have predefined common characteristics together as a single unit. Workload groups allow you to define and monitor specific attributes for each individual workload group, as you will see in the "Monitoring Resource Governor" section. You can also dynamically move workload groups between resource groups if you determine they would be better suited for a different resource pool based on your monitoring statistics. Workload groups consist of two predefined groups that map to the corresponding resource pool: internal and default. The same rules apply to the internal and default workload groups that we discussed for the internal and default resource pools. You can set the following properties when creating a workload group:

- IMPORTANCE: The weight of importance a workload group is given within a resource pool. Workload groups with different levels of importance do not affect each other outside of each resource pool. Valid values are LOW, MEDIUM, and HIGH with the default being MEDIUM.

- REQUEST_MAX_MEMORY_GRANT_PERCENT: The maximum percentage of memory that a single request is allowed to consume from a given resource pool. The valid range is from 0 to 100 with a default setting of 25.

- REQUEST_MAX_CPU_TIME_SEC: The maximum amount of time (in seconds) that a request will run before generating the CPU Threshold Exceeded event. Resource Governor will not prevent the query from running; it will just raise the event so you can capture requests that exceed your defined threshold. Valid values are 0 or greater with a default setting of 0, which is unlimited.

- REQUEST_MEMORY_GRANT_TIMEOUT_SEC: The maximum amount of time a query will wait (in seconds) for a memory grant to become available. Valid values are 0 or greater with a default setting of 0, which means an internal calculation based on the query cost will be used to determine the maximum time.

- MAX_DOP: The maximum degree of parallelism for the workload group. The default is 0, which uses the global SQL Server setting for MAX_DOP.

- GROUP_MAX_REQUESTS: Maximum number of simultaneous requests the workload group can execute at any given time. Valid values are 0 or greater with a default setting of 0, which is unlimited.

Let's create the workload groups shown in Figure 16-15 and assign them to their respective resource pools. The script in Listing 16-15 will create the BackupGroup, ReportingGroup, and the TestingGroup and reconfigure the Resource Governor so they will be immediately active and awaiting processes.

Listing 16-15. *Script to Create the Backup, Reporting, and Testing Workload Groups*

```
CREATE WORKLOAD GROUP BackupGroup
USING BackupPool
GO

CREATE WORKLOAD GROUP ReportingGroup
WITH
 (IMPORTANCE = MEDIUM,
 REQUEST_MAX_MEMORY_GRANT_PERCENT = 30,
 REQUEST_MAX_CPU_TIME_SEC = 0,
 REQUEST_MEMORY_GRANT_TIMEOUT_SEC = 0,
 MAX_DOP = 0,
 GROUP_MAX_REQUESTS = 0)
USING ReportingPool
GO

CREATE WORKLOAD GROUP TestingGroup
WITH
 (IMPORTANCE = LOW,
 REQUEST_MAX_MEMORY_GRANT_PERCENT = 20,
 REQUEST_MAX_CPU_TIME_SEC = 180,
 REQUEST_MEMORY_GRANT_TIMEOUT_SEC = 0,
 MAX_DOP = 1,
 GROUP_MAX_REQUESTS = 20)
GO

ALTER RESOURCE GOVERNOR RECONFIGURE
GO
```

If you look at the BackupGroup, you will see that all of the parameters are optional; you are not even required to specify the resource pool. If you do not manually assign a workload group to use a specific resource pool, it will automatically be assigned to the default resource pool. If you look at the TestingGroup, you can see that we did not assign it to a specific resource pool, since we want to create it in the default resource pool. We have throttled back the TestingGroup quite a bit, giving it low priority, only 20% of the resource pool for a single request, only one processor, and allowing it to run only 20 processes at any given time. We have also configured the TestingGroup to raise an event every time it executes a query that takes longer than 180 seconds. At this point, your workload groups are configured and waiting for incoming processes. Your current configuration in SQL Server Management Studio should mirror the configuration shown in Figure 16-16. The next step is to configure the classifier function to send the processes to the appropriate workload groups.

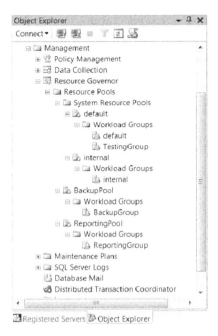

Figure 16-16. *Resource Governor configuration in SQL Server Management Studio*

Classifier Function

The classifier function is a T-SQL function that is executed for each login, which allows you to write logic to route incoming requests to the appropriate workload group. You must create the classifier function in the `master` database, and the Resource Governor can only use one classifier function at any given time. You can, however, create multiple classifier functions and dynamically change which function the Resource Governor uses. You can use the following functions to help you create your classifier function:

- `HOST_NAME()`
- `APP_NAME()`
- `SUSER_NAME()`
- `SUSER_SNAME()`
- `IS_SRVROLEMEMBER()`
- `IS_MEMBER()`
- `LOGINPROPERTY(suser_name(),'DefaultDatabase')`
- `LOGINPROPERTY(suser_name(),'DefaultLanguage')`
- `ORIGINAL_DB_NAME()`
- `CONNECTIONPROPERTY(<PropertyName>)`

You can also create a lookup table to help you with your classifier function. For example, you may want to send certain processes to a different workload group, depending on a schedule you have defined in your lookup table. However, you need to keep in mind that SQL Server will execute the classifier function for each login, so it should be as efficient as possible in order to prevent performance issues. A good thing to keep in mind is that the dedicated administrator connection will never be classified, so you can always log in using this connection to fix any issues you may encounter.

Caution The workload groups used in the classifier function are case sensitive. If you do not use the correct case when referencing the workload groups, the requests will be routed to the default workload group.

Let's create a classifier function that will route the incoming requests to the workload groups shown in Figure 16-15 by running the script in Listing 16-16.

Listing 16-16. *Code to Create and Enable a Classifier Function*

```
USE master
GO

CREATE FUNCTION RG_Classifier_V1 ()
RETURNS sysname
WITH SCHEMABINDING
AS
BEGIN

    DECLARE @GroupName sysname

    IF (IS_MEMBER('KEN-PC\TestingGroup') = 1)
        SET @GroupName = 'TestingGroup'

     ELSE IF (APP_NAME() LIKE '%REPORT SERVER%')
        SET @GroupName = 'ReportingGroup'

     ELSE IF (SUSER_NAME() = 'BackupUser')
        SET @GroupName = 'BackupGroup'

     ELSE
        SET @GroupName = 'default'

    RETURN @GroupName

END
GO
```

```
--Assign the function to the Resource Governor and reconfigure
ALTER RESOURCE GOVERNOR WITH (CLASSIFIER_FUNCTION = dbo.RG_Classifier_V1)
GO
ALTER RESOURCE GOVERNOR RECONFIGURE
GO
```

You can see the completed configuration (shown in Figure 16-17) by right-clicking on Resource Governor in SQL Server Management Studio and selecting Properties from the context menu.

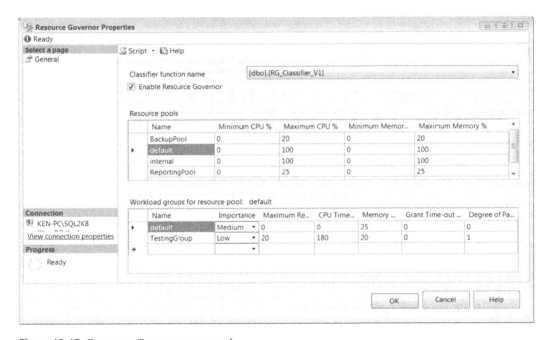

Figure 16-17. *Resource Governor properties*

In order to remove a classifier function from the Resource Governor, you can run the ALTER RESOURCE GOVERNOR statement and specify the new classifier name, or NULL if you want to remove all classifier functions and send all requests to the default workload group. The statement in Listing 16-17 will remove all classifier functions from the Resource Governor.

Listing 16-17. *Code to Remove All Classifier Functions from the Resource Governor*

```
ALTER RESOURCE GOVERNOR WITH (CLASSIFIER_FUNCTION = NULL);
GO
ALTER RESOURCE GOVERNOR RECONFIGURE;
```

Monitoring Resource Governor

Knowing how to monitor your Resource Governor configuration allows you to validate the choices you made during the setup process. Resource Governor monitors provide you with the essential data needed to alter and adapt your configuration based on informed decisions instead of just making random configuration changes and hoping for the best. You can monitor your Resource Governor configuration using performance counters, trace events, and views.

Performance Counters

There are two new performance counters you can use to collect information about resource groups and workload groups: SQLServer:Workload Group Stats and SQLServer:Resource Pool Stats. Both of these performance counters expose several properties in PerfMon and the sys.dm_os_performance_counters DMV. You can run the query in Listing 16-18 to see a list of properties returned for both of these performance counters for the default workload group and resource pool.

Listing 16-18. *Performance Counters for the Default Workload Group and Resource Pool*

```
SELECT *
FROM sys.dm_os_performance_counters
WHERE object_name IN
  ('MSSQL$SQL2K8:Workload Group Stats','MSSQL$SQL2K8:Resource Pool Stats')
  AND instance_name = 'default'
```

The results of Listing 16-18 are displayed in Figure 16-18. As you can see, there is a lot of valuable information you can gather using these performance counters.

	object_name	counter_name	instance_name	cntr_value	cntr_type
1	MSSQL$SQL2K8:Workload Group Stats	CPU usage %	default	0	537003264
2	MSSQL$SQL2K8:Workload Group Stats	CPU usage % base	default	2054	1073939712
3	MSSQL$SQL2K8:Workload Group Stats	Queued requests	default	0	65792
4	MSSQL$SQL2K8:Workload Group Stats	Active requests	default	0	65792
5	MSSQL$SQL2K8:Workload Group Stats	Requests completed/sec	default	0	65792
6	MSSQL$SQL2K8:Workload Group Stats	Max request cpu time (ms)	default	0	65792
7	MSSQL$SQL2K8:Workload Group Stats	Blocked tasks	default	0	65792
8	MSSQL$SQL2K8:Workload Group Stats	Reduced memory grants/sec	default	0	272696576
9	MSSQL$SQL2K8:Workload Group Stats	Max request memory grant (KB)	default	14736	65792
10	MSSQL$SQL2K8:Workload Group Stats	Query optimizations/sec	default	110	272696576
11	MSSQL$SQL2K8:Workload Group Stats	Suboptimal plans/sec	default	6	272696576
12	MSSQL$SQL2K8:Workload Group Stats	Active parallel threads	default	0	65792
13	MSSQL$SQL2K8:Resource Pool Stats	CPU usage %	default	0	537003264
14	MSSQL$SQL2K8:Resource Pool Stats	CPU usage % base	default	2054	1073939712
15	MSSQL$SQL2K8:Resource Pool Stats	CPU usage target %	default	0	65792
16	MSSQL$SQL2K8:Resource Pool Stats	CPU control effect %	default	0	65792
17	MSSQL$SQL2K8:Resource Pool Stats	Compile memory target (KB)	default	1101096	65792
18	MSSQL$SQL2K8:Resource Pool Stats	Cache memory target (KB)	default	1101096	65792
19	MSSQL$SQL2K8:Resource Pool Stats	Query exec memory target (KB)	default	1032240	65792
20	MSSQL$SQL2K8:Resource Pool Stats	Memory grants/sec	default	50	272696576
21	MSSQL$SQL2K8:Resource Pool Stats	Active memory grants count	default	0	65792
22	MSSQL$SQL2K8:Resource Pool Stats	Memory grant timeouts/sec	default	0	272696576
23	MSSQL$SQL2K8:Resource Pool Stats	Active memory grant amount (KB)	default	0	65792
24	MSSQL$SQL2K8:Resource Pool Stats	Pending memory grants count	default	0	65792
25	MSSQL$SQL2K8:Resource Pool Stats	Max memory (KB)	default	1305008	65792
26	MSSQL$SQL2K8:Resource Pool Stats	Used memory (KB)	default	22296	65792
27	MSSQL$SQL2K8:Resource Pool Stats	Target memory (KB)	default	1305008	65792

Figure 16-18. *Resource Governor performance counters*

Using these counters in PerfMon will provide a more interactive experience showing changes in real time. If you alter your Resource Governor configuration, the PerfMon counters will reflect the changes immediately. Using PerfMon is extremely useful when adding and comparing counters from different workload groups and resource pools.

Trace Events

There are three valuable trace events that you can use to obtain information about Resource Governor: CPU Threshold Exceeded, PreConnect:Starting, and PreConnect:Completed. The CPU Threshold Exceeded event will fire whenever a query exceeds the REQUEST_MAX_CPU_TIME_SEC value you set for a workload group. From the CPU Threshold Exceeded event, you can obtain the workload group where the violation occurred, the spid of the process that caused the violation, and when the violation occurred. The CPU Threshold Exceeded event occurs every five seconds, so there is a slight chance that you could exceed the query threshold and not trigger the event. You can use the PreConnect:Starting and PreConnect:Completed events to determine how efficient your classifier function is operating. The PreConnect:Starting event fires when the classifier function begins execution, and the PreConnect:Completed event fires after it has finished. As you can see in Figure 16-19, the CPU Threshold Exceeded event is located under Errors and Warnings, and the PreConnect:Starting and PreConnect:Completed events are located in the Sessions section in SQL Server Profiler.

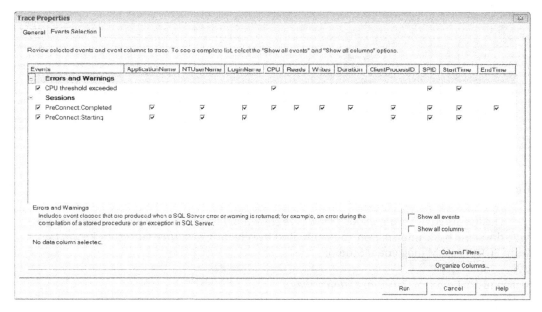

Figure 16-19. *Resource Governor trace events*

Views

There are six views, three DMVs, and three catalog views, all of which provide insight into your Resource Governor configuration. The DMVs provide statistical information, while the catalog views provide information about your current configuration. The Resource Governor DMVs are shown in Listing 16-19.

Listing 16-19. *Resource Governor Dynamic Management Views*

```
SELECT * FROM sys.dm_resource_governor_workload_groups
SELECT * FROM sys.dm_resource_governor_resource_pools
SELECT * FROM sys.dm_resource_governor_configuration
```

If you execute the code in Listing 16-19, you should receive results similar to the output shown in Figure 16-20. You can run the ALTER RESOURCE GOVERNOR RESET STATISTICS statement in order to reset the DMV statistics.

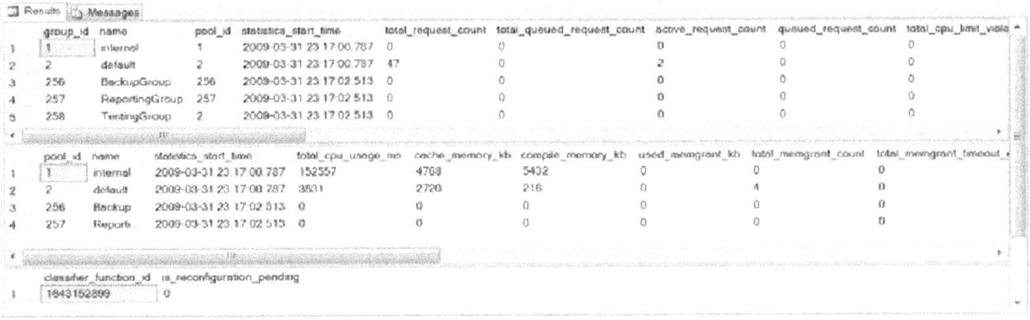

	group_id	name	pool_id	statistics_start_time	total_request_count	total_queued_request_count	active_request_count	queued_request_count	total_cpu_limit_viola
1	1	internal	1	2009-03-31 23:17:00.787	0	0	0	0	0
2	2	default	2	2009-03-31 23:17:00.787	47	0	2	0	0
3	256	BackupGroup	256	2009-03-31 23:17:02.513	0	0	0	0	0
4	257	ReportingGroup	257	2009-03-31 23:17:02.513	0	0	0	0	0
5	258	TestingGroup	2	2009-03-31 23:17:02.513	0	0	0	0	0

	pool_id	name	statistics_start_time	total_cpu_usage_ms	cache_memory_kb	compile_memory_kb	used_memgrant_kb	total_memgrant_count	total_memgrant_timeout_
1	1	internal	2009-03-31 23:17:00.787	152557	4768	5432	0	0	0
2	2	default	2009-03-31 23:17:00.787	3831	2720	216	0	4	0
3	256	Backup	2009-03-31 23:17:02.513	0	0	0	0	0	0
4	257	Report...	2009-03-31 23:17:02.513	0	0	0	0	0	0

	classifier_function_id	is_reconfiguration_pending
1	1643152899	0

Figure 16-20. *Resource Governor DMV sample output*

The Resource Governor catalog views are shown in Listing 16-20. The catalog views provide the same basic information you could find by selecting Resource Governor Properties from SQL Server Management Studio.

Listing 16-20. *Resource Governor Catalog Views*

```
SELECT * FROM sys.resource_governor_workload_groups
SELECT * FROM sys.resource_governor_resource_pools
SELECT * FROM sys.resource_governor_configuration
```

Figure 16-21 shows the output returned from running the code in Listing 16-20. This is just an alternative way to get information about your current configuration without having to dig through SQL Server Management Studio.

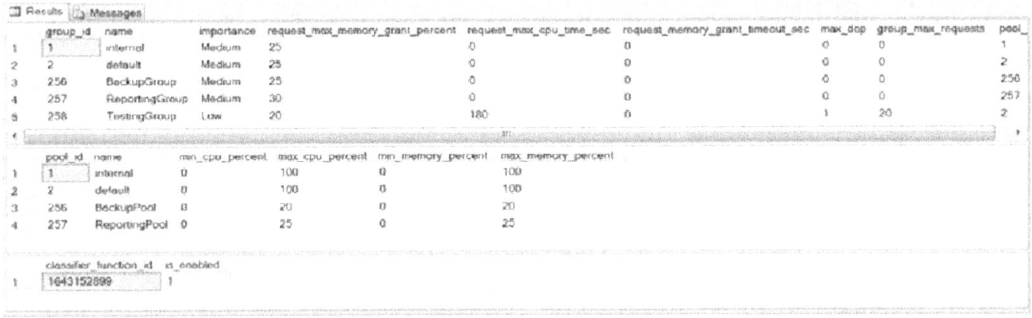

	group_id	name	importance	request_max_memory_grant_percent	request_max_cpu_time_sec	request_memory_grant_timeout_sec	max_dop	group_max_requests	pool_
1	1	internal	Medium	25	0	0	0	0	1
2	2	default	Medium	25	0	0	0	0	2
3	256	BackupGroup	Medium	25	0	0	0	0	256
4	257	ReportingGroup	Medium	30	0	0	0	0	257
5	258	TestingGroup	Low	20	180	0	1	20	2

	pool_id	name	min_cpu_percent	max_cpu_percent	min_memory_percent	max_memory_percent
1	1	internal	0	100	0	100
2	2	default	0	100	0	100
3	256	BackupPool	0	20	0	20
4	257	ReportingPool	0	25	0	25

	classifier_function_id	is_enabled
1	1643152899	1

Figure 16-21. *Resource Governor catalog view sample output*

Summary

SQL Server 2008 provides many enhancements to help you manage query performance. Many of the enhancements shown in this chapter were introduced in SQL Server 2005 and built upon in SQL 2008 to provide you with more granular control over your queries. Some enhancements, such as the Resource Governor, lay an entirely new foundation for managing query performance. By providing more granular control over your query performance, SQL Server 2008 allows you to maintain a more robust and predictable environment; which results in fewer phone calls because of rogue queries running out of control.

PART 5

Conclusion

CHAPTER 17

■ ■ ■

Secrets to Excelling As a Professional DBA

This chapter focuses on developing non-technical skills that can help separate you from every other DBA within your organization. Why is this important? In our opinion, the non-technical skills place you in the top tier of DBAs and ultimately help you make more money. We have both been successful professionally in a short period. We would like to share with you some of the things that we have done to grow rapidly in our profession.

Be Good at What You Do

In order to excel in any profession, you have to be good at it. There are no ifs, ands, or buts about it; if you're not a good database administrator, then you will not excel in the DBA role. Just because you're not a good DBA today, does not mean you can't be an outstanding DBA within a couple of years. You just have to set your sights on the goals you want to achieve and work hard to accomplish them.

Face Reality

Part of being a good DBA is to face reality. Be honest with yourself about what you know and what you do not know. Be honest with others as well. Know when you can do something, and know when to ask for help. And be prepared to compromise.

Accept That You Are Not the Best

You do not have to be the best DBA within your organization in order to surpass the other DBAs. There is nothing wrong with striving to be the best. Understand that there will be DBAs who know more about a topic within SQL Server than you do. SQL Server is too large for you to be an expert in everything. So strive to have more overall knowledge about SQL Server than most, be able to discuss various SQL Server topics intelligently, and be really good at *some topic* within SQL Server—find a niche that interests you, in which you can develop a deep expertise and be recognized for it.

Accept and Learn from Criticism

Throughout your career, you will perform actions that are not necessarily the best and someone will criticize you for those actions. Depending on what you did, who caught it, and how bad it was, you may be heavily criticized in an unfriendly way. In order to excel as a DBA, you have to take in those words, regardless of how harsh they are, learn from them, and move on. Whatever you do, don't take criticism personally and start doubting your ability or skill set. As good as you are, you can't do everything right the first time. There is no shame in making a mistake; just don't make the same mistake over and over again.

Accept That Things Won't Always Go Your Way

Unless you run your own company, you might as well accept the fact that things will not always go your way. As strong-minded as DBAs are sometimes, it can be hard to realize that the decision makers will not always agree with you. When that happens, don't let it bother you. Your job is to provide your recommendation, but the decision makers will ultimately make the decision. There are two things that we want you to keep in mind when you see that things aren't going your way:

- *Learn to compromise*: When it appears that things will not be going your way, then it's wise to start compromising. One tactic you can use is to figure out what you like about a proposed plan that the decision makers are leaning toward, then start talking positively about that aspect of the plan. When it appears that you are coming around to their side, try to rally for a little piece of your plan, the part that you can't live without. Don't be as aggressive as you might have been initially; just try to make a good case for why the process will benefit as a whole if that piece of your plan is added to their plan.

- *Remember the pecking order*: Regardless of how much you disagree with the plan that the decision makers come up with, the only thing you can do is provide your recommendation. At the point when you realize that their minds are made up, try to figure out how to make their plan better rather than talking until you're blue in the face. At the end of the day, they are paid the big bucks to make the big decisions. Your job is to make sure they are successful.

As long as you can accept the points discussed in this section, then you shouldn't have a problem excelling as a DBA. These are points that we have learned over time and wished someone would have shared with us early on.

Build Your Reputation

While you are increasing your knowledge of SQL Server, you should work on developing a reputation within your organization. Do you want to be known as the DBA who always needs help solving problems and never gets your work done on time? Or do you want to be known as the go-to person who will get the work done and solve problems? You're reading this book, so we know the option you have chosen. The following list contains some ideas that will help you on your way to building the reputation that you want:

- *Be dependable*: Your customers, your manager, and your team all need to know that they can depend on you. From completing your assignments on time to helping out other team members with their work (even when you are not asked and when it requires you to work on weekends), make sure you are a person who everyone knows they can count on. If you say you're going to do something at a certain time but forget, then you won't be representing yourself very well. Find a way in your environment to continuously show your management, team, and customers that you are a dependable member of the team.

- *Be accountable*: You are not perfect. You will make mistakes. But as long as you always admit your mistakes, you're more likely to be believed when bad things happen and you say that you did not cause the problem.

  Being accountable also means that you may have to accept responsibility for problems that you don't think you caused but cannot prove that someone or something else caused it. People will always blame the database for problems. That means, as a DBA, they will blame you for those problems. We know that the database is not the problem in most cases, but proving that is sometimes a little more challenging. You must choose your battles; without proof, accept responsibility and don't point fingers.

- *Be the go-to person*: You should always strive to be the go-to person within your team. When management, customers, or other members of your team start to depend on you to help them through tough situations, then you can tell you're becoming that go-to person.

- *Be the problem solver*: Strive to be the person who everyone seeks out to solve tough problems. If you want to specialize in one area, like performance, then become the performance problem solver. However, if you want to be the best of the best, then work hard at being a problem solver in all areas within your environment.

- *Achieve the unachievable*: We know that projects will come down the pipeline without enough time to accomplish the tasks. Work hard to become the person who's requested to work on projects with impossible timelines. Everyone respects the person who completes the impossible assignment and gets management or customers out of a jam. On your way to becoming one of the best DBAs in your organization, you will need to pull off a couple of projects like this.

As we conclude this section, we hope you understand how important it is to be good at what you do in order to excel as a DBA. Your reputation is what will play a heavy role in determining promotions and pay increases. Work hard at creating a reputation that you can be proud of.

Go Above and Beyond

In order to excel as a DBA, you have to be willing to go above and beyond your required duties. Going above and beyond means you have to be willing to work long hours, work on assignments or projects outside of your job description (if you are a DBA II, do senior DBA work), and put forth an extreme amount of effort in everything you do. Going above and beyond means you don't do just the minimum to accomplish assignments. Add all the bells and whistles to make sure the process you create stands out.

Going above and beyond also means taking the initiative. Following are some types of projects you can take on to show management and your teammates that you are serious about doing more:

- *Take on new projects*: Perhaps there is a problem that needs a solution. Because you and your teammates are busy, no one does anything to resolve the problem or come up with a solution. That is where you come into play. Take on those types of projects on your own time. Come up with solutions—not just a solution to the problem, but also a solution that blows everyone away with your in-depth knowledge of different technologies and concepts. Take advantage of the projects that need work and that everyone else ignores.

- *Challenge the norms*: In most organizations, processes and procedures created years ago are still in place. Technology has changed so much over the years that the processes are inefficient and need to be rewritten. Unfortunately, most people are hesitant to change processes that are "not broken," even if it's known that those processes need improvement. Grab the opportunity to show your team and management the way these processes *should* run. Don't make the mistake of trying to convince everyone verbally that your way is the best way—show them. Find a way to compare the old process against your new process, and let the statistics speak for themselves.

But we're going to warn you: Trying to change existing processes won't be easy. There are a lot of people attached to existing processes, and people are usually against change. Don't get discouraged when they resist. However, it's hard for anyone to resist when the performance of your newly created process is substantially better than the old process. So gather statistics on both processes, and show everyone why your way is the best. Let your results convince them.

Communicate Effectively

Communicating effectively is another way for you to distinguish yourself from many other DBAs. Many DBAs do not communicate well with non-technical people. Some even struggle to communicate with fellow DBAs. In most cases, the problem isn't a lack of communication skills. The problem stems from an inability to explain a point at a level that the target audience can completely comprehend. The following sections give some tips that may help.

Talk to Your Target Audience

To prevent yourself from using too many technical details, you should try to talk to the technical level of the majority of your audience or the most important members of the group (which may consist of some end users on a conference call, a customer, or a meeting of various people). Make sure those people clearly understand what you are discussing before the conversation ends. You can always clarify things for the smaller group that may not have caught all of the presented information.

Think about the information needed to fulfill the expectations of the majority of the group. If the majority of the group in question consists of non-technical people, then you should provide them with a high-level overview of the content you are discussing. Most of the time, non-technical users want the result. They are less concerned with the details surrounding how the process will work. They pay you the big bucks to figure that out. On the flip side, if you are in a meeting with a group of DBAs discussing an issue where they are expecting detailed information, then you should not discuss the issues at an overview level. For all of the levels in between non-technical people and other DBAs, you should adjust your content accordingly. You should set a goal to become knowledgeable enough such that you can present the content at varying levels of technical detail, but still get the point across effectively to the various people you communicate with.

Know When You Aren't Getting Through

Sometimes, when you are talking to your target audience, you may have thought that their technical level is greater on a topic than it really is. Other times, you may explain something in a manner that is not clear enough for the group to understand your point. Regardless of the cause, you need to be able to determine when the group you are talking to doesn't "get it." You all know the look—blank faces, consistent nods, no follow-up questions, and other empty methods of them agreeing with you.

If you want to be in the top tier of DBAs, then you need to recognize the look and be knowledgeable enough about the topic to explain it differently. You should also be patient and ensure the group that it does not bother you to explain the content so that they will understand it. Patience is really important. Depending on the group, it may take time for them to figure out what you are talking about. Regardless of how long it takes, spend the time asking questions of the group to make sure that they really do understand the information you are presenting. They will appreciate your efforts.

Know When They Don't Care

There's also a danger sometimes in explaining too much detail. Many of us are so passionate about SQL Server that we sometimes provide too much information when asked a question. When asked questions about what columns to add an index on, we provide detailed explanations about reviewing the execution plan, checking the indexes that are currently available, comparing the reads versus writes on the table, and 30 minutes later we have bored the developer to death. Sometimes it's enough to say, "Add an index to columns A and B with an INCLUDE column of C."

Your audience really does care about what you have to say, but often not at the same level of detail that matters to you. Look for signs of restlessness and boredom. Learn when to summarize. Learn when to say simply that a given approach to a database problem will perform better, and when to launch into great detail about why that is the case.

A good strategy is to summarize first, while being prepared with hard facts to back up your statement. When you tell developers that you need to include a column, be prepared to explain why that is the case, should they care enough to ask. Some will be very interested in that level of detail. Others will not be interested at all. The trick is to learn to detect the level of interest from your specific audience and to respond appropriately.

Be a Good Listener

One aspect of being a good communicator is the ability to be a good listener. You have to pay attention to what people are saying in order to accurately and effectively answer their questions and concerns. Let's be honest—sometimes we have a hard time listening to what other people are saying. We over talk them, assume we know what they want, and then just start talking. Oftentimes, if we would just listen to people, we could solve more problems and answer more questions.

To be a good listener, you have to be an active participant in a conversation. Follow along with the conversation, ask questions, and provide feedback. If you are not interested in the conversation, then try to find a way to make yourself interested.

Remain Calm Under Pressure

As you probably know by now, being a DBA can be stressful. Processes will break, systems will go down, and you will experience major performance problems at times throughout your career. As you continue to excel as a DBA, you will have to learn how to handle the pressures of dealing with high-stress situations.

Prepare for Pressure Situations

Prepare in advance for stressful situations, and you will increase your chances of not panicking when it is time for you to perform. What do you need to prepare for? Chapter 12 discussed practicing your recovery strategy and documenting information needed to recover if your server goes down. Use the monitoring techniques in Chapter 14 to proactively monitor your server and hopefully prevent performance problems from occurring in your system. Lastly, you have to prepare for the unexpected.

Understand that you cannot prepare for everything. You will sometimes experience problems that you haven't experienced before. The best way to overcome a lack of experience is to read more blogs and participate in the SQL Server community (also refer to Chapter 18). That way, you minimize the types of issues that you haven't seen before.

Deal with Pressure Situations

Unfortunately, the day will come when you have to deal with a disaster. Management and others will remember how you handle these situations, so take advantage of the opportunity. Depending on the criticality of the situation, you may not have time to implement or practice some of the things that we list in this section. Just keep them in mind and utilize what you can when you can.

- *Stay calm*: It is important to make sure you remain calm throughout a crisis. Depending on the application and the amount of money lost while the systems are down will ultimately determine how much pressure you get from management during the outage. Stay confident in your ability to handle the situation and that should help management deal with some of their nervousness. The only person you can control during a crisis is yourself. When everyone around you loses control, remember you are prepared. You can do it. And don't let the people around you impact your ability to remain calm.

- *Get management out of the room*: In a crisis, your boss may want to hover about as you try to diagnose and solve the problem. For many, such hovering is akin to placing a huge mental block in the path of their otherwise clear thinking. If you can tactfully get your boss out of the room, do so. Explain that it will help you think clearly if you can have some time alone or with whatever technical colleagues you want at your side. Many managers will respect that argument if you put it to them in a calm and tactful manner.

- *Identify the problem*: Before you start resolving the issue or providing estimates for the amount of time it will take you to get the system back up, make sure you clearly identify the problem. If you don't research the problem for yourself, you could end up resolving one issue and not all of the issues. That will just increase your downtime and make management unhappy. So spend a little time researching the issues prior to providing solutions. Don't make the mistake of providing false estimates because you didn't do the research up front.

- *Determine the solution*: Once you have identified all of the issues, discuss your resolution before you start fixing things. If you work with a team of DBAs or other IT staff, discuss your possible resolution to make sure you cover everything. There is nothing worse than thinking you have the issue resolved just to create another problem. Talking about an issue does not appear to management that you are resolving the issue. However, discussing the issue with staff and colleagues will lead to better and safer resolutions, so don't skip this step.

- *Create a backup plan*: Based on the severity of the issue, you should come up with a backup plan to your original plan. Granted, you will not be able to plan for every possible failure, and you should not spend time doing so. However, it is important to make sure you have an immediate backup plan just in case your primary option does not work out. That way, you don't have to get everyone back together to discuss your next steps.

- *Work simultaneously*: Once you have determined your plan of action, distribute the work if you can. In other words, assign tasks to multiple DBAs to help get the system back up faster. There is no reason to have everyone sitting around one computer if there are tasks that each can do.

- *Have someone stand over your shoulder*: During a crisis, mistakes are costly. Don't make assumptions. Make sure your actions will successfully accomplish the agreed-upon plan. Performing the wrong action, like restoring the wrong database file, could double your downtime and really upset management and customers. When executing important processes, have another DBA stand over your shoulder to make sure you are doing what you all planned. That way, one of you will likely catch an error before you lose too much time.

  There is nothing wrong with asking someone to stand over your shoulder. With the pressures of a crisis, you are more likely not to be thinking as clearly as you normally do. Depending on the time of the issue and the number of hours you have been working, fatigue may start to set in. That can also cause you to make more errors than normal. Take advantage of having a second pair of eyes to validate the decisions you make, especially the important ones.

- *Provide status updates*: Throughout the disaster, you will have to provide updates to management. Make sure you don't provide an estimated time that the system will be available until you know what the issue is and your solution. Always over estimate the amount of time you think it will take to recover from the issue. When unexpected problems occur with your solution, make sure you communicate to management the impact to the estimated system availability time. (Hopefully, you followed some of the tips in the section "Prepare for Pressure Situations" and have good statistical information to provide better estimates on the amount of time it will take to perform certain actions.)

- *Remember to eat*: During a crisis, especially an extended crisis, make sure you take care of yourself. As much as you can, try to follow your normal routine. If you normally leave work for lunch, then strive to make time to leave work and grab a quick bite to eat. If you frequently leave your desk for a beverage and a little chit-chat around the water cooler, then sneak away to the water cooler every now and again. You aren't only making sure you stay hydrated and nourished during the crisis; you are also giving yourself a chance to step away from the problem to clear your head. You will be amazed at the number of problems that you will solve when you are away from your computer giving your mind a well-deserved break.

Wrap Up the Pressure Situation

After you have the system back up and running, you need to make sure you wrap up the situation properly. The following list contains some of the steps that we follow after the dust settles.

- *Set up a post-mortem meeting*: Make sure you have a meeting with all of parties involved, including management, to discuss the situation. Make sure the meeting at least addresses the following questions:

  - What caused the issue?

  - What did you do to fix the issue? Recap the events in the order that they happened.

  - What are the negative repercussions of your actions? For example, did we lose any data?

  - How do we prevent the issue from happening in the future?

- *Complete unfinished tasks*: Often, when you are in the middle of a crisis, you work on the most critical tasks needed to get the system back up for users to connect to it. After users are connected again, make sure you go back and finish the less important tasks that you may have skipped during the crisis.

- *Take a look back*: Shortly after the crisis, get together with everyone involved in the recovery process and discuss the things that you all did well versus the things that need to be improved upon before the next crisis. Talk about everything—communication, processes that you all followed, the amount of time it took to resolve the issue, any mistakes that were made, things that you all did right, and everything else that you can think of. Whatever you do, don't make this meeting a finger-pointing session. Just make sure you all figure out the things you can do better the next time a crisis occurs.

We know you may not have a lot of time to spend preparing for a situation that may never happen. However, those of you who prepare for different situations and have a plan for dealing with a crisis will often solve the problems faster and remain calm during the crisis.

Be an Effective Leader

It is important to have excellent leadership qualities to excel as a DBA. Regardless of your career ambitions, as a manager of DBAs or a lead DBA, you have to be an effective leader to make it to the top. A promotion to a leadership role does not make you a leader. You cannot force people to follow you. You can find leadership characteristics all over the Internet; however, the following sections provide you with some information that we feel will help you become a leader in the eyes of other DBAs.

Make Tough Decisions

In order to be a leader, you have to be able to make tough decisions. There is no easy way, but someone has to do it. We all know what those decisions are—decisions where you struggle to make up your mind about what the best course of action is, decisions where you are going to be appreciated for making the right choice and getting the system back up quickly, or cursed for making the wrong decision and increasing the downtime of the application. If you want to excel as a DBA, then you are going to have to be ready to make the tough decision when the time comes, and then justify your recommendation.

Situations will arise where you have to defend your recommendation against another. Make sure you can back it up thoroughly, but be prepared to consider opposing points of view. Don't let the person against whom you are defending your recommendation intimidate you. No one is perfect; no one knows it all. If you support your argument well enough, then you have accomplished your mission. Your recommendation doesn't have to be chosen in order to prove that you are ready to make tough decisions. You just have to show the decision makers that you are ready to take on that role. Do a good job supporting your argument, and the decision makers will listen to you a little more the next time.

One thing that you must do when discussing your recommendation is keep your ears open. Often, DBAs have a habit of not listening to other people when they disagree on the best approach to solving a problem. If you fall into that category, then you cannot be that way if you want to be a leader. If you aren't listening to the point that others are making, then you may end up making the wrong decision. Being the decision maker doesn't mean that you have to use your ideas all the time. It means that you have the responsibility of making the best decision for the situation that you are in. That recommendation can come from anyone. If you aren't listening to what they are saying, then you will likely miss that information.

Make Others Around You Better

A good leader will make other DBAs better. You can do this with a variety of methods, like sharing with them the cool things that you learned from reading this book or other articles online. The following list provides you with some of the different things you could do make the other DBAs around you better.

- *Be a good teacher:* One skill set that some DBAs lack that you could take advantage of is being a good teacher. Take the time to work with other DBAs to show them some of the methods that you use to solve problems. When you work on something cool that you think they can benefit from, then share the information. Make the time to work with them to help solve their problems. Don't try to make them solve problems the way that you do. Just help them solve it their own way. Strive to help others as much as possible, and it will be appreciated.

- *Be a mentor*: If the opportunity presents itself, then take advantage of it. Mentoring other DBAs, both seasoned or junior, can be rewarding for both of you. Mentor another DBA even if your job description does not require you to. Mentor another DBA even if you don't think you have the time. Management and the rest of the team will notice and appreciate it.

- *Learn from others*: You will make other DBAs around you better if you ask for help when you need it. Give them the opportunity to work on being a good teacher and a mentor to you. That is a great way to make sure you have a mutual relationship of giving and taking information from the other DBAs. Learning from other DBAs also gives you a chance to show them that you don't think you know it all and gladly welcome their help. Don't be too proud to learn from others.

- *Create healthy competition*: Healthy competition among DBAs can be beneficial for all of you. As long as you are competing, then all of you will push yourselves to get better. That is a win-win situation for everyone, including the company. Converting cursors to set theory or tuning poorly performing queries are great examples of competitions that everyone can participate in.

We can't talk about many things you can do to make others around you better. However, the point we are making is that you shouldn't purposely try to create a gap between yourself and the team. Don't keep all of your knowledge and experience bundled inside of your brain. Share the information; don't intentionally create a knowledge gap between you and everyone else. Sharing information will make a stronger team, and management will recognize that you are the source of its strength and reward you accordingly.

Summary

As we conclude this chapter, we hope that we provided you with some good information to help you get to the next level professionally. We implemented a large number of these steps in our careers, and that is what helped us get to where we are today. We hope that this information benefits you as well.

You should always strive to constantly become better at what you do. Chapter 18 talks about being an active member of the SQL Server community and other methods for learning outside of work. Combine the information that you learned in this chapter along with the information you will learn in Chapter 18 to help you put together a plan to excel as a DBA.

CHAPTER 18

What's Next?

I am sure you know by now that being a DBA requires a huge skill set covering a wide spectrum of technologies. DBAs are expected to know a little bit about everything. But what makes being a DBA even harder is that technology is a fast-paced industry, with rapid advancements that seem to outdate what you thought of as new before you've even had a chance to learn it. The days are over when you learned a skill and then worked for several years before you needed to upgrade your skill set. You have to learn new things constantly and stay on top of the latest industry news in order to excel as a DBA.

Ongoing Experimentation and Learning

You should take a little time to learn something new at least once a week. Just pick a topic you like and do a little research. We like to look over the topics in SQL Server Books Online, read a blog entry or two, find a webcast, and then do some experimentation to get hands-on experience. What's good about blog entries is that you can get some real-world feedback on a topic based on someone else's experience.

If you are not sure where to start, Microsoft has a great learning web site at www.microsoft.com/Learning/. One of our favorite features is the ability to select a learning plan. This is a predefined plan created by Microsoft that consists of a collection of articles, books, webcasts, online training, classroom training, and anything else that will help you learn a specific area of interest. As you follow the learning plan, you can mark items complete so you can track your progress throughout the plan. Another great resource on the Microsoft Learning web site is the Microsoft SQL Server Training Portal located at www.microsoft.com/learning/en/us/training/sql-server.aspx. The SQL Server 2008 Training Portal contains a compiled list of links dedicated to learning SQL Server 2008, including special offers and certification information.

Studying for a Microsoft certification exam is another good way to guide your training and keep you on track. You can find an exam guide for each certification offered by Microsoft to help you prepare for the test. In every exam guide there is a Skills Measured section. You should print out this section and work your way down the list, making sure that you have mastered each item. Don't just read about each topic and think you have mastered it. You really need to do some hands-on testing in order to ensure you fully understand each topic. A certification is not only an excellent way to learn new things, but it also gives you another bullet point on your resume.

You can also sign up for a daily newsletter from web sites (such as SQLServerCentral.com and MSSQLTips.com) and read them as a part of your daily routine. If you find a particular topic of interest, you can take a few minutes and read an article or two. Newsletters are a daily reminder that you should take some time out of your busy schedule and learn something new. The SQL Channel at JumpstartTV.com (`www.jumpstarttv.com/channels/SQL.aspx`) has several videos that are generally less than five minutes each. You can create a free account and add videos to watch that pique your interest. Even on your busiest days, you should be able to take a five-minute break and watch a video.

Podcasts

Podcasts are another great resource that many people often overlook. Podcasts are a great way to learn things while you are on the go (driving, on a plane, and so forth). Don't worry, podcasts come in both video and audio form, so you don't have to watch and drive at the same time. Some of the available podcasts include the following:

- Voice of the DBA (`http://sqlservercentral.mevio.com`)

- SSWUG.org (`www.sswug.org/media/`)

- SQL Down Under (`www.sqldownunder.com`)

- Microsoft Events and Webcasts (`www.microsoft.com/events/podcasts/`)

- SQLServerPedia (`http://sqlserverpedia.com/wiki/SQL_Server_Tutorials`)

Free Training Events

Always be on the lookout for free training events in your area. Many times Microsoft has a road show to present some of the latest technology. However, these don't happen year round; they usually coincide with product release schedules, so keep checking the Microsoft web site periodically. SQL Saturday is another way to get free training. SQL Saturday is a one-day training event on (you guessed it) Saturday, packed full of sessions dealing with all aspects of SQL Server. Finally, find a local users group and get involved. Users groups generally have monthly meetings with a one-hour session that covers various topics within SQL Server. A local users group is also a good way to network with other SQL Server professionals in your area and learn something new in the process. You can find more information at the following links:

- `www.msdnevents.com/default.aspx`

- `www.sqlsaturday.com`

- `www.sqlpass.org/PASSChapters.aspx`

SQL Support Options

There are numerous support options available to help you with the SQL Server learning process along the way. You can even find the right support if you are trying to learn a new feature and just have a few questions. You can group SQL support into two basic categories: free support and paid support. For obvious reasons, you should exhaust your free support options before contacting Microsoft support. If you are stuck or have an issue, chances are good that someone else has had the same issue and there is already a documented resolution on the Internet.

Free Support

You would be amazed at the number of people who are willing to help you solve your SQL Server issues; all you have to do is know where to find those people. We have actually seen three different answers (each one being correct) in response to a forum post, all within five minutes. However, you should still do your homework before posting out to forums and newsgroups. Many times a simple search in the right place will provide the answer to your question. Also, you will receive a faster and more accurate response by providing a detailed explanation of your issue, including the things you have already tried to do to resolve the issue.

Product Solution Center

The product solution center for SQL Server is located at `http://msdn.microsoft.com/en-us/sqlserver/bb895923.aspx` and is kind of like a support dashboard for SQL Server, providing you with a centralized support hub. The SQL Server Troubleshooting and Support web site provides you with many important resources on a single web page, such as the following:

- Knowledgebase search functionality
- Latest updates and service packs
- Knowledge base articles addressing top issues
- SQL Server forums
- Microsoft professional support
- Upcoming webcasts
- Technical articles and tutorials

As you can see in Figure 18-1, the SQL Server Troubleshooting and Support web site provides a great interface for you to find the help you need quickly.

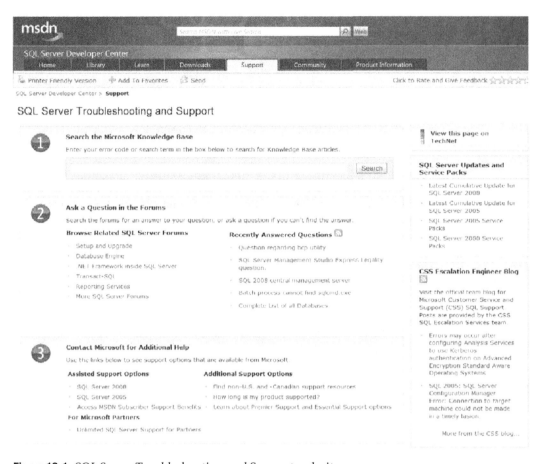

Figure 18-1. *SQL Server Troubleshooting and Support web site*

Microsoft Community Resources

The Microsoft Technical Communities web site is located at www.microsoft.com/communities/
default.mspx. It provides several links that will connect you with other SQL Server users,
including peers and Microsoft employees. The web site contains the following links:

- *Forums*: This link will direct you to forums that are hosted by Microsoft. Some of the
  best names in the business, both Microsoft and non-Microsoft employees, actively
  monitor these forums to answer your questions.

- *Blogs*: This link will allow you to search Microsoft Community blogs posted by Microsoft employees.

- *Technical Chats*: This link will allow you to view upcoming live chats hosted by Microsoft experts.

- *Newsgroups*: This link will allow you to post a question in one of the 2,000-plus newsgroups dedicated to Microsoft products.

- *Webcasts*: This link will allow you to search for an upcoming live webcast or pick from a wide selection of on-demand webcasts hosted by an industry specialist.

- *Find a Community Web Site*: This link connects you with other web sites and resources, usually hosted by a SQL Server MVP.

- *User Groups*: This link will allow you to search for user groups in your area dedicated to your technology interests.

Paid Support

Microsoft offers several options in the form of paid support that covers everything from a single call for help to an entire Enterprise support program. You can find the option that meets your needs on the Microsoft Help and Support web site located at `http://support.microsoft.com/default.aspx?scid=fh;EN-US;OfferProPhone`. Table 18-1 shows the Problem Resolution Services support options at the of this writing. Business hours are Monday through Friday from 6:00 AM to 6:00 PM Pacific Time.

Table 18-1. *Microsoft Problem Resolution Services Support Options*

Support Option	Price
E-mail only support	$99 USD (one incident)
Business hours telephone support	$259 USD (one incident)
Business hours telephone support	$1,289 USD (5 pack of incidents)
Business-critical after hours telephone support	$515 USD (one incident)

Advisory Services

Contacting Microsoft Advisory Services is like hiring an offsite consultant for a rate of $210 USD per hour. Microsoft Advisory Services consist of a short-term agreement that allows you to work with the same technician. This provides a higher level of support, offering analysis and recommendations that go beyond the scope of Problem Resolution Services. You can use Microsoft Advisory Services with consultation pertaining to the following:

- Code reviews

- Installation and configuration technologies

- Performance tuning

- System management server deployments

- Migrations

You can read more about Advisory Services by visiting Microsoft's web site located at `http://support.microsoft.com/gp/advisoryservice`. If you have Enterprise Support needs that go beyond Advisory Services, you can visit the Enterprise Support web site located at `www.microsoft.com/services/microsoftservices/srv_enterprise.mspx`.

Web Sites Dedicated to SQL Server

There are many web sites completely dedicated to SQL Server. Not only do these sites offer forums, articles, blogs, newsletters, sample scripts, and job postings, but they also offer a place for SQL Server professionals of all skill levels to collaborate with each other and exchange knowledge and ideas. If you frequent these web sites, you will begin to recognize many of the same names. As you start contributing to these web sites, you can make many valuable connections with other SQL Server professionals as well.

Some of these web sites include the following:

- Professional Association for SQL Server (`www.sqlpass.org`)

- SQL Server Central (`www.sqlservercentral.com`)

- Simple-Talk (`www.simple-talk.com/sql/`)

- SQLServerPedia (`http://sqlserverpedia.com`)

- MSSQLTips.com (`www.mssqltips.com`)

- SQLTeam.com (`www.sqlteam.com`)

- SQL Server Performance (`www.sql-server-performance.com/index.aspx`)

- SQL Server Community (`http://sqlcommunity.com`)

Microsoft even has a web site called SQL Server Connect located at `http://connect.microsoft.com/SQLServer` that allows you to collaborate with Microsoft employees and other members of the SQL Server community to provide feedback about SQL Server and submit ideas for the next release.

Apress Titles for Specialized Topics

Apress offers a wide variety of books that dive deep into the specific technology of your choice. If you recall in Chapter 3, we said that high availability deserves a book of its own. Well, at the time this chapter was written, there were actually three books on the subject, each one focusing on a specific high-availability technique.

- *Pro SQL Server 2008 Mirroring* by Robert Davis and Ken Simmons (Apress, 2009)

- *Pro SQL Server 2008 Failover Clustering* by Allan Hirt (Apress, 2009)

- *Pro SQL Server 2008 Replication* by Sujoy Paul (Apress, 2009)

These individual books provide the detailed coverage you need in order to master specific areas within SQL Server. For example, business intelligence can be broken into three key areas: Reporting Services, Analysis Services, and Integration Services. Apress has dedicated a book to each of them.

- *Pro SQL Server 2008 Reporting Services* by Rodney Landrum, Shawn McGehee, and Walter J. Voytek II (Apress, 2008)

- *Pro SQL Server 2008 Analysis Services* by Philo Janus (Apress, 2009)

- *Pro SQL Server 2008 Integration Services* by Dandy Weyn (Apress, 2009)

There are also some good books to help you ramp up your development skills. Even if programming is not your specialty, every DBA needs enough programming knowledge to do a little development here and there. You also need a good understanding of how to design a database so that it doesn't cause you, the DBA, an administrative nightmare. And let's face it: XML has been around for a long time now, and it is more tightly integrated with SQL Server in each release. XML is an area that many DBAs need to work on—XML looks intimidating, and many DBAs avoid it altogether. If you learn to use XML correctly, you will find it can provide an advantage over straight T-SQL in many areas of SQL Server.

- *Pro T-SQL 2008 Programmer's Guide* by Michael Coles (Apress, 2008)
- *Pro SQL Server 2008 Relational Database Design and Implementation* by Louis Davidson, with Kevin Kline, Scott Klein, and Kurt Windisch (Apress, 2008)
- *Pro SQL Server 2008 XML* by Michael Coles (Apress, 2008)

In Chapter 16 we mentioned the need for every DBA to have a solid understanding of performance tuning. If you want to keep your job, you should have a vested interest in disaster recovery as well. Here are a couple of books we would recommend you add to your shelf (after you read them of course) from a purely administrative perspective.

- *SQL Server 2008 Query Performance Tuning Distilled* by Grant Fritchey and Sajal Dam (Apress, 2009)
- *Pro SQL Server Disaster Recovery* by James Luetkehoelter (Apress, 2008)

Summary

As you can see, there is more information available than you will ever have time to consume. It is valuable to have a basic working knowledge of all the components in SQL Server, while really digging in and mastering your specific areas of interest. For example, you may never have the interest or need to learn Reporting Services, but you may enjoy writing the most complex and efficient queries in your organization. What is important is that you realize you cannot be an expert in every aspect of SQL Server; however, if you continuously read and practice new techniques, you will become an expert doing the things you like to do best.

Index